Notes on the Gospels – Matthew

Other Jacobus Volumes from Solid Ground

We are presently honored to offer the following four volumes from the pen and heart of Melancthon Jacobus –

NOTES ON THE GOSPELS – Matthew
"The aim of these notes has been to bring together the results of Biblical investigation, and to lay them in the very path of the Sabbath school teachers and students, for their weekly lessons." – the author

NOTES ON THE GOSPELS – Mark & Luke
Charles Hodge, William Henry Green, J.W. Alexander and others from Princeton Seminary said, "The excellent Commentaries of Dr. Melancthon Jacobus have deservedly attained a high reputation, and their wide circulation proves how well they are adapted to the wants of both ministers and laymen. They present, in a brief compass, the results of extensive erudition, abound in judicious exposition and pertinent illustration, and are, moreover, distinguished by doctrinal soundness, evangelical character, and an eminently devout spirit."

NOTES ON THE GOSPELS – John
"The ancients gave to this Evangelist the symbol of *the Eagle*. He is so lofty in doctrine, and so rich in the discourses of our Lord, while his narrative is so additional to the foregoing, that John, of all the four, could best claim a volume of exposition… The study of its contents, with an understanding of its relation to the other Evangelists, will show it to be a *new* Gospel narrative, and yet not 'another Gospel'–a crowing exhibition of the Person and Work of our Lord, out of the richest experience of His love, and with patriarchal feet already stepping into the New Jerusalem–the aged Apostle seeming already to get a vision of the Lamb, and to hear the anthems of the redeemed; and bearing a testimony, the substance of which is, "WE LOVE HIM BECAUSE HE FIRST LOVED US."–from the Author's Preface

NOTES ON THE ACTS OF THE APOSTLES
Jacobus wrote this outstanding work on the Acts of the Apostles in 1859. In his own words (taken from the Preface) "As the only Inspired History of the New Testament Church is here given, it becomes most deeply interesting and useful to Christians of all time to mark the great principles here illustrated; to observe the true nature of Christ's Kingdom, as here set forth, and to note the true Idea of the Church, and the laws of its progress. The important use of this Book to the Church in all time cannot be over-rated."

Notes on the Gospels

Critical and Explanatory

Incorporating with the Notes, on a New Plan
the Most Improved Harmony
of the Four Gospels

MATTHEW

BY

Melancthon W. Jacobus
Then Professor of Biblical Literature
in the Western Theological Seminary
at Alleghany City, PA

Solid Ground Christian Books
Birmingham, Alabama USA

Solid Ground Christian Books
6749 Remington Circle
Pelham AL 35124
205-443-0311
mike.sgcb@gmail.com
www.solid-ground-books.com

NOTES ON THE GOSPELS
Critical and Explanatory: MATTHEW

by Melancthon W. Jacobus (1816-1876)

First published in 1848

First Solid Ground Edition: February 2013

Cover design by Borgo Design

ISBN- 978-159925-333-6

PREFACE.

The aim of these Notes has been to bring together the results of Biblical investigation (so much increased of late), and to lay them in the very path of Sabbath school teachers and scholars, for their weekly lessons. It is believed that the plan of furnishing to their hand, from various and voluminous sources, the apparatus and material called for, will make the exercise attractive, and will both encourage and facilitate the study of God's word. This plan, therefore, takes up the Questions of the American Sunday School Union, so extensively in use, and especially the "Consecutive Union Question Book," lately issued, on the Gospels, to prepare Notes *with the Questions in eye*, and to weave around these Questions the material for more. The book accompanies the Questions without being dependent on them. The author hopes to stand thus in the avenue of so much scriptural instruction, and to be himself a party in the pleasant work, if so be he may be partaker, also, of the reward. He has not done the teacher's work for him, but has gathered for his use that which shall help him in his study, and make it satisfactory; while he has planned, by this means, to introduce to his notice what he needs to know, beyond all that the Questions call for.

Teachers so often have not the time for searching commentaries, or for reading discussions and diffuse annotations, that they may easily slight the study, or be discouraged in the good work. Such a Hand-Book, therefore, has been welcomed by many ministers, teachers and superintendents, with whom the author has conversed in the course of its preparation. And while the *pupils* in Sabbath schools and Bible classes have been mainly afloat, with Questions which are often themselves dark, and oftener such as no one seems precisely to answer, it is believed that an important good may be hereby attained, in bringing *scholars* to their classes well prepared—and *that* not only on the Questions, but on other collateral questions suggested by the Notes.

May it not also lead to the systematic study of the Gospel Histories, in parochial and other schools, and in family instruction, that the *Notes* have the advantage of *Questions* so well approved and every where so accessible as those of the S. S. Union—and these Questions arranged in short *Lessons*, within the reach of a daily or weekly exercise?

Another novel feature of these Notes is, the method of bringing to view a Harmony of the Four Gospel narratives. The common plan has been that of Calvin, Doddridge, Townsend and others—to bring together the parallel passages from the different Evangelists, and to comment on them, thus, in their order. Such a plan must always have the disadvantage of breaking the text, omitting some portions from each Evangelist, and destroying their respective characteristics. But *this* plan brings a Harmony into practical use, *by placing it where it applies*, and where it must all along suggest to the reader, in Captions of the Notes, the many important hints it gives. Furthermore, it goes over the other three Evangelists in the very act of examining one—bringing to view, in their place, the additional records of the others—and thus keeps up the thread of the whole history. It has also this advantage, of giving plain, brief captions to each paragraph, which call attention to the items, and of showing their order by the sections numbered throughout.

Dr. Robinson's Harmony, as corrected from Newcome, and followed by Greenleaf in his "Testimony of the Evangelists," has been adopted, with slight alterations, as being quite the best. This method has thrown the Notes into paragraphs, which have furnished an opportunity for briefly eliciting and summing up the inspired teachings under many sections, in short observations at the close of each, as much more likely to be useful than the usual sundries of remarks at a chapter's end.

Besides the more accessible and familiar works which have been constantly consulted, free use has been made of rarer helps, as, Calvin's Commentaries; Trench's Notes on the Parables, Miracles, and Sermon on the Mount; Bengel's Gnomon; Greenleaf's Testimony of the Evangelists; Englishman's Greek Concordance; Kitto's Biblical Encyclopedia; Trollope's Analecta Theologica; Hengstenberg's Christology; Blunt's Coincidences; Winer's Idioms of the New Testament; Olshausen, Townsend, &c.

Special acknowledgments are here due to the Publisher of Kitto's Biblical Encyclopedia—MARK H. NEWMAN, Broadway, New York—for access to the plates of that valuable work, from which there have been obtained many useful pictorial illustrations.

The author could scarcely have pressed this undertaking to completion, amidst the laborious duties of his parochial charge, but for the strong hope of promoting sound scriptural instruction through this channel also. In this, he has been constantly encouraged by the good opinions of his plan which have been widely expressed to him from the beginning. He can freely say, in the sentiment of that pious commentator on the Psalms, Bishop Horne, that the labour itself has been most profitable and pleasant. And now, the Divine and Gracious Author of the Gospel, in whose strength it has been prosecuted, and in whose name it is sent forth, can bless it to many for edification and for salvation.

MELANCTHON W. JACOBUS.

BROOKLYN, N. Y., *March*, 1848.

MATTHEW THE APOSTLE AND EVANGELIST.

There are four inspired histories of our Lord Jesus Christ in the New Testament. These refer to the same great subject of salvation by a Redeemer; though the authors do not relate precisely the same things. Each gives his own narrative. The history is to be gathered from them all, and their statements are found to be harmonious. Hence, the testimony is *fourfold*. It is THE GOSPEL by Matthew, by Mark, by Luke, and by John—written by these severally, yet *one Gospel* by all, and in all (see Matt. 4. 23. Mark 1. 1. Luke 9. 6).

Two of these Evangelists—the first and last—were apostles. It has been well remarked, also, that "two—Mark and John—were too unlearned to forge the narratives; and the other two—Matthew and Luke—were too learned to be deceived by imposture."

The term for "Gospel," in Greek, which is anglicized in the old English, "evangel," gives rise to the title "Evangelist," which has the sense of *gospelizer*, or publisher of the Gospel. The Greek term, in its derivation, signifies the same as the Anglo-Saxon "Godspell"—*good tidings*—from which we have our word "Gospel."

These four histories may be regarded as *the inspired summaries of the apostles' preaching*. Immediately after the ascension of our Lord, "they went forth and preached every where," according to their Divine commission. Matthew, doubtless, laboured chiefly in Judea. When it became needful to have a permanent history of our Lord's life and death—His teachings and doings—and to give it the widest circulation for a witness, before Jerusalem should be destroyed (see ch. 24. 14, and ch. 28. 19), Matthew wrote, under the Divine inspiration, more particularly for the Jews. Soon after, Mark wrote for the Romans, as would seem from the Latin terms which he introduces, and from his gospel being written at Rome. Luke wrote for the Gentiles *more generally*, exhibiting Christ as "the seed of the woman." And John wrote last of all, supplying what might be added to the rest, and setting forth Jesus as the co-equal Son—who "was with God," and "was God."

Though different authorities have assigned various dates to this gospel, ranging from A.D. 38, to A.D. 68, the strong internal and external evidence favours the later time. It may safely be dated at A.D. 62, about eight years before the destruction of Jerusalem. It was not so necessary at an earlier period, while the apostles themselves could preach, and while "they went forth and preached every where" (Mark 16. 20). "About this time," says Lardner, "the Gospel had been propagated in many Gentile countries; the times were troublesome in Judea (under Nero), and the war was coming on. Several of the apostles were dead, and others of them who survived, were gone or going abroad, and many of the Jewish believers were about to seek shelter elsewhere. Now, was therefore a proper time to write a history of Christ and His miracles. Moreover, in this Gospel are recorded divers plain predictions of the coming overthrow of Jerusalem and the Jewish state, which could not be well published to all the world in writing, till about this time."—*Lardner's Works*, vol. 5, p. 305.

It has been argued by many, that this Evangelist, unlike the rest, wrote in Hebrew—a corrupt Hebrew or Syro-Chaldaic being the vernacular tongue in Palestine, in the time of our Lord. But though he wrote mainly for the Jews, they had already become familiar with the Greek language, which had spread abroad since the reign of Alexander. The many Jews resident in Egypt, had required a Greek version of their Old Testament Scriptures, more than 300 years before. And as this Gospel History was intended to circulate most widely, and, in the mind of the Spirit, was designed to go abroad among Gentiles also—we find sufficient reason for regarding this prevalent tongue as the original. Besides, it is confessed that other portions of the New Testament Scriptures written at and about this time, were in the Greek language. "The Epistle of James," which is supposed to date A.D. 60, and which was addressed "*to the twelve tribes scattered abroad*," was written in Greek. This Jewish Greek was not indeed the pure tongue, but mixed with Hebraisms (see Winer's Idioms of the New Testament). Lardner, after citing the testimonies which have been urged for the Hebrew original of this gospel, concludes against them, and argues that this cannot be a Greek translation, because the same reason which would have made a translation into Greek necessary, would have induced Matthew himself to write in Greek.

It is further to be observed, that this apostle had early become familiar with the Greek tongue by his intercourse in the office of collector, and that it was already spoken extensively among the Jews of Judea, among whom he preached immediately after the ascension. The Jewish authors, Philo and Josephus, cotemporaries of the apostles, wrote in Greek. The mere fact that, by all confession, this Greek Gospel as we have it, was universally circulated, while no trace of a Hebrew Gospel is found, would weigh strongly in favour of the Greek original—since we might suppose that it would be written in the tongue in which it would be most needed, and most circulated. That the oldest Fathers of the church (says Olshausen) did not possess Matthew's Gospel in any other form than that in which we now have it, is fully settled. It is clear from the character of the citations out of the Old Testament, that this must be something else than a mere version. Besides, there is not the slightest trace of any opposition to it, as there must have been if the apostle had written in Hebrew, and a Greek *translation* was crowding it out, as though itself the *original*. Yet there is frequent mention early made of a Hebrew Gospel by Matthew. Lardner best accounts for this, by supposing that a Hebrew translation was made for limited use, which some came to consider as the original. Olshausen concludes that Matthew wrote in Hebrew, and afterward himself wrote in Greek.

MATTHEW was a Jew of Galilee. He was an inferior collector of customs under the Roman government, to whom the Jews were now tributary. His station was at the port of Capernaum, or, as some have thought, on the high road from Capernaum to Damascus. He is also called LEVI (Mark 2. 14. Luke 5. 27, 28) and "*the publican*," in his own list of the apostles. Matt. 10. 3. It was common among the Jews to have two names: as Lebbeus, whose surname was Thaddeus"—Matt. 10. 3—and "Simon, who is called Peter." Matt. 10. 2. When a Jew became a Roman citizen, he usually assumed a Roman name. It is, therefore, supposed that "Levi" was the original Hebrew, and "Matthew" the assumed Roman name of this Evangelist.

This gospel was evidently written with a special aim to evangelize the Jews. Hence the apostle brings forward the convincing proofs, that Jesus was the Christ, and even *that Messiah* whom their prophets had foretold. Hence he constantly refers them to their Scriptures of the Old Testament as fulfilled in Him. But this would be a leading argument for Christianity with the Gentiles also. He constantly considers John the Baptist in reference to Malachi's predictions, and recognizes his person and work as their direct accomplishment. Besides this, Matthew abounds in citations from the prophets, which some authors here, and many in Germany, have regarded as mere "accommodations," or *happy applications*, of the prophetic language. It requires no very high view of inspiration, to take them as so many inspired notices of inspired predictions fulfilled in the events.

In choosing Matthew for an apostle, our Lord adopted a striking memorial of Judah's low estate, the country being now tributary, and an officer of the tribute, one of the twelve! It was at such a time of the chosen tribe's declension, that the Messiah was predicted as to come. Genesis 49. 10. Zech. 9. 9.

Our received English version of the Scriptures is a most elaborate correction of the previous translations, and that from the *original tongues*. Forty-seven men of the highest abilities were employed in the work for the space of three years, by authority of the King (James I). They were divided into six companies, and were assigned different portions. The work of each group underwent the revision of all the others, after having been first thoroughly sifted in their own immediate circle. The whole was then finally revised by twelve men—these being a committee of two from each company. Thus most learnedly and laboriously prepared, it was issued at London. A.D. 1611. After many ineffectual attempts to improve upon it, by new versions, it is admitted among scholars, that a more faithful and true translation, all in all, cannot be expected, and need not be desired

CONTENTS

AND

SYNOPSIS OF THE HARMONY.

	CONTENTS.	MATT.	MARK.	LUKE.	JOHN.
Sect.	**PART I.**				
	EVENTS CONNECTED WITH THE BIRTH AND CHILDHOOD OF OUR LORD.				
	TIME: *About thirteen and a half years.*				
1.	Preface to Luke's Gospel.	………	………	1. 1–4	
2.	An Angel appears to Zacharias. *Jerusalem.*	………	………	1. 5–25	
3.	An Angel appears to Mary. *Nazareth.*	………	………	1. 26–38	
4.	Mary visits Elizabeth. *Jutta.*	………	………	1. 39–56	
5.	BIRTH OF JOHN THE BAPTIST. *Jutta.*	………	………	1. 57–80	
6.	Genealogies.	1. 1–17	………	3. 28–38	
7.	An Angel appears to Joseph. *Nazareth.*	1. 18–25			
8.	THE BIRTH OF JESUS. *Bethlehem.*	………	………	2. 1–7	
9.	An Angel appears to the Shepherds. *Near Bethlehem.*	………	………	2. 8–20	
10.	The circumcision of Jesus, and his presentation in the Temple. *Bethlehem. Jerusalem.*	………	………	2. 21–38	
11.	The Magi. *Jerusalem. Bethlehem.*	2. 1–12			
12.	The flight into Egypt. Herod's cruelty. The return. *Bethlehem. Nazareth.*	2. 13–23	………	2. 39–40	
13.	At twelve years of age Jesus goes to the Passover. *Jerusalem.*	………	………	2. 41–52	
	PART II.				
	ANNOUNCEMENT AND INTRODUCTION OF OUR LORD'S PUBLIC MINISTRY.				
	TIME: *About one year.*				
14.	THE MINISTRY OF JOHN THE BAPTIST. *The Desert. The Jordan.*	3. 1–12	1. 1–8	3. 1–18	

CONTENTS.	MATT.	MARK.	LUKE.	JOHN.
Sect.				
15. THE BAPTISM OF JESUS. *The Jordan.*	3. 13–17	1. 9–11	3. 21–23	
16. THE TEMPTATION. *Desert of Judea.*	4. 1–11	1. 12, 13	4. 1–13	
17. Preface to John's Gospel.				1. 1–18
18. Testimony of John the Baptist to Jesus. *Bethany beyond Jordan.*				1. 19–34
19. Jesus gains Disciples. *The Jordan. Galilee?*				1. 35–25
20. The Marriage at Cana of Galilee.				2. 1–12

PART III.

OUR LORD'S FIRST PASSOVER, AND THE SUBSEQUENT TRANSACTIONS UNTIL THE SECOND.

TIME: *One year.*

CONTENTS.	MATT.	MARK.	LUKE.	JOHN.
21. At the Passover Jesus drives the Traders out of the Temple. *Jerusalem.*				2. 13–25
22. Our Lord's discourse with Nicodemus. *Jerusalem.*				3. 1–21
23. Jesus remains in Judea and baptizes. FURTHER TESTIMONY OF JOHN THE BAPTIST.				3. 22–36
24. JOHN'S IMPRISONMENT, AND JESUS' DEPARTURE INTO GALILEE.	4. 12	6. 17–20 1. 14	3. 19, 20 4. 14	4. 1–3
25. Our Lord's discourse with the Samaritan woman. Many of the Samaritans believe on him. *Shechem or Neapolis.*				4. 4–42
26. Jesus teaches PUBLICLY *in Galilee.*	4. 17	1. 14–15	4. 14, 15	4. 43–45
27. Jesus again at Cana, where he HEALS the son of a nobleman lying ill at Capernaum. *Cana of Galilee.*				4. 46–54
28. Jesus at Nazareth; he is there rejected, and fixes his abode at Capernaum.	4. 13–16		4. 16–31	
29. The CALL of Simon Peter and Andrew, and of James and John, with the miraculous draught of fishes. *Near Capernaum.*	4. 18–22	1. 16–20	5. 1–11	
30. The healing of a Demoniac in the Synagogue. *Capernaum.*		1. 21–28	4. 31–37	
31. The healing of Peter's wife's mother, and many others. *Capernaum.*	8. 14–17	1. 29–34	4. 38–41	
32. Jesus with his Disciples goes from Capernaum throughout Galilee.	4. 23–25	1. 35–39	4. 42–44	
33. The healing of a Leper. *Galilee.*	8. 1–4	1. 40–45	5. 12–16	
34. The healing of a Paralytic. *Capernaum.*	9. 2–8	2. 1–12	5. 17–26	
35. The call of Matthew. *Capernaum.*	9. 9	2. 13, 14	5. 27, 28	

SYNOPSIS OF THE HARMONY. 9

Sect.	CONTENTS.	MATT.	MARK.	LUKE.	JOHN.
	PART IV.				
	OUR LORD'S SECOND PASSOVER, AND THE SUBSEQUENT TRANSACTIONS UNTIL THE THIRD.				
	TIME: *One year.*				
36.	The Pool of Bethesda; the healing of the infirm man; and our Lord's subsequent discourse. *Jerusalem.*	....	....	....	5. 1–47
37.	The Disciples pluck ears of grain on the Sabbath. *On the way to Galilee?*	12. 1–8	2. 23–28	6. 1–5	
38.	The healing of the withered hand on the Sabbath. *Galilee.*	12. 9–14	3. 1–6	6. 6–11	
39.	Jesus arrives at the Sea of Tiberias, and is followed by multitudes. *Lake of Galilee.*	12.15–21	3. 7–12		
40.	Jesus withdraws to the Mountain, and CHOOSES THE TWELVE; the multitudes follow him. *Near Capernaum.*	....	3. 13–19	6. 12–19	
41.	THE SERMON ON THE MOUNT. *Near Capernaum.*	5.1,—8.1	....	6. 20–49	
42.	The healing of the Centurion's servant. *Capernaum.*	8. 5–13	....	7. 1–10	
43.	The raising of the Widow's son. *Nain.*	....	....	7. 11–17	
44.	John the Baptist in prison sends Disciples to Jesus. *Galilee. Capernaum?*	11. 2–19	....	7. 18–35	
45.	Reflections of Jesus on appealing to his mighty Works. *Capernaum.*	11.20–30			
46.	While sitting at meat with a Pharisee, Jesus is anointed by a woman who had been a sinner. *Capernaum?*	....	....	7. 36–50	
47.	Jesus, with the Twelve, makes a second circuit in Galilee.	....	....	8. 1–3	
48.	The healing of a Demoniac. The Scribes and Pharisees blaspheme. *Galilee.*	12.22–37	3. 19–30	11.14,15, 17–23	
49.	The Scribes and Pharisees seek a sign. Our Lord's reflections. *Galilee.*	12.38–45	....	11. 16, 24–36	
50.	The true Disciples of Christ his nearest relatives. *Galilee.*	12.46–50	3. 31–35	8. 19–21	
51.	At a Pharisee's table, Jesus denounces woes against the Pharisees and others. *Galilee.*	....	....	11.37–54	
52.	Jesus discourses to his Disciples and the multitude. *Galilee.*	....	....	12. 1–59	
53.	The slaughter of certain Galileans. Parable of the barren Fig-tree. *Galilee.*	....	....	13. 1–9	

SYNOPSIS OF THE HARMONY.

CONTENTS.	MATT.	MARK.	LUKE.	JOHN.
54. PARABLE of the Sower. *Lake of Galilee. Near Capernaum?*	13. 1–23	4. 1–25	8. 4–18	
55. Parable of the Tares. Other Parables. *Near Capernaum?*	13.24–53	4. 26–34		
56. Jesus directs to cross the Lake. Incidents. The tempest stilled. *Lake of Galilee.*	8. 18–27	4. 35–41	8. 22–25 9. 57–62	
57. The two Demoniacs of Gadara. *S.E. coast of the Lake of Galilee.*	8.28–34 9. 1	5. 1–21	8. 26–40	
58. Levi's Feast. *Capernaum.*	9. 10–17	2. 15–22	5. 29–39	
59. The raising of Jairus' daughter. The woman with a bloody flux. *Capernaum.*	9. 18–26	5. 22–43	8. 41–56	
60. Two blind men healed, and a dumb spirit cast out. *Capernaum.*	9. 27–34			
61. Jesus again at Nazareth, and again rejected.	13.54–58	6. 1–6		
62. A third circuit in Galilee. THE TWELVE INSTRUCTED AND SENT FORTH. *Galilee.*	9.35–38 10. 1–42 11. 1	6. 6–13	9. 1–6	
63. Herod holds Jesus to be John the Baptist, whom he had just before beheaded. *Galilee? Perea.*	14. 1–12	6. 14–16, 21–29	9. 7–9	
64. The Twelve return, and Jesus retires with them across the Lake. Five thousand are fed. *Capernaum. N.E. coast of the Lake of Galilee.*	14.13–21	6. 30–44	9. 10–17	6. 1–14
65. Jesus walks upon the water. *Lake of Galilee. Gennesareth.*	14.22–36	6. 45–56		6. 15–21
66. Our Lord's discourse to the multitude in the Synagogue at Capernaum. Many Disciples turn back. Peter's profession of faith. *Capernaum.*	....	....	....	6. 22–71 7. 1

PART V.

FROM OUR LORD'S THIRD PASSOVER UNTIL HIS FINAL DEPARTURE FROM GALILEE AT THE FESTIVAL OF TABERNACLES.

TIME: *Six months.*

67. Our Lord justifies his disciples for eating with unwashen hands. Pharisaic Traditions. *Capernaum.*	15. 1–20	7. 1–23		
68. The daughter of a Syrophenician woman is healed. *Region of Tyre and Sidon.*	15.21–28	7. 24–30		
69. A deaf and dumb man healed; also many others. Four thousand are fed. *The Decapolis.*	15.29–39	7. 31–37 8. 1–9		

SYNOPSIS OF THE HARMONY. 11

Sect. CONTENTS.	MATT.	MARK.	LUKE.	JOHN.
70. The Pharisees and Sadducees again require a sign. [See § 49.] *Near Magdala.*	16. 1–4	8. 10–12		
71. The Disciples cautioned against the leaven of the Pharisees, etc. *N.E. coast of the Lake of Galilee.*	16. 5–12	8. 13–21		
72. A blind man healed. *Bethsaida (Julias).*	....	8. 22–26		
73. Peter and the rest again profess their faith in Christ. [See § 66.] *Region of Cesarea Philippi.*	16.13–20	8. 27–30	9. 18–21	
74. Our Lord FORETELLS HIS OWN DEATH AND RESURRECTION, and the trials of his followers. *Region of Cesarea Philippi.*	16.21–28	8. 31–38 9. 1	9. 22–27	
75. THE TRANSFIGURATION. Our Lord's subsequent discourse with the three Disciples. *Region of Cesarea Philippi.*	17. 1–13	9. 2–13	9. 28–36	
76. The healing of a Demoniac, whom the Disciples could not heal. *Region of Cesarea Philippi.*	17.14–21	9. 14–29	9. 37–43	
77. Jesus AGAIN FORETELLS HIS OWN DEATH AND RESURRECTION. [See § 74.] *Galilee.*	17.22, 23	9. 30–32	9. 43–45	
78. The tribute-money miraculously provided. *Capernaum.*	17.24–27	9. 33		
79. The Disciples contend who should be greatest. Jesus exhorts to humility, forbearance and brotherly love. *Capernaum.*	18. 1–35	9. 33–50	9. 46–50	
80. THE SEVENTY INSTRUCTED AND SENT OUT. *Capernaum.*	....	....	10. 1–16	
81. Jesus goes up to the Festival of Tabernacles. His final departure from Galilee. Incidents in Samaria.	....	....	9. 51–56	7. 2–10
82. Ten Lepers cleansed. *Samaria.*	....	....	17.11–19	

PART VI.

THE FESTIVAL OF TABERNACLES, AND THE SUBSEQUENT TRANSACTIONS UNTIL OUR LORD'S ARRIVAL AT BETHANY, SIX DAYS BEFORE THE FOURTH PASSOVER.

TIME: *Six months less one week.*

83. Jesus at the Festival of Tabernacles. His public teaching. *Jerusalem.*	....	....	....	7. 11–53 8. 1
84. The woman taken in Adultery. *Jerusalem.*	....	....	....	8. 2–11

SYNOPSIS OF THE HARMONY.

CONTENTS.	MATT	MARK.	LUKE.	JOHN.
Sect.				
85. Further public teaching of our Lord. He reproves the unbelieving Jews, and escapes from their hands. *Jerusalem.*	....	....	....	8. 12–59
86. A lawyer instructed. Love to our neighbour defined. Parable of the Good Samaritan. *Near Jerusalem.*	....	....	10.25–37	
87. Jesus in the house of Martha and Mary. *Bethany.*	....	....	10.38–42	
88. The Disciples again taught how to pray. *Near Jerusalem.*	....	....	11. 1–13	
89. The Seventy return. *Jerusalem?*	....	....	10.17–24	
90. A man born blind is healed on the Sabbath. Our Lord's subsequent discourses. *Jerusalem.*	....	....	....	9. 1–41 10. 1–21
91. Jesus in Jerusalem at the Festival of Dedication. He retires beyond Jordan. *Jerusalem. Bethany beyond Jordan.*	....	....	....	10.22–42
92. The raising of Lazarus. *Bethany.*	....	....	....	11. 1–46
93. The counsel of Caiaphas against Jesus. He retires from Jerusalem. *Jerusalem. Ephraim.*	....	....	....	11.47–54
94. Jesus beyond Jordan is followed by multitudes. The healing of the infirm woman on the Sabbath. *Valley of Jordan. Perea.*	19. 1, 2	10. 1	13.10–21	
95. Our Lord goes teaching and journeying towards Jerusalem. He is warned against Herod. *Perea.*	....	....	13.22–35	
96. Our Lord dines with a chief Pharisee on the Sabbath. Incidents. *Perea.*	....	....	14. 1–24	
97. What is required of true Disciples. *Perea.*	....	....	14.25–35	
98. Parable of the Lost Sheep, etc. Parable of the Prodigal Son. *Perea.*	....	....	15. 1–32	
99. Parable of the Unjust Steward. *Perea.*	....	....	16. 1–13	
100. The Pharisees reproved. Parable of the Rich Man and Lazarus. *Perea.*	....	....	16.14–31	
101. Jesus inculcates forbearance, faith, humility. *Perea.*	....	....	17. 1–10	
102. Christ's coming will be sudden. *Perea.*	....	....	17.20–37	
103. Parables. The importunate Widow. The Pharisee and Publican. *Perea.*	....	....	18. 1–14	
104. Precepts respecting divorce. *Perea.*	19. 3–12	10. 2–12		
105. Jesus receives and blesses little Children. *Perea.*	19.13–15	10.13–16	18.15–17	

SYNOPSIS OF THE HARMONY.

CONTENTS.	MATT.	MARK.	LUKE.	JOHN.
Sect.				
106. The rich Young Man. Parable of the Labourers in the Vineyard. *Perea.*	19.16–30 20. 1–16	10:17–31	18.18–30	
107. JESUS A THIRD TIME FORETELLS HIS DEATH AND RESURRECTION. [See § 74, § 77.] *Perea.*	20.17–19	10.32–34	18.31–34	
108. James and John prefer their ambitious request. *Perea.*	20.20–28	10.35–45		
109. The healing of two blind men near Jericho.	20.29–34	10.46–52	18.35–43 19.1	
110. The visit to Zaccheus. Parable of the ten Minæ. *Jericho.*	....	....	19. 2–28	
111. Jesus arrives at Bethany six days before the Passover. *Bethany.*	....	....	....	11.55–57 12.1,9-16

PART VII.

OUR LORD'S PUBLIC ENTRY INTO JERUSALEM, AND THE SUBSEQUENT TRANSACTIONS BEFORE THE FOURTH PASSOVER.

TIME: *Five Days.*

112. Our Lord's PUBLIC ENTRY INTO JERUSALEM. *Bethany. Jerusalem.*	21. 1–11, 14–17	11. 1–11	19.29–44	12 12–19
113. The barren Fig-tree. THE CLEANSING OF THE TEMPLE. *Bethany. Jerusalem.*	21.12,13, 18, 19	11.12–19	19.45–48 21.37, 38	
114. The barren Fig-tree withers away. *Between Bethany and Jerusalem.*	21.20–22	11.20, 26		
115. Christ's authority questioned. Parable of the Two Sons. *Jerusalem.*	21.23–32	11.27–33	20. 1–8	
116. Parable of the wicked husbandmen. *Jerusalem.*	21.33–46	12. 1–12	20. 9–19	
117. Parable of the Marriage of the King's Son. *Jerusalem.*	22. 1–14			
118. Insidious question of the Pharisees: Tribute to Cesar. *Jerusalem.*	22.15–22	12.13–17	20.20–26	
119. Insidious question of the Sadducees: Resurrection. *Jerusalem.*	22.23–33	12.18–27	20.27–40	
120. A lawyer questions Jesus. The two great Commandments. *Jerusalem.*	22.34–40	12.28–34		
121. How is Christ the son of David? *Jerusalem.*	22.41–46	12.35–37	20.41–44	
122. Warnings against the evil example of the Scribes and Pharisees. *Jerusalem.*	23. 1–12	12.38, 39	20.45, 46	
123. Woes against the Scribes and Pharisees. Lamentation over Jerusalem. *Jerusalem.*	23.13–39	12. 40	20. 47	
124. The Widow's mite. *Jerusalem.*	....	12.41–44	21. 1–4	

CONTENTS.	MATT.	MARK.	LUKE.	JOHN.
Sect.				
125. Certain Greeks desire to see Jesus. *Jerusalem.*	....	....	....	12.20–36
126. Reflections upon the unbelief of the Jews. *Jerusalem.*	....	....	....	12.37–50
127. Jesus, ON TAKING LEAVE OF THE TEMPLE, FORETELLS ITS DESTRUCTION AND THE PERSECUTION OF HIS DISCIPLES. *Jerusalem. Mount of Olives.*	24. 1–14	13. 1–13	21. 5–19	
128. The signs of Christ's coming to destroy Jerusalem, and put an end to the Jewish State and Dispensation. *Mount of Olives.*	24.15–42	13.14–37	21.20–36	
129. Transition to Christ's final coming at the Day of Judgment. Exhortation to watchfulness. Parables: The ten Virgins. The five Talents. *Mount of Olives.*	24.43–51 25. 1–30			
130. Scenes of the Judgment Day. *Mount of Olives.*	25.31–46			
131. The Rulers conspire. The supper at Bethany. Treachery of Judas. *Jerusalem. Bethany.*	26. 1–16	14. 1–11	22. 1–6	12. 2–8
132. Preparation for the Passover. *Bethany. Jerusalem.*	26.17–19	14.12–16	22. 7–13	

PART VIII.

THE FOURTH PASSOVER; OUR LORD'S PASSION; AND THE ACCOMPANYING EVENTS UNTIL THE END OF THE JEWISH SABBATH.

TIME: *Two Days.*

CONTENTS.	MATT.	MARK.	LUKE.	JOHN.
133. The Passover Meal. Contention among the Twelve. *Jerusalem.*	26. 20	14. 17	22.14–18, 24–30	
134. Jesus washes the feet of his disciples. *Jerusalem.*	....	....	....	13. 1–20
135. Jesus points out the Traitor. Judas withdraws. *Jerusalem.*	26.21–25	14.18–21	22.21–23	13.21–35
136. Jesus foretells the fall of Peter, and the dispersion of the Twelve. *Jerusalem.*	26.31–35	14.27–31	22.31–38	13.36–38
137. THE LORD'S SUPPER. *Jerusalem.*	26.26–29	14.22–25	22.19, 20	.
138. Jesus comforts his Disciples. THE HOLY SPIRIT PROMISED. *Jerusalem.*	....	....	....	14. 1–31
139. Christ the true Vine. His Disciples hated by the world. *Jerusalem.*	....	....	....	15. 1–27
140. Persecution foretold. Further PROMISE of the Holy Spirit. Prayer in the name of Christ. *Jerusalem.*	....	....	....	16. 1–33

SYNOPSIS OF THE HARMONY.

CONTENTS.	MATT.	MARK	LUKE.	JOHN.
Sect.				
141. Christ's last prayer with his disciples. *Jeruaslem.*	....	....	....	17. 1–26
141½. Departure to the Mount of Olives. *Mount of Olives.*	26. 30	14. 26	22.39	18. 1
142. THE AGONY IN GETHSEMANE. *Mount of Olives.*	26.36–46	14.32–42	22.40–46	
143. Jesus betrayed, and made prisoner. *Mount of Olives.*	26.47–56	14.43–52	22.47–53	18. 2–12
144. Jesus before Caiaphas. Peter thrice denies him. *Jerusalem.*	26.57,58, 69–75	14.53,54, 66–72	22.54–62	18.13-18, 25–27
145. Jesus before Caiaphas and the Sanhedrim. He declares himself to be the CHRIST; is condemned and mocked. *Jerusalem.*	26.59–68	14.55–65	22.63–71	18.19–24
146. The Sanhedrim lead Jesus away to Pilate. *Jerusalem.*	27. 1, 2	15. 1–5	23. 1–5	18.28–38
146½. Christ before the Governor. *Jerusalem.*	27.11–14			
147. Jesus before Herod. *Jerusalem.*	....	....	23. 6–12	
148. Pilate seeks to release Jesus. The Jews demand Barabbas. *Jerusalem.*	27.15–26	15. 6–15	23.13–25	18.39, 40
149. Pilate delivers up Jesus to death. He is scourged and mocked. *Jerusalem.*	27.26–30	15.15–19	....	19. 1–3
150. Pilate again seeks to release Jesus. *Jerusalem.*	....	....	....	19. 4–16
151. Judas repents and hangs himself. *Jerusalem.*	27. 3–10			
152. Jesus is led away to be crucified. *Jerusalem.*	27.31–34	15.20–23	23.26–33	19.16, 17
153. THE CRUCIFIXION. *Jerusalem.*	27.35–38	15.24–28	23.33, 34	19.18–24
154. The Jews mock at Jesus on the Cross. He commends his mother to John. *Jerusalem.*	27.39–44	15.29–32	23.35–37, 39–43	19.25–27
155. Darkness prevails. Christ EXPIRES ON THE CROSS. *Jerusalem.*	27.45–50	15.33–37	23.44–46	19.28–30
156. The vail of the Temple rent, and graves opened. Judgment of the Centurion. The Women at the Cross. *Jerusalem.*	27.51–56	15.38–41	23. 45, 47–49	
157. The taking down from the Cross. The burial. *Jerusalem.*	27.57–61	15.42–47	23.50–56	19.31–42
158 The Watch at the Sepulchre. *Jerusalem.*	27.62–66			

SYNOPSIS OF THE HARMONY.

Sect. CONTENTS.	MATT.	MARK.	LUKE.	JOHN.
PART IX.				
OUR LORD'S RESURRECTION, HIS SUBSEQUENT APPEARANCES, AND HIS ASCENSION.				
TIME: *Forty Days.*				
159. The Morning of THE RESURRECTION. *Jerusalem.*	28. 2–4	16. 1		
160. Visit of the Women to the Sepulchre. Mary Magdalene returns. *Jerusalem.*	28. 1	16. 2–4	24. 1–3	20. 1, 2
161. Vision of Angels in the Sepulchre. *Jerusalem.*	28. 5–7	16. 5–7	24. 4–8	
162. The Women return to the City. JESUS MEETS THEM. *Jerusalem.*	28. 8–10	16. 8	24. 9–11	
163. Peter and John run to the Sepulchre. *Jerusalem.*	....	....	24. 12	20. 3–10
164. Our Lord is seen by Mary Magdalene at the Sepulchre. *Jerusalem.*	....	16. 9–11	....	20.11–18
165. Report of the Watch. *Jerusalem.*	28.11–15			
166. Our Lord is seen of Peter. Then by two Disciples on the way to Emmaus. *Jerusalem. Emmaus.*	....	16.12, 13	24.13–35	
167. Jesus appears in the midst of the Apostles, Thomas being absent. *Jerusalem.*	....	16.14–18	24.36–49	20.19–23
168. Jesus appears in the midst of the Apostles, Thomas being present. *Jerusalem.*	....	....	....	20.24–29
169. The Apostles go away into Galilee. Jesus shows himself to seven of them at the Sea of Tiberias. *Galilee.*	28. 16	....	....	21. 1–24
170. Jesus meets the Apostles and above five hundred Brethren on a Mountain in Galilee. *Galilee.*	28.16–20			
171. Our Lord is seen of James; then of all the Apostles. *Jerusalem.*				
172. THE ASCENSION. *Bethany.*	....	16.19, 20	24.50–53	20.30, 31
173. Conclusion of John's Gospel.	....	....	....	21. 25

N. B.—The "A.D." in the book, at the top of the page, indicates the *year of Christ*, and not of the period called ANNO DOMINI. That period—or the common Christian era, which was introduced by Dionysius (as is supposed) about A.D. 516—is computed to have been set four years too late. So that Christ was born four years before this era begins to reckon. Confusion had often arisen from not distinctly noting this.

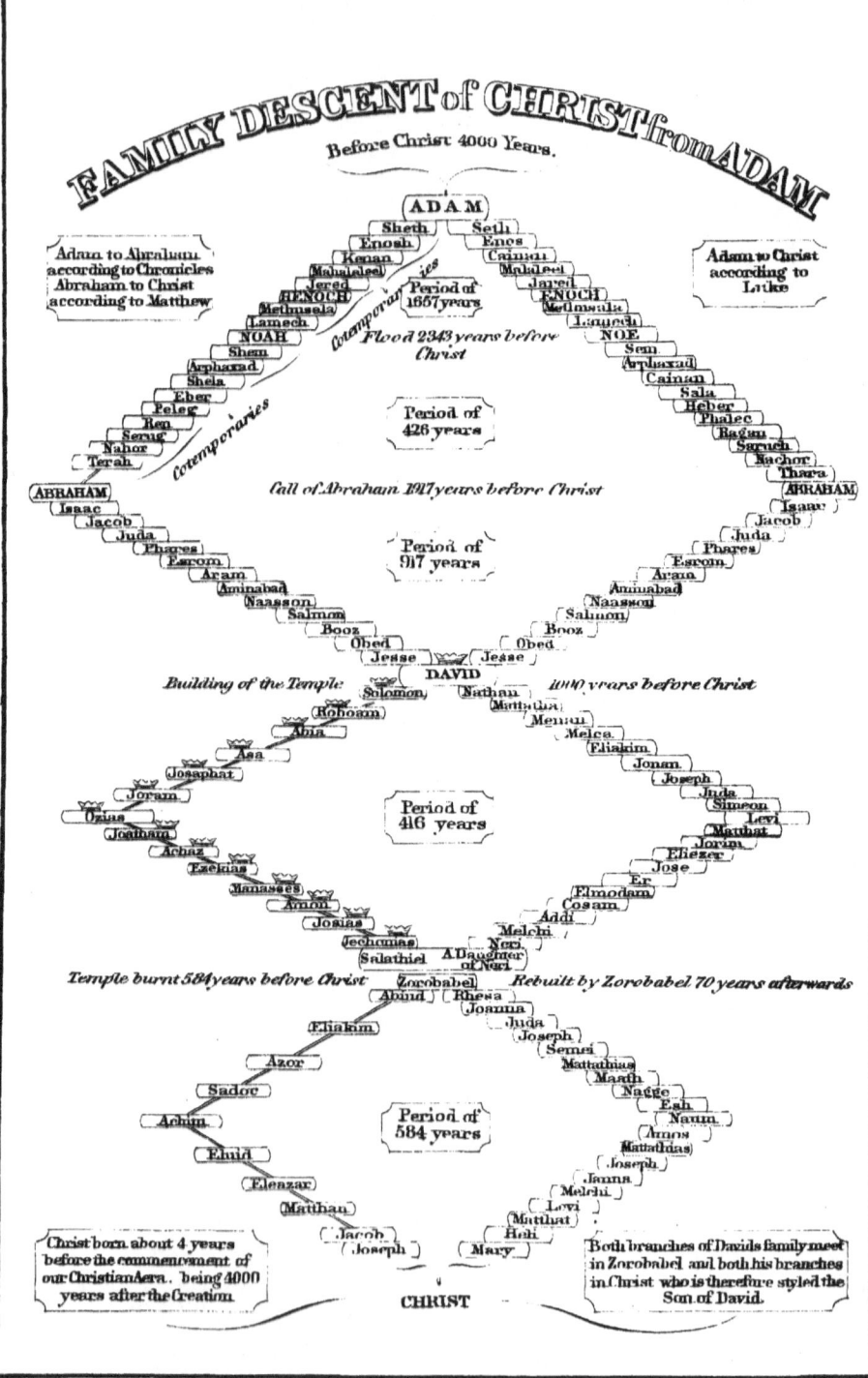

THE GOSPEL ACCORDING TO MATTHEW.

CHAPTER I.

THE book of the generation^a of Jesus Christ, the son of^b David,^c the son of Abraham.

<sub>a Lu. 3.23,&c.　b Ps. 132.11.　c. 22.45.　Ac. 2.30.
c Ge. 22.18.　Ga. 3.16.</sub>

2 Abraham^d begat Isaac; and Isaac^e begat Jacob; and Jacob^f begat Judas and his brethren.

3 And Judas begat^g Phares

_{d Ge. 21.2-5.　e Ge. 25.26.　f Ge. 29.35, &c.　g Ge. 38.29,30,&c.}

CHAPTER I.

Sections 1 to 5 inclusive, of the Gospel History are connected with the birth of John the Baptist. See Luke 1. 1-80, and see Synopsis of the Harmony.

§ 6. GENEALOGIES.

Matt.	Mark.	Luke.	John.
1. 1-17.		3. 23-38.	

1-17. *The book of the generation* is a phrase corresponding with the word genealogy. It is meant here to introduce the genealogical record by which the parentage and descent of our Lord, through Joseph, was to be shown. The Jews kept such tables, public and private, with great care, to show their families and tribes. Ezra, ch 2. Nehemiah, ch. 7. Matthew, writing his history for the Jews, aimed to show that Christ was descended from David and Abraham, their most noted and sacred names. This was most necessary for his object, which was to convince them that Christ was the true Messiah, such as they looked for—the son of Abraham, a Jew, and the son or descendant of king David, a king of David's line, according to their prophets. See v. 6. Isa. 9. 7; 11. 1. Jer. 23. 5. Matt. 9. 27; 12. 23; 15. 22; 21. 9, 15; 22. 42, 45. Luke 18. 38. Accordingly our Lord is shown to have come in the direct line of kings, as a rightful successor to the throne. See the Annunciation, Luke 1. 32, 33. So He was understood to claim this title (John 1. 49, and 19. 21), and it was written over His head at the crucifixion (John 19. 19), "The King of the Jews" Zech. 9. 9. The promise was made to David of a Son to sit perpetually on his throne, and this could be completely realized only in Christ. Compare 2 Sam. 7. 13, 14, with Heb. 1. 5. See also 1 Kings 2. 4 and 8. 25. Jer. 33. 17. Compare Acts 2. 30.

"Now to Abraham and his seed were the promises made. He saith not, And to seeds, as of many; but as of one, And to thy seed, which is Christ." Gal. 3. 16. See Gen. 22. 18.

The genealogies of Matthew and Luke differ, and we find that it is not without design. The explanations are hinted at by the evangelists themselves in their respective records. Matthew traces out the line of "Joseph, the husband of Mary" (v. 16), intimating, that because Joseph stood to Mary *in the legal relation* of husband, he would show Christ's legal descent through him according to the tables. Luke traces out the line of "*Jesus, being as was supposed the son of Joseph*" (ch. 3. 23). He intimates thus, that because Jesus was in reality the son of Mary, he would trace her parentage, as he does, through Heli her father, and Christ's natural descent through her. In Matthew, observe the language is direct, " Jacob *begat* Joseph." In Luke it is "*Jesus, being as was supposed the son of Joseph—of Heli.*" Thus Christ is traced back to David and Abraham by Matthew, for the special benefit of the Jews, and by Luke he is traced even to Adam, for the benefit of the Gentile world. By Matthew he is found to be the son of David (Isa. 11. 1), and the seed of Abraham (Gal. 3. 16), and by Luke, the seed of the woman (Gen. 3. 15), and the Son of

and Zara of Thamar; and Phares begat ʰ Esrom; and Esrom begat ⁱ Aram;

4 And Aram begat Aminadab; and Aminadab begat ʲ Naasson; and Naasson begat Salmon; ᵏ

5 And Salmon begat Booz of ˡ Rachab; and Booz begat Obed ᵐ of Ruth; and Obed begat Jesse;

6 And Jesse begat ⁿ David the king; and David the king begat ᵒ Solomon of her *that had been the wife* of Urias;

7 And Solomon begat ᵖ Roboam; and Roboam begat Abia; and Abia begat Asa;

8 And Asa begat Josaphat; and Josaphat begat Joram; and Joram begat Ozias;

9 And Ozias begat Joatham; and Joatham begat Achaz; and Achaz begat Ezekias;

10 And Ezekias ᵠ begat Manasses; and Manasses begat Amon; and Amon begat Josias;

11 And ¹ Josias begat Jechonias and his brethren, about the time they were carried away to Babylon;

12 And after they were brought to Babylon, Jechonias begat ʳ Salathiel; and Salathiel begat Zorobabel; ˢ

13 And Zorobabel begat Abiud; and Abiud begat Eliakim; and Eliakim begat Azor;

14 And Azor begat Sadoc and Sadoc begat Achim; and Achim begat Eliud;

15 And Eliud begat Eleazar; and Eleazar begat Matthan; and Matthan begat Jacob;

16 And Jacob begat Joseph the husband of Mary, of whom was born Jesus, who is called Christ.

17 So all the generations from Abraham to David *are* fourteen generations; and from David until the carrying away into

h Ge.46.12. *i* Ru.4.19. *j* 1 Ch.2.10. Nu.1.7. *k* Ru. 4.20. *l* Jos.6.25. Ru.4.21. *m* Ru.4.13. *n* 1 Sa.17.12. *o* 2 Sa.12.24. *p* 1 Ch.3.10,&c. *q* 2 Ki.20.21. 1 Ch.3.13.

1 Some read, *Josias begat Jakim, and Jakim begat Jechonias.*
r 1 Ch.3.17,&c. *s* Ne.12.1.

Man (Luke 9. 56). See Plate, that Mary is descended in a right line from Solomon. Luke 1. 32; 2. 5. Rom. 1. 3. Calvin holds this to be most important.

Jesus Christ. This is the ordinary name given in Scripture to the incarnate Son of God. Both evangelists remind us, in the genealogies, of Christ's miraculous conception. Matthew passes to it thus remarkably, "Joseph, the husband of Mary, *of whom* (that is, of Mary, for the pronoun in the Greek is feminine) was born Jesus, who is called Christ." (v. 16.) And Luke has it in equally striking terms, "Jesus being, *as was supposed*, the Son of Joseph, &c. *Jesus* is a proper name (v. 21); and *Christ* is an official title, meaning, "the *Anointed.*" Acts 2. 36. It corresponds with the Hebrew word *Messiah.* This name, therefore, asserts the Messiahship of Jesus. And all the functions of that office were associated in the mind of the Jew with *anointing*, by which their kings and priests were consecrated, or set apart. See Psalm 45. 7. Isa. 61. 1.

The son of David, the son of Abraham, means the *descendant* of these. So Joseph is called in v. 20, "Thou *son of David.*" But David's greater son was Christ.

17. *Fourteen generations.* "In the first fourteen generations, the people of Israel were under prophets; in the second, under kings; in the third, under the Asmonean princes. The first fourteen brought their kingdom to glory under the reign of David; the second, to misery, in the captivity of Babylon; and the third, to glory again under the Messiahship of Christ. The

Babylon *are* fourteen generations; and from the carrying away into Babylon unto Christ *are* fourteen generations.

18 Now the birth† of Jesus Christ was on this wise: When

† Lu.1.27,&c.

as his mother Mary was espoused to Joseph,* before they came together, she was found with child of the Holy Ghost.

19 Then Joseph her husband, being a just *man*, and not wil-

* 5th year before the account called *A. D.*

---

first division begins with Abraham, who received the promise, and ends with David, who received it again with greater clearness. The second begins with the building of the temple, and ends with its destruction. The third opens with a deliverance from temporal enemies and return from captivity, and terminates in their spiritual delivery from every enemy by Christ, to whom each successive generation pointed as the Prophet, King, and Priest of His people."— Townsend's Arrangement of N. T. Lightfoot, 1. 418.

§ 7. AN ANGEL APPEARS TO JOSEPH.—
Nazareth.

| Matt. | Mark. | Luke. | John. |
| 1. 18-25. | | | |

18. *On this wise*—thus.——¶ *His mother Mary.* She is spoken of also in Matt. 2.11, 13, 14, 20, 21; in Luke 1. 22—and 1. 43 the salutation of Elizabeth, which explains itself—Luke 2. 39, 48 and 51, on occasion of their visit to Jerusalem at the Passover—in John 2. 1, at the marriage of Cana in Galilee— in Matt. 12. 46, and in John 19. 25, 26, when she stood at the cross. But no where is she mentioned as entitled to worship. She is no where called in Scripture, the Virgin Mary, as a title or worshipful name. We have no account of any peculiar honours being paid her earlier than the 5th century. Luke 1. 28, is the usual form of salutation, employed by the angel (see Judges 5. 24), in reference to the announcement he was about to make. As to invoking her mediation, it is expressly declared in Scripture, that there is one Mediator, 1 Tim. 2. 5, the man Christ Jesus (1 John 2, 1). See also Matt. 4. 10. Rev. 19. 10. And God alone is the proper object of religious worship. Exodus 20. 3. In Acts 1. 14, after the ascension, she appears with the disciples as one of the social worshippers in the upper room at Jerusalem, waiting for the promise of the Father. The wise men found Mary, his mother, with the child, at Bethlehem, but they worshipped only the child, ch. 2. 11.——¶ *Espoused*— pledged to be married. They were bound, by this, as man and wife, among the Jews. Deut. 20. 7; 22. 25, 28. And the espousal or pledge was made usually ten or twelve months before marriage. (Gen. 24. 55, margin.) Judges 14. 8.——¶ *Before they came together.* The virgin had not yet been delivered by her parents to her husband, but still remained under their roof. The marriage ceremony had not yet taken place; and as yet Joseph knew her not (v. 25). In these circumstances "she was found with child." And it is here stated that this was "*of the Holy Ghost*," according to the angel's announcement. Luke 1. 26, 28. The most virtuous will be liable to unjust suspicion, and to undeserved reproach.

19. *Joseph her husband*—" being a *just one*," literally. This is in reference to the law. The old Wicklif version reads *righteous*. Being a strict observer of the rites of his nation, he was unwilling to company with a woman who seemed to have been defiled. He was not a man disposed to connive at sin, and yet he was inclined to avail himself of a provision in the law for having her disgrace private. He was not willing to make her case one of publicity, and of prosecution as an adulteress. Deut. 22. 23, 24. Lev. 20. 10. Ezek. 16. 38, 40. John 8. 5. Good men, we see, are liable to form erroneous judgments of others' character and conduct.——¶ *To put her*

22 MATTHEW. [A. M. 4000

ling to make her a public example, was minded ᵘ to put her away privily.

20 But while he thought on these things, behold, the angel of the Lord appeared unto him in a ᵛ dream, saying, Joseph, thou son of David, fear not to take unto thee Mary thy wife; for that which is ¹ conceived in her is of the Holy Ghost.

21 And she shall bring forth a son, and thou shalt call his name ² JESUS: for he shall

---

ᵘ De. 24. 1.　ᵛ ver. 16.　　　¹ Begotten.　² i. e., Saviour.

---

away privily (or privately)—to give her a bill of divorce, in private (Deut. 24. 1), delivering it into her hand or bosom, as was the custom. In such case, two witnesses only were necessary; and they witnessed only the act of divorce, and need not know the reason. We should always judge charitably, and choose lenient rather than severe measures, where there is the least room for doubt.

20. *But while he thought, &c.* Here God interposed, at the very critical moment, so as to secure satisfaction to Joseph, and to shield the reputation of Mary.——¶ *The angel of the Lord.* This definite reference is naturally to the angel Gabriel, who had officiated in this matter, announcing the birth to Mary (Luke 1. 26–28).——¶ *Appeared*—manifested himself to Joseph as being from God, so as at least *to leave him in no doubt* of the message being from heaven. Our necessity is God's opportunity. When we are anxiously seeking out our duty, God will show us the way.——¶ *In a dream.* This was a common method of divine communication under the Old Testament (Gen. 31. 24. 1 Kings 3. 5), before the full revelation of God had come to us in the Scriptures. We have no right to suppose that there is any such communication now. A superstitious faith in dreams has led to many mischievous results. The scriptural explanation is, that "a dream cometh through the multitude of business." Eccles. 5. 3. To receive new revelations, as those of Swedenborg, is to set aside the authority of Scripture. "*Filthy dreamers*" (Jude 8) will only multiply, and still demand our faith.——¶ *Thou son of David.* " He was of the house and lineage of David." Luke 2. 4. The angel calls Joseph by this title as *emphatically* a descendant of David, in the relation he was to bear to Christ. This address would open his mind to receive the astounding declaration that follows. It is not improbable that Joseph and Mary were the only survivors of David's race; for though they had relatives, yet these, as far as the record informs us, were intermixed with other families and tribes in Israel; and if so, Jesus was the only remaining sprout of the root of Jesse.—Davidson's Connection, Vol. iii. p. 21. ——¶ *Fear not*—of being implicated in any crime; *for* (compare Luke 1. 35) the truth of the case makes her innocent and you honoured.

21. *And she shall bring forth.* The angel now announces both the future birth, and the name appointed for the Son by divine authority. *Jesus* means *Saviour.* In Hebrew the name Joshua means the same thing; and hence, in Acts 7. 45, and Heb. 4. 8, our translation reads *Jesus*, where it should read *Joshua*, i. e., the leader of the Jews into Canaan. The name was given for the reason stated here.——¶ *For He shall save His people.* This shall be His office work, and this is His design in coming into the world. His people are such as are given to Him by the Father (John 6. 37; 17. 6). They are elsewhere called His chosen. 1 Pet. 2. 9. His elect, Mark 13. 20. His children, 1 John 3. 10. A peculiar people, Tit. 2. 14. The Jews were known of old as the people of God. They were chosen by Him, and separated from the nations — regarded and treated as His. Comp. Deut. 14. 2 and 1 Pet. 2. 9. So, Christ's people now are such as belong to Him by the

save ʷ his people from their sins.

22 Now all this was done, that it might be fulfilled which was spoken of the Lord by the prophet, ˣ saying,

23 Behold, a virgin shall be with child, and shall bring forth a son, and ¹ they shall call his name Emmanuel; which being interpreted, is, God ʸ with us.

w Ac.5.31; 13.23,38.   *x* Is.7.14.

1 Or, *his name shall be called.*   *y* Jno.1.14.

Father's gift, John 6. 37, and by His own redemption. 1 Pet. 1. 18, 21. These He shall securely save.—— ¶ *From their sins.* We are lost by sin. He saves His people from the curse of sin, and from its controlling power (Rom. ch. 6). This he does, by making a complete atonement, such as brings a free pardon and saves from the condemnation of sin (1 Pet. 3. 18); and by providing such an operation of the Holy Ghost in the heart, as subdues sin and removes it. John 15. 16; 16. 13.

22. *That it might be fulfilled.* It is here expressly declared, that this event was brought about in fulfilment of Isaiah's prophecy (7. 14), and in order to fulfil it. Of course the prophecy must have contemplated this event, and could not have had a complete fulfilment short of it. Ahaz refused to ask a sign as to the deliverance then at hand. But a sign was given. And, observe, it was *given to the "house of David"* (that is, the Jewish nation), and for a remoter purpose (see Isaiah 7. 13). A miraculous birth is evidently referred to, in the language of the prophet, "*A virgin, &c.*" And here there was thrown in, for the Jewish people, a remarkable prediction of Christ, that should stand on record to confirm His claims. As to Ahaz, it was quite sufficient to indicate the *interval* of the deliverance; viz., the time of a child's minority. This could be shown in the case of any child, and was sufficiently indicated in the general terms, without any further sign to him, saving the fare of " butter (or curds) and honey," as signifying the state of the land, waste and uncultivated, until that deliverance. Besides, a promise of Christ to the Jews, was always a constructive pledge or sign that the nation should be delivered and not destroyed, since the Jews held that they existed as a nation for the Messiah's sake. From the prophet Micah (5. 2, 3) it is plain that some virgin birth was expected, as a miraculous fulfilment of Isaiah's prediction.——¶ *A virgin.* This explains to Joseph her supposed adultery. The prophet had distinctly declared the virginity of our Lord's mother. Hence, it was to be understood as a purely miraculous event. Yet why impossible, any more than the creation of Adam or Eve? "A body hast thou prepared me," saith Christ, when He cometh into the world (Heb. 10. 5). There is no good ground for the Romish tenet of Mary's perpetual virginity. The last verse of this chapter goes to contradict it. Besides, Christ is called her *first-born*, and this is a term commonly used to indicate the primogeniture, and in such connexion implies the order of birth, with reference to other children (Gen. 27. 32). Besides, the brethren and sisters of our Lord are spoken of. Mark 6. 3. Matt. 12. 46. " James, the Lord's brother." Gal. 1. 19.——¶ *Emmanuel.* This is the Hebrew name from the prophecy. It means, literally, *God with us.* In this sense, this must have been the fulfilment to which the prophecy ultimately looked. This referred Joseph more distinctly to the miracle as the explanation. So it directly proves the union of the divine and human natures in Christ.—— ¶ *They shall call his name;* i. e., this shall be His nature and character. He shall be *God with us.* The force of the phrase includes this; as in Isa. 9. 6. " His name shall be called Wonderful." Christ is the God-man prophesied as to come. " The Word was made flesh." John 1. 14. This incarnation is the grand sign of deliver-

24 Then Joseph, being raised from sleep, did as the angel of the Lord had bidden him, and took unto him his wife:

25 And knew her not till she had brought forth her first-born ᶻ

z Ex.13.2. a Lu.2.21.

son: and he called his name JESUS.ᵃ

CHAPTER II.

NOW when Jesus was born* in Bethlehem of Judea, in the days of Herod the king, be-

* 4th year before the account called A. D.

---

ance to His people, and the divine explanation of all that is miraculous in Christ's birth, or wonderful in Himself or in His work. If we are united to Christ by faith, says Calvin, we possess God. Jesus Christ is God equally with the Father.

24. Joseph is here represented as at once assured in faith and prompt in obedience. He could believe the divine message, though he had nothing for it but God's word. Hence, his convictions and purposes were entirely changed, and cheerfully he enters upon the course divinely prescribed.

This is the faith of the Gospel. In all this, Joseph showed the temper of every true Christian. Believing is followed by repentance, and instant obedience is the proper mark of sincerity.

25. *Knew her not till, &c.* The perpetual virginity of Mary finds no warrant here. It is meant here to be asserted, that Christ was not Joseph's own son; and it is *implied*, that Joseph had children afterward.——¶ *Jesus.* This name was given by direction of God, v. 21, and on the eighth day, Luke 2. 21.

	Matt.	Mark.	Luke.	John.
§ 8. The Birth of Jesus.—*Bethlehem*..................	....	....	2. 1-7	
§ 9. An Angel appears to the Shepherds.—*Near Bethlehem*..	....	....	2. 8-20	
§ 10. The Circumcision of Jesus.—*Bethlehem*....... His presentation in the Temple.—*Jerusalem*..	....	....	2. 21-38	
CHAPTER II. § 11. *The* **Magi,** *or* **Wise Men.**—*Jerusalem, Bethlehem.*	2. 1-12			

1-12. *When Jesus was born.* (See Luke 2. 1-20, and note also the intermediate events, §§ 8, 9, and 10, in the Harmony.)——¶ *Bethlehem of Judea*—a town six miles southward from Jerusalem, on the road to Hebron. It was generally called Bethlehem-judah, so designated to distinguish it from a Bethlehem in Galilee, tribe of Zebulon. Hither Joseph and Mary had come up from Nazareth, at the decree of the Roman emperor, Augustus, to be taxed (or enrolled), Luke 2. 1-7, for they were of the house and lineage of David, and they belonged to Bethlehem in the family registry, as David was born there. The name Beth-

lehem means, literally, "house of bread," and was so called, perhaps, on account of the fertility there, which travellers describe as being remarkable. A more sacred reference we may find in "that Bread of Life" (John 6. 48) having been there brought forth. This place was called, also, the city of David, because it was David's birth-place (1 Sam. 16. 18), "a son of Jesse, the Bethlehemite."——¶ *In the days of Herod, the king.* This civil condition of things at Christ's birth, was as important to be noticed as the place—both as in fulfilment of prophecy. This Herod was a foreigner, and made

A. D. 1.] CHAPTER II. 25

hold, there came wise men from the east to Jerusalem,

2 Saying, Where is he that is born ᵇ King of the Jews? for we have seen his ᶜ star in the east, and are come to ᵈ worship him.

b Ze.9.9. *c* Nu.24.17. Is.60.3. *d* Jno.5.23.

king by the Romans, who now held the Jews in subjection. And in him was fulfilled Jacob's prophecy. Gen. 49. 10. But the sceptre had not departed from Judah, until the Shiloh had come. Herod was the son of Antipater. He was now established in the kingdom of Judea, which had been over sixty years under the Roman power. Augustus was emperor of Rome, and this Herod had now reigned, though in dependence on the Roman government, about thirty-four years. Now the decree from Rome for an enrollment of the people, as tributary to the foreign power, was a mark of their actual subjection. Cæsar's penny showed their subserviency. Matt. 22. 20. (See Luke 2. 1.) Herod had gained a character for bravery and cruelty, while he had restored Jerusalem to much of its ancient magnificence by his splendid projects. He was called "the Great," and it was he who had repaired the temple, so as to give it much of its former glory.——¶ *Wise men.* Wicklif's version, 1380, reads "*astromyens*" (or *astronomers*), also called *magi* from the Greek term *magoi*, whence also our word *magicians.* These men were of an ancient and sacred order, the most influential in the civil, religious, and literary world. Among the Medes, they were, like the Levites under the Mosaic institutions, intrusted with the care of religion. They had also the arts and sciences, and all philosophy under their charge. They paid much attention to astronomy. Their name denotes their priestly character. (Mag, or Mog, in the Pehlvi, denotes priest.) This Magian learning was known in history as the law of the Medes and Persians. It was a necessary part of a princely education to be taught in their learning; and this was the privilege of none but kings. They were spread over other eastern countries. Such are spoken of in Daniel 1. 20, &c., as "*magicians and astrologers,*"—different classes of this order. See Daniel 2. 18. Their visit here may be regarded as an homage paid by the highest order in the world, to the *day-star* risen upon earth. In this was immediately fulfilled the prediction of Malachi, "From *the rising of the sun* (or the East), even unto the going down of the same, my name shall be great among the Gentiles," &c. (Mal. 1. 11). So, Isa. 60. 3, "The Gentiles shall come to thy light, and kings to the brightness of thy rising."
——¶ *The east.* Oriental countries, are generally understood by this term. East of Judea is here meant. From the land of the Chaldees whence Abraham was called, they may have come. Jer. 1. 35. Dan. 2. 12.——¶ *To Jerusalem.* Because here was the temple; and this was the holy city; and here were the sacred oracles and officers from whom they could ascertain the prophecies. It might appear that they had derived their knowledge of "the *King of the Jews*" from the Jewish Scriptures, or from scattered Jews, who had so far informed them of the expected Messiah. But how then did they know the star, and not know where He should be born? Though a general expectation was spread abroad, that some great King should arise in Judea, yet this would not account for their amount of information. Virgil, who lived a little before this, owns that a child from Heaven was looked for, who should restore the golden age, and take away sin. But these Magi were moved, doubtless, by a divine impulse. They received special illumination and direction from Heaven, leading them to follow the star, and to inquire at Jerusalem. A revelation from God is not enough of itself. The Spirit must lead us to seek Christ, and direct us to the spot.

2. *We have seen his star.* Though

3 When Herod the king had heard *these things*, he was troubled, and all Jerusalem with him.

4 And when he had gathered [e] all the chief priests and scribes of the people together, he demanded of them where Christ should be born.

[e] Ps. 2. 2.

---

a comet, or eclipse, or meteor, was regarded as the portent of some great event, yet we do not read of any such general impression made by this singular appearance. Hence, we conclude that it was a sign granted to these. They were otherwise "*warned of God*" afterward. (See v. 12.) Around the shepherds shone "the glory of the Lord." To the wise men rose this "star," which they were assured of as "*His.*" To Saul of Tarsus "a light beyond the brightness of the sun" appeared at mid-day. We do not read of others going to Jerusalem, attracted by this sight in the sky. Yet it was a powerful revelation to *these*, bringing them from the East, the representatives of the highest earthly order. Balaam had prophesied of Christ (Numbers 24. 17), "There shall come a star out of Jacob," &c.; and this sign they saw. An expectation was abroad that a mighty king should arise in Judea; and doubtless such a prophecy was current, as the ground of it, among the Jews. Kepler has calculated that a remarkable conjunction of Jupiter and Saturn occurred about that time. But such a sight seems not to suit the narrative. They made themselves known as visitants and inquirers from the oriental world. "We, in the East, have seen his star." Herein was a testimony to the Jews at Jerusalem, that the Messiah had indeed come. The star was a token to the Magi. The visit of the Magi was a token to the Jews. Christ must be revealed to the soul by His appropriate marks, or we shall never set out after Him.—— ¶ *To worship Him.* The word refers rather to a civil homage (Luke 14. 10), than to a religious act, though it may include both. It means to acknowledge and honour Him as King, by prostration before Him, and by presents. This was the custom of that day, in paying homage to kings. They saw *His star*, and sought for *Him.* We should not be content with anything short of Christ himself. It has been calculated by Benson, that they came from the thirty-ninth to the forty-second day after the birth of Jesus.

3. *When Herod the king had heard, &c.* Their visit and inquiry were soon made known to Herod. He was startled and troubled, because all this confirmed to him the general expectation. And such a royal advent was the peril of his throne. He was himself "king of the Jews." Besides, he was now about seventy years old. He had reached the throne through violence and blood. He had murdered his wife, Mariamne, and two of his sons, and he had reason to expect retribution. The alarm was general. All Jerusalem, it might be said, was troubled with him. Some feared new upturnings, with the slaughter and confusion of revolutionary times. Some dreaded the rapacity and malice of Herod, which might break out by this means.

4. *The chief priests and scribes.* The Sanhedrim was composed of these. It was the court of highest civil and ecclesiastical authority among the Jews; and this body of seventy was doubtless appealed to in this important case. The scribes, who were lawyers of the Mosaic code, kept the public records, and were writers or scribes of the Scriptures, besides being teachers or schoolmasters, called "doctors of the law." Being most familiar with all the Jewish Scriptures, they would be able at once to tell where the prophecies had appointed the birth of Christ. The class of *chief priests* included, besides the acting High Priest, all that had already acted as such, besides the heads or chiefs of the twenty-four courses into

5 And they said unto him, In Bethlehem of Judea: for thus it is written ᶠ by the prophet;

6 And thou Bethlehem, *in* the land of Juda, art not the least among the princes of Juda: for out of thee shall come a governor, that shall ¹ rule ᵍ my people Israel.

7 Then Herod, when he had privily called the wise men, inquired of them diligently what time the star appeared.

8 And he sent them to Bethle-

hem; and said, Go and search diligently for the young child; and when ye have found *him*, bring me word again, that I may come ʰ and worship him also.

9 When they had heard the king, they departed: and, lo, the star, which they saw ⁱ in the east, went before them, till it came and stood over where the young child was.

10 When they saw the star, they ʲ rejoiced with exceeding great joy.

f Mi.5.2. Jno.7.42. 1 Or, *feed.* Is.40.11. *g* Re.2.27.   *h* Pro. 26.24. *i* ver. 2. *j* Ps.67.4.

---

which the priesthood had been divided by David (2 Chron. 8. 14). The Jews looked for Christ at this time—but as a temporal king.——¶ *Demanded.* Inquired, or required to know. All the circumstances forced conviction on his mind of Christ's having come. He wished to act promptly in his cruel designs against such a rival. Hence he would know where Christ could be found.

5. They replied immediately and distinctly, and cited their authority from the Scripture.

6. They refer to Micah, 5. 2, sufficiently to inform him of the place, as "Bethlehem in the land of Judah." This was the point; and as to the rest of the passage, only the substance of the prophet's words is given, or need be, viz., That this town, though small in civil distinction—"though thou be little among the thousands (princes) of Judah"—should be highly honoured as the birth-place of the Messiah—the Ruler of Israel—the King of the Jews. The term "thousands," refers to the civil divisions of the tribes into *thousands*," 1 Sam. 10. 19; and "princes" were the chiefs or rulers of these.

7, 8. Herod now summoned the wise men *privily*, (that is, privately,) not willing to show his anxiety, or to produce political agitation. He took secret counsel of them—inquiring diligently (sparing no pains to discover

of them), as to the time of the star's appearance. His object was to infer the age of the child; for his dreadful plot was to make sure its destruction, by destroying all the children within or about that age.——¶ *Search diligently.* He would feign now to fall in with their devout purpose of finding the child; and he even pretends to wish an opportunity of worshipping also. But he wished to lay violent hands upon him. God saw and heard these plans of Herod, and He knows all the secret devices of iniquity, and all the motives and purposes of every heart.

9. *They departed.* It is not likely that they were led by the star to Jerusalem. They went to the holy city because they were warned of God so to do, or because they knew that this was the place to inquire, as the seat of the Jewish religion. And behold, the token, whatever it was, that first appeared to them, now unexpectedly re-appeared, and moved perceptibly on, till it took a marked station over tne very house. It was all a peculiar arrangement to suit the case. It must have been near the earth to indicate the dwelling, and yet it could not have appeared to others as it did to them. It was most important that they should be notified of the house, because they could not have ascertained that from any inquiries. God's directions are

MATTHEW. [A. D. 1.

11 And when they were come into the house, they saw the young child with Mary his mother, and fell down, and worshipped him: and when they had opened their treasures, they ¹ presented unto him ᵏ gifts; gold, and frankincense, and myrrh.

<small>1 Or, *offered*. k Ps.72.10. Is.60.6.</small>

12 And being warned of God ˡ in a dream that they should not return to Herod, they departed into their own country another way.

13 And when they were departed, behold, the angel of the Lord appeareth to Joseph in a dream, saying, Arise, and take

<small>l c.1.20.</small>

---

most particular, and as definite as the case requires.

10. *They rejoiced.* This was, most of all, a revelation to their souls, and it filled them with joy. Every indication of God's guidance is a source of joy to his followers. The same mark that had been given them at first, was again vouchsafed, and they were doubly assured. "Then shall we know if ye follow on to know the Lord."

11. *Fell down.* This was the attitude of homage to kings—pros-

tiation before them. (Esther 8. 3.) "Mary his mother" only is named, to show that Joseph's relation was not that of an own father. Yet, though they saw "the child and his mother," they worshipped only the child! They never thought of "*the virgin Mary*" as an object of worship. The mother is mentioned only to identify the child —the seed of the woman—the Emmanuel of *virgin birth.*——¶ *Gifts.* This was customary homage to a prince. See 1 Sam. 10. 27. 1 Kings 10. 2. They treated this babe of Bethlehem, though so obscurely born, as a royal child. These articles were presented as the most valuable products of the country, or as the most appropriate gifts. They were such as the Queen of Sheba presented to Solomon. Here was incense and a pure offering.

(Mal. 1. 11.)——¶ *Gold.* To devote our wealth to the Lord, is a proper act of worship, and should never be considered a mean service for the sanctuary.——¶ *Frankincense.* A gum from the trunk of a tree, obtained by slitting the bark. It was used for incense in worship, and is very fragrant when burned. Levit. 16. 12. It was found chiefly in Arabia.—— ¶ *Myrrh* was obtained in the same way, though it sometimes dropped from the tree. It was valued mainly for embalming the dead. John 19. 39. We should offer Christ our best gifts. "Let all that are round about Him bring presents."

12. *Warned of God.* They had a special direction from God in vision, to keep aloof from Herod and from his plans. He expected them to return by way of Jerusalem (vs. 8). Such a revelation they doubtless had of Christ's birth at first, of which the star was only confirmatory. How faithfully God takes care of his children, and baffles the counsels of the wicked.

§ 12. THE FLIGHT INTO EGYPT. HEROD'S CRUELTY. THE RETURN.— *Bethlehem. Nazareth.*

Matt.	Mark.	Luke.	John.
2. 13–23.		2. 39–40.	

13. *Appeareth to Joseph.* It is not said whether the wise men saw him at all. He is kept back in the history, as sustaining no important part in an evangelical view. Yet he was the husband of Mary, and he would be necessary to lead their flight. Egypt was within three or four days' reach

A. D. 2.] CHAPTER II. 29

the young child and his mother, and flee into Egypt, and be thou there until I bring thee word: for Herod ᵐ will seek the young child, to destroy him.

14 When he arose, he took the young child and his mother by night, and departed into Egypt:

15 And was there until the death of Herod, that it might be fulfilled which was spoken of the Lord by the prophet, saying, ⁿ Out of Egypt have I called my son.

16 Then Herod, when he saw that he was mocked of the wise men, was exceeding wroth, and sent forth, and slew all the children that were in Bethlehem, and in all the coasts thereof, from two years old and under, according to the time which he had diligently inquired º of the wise men.

17 Then was fulfilled that which was spoken by Jeremy ᵖ the prophet, saying,

18 In Rama was there a voice

m Job 33.15,17. *n* Hos.11.1.   *o* Ver.7. *p* Je.31.15.

---

of Joseph's family, S. W. of Bethlehem, and yet it was out of Herod's jurisdiction, and many Jews were living there. Besides, it was the land where Abraham and Sarah had been saved from Pharaoh (Gen. 13. 1); where Jacob had taken refuge from famine, and Joseph had saved the holy seed (Gen. ch. 45); where Israel had been oppressed by Pharaoh, and whence they had set out under Moses for the promised land (Exod. 5. 6, and 12. 41).

15. *Until the death of Herod.* Herod died a most remarkable and loathsome death (Josephus' Antiq. 17. 10), in evident visitation of God, and about the thirty-seventh year of his reign. It is not probable that the family of Joseph remained more than a year in Egypt. The child was clearly under two years when Herod sought his life. He waited a sufficient time for the return of the wise men, and died soon after the brutal massacre of the infants. The whole occurred likely within about two years. "The wicked is driven away in his wickedness." Prov. 14. 32.——
¶ *That it might be fulfilled.* Though this prophecy, in Hosea 11. 1, was applicable originally to the Exodus of Israel from Egypt, yet it had also a reference to this event, viz., the Exodus of Christ from Egypt. The events are to be regarded as one in the plan of Jehovah, for preserving His church and defeating its oppressors. And Israel's departure out of Egypt foreshadowed the subsequent departure of Christ, so that in the mind of the Spirit dictating the record, they could both be couched under the same prophecy. How marvellously God's plans are fulfilled, while those of his enemies are frustrated.

16. *Mocked.* Foiled—baffled in this plot. He now devised another method, prompted by his rage at this vexatious disappointment. He determined now to make sure of destroying Christ, by putting to death all the male children in all the region, or coasts, from two years old and under, as he understood this child to be within two years of age.——¶ *According to the time.* So he had calculated from all that he could ascertain of the wise men. He took the time of the star's appearing, and reckoned the interval since. Bethlehem had about two thousand inhabitants in and around the village, and Townsend calculates that about fifty infants were slain.

17. *Then was fulfilled, &c.* This event was in fulfilment of the prophecy in Jer. 31. 15, and 40. 1. It is not a mere accommodation of the language. The first and immediate reference was, indeed, to another event. But this more remote occurrence was included also. Like lights far off and in a row, the distant objects could be re-

heard, lamentation, and weeping, and great mourning, Rachel weeping *for* her children, and would not be comforted, because they are not.

19 But when Herod was dead, behold, an angel of the Lord appeareth in a dream to Joseph in Egypt,

20 Saying, Arise, and take the young child and his mother, and go into the land of Israel: for they are dead q which sought the young child's life.

21 And he arose, and took the young child and his mother, and came into the land of Israel.

22 But when he heard that Ar-

q Ex.4.19.

---

ferred to as one. At Rama, a small town six miles north of Jerusalem, the Jewish captives were gathered in chains after the conquest of Jerusalem by Nebuzar-adan. The town was in Benjamin—and Rachel, the mother of Benjamin, is depicted by Jeremiah—himself a chained captive among them—as rising from her grave, which was between Bethel and Bethlehem (Gen. 35. 16), and weeping for her children or descendants—refusing consolation because of their death. The prophet is made to use language which should contain also a reference to this sad event. Both calamities were full of wo for the Jewish people, and the Holy Ghost referred to both in one. How comprehensive is God's foreknowledge, "who declares the end from the beginning, and from ancient times the things that are not yet done" (Isa. 46. 10). Are not these slaughtered innocents the first martyrs for Christ?

19. See note, v. 15. Herod had died, and it was now safe for the family to return. Joseph is so instructed by an angel. All his path is under direction of God, and under guardianship of angels (Psalm 91). It seems likely that Herod's son, Antipater, had shared in the father's malicious designs, but Herod had put him to death a few days before his own decease. How the families of the wicked are swept away! "The name of the wicked shall rot." *See cuts below.*

20. God had promised him word (v. 13). Joseph accordingly returned to the holy land, or land of Israel, but not to Judea.

21. See Map.

22, 23. *Archelaus.* Herod had made

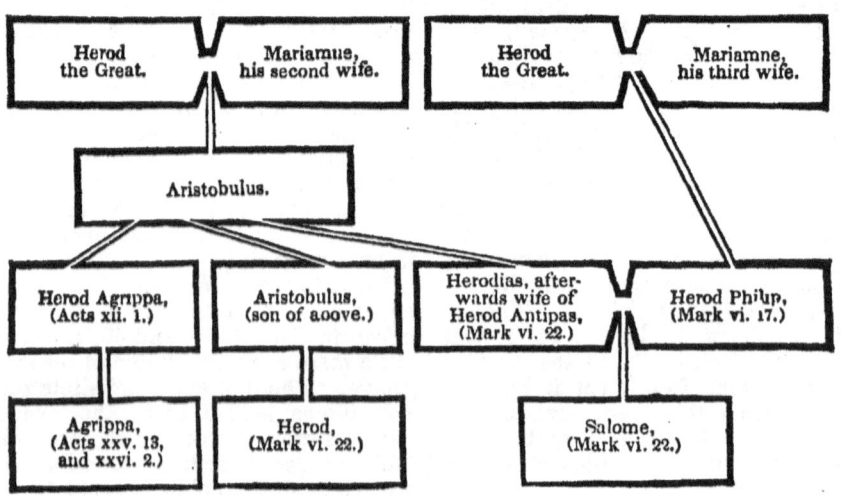

[A.D. 3.] CHAPTER II. 31

chelaus did reign in Judea in the room of his father Herod, he was afraid to go thither: notwithstanding, being warned of God in a dream, he turned aside into the parts of *r* Galilee:

r c.3.13. Lu.2.39.

23 And he came and dwelt in a city called *s* Nazareth : that it might be fulfilled which was spoken by the prophets, He shall be called a Nazarene.*t*

s Jno.1.45. *t* Nu.6.13. Ju.13.5. 1 Sa.1.11. Am.2. 10-12. Ac.24.5.

his surviving sons heirs to his kingdom. They were called Herod also, and are so known in Scripture. To Herod *Antipas* fell Galilee and Perea. To Herod *Archelaus* fell Judea, Samaria, and Idumea. Joseph heard of this Archelaus, upon the throne in Judea, resembling his father in cruelty—having slaughtered three thousand persons at the first passover after Herod's death— and *he was afraid* to go within his juriodiction. While in this perplexity he was specially directed by God, and turned aside into the parts or country of Galilee, where Herod Antipas reigned, who was a milder prince, and under whom Joseph could feel more secure. Galilee was the northern section of Palestine, Samaria being the middle, and Judea the south. See Map, and Bible Dictionary.—¶ *Nazareth* was the place of Mary's former residence (Luke 1. 26). This naturally influenced Joseph's course, and thither he would naturally have gone. Yet for this he had a higher direction, and a reason that had needs be stated here, to show the constant perils and persecutions of the holy child. Nazareth was a town in the lower part of Galilee, about sixty miles N. from Bethlehem. It was an obscure and despised place, which led Nathanael to ask, "Can there any good thing come out of Nazareth?" John 1. 46. And hence, Christ being a Nazarene, it is noted by way of reproach, as fulfilling not any one prophecy, but the substance of them all—"A reproach of men, and despised of the people." Psalm 22. 6. Isa. 53. 2, 3, 4. "Jesus of Nazareth' was used as a title of contempt; and Matthew, writing for the Jews, brings out the Old Testament points, and the ample fulfilment of their prophetic Scriptures. Here, at Nazareth, our Lord remained till he was about twenty-nine years old, in comparative obscurity; and then, at thirty, entered upon His public ministry. Six months previously, John the Baptist appeared as His herald and forerunner, to which our evangelist now passes, in chapter 3. Meanwhile, Luke records an intermediate event.

§ 13. At twelve years of age Jesus goes to the Passover.—*Jerusalem*.

Matt.	Mark.	Luke.	John.
		2. 41-52.	

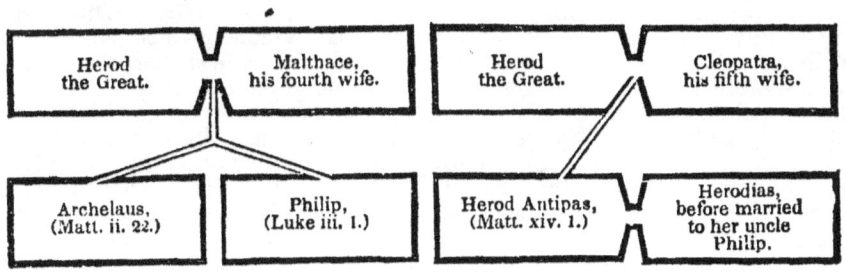

CHAPTER III.

IN those days came ᵃ John the Baptist, preaching in the wilderness of Judea,

a Lu.3.2. Jno.1.18.

PART II.

Announcement and Introduction of our Lord's Public Ministry.

Time, about one year.

§ 14. THE MINISTRY OF JOHN THE BAPTIST.—*The Desert. Jordan.*

| Matt. | Mark. | Luke. | John. |
| 3. 1-12. | 1. 1-8. | 3. 1-18. | |

CHAPTER III.

1. *In those days.* This phrase hints to the reader, that a long interval of time is passed over in the history, as unimportant to be noticed. This covers the period of Christ's minority, which He spent at Nazareth, following His father Joseph's trade of carpenter (compare Matt. 13. 55 with Mark 6. 3), and attracting no special public notice, save in the visit to Jerusalem and the temple, at *twelve years of age.* (§ 13.) This was the period fixed, by common consent, as the age of discretion with males, when Jewish youth became "sons of commandment," and were bound to the observances of the ceremonial law. The object of the evangelists was to record Christ's public ministry. Hence they pass over a period of some seventeen years altogether—from his twelfth to his twenty-ninth. And Matthew here skips a space of over twenty-five years—from the return from Egypt until the public appearance of John the Baptist. Luke gives the time from the national data (ch. 3. 1). These events are connected with civil history. John was six months older than Jesus. For an account of his parentage and birth, see Luke, ch. 1. His parents were Zacharias and Elizabeth. He was called "the Baptist," because this was his office, as distinct from Christ's—baptizing and preaching the baptism of repentance for the

2 And saying, Repent ye: for the kingdom of heaven is at hand.

3 For this is he that was spoken

remission of sins. Mark 1. 4. Paul distinguishes the two offices, 1 Cor. 1. 17, "Christ sent me not to baptize, but to preach the gospel." Baptism had been familiarly practised among the Jews, and known as the initiatory rite, and John came to introduce men to the gospel dispensation. (See Malachi 3. 1, and Mark 1. 2.) Baptism formerly admitted proselytes to the Jewish religion—now it admitted Jews to the gospel religion.——¶ *In the wilderness of Judea.* A rough, mountainous, and thinly populated district, along the Jordan. Luke says, "He came into all the country around Jordan."

2. John's message was, *Repent ye.* Malachi, the last prophet of the Jews, had pointed him out, as acting in just such a capacity, as Christ's messenger (3. 1)—as the Elias (4. 5)— *preaching repentance*—"turning the hearts of the fathers to the children, and of the children to the fathers" (4. 6). His business was to call for a general reformation among the Jews, who had become degraded and corrupt. His exhortation was based upon doctrine—"Repent ye, for the kingdom of heaven is at hand." (See also Mark 1. 4). He heralded the remission of sins in Christ who was to come; the approach of Christ's prophesied kingdom—not earthly and carnal, as the Jews had thought, but spiritual and heavenly; and on this ground, and in keeping with this new state of things, he charged them to alter their views, their hopes, and their conduct. This is *to repent.* The Jews held that the Messiah would expect "a repenting generation." And in one of their books they have this sentiment, "If Israel repent but one day, presently the Messias cometh." There are two senses of the term, repentance. The one is this thorough *change of mind*—of the hopes, pur-

of ᵛ by the prophet Esaias, saying, The voice of one crying in

v Is. 40. 3.

poses, and course of life. The other is *remorse*. Judas repented in the last sense. It was "the sorrow of the world that worketh death." No anguish of feeling is anything, save as leading to Christ and to a change of life. And a hearty change *implies* substantial sorrow for past impenitence and depravity. Every one should repent because he has a wicked nature—because he has lived wickedly; and because forgiveness is proclaimed to sinners in Christ; while Christ himself, the Saviour and Judge, is *at hand*. And there is no valuable sign of true repentance apart from a thorough reform of character and conduct. Repentance is not the ground of forgiveness. Yet sinners should repent of their sins if they would obtain forgiveness, because this is most fit and requisite, that the renunciation and confession of sin should go before the assurance of forgiveness, even as John the Baptist's work goes before Christ's. Though the forgiveness is proclaimed freely, and the goodness of God is urged as an incentive to repentance, yet only they who repent of sin can enjoy a sense of pardon, or know the meaning of forgiveness for themselves; and only they are actually forgiven. So, wise parents require of their children repentance. Yet often the parent's willingness to forgive freely, is that which provokes the heartiest repentance in the child. There is nothing in a sinner's repentance which obligates God to forgive. It does not take away sin. Neither is it *because* he repents, but *because Christ has died*, that he is forgiven. Hence, the message is, "Repent ye, for the kingdom of heaven is at hand. John preached the baptism of repentance, (for) *in reference to* the remission of sins by Christ, who was at hand. Mark 1. 4. The coming of Christ is so spoken of, because this was what the prophets had pointed to. (Dan. 7. 13, 14.) David the king was to have a son and successor greater than Solomon, to sit forever on his throne. 1 Kings 2. 4; 8. 25. Jer. 33. 17. By *the kingdom of heaven*, is meant the gospel dispensation as the kingdom of Christ upon earth. It was now no longer distant, as it had been to prophets, but *at hand*, and very near. It was to be established in the death and resurrection of Christ. John was its immediate forerunner, to announce its coming; and so it was to be immediately expected. That kingdom is now set up. Since John's time the kingdom of God is preached, and every man (of all nations) presseth into it (Luke 16. 16). "For from the days of John the Baptist until now the kingdom of heaven suffereth violence, and the violent take it by force" (Matt. 11. 12). They who urgently press into it, and earnestly lay hold of its benefits, are true Christians, and only they belong to it. "The word is nigh thee." Rom. 10. 8. The *gospel of the kingdom* is now preached. This kingdom, though set up, and proclaimed, and already come in its plans *and offers*, has not yet fully come in its results. So we are to pray, "Thy kingdom come," "that the kingdom of grace may be advanced, ourselves and others brought into it, and that the kingdom of glory may be hastened."—*Shorter Catechism.*

3. *This is he.* Esaias (called Isaiah in the Old Testament or Hebrew tongue, this being the Greek) had spoken of John distinctly, though not by name. It was more than seven hundred years before John's time that Isaiah prophesied. Here is another instance of a prophecy, referring just as truly to an event far subsequent as to the one nearer at hand. Though the passage in Isaiah (40. 3) referred more immediately to the deliverance and return of the Jews from the Babylonish captivity, yet the fuller application was to this greater event. And the subjects of the prophecy were kindred in themselves. The chosen people coming out of that captivity which so represented the bondage of sin; and the same covenant people

34 MATTHEW. [A. D. 29.

the wilderness, Prepare ye the way of the Lord, make his paths straight.

4 And the same John had his ^w raiment of camel's hair, and a

w 2 Ki.1.8. Mat.11.8.

leathern girdle about his loins; and his meat was locusts ^x and wild honey.

5 Then went out to him Jerusalem, and all Judea, and

x Le.11.22.

coming out now from that legal dispensation "*which gendereth to bondage.*" Galatians. Hence both events could bear to be couched under the same prophetic language. We learn now, from this evangelist, that John was *he* whom the prophet announced, though *then* the prophecy seemed to apply only to the events more immediately at hand. *The Lord,* of whose coming John gave notice, was Christ himself. The prophet Isaiah seemed to hear the voice of the wilderness preacher.——¶ *Prepare ye the way.* This is an image drawn from Eastern customs. Monarchs on a march sent a herald before them, to prepare their way, to have their path levelled and straightened, and to announce their coming. John preached this preparation of Christ's way, as he was to "turn the hearts of the fathers to the children, and of the children to the fathers, lest He come and smite the earth with a curse" (Mal. 4. 6). He stirred up the people to expect Him "suddenly," Mal. 3. 1, and he called for a removal of all obstructions out of the way of His coming. He made His paths straight, as he notified them of the nature of His reign, so different from that which they had thought; and he exhorted them to make ready for His direct ministry of grace among them.

4. *Camel's hair.* John's clothing is here described as an expressive symbol of his work. To the Jews all this mode of living in the wilderness, and with coarsest clothes, strikingly indicated his work of preaching repentance. So the prophets wore this clothing (2 Kings 1. 8. Zech. 13. 4). So Christ intimates (Matt. 11. 8), " They that wear soft clothing are in king's houses." This camel's hair was woven into a coarse fabric, and served for clothing to the poorer classes. As a kind of sackcloth, it was the garb of mourning and penitence. John comes forward, therefore, as repentance personified. "In that which he does, he shows the people what they should do."—*Hengstenberg.* As he was "the Elias which was to come," reference is also made to the garb of the prophet Elijah, whose work he represents. See 1 Kings 21. 27, where Ahab copies the repentance which the prophet set before him. See also 2 Kings 1. 8, " He (Elijah) was a hairy man, and girt with a girdle of leather about his loins."——¶ *His meat* (or *food*) *was locusts,* Levit. 11. 22, which the Jews were expressly allowed to eat. This was the coarsest fare, and all in keeping. It was significant of his work. The prophet Elijah was fed by ravens. The Saviour represents this fare of John as a continual fasting, Matt. 11. 18, " *John came neither eating nor drinking.*" Locusts were eaten by the poor, mostly without much preparation, roasted and taken with salt. See *Union Bib. Dictionary.*——¶ *Wild honey.* This was either taken from rocks and stumps of trees, or it was such as is sometimes found in the East, collecting on the foliage of a *honey tree,* of which we are told, 1 Sam. 14. 25, 26, and 27, and flows profusely. Locusts might sometimes fail. This was a food belonging to a wild and waste region. See Isa. 7. 15.

5. *Jerusalem, &c.* A great multitude thronged to receive John's baptism. The inhabitants of Jerusalem in large numbers, and crowds from different parts of Judea, and all about the river and valley of Jordan, attended upon his preaching, and received his ordinance. Many had such expectations of Christ's coming, and so remembered what was declared by their last prophet, of the herald,

all the region round about Jordan,

6 And were baptized of him in Jordan, confessing ʸ their sins.

y Ac.1.5; 2.38; 19.4,5,18.

and of his preparatory work, that they went out to him at once. Many others had been drawn after him by the novelty of his dress and of his doctrine. So Christ intimates in Matt. 11. 7, when " He inquired of the multitudes concerning John, What went ye out for to see ?"

Jerusalem. The capital of the kingdom of Judah; called also *Salem,* Gen. 14. 18 and Ps. 76. 2; and *Jebus,* from the Jebusites, who held it before it was possessed by Israel (Josh. 18. 28). The name means, " habitation or inheritance of peace." The city was built on four principal hills: *Bezetha,* on the north ; *Moriah,* on the east; *Zion,* on the south; *Acra,* on the west. Across the valley or ravine, by which Moriah was separated from Zion, a bridge was built, for easier access to the temple, which stood on Mount Moriah. " The mountains round about Jerusalem" were highest on the east, where lay the Mount of Olives, commanding the finest view of the city, and from which our Lord beheld it and wept. The temple was on that side; and the valley separating Moriah from Olivet was the valley of the Kedron ; and there, at the foot of Mount Olivet, across the brook from the city, was the garden of Gethsemane. The valley of Jehoshaphat lies along the south-east, and the valley of Hinnom toward the southwest, separating the city respectively from the " Hill of Offence" and the " Hill of Evil Counsel." See Plate. The circumference of the ancient city was nearly three and a half geographical miles. The circumference of the present walls does not exceed two and a half—though Mount Zion is now unenclosed, and a portion also at the north. The population is estimated most correctly at fifteen thousand.──¶ *Jordan.* The only river of any note in Palestine, gives the name to a broad valley through which it flows. This valley is some sixty miles in length, and from five to ten miles in breadth.

6. *Were baptized.* This ordinance had formerly been in use among the Jews. It was known as an initiatory rite. Proselytes to the Jewish religion were received in this way. Hence, they understood the ordinance as signifying an espousal of a new religion, and so it was a mode of public profession. More or less the outward rite involved the idea of cleansing. The use of water had this significance. In the Christian church it is plainly symbolical of the Spirit's agency, and of this Divine influence graciously imparted from above. "Except a man be born *again*" (margin, *from above*). " Then will I sprinkle clean water upon you, and ye shall be clean." Ezek. 36. 25. The word *baptize,* is the Greek term *baptizo,* not translated, but transferred to our language. Therefore it tells nothing of the *mode.* Observe the terms. Two elements are mentioned in the New Testament baptizing, viz., water, and the Holy Ghost. "I indeed baptize you *with water,* but He shall baptize you with the Holy Ghost." From knowing of the mode in the use of one of these elements, we may infer the mode in the use of the other. The baptizing with the Holy Ghost is elsewhere spoken of, as by the Spirit's being *poured out*—" Until the Spirit be poured upon us from on high." Isa. 32. 15. " I will pour out my Spirit upon you." Prov. 1. 23. " I will pour out my Spirit upon all flesh." Joel 2. 28. Zech. 12. 10. Or its *being sent*— " I will send the Comforter." Or its *descending*—as at Christ's baptism, where the sign and thing signified met—" The Holy Ghost descended like a dove and rested upon Him." Or its *being sprinkled upon* the person. Ezek. 36. 25. " So shall He sprinkle many nations." Isa. 52. 15. And *rain* was a common emblem of it in the Old Testament. Hence, we conclude,

7 But when he saw many of the Pharisees and Sadducees come to his baptism, he said unto them, O generation *of vipers, who hath warned you to* flee from the wrath to come?

z Is.59.5. c.12.34; 23.33. Lu.3.7. a Je.51.6. Ro.1.18.

that the baptizing with water is by its descent, outpouring, sprinkling upon the person. The doctrine of the ordinance requires it to be administered, not by applying the person to the water, but the water to the person. This is the symbolical purport. The element denotes, not the atoning, but the cleansing influence. It is the water, not the blood. And renewing grace is to be received only at the sovereign hand of God. And the children of God are described in the Revelation, as having His name in their foreheads. It may here be mentioned, that the word *baptisterium*, from which the term *baptistery* is had, signifies, "not a bath sufficiently large to immerse the whole body, but a vessel or labrum containing water for pouring over the head (Plin. Ep. 6). See Smith's Dictionary of Greek and Roman Antiquities. John's baptism was not fully the same as that in the Christian church; for some of John's disciples were re-baptized. Acts ch. 19. And the commission for the Christian church, was to baptize in the name of the Father, and of the Son, and of the Holy Ghost." Matt. 28. 19. (See notes on verse 11.)——¶ *Confessing their sins.* In the baptism of repentance (says Bengel) they confessed their sins. In the baptism of Christ they confessed Christ. John preached repentance; and they who received his baptism owned their sinfulness, and professed a change of mind and conduct. They put off former things, and gave an indication, and admitted a sign, of *newness of life.* This confession was open and free, as the term in Greek implies—not private and auricular, and not constrained, but voluntary. Yet all this *looked toward* Christ, "in whom we have forgiveness of sins." "*Sin* is any want of conformity unto, or transgression of, the law of God."—*Shorter Catechism.* "All unrighteousness is sin." 1 John 5. 17. "Sin is a transgression of the law." 1 John 3. 4. And where persons of riper years receive baptism (and to such, of course, the ordinance was first offered), they should sincerely acknowledge past sin, with purposes and promises of a new life. The following verses show that this was John's view of it.

7. *The* PHARISEES were a powerful religious sect, of predominant influence in the Jewish state. They were the recognized teachers, proud of their legal knowledge, and boasting a superior sanctity; outwardly practising austerities, but inwardly indulging the worst passions. They believed in the resurrection, and in angels good and bad, as the *Sadducees* did nct. Acts 23. 8. They held also to a divine government of *fate*, and they claimed favour of God, on the ground of descent from Abraham. They observed the strictest letter of the Mosaic law; and besides held to various traditions (ch. 15. 2), washed themselves religiously before meals, fasted twice a week, on Thursdays and Mondays (see ch. 9. 14, and ch. 23. 15, 23), made much of vestments and of sacred appendages (ch. 6. 1, ch. 23. 3, 24), but were hypocritical (ch. 23. 14, 27, &c.), narrow-minded, selfish, bigoted, and vain, fond of pleasures and lax in morals (ch. 5. 20, ch. 15. 4, 8, ch. 23. 3, 14, 23, 25). And a religion such as theirs, was declared by our Lord wholly worthless for admittance to heaven (Matt. 5. 20). Their name is from the Hebrew word, *pharash*, which means, to *separate*; and these, and such as "these, are they that separate themselves, having not the Spirit." Jude v. 19. Josephus says they were akin to the Stoics among the Greeks (Vita Joseph., § 2). See Matt. 9. 11, and 23. 5, 15, 29. The SADDUCEES were fewer, but more wealthy, and of higher rank, yet had no influence with the multitude.

8 Bring forth therefore fruits [1] meet for repentance:

9 And think not to say within yourselves, We have Abraham to *our* father: for I say unto you, that God is able of these stones to raise up children unto Abraham.

10 And now also the axe is laid unto the root of the trees:

[1] Or, *answerable to amendment of life.*

They were bitter opposers of Christ, and denied the immortality of the soul, and all the doctrines of another life (Acts 23. 8). This being the character of these sects, John was surprised at their coming to his baptism. Hence he calls them by a name descriptive of their real disposition, "A generation of *vipers*," Isa. 14. 29, rather than the generation of faithful Abraham, which they claimed to be. A viper was a venomous serpent. And so they were children of the old serpent (Rev. 12. 9), who is the devil, "the father of lies." Cunning and poisonous with their doctrines, and ready to dart their malicious venom at everything good.——¶ *The wrath to come.* He preached the wrath of God to come upon the wicked (2 Thess. 1. 10, 11). He alludes to Malachi 4. 6, as the wrath expected. Their coming to him, looked like a disposition to flee from that wrath, by receiving the baptism of repentance for the remission of sins. Observe, it was not a mere *water baptism* that John preached, but one which implied a fleeing from the wrath to come upon sin, by taking the warning of repentance. And sinners are saved from the wrath to come, not by any baptism of water, but by fleeing for refuge to lay hold on the hope set before us.

8. *Fruits.* He tells them, therefore, to bring forth fruits meet for repentance; that is, to begin with their conduct and principles, in a way appropriate to repentance, and to show in their lives the appropriate results of such a change. And as fruit is the best evidence of the nature and quality of a tree, so they should thus best evince their sincerity.——¶ *Repentance*, is a change of mind which is best proved by turning away from sin and Satan to God.

9. *Abraham to our father.* The Jews boasted in Abraham. They were his descendants according to the flesh, and he was "the friend of God," and the covenant was to him and *to his seed.* So these boasted in their mere hereditary descent, as a sufficient righteousness before God. But "God is able of these stones to raise up children unto Abraham." He is not confined to nations, or to means, or to a law of succession in the church. They should not think that He was confined to Abraham's natural seed. The true succession now, is that of true piety; and Abraham's true children are such as God has raised up and created anew. (See John 8. 39.) "If ye be Christ's, then are ye Abraham's seed, and heirs according to the promise" (Gal. 3. 29). God can, and will, gather a chosen people from the Gentiles, which the Jews thought to be quite as impossible as that He should make church members out of stones. They mistook and perverted the Abrahamic covenant, which was to be of permanent force in the church, and which now includes, with believing parents, their infant offspring. But we cannot be saved, if we continue in sin, even though our parents be pious.

10. *And now.* This is the doctrine—that the time had come for getting at the root of things. Men's hearts should be laid open, and so they should be judged, and not according to the mere outward appearance. John notifies them of this new state of things. They were to be treated as trees are by the woodman.——¶ *Unto the root.* The axe laid unto the root, denotes that every thing is ready now for cutting down such as are heartless and fruitless. That the trial shall be of the heart and life. Men cannot hope any longer to stand upon a mere profession, or external relation, or upon

therefore every tree which bringeth not forth good fruit, is *b* hewn down, and cast into the fire.

11 I indeed baptize you with water *c* unto repentance: but he that cometh after me is mightier than I, whose shoes I am not worthy to bear: he shall baptize you *d* with the Holy Ghost, and *with* fire:

12 Whose fan *is* in his hand,

b Jno.15.6. *c* Lu.3.16. Ac.19.4. *d* Ac.1.5.

---

an outward show of ceremonies and pretensions. Now, the rule that is to be pressed is this, "By their fruits ye shall know them." Men must give substantial and actual evidence of their being Christians, or they will be cut down. Nor is this a dispensation for mere outward reform—lopping off bad branches—putting aside offensive habits—as the end to be reached. But it is a time for judging of real character, and for coming to final decisions.——¶ *Every tree.* A man that lacks piety is here represented by the tree that bears no good fruit. Corruption and wickedness are the natural fruits of the human heart (Mark 7. 21-23); and he on whom the good fruit of true piety is not found, will be cut down and cast into the fire, as rotten and worthless trees are used for *fire-wood.* Still the reference to Malachi's prophecy is kept up (Mal. 4. 1). "The day cometh that shall burn as an oven; and all the proud, yea, and all that do wickedly, shall be *as stubble:* and the day that cometh shall burn them up, that it shall leave them *neither root nor branch.*" In Luke's narrative, we find that this sentiment started a general inquiry, "*What shall we do, then?*" He directed them to honesty, benevolence, and mercy.

11. *Cometh after me.* "The messenger of the covenant," of whom John was the forerunner. Mal. 3. 1. ——¶ *Mightier.* His extra prerogative and power are pointed to. He is the Master whom John only served, and whose greater work he introduced. The difference between the two baptisms is, that John's is outward—Christ's inward. John sprinkles nothing but water, and cannot reach the heart. The ordinance he uses looks toward a repentance which he cannot impart. Christ shall pour out the *Holy Ghost,* who shall renew the heart; and He shall come with fire, which shall try and purify the reins. Again the reference is to Malachi. "He shall sit as a refiner and purifier of silver." Mal. 3. 3. "He is like a refiner's fire," &c. (3. 2). Acts 1. 5, and 11. 16. And He shall consume the incorrigible and worthless—"shall burn as an oven." Mal. 4. 1.——¶ *Shoes.* The shoes or sandals then worn were loose slippers, consisting of a piece of wood or leather, like the sole of a shoe, bound to the bottom of the feet by thongs (called *the latchet*, Mark 1. 7), as a boy's skate is fastened. These were put off on entering the house, and to unloose them was the most menial work—troublesome, and often filthy. John declares that he is not worthy to do even this lowest service to such a one as Christ (John 3. 30).

This cut is taken from the **Union Bible Dictionary.**

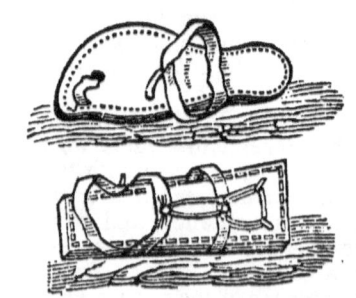

12. *Whose fan.* This carries out the idea. This is a winnowing instrument (Jer. 15. 7). A hand-scoop by which the grain could be so thrown up and exposed to the wind,

and he will thoroughly purge [e] his floor, and gather his wheat into the garner; but he will burn up the chaff [f] with unquenchable fire.

<small>e Mal.3 2,3. f Ps.1.4. Mal.4.1. Mar.9.44.</small>

as to separate the chaff. Wheat and chaff were to be most strictly separated. Again the reference is to Malachi. " Then shall ye return and discern between the righteous and the wicked," &c. (Mal. 3. 18). "For behold the day cometh that shall burn as an oven (Mal. 4. 1), &c. Thus He will *thoroughly cleanse His* threshing-*floor* (Isa. 21. 10)—that is, His church, so as to have it pure; and the merely nominal and hollow professors should be sifted out, and blown away like chaff before the wind. Jer. 15. 7. Luke 22. 31.——¶ *His wheat.* The sincere and true children of God should be gathered like good grain into the granary, or place of preservation. God will *house* His people. "They shall be kept (or garrisoned, as the term is) by the power of God through faith unto salvation" (1 Pet. 1. 5). But the *chaff*—the wicked that are mixed with the good in the church —He shall burn (Isa. 5. 24) with inextinguishable fire (parable of the tares, Matt. 11); which, because it is *unquenchable*, must be *eternal*. Matt. 25. 41, 46. Mark 9. 48. 2 Thess. 1. 8, 9. See Job 26. "A fire not blown (not to be blown out), shall consume him." "The ungodly are not so: but are like the chaff which the wind driveth away." Ps. 1. 4. This was the last process of cleansing grain "thoroughly."

13 Then cometh Jesus from Galilee to Jordan, unto John, to be baptized [g] of him.

14 But John forbad him, saying, I have need to be baptized

<small>g Mar.1.9. Lu.3.21.</small>

"The fan doth cause light chaff to fly away:
So shall the ungodly in God's winnowing day."
Flavel.

The preceding cut is from Kitto's Encyclopedia, showing the mode of using the *fan.*

§ 15. THE BAPTISM OF JESUS.—*The Jordan.*

Matt.	Mark.	Luke.	John.
3. 13-17.	1. 9-11.	3. 21-23.	

13. *Then cometh Jesus from Galilee* We learn from John 1. 28, that John the Baptist was baptizing at Bethabara, beyond Jordan. This was a town in the tribe of Reuben, and near the Dead Sea. Here, it is supposed, over against Jericho, the Jordan was crossed by the Israelites, under Joshua. The name means, "*a place of passage.*" From Galilee, in a southerly direction, Christ came. He had been at Nazareth till now. He was entering His thirtieth year (Luke 3. 23) And here we have his submission to John's ordinance, to "fulfil all (legal) righteousness." See Exodus 29. 4. It was also a formal inauguration, and public entrance upon His gospel offices, as sanctioned by the law. John could introduce Christ. His office was that of a forerunner and herald. Our Lord was now at the age of the priests at their entrance into office (Numbers 4. 3). There was an analogy also in the personal types. It was the age of *Joseph* at his appearing before Pharaoh (Gen. 41. 46), and the age of *David* when he began to reign (2 Sam. 5. 4). This was now about the feast of Tabernacles, at which time of the year Christ was born. The most exalted piety will earnestly seek the appointed ordinances. Psalm 27. 4.

14. *I have need, &c.* John evidently looked for Christ, and was led to recognize Him, before the baptism, on

of thee, and comest thou to me?

15 And Jesus answering, said unto him, Suffer *it to be so* now: for thus it becometh us to fulfil all righteousness. Then he suffered him.

16 And Jesus, when he was

His application for the ordinance. But there was yet a Divine certificate to be given, for his own full assurance, and for the faith of ages. In John 1. 31, he says, "*I knew Him not*," which refers to the fact of their having been personally apart—that Christ had a long time come, yet had not presented himself, and was dwelling so many years in Galilee, unknown to the people, or even to John, His forerunner, as the Messiah—not yet manifested, but to *be manifested*. He alludes to the fact, that His obscurity at Nazareth had almost obliterated the impressions of His miraculous birth and its circumstances. John knows Him *now*, and objects to the request, on the ground of Christ's superiority to him, and especially of His superior *office work*. "If one of us is to be baptized of the other, I am the one that needs to be baptized of thee." He knows him now, but not as he shall know Him soon from heaven. John recognized Christ's work as better than his. The gospel baptism is better than that of the law. The gospel hope is better than that of Sinai.

15. *Suffer it.* Our Lord insisted, and it was not in John's right or power to refuse. A sense of personal unfitness should never keep us from performing any enjoined duty. He who commands, also warrants and helps. It became them both, for in the great plan of redemption they co-operated. This act was now required. It was admitted because of its propriety in the view of our Lord. He was not obligated to the law, but put himself voluntarily under it. He was "made of a woman, made under the law" (Gal. 4. 4). Yet He was no *mere man*, but the God-man. He submitted to the law's requiremenst in His official work.——¶ *It becometh us.* It was *becoming* as they were related, and as they held their respective offices, thus to do.——¶ *To fulfil all righteousness.* That is, to comply with all the legal ceremonial requirements. This was the legal ceremony for induction to the priest's office. He would honour the typical ordinance, and submit himself to that appointed institution. "Jesus Christ was a minister of the circumcision." Rom. 15. 8. He would also consecrate the ordinance, as a perpetual institution in the church, for the Christian membership, who are declared to be "a *royal priesthood*" (1 Pet. 2. 9), and so, He would put himself among the baptized. Let none regard this as a needless ceremony.—— ¶ *Then he suffered him*—or allowed Him to be baptized.

16. *Out of the water*—literally, *ascended from the water*. The same words are used as in Luke 2. 4, "Joseph went *up from Galilee*." And Acts 25. 1, " He ascended *from Cæsarea* to Jerusalem." Hence there is no proof in this of their having gone the farther *into* the water, much less of Christ's having gone *under* the water. We may readily suppose, that in that hot country, they even walked into the shallow edge of the stream, for the greater convenience of applying the water by sprinkling. So Philip and the eunuch went *both* into the water. Acts 8. 38.——¶ *And, lo.* Christ prayed at His baptism (see Luke 3. 21), and possibly it was for some open and public recognition, such as this which He received from heaven, "while He was praying."——¶ *The heavens were opened unto him.* This was given for His own assurance, and personal recognition, while it served also as a testimony to his Divine Sonship, and the acceptance of His official work. Mark 1. 11, presents it as occurring to Christ, with this additional, that the language is addressed personally to Him, "*Thou* art my beloved Son, in *Thee* I am well pleased." John the Baptist also saw the descent of the Spirit upon

[A. D. 30.] CHAPTER IV. 41

baptized, went up straightway out of the water: and, lo, the heavens were opened unto him, and he saw the Spirit of God [h] descending like a dove, and lighting upon him:

17 And, lo, a voice from heaven, saying, This is my beloved [i] Son, in whom I am well pleased.

[h] Is.11.2; 42.1; 61.1. Jno.3.34. [i] Ps.2.7. Lu.9.35. Ep.1.6. 2 Pe.1.17.

CHAPTER IV.

THEN was Jesus led up of [j] the Spirit into the wilderness, to be [k] tempted of the devil.

2 And when he had fasted forty days and forty nights, he was afterward an hungered.

3 And when the tempter came to him, he said, If thou be the

[j] 1 Ki.18.12. Ez.11.1,24. Ac.8.39. [k] Mar.1.12. Lu.4.1.

Him. John 1. 32. Christ sets us an example of prayer, and the splendid answer is our encouragement.—— ¶ *The Spirit of God.* The Holy Ghost, Third Person of the Blessed Trinity. This was His special anointing by the Spirit, for the Messianic offices (Isaiah 61. 1). Here the symbol and its signification met. The descent upon Him was "*in a bodily shape like a dove*" (Luke 3. 22), so that John could be witness to it, and have his confidence assured by this most remarkable phenomenon. Note the personality of the Holy Ghost. Christ *saw the Spirit* descending. The voice of God the Father out of heaven was doubtless heard by all, as a public testimony (See John 12. 28–30). This formula of recognition was repeated when Christ was transfigured. Matt. 17. 5. Luke 9. 35, 36. 2 Pet. 1. 17. It was an open declaration of Christ's being the Messiah predicted, and *that He was accepted in heaven as Mediator*. Thus, at the opening of His public work, a public exhibition is given of the adorable Trinity. The Father speaks—the Son is baptized—the Holy Ghost alights upon Him. The Father is here declared as fully satisfied with Christ's official work of mediation for sinners. Observe, "*In him,*" not *in us*—in the Saviour, not in the sinner —God is *well pleased.* Observe, Christ's atoning office, and the Spirit's quickening, renewing work, go together. "*He* shall baptize you with the *Holy Ghost.*"

CHAPTER IV.

§ 16. THE TEMPTATION OF CHRIST.— *Desert of Judea.*

Matt.	Mark.	Luke.	John.
4. 1–11.	1. 12, 13.	4. 1–13.	

1. Jesus, after thus being openly acknowledged and inducted, both personally and officially, at His baptism, enters at once upon His work, and enters into temptation. He was "*led up by the Spirit*" (i. e., the Holy Ghost), which shows that this whole transaction was founded in the plan of God. He "was full of the Holy Ghost" (Luke 4. 1), who had ministered so prominently at His conception and baptism, and had just appeared descending on Him. And as "for this purpose the Son of God was manifested, that He might destroy the works of the devil" (1 John 3. 8), the conflict opens at once.——¶ *Led up.* This term is the same used in Luke 4. 5, of the tempter's agency. This temptation was an act of Christ's sacrificial work, "*Who, through the eternal Spirit, offered himself without spot to God.*" Heb. 9. 14. ——¶ *To be tempted.* Not as "a man is tempted when he is drawn away of his own lust and enticed" (James 1. 14), but to be tried, proved, and especially here to be assaulted with most malignant efforts to seduce Him to evil. This was done by *the devil*— the adversary, accuser, and enemy of mankind. He is a real person, and not merely an influence. He is called the Old Serpent (Rev. 12. 9); Satan

Son of God, command that these stones be made bread

4 But he answered and said, It is written, [1] Man shall not live

l De.8.3.

(Job 1. 6–12); Beelzebub (Matt. 12. 24); The Prince of the power of the air (Ephes. 2. 2). He is the leader of the legions of fallen angels, and of the wicked spirits in hell (Rev. 12. 9. and 20. 10). He tempts men by suggesting evil thoughts, or stirring up evil desires through the senses (as our first parents, Gen. 3)—the children of disobedience (Ephes. 2. 2)—and David to number the people (1 Chron. 21. 1). Or by instigating to wicked acts, as *Judas* (Luke 22. 3)—*Ananias* (Acts 5. 3). Or by deceiving (Rev. 12. 9). See 1 Pet. 5. 8. Our depraved nature aids him in his temptation. We fall in, naturally, with his schemes, and yield to the motives he urges. He gets an advantage of us if we are not constantly on the watch against his devices (2 Cor. 2 11). Hence, in the Scripture, we are charged to " watch and pray, that we enter not into temptation," and to " resist the devil" (1 Pet. 5. 9), with the promise, that so doing, " he shall flee from us " (James 4. 7). Christ was tempted, so as " to be able to succour them that are tempted " (Heb. 2. 18). As the first Adam had been tempted, and had fallen, the second Adam enters (by the Divine plan) into temptation, to show His steadfastness and superiority to the first Adam. " He was tempted in all points, like as we are, yet without sin." See Heb. 2. 18 and 4. 15.

2. *Fasted.* Abstained from food. There was a fast required by the Mosaic law, on the great day of annual atonement (Levit. 23. 27, 29). This exercise of fasting seems always to have retained some prominence (Acts 27. 9). There were also private fasts, though the law did not require them. After the exile, fasts became very frequent, as a regular part of the current religious worship. Fasts were regarded as a useful exercise, to prepare the mind for special religious impressions (Dan. 10. 2, sq. Matt. 27. 21. Acts 13. 3; 14. 23). From one day to forty days had been observed; but the last period, with a special sanctity, in reference to certain events in Jewish history. Thus Moses fasted on the Mount (Exod. 34. 28, Deut. 9. 9, 18); and Elijah (1 Kings 19. 8). Yet it was greatly abused in the prophet's day (Isa. 58. 4), and by the Pharisees in our Saviour's time (Matt. 6. 16). It may be abused by its excesses, in weakening the flesh—by making a virtue or merit of the exercise—and by mistaking the outward humiliation for the inward mortification before God. Our Lord seems to have abstained utterly from food, as Luke declares expressly, that " *He did eat nothing* (Luke 4. 2). This was part of Christ's humiliation—Being found in fashion as a man, He humbled himself even beneath the common lot of men. It was also part of His induction to office—" A prophet like unto Moses." And He submitted to our personal woes as part of His mediatorial work—" Himself took our infirmities and bare our sicknesses." Matt. 8. 17. The first Adam *fell* by *eating*—Christ *begins* by *fasting.*

3. Satan is here called *the tempter,* as his business was temptation; and by this work he is known among men. So he assaulted the first Adam (Gen. 3). Hence we may know that solicitations to *evil* are always of the *devil.* Observe, he suits himself to our circumstances, and we need always to be on our guard. We should specially fear his suggestions when he pretends friendship, and offers his plans for our help. We should pray not to be *led into temptation,* because we are not yet *delivered from evil.* As to the temptation of Christ, we are to remember that it was by the Divine plan for His official work, and that He was " *led by the Spirit* into the wilderness" *with this in view.*——¶ *If thou be the Son of God.* He had just been proclaimed the Son of God by a

by bread alone, but by every word that proceedeth out of the mouth of God.

5 Then the devil taketh him up into the holy city, ᵐ and setteth him on a pinnacle of the temple,

6 And saith unto him, If thou be the Son of God, cast thyself down: for it is written, ⁿ He

m Ne.11.1. c.27.53.

n Ps.91.11,12.

---

voice from heaven. It was a fundamental point, involving a recognition of His person and work, and the acceptance of His offices in heaven. Wherefore Satan joins issue upon this. Observe, this point of Christ's true and proper Divinity involves the whole Christian religion. Satan and all Christ's enemies will principally contest this. They who deny that Christ is God, must repudiate *all His claims*, as did the Jews.——¶ *Command.* The devil acknowledges that He who is the Son of God must be omnipotent—God himself. *If thou be—command.* This was a temptation to Christ, only as an *assault* from the devil—not as an attraction in itself. It challenged Him to distrust the plan and promise of the Father. The act would have been wrong, *as it was proposed and understood, viz., to break through the Divine plan.*

4. *But he answered.* This is quoted from Deut. 8. 3. These are the words of Moses, spoken of the *manna*, which was furnished Israel when a hungered in the wilderness, and which was so extraordinarily supplied. This was sent to show, that beyond all common resources, God has boundless means of providence, and that *He* is to be lived upon, in His word of promise and in His work of power and grace. "I am *that bread.*" John 6. Give us day by day the bread which every day requires. Only *they* know how to live, who live upon God's covenant. He gives himself to us for a portion, "I am the Lord thy God." Temptation often assaults us *through the appetites,* and appeals to us on the ground of *necessity.* But always is it to be resisted by the express word of Scripture.

5. *Taketh Him up.* Not against His will, for the word has no such meaning. There was a personal agency of the devil; and Christ, though led to the holy city, was not led into sin. Christ submitted to this as He submitted to death. The city of Jerusalem was called the holy city, as it was the seat of the Jewish religion; and "holy" in the ceremonial sense of being set apart for a sacred use. The inscription on their coins was, "*Jerusalem the holy.*——¶ *Pinnacle* (or *wing*) *of the temple.* The temple was that immense building on the top of Mount Moriah, which had been rebuilt and adorned till it rivalled that of Solomon on the same site. This wing was probably the projecting tower, called the king's portico, which, says Josephus (lib. xv., ch. 2, § 5), "was one of the most remarkable works ever seen under the sun. For, whereas, the valley (of Jehoshaphat or Cedron) was so deep and precipitous that one could not bear to look down it, on the very edge of this precipice Herod raised the immense height of this tower, so that if any one from the peak of this roof should look down through both these depths at once, he would be seized with dizziness," &c. This was some seven hundred feet in height. (See Union Bib. Dictionary, and Plate of Ancient Jerusalem.)

6. From this height Christ was challenged by Satan to cast himself down; and now the challenge was based upon Scripture. It is found in Psalm 91. 11, 12. It was an attack upon Christ on the *Scriptural* ground, where He had just resisted the tempter. It was a challenge to *presumption,* as before it had been to *distrust.* This passage is a promise to the righteous, of God's providential care extending to all their steps (Ps. 91. 1). Satan now dares the Saviour to test the truth of that promise, and as He

shall give his angels charge concerning thee: and in *their* hands they shall bear thee up, lest at any time thou dash thy foot against a stone.

7 Jesus said unto him, It is written again, Thou ᵒ shalt not tempt the Lord thy God.

8 Again, the devil taketh him up into an exceeding high mountain, and sheweth him all the

kingdoms of the world, and the glory of them;

9 And saith unto him, All these things will I give thee, if thou wilt fall down and worship me.

10 Then saith Jesus unto him, Get thee hence, Satan; for it is written, Thou ᵖ shalt worship the Lord thy God, and him only shalt thou serve.

o De.6.16.   p De.6.13. 1 Sa.7.3.

---

had just expressed His implicit confidence in God's word to this effect, to give a signal proof of it now. And again observe, he dares Him to prove His *divinity*. But God's promises are not to the presumptuous; nor will they encourage presumption. As Christ here encounters *temptation* for His people, so He sets a pattern of resistance, and draws for them the lessons which are to serve them in all their life. The angels have doubtless many services of protection and deliverance to perform for the righteous. They are the pure, unfallen spirits in heaven. See the case of Daniel (3. 28); of Peter (Acts 5. 19).

7. *It is written again.* Christ replies by another quotation of Scripture (Deut. 6. 16). To *tempt* means to *try*—to dare. Thou shalt not PROVOKE God by a vain foolhardiness, and by putting His promises to a rash and daring test. This is vastly different from an humble trust.

8. *An exceeding high mountain.* This is Christ's next position in the assault of Satan. There were lofty peaks, as Nebo (Deut. 34. 1–3), which commanded a most extensive view. And here the suggestion was made to Him of universal, temporal power. "All the kingdoms of the world" could not have been seen with the natural eye—even the kingdoms of Palestine—"*in a moment of time*" (as Luke has it), even if a point of observation could have been found. Nor could even the widest view from any known peak have been surveyed so instantaneously. The temptation lay in the *foul suggestion*, which Christ so instantly repelled. The *glory* of the kingdoms (their wealth, and pride, and power) was shown Him. It was most likely, when He was on some such commanding summit, with vast worldly greatness lying in the view, that this suggestion of the adversary was made. It implied no sin in Christ, and it led to none. Christ had not where to lay His head.

9. *Will I give thee.* Satan claimed all earthly glory as his (Luke 4. 6), to keep or to give away, and as *given to him*. Though Satan is "the prince of this world," as having a temporary dominion here, and having many subjects, yet the kingdoms belong to Christ (Ps. 22. 28), "and he is the Governor among the nations." "All power is given unto Him in heaven and on earth." Satan's promises are impious delusions. "He is a liar, and the father of it" (John 8. 44).

10. Christ again resists, with the Scripture. He shows from the law (Deut. 6. 13; 10. 20), that as a man He could not warrantably worship any but God himself, because there was no other proper object of religious worship, and no man can serve two masters (Matt. 6. 24). The *first* commandment involves the whole law. Even devil-worship is here proposed to Christ by offers of the world! Even the best on earth may be assailed by the most horrible temptations. And worldly offers often involve such horrid things. Yet Satan succeeds

A. D. 30.]   CHAPTER IV.   45

11 Then the devil leaveth him, and behold, angels q came and ministered unto him.

q He.1.6,14.

12 Now when **Jesus** had heard that John was ¹ cast into prison, he departed into Galilee:

1 Or, *delivered up*.

with men in these. But "whosoever will be a friend of the world is the enemy of God." We should repel them at once, on the authority of the Most High, and with "the sword of the Spirit, which is the Word of God" (Ephes. 6. 17).

11. *Leaveth Him.* Luke adds, "*for a season*" (ch. 4. 13). There was a victory. But it did not annihilate Satan, or chain him down as yet. Only God's covenant preserves the Christian from the worst effects of Satan's rage and malice, and He will not suffer them to be tempted above what they are able to bear. 1 Cor. 10. 13. 2 Pet. 2. 9. John 10. 28, 29. Observe the condescension of Christ to be tempted for us. The holiest on earth may fall into temptation. vs. 1. Resistance has a promise of success, now, by virtue of Christ's triumph. Heb. 2. 17, 18; 4. 15, 16. We may expect repeated assaults and buffetings. They were thrice repeated here, and then, the devil departed only for a season. Those especially who have had tokens of acceptance from above, may expect the adversary. vs. 1–2. There is, in the Scripture, a direction and reply for every form of Satan's attack (vs. 4, 7, and 10), and the Word of God is the sword of the Spirit, vs. 11.

	Matt.	Mark.	Luke.	John.
§ 17. Preface to John's Gospel.	....	....	....	1. 1–18
§ 18. Testimony of John the Baptist to Jesus.—*Bethabara, or Bethany, beyond Jordan.*	....	....	....	1. 19–34
§ 19. Jesus gains Disciples.—*The Jordan—Galilee.*	....	....	....	1. 35–52
§ 20. The Marriage at Cana of Galilee.	....	....	....	2. 1–12

PART III.

Our Lord's first Passover, and the subsequent transactions until the second.

Time. One year.

	Matt.	Mark.	Luke.	John.
§ 21. At the Passover Jesus drives the traders out of the temple.—*Jerusalem.*	....	....	....	2. 13–25
§ 22. Our Lord's Discourse with Nicodemus.—*Jerusalem.*	....	....	....	3. 1–21
§ 23. Jesus remains in Judea and baptizes. Further testimony of John the Baptist.	....	....	....	3. 22–36
§ 24. JOHN'S IMPRISONMENT AND CHRIST'S DEPARTURE INTO GALILEE.	4. 12	6. 17–20 1. 14	3. 19–20 4. 14	4. 1–3

12. John's imprisonment is a leading event in this part of the history. It gives, now, the avowed occasion for Christ's commencing his public work. This verse connects these two ministries, and shows their relation. It marks a period in the history. At this important juncture, and in order

13 And leaving Nazareth, he came and dwelt in Capernaum, which is upon the sea-coast, in the borders of Zabulon and Nephthalim:

14 That it might be fulfilled

---

to keep the harmony of the subsequent events more clearly in view, we refer here to Parts III. and IV. of the "Synopsis." The particulars of the Harmony, as they occur in the Notes, should be compared with this table. These memoirs of our Lord are given by Matthew with little regard to their order in the narrative. Hence these Parts (III. and IV.) will need the closer attention.

NOTE.— *When a passage is to be commented on that has already been passed in the Harmony, the caption will be put* IN BRACKETS.—*See* § 26, p. 47.

The important point of order here to be noted is, that Christ's preaching appears as depending on the cessation of that of John. This was John *the Baptist*, as distinguished from John *the Evangelist*. For an account of his imprisonment, see ch. 14. 3–5. Mark 6. 17–19. John had reproved Herod for marrying his brother Philip's wife; to do which, he had put away his own wife, and Herodias had put away her own husband. See Mark 10. 12. As John decreased Christ increased. The kingdom of this Herod (Antipas) was Galilee and Perea.

	Matt.	Mark.	Luke.	John.
§ 25. Our Lord's Discourse with the Samaritan woman. Many of the Samaritans believe on Him.—*Shechem or Neapolis*.	. . . .	. . . .	. . . .	4. 4–42
§ 26. Jesus teaches publicly in Galilee. . .	4. 17	1.14, 15	4.14, 15	4. 43–45
§ 27. Jesus again at Cana, where he heals the son of a nobleman lying ill at Capernaum.—*Cana of Galilee*. . .	. . . .	. . . .	. . . .	4. 46–54
§ 28. JESUS AT NAZARETH. HE IS REJECTED, AND DWELLS AT CAPERNAUM.	4.13–16	. . . .	4.16–31	

13. The intermediate passages show Christ's work of teaching and baptizing in Judea. Hearing of John's imprisonment, He departed thence into Galilee, where He had formerly resided, and whence He had come to be baptized by John (ch. 3. 13). In John 4. 1–3 a further reason for this movement is given, connected with John's work. It was the rumor among the Pharisees of His works, that led Him to retire. He had done sufficiently for the time, and He would not prematurely excite their fears and malice.——¶ *Nazareth*. Hither He first came, and here He preached. This was the place "where He had been brought up." His countrymen disliked his doctrine of distinguishing grace, and would not receive His message, but cast Him out (Luke 4. 14–30). It is more natural to reject Christ and His doctrines of grace, than it is to love our own flesh and blood—"for neither did His brethren believe in Him." John 7. 5.——¶ *Capernaum*, i. e., "*the town of consolation*," was situated near the N. W. corner of the Sea of Gennesareth, or Galilee (John 6. 17), in the confines of the tribes of Zabulon and Nephthalim, in the neighbourhood of Bethsaida, not far from the junction of the river Jordan with the sea. It lay N. E. from Nazareth. Zabulon and Nephthalim were adjacent tribes, composing a part of Galilee. (See Gen. 49. 13. Joshua 19. 20, 32. And see Map.) Capernaum was in the borders or near the boundary of these lands. Here he dwelt, passing here most of the three years and over of His public ministry.

14–16. This prophecy, which was

which was spoken by Esaias the prophet, ʳ saying,

15 The land of Zabulon, and the land of Nephthalim, *by the way* of the sea, beyond Jordan, Galilee of the Gentiles;

16 The people which sat in darkness ˢ saw great light: and to them which sat in the region and shadow of death, light is sprung up.

17 From that time Jesus began

ʳ Is.9.1,2.   ˢ Is.42.6,7. Lu.2.32.

---

thus fulfilled, is found in Isaiah 9. 1, 2. The sense of the passage is, that the land which in the former time He debased—the land of Zabulon and the land of Nephthalim—the maritime district—the country adjacent to the sea, and *beyond* the Jordan (or *around its head*), called "Galilee of the Gentiles"—this land he shall make, or hath made glorious. This was the district which first suffered in the Assyrian invasion. This district, or Upper Galilee, was bounded N. by Mount Lebanon and the countries of Tyre and Sidon, W. by the Mediterranean Sea, E. by Abilene, Ithurea, and Decapolis, and S. by Lower Galilee. It was called Galilee *of the Gentiles* (or the nations), from its having a more mixed population—less purely Jewish than the others. Cæsarea Philippi was its principal city. See 1 Kings 9. 11.—¶ *Sat in darkness.* This expresses spiritual blindness and extreme distress. They were involved in ignorance of true religion, most distressing and destructive, in which, if they continued, they must perish. Hence it was fitly called, the region and shadow of death—like the grave, a region where moral death dwelt and cast his dreadful shadow. The country of Galilee was noted for a turbulent, coarse, rebellious, and benighted people. See Luke 13. 1 and 23. 6. The Gospel of Christ was the great light which had sprung up. Christ is "the true light." John 1. 9 and 3. 19. 1 Pet. 2. 9. 1 John 1. 5 and 2. 8. Heathen lands—Pagan and Mohammedan—may now be said o be in this condition. Nothing but the Gospel can enlighten them. Many of these countries are now open to receive it. Yet multitudes in Christian lands, who have the Gospel, are sitting in darkness. And this is the condemnation. John 3. 19. Christ himself is the great source of all the light that men need. John 8. 12. "*The light of the world.*" John 1. 8. Isa. 42. 6; 49. 6. Mal. 4. 2. Christians are described accordingly, as "in the midst of a crooked and perverse generation, among whom they shine (or, SHINE YE) as lights (or light bearers) in the world, holding forth the word of life." Phil. 2. 15. Observe, that sin and misery go together, and Christ is the only salvation. What a privilege is the light of the Gospel. See Isa. 60. 2. The most enlightened are in darkness until Christ arise upon their souls. Only He who commanded the light to shine out of darkness can shine in our hearts. 2 Cor. 4. 6.

[§ 26. JESUS TEACHES PUBLICLY IN GALILEE.]

Matt.	Mark.	Luke.	John.
4. 17	1. 14–15	4. 14–15	4. 43–45

17. *From that time.* This calls more direct attention to the commencement of Christ's preaching. It was important, as connected with John's ceasing. But here it is, as yet, stated only in general terms. Hence this announcement may be regarded as coming in order, properly, before the account at Nazareth (vs. 13–16). Peter, at Cæsarea, after the resurrection, preaches the Gospel as "that word which was published throughout all Judea, and *began from Galilee after the baptism which John preached.*" Acts 11. 37.—¶ *To preach.* is to proclaim a message on a religious subject (as, "preaching the Gospel," Luke 9. 6). Christ usually went about from place to place, preaching in their houses of worship. Luke 4. 15. Mark 4. 15. "And He taught in their synagogues." "He went about teaching

to preach, and to say, Repent: *t* for the kingdom of heaven is at hand.

18 And Jesus walking by the sea of Galilee, saw two brethren, Simon *u* called Peter, and Andrew his brother, casting a net into the sea: for they were fishers.

19 And he saith unto them, Follow me, and I will make you *v* fishers of men.

20 And they straightway left *w* their nets, and followed him.

21 And going on from thence, he saw other two brethren, *x* James *the son* of Zebedee, and John his brother, in a ship with

t c.3.2; 10.7. *u* Jno.1.42.

v Lu.5.10. 1 Co.9.20-22. 2 Co.12.16. *w* Mar 10 v.28-31. *x* Mar.1.19,20.

in their synagogues, and preaching the gospel of the kingdom." Matt. 4. 23. Mark 1. 14.——¶ *Repent*. He commanded them to repent. This is to *turn from* former views, and trusts, and ways of wickedness, and embrace His doctrines and practice. Mark has it, "The time is fulfilled, and the kingdom of God is at hand: repent ye, and believe the gospel." Ch. 1. 15. Sinners should repent because God commands it, and because all sin is heinous and ruinous, and because repentance toward God is their highest interest and duty. Christ used a Gospel motive. Repent, *because* the Gospel of the kingdom is preached, and free forgiveness is proclaimed. Because this method of grace, with its dispensation of the Spirit, is here at hand, they should turn to it from their sins and errors. It was *at hand*, as He was then announcing it and setting it up. This command must still be preached to all, for God "now commandeth all men every where to repent. Acts 17. 30. Men are to *believe the gospel;* that is, they are to receive with thankfulness and confidence the glad tidings of atonement and pardon by Christ. Faith is required of men, not as a mitigated task-work—not at all as a performance—but as the only means of receiving the great salvation, which has been freely and fully provided in Christ. Repentance is demanded, not as a meritorious service, but as a hearty response to this gospel news; not as a price wherewith to obtain the hope, but as the necessary "*fleeing*

for refuge to lay hold on the hope set before us." This secures a new life.

§ 29. THE CALL OF SIMON PETER AND ANDREW, AND OF JAMES AND JOHN, WITH THE MIRACULOUS DRAUGHT OF FISHES.—*Near Capernaum.*

Matt.	Mark.	Luke.	John.
4. 18-22	1. 16-20	5. 1-11	

18. *The Sea of Galilee.* This sheet of water lies near the sources of the Jordan, bordering on Galilee. It is also called the Sea of Chinnereth (Numbers 34. 11), and in the New Testament, the Sea of Galilee (Matt 4. 18), the Sea of Tiberias (John 21 1), and the Sea or Lake of Gennesaret or Gennesareth (Luke 5. 1), which last is but a variation of the Hebrew name. Its length is about eleven or twelve miles, and its breadth from five to six. For the calling of the four apostles, Simon and Andrew (brothers), and James and John (brothers), see Luke ch. 5.——¶ *Simon called Peter* (or Cephas)—*Peter* being the Greek word for a stone, and Cephas being the Syriac for the same. John 1. 42. Here the four are spoken of as called in the same connexion. Luke has mentioned only the two, without denying of the other two. A comparison of the narratives shows a striking harmony, which argues for their respective veracity. By Matthew they are spoken of as casting a net into the sea. Luke tells how they cast the net at Christ's bidding. Matthew speaks of James and John mending their nets. Luke tells how they

Zebedee their father, mending their nets; and he called them.

22 And they immediately left the ship and their father, and followed him.

23 And Jesus went about all

y c.9.35. Lu.4.15,44.

Galilee, teaching ⸱ in their synagogues, and preaching the gospel ᶻ of the kingdom, and healing all manner of sickness, and all manner of disease ᵃ among the people.

z c.24.14. Mar.1 14. *a* Ps.103.3. c.8.16,17.

---

were broken by the exceeding draught. And Luke tells us that Christ saw *two ships*, ch. 5. 2, and that these pairs of brothers were partners (ch. 5. 7). It was not of chance that Christ met these, who should be his apostles. Who can doubt that the Shepherd was out seeking His sheep?

19. *Follow me.* This was the brief but significant command which Christ commonly gave to those whom He called as disciples. As they were engaged in their ordinary business, this called them to accompany Christ at whatever sacrifice, and to become His steadfast followers. They were first effectually called as disciples, and then made apostles (Mark 3. 13–19). See § 40, p. 52. They became, by His appointment, *fishers of men*, as it was their business to preach the gospel, and to win souls to Christ. (See Jer. 16. 16.) "Thou shalt catch men;" Luke 5. 10; that is, "draw men over to the gospel." Christ's ministers must first be Christians. The office has no such virtue as can dispense with piety.

20. They complied *straightway*—immediately. See Ps. 119. 60. Their *nets* were their means of livelihood. This was an effectual calling. And we are to learn from their promptitude, to follow instantly at Christ's call, whether it be to the great duty of repentance, or to any particular work. We are required to leave all and follow Christ. That is, to let nothing keep us back from Christ, or divert our interest from Him. And we are to follow His direction in all duty, and His plan of salvation by grace alone, and His holy example in all things.

21. *John his brother.* This was "the beloved disciple."——¶ *With Zebedee their father.* On comparing this verse with ch. 8. 21, ch. 20. 20, and ch. 26. 55, it is inferred that there is an undesigned coincidence, which attests the veracity of the evangelist. Now Zebedee is alive; but the next passage quoted shows that one of the *disciples* (few as yet) had lost his father, and wished to bury him; and the next passages cited speak of "*the mother of Zebedee's children*," showing incidentally that the father had died.—*See Blunt's Veracity.*

22. *Left the ship and their father* Luke has it, "When they had brough, their ships to land" (ch. 5. 11). Christ's call is superior to that of business, and His authority is higher even than that of a parent. We must obey God rather than men. We are even promised rewards, here and hereafter, for such a forsaking of friends and possessions, where this is the only choice. Matt. 19. 29. This is not to induce disobedience in children, or to encourage disrespect to parents. A needless and headstrong resistance of parental authority, even in religious things, is to be condemned. Yet it will sometimes be the effect of true religion in a family to separate the membership. In Matt. 10. 35, it is declared by Christ, as a foreseen result of His work, that He has come "to set a man at variance against his father," &c. Where there is no way left, but either to forsake parents or to forsake Christ, we are to part with father and mother rather than with the Saviour. It is not often, in a Christian land, that children, who act kindly and discreetly in following Christ, are driven to forsake their parents for Him. They should seek to show the excellence of their religion, and win their parents to the Saviour.

50 MATTHEW. [A. D. 31]

24 And his fame went throughout all Syria: and they brought unto him all sick people that were taken with divers diseases

	Matt.	Mark.	Luke.	John.
§ 30. The healing of a demoniac in the Synagogue.—*Capernaum*.	. . . .	1.21–28	4.31–37	
§ 31. The healing of Peter's wife's mother, and many others.—*Capernaum*. .	3.14–17	1.29–34	4.38–41	
§ 32 JESUS, WITH HIS DISCIPLES, GOES FROM CAPERNAUM THROUGHOUT GALILEE. .	4.23–25	1.35–39	4.42–44	

23. This was a second circuit in Galilee. The third is recorded, Matt. 9. 35. The day after healing Peter's wife's mother (§ 31), He went out to a retired place for prayer. Mark 1. 35. ——¶ *Synagogue*, is so called from a Greek word, *sunagoge*, meaning an *assembly*. Our word "*church*" has, in the Greek, a similar derivation from a word meaning to *call out from*, and so to gather into a body, a separate community. This place of worship, in our Saviour's time, was not of any recent establishment among the Jews. Little is said about synagogues in the Old Testament. There were "high places," spoken of commendably, as 1 Sam. 9. 19, and 10. 5, 13, 1 Kings 3. 4, &c., which may have been the synagogues. The temple was the exclusive place for *sacrificing*. But for keeping the Sabbath as a day of holy convocation (Psalm 26. 12 and 68. 26), in different communities, and for celebrating those solemnities obligatory, besides the three festivals at Jerusalem, must there not have been synagogues—places of worship—else must they not have lost the law, the Sabbath, and their religion? In the synagogue service, the Old Testament was read and expounded, and prayer was offered. The books of Moses, and part of the prophetic books, were systematically read through each year. These were the parish churches in our Saviour's time. Christ found them in universal use. Nearly five hundred of them were in the single city of Jerusalem before it was destroyed by the Romans. It is not wonderful that the Christian church, which our Lord instituted, should have been constructed after this model, and not after that of the temple. He attended with the apostles at these churches, and there they addressed the people from the Scriptures read. Luke 4. 15–22. Acts 13. 14, 15. The great advantage derived from the synagogues was *the preservation of the true religion among the people*. The law was thus preserved, and the Sabbath, and all the institutions of their religion. The truths of Scripture were circulated among the people by this means, where otherwise they must have been kept back. Hence we find that in Ezra's time a reformation in this respect was needed, because the people had been without their houses of worship and habits of worship during the captivity. Nehem. ch. 8.—— ¶ *Gospel of the kingdom*. By this is meant, that gospel which proclaims the reign of Christ, and by the preaching of which the kingdom of Christ is set up and established among men. The gospel belongs to this kingdom, as the grand feature of this new dispensation. The coming of this kingdom was mainly in the preaching and power of the gospel among men.—— ¶ *Teaching*. Instructing—expounding the Scripture; which was done in a sitting posture, after it had been read *standing*. He *taught* them the law, and *preached* to them the gospel. He healed the sick by the word of His power, to give proof of the gracious nature and Divine authority of His work.

24. *Syria*. In the New Testament it is the name of the Roman province (Matt. 4. 24. Luke 2. 2. Acts 15. 23, 41, and 18. 18, and 20. 3. and 21. 3. Gal. 1. 21), which was governed by Presidents, and to which Phenicia

and torments, and those which were possessed with devils, and those which were lunatic, and those that had the palsy; and he healed them.

25 And there followed him

and, with slight interruption, Judea also were attached. It included the country between the Euphrates and the Mediterranean, from the mountains of Taurus and Amanus in the N., to the desert of Suez and the borders of Egypt on the S. Mark (1. 28) reads, " into the country surrounding Galilee."——¶ *Lunatic.* Those afflicted with epilepsy or a mental derangement, which was supposed to increase with the increase of the moon—moonstruck. Hence our word has a Latin derivation from *luna*, which signifies the *moon*, and the Greek term here is similarly derived.——¶ *The palsy.* A paralysis, either of the whole system or of one side, or of the trunk and limbs, or a cramp or contraction and stiffening of the parts. Various diseases of this nature are included under this term in the New Testament. It is known at the East as a very fearful and fatal disease, which terminates suddenly after the most racking pains.——¶ *Possessed with devils.* Some are fond of making this a mere popular theory, and one which our Saviour and his apostles only chose not to contradict—speaking of diseases *as though* they were from a possession of evil spirits. But Jesus addresses the demons as such (Matt. 8. 32. Mark 5. 19. Luke 4. 35). So does Paul. Acts 16. 18. Jesus bids them be silent, Mark 1. 25—to depart and enter no more into the person. Mark 9. 25. See Luke 10. 18, and the context; and Matt. 12. 25—context; and Matt. 12. 43, 44—context; in all which places the demons are spoken of, in connexion with Satan, as satanic beings, and their nature is explained. The New Testament writers distinguished between the diseased and the demoniacs. Mark 1. 32. Luke 6. 17, 18. And Jesus himself does so. Matt. 10. 8. The demons knew Christ to be the Son of God. Matt. 8. 29. Mark 1. 24; 5. 7. And "the Christ." Luke 4. 41. The demoniacs confess that they were possessed with demons. Mark 5. 9. So do their relatives. Matt. 15. 22. The sacred writers assert that such were brought unto Jesus, Matt. 4. 24. Mark 1. 32—or met Him. Luke 8. 27. Jesus commands them not to make Him known as Messiah. Mark 1. 24. He rebuked them. Matt. 17. 18. The evangelists declare that the demons departed from the victims at His command. Matt. 17. 18. Mark 9. 25, 26. Luke 4. 35; 11. 14. And Christ himself so asserts. Luke 13. 32. To the demons themselves were ascribed personal acts. They spake, conversed, asked questions, gave answers, asserted their personal knowledge of Christ, and their dread of Him. Matt. 8. 29. Luke 8. 28. They are spoken of as having locomotion; changing their locality; going out of one person possessed; and entering into other bodies. Matt. 8. 32. This only shows us what influence over men is held by the prince of the power of the air; and Christ, by this means, exhibited His supremacy over the legions of darkness. Christ *healed* the people by miraculous power, and this power He exerted to attest His divinity, and to prove His claims and work. " Believe me for the *very works' sake*" (John 14. 11).——A *miracle*, is a supernatural work—an effect produced above, or against the laws of nature—requiring the same Divine power as instituted those laws, to suspend or contravene them. Christ wrought miracles *by His own power*, and this proved Him to be God. The apostles wrought miracles *in His name*, Acts 3. 6, which also attested His divinity as the source of their work. The argument is, that a miracle is of God, and that this stamp of Divine prerogative would not be set upon any doctrines or claims that were false. Hence, a miracle wrought, as the raising of Lazarus from the grave by a word, after several days' burial—or of

great multitudes [b] of people from Galilee, and *from* Decapolis, and *from* Jerusalem, and *from* Judea, and *from* beyond Jordan.

b Lu.6.17,19.

the widow's son from the bier—or the feeding of thousands from a few loaves — was sufficient proof of Christ's word and work, and this has always been a leading external evidence of Christianity. How gracious is the work of our Lord. He would heal diseases, to show how He came to take away the curse.

25. *Decapolis.* From *deka*—ten, and *polis*—city; designating, not the country, but certain *ten cities*, which resembled each other in being inhabited mostly by Gentiles, and in having peculiar institutions and privileges. Pliny gives the list—Damascus, Philadelphia, Raphana, Scythopolis, Ga-

CHAPTER V.

AND seeing the multitudes, he went up into a mountain: and when he was set, his disciples came unto him.

dara, Gerasa, Hippos, Dion, Pella, Canatha. But authors are not agreed as to all these. In the time of our Lord, the Decapolitan towns were not far from the Sea of Galilee (Mark 5. 20; 7. 31). They were mostly, if not altogether, east of Jordan.

Of these "*great multitudes*," few, probably, were true disciples. Most followed Him for curiosity, from the novelty of His teachings and doings. After this we find our Lord at Capernaum and elsewhere, healing and working miracles, calling Matthew, and afterward choosing the twelve, and *on that occasion* delivering His Sermon on the Mount. Note the Harmony.

	Matt.	Mark.	Luke.	John.
§ 33. The healing of a leper.—*Galilee*. . . .	8.2–4	1.40–45	5.12–16	
§ 34. The healing of a paralytic.—*Capernaum*.	9.2–8	2.1–12	5.17–26	
§ 35. The call of Matthew.—*Capernaum*.	9.9	2.13–14	5.27–28	

PART IV.

Our Lord's second Passover, and the subsequent transactions until the third.

Time. One year.

	Matt.	Mark.	Luke.	John.
§ 36. The pool of Bethesda; the healing of the infirm man; and our Lord's subsequent discourse.—*Jerusalem*.	. . . .	. . . .	. . . .	5.1–47
§ 37. The Disciples pluck the ears of grain on the Sabbath—*on the way to Galilee*.	12.1–8	2.23–28	6.1–5	
§ 38. The healing of the withered hand on the Sabbath.—*Galilee*.	12.9–14	3.1–6	6.6–11	
§ 39. Jesus arrives at the Sea of Tiberias, and is followed by multitudes.—*Lake of Galilee*.	12.15–21	3.7–12		
§ 40. Jesus withdraws to the Mountain and chooses the Twelve—the multitudes follow him.—*Near Capernaum*. . .	. . . .	3.13–19	6.12–19	
§ 41. THE SERMON ON THE MOUNT.—*Near Capernaum.*	5.1 to 8.1		6.20–49	

CHAPTER V.

1. It must be observed that some space of history has intervened between these chapters. Christ, meanwhile, has wrought miracles, recorded by the other evangelists, as seen in the Har-

[A. D. 31.] CHAPTER V. 53

2 And he opened his mouth, and taught them, saying,*c*
3 Blessed *are* the poor *d* in spirit: *e* for theirs is the kingdom of heaven.
4 Blessed *are* they that mourn:

c Lu.6.20,&c. *d* Is.57.15; 66.2. *e* Ja.2.5.

---

mony, viz., at Jerusalem, Capernaum, and elsewhere in Galilee (§ 33 to § 40). He has called Matthew, and has chosen the twelve.——¶ *The multitudes.* These are not those mentioned in verse 25, preceding, but *other multitudes,* spoken of in Matt. 12. 15, 21, and Mark 3. 7, 12. See § 39, p. 52. The common mistake on such points, shows how important it is to study this evangelical history *harmonized,* and not as though it were a consecutive record of events. This discourse of our Lord is commonly known as " the *Sermon on the Mount,*" because it was a set discourse, expository of the law and the gospel, pronounced by Him from the slope or summit of a hill, in the suburbs of *Capernaum.*——¶ *His disciples* are now spoken of as a class who had become His regular attendants and followers. All the multitude were not His disciples, yet He meant to instruct them, and especially His followers.——¶ *When he was set.* This was the custom of the Jewish doctors, who *sat,* in token of their authority.

2. *Opened his mouth.* This hints of a weighty doctrine, and a special discourse. (See Job 3. 1. Acts 8. 35). Christ here set forth the spiritual nature of His kingdom, and its accordance with the true spirit of the law and prophets.

3. *Blessed.* This is Christ's *benediction.* It supposes His authority to bless. Such are *happy* who are blessed of Him, for *theirs is the kingdom of heaven.* This includes all the gospel blessings—"grace, mercy, and peace."

——¶ *Poor in spirit.* Luke says, Blessed *be ye poor,* or the poor (6. 20). These things are often connected. A gracious poverty of spirit is remarked as being associated, in God's plans of grace, with poverty of worldly lot. " For he hath chosen the poor of this world, rich in faith." And there are facilities noticed in Scripture which such have for salvation (Matt. 19. 23. Zeph. 3. 12. Luke 18. 24. Ps. 10. 14), though often the poorest are the proudest—for true religion is not the growth of outward circumstances. Worldly poverty cannot produce piety. This disposition here called " BLESSED," is that *humility* which is characteristic of Christians—that lowliness and meekness which Christ himself patterned for us in the flesh, and which we are exhorted to *put on, and to be clothed with.* It is unpretending—not boastful of desert before God—submissive to His will and plan, and the opposite of high looks and high mindedness. This would show that His gospel makes the lowly, who are judged badly off, truly happy. Such are " blessed"—*or happy,* as the term more literally is. They are *happy* in the nature of the case, and Christ pronounces them *blessed,* as His benediction. This is a vital element of Christian character.——¶ *For theirs.* Such *have* the kingdom of heaven already set up in their hearts. " He that believeth *hath* everlasting life," and to such Christ accords the benefits of His kingdom (Ps. 132. 15, and 138. 6). Men should be humble, because they are frail and empty, and in the hands of God; because they have nothing sure, but are liable to adversity and death; and because they are sinners, and deserve nothing but wrath. Besides, the truly humble have the greatest blessings promised them; even that with them God himself *dwelleth,* as in His honoured and favoured abode. Poverty can be a blessing only, as leading us to such durable riches and righteousness. Ps. 9. 18; 10. 14; 68. 10; 69. 32; 72. 4; 107. 41; 140. 12. Matt. 11. 5. James 2. 5. " He giveth grace unto the humble." James 4. 6. This poverty of spirit is not a mere melancholy, or a mere sanctimony, but the very essence of inward piety, which is most

54 MATTHEW. [A. D. 31.

f for they shall be comforted.*g*

f Is.61.3. Eze.7.16. *g* Jno.16.20. 2 Cor.1.7.

5 Blessed *are* the meek: for they *h* shall inherit the earth.

h Ps.37.11.

opposite to the self-sufficiency and pride of nature. It may be assumed and counterfeited, but can be really had only by the Spirit of the Lord. The characteristic temper and style of the poor man, applied to spiritual things, gives the portrait of a true Christian.

4. *They that mourn.* Primarily, those who mourn for their sins. Affliction and earthly sorrow do not give claim to the Divine favour, as some would think. Any cup, however bitter in this life, can never entitle us to comfort in the life to come. Some think they have had their share of evil things here, and they look on this account for happiness hereafter. But this is a false hope. The mourning cannot fall short of a godly sorrow *to be blessed*. Yet mourners, who in their affliction look for relief and comfort to Him who speaks the promises, shall find consolation. It is blessed to mourn for sin, not because this merits anything—as though penance and penitence were deserving of God's love, or even of forgiveness—but because such a sense of sin comports with God's own estimate of it, and so falls in with His method of salvation by a Redeemer. It bewails and flees from sin, and looks for a Saviour from its penalties and power.──¶ *They shall be comforted* with the grateful tidings of pardon, and news of salvation in the gospel (ch. 11. 28–30). And Christ here sets forth this as one of the peculiar benefits of His regard. *Christians* are blessed when they mourn in affliction, because they have the Comforter (John 14. 26, &c.), the Holy Ghost, to take of the things of Christ and show them unto them. Christ would show that his gospel can give a happiness to mourning itself—a rare plan that can turn stones to gold (Rom. 5. 3, 5). *His* sufferings and sorrows have made ours sacred and sweet. See Isaiah 40. 1, 2.

5. *The meek.* The unresentful, and patient under abuse. This is not insensibility to our just claims, but a subdued temper that is enjoined. See John 18. 23, where Christ contended for His rights; and Acts 16. 37, where Paul strenuously demanded his. Moses was the Old Testament pattern of meekness (Numb. 12. 3). Israel murmured at him for bringing them out of Egypt to die in the wilderness, but he bore it meekly, and prayed for them. We should "show all meekness unto all men, for we ourselves were also sometime foolish, disobedient," &c. Titus 3. 23. But Christ is the great model of this grace. He represents himself in this attractive character, Matt. 11. 19, "I am meek and lowly in heart." The passions of our evil nature are to be restrained toward our fellow-men. His yoke is to be taken upon us, and so we "shall find rest to our souls."──¶ *Inherit the earth*—or the land; alluding to the land of promise, which was Canaan of old, comprehending all good in the eye of the Jews. The land of promise now, is the inheritance of the promises, including all good here, and heaven itself hereafter. Though the meek give up their rights sometimes, rather than contend, yet they get more by inheritance—the earth—the land. This is *rest*—a single term for the whole world of benefits and blessings. As to temporal things, the meek man has an advantage in his equanimity and peace. He saves himself the troubles that come from hot haste and strife. An inward satisfaction in his Christian hope is the world to him. A man that will resent every affront, will never lack affronts to resent. He will always be unhappy. Prov. 22. 24, 25; 15. 1; 25. 8, 15. The same promise is found in Psalm 37. 11. The true Christian temper is the only security for earthly happiness.

6. *Hunger and thirst.* This expresses a very earnest and ardent desire. This is Scripture usage. Ps. 42.

6 Blessed *are* they which do hunger and thirst after righteousness: for *i* they shall be filled.

7 Blessed *are* the merciful: for *j* they shall obtain mercy.

8 Blessed *are* the pure in *k* heart: for they shall see God.

i Ps.145.19. Is.65.13.

j Ps.41.1,2. *k* Ps.24.3,4. He.12.14. 1 Jno.3.2,3.

1, 2; 63. 1, 2. Those who ardently pursue and earnestly seek after righteousness, as men naturally strive to satisfy hunger and thirst, shall be filled. This is the principle of the gospel dispensation. "He satisfieth the longing soul, and filleth the hungry soul with goodness." This longing, says Augustine, is the dilating of the vessel that it may contain the more. Righteousness, understood either as godly living or as justification with God, should be most strenuously longed for, because it is the highest possible good. The righteousness of Christ is our only hope, and holiness is our true happiness. They who do not so long for righteousness must be quite content with their character and standing before God, and they seek no Saviour.—— ¶ *Shall be filled.* They who strongly desire holiness and pardon, shall most assuredly be supplied, because all God's vast arrangements of grace are for this end. He has blessings abundantly to give, and it is most agreeable to all His counsels, and plans, and promises, to give freely. No desire, therefore, of the human heart is so sure of being met and filled as this. Luke 1. 53. Isa. 55, and 65. 13. Jno. 4. 14; 6. 35; 7. 37, 38. Ps. 17. 15. Such are *filled* in this life with a gratification of their devout wishes. They receive of Christ's fulness, grace for grace. They are enabled to fulfil duty, and shall have the pasture that Christ gives. Rom. 14. 17. Jno. 4. 34. Comp. Matt. 3. 15. And hereafter they shall be filled with salvation, and triumph, and all blessedness. The invitation now is,"Come, buy and eat, without money and without price." Isa. 55. 1. "Open thy mouth wide, and I will fill it."

7. *The merciful.* They who take a share in the sorrows of others. Though it would seem to increase their own troubles, yet God gives a blessing to go with it, that can make it, contrary to all worldly opinions, a source of happiness. To our fellow-men who are in distress we should show mercy, accounting such as we meet in affliction to be our neighbours. "Blessed is he that considereth the poor, the Lord will deliver him in time of trouble" (Ps. 41. 1). Matt. 10. 42. A cup of cold water to a disciple shall not lose its *reward.*——
¶ *Shall obtain mercy.* Such shall obtain mercy from God, not only, but from man also, whom God will dispose to compassionate such in their times of distress. Mere benevolence to our fellow-men can never gain us pardon of sin and salvation with God. We cannot so merit heaven. But God will, in providence, reward with mercy those who show mercy. Ps. 37. 26. And when benevolence is exercised out of love to God (Ps. 112. 15), in thankfulness for His distinguishing favours, and in imitation of Christ, it will be regarded as done on His account. And he that giveth to the poor on such principle, will be considered as lending to the Lord (Prov. 19. 17). Our Lord has taught us to show mercy, by an instructive parable of the good Samaritan, Luke 10. 35; and of the two servants, Matt. 18. 23. What mercy has He shown to us all. They who so constantly experience the mercies of God, should be merciful to their fellow-men. And it is a disposition the most important to cultivate. Hence Christ's arrangement for the church—"The poor ye have always with you, and whensoever ye will, ye may do them good" (Mark 14. 7). It is more blessed to give than to receive. Acts 20. 35 *Our* reward is *mercy*, and not wages. A true Christian cannot be unmerciful. The overbearing, and severe, and heartless, have no promise here.

8. *Pure in heart.* (As opposed to

56 MATTHEW. [A. D. 31.

9 Blessed *are* the ¹ peacemakers: for they shall be called the children of God.

10 Blessed *are* they which are persecuted for righteousness' ᵐ sake: for theirs is the kingdom of heaven.

11 Blessed are ye, when *men*

l Ps. 34. 14.   *m* 1 Pe. 3. 13, 14.

---

the mock purity of the Pharisees.) Those whose thoughts, feelings, motives, and principles are pure. If only the outward conduct should be guarded and governed by the gospel, the kingdom would but very partially come. This purity of heart is the distinction of true Christians. However men may pretend to it, and flatter themselves of having it, none are righteous by nature, no not one. Rom. 3. 10. The Spirit of God alone can cleanse the heart. Ps. 51. Christ purifies unto himself a peculiar people, zealous of good works, and this He does by sending the Holy Ghost into their hearts. A person may be pure in his conduct to the eye of man, and not pure in heart to the eye of God. So a man may be pure in heart, and do what is wrong unintentionally. But to be good at heart, and wicked in life, is impossible. "By their fruits ye shall know them" (See ch. 7. 20).—¶ *They shall see God*, as a friend into whose presence they shall come (Rev. 32. 4). It was counted a privilege and honour, among eastern nations, to see the face of kings—to "stand before kings," Prov. 22. 29, and to stand in the king's presence. 2 Kings 25. 19, margin. *To see God*, includes the blessedness of knowing Him here, and of being "ever with the Lord" hereafter. "To *lift up the face of one*," is a common Hebrew expression for acquittal and approval in judgment. So these shall be pronounced the people of God at the judgment day. See Heb. 13. 14. They shall be admitted to favour. His sceptre shall be stretched out. See Esther 5. 2. In the East, where monarchs were seldom seen, and seldomer approached by their subjects, it is no wonder that an introduction to them should have been an image of high honour and happiness. (Bloomfield.) Our word *sincere*, is derived from the Latin, signifying *without wax*, alluding to honey that has no admixture of the comb.

9. *The peacemakers*. Those who, "as much as lieth in them, live peaceably with all men," and also seek by all means to promote peace among others. There are such who strive to conciliate where there is variance, and who are noted as the healers of many a breach. They often encounter the reproach of their fellow-men, but they have this promise from God.——¶ *They shall be called the children of God*—partakers of His nature who is "the God of peace." (See Rom. 15. 33. 2 Cor. 13. 11.) This is on the ground, that any genuine likeness to God indicates the new creature. The temper is lovely in itself. But the motives and principles must be God-like. We should live peaceably because we are all sinners. Christians are commanded to show all meekness unto all men, because they also were once foolish, &c. (Titus 3. 2). A peaceable temper and example, springing from peace with God, will do much to cultivate peaceableness around us; and Christians are enjoined to follow peace with all men (Heb. 12. 14); and by all means in their power to have men make their peace with God.

10. *Persecuted*. This is what the Christian is led to expect. "All that will live godly in Christ Jesus shall suffer persecution" (2 Tim. 3. 12). "Marvel not, my brethren, if the world hate you." Yet more. To be followed with abuse, and to have men seek to do them injury, because of their religion, or their performance of duty, is the lot of the righteous often. But it must be truly for righteousness' sake, and not for the sake of ambitious plans, or strange doctrines, or censorious language, or proud and exclusive pretensions, if

shall revile you, and persecute you, and shall say all manner of evil against you ¹ falsely, for my sake.

12 Rejoice, and be exceeding glad: for great *is* your reward ⁿ

1 *Lying.* n 2 Co. 4. 17.

in heaven ‹ for so persecuted they the prophets which were before you.

13 Ye are the salt º of the earth: but if the salt have lost his savour, wherewith shall it

o Mar. 9. 50.

---

the promise annexed would be secured. If men are really persecuted for righteousness' sake, they must be truly righteous; and so it may be said that theirs is the kingdom of heaven. They have the kingdom of grace set up in their hearts, and through faith and patience they shall inherit the promises.

11. *Revile you.* To say hard and bitter things of you—cast reproaches upon you—set you out as vile—give you a vile character –this is a kind of persecution. Calumny, hard speeches, and mockery are here meant, and these Christ suffered. But He reviled not again (1 Pet. 2. 23). We ought not to court abuse, or to glory in it, as though it were necessarily a credit. Nor is it allowable to speak disparagingly of men with a view to their disparagement, even though we may speak the truth. Yet if a bad character is given us, and not falsely, but in truth, we have ourselves to blame (1 Pet. 2. 20). And in such case there is no comfort for us in this blessing. If our names are cast out as evil for Christ's sake, in performance of plain duty, and because we follow Christ, then we are blessed in the consciousness of rectitude, and in the promise of Divine favour. Augustine says, "It is the *cause* which makes the *martyr*." Our only comfort under reproaches and accusations of men is, that they are false, and suffered in Christ's cause, and as He suffered them in the way of duty, and with a Christian spirit of meekness and love. But it is no certain mark of a good cause that it meets with strong opposition.

12. *Rejoice and (exult).* The *reward* is at hand, not as though it were in payment of debt, but all of grace which shall crown the sufferings of the Christian with great glory, and with all that shall abundantly recompense him. "Take my servants, the prophets, which have spoken in the name of Christ, as an example" (Jas. 5. 10).——¶ *The prophets* were the religious teachers of the Jews, and were sent by God with special messages and predictions to the people. But the Jews persecuted them. So Christ complained—"O Jerusalem, Jerusalem, thou that killest the prophets," &c. Ch. 24. 37. See the case of Elijah (1 Kings 18. 17; 19. 1–18; 21. 20); Elisha (2 Kings 2. 23); Jeremiah (Jer. 20. 2, 10; 26. 8–15; 32. 3; 37. 11–15; 38. 4–13); Daniel (Dan. 6. 1-17), who was persecuted for speaking the plain truth. And Christ testified that the people hated Him because He told them the truth (John 8. 40); and they even sought to kill Him. They stoned Him—drove Him out of their midst—falsely accused Him—and finally scourged and crucified Him, on this avowed account. And the wicked take such offence at this truth being told to them, because it condemns them, and would make them discontented with themselves. We should behave respectfully and kindly toward those who tell us of our sins and faults.

13. *The salt.* Salt has the quality of preserving and purifying what would otherwise rot. It also gives savour or relish to food—seasoning it. It has also a penetrating power. Christ applied His discourse now to the apostles, to whom the dispensing of religious doctrines would soon be committed. It would be their part to "*salt the earth*," not to infect it with a depraved and vicious taste. So Christians should cast a healthful savour

be salted ? it is thenceforth good for nothing, but to be cast out, and to be trodden under foot of men.

14 Ye are the light ᵖ of the world. A city that is set on an hill cannot be hid.

15 Neither do men light a can-

p Ph.2.15.

---

of true piety around them, maintaining sound doctrine, sober conduct and conversation, and earnest prayer, which would tend to preserve and purify the world. The church should be to society what salt is to daily food. The church is the only adequate means for preserving the world from destruction. The gospel ministry salts the earth. The offerings on the altar were salted with salt. Leviticus 2. 13.——¶ *Lost his savour*—or quality. This would often be the case with salt, such as was used at the East. It was taken out of mines, mixed with much foreign substance, and when exposed to the elements would lose its saltness, and would thenceforth be good for nothing but for hardening paths, and for being trodden under foot of men. Christians are like this, when they have lost their humility and life, and do not show any power in their religion. Then the case is excessively bad. Like rotten branches on the vine, men gather them and cast them into the fire, and they are burned. "Men *cast them out.*" They do no good any longer, and are only a reproach to Christ's cause, and an irreparable damage is done. Young Christians may so live as to grow in grace, and gain great maturity and power in their religious course, by hungering and thirsting after righteousness, and by pressing forth constantly to the things that are before—overcoming the world by their faith, and winning others by their humble piety. "Let your speech be alway with grace, seasoned with salt." Col. iv. 6.—— ¶ *Good for nothing.* The loss of the salt, or genuine spirit of Christianity, cannot be supplied by any expedient whatsoever; and whatever the profession of such, they are utterly worthless, insipid, rotten. Luke 14. 35.

14. *The light of the world.* This is spoken of Christians generally, and of Christian ministers especially. They are not the original and true light. This Christ is (John 1); as distinct from any messenger, as John the Baptist. "John was the lamp, and Christ the light; as John was the voice, and Christ the Word."—*Augustine.* Light enables us to see persons and things, and shows us the world around—our path, our dangers and prospects—and helps us to discriminate. Christians are said to shine in the midst of a crooked and perverse generation, as lights in the world, holding forth the word of life. They are "light in the Lord" (Ephes. 5. 8). It is by maintaining the truth, and exemplifying true piety, and representing the way to heaven, that Christ's people are luminaries. They receive their light from Christ, and should show it by good works and a manifest sincerity. They should labour to diffuse it.—The Jews applied this title to their Rabbins, and among the Greeks and Romans, celebrated persons, especially teachers, were called "*Lights* of the world." Christians are the luminaries which God has set in the world to give light, and He would enlighten others by their instrumentality. They are charged with the duty of sending the light of the gospel all over the world, and of setting a bright example. But they were not only set to give light; they are objects of universal notice, remarked by all.——¶ *A city, &c.* Such a spectacle as a city on a high summit must command attention. Many cities are built on a height—on a crown or a slope of a hill. They can be seen from afar; and the public buildings and towers attract special notice. So with Jerusalem. It was a great city—a noble sight—the city of the great king—its palaces and bulwarks on an eminence. Christians

dle, and put it under ¹ a bushel, but on a candlestick; and it giveth light unto all that are in the house.

1 The word, in the original, signifieth, *a measure containing about a pint less than a peck.*

16 Let your light so shine before men, that they may see your good works, and glorify ᵠ your Father which is in heaven.

q 1 Pe.2.12.

are like such a city. All their actions are watched, and their example is prominent and important, and cannot be hid; and hence, if they fall into sins, the mischief must be widespread, and multitudes must suffer. Like such a city on fire, their ruin must be seen all abroad.

15. The use of light is, not to be hidden, but to reveal itself and things around it. The use of their religion was to enlighten others. Christ would not have given them light to have them hide it, and make no proper use of it, any more than men would light a candle to hide it under a basket or bushel. It is here hinted, that disciples of Christ are in danger of putting their Christian light under their corn measure, and of having their good example, and Christian influence, obscured by worldly objects. (Compare Luke 11. 33, 36 with this.) One Christian lights a house.

16. *Let your light so shine.* Christ's disciples can let their light shine by a holy example in all points, and by a consistent course of conduct. Christians should walk with this object in view, that men may see the power of true piety in their life, so as to be won to follow them as they follow Christ. The good example of a Christian proves the truth against all gainsaying, and furnishes a living argument for Christianity, which has led many to embrace the religion of Christ and to glorify God. Thus the disciples are to "show forth the praises of Him who called them out of darkness into his marvellous light." They are not to parade their good deeds boastfully before the world (see Matt. 6. 1); but since their example must so powerfully operate, as they are seen from afar, and known, they must not be careless of their influence with others, but must strive to have it uniformly good, enlightening in duty and true happiness, and winning to Christ.

On verses 13–16, OBSERVE, (1.) The Christian church, in its ministry and membership, is ordained to be the conservative element of society—to season, purify, and preserve the world, by holy character, sound doctrine, good example, personal exertion in every good cause, and earnest prayer for men. (2.) It is the quality of true religion to season and preserve whatever it touches. This healthful influence is shown in the facts. How salutary and savoury is the smallest measure of Christian influence in daily life, as a seasoning of salt at the table. (3.) If the professing Christian has lost this quality, and does not exert this peculiar power, there is no earthly remedy. The Christian name, without the power, is the poorest thing on earth. (4.) The Christian church is the grand illuminating agency for the world. Gross darkness would reign without the Scriptures, which it keeps and promulgates, and without the various lights of science, and learning, and universal truth, which it affords. I, is the essential quality of true religion to be *luminous.* It cannot exist without giving light. It only quite ceases to illuminate when it has gone out in darkness. (5.) A Christian, from *his exalted station,* must have a wide influence; and so his light, like that of a beacon or light-house (Phil. 2. 15), must have broad effect. A profession of religion is watched, and must be powerful for good if consistent. But a beacon that is not lighted does harm. Vessels run on the rocks or shore, where, if it had been kept bright, it would have directed them. The Christian life is an abiding and living testimony, a bright example, and a lure to heaven. A true Chris-

60 MATTHEW. [A. D. 31.

17 Think not that I am come to destroy *r* the law or the *s* prophets: I am not come to destroy, but to *t* fulfil.

18 For verily I say unto you,

_{r Mat.3.15. s Is.42.21. t Ps.40.6–8.}

Till heaven and earth pass, one jot or one tittle *u* shall in no wise pass from the law, till all be fulfilled.

19 Whosoever therefore shall

_{u Lu.16.17.}

---

tian must have commanding power with men, even when unconscious of it himself. So prominent an object, like a city built on a hill, cannot be hid.

17. *Think not.* They might easily think so. Our Lord invited the Jews to receive a religion which should greatly interfere with all their carnal notions of the Mosaic economy. Their objection would be, that this would really abrogate or make void their old faith and that of their fathers. The law and the prophets was that system of faith and practice taught by Moses in the law, and by the prophets in their messages. He assures them that his doctrine agrees perfectly with them—that it even *fulfilled* them, and was necessary to them for their completion. They must not be alarmed, then, as though this preaching and teaching were a revolt from their religion. Christ came to fulfil the law—to open its full sense by His exposition of it—to magnify the law by His obedience of its requirements in His life, and by His endurance of its penalty in His death, and to fulfil it " as *the end of the law,*" or the aim and accomplishment of it, for justifying righteousness to the believer. So there is nothing in the gospel which derogates in the least from the law; but even its plan of justification by faith without works, establishes the law (Rom. 3. 31). And so He fulfilled the prophets, by showing the truth of their predictions, and bringing them to pass in himself; for He was the great object of prophecy. " The testimony of Jesus is the spirit of prophecy." The moral law is of perpetual force, and the full sense of the old economy is brought out in the new. Grace to obey comes by Christ.

18. *Till heaven and earth pass.* This is a proverbial phrase often occurring in Scripture, and sometimes in the classics, to signify that a thing can never happen. Ps. 120. 26. Luke 16. 17. Matt. 24. 35, &c. Luke has it, " *It is easier,*" *&c.* It was a received opinion among the Jews, that the visible universe would never pass away, but be renovated, and so last forever. We often say that a thing will never happen *so long as the world stands.* Christ would strongly express to the Jews His deference to the law, and His determination to maintain it, in every part of it, without any fail. This was necessary to correct their prejudices and meet their objections. The gospel is not understood or appreciated, except it be seen as fulfilling the law (Romans 3. 31). —¶ *One jot or tittle.* The least possible part. *Jot* is the name of the smallest letter in the Hebrew alphabet (י), and so it is used to express the smallest possible thing. So 'alpha' and 'omega' are the first and last letters of the Greek alphabet, whence Christ is called the alpha (α) and the omega (ω)—the first and the last. So *tittle* is a minute *point* by which one Hebrew letter is often distinguished from another (as ט from ם). See James 2. 10, " offend in one *point.*" The sense is, that not so much as the dot of an (i) or the cross of a (t) shall fail from the law. All shall be fulfilled. The phrase, " *Till* heaven and earth pass," does not allow us to infer that there is a definite limit set to the law's enforcement, and that we are to look forward to any such a time as the passing away of the visible universe, for the passing away of the law.—The law to which Christ referred was the *moral law;* for this it is that He proceeds at once to expound, and to show how the gospel fulfils it. To know what law of Moses is not abrogated, we have only to ask whether it is such as is founded on

A. D. 31.] CHAPTER V. 61

break one of these least commandments, and shall teach men so, he shall be called the least in the kingdom of heaven : but whosoever shall do and teach *them*, the same shall be called great ᵛ in the kingdom of heaven.

20 For I say unto you, That except your righteousness shall exceed ʷ *the righteousness* of the scribes and Pharisees, ye

v 1 Sa. 2. 30.　*w* c. 23. 23–28.　Ph. 3. 9.

---

moral principles, and so equally binding upon all nations and all times, or whether it is local and national. The ceremonial law was constructed to meet the peculiar case of the Jews, and so it was ordained for that people. So far as it contained doctrine, as in its types and shadows, it is fulfilled in Christ. This Paul proves in the Epistle to the Hebrews (see 9. 10 and 10. 1). And so far as it was a system of religious ceremonies, it has passed away. So the *judicial* law of the Jews was governmental and political. This passed away with the Jewish state so far as it was local. But where it contained statutes of moral and universal force, they remain binding. But the *moral* law was founded in the nature of things, and confirmed and enforced by Christ's gospel, and can never pass away. This law, no mere man since the fall has ever perfectly obeyed. But Jesus Christ most entirely obeyed it, and in Him have we righteousness and strength. No sinner can be saved but by the merit of His obedience and death. This we must humbly apply for, and heartily rest in, for salvation. Though " some sins in themselves, and by reason of several aggravations, are more heinous in the sight of God than others," yet "every sin deserveth God's wrath and curse, both in this life and that which is to come."—*Shorter Catechism*.

19. Sin or error, *taught*, is worst. No command of God is little in itself. For " whosoever shall keep the whole law, and yet offend in one *point* (one jot or little), he is guilty of all" (James 2. 10). The Pharisees made void the law by their traditions. They made distinctions, too, between great and small commandments. The Jews reckon the least commandment of the law to be that of the bird's nest (Deut. 22. 6, 7). And they omitted the weightier matters of the law—judgment, mercy, and faith—while they strictly tithed the mint, anise and cummin. No duty is to be despised. By these least commandments, our Lord meant those which the Pharisees counted least, and which men are wont to count of least importance. —— ¶ *Shall be called least.* As he disparages the law, so shall he be disparaged under the gospel. In the kingdom of heaven, or in the church under this economy of Christ, he shall be set at nought. As he makes void the law, so his profession shall be made void. See Isa. 9. 15. Mal. 2. 8, 9. Our duty is to do and teach all that God has commanded. Professing Christians cannot indulge "small sins," and find favour with God. Ministers cannot shun to declare the whole counsel of God. Practice and precept, too, must go together. It is not enough to do what is right between man and man. We must set an example of piety toward God; and we may all teach others by this means. To ' *do and teach* ' the truth, gives a high grade under the gospel dispensation.

20. Here the drift of the former verses is explained. Our Lord demanded higher views of the Divine requirements, and a better course of conduct than the scribes and Pharisees showed. They had a corrupt doctrine of righteousness, and made a hypocritical parade of self-righteousness.—— ¶ *Exceed.* Literally—*abound more than.* The Wicklif translation, 1380, has it, " *be more plenteous.*" Abel's sacrifice (Heb. 11, 4) is literally a more abounding or fuller sacrifice—translated, *more excellent.*

shall in no case enter into the kingdom of heaven.

21 Ye have heard that it was said ¹ by them of 'old time, ˣ Thou shalt not kill; and whosoever shall kill shall be in danger of the judgment:

22 But I say unto you, That whosoever is angry with his brother without a cause, ʸ shall

1 Or, *to them.* x Ex.20.13. De.5.17.

y 1 Jno.3 15.

It is the same idea found in both passages, and in both to show the defectiveness of the opposite. Whether Cain's or the Pharisees', something was essentially lacked. Unless your doctrine and practice go beyond that of mere formalists and time-servers, ye shall have no part nor lot in the gospel. *True righteousness* " is that of the heart, in the spirit, and not in the letter, whose praise is not of men, but of God" (Rom. 2. 29). It is composed of such tempers as Christ had just pronounced blessed, as humility, meekness, holiness, mercy, purity, &c. And we must have such views of God's requirements, and of our own lives, as to see that in Christ alone we have complete righteousness and strength. Observe, our Lord now proceeds to point out the true force and meaning of the law, and to expose the vain traditions of the Pharisees—to show how it was *they* who would destroy, and *He* that would fulfil. They who are not fit for the kingdom by an embrace of Christ, and imitation of Him, must perish.

21. *Ye have heard.* He first takes the sixth command (Exod. 20. 13), and refers them to the exposition of it that was familiar among them, and of old standing. This command was the first broken openly by Adam's race. And its violation stands first on the list of natural depravities. " Out of the heart proceed evil thoughts— *murders"* (ch. 15. 19). The sum of the commandments is love. Their ideas of this law went no further than the clause which they added to explain it. So it applied only to actual murder, and subjected the murderer to an inferior punishment.——¶ *The judgment.* This was a lower court of the Jews, deciding causes of small or moment. The actual murderer was held liable to this court, and that was all.

22. *But I say unto you.* Christ now puts forward His exposition of the law, as in contrast with that which had been received among them. He was the law's authorized expounder. He was God in the flesh; and who could explain the law as well as he? He shows that the precept extends properly to the thoughts, and feelings, and language, as well as to outward acts. This is the great point. " He judgeth not according to outward appearance, but looketh on the heart."

1st. As to the feeling. Because anger, indulged and carried out, leads to murder; and because with God the inward feeling has the essence of the outward act; therefore it comes under the condemnation. Not only the act, but whatsoever tendeth thereunto, is condemned (1 John 3. 15). See the case of Cain, and of Joseph's brethren, where the evil passion led on to murderous deeds.——¶ *His brother.* His fellow-man. All men are our brethren, as of the same human family. Mal. 2. 10. 1 Cor. 8. 6. The idiom arose from the Jews regarding all Israelites as brethren. So the word *neighbour,* as Christ explained it in the parable of the good Samaritan. It is not taught here, that anger may be indulged where men think they *have a cause.* It is rather hinted, that anger at a brother is causeless. See Psalm 7. 4; 25. 3; 119. 78. We may be angry at the sin, but not at the person. The general idea is clear. He that is easily angry, or bitterly angry, and more at *persons* than at *things,* is to be condemned.

2d. As to the language of anger.—— ¶ *Raca.* A term of reproach, meaning a contemptible, worthless fellow

[A. D. 31.] CHAPTER V. 63

be in danger of the judgment: and whosoever shall say to his brother, ¹ Raca, shall be in danger of the council: but whosoever shall say, Thou fool, shall be in danger of hell fire.

1 i. e., *vain fellow.* 2 Sa. 6. 20.

To use scornful language towards others, is an offence before God, though it is thought so lightly of, and is so frequently done, as though it were no harm. But it is here shown to be included under the sixth commandment. The religion of Christ enjoins kindness, gentleness, and courteousness to all. "Let all bitterness, and wrath, and anger, and clamour, and all evil speaking, be put away from you."—¶ *The council.* Literally, the *Sanhedrim,* before whom weightiest matters came—the highest court of the Jews. The idea is, that this offence, counted so slight by the Pharisees, as though it had nothing at all to do with the commandment, is reckoned by Him a Sanhedrim offence, worthy of being brought before that highest tribunal — an offence weighty as those they referred to that highest court. This council was composed of seventy members, from the chief priests, elders, and scribes. The acting high priest was usually president of the Sanhedrim. This tribunal could pass sentence of death, but could not execute, now that Judea was under the Romans. They could only pronounce a decision, and transmit it to the procurator, with whom it rested to execute or not.—We learn that abusive language will be taken notice of by God, and that it renders a man liable to the highest judgment, though he may have thought it would never come into account. "Every idle word that men shall speak, they shall give account thereof in the day of judgment" (ch. 12. 36).——¶ *Thou fool.* This term, in the Scripture sense, carries with it an accusation of depravity and wickedness. Thou *wretch* or *sinner* (Ps. 14. 1. Josh. 7. 15).——¶ *Shall be in danger of hell fire.* Literally—*shall be worthy of the Gehenna of fire.* The object here was to classify these offences, and to show that this last, though judged so trivial among them, was worthy the severest doom of which they knew, called the *Gehenna of fire.* Among the Jews there were three grades of condemnation—the judgment, the council, the fire of Hinnom. The word *Gehenna* is made up of two Hebrew words, meaning together *the valley of Hinnom.* This lay at the south-west of Jerusalem, below Mount Zion, and was the infamous place where human sacrifices were offered to the idol Moloch (2 Kings 16. 3. Jer. 7. 31. 2 Chron. 28. 3; 33. 6). The Rabbins tell us that a statue of the idol, made of brass, was placed on a brazen throne, having the head of a calf, with a crown upon it. The whole structure was hollow, and in the pedestal, as a furnace or oven, a fierce fire was kindled. When the image became heated red hot, the infant victim was thrown into its arms. This place was also called Tophet, Jer. 7. 31, 32, from *toph, a drum,* because drums were beaten furiously to drown the cries of the tormented victims. This horrid worship afterward became discarded (2 Kings 23. 10), and the place was used as a receptacle for all the filth of the city. Carcasses were thrown out there. The bodies of vilest criminals were cast into that sink of pollution. Some were also executed there, as a distinction of vileness. And on account of the awful pestilential stench that the place threw up, from so much rottenness, fires were kept perpetually burning. Hence it is called the Gehenna of fire —a fit symbol of hell. The word Gehenna was used by our Lord most distinctly for hell itself. It is used in the New Testament twelve times; always by our Lord, except once by James (3. 6); and always as meaning the place of eternal torment, except here, where it refers distinctly to the valley of Hinnom, as *representing* that abode of the lost. These three

23 Therefore, if thou bring thy gift ᶻ to the altar, and there rememberest that thy brother hath aught against thee,

z De.16.16.17.

24 Leave there thy gift before the altar, and go thy way; first be reconciled to thy brother, and then come and offer thy gift.

grades of condemnation among the Jews were here used by our Lord, to show divers grades of offences under the sixth commandment, which the Pharisees did not at all allow. In the eye of God's broad and searching law, these forms of evil passions, though they issued not in actual murder, should be held equal to those crimes which they condemned by "the judgment," "the council," and the "fire of Hinnom." And harboured or concealed anger, contemptuous and abusive language, and bitter reviling and imprecations, should be adjudged to condign punishment in the world to come, such as these earthly verdicts could only in a manner represent. If we have anything against our neighbour, the Scripture directs us what to do. We are to go and tell him, and seek reconciliation (ch. 18. 15-17).

23, 24. DUTY TO GOD.—Our Lord would teach, that the sixth command is obeyed only by maintaining kindness and good understandings with our neighbour. The Pharisees thought that if sacrifices were offered, and external rites observed, they did well. But here is a *first* duty to God. As to outward worship, we should not put *it* first, as though it were enough and every thing. We should make it our very first business to promote conciliation and love. If we have even gone so far as to begin our religious worship, and *there* remember that another *has ground of complaint against us*, we are to go about the settlement of this first of all, for the worship will be rejected of God if we have not *followed peace with all men*. "*Put on* (love) charity, which is the bond of perfectness."——¶ *If thou bring thy gift to the altar*. This was the prominent act of external worship, among the Jews. The altar was the place where they presented their offerings, and whatever they brought was called a GIFT. The representation here given of the altar is from *Kitto*. For another form, see under Matthew 23. 18, taken from the same work.——¶ *Be reconciled*. Be agreed. OBSERVE, The *offender* is enjoined to be reconciled. So sinners are urged to be reconciled to God. The meaning here is, to seek reconcilement and agreement—to make acknowledgment of the wrong, and apply for favour. " Seek peace and pursue it." Philo says, that when

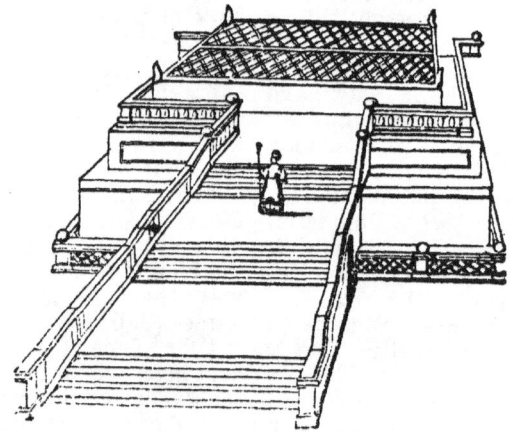

A. D. 31.] CHAPTER V. 65

25 Agree with thine adversary quickly, while thou art in the way with him; lest at any time the adversary deliver thee ᵃ to the judge, and the judge deliver thee to the officer, and thou be cast into prison.

26 Verily I say unto thee, Thou shalt by no means come out thence, till thou hast paid the uttermost farthing.

a Pr.25.8. Lu.12.58.59.

27 ¶ Ye have heard that it was said by them of old time, Thou shalt not commit adultery:

28 But I say unto you, That whosoever looketh ᵇ on a woman to lust after her, hath committed adultery with her already in his heart.

29 And if thy right eye [1] offend thee, pluck it out, and cast *it* from thee: for it is profitable

b Job 31.1. Pr.6.25. 1 or, *do cause thee to offend.*

---

a man injured his brother, and, repenting of his fault, voluntarily acknowledged it, he was first to make restitution, and then to come into the temple, presenting his sacrifice and asking pardon. Thus we are here taught that no worship of God is acceptable, while we neglect our duties to one another, and live in discord with our fellow-men.

25. THE PART OF PRUDENCE.—This verse exhorts to a speedy settlement of difficulties, and inculcates a placable spirit and a promptness to make amends. Long and grievous strifes at law come often from men's being too tenacious of their own rights, and too regardless of others'; being obstinate and unyielding in settlement.—— ¶ *Adversary*—accuser or creditor.—— ¶ *In the way*—that is, on the road to the court or judge. By the Roman law, the aggrieved could compel the other party to go with him before the Prætor—but they might agree by the way to settle, which was often done. Do not be slow to do justice, for the matter will grow more serious. "How great a matter a little fire kindleth." "The beginning of strife is as when one letteth out water" (Prov. 17. 14). That personal difficulties grow serious by delaying the settlement, is here set forth by taking a case of debt, where, if the claim is not attended to, the creditor or adversary may deliver the debtor to the judge, and the judge to the officer or sheriff, and the sheriff to the prison—and so from step to step it reaches extremes. No purgatory is taught here, for this relates wholly to dealings with fellow-men. Children are to understand, that they often sin by not making up at once, when there is any wrong done. If any one has wronged them, they are quickly to forgive, and if they have done any thing wrong to others, they are quickly to own it, and ask pardon, and promise to do so no more. Augustine interprets this of *the Law,* as the adversary, with a spiritual application which it may include.

26. *Not come out thence.* This shows the serious consequence of letting difficulties grow by delaying to settle them. Our Lord speaks of various strifes that arise among men, and uses these phrases of court to illustrate the subject. How much better, even as the part of prudence, to agree with the creditor, or attend to any claim upon us, than have things come to such an issue. How wise, also, to be reconciled to God, before it is too late. See ch. 18. 34; 25. 46.

27–30. The seventh commandment (Exodus 20. 14), our Lord expounds on the same great principles. He judgeth not according to the outward appearance, but looketh on the heart. The lust of the flesh and the lust of the eye are here condemned as a violation of the commandment. Not only the act of adultery, but the unchaste desire (or the adulterous eye, 2 Pet. 2. 14). Even the looking, that is to indulge these impure thoughts and passions, is a breaking of the

for thee that one of thy members should perish, and not *that* thy whole body should be cast into hell. c

30 And if thy right hand offend thee, cut it off, and cast *it* from thee: for it is profitable for thee that one of thy members should perish, and not *that* thy whole body should be cast into hell.

c Ro.8.13. 1Cor.9.27.

31 It hath been said, Whosoever shall put away his wife, let him give her a writing of divorcement: d

32 But I say unto you, that whosoever shall put away his wife, e saving for the cause of fornication, causeth her to commit adultery: and whosoever shall marry her that is divorced, committeth adultery.

d De.24.1. Je.3.1. Mar.10.2-9. e c.19.9. 1Cor.7 10,11.

---

command. That looking with a lustful eye was the crime of David, which led on to adultery, and that, to murder. 2 Sam. 11. Psalm 51.——¶ *Thy right eye.* The most important organ of sense. See Zach. 11. 17.——¶ *Offend.* The Greek word is *scandalizo.* The Cranmer translation, 1539, has it "*hynder.*" The Geneva, 1557, has it "*cause thee to offend.*" This is the true sense. Some would argue that they could not avoid this entering of sin at the eyes. But better part with your very right eye than sin. Therefore strive most earnestly to crucify the flesh (Gal. 5. 24), and mortify the members (Col. 3. 5), and "abstain from fleshly lusts which war against the soul" (1 Pet. 2. 11).——¶ *Pluck it out.* This indicates the strongest opposition. Not surely to mutilate our bodies, but to deny ourselves severely, lest we go into temptation; and to put away all occasions of sin—to crucify not only the flesh, but the affections and lusts, striving by all means to lay aside the sins which most easily beset us, and sacrifice the dearest things that prove occasions to sin. Submit to denials, and use even violent means that would be like putting out the eye itself, rather than yield. "The metaphor" (says Flavel) "is from chyrurgeons, whose manner it is, when the whole is in danger by any part, to cut it off, lest all perish."

30. The same sentiment is here repeated. It teaches that we had better lose our *limbs* than sin with them, and that no loss or damage is so grievous as the loss of God's favour—that therefore we must not yield our members as instruments of unrighteousness unto sin, nor by any means let sin reign in our mortal body, that we should obey it in the lusts thereof. Rom. 6. 12, 13.——¶ *It is profitable*— it will be to your advantage to give up this source or means of sinful gratification, whatever it be, rather than be cast, with all the unmortified passions of the flesh, into hell.

31, 32. Moses had said it (Deut. 24. 1). And this had been so construed by the Jewish teachers, as to admit of separation between husband and wife on the slightest grounds, if only a bill of divorce was given. How this evil prevailed in the time of Malachi, see Mal. 2. 14–16. They were "suffered" by the judicial statute, or magistrate's rule, to put away the wife on account of ceremonial uncleanness. This, because of their social condition and hardness of heart, was tolerated then. But the permission (says Scott) was construed into a command, and sadly abused. What had been allowed as a civil matter under Moses, to avoid a greater evil, had been pronounced by them every way right, and thus the original institution of marriage had been degraded and disesteemed. Yet, as the legal writing of divorcement was required by Moses, and a wife could not be put away without the formality and delay of this, *it was a lower witness to the sanctity of marriage;* so that Christ and Moses legislate in the same direction

[A. D. 31.] CHAPTER V. 67

33 ¶ Again, ye have heard that it hath been said by them of old time, Thou shalt not forswear thyself, ᶠ but shalt perform unto the Lord thine oaths:
34 But I say unto you, Swear not at all : ᵍ neither by heaven; for it is God's throne :
35 Nor by the earth ; for it is his footstool: neither by Jerusalem ; for it is ʰ the city of the great King.

f Le.19.12. Nu.30.2. De.23.23.   *g* c.23.16–22. Ja.5.12. *h* Re.21.2,10.

But Christ here laid down the rule, that divorce, saving for one cause, fornication, does not break the marriage covenant—the woman is counted by Him a *married woman* still! He that marries her, commits adultery, and *she is caused to commit adultery* by this unlawful divorce. They that give divorces or grant them for any other cause than fornication, come under this sentence of our Lord. They who grasp at every liberty they can find, will never keep God's commandments. How little will such regard their duty, or guard their hearts from sin. Marriage is most sacred as a standing symbol in the world, of Christ's union with the Church.

33. *Forswear thyself*—swear falsely – perjure thyself. See Levit. 19. 12. Deut. 23. 23. They interpreted the law as applicable to false swearing only where the proper name of Jehovah was used. If this were omitted in the oath, they counted the perjury a small offence. So they distinguished oaths into weightier and lighter, making an exact scale of their obligation on the conscience. And they deemed the perjury, or false swearing, the only profanity. An *oath* is a solemn affirmation, in which God is called to witness to the truth of what is said, and to visit with His vengeance if the oath be false.——¶ *Perform unto the Lord*. Sacredly to stand by and fulfil what is engaged in the oath. Our Lord would teach that light swearing, as well as false swearing, was forbidden—that taking His name in vain (Exodus 20. 7), applies to all irreverent oaths, even where His proper name is not introduced. For His name is that whereby He maketh Himself known, and includes His "titles, attributes, ordinances, words, and works." Instances are given to this effect in the verses following.

34. *Swear*—take oath—*not at all*. This is not to forbid all oaths, but of such kind as are named. They used various forms of swearing by solemn objects, as by the temple, by heaven, by the head, by Jerusalem; and they made the most capricious distinctions in these oaths—as that it was right to swear by the temple, but not by the gold of it—and by the altar, but not by the gift upon it. (See ch. 23. 16–23.) Our Lord would teach that this was indirectly swearing by God—for the Heaven was *His throne*, and the earth was *His footstool*. He does not here forbid judicial oaths, but mainly these conversational oaths which he instances, and others only as verging toward such. He teaches that an oath, if it be any thing but a wanton mockery and profanity, is in substance a solemn appeal to God. And hence, though a man may swear lightly by some inferior object, or though the law under which he swears may not require him to believe in God, and eternity, and a judgment, yet an oath is an oath, however it be called, and those who make light of it do profane God's name. Besides, in swearing by an inferior object, we ascribe to it the prerogative of God. "He that sweareth in the earth, shall swear by the God of truth" (Isa. 65. 16).

35. *Jerusalem*. This city had its sanctity from being the seat of His majesty and the place of His holy temple. God is the great King and Governor of the nations. Psalms 47. 7; 48. 2 ; 95. 3. Job 13. 9.——¶ *By thy head*—or by thy life. "As I live," "may I die if it be not true." We

MATTHEW. [A. D. 31.

36 Neither shalt thou swear by thy head, because thou canst not make one hair white or black:

37 But let your communication be, Yea, yea; Nay, nay: for whatsoever is more than these, cometh of evil.*i*

38 ¶ Ye have heard that it hath been said, An *j* eye for an eye, and a tooth for a tooth:

39 But I say unto you *k* that ye resist not evil: but whosoever shall smite thee *l* on thy right cheek, turn to him the other also.

40 And if any man will sue thee at the law, and take away

i Ja.5.12.   *j* Ex.21.24. *k* Pr.20.22; 24.29. Ro.12.17-19. *l* Is.50.6.

---

have not our lives in our power, even to alter the essential colour of a hair. Therefore we have no right to pledge our lives for our sincerity. And to use such oaths in conversation is the grossest trifling with God and sacred things. But many profane people now use a list of such oaths, which they flatter themselves do not violate the third commandment, because the name of God is not used. Such persons are ungodly and condemned. Profane swearers are generally of low, debased character in every important respect.

37. *Your communication.* Your talk. Be content with a solemn, honest, explicit, yes or no. There is really no need of more. Extravagant talk and profuse appeals and affirmations to establish what we say, come of evil. They spring from bad dispositions, wrong views, evil motives or habits, and are from the Evil one. The oath of itself, is a recognition of man's untruthfulness.

38. *An eye for an eye.* God had enjoined this (Deut. 19. 21. Levit. 24. 20. Exod. 21. 24) as a rule for magistrates to punish personal injuries by inflicting the like, and not more or less at their pleasure. But this rule was seized upon by individuals to gratify private revenge, and to do to others as others did to them. This *lex talionis,* or law of retaliation, was mostly in private hands, according to their customs, and was a source of great mischief.

1. As to personal indignity. 39. *Resist not evil,* or the evil-doer who affronts you. This is against rendering evil for evil to any man, and even more against taking a stand of hostile opposition to match another's misconduct. As in the former passages, the doctrine laid down is not absolute, but qualified by what immediately follows. To practice non-resistance in all cases, is often to encourage the wicked.——¶ *Smite thee.* Greek - *rapisei—rap* or *slap thee.* This was regarded as a special affront. 2 Cor. 11. 20. The phrase is used here proverbially. We are to present a front of greatest patience and forbearance. Instead of *smiting back,* as is common among men, it had better be borne meekly. "This one staff of Moses shivers the ten thousand spears of Pharaoh." A personal indignity had rather be suffered than to *pay back in the same coin.* This does not refer to self-defence for protection of life and family. Our Lord's example is to the point, "Who when he was reviled, reviled not again." 1 Pet. 2. 23. Micah 5. 1. See Rom. 12. 17-19.

2. As to injury of estate. 40. *Sue thee at the law.* The principle is here applied to property. Where an ill-designing and malicious man takes every opportunity to wrong by lawsuits, and gets an advantage so far as to take away your *coat,* let him have your cloak also, rather than contend. These were the two chief garments in use at that time. The coat was the *under,* and the cloak the *upper* or *over,* a sort of wrapper, and loose. See Cuts 1–3. It was often used by the poor at night for a covering. Hence the law of Moses provided that in case it was given as a

thy coat, let him have *thy* cloak also.

41 And whosoever shall compel thee to go a mile, go with him twain.

42 Give to him that asketh

pledge, it should not be retained over night. So it was valued more than the other. And the sentiment here is, that even besides your coat, you had better give up your cloak than contend with such a man. Even on temporal grounds this is often found to be the best plan, rather to lose something than quarrel at law with malicious and wicked men. The cuts below are from Kitto's Encyclopedia, showing the *coat* (under) and *cloak* (over), also the fringe (fig. 4) on the hem or border of the outside garment, not at the feet, but midway.

3. As to personal liberty. 41. *Compel.* The term here used is from a word signifying a king's courier, who could compel (see the word chap. 27. 32) into the public service, especially to carry the king's commands through the empire. This was a custom of Persian origin, and the duty taught is, that if compelled or pressed into service by such public authority, and made to go a mile, we should go *twain*, that is, two miles, rather than quarrel. The spirit here enjoined is, wherever it is possible, and as much as lieth in us (that is, *for our part*), to live peaceably with all men. Rom.

12. 18 and 13. 1. Patience and gentleness under the severe exactions of men, are inculcated.

42. *Give.* A broad rule of benevolence is here laid down, which will be safe for all cases. The heart must be open to give. We should cultivate the habit of giving. This is meant as a rule against the rule of many, *not to give*. We had better even give to one that shall prove undeserving, than turn away the worthy poor unhelped. Many object that there are impostors; but this does not discharge us of our obligation. Such a general presumption in favour of giving should be set aside only by a weighty and sufficient reason. The spirit noticed in James 2. 15, 16, is rebuked that says, " Be ye warmed," &c., but gives nothing. Christians should ask themselves what they have that they have not received. "Every good gift and every perfect gift is from above (James 1. 17), and cometh down from the Father of lights." He gives us more than others, that we may have wherewith to dispense His bounties. So He makes us stewards, and will hold us to account. We should take all

Exod 22. 26.

Numbers 15. 38.

thee, and from him that would borrow of thee turn not thou ᵐ away.

43 ¶ Ye have heard that it hath been said, ⁿ Thou shalt love thy neighbour, and hate thine enemy:

44 But I say unto you, Love ᵒ your enemies, bless them that curse you, do good to them that hate you, and pray ᵖ for them which despitefully use you, and persecute you;

m De.15.7,11. *n* De.23.6.

o Ro.12.14,20. *p* Lu.23.34. Ac.7.60.

fit means for applying our liberality in the best way. Augustine says that the point lies here, " *We are to give to every man, but not to give every thing* "—not always to give what is asked, but to send none away without some good word or deed from us.——¶ *Borrow*. We should be ready to lend. This is another shape of liberality. The poor may be helped in this way, where they are worthy and industrious, and ask no more. Luke has it, " and lend, *hoping for nothing again* (6. 35).——¶ *Turn not thou away*—from such an application; but show a disposition to entertain it in Christian kindness. Christians should be liberal, considering how great things God hath done for them, and how destitute they would be without the special, distinguishing liberality of God.

43. *It hath been said*. See Levit. 19. 18, where only the first clause is found in the law, "Thou shalt love thy neighbour (as thyself"). They had added the following clause. As the Theocratic people, they were to hate their enemies only as God's enemies. So we find David often praying for destruction to come upon his enemies. Yet not his private foes so much as God's. Here Christ teaches us that we must love the man while hating the evil that is in him. But the Jews indulged private hatred. It was their carnal inference, and they had made it part of the law. They pretended that the command to love their neighbour bound them to hate their enemies. And while God called their fellow-man their neighbour, they contended that none but Jews and friends were such. They termed all the heathen their enemies, and their hatred toward them was proverbial.

And this they pretended to have deduced from God's command for avoiding and driving out the heathen.

44. *Love your enemies*—in the sense explained, blessing, benefitting, and praying for them. An enemy is one who hates us, and seeks to injure us. Bear good-will toward such, not rendering evil for evil to any man, but contrariwise blessing. See David's treatment of Saul, and its effect upon his enemy, who exclaimed, " Thou art more righteous than I, for thou hast rewarded me good, whereas I have rewarded thee evil" (1 Sam. 24. 17). We are not required to cherish and treat them as friends. Yet we must not treat them as enemies, but rather regard them as fellow-sinners.——¶ *Bless them*. Give them good words. See Acts 7. 60. We should remember how God treats us, " for he is kind unto the unthankful and evil," and by so doing we shall heap coals of fire on their heads.——¶ *Do good*. Be disposed to benefit them that are ill-disposed toward you and seek your injury.—— ¶*Despitefully use you*—insult and abuse you. Pray for such as execrate you. By this means they may be made better, for God can renew their hearts in answer to your requests. Pray for blessings upon such as pour abuses and imprecations upon you. Return the opposite conduct, good for evil, " contrariwise blessing." 1 Pet. 3. 9.——¶ *Persecute you*—injure you and *follow* you with wrongs. One of the most beautiful gems of oriental literature is contained in a passage from the Persian poet Sadi, quoted by Sir William Jones, teh sentiment of which is embodied in the following lines:

45 That ye may be the children of your Father which is in heaven: for he maketh his sun to rise ⁹ on the evil and on the good, and sendeth rain on the just and on the unjust.

46 For if ye love them which

q Job 23.3

love you, what reward have ye? do not even the publicans the same?

47 And if ye salute your brethren only, what do ye more *than others?* do not even the publicans so?

48 Be ye therefore perfect, ʳ

r Ge.17.1. De.18.13. Lu.6.36,40. Col.1.28.

The sandal tree perfumes, when riven,
The axe that laid it low;
Let man who hopes to be forgiven,
Forgive and bless his foe.

45. *That ye may be the children.* This is the temper of God, and to resemble Him, or to have evidence of being born of Him, we must show such a disposition. "He is kind to the unthankful and to the evil." This is shown in the sunshine and the rain, which are His. He sends daily a thousand mercies upon the vilest sinners. And as we see daily this goodness of God to offenders, we should practise accordingly. This is contrary to carnal nature. Yet this is God's plan in the world. To show His wrath, and to make His power known, He endures with much long-suffering the vessels of wrath fitted to destruction (Rom. 9. 22). But at the judgment He will make the closest distinction. "Then shall ye return and discern between the righteous and the wicked" (Mal. 3. 18. Matt. 25. 46).

46. *For if.* To return good for good is natural, and a mere exchange which none are too bad to make, as it suits their interest; but to render good for evil is most contrary to nature, and is the Christian's temper as distinct from the world.——¶ *Publicans.* Luke says *sinners.* The Publicans were tax-gatherers, and their business was to get from every body and not to give—to take in, and not to give out; and yet even these, who only knew of exacting dues from every man, even they would render love for love, and pay back in the same coin the kindness shown to them. Publicans and sinners (or heathens) are terms often associated.

They were counted a vile class, partly because they were covetous and rapacious—deceitful and cruel as a class. It is our natural pleasure and interest to love those who love us. It is our Christian duty and privilege to love those who do not love us. Otherwise, what do we more than others? What special triumph is it over evil passions? What gain is our religion to us? Especially, what *reward* have we by this rule? What treatment could we expect of God on the same principle?

47. *Salute.* This word is often rendered *greet,* and sometimes *embrace,* as a token of friendship and affection. It is meant to express the common offices of civility and good understanding, being on *good terms* and treating kindly. If you greet none but your friends with marks of favour, what do ye *special,* or extra, or beyond others, to show the power and value of your religion? A follower of Christ is bound to do more than others, because the religion of Christ is better than others, and makes men better.

48. *Be ye, &c.* This is the language of the law. Deut. 18. 13. "Thou shalt be *perfect* (marg. *upright,* or *sincere*) with the Lord thy God." Therefore adopt no such false standard as the Pharisees, who qualify the law and make it void by their traditions. Be ye consistent and complete in your piety, in like manner as your Father in heaven.——¶ *Perfect.* There is nothing here to prove that sinless perfection is attained in this life. Paul constantly uses this term (τελειοι) to denote an advanced, matured piety, as distinguished from *babes* (νηπιοι) in

even as your Father which is in heaven is perfect.

CHAPTER VI.

TAKE heed that ye do not your ¹ alms before men, to be seen of them: otherwise ye have no reward ² of your Father which is in heaven.

1 or, *righteousness*. Ps.112.9.   2 or, *with*.

2 Therefore when thou doest *thine* alms, ³ do not sound a trumpet before thee, as the hypocrites do in the synagogues and in the streets, that they may have glory of men. Verily I say unto you, They have their reward.

3 or, *cause a trumpet to be sounded*.

Christ. These were "men of full age." "Leaving the principles or elements (rudiments), let us go on unto *perfection*." Noah is spoken of as "a just man and *perfect* (or *upright*, margin) in his generation," where the latter clause is explanatory. (Gen. 6.9.) He was pious in all his relations of life. Luke reads, "Be ye therefore *merciful*" (6. 36). ——¶ *Even as.* (ὥσπερ, Gr.) *In like manner as, &c.* We are to have a holy God—our Father in heaven —for a pattern; and we are never to rest satisfied with our attainments until we reach His spotless perfection in the heavens. "He that dwelleth in God, dwelleth in love, for God is love."

CHAPTER VI.

1. *Your alms.* Our Lord having taught us what we are to do, proceeds now to teach us how we are to do it. Doing alms is giving money, food, clothing, or any such supply to the destitute. Those bounties to the poor which you commonly give, give with the right spirit. Our Lord would correct evil motives in doing good things. He would teach that the virtue lies not in the outward act, for the inward temper and aim may destroy all the goodness in His sight. "Ambition maketh alms vain." Doing alms, or distributing supplies among the poor, to be *seen of men*, where the object is to make a show, and attract public notice—this has no praise-worthiness before God. A Christian should let his light shine. He should therefore be willing that others should know of his doings, for example's sake. But this is plainly different from noising them abroad. Augustine likens those who boast their good deeds, to the foolish hen, who has no sooner laid her egg, than by her cackling she calls some one to take it away.——¶ *Otherwise*, or *else*, he loses God's approbation of the act. The merciful, who are humbly and heartily so, out of Christian charity, shall obtain mercy (Matt. 5. 7).

2. *Do not sound a trumpet.* This is a phrase used in many languages to express boasting and parade. We need not suppose that any trumpet was actually blown.——¶ *Hypocrites*, pretenders, dissemblers, false characters. The term was first used for *stage-actors*, who often wore masks, and whose business it was to act a false part, to assume the character of another, and counterfeit his conduct. It may be remarked that stage-players and gladiators were introduced to the public by sounding of trumpets.—— ¶ *Synagogues*, and streets. Alms were specially distributed in the synagogues or places of religious concourse. The poor would flock there, naturally hoping for charities from the good. So, the lame man at the temple gate (Acts 3). In the Apostles' time, collections for the poor and needy formed part of the worship on the Sabbath. The *streets*, also, at the corners, and where roads met, served as a resort; and there, amongst the crowd, the utmost ostentation was shown by the proud and heartless donors.——¶ *Their reward.* This noisy praise in the streets they look for, and they get it to their heart's content; and this is all they shall get. God gives them their request, but sends leanness into their

3 But when thou doest alms, let not thy left hand know what thy right hand doeth:

4 That thine alms may be in secret: and thy Father, which seeth in secret, himself shall reward *a* thee openly.

5 ¶ And when thou prayest, thou shalt not be as the hypocrites *are:* for they love to pray, standing in the synagogues and in the corners of the streets, that they may be seen of men. Verily, I say unto you, They have their reward.*b*

6 But thou, when thou prayest, enter into thy closet, and when thou hast shut thy door, pray to thy Father which is in secret; and thy Father, which seeth in secret, *c* shall reward thee openly.

7 But when ye pray, use not

a Lu.8.17; 14.14.   *b* Pr.16.5. Ja.4.6.   *c* Ps.34.15. Is.65.24.

soul (Psalm 106. 15). These cuts are taken from the plates of Kitto's Encyclopedia, showing the postures prevalent among the Orientals. *Standing* in prayer is doubtless the scriptural mode for public worship. 1 Ki. 8. 14.

3. Alms should be given *in secret;* that is, *unostentatiously,* without a disposition to blaze the good act abroad.——¶ *Let not thy left hand know* is a proverbial phrase, to express a modest privacy—not making it known even to ourselves—not making it a merit, or taking the praise to ourselves. This non-appropriation of it—this internal, humble unconsciousness of a good work, contrasts essentially with the trumpeting forth of the Pharisees. Such vain ambition is to be cured by remembering God's omniscience. He needs no proclamation of our good deeds to inform Him, and He looketh on the heart. *He sees,* and shall reward thee openly when the secrets of all hearts shall be revealed (25. 34).

5. The same warning is directed against their showy habits of prayer. It is not the place that is here condemned, but the feeling that gives the act such vain prominence. Pomp and parade in prayer for vain-glory is an awful abomination before God. They chose the most thronged places, and had no relish for secret prayer: they wished to be seen of men, so as to get the character of great devoutness and piety.

6. *Thy closet*—a retired apartment for prayer. This was commonly, among Orientals, a room rising, like an observatory of a modern house, above the main building. It sometimes had two or three apartments. "The little chamber" (2 Kings 4. 10), "the summer chamber" (Judges 3. 20), "the upper chamber" (2 Kings 23. 12), "the inner chamber" (1 Kings 20. 30), may refer to this. It was a place for retirement and undisturbed devotion in private. Christ would teach that we should rather seek secrecy, than court a vain publicity. We should pray *alone,* because we

vain repetitions, ᵈ as the heathen *do:* for they think that they shall be heard for ᵉ their much speaking.

8 Be not ye therefore like unto them: for your Father knoweth ᶠ what things ye have need of before ye ask him.

9 After this manner therefore pray ye: Our ᵍ Father ʰ

d Ec.5.2. e 1K.18.26,&c.   f Lu.12.30. Jno.16.23-27. g Lu.11.2,&c. h Ro.8.15.

have private business with God, and every one of us must give account of himself to God. Besides, the advantage is, that one alone can better command his thoughts, and pour them out more freely and fully "where none but God can hear." It is called *secret* prayer, because it is secluded and apart from the notice of men. But social and public prayer are no less a duty. The main object here is to rebuke pretension and parade in prayer. We read of Christians being gathered for prayer (comp. Acts 1. 4, and 2. 1. Acts 1. 24; 12. 5, 12). In prayer we are to shut out the world and all vain thoughts.

7. *Vain repetitions* — an empty round of phrases recited, parrot-like, or an idle repeating of the same words, without thought. The term (*battologesete*) is supposed to be taken from the primary sounds of infancy—an incoherent babble. The Old English translation renders it here "Babble not too much." "An endless tumult and hubbub of words," says Augustine, "is often substituted for the unspeakable utterances of the spirit."——¶ *The heathen*—the Gentiles, or the nations, as the term is, who were foreigners and aliens from the commonwealth of Israel. Jews should not *be* or *do* as the unenlightaned heathen. Christians should not act like the world. It was not against *repetition,* but *vain repetition,* that our Lord here spake. This the Gentiles often practised; and the merely formal among nominal Christians will often copy the Pagans. We may pray and pray again for the same thing. We may repeat our desires and words in the same prayer. This sometimes is done devoutly from very earnestness, and in the way of importunity. It is against idle and empty words repeated to spin out a heartless prayer, or to make a merit of long prayer, that Christ is speaking. Those to whom he alluded calculated "to be heard for *their much speaking.*" Much praying is a different thing, and is commanded.

8. A Jew ought to know and do better than a Gentile. God was his Father. How consoling to a sincere heart, that God knows its real desires, beyond the poor clothing of words. But though He knows what we need, before we ask, it is right to ask what we want. God's knowing about it does not alter our duty to ask for it: and He has made His promises with this requirement, that we shall ask if we would receive. "That which is unsought would mostly remain unacknowledged also." "Ask and ye shall receive," is a command no less than a promise. "We are to pray," says Bengel, "not that we may teach the Father, but worship Him."

9. Here follows the "LORD's PRAYER," so called because dictated by Christ to His disciples, and so having the Lord for its author. John had delivered some frame-work of prayer to his disciples, and one of Christ's followers requested the same from Him (Luke 11. 1). This was very commonly done by the Jewish teachers.——¶ *After this manner*—like this—in this style—not as the Gentiles or Pharisees. This was intended as a *guide* to devotion. A skeleton and frame-work of all prayer—a normal petition. Our Lord was teaching them *how* to pray, not *what* to pray. He did not mean that all our prayers should be in these exact words. Luke has given the same prayer in *different* words (Luke 11). Christ and the Apostles used other words of prayer (Matt. 26 39; 42. 44.

which art in ¹ heaven, hallowed be ʲ thy name:

10 Thy kingdom ᵏ come: thy will be done, in earth ¹ as *it is* in heaven.

11 Give us this day our ᵐ daily bread:

i Ps.115.3. *j* Ps.111.9; 139.20. *k* c.16.28. Re.11.15. *l* Ps.103.20,21. *m* Pr.30.8. Is.33.16.

Acts 1. 24, 25). This should always be the substance of a well-ordered prayer; brief, concise, comprehensive, and to the point. It consists of a preface, six petitions, and a doxology, and it is found substantially in the 19 prayers of the Jewish Liturgy, except the clause, "as we forgive our debtors."——¶ *Our Father*. God will, first of all, be owned in his true character, as the paternal source of all His creatures — Creator, Preserver, Governor, Benefactor, and the covenant Father of believers. And we cannot go on with our prayer until we recognize Him in His endearing relations to us. We never have the heart to pray, nor can we ask aright, until we see Him as our reconciled Father in Christ Jesus. Under the old Covenant, they could only say Master; under the new, we say *Abba Father* (Rom. 8. 15. John 1. 12). It is *our* Father, not *my* Father. It is meant to be the prayer of brethren, who in Christ are knit together into one body, adopted in Him into the same family.——¶ *In heaven*. Most Exalted, the High and Lofty One. This expresses utmost reverence, and acknowledges His omniscience, omnipresence, omnipotence, and all His loftiest attributes. (See Psalms 2. 4; 115. 3.) This address was common in the Jewish prayers with the same meaning; yet God is every where present as a spirit, and a dispenser of spiritual blessings to His worshippers. "Where two or three are gathered together in my name, there am I in the midst of them," &c. His glory is such that the "heaven of heavens cannot contain Him" (2 Chron. 2. 6). We are thus taught to look for God, not in ourselves, but out of and above ourselves. "This is a protest," says Augustine, "against pantheistic notions, against all philosophical schemes, of the identity of our spirit and the Spirit of God." The Spirit witnesseth with the spirits of believers that they are the children of God.——¶ *Hallowed be thy name.* Let that whereby thou makest thyself known be held sacred, kept holy, and every where revered. God's name means "His titles, attributes, ordinances, words and works;" because a name is that whereby any one is made known; and this first petition begs that God and all divine things may be held sacred, venerated and adored among men and in all the universe. We are, first of all, and in all our conduct, and all our prayers, to have respect to God's glory. To keep the Sabbath holy is to hallow it; and so of all that belongs to true religion.——¶ *Thy kingdom come*. The kingdom spoken of in Scripture, is the kingdom of Christ—the reign of grace which He has set up in the world, called the kingdom of heaven, and the kingdom of God. This petition recognizes His Divinity, and shows that He is to be regarded as one with the Father. Let Satan's kingdom be destroyed, and the kingdom of grace be advanced, ourselves and others brought into it and kept in it, and let the kingdom of glory be hastened (see Shorter Catechism). Men oppose this kingdom because they dislike its holy restraints and pure government, and so they help on the kingdom of Satan by serving sin. The darkness, degradation and vices of heathen countries show that this kingdom has not come among them, because it is "righteousness, and peace and joy in the Holy Ghost" (Rom. 14. 17). We can help forward every Christian enterprize as we have opportunity and ability, and we can always put up his petition, and so we can extend the kingdom by our labours and our prayers.——¶ *Thy will be done*. God's will is the only true

12 And forgive us our debts, n **as we forgive our debtors:**

n C.18.21-35. Lu.7.40-48.

13 And lead us not into temptation, but deliver us p **from**

o C.26.41. Lu.22.40,46. p Jno.17.15.

standard of conduct for all creatures; and on this fallen earth we must have from Him the power to do His will. We must pray for ability "to know, obey, and submit to His will in all things, as the angels do in heaven." The Scriptures contain His will as here spoken of. We are to seek the circulation of the Scriptures, and their widest influence, and the most complete subjection of men to their divine rules. Most men seek their own, not the things which are Jesus Christ's. Yet, if they had their desire, it would end in their own ruin not only, but in that of the universe. On the other hand, if God's will were done by all as by angels, this earth would be like heaven, where the angels dwell. They do His will most perfectly (Psalm 103. 20). And we are here taught not to be content with doing our duty as others do it, but *as angels do it* (chap. 5. 48). We are to aim at being perfect, "like as our Father in heaven" and "the angels in heaven are perfect;" and we are to pray that more and more God's will may be everywhere and in every way obeyed. Christ had a human will subordinated to the Divine will in Him, yet not abolished by it.

11. After having first sought the glory of God in our petitions, we may pray even for *bread*. Whatever we need for our daily sustenance we may ask of Him. Unless He favour us, we cannot obtain a morsel by greatest industry and toil; therefore we ought daily to thank *Him* for all that we get. We should feel this dependence upon Him for every thing, and we should desire to receive every good gift as from His hand, even though we may earn it from others. Every good gift is from above, and cometh down from the Father of lights. Jas. 1. 17. This brief prayer covers all temporal mercies, and includes all that we need ask. Such a style of petition for earthly things, teaches us *moderation*.

—¶ *Daily*. This word means *essential*—sufficient for our support. Luke says, "Give us day by day our daily (or sufficient) bread." It is meant to include all daily supplies, as well for the body as for the soul. This whole prayer is meant for more than one. "*Our* Father"—"give *us*"—"forgive *us*"—"deliver *us*," &c.; and being here set forth for a style of daily prayer, we are taught to *pray socially*, day by day. This can be done in the family; and it is daily, family prayer that seems supposed here, where the family head asks daily for such bounties as are needed. "Having food and raiment, let us be therewith content" (1 Tim. 6. 8). Daily piety is requisite—we are to live daily and hourly upon God.

12. *Debts*. In Luke another word is used, which reads "trespasses." That is here the meaning (see vs. 14). The Scriptures often speak of sin in this light. Trespasses, or sins, are debts. Sinners are debtors. They owe God vast amounts of love and service, which they have never paid Him, and never can pay. "What shall I render unto the Lord for all his benefits toward me" (Psalm 116. 12). To forgive a debt is to free the debtor from payment, and blot out the charges against him. God forgives the debts or sins of His people, by blotting them out, and not *remembering against them their iniquities*, of which they repent. Christ has satisfied the claims of Justice for all who trust in Him, and He can claim forgiveness for all who are His, while it is all of grace to them. He has taken away the condemnation (Rom. 8. 1), and now God can be just and yet justify. Reference is here made to daily trespasses, for no man liveth and sinneth not.——¶ *As we forgive*. We must be able to say, as it reads in Luke, "for we also forgive." Our Lord dwells here on this duty (see vss. 14 and 15). God confines us in st

evil: for thine ᑫ is the kingdom, and the power, and the glory, for ever, Amen.

q Re.5.12,13.

14 For if ye forgive men their trespasses, your heavenly Father will also forgive you.

---

specially and solemnly here to the great gospel law of forgiveness. Our forgiving others will not, of itself, save us; no virtue can atone, and no worship is acceptable with hatred or ill-will in our hearts, or wilful quarrels with others (vs. 23); and no prayer for forgiveness need be offered unless we are ready to forgive. Matt. 18. 35. Mark 11. 25, 26. So Christ has joined together this important duty of forgiving others, and this most important prayer of a sinner to be forgiven. Christ, in forgiving us, sets us the most perfect example of forgiving injuries. "How terrible may this prayer become to us (says Augustine), if we be unforgiving." We are taught, in all our prayers, to examine well our own tempers. How important to put up this prayer in the right spirit! If we are unforgiven or unforgiving, we must surely perish! "Depart from me, ye workers of iniquity" (Matt. 25). This petition alludes to daily trespasses as the bread to daily bread. How can perfectionists use the Lord's prayer? 1 John 1. 8.

13. *Temptation.* Let not our course lie through temptation. *Christ was led up by the Spirit* into the wilderness, to be tempted—yet He was tempted "*of the devil;*" and in the execution of His official work, His mediatorial course was marked out through that field of trial. And as we know our sinfulness and weakness, it is fit that we should not ask forgiveness for the past, without imploring this exemption from trial for the future. This is an implied confession of our frail and erring nature, and of our imperfect state. It is the sin of many that they do not dread and deprecate temptation, but run into it. If they prayed against it, as Christ has taught, they would be more watchful of it (Matt. 26. 41). The young are especially exposed. Young professors of Christ often fall. Gay amusements and vain companions surround them, and they apologize for these allowances. They often feel strong, and think there is no danger; but they run into the temptations, and are led astray by an enticing world. There is no safe rule but this—to dread and pray against all forms of temptations, and so to deny ourselves those occasions, companions, and employments which are calculated to ensnare our souls. "As strangers and pilgrims, abstain from fleshly lusts that war against the soul." 1 Pet. 2. 11.——¶ *Evil.* Literally, "*the evil;*" that is, the evil or dreadful consequence of temptation. Or, it may mean, "*the Evil One,*" Satan (Matt. 15. 19. 1 John 2. 13), and so include all sin and misery in the widest sense. We may and ought to pray for deliverance from all that belongs to sin. God alone is the Deliverer. To be delivered or *set free* from our evil natures, from Satan's snares, from sorrow, and suffering, and sins, is matter for daily prayer. Sin is the greatest evil, and the *source* of all beside. Christ has come to bring us deliverance from the bondage of corruption, into the glorious liberty of the children of God.——¶ *Kingdom.* Here follows the doxology, ascribing to God all the power to perform these things, and all the praise and glory for their performance, and from it.——¶ *Amen.* This word is from the Hebrew verb, *to be firm, sure.* It means, *so let it be!* or, *may it be made sure!* It is added at the close, to express the strong desire of the petitioner for all that he has asked. It is a form of subscription and seal set to the prayer, confirming it as the hearty wish of the suppliant, or it is a general enforcement of the request. Such phrases are common— as in memorials to government we say, "So your petitioners will ever pray." This word, *amen,* though often spoken lightly, is properly a

15 But if ye forgive not men their trespasses, neither will your Father forgive your trespasses. ʳ

16 ¶ Moreover, when ye fast, be not, as the hypocrites, of a sad countenance: for they disfigure their faces, that they may appear unto men ˢ to fast. Verily I say unto you They have their reward.

17 But thou, when thou fastest, anoint thine head, and wash thy face;

18 That thou appear not unto men to fast, but unto thy Father which is in secret: and thy Father, which seeth in secret, shall reward thee openly.

ʳ Ep.4.31. Ja.2.13.   ˢ Is.58.3,5.

---

solemn form of prayer to God, who only can make anything sure. It was sometimes used to express the uniting of a company in a social prayer (1 Cor. 14. 16). It occurs very often in the Gospels, rendered "*verily*," or repeated, "*verily, verily*."

14. This refers to the fifth petition. It would indicate, that as forgiveness is the great message of the Gospel, so it is the leading duty of fellow-sinners toward each other. This would account for this particular subject being here taken up out of all the topics presented in the Lord's Prayer. Besides, the fifth petition was peculiar, as having this sort of condition annexed, "*as we forgive;*" and here the reason is assigned for such a proviso. ——¶ *For, if ye forgive*, &c. The true spirit of forgiveness, in imitation of Christ, is a pledge of forgiveness being obtained of Christ. A uniform temper of forgiveness is characteristically Christian, and Christians who have obtained pardon through Christ, are charged to expect that measure of forgiveness from God which they mete out to others. No one virtue can save, but it can give evidence of our regeneration. An unforgiving spirit has no evidence of pardon from God.

16. *Moreover, when ye fast.* The great Teacher here lays down again the doctrine of sincerity and simplicity in religious devotions, and applies it to fasting, as He had done to alms and prayer. This alludes to their private and voluntary abstaining from food. The Jews had four annual fasts, and many private fasts.

The Pharisees fasted twice a week (Luke 18. 12), to wear the appearance of extra sanctity and devotion. This was on the second day of the week, when Moses ascended Mount Sinai, and on the fifth day, when he came down.——¶ *A sad countenance*, More literally, a *scowling face*—a sullen, morose look.——¶ *They disfigure*. They spoil the appearance of their faces, neglecting to wash, and comb, and anoint themselves as usual—throwing ashes and earth upon their heads. They strove to look as squalid and wretched as possible. The Searcher of hearts knew that their object was only to *appear* self-denied, humble, and devout in the sight of men.

17. *Anoint thy head.* It was THEIR custom to wash at every meal, and to anoint freely with olive oil, *except* on days of fasting. Christ teaches that they should not make such alteration in their appearance, but anoint and wash *as usual*, having for their object, not to show themselves to men as fasting, for this is hypocrisy and mockery, but to appear acceptably before God. In all these precepts, Christ would guard His disciples against a vain show and empty parade in their devotions and duties.

19. Christ had enjoined sincerity toward God in almsgiving and fasting—in charity to others and piety toward Him. He had also taught them to pray and how to pray. Now he proceeds to discourse against worldliness, which is so hostile to benevolence and confidence in Him. We should not seek independence of

19 ¶ Lay not up for yourselves treasures upon *t* earth, where moth and rust doth corrupt, and where thieves break through and steal:
20 But lay up for yourselves treasures in *u* heaven, where neither moth nor rust doth corrupt, and where thieves do not break through nor steal:
21 For where your treasure is, there will your heart be also.
22 The light of the body is the eye: *v* If therefore thine eye be single, thy whole body shall be full of light:

t Pr. 23.4. Lu.18.24,25. He. 13.5. *u* Is.33. 6. Lu.12.33,34. 1 Ti.6.19. *v* Lu.11.34,36.

His providence, or prefer earthly to heavenly wealth.——¶ *Treasures.* Valuable articles—money, raiment, corn, wine, oil. This was the wealth of the rich in the East. The language here is, Do not *treasure up treasures,* or store away stores for yourselves upon earth—that is, Do not make it your chief aim to hoard up large possessions here below. The great hinderance to spirituality is worldliness.——¶ *Upon earth.* This is not the *place* for laying up possessions—because it is full of destructive agents, moth, rust and robbers.——¶ *Moth.* As a principal article of wealth was in goodly garments and changes of raiment, and as moth is a small worm which ruins clothing, it is meant that their possessions are perishable, and will be destroyed.——¶ *Rust.* By the rust that destroys metals, is meant that which would render their other valuables worthless. In general, it alludes to the gnawing tooth of Time. All earthly treasures are liable to perish by treachery of men, disasters of Providence, and their own perishable nature. They shall fade away and fail at last, and often while the owners are alive. "Riches take to themselves wings."——¶ *Treasures in heaven.* Provide for your soul's interests. This is more than the body. Lay hold on the hope set before you. Set your affection upon things above. Seek an inheritance incorruptible and undefiled. Heaven is the place for laying up an enduring portion. These treasures are such, and the place is such, that they can never be invaded, much less destroyed. God offers to take into His own secure keeping that which we otherwise could not retain. We are charged to send it before us to that world where we are certainly going, that we may find it there.

21. The heart will be where the treasure is. This duty is urged here, from the consideration that the *heart* will cleave to the treasure wherever and whatever it be. We may know where we have our treasure laid up, if we notice where our affections are set. The heart follows and fixes on its treasures, whatever they be, or wherever. "If riches increase, set not your heart upon them." We should employ our earthly treasures in heavenly deeds of benevolence and piety. *And we should take care of our hearts,* for they shall be corrupted and worn by cleaving to earthly treasures. We can properly and safely cleave only to that which is true and eternal. "Keep thy heart with all diligence, for out of it are the issues of life."

22. *The light of the body.* All light enters by the eye. Every thing depends upon the condition and action of this organ. This is an adage. Our chief impressions abroad in the world depend upon the eyesight, what the eye is set upon, and what it sees, and how. Our actions mostly depend on this.——¶ *Single*—simple, set on one object, or seeing clearly and not confusedly. The eye, here, is the *intention or motive.* In general, it means the disposition.——¶ *Full of light.* "*Lucid as if all an eye.*"—Bengel. All your actions should be well advised, and full of wisdom and spiritual understanding in the knowledge and service of Christ, by having the eye singly or supremely directed upon Divine things. "This one thing I

23 But if thine eye be evil, thy whole body shall be full of darkness. If therefore the light that is in thee be darkness, how great *is* that darkness!

24 ¶ No man can serve two

---

do." "Looking unto Jesus." So racers run with an eye singly on the goal. This singleness of purpose and feeling makes our course straight and plain.

23. *Evil.* As a single eye is good, so an evil eye is double. "A double-minded man is unstable in all his ways." A blurred or double sight sees nothing plainly, but all confusedly, and the result will appear in all the conduct.——¶ *Darkness.* Ignorance and sin belong to a depraved aim, and an unfixed and wavering sight. "Having the understanding darkened—being alienated from the life of God through the ignorance that is in them because of the blindness of their hearts." (ch. 20. 15. Eph. 4. 18. Deut. 15. 10. Prov. 25. 6.) There is no security for holy living but in the utmost singleness and steadfastness of purpose to serve God, and in the fixedness of thought and faith and affection upon things above. ——¶ *The light that is in thee.* The light of understanding and conscience. The conscience enlightened is God's command within us. If this be darkness, how total is the darkness, and how dreadful and how fatal. "Even their mind and conscience is defiled." Sin darkens the mind more and more. Men are totally depraved. Sin is not merely in the act, but in the nature. It is not merely in the *will*, but in the *eye*. Having the understanding and conscience darkened, they plead a kind of Divine authority for sin, and then how great is the darkness—they even walk by darkness—*are guided by a wrong light*—the torch-light of Judas. Spiritual light is imparted only by that power which made the light of the natural world to shine out of darkness. Sinners are blind to their own interest and duty and destiny; "having eyes they see not" the plainest truths of God's word and providence. Paul was chosen as a messenger of truth to open the blind eyes. "The love of money is the root of all evil." Covetousness leads men into a snare, and when wealth is so avariciously sought after, it stands in the way of seeing any thing else. So it blinds men. As to earthly and heavenly wealth, we do supremely seek after one or the other, even as a servant cannot hold himself at the call of two masters, and cannot be said to render both his service, because each master requires all. The parable of the unjust steward (Luke 16. 1–3.) was spoken by our Lord, to impress this sentiment.

On verses 19–34, OBSERVE (1.) Worldliness is the great hinderance to spirituality, and the opposite to internal purity. It is contrary to the spirit of prayer and true benevolence, as just insisted on by our Lord. (2.) Laying up, as opposed to distributing, and laying up for self, instead of dispensing to others and using for the Lord, are here condemned (vss. 19 and 20). Laying up *earthly* treasures instead of *heavenly*, is the evil—and usually the result is an aim to be independent of God's providence, so as not to plead the fourth petition, "Give us day by day our daily bread." It seeks at length to live on something besides God. It lays up the sources of disappointment. It is laying up of our valuables *upon earth*, where every thing is unsafe. Moth and rust are there, and the valuables that are treasured up are of themselves perishable. There are destructive agents, as *insidious* as the *moth*; and there is the element of corrosion in their very nature, just as some metals rust for want of use. And there are thieves besides ready to steal valuables of this kind—robbers, whose occupation is to plunder such stored treasures. Spiritual treasures laid up are out of such reach in heaven, "an inheritance incorruptible and undefiled." Hence our true wisdom is to make such an investment, which is so superior in

[A. D. 31.]   CHAPTER VI.   81

masters: *for either he will hate the one, and love the other; or else he will hold to 'the one, and despise the other. Ye cannot *serve God and Mammon.

w Lu. 16.13.   *x* Ga. 1.10. 2 Ti.4.10. Ja. 4.4.

25 Therefore I say unto you, Take no thought *y* for your life, what ye shall eat, or what ye shall drink; nor yet for your body, what ye shall put on. Is

y 1 Cor.7.32. Ph. 4.6.

itself, and so much more safe from harm. *And as to our hearts* (vs. 21), there is this moral objection against having our valuables in such worldly goods. Not only is it not *real estate*, it is not *fast property*. But as the *heart* of the worldling cleaves to the object of affection and aim, the heart itself will suffer injury by holding to such perishable and unworthy objects. It will be more and more corrupted and *worn*. For such "love of money is the root of all evil, which while some coveted after, they have erred from the faith, and *pierced themselves through with many sorrows*." Covetousness is idolatry, and it leads to disobedience of God, and often, also, to dishonesty toward men. Hence the *next* (vs. 22): If the heart be simple and single, the whole mind will be illuminated and luminous to others. This sincerity or singleness of service as unto God is taught in regard to alms and fasting and prayer in the first part of the chapter, and it is essential. But in *double-seeking* (vs. 23), as of God and mammon, there is all the warping of judgment and bending of principle and stretching of conscience that belongs to a worldly, avaricious course. All is darkness—conscience is darkened —the mind is not clear—the soul is in darkness—the life is dark. The candle which God has given to shine, is put under this bushel measure. Then a man at length *walks by darkness*—a depraved conscience directs him: "a deceived heart hath turned him aside, so that he cannot deliver his soul, nor say, Is there not a lie in my right hand." We cannot be both worldly and heavenly. We may know where our treasure is, by marking where our heart's affections are

set. We may so live as to lay up treasures in heaven, even as the worldling daily stores away his empty treasures on earth.

24. The essential difficulty and folly of attempting this double service are here pointed out as a warning. The man will either hate Satan and love God—or else he will hold to Satan and despise God.——¶ *Mammon.* This is a Syriac word meaning riches or worldly lucre. To serve mammon, is to labour for it as a servant labours for his master; to be devoted to gain, and to have the heart set supremely upon the world, making every thing bend to the attainment of property, The poor may be as worldly-minded and avaricious as the rich. To serve God is to obey him, to labour for his cause, and to have the heart set upon Him—to regard His will in all things, and to devote ourselves to the practice and pursuit of godliness. We may know whether we are servants of the one or of the other, by observing the course of our thoughts and desires and actions, and watching which object we are wont to prefer. "To whom ye yield yourselves servants to obey, his servants ye are to whom ye obey." Rom. 6. 16. We should serve God and not mammon, and we should do it by studying to know our duty from His word, and by striving daily to follow His commandments, setting our affections upon things above and not on things on the earth.

25. *Take no thought* for your life. Be not *over-anxious* about your living—livelihood. So the English word *thought* is used by our translators in 1 Sam. 9. 5. for *over-solicitude*, and it is found with this sense in the old English writers. Parkhurst says, the

not the life more than meat, and the body than raiment?

26 Behold the fowls of the air: for they sow not, neither do they reap, nor gather into barns; yet your heavenly Father *z* feedeth them. Are ye not much better than they?

27 Which of you by taking thought can add one cubit unto his stature?

z Job 38.41. Lu.12.24,&c.

Greek term in its derivation means a distracting, heart-dividing carefulness. It is the same word in Phil. "Be *careful* for nothing," and our Saviour's word to Martha, "Thou art *careful* and troubled about many things." This is the enforcement of the precept against worldliness and worldly-mindedness, in the former verses. This command does not forbid a moderate and well-regulated attention to our worldly interests, but instead of such an over-solicitude for this world's goods as would crowd out divine things, or make them subordinate, we are to look more to God, and trust more in his power and promises. The scriptures often exhort to diligence in our worldly pursuits (1 Tim. 5. 8. 2 Thess. 3. 10. Rom. 12. 11). As the early disciples often *forsook all* to follow Christ, they would have grievous *cares*.

25. *Is not the life more than meat?* If He can give you life, He can give you means to support it; and would He furnish the *greater*, and not the *less?* Is not the life more important in His sight than the food it requires? And did He not give you life, the greater blessing, without your care, and what value is raiment in comparison with the body itself? It is not all of life to live. "A man's life consisteth not in the abundance of the things which he possesseth." Is there not every encouragement to expect His care for your bodily wants, and to look to Him accordingly? The idea is that He has given you life, and a body without your care. He will give you food and raiment which are the lesser gifts; and food and raiment He gives to the fowls and lilies, and shall He not much more, to you? "Man must be sent to school to the fowls of the air." *Henry.*

26. As to *food*, a very plain case, which all can behold, and most fit to inspire confidence in God, is His care of the birds. He provides for them—furnishes their food—they seldom or never starve in hardest weather—no famine reaches them. See Psalm 147. 9, where the term is *ravens* (which Luke uses), and as some think because the young ravens are immediately deserted by their parents, and must be specially provided for by God. This would make the case more marked. It applies to all birds. And the argument from less to greater holds here as before. We are better than the birds of the air, not as serving God better, but as of more importance in the scale of being—having souls, and being immortal. Trust in Christ.

27. The next argument is from the *fruitlessness* of such over-anxiety. What can it accomplish at best? Suppose you indulge such distracting solicitude, what can you achieve with it all?——¶ *For which of you by taking thought*—with all his thought and anxiety. A striking question is here put to show how utterly vain it is to fret and drudge independently of God's providence. *Who* can add to his stature or height by any amount of painstaking or anxious endeavours? Who can make himself a cubit taller than he is? How impossible! God has this matter entirely in His hands, and it is a thing which no one ever attempted, so utterly is it beyond our reach.——¶ *One cubit.* From 18 to 22 inches. Originally it marked the length of the arm, from the elbow to the farthest point of the hand. The word in Latin means the lower arm. (See Deut. 3. 11.) This is not a distinct item of care proposed as ranking with food and raiment, but a *question put*, to show the folly of self-de-

28 And why take ye thought for raiment? Consider the lilies of the field, how they grow; they toil not, neither do they spin:

29 And yet I say unto you, that even Solomon in all his glory was not arrayed like one of these.

30 Wherefore, if God so clothe the grass of the field, which to-day is, and to-morrow is cast into the oven, *shall he* not muhc more *clothe* you, O ye of little faith?

31 Therefore take no thought,[a] saying, What shall we eat? or,

a Ps. 37.3; 55.22. 1 Pe.5.7.

---

pendence and distracting care from not putting trust in God, the sovereign disposer of all. Therefore it need not relate to the measure of life, which, as Bengel remarks, is not measured by cubits. *A cubit to the stature*, is put, as the most impossible thing—for it were impossible *to add an inch!* Yet the height is "*that which is least*." Luke 12. 26.

28. As to *raiment* or clothing, the argument is taken from God's care of the flowers and fields, in clothing them with their verdure and beauty. ——¶ *Consider*, or attentively survey them. They do not *toil* or *labour*. They use none of the means for their clothing which men employ. Who *arrays* them, or beautifully dresses them? Kings of the East wore very rich and elegant robes of purple and white. And Solomon, we know, had great splendour in his court. But even *he*, in all his most gorgeous apparel, was not as splendidly clad as the lily. The lily of Palestine is a beautiful scarlet—its size about half the com on tiger-lily—the flowers are turban-like. It grows in the locality where Christ delivered His discourse, and it blooms at the very season when this sermon was supposed to have been delivered. *Kitto.* He is over all, God blessed forever.

30. *Wherefore.* If such care is taken for clothing the *short-lived* grass that grows to-day, but to-morrow is burned for fuel, how much more will He clothe you? How little consequence what clothing the grass of the field has? The *grass* is a term used in the East to include flowers and herbs, and every thing in the field but trees. Where fuel is scarce, withered stalks and dried grass are used for the fire. In these countries, also, baking is done by heating an oven with such fuel. A hole is dug in the earth about the size of our common ovens, and paved with stones. When these stones are heated by the fire, the ashes are removed and the dough is spread upon the stones. These ovens were most commonly in use (comp. Ezek. 15. 4). They had a way of baking also on the heated sand, and they used portable ovens made of clay or plates of iron.——¶ *Much more.* This refers to the *certainty*, not to the *quality* of the clothing. Here we may have rude apparel, and yet be faithfully clothed. In heaven our raiment shall be more splendid than Solomon's.——¶ *O ye of little faith.* Such undue anxiety for our temporal affairs shows a want of trust in Divine Providence. If Christians confided more in Christ, believing in His universal power and care, and relying on His abundant promises, and living on His covenant, they would not give way to such distracting anxieties. And Christ complains most of our *not trusting Him for all things.*

31. *Therefore.* Do not worry about food and clothing. We must have *cares*, and we should be careful. But we have no right to fret and teaze ourselves about these matters, that are so in the hands of God. We must own His supremacy and trust His fatherly covenant love.

32. *Gentiles.* In Luke it is "*the nations of the world*"—the unenlightened heathens. The Jews, who knew of the true God, ought to live differently

What shall we drink? or, Wherewithal shall we be clothed?

32 (For after all these things do the Gentiles seek:) for your heavenly Father knoweth that ye have need of all these things.

33 But seek ye first ᵇ the kingdom of God, and his righteousness; and all these things shall be added ᶜ unto you.

b 1 Ti. 4.8. *c* Le. 25.20,21. 1 Ki. 3.13. Ps. 37.25. Mar. 10.30.

34 Take therefore no thought for the morrow: for the morrow shall take thought for the things of itself.ᵈ Sufficient unto the day *is* the evil thereof.

CHAPTER VII.

JUDGE ᵉ not, that ye be not judged.

2 For with what judgment ye judge, ye shall be judged; and

d De. 33. 25. He. 13. 5,6. *e* Lu. 6. 37. Ro. 2. 1 1 Cor. 4.5.

---

from the dark pagans who were ignorant of His providence, and bowed down to idols. But above all, Christians should remember that their own Father in Heaven knows all their wants, and can supply them, and can they not confide in His love?

33. *Seek first.* Instead of caring supremely for your daily living—food and raiment—give first attention to the religion of Christ; seek it diligently and earnestly—make it the first concern. Strive, above all things, to embrace the offers of the Gospel, and to become interested in Christ by applying for His righteousness, and as well for the holiness which He requires as for the pardoning grace which He provides. Seek the merit of His death, and the spirit of His life, and the only justification by His plan of grace. Then you shall be interested in His *covenant*, which covers all good things, and even " our daily bread," for which Christ had just taught them to pray. " No good thing will He withhold from them that walk uprightly." Psalm 84. 11.

34. *For the morrow.* Do not give yourself such excessive anxiety for the future here. God has furnished *promises*, exceeding great and precious, to satisfy us about this; and to-morrow belongs to itself. Let it alone to itself. If it bring its own cares, it will also have its own supplies. Do not borrow trouble. To-day's troubles are enough for to-day, and every day has sufficient cares for itself without adding those of to-morrow. Besides, to-morrow may find us in eternity.

CHAPTER VII.

In the last paragraph our Lord discoursed about Divine Providence and grace—showed the wisdom of trusting in Him, and the folly of vexing and perplexing our minds too much with earthly cares, apart from Him, when the soul is so much more important, and faith so much more excellent. We should *cast all our care upon Him*, for He careth for us.

1. *Judge not*, that is, rashly or harshly, or hastily, for the sake of judging—or with a spirit of severe judgment. This applies to backbiting and slandering the character and conduct. The Pharisees were notoriously prone to this, and it is a natural disease. We may form opinions of others, but not censoriously, or enviously, or unfairly. It is unkind and unjust to harbour such judgment, and in true piety there is a disposition to be lenient toward others' faults, remembering our own. We have no right to injure the character of others by any such criticism or disparaging opinion without a necessity, and to gratify a bad feeling toward them. It is especially odious where it is in a way of pharisaical self-sufficiency.——¶ *That ye be not judged.* One reason why we should abstain from any such treatment of others is this: that if we judge them, we may expect the like ourselves. And the presumption is all against us in exercising such a temper, and God will judge us with the severity of His law for such a malicious feeling and practice. Luke adds the positive duties of giving and for-

with what measure ye mete, *f* it shall be measured to you again.

3 And why beholdest thou the mote that is in thy brother's eye, but considerest not the beam that is in thine own eye?

4 Or how wilt thou say to thy brother, Let me pull out the mote out of thine eye: and behold, a beam *is* in thine own eye?

5 Thou hypocrite, first cast out the beam *g* out of thine own eye; and then shalt thou see clearly to cast out the mote out of thy brother's eye.

6 ¶ Give not that which is holy unto the dogs, neither *h* cast

f Ju. 1.7.

g Ga. 6.1. *h* Pr. 9. 7,8; 23.9.

giving.——¶ *For*. This is a proverb which was common among the Jews, and expresses the sentiment just noticed in the preceding clause. Men will deal out to us the same kind of judgment which we pass upon others, and God also will visit us accordingly. Even in this world, He treats men, often, as they treat others. (See Isa. 33. 1.) Haman was hanged on the gallows he had prepared for Mordecai. Esther 6. "As I have done, so God hath requited me." See the case of ADONI-BEZEC (Judges 1. 7). And especially when we condemn in others the same sins that we ourselves commit, we condemn ourselves most severely (Romans 2. 1). Christ condemns our taking satisfaction in judging others, and our indulging sin in ourselves; for these things commonly go together.

3. *And why*. It is unreasonable. This refers to a proverb common among the Jews and others, about men who censured their neighbours and were more grossly guilty themselves.——¶ *Mote*. The *merest straw* or *splinter*, as opposed to the *beam*. The mote was the lightest, tiniest chaff.——¶ *The beam* was a huge timber. How is it, asks our Lord, that you look at a neighbour, and see sharply the smallest offences or faults of his, and do not see your own disposition or conduct? In the very temper in which you judge him, there is a more grievous wrong, than the small failings which you find out in your neighbour. We should first correct our own faults, because only then can we consistently criticise others (comp. Gal. 6. 4). In Luke we find this enforced by a parable, "Can the blind lead the blind?"

4. *Thy brother*—or neighbour, fellow-man. What consistency is there in offering to correct the fault of another, and behold you are more in fault? Such censoriousness God hates.

5. *Hypocrite*. See note on ch. 6. 2. He is a hypocrite in pretending to be so much better than he is, covering his own faults, while he sets himself up as a judge of others.——¶ *See clearly*. Correcting his own failings first, especially his bad tempers, he will get rid of an evil eye—the beam will be removed, and he can better see to inspect others' characters and conduct. He will judge more tenderly and truly: and finding out his own failings, he will judge most moderately and modestly. Luke adds the doctrine of a tree and its fruit as a safe rule of judging—yet we are to consider one another, to provoke unto love and good works in a Christian, mutual watch and care.

6. Lest all judging might seem prohibited, our Lord here teaches that we should not expose our religion to the scorn of bad men. "Let not your good be evil spoken of." And in judging others, we must still consider dogs as dogs, and swine as swine, in self-defence, otherwise sacred things will be abused by being held indiscriminate. While we are not to be too severe, we are not to be too lax in judgment. Here are two adages or common sayings which our Lord applies to this subject.——¶ *That which is holy*—sacred things. "The holy

86 MATTHEW. [A. D. 31.

ye your pearls before swine, lest they trample them under their feet, and turn again and rend you.

7 ¶ Ask, and it shall be given you; *i* seek, and ye shall find; knock, and it shall be opened unto you:

i Is. 55. 6. Lu. 18. 1.

8 For every one that asketh receiveth; and he that seeketh *k* findeth; and to him that knocketh it shall be opened.

9 Or what man is there of you, whom if his son ask bread, will he give him a stone?

j Ps. 81. 10, 16. Jno. 14. 13, 14; 16. 23, 24. 1 Jno. 3. 22; 5. 14, 15. *k* Pr. 8. 17. Je. 29. 12, 13.

---

thing" under the Old Testament, was the flesh of the altar.——¶ *Dogs*—and swine are the profane and sensual, or the malicious and debased. Dogs are they who turn the grace of God into lasciviousness. In our judgment of others, we are not to be so lax as to consider dogs or evil-workers, as holy. (See Phil. 3. 2. "Beware of dogs.") See Rev. 22. 15. "Without are dogs." We are not to give such offensive and malicious people a good character, nor apply the promises indiscriminately to them, lest we may wound the cause of religion. Nor are we to expose sacred things to the *ill-treatment* or abuse of outrageous and impious men. 2 Pet. 2. 22. Matt. 15. 27. There is nothing here to excuse such as fear to rebuke iniquity or refuse to engage in active duty—unwilling to testify for Christ. By neglecting altogether the rules of prudence and sound judgment, we might rudely cast the doctrines and precepts of religion before the most debased and grovelling men, only to have these pearls trampled on, in common with the filth of the sty. *Pearls* are precious stones taken from shell-fish of the oyster species. Pearl oysters are found in clusters, on rocks or pearl banks in the Persian Gulf, and near Ceylon and Java. By "*your pearls*" are here meant the privileges and doctrines of their religion. Matt. 13. 45.

7, 8. *Ask.* Fundamental directions are now given, and the discourse is summed up. These are the summary commands and promises in regard to prayer. There are three various assurances here to encourage prayer; and prayer is a leading duty. In the Lord's prayer He had just given an idea of what is to be asked for; and we are to ask with earnestness, diligence and perseverance, as these words would seem to indicate. To *ask* signifies a *personal address*. We must believe that *He is*. To *seek*, signifies an object earnestly in view. To *knock* signifies an application at the door, and an embrace of the promise in the appointed way—("We have boldness and access with confidence by the faith of Him." Ephes. 3. 11, 12.)——¶ *Seek.* Search for Divine things. They are hid to the natural heart. "The secret of the Lord is with them that fear Him." "Then shall ye find me, when ye shall search for me with all your hearts."—— ¶ *Knock*—that you may enter by the door. John 10. Make application to Christ to be admitted fully into the mysteries of His kingdom. 2 Cor. 6. 18. Luke 13. 25. You are brought to the very door of heaven by the Gospel. Knock for entrance. It is not enough to say our prayers. We must ask with a view of receiving—we must seek as those that are anxious to find—we must knock with importunity as taking no denial. See Luke 11. 8.——¶ *For every one.* For strongest encouragement, we are now pointed to the grace of our Heavenly Father as it is actually experienced among men. "The Lord is nigh unto all them that call upon Him." "Whosoever shall call upon the name of the Lord shall be saved." This is the established rule of His grace; and this is the fact attested by all experience. Praying men and seekers of God do receive and find. Psalm 22. 26. Yet it is to be remembered that if we ask not with filial confi-

10 Or if he ask a fish, will he give him a serpent?

11 If ye then, being evil, know how to give good gifts unto your children,[l] how much more shall your Father which is in heaven give good things to them that ask him?

12 Therefore all things what- soever ye would that men should do to you, do ye even so to them: for [m] this is the law and the prophets.

13 ¶ Enter ye in [n] at the strait gate: for wide *is* the gate, and broad *is* the way, that leadeth to destruction, and many there be which go in thereat:

[l] Lu.11.11.&c.

[m] Le. 19.18. Ro.13.8-10. Ga. 5.14. [n] Lu.13.24.

---

dence ("Our Father") and with humility ("Thy will be done") the prayer is not complete: remembering always to lay every thing at the feet of Him who has all right, and whose is "the kingdom and the power and the glory." See Jas. 4. 3. *Observe,* prayerless men are found out by their lack of graces. As they have not the spirit—so they cannot have asked.

9. *Or what man.* Our Lord chooses farther to illustrate and enforce this by the conduct of parents. What father will so badly treat a child's request as to deny him what he needs— or to give him what is evil. God will withhold no good thing from them that walk uprightly, and blessed is the man that trusteth in Him, so as to look to Him for blessings, and leave Him to judge of what is best.

11. *Evil.* Naturally corrupt—as distinguished from the heavenly Father, who is essentially holy.—— *How much more* shall God show parental affection toward the prayers of them that ask Him, than earthly parents who are naturally evil. This freeness and fulness of the Gospel offer, must leave men utterly without excuse. Why should they be prayerless or godless?——¶ *Good things.* (Luke 11. 13. '*The Holy Spirit*.') The gift of the Spirit includes all good. The meek shall inherit the earth.

12. *Therefore.* One of the closing deductions of our Lord is this GOLDEN RULE of the Gospel. This stands, here, for a summary of our relative duties, as they are taught in the moral law. This, therefore, at the same time, concludes His teaching on these points here, and proves what he set out to establish (ch. 5. 17), that He "came not to destroy the law but to fulfil." Every one can tell how he wishes to be treated by others—kindly and with allowance for his faults. He carries this rule, therefore, within him, and has no excuse for neglecting or violating or misunderstanding it. Let him treat others kindly, and with allowance for their faults, as Christ has taught. This is the sum of the law and the prophets, as to our relative duties, and the world would be peace and happiness and good-will, if this rule prevailed in its true spirit among men. But all this has a special connexion with the Gospel plan—as follows:

13. Our Lord exhorts men beyond all their mutual moralities to *embrace the Gospel.* And here He distinctly teaches that to enter the gate of life, is something besides the cultivation of such mutual kindness and good-will. This *entrance,* therefore, is to be their great business. The gate is not an easy, but a difficult passage, because of our evil hearts. In the Gospel plan of salvation there is but one way, and one gate. "I am the way" —"I am the door," of the sheepfold (John). *The gate* of the city (Revelation).——¶ *Strait,* narrow. The word is sometimes mistaken for *straight*— direct, or not crooked. The reference is here to the narrow gate for foot-passengers in walled cities, as distinguished from the broad, double, public gate for vehicles, processions and the crowd. Such a gate was sometimes called the *needle's eye*—as being

88 MATTHEW. [A. D. 31.

14 ¹ Because strait *is* the gate, and narrow *is* the way, which leadeth unto life; and few ᵒ there be that find it.

1 Or, *how.* o c.20.16; 25.1-12. Ro. 9.27,29.

15 ¶ Beware of false prophets, ᵖ which come to you in sheep's clothing, but inwardly they are ravening ᵠ wolves.

p De.13.1-3. Je.23.13-16. 1Jno.4.1. q Ac.20.29-31.

the most limited opening—which a loaded camel of course could not possibly get through, but would need to take the other and wide gate. And the difficulty would be as well in the back as in the burden. (See ch. 19. 24.) At a wedding feast, also, the entrance was by a narrow wicket gate, at which the janitor sat, to admit one at a time, that only guests might enter; and that there each man might get his wedding garment as furnished by the lord of the feast.—— ¶ *For wide is the gate.* The common course of carelessness and sin is roomy. The entrance is wide. It is easy at the opening. People enter it most naturally; and the way itself is broad. It gives license to the carnal heart. But just so certainly does it lead to destruction—" everlasting destruction from the presence of God." All unrenewed men walk in this way. A change of heart and life is requisite for salvation. " Thou wilt shew me the path of life."

14. *Unto life.* The life eternal in glory—everlasting salvation—the *perfect day* to which the path of the just leads. Our evil hearts, low desires, and carnal principles, make the way difficult. "If the righteous scarcely be saved," &c. (1 Pet. 4. 18). But because it is wisdom's way as our only proper course, and highest interest, it is pleasantness and peace. So few find it because they are "alienated from the life of God, through the ignorance that is in them, because of the blindness of their heart" (Eph. 4. 18). Gibbon boasted that Christ's golden rule could be found substantially in Isocrates 400 years before. But it is not the same. *That* only taught to avoid doing others the *injuries* which we would not have them do to us. It said nothing of this active love. And if it were fully the same, it would only be found to be the old precept which this very passage declares it to be—the substance of " the law and the prophets." As to the strait gate, Augustine here makes use of a legend concerning the artifice by which the serpent was believed to get rid of its old skin, by forcing itself through some narrow aperture, and so leaving behind the old, and coming out in all the splendour and freshness of the new. *Trench.*

15. On this vital subject of salvation, they had need to be cautioned against false directions, else they might mistake the way—and follow the broad instead of the narrow. There is great danger of the wide gate.—— ¶ *False prophets.* False teachers might boast that they were *the few* in the right. By *prophets* were originally understood, those who foretold future events. They were also teachers. Here the caution is against those who teach falsely about the future, "who prophesy smooth things" (See Jer. 23. 17. 26).—— ¶ *Sheep's clothing.* The false prophets not improbably clothed themselves with a cloak made of sheep skins, or of the fleece roughly made up, to imitate the garb of the true prophets. The idea is, they come to you in the garb of meekness and sincerity and harmlessness, in the very dress of Christ, who is the Lamb, claiming to teach of Christ and to teach like Him.—— ¶ *Ravening wolves.* They are really the very opposite to what they pretend —rapacious—insincere and mischievous. As wolves, instead of being sheep, tear and devour the flock, so these are the bitter enemies of Christians, and would ruin them if possible. We should beware of such as teach untruth and error. It is a false charity to be indiscriminate in so vital a matter. We may judge usually of doctrines from their effects upon the life. We are to be most particu-

16 Ye shall know them by their ʳ fruits. Do men gather grapes of thorns, or figs of thistles?

17 Even so every good tree ˢ bringeth forth good fruit; but a corrupt tree bringeth forth evil fruit.

18 A good tree cannot bring forth evil fruit, neither *can* a corrupt tree bring forth good fruit.

19 Every ᵗ tree that bringeth not forth good fruit, is hewn down, and cast into the fire.

20 Wherefore by their fruits ye shall know them.

21 ¶ Not every one that saith unto me, Lord, Lord, ᵘ shall en-

ʳ c.12.33. ˢ Lu.6.43,45.
ᵗ c.3.10. Jno.15.2,6. ᵘ Is.48.1,2. c.25.11,12. Lu.6. 46; 13.25. Ro.2.13.

---

lar, for the gate is *strait*—most narrow. The way is most precise, as well as most private.

16. *Their fruits*—conduct. The teachers themselves commonly show the effects of their faith in their conduct. This is natural, as that trees should yield their own fruit and not another kind. Yet in so judging, we are to " beware of the leaven of the Pharisees and the Sadducees, which is hypocrisy." The pure word of God circulated in the scriptures, will serve to confound error of every kind.

17, 18. *Even so.* It is so in vegetable nature. You can tell a tree from the fruit it bears, and so you can tell a teacher from the fruit his doctrines yield; and so you can tell every good man from his habitual good actions. As a *corrupt tree* of bad nature and quality brings forth an evil kind of fruit, so a bad doctrine brings forth bad results. Error cannot save men. So the natural, unrenewed heart must show itself somehow in the life. It is not possible in the nature of things that it should be otherwise. " The carnal mind is enmity against God, and is not subject to the law of God, *neither indeed can be.*" Augustine says, on this subject, "I praise the fruit of a good work, but in faith I acknowledge the root." The degenerate tree is not capable of restoring itself by its own unaided power. The law of human living is as the law of fruit-bearing trees, that according to their kind, so they must produce. Isolated acts of men may seem every way righteous, while they are not Christian. The question cannot be upon detached doings. But was the man righteous? Was the tree good? Leaves may deceive often from a close resemblance. But what is the stalk and the root? Has there been a positive engrafting into Christ?

19. *Hewn down.* So in Matt. 3.10. Repentance and regeneration are necessary, because the heart is naturally evil, and there must be a radical change. " And now the axe is laid unto the root of the trees." The wild and bitter stock that was removed from Eden, can only be restored by being grafted anew upon one of that stock from which it originally fell, and by this re-engrafting becoming partaker of the better life. *Trench.*

21. *Not every one.* Christ, as the great searcher of the heart, will distinguish. Not all shall enter into life who profess Christ, however repeatedly and loudly and familiarly saying, *Lord, Lord,* as though they were His followers. He demands a profession of His name, but those who have only this, He will exclude and reject. Those who enter, must do the will of God, must be His obedient and faithful disciples. The workers of iniquity are unfit for heaven, because that is a place of perfect obedience to His will, and true Christians pray daily that they may do His will on earth as it is done in heaven. Those who do not sincerely aim to do and submit to His will in all things, do not belong to Christ. (" He that doeth the will of God, the same is my brother," &c.)

ter into the kingdom of heaven; but he that doeth the will of my Father which is in heaven.

22 Many will say to me in that day, Lord, Lord, have we not prophesied *v* in thy name? and in thy name have cast out devils? and in thy name done many wonderful works?

23 And then will I profess unto them, I never knew you: depart from me, *w* ye that work iniquity.

24 ¶ Therefore *x* whosoever heareth these sayings of mine, and doeth them, I will liken him unto a wise *y* man, which built his house upon a rock:

25 And the rain descended, and the floods came, and the winds blew, and beat upon that house; and it fell not; for it was founded upon a rock.*z*

26 And every one that heareth these sayings of mine, and doeth them not, shall be likened unto a foolish *a* man, which built his house upon the sand:

27 And the rain descended, and the floods came, and the winds blew,*b* and beat upon that house; and it fell: and great was *c* the fall of it.

28 ¶ And it came to pass, when Jesus had ended these sayings,

v Nu.24.4. 1 K. 22.11, &c. Je.23.13,&c. Ac.19.13-15. 1Co.13.2. *w* Ps.5.5. c.25.41. Re.22.15. *x* Lu.6.47,&c. *y* Ps.111.10; 119.99,130.

z Ps.92.13-15. *a* 1Sa.2.30. Je.8.9. *b* 1Co.3.13. *c* He.10.26,27.

---

22. *In that day.* The day of final and general judgment, see Luke 13. 25. Though they may have done all these things that seem so religious, yet they have an evil heart of unbelief, in "departing from the living God." It is not merely what we have *done*, but what we have *been* that shall be required.

23. *Profess*—openly declare.——¶ *I never knew you:* never approved or recognized you as my followers. This is the sense of the word in many passages. Ps. 1. 6, &c. 1 Cor. 8. 3.——¶ *Depart from me.* Unbelief departs from the living God—refuses to follow, obey, and love Christ. And so unbelievers must forever depart—must go down to their destruction from the presence of God, and from the glory of His power—outcast "into outer darkness."

24-27. Christ closes this sermon on the Mount by an impressive and forcible comparison. He was the great Teacher of unadulterated truth, and they should carefully distinguish His teachings from those of false prophets, who should plausibly come to them, ready to deceive and devour.

To hear these doctrines of His, which he had just taught, and to obey them, is the only true wisdom. We are building for eternity—and how foolish is that man who builds his house upon the sand. He has no foundation. Every Jew could understand the simile. In that country they were liable to sudden and heavy rains, which would swell the Jordan, and its overflow, rapid and powerful, would sweep away every tenement situated on its banks.——¶ *Rains,* winds and floods, make it wise to build on a good foundation, to "lay up in store a good foundation against the time to come." We are all liable to afflictions, sudden fears, and death: and the man whose hopes are at loose ends, and on a sandy foundation, must expect his house to fall. This is the case of unconverted sinners. Their destruction shall come as a mighty whirlwind (Prov. 1. 27), and it shall be great because it is *the soul's* eternal loss. None are safe whose hopes are not built on Christ, the Rock of Ages. Some have a secret hope, but cannot give a reason of it. They should look well to its grounds.

[A. D. 31.] CHAPTER VIII. 91

the people were astonished d at his doctrine:

29 For he taught them as *one* having authority, and not as the scribes.

d Je. 23.29. Mar.6.2.

---

28. *His doctrine.* His sayings or teachings.

29. *Having authority.* As having the *right* to say what is truth. Not like the Scribes, telling what the Jewish Rabbins or doctors taught. The Scribes were the Jewish lawyers, as the term indicates, who had to do with the Scriptures—to copy and preserve them. But Christ's teaching was like that of a master who owned none higher than Himself, and who, in all His words and actions, plainly showed His inherent authority to speak, both as lawgiver and interpreter. The ruin of those is great who, under the teaching of the Gospel, refuse to hear and obey.

OBSERVE: *Three* principles are laid down in the Sermon on the Mount:
(1.) True happiness is not where the world would place it. ch. 5. 1–17.
(2.) The Gospel establishes the Law. ch. 5. 17, to ch. 6.
(3.) A mere outward religion is vain. ch. 6 to ch. 8.

[§ 33. THE HEALING OF A LEPER.]
Galilee.

Matt.	Mark.	Luke.	John.
8. 2–4	1. 40–45	5. 12–16	

It would seem, from comparing the narratives, that this case of a leper is briefly introduced here by the way, without regard to the time and order of events. It is probably the same as Mark and Luke record, which seems to have belonged to our Lord's tour in Galilee, previously to this, but is mentioned here by Matthew briefly, in passing. St. Ambrose has called this chapter, a chapter of miracles. Observe, they were wrought at very different times, but Matthew collects them here into one narrative.

2. *A leper.* Luke has it, "a man full of leprosy." The leprosy was a distemper of the most loathsome kind,

CHAPTER VIII.

WHEN he was come down from the mountain, great multitudes followed him.

2 And behold, there came a

and broke out on the skin ultimately, sometimes after being for years in the system. It came out in blotches, mostly circular, like a ring-worm. It formed at length into scales, and sometimes covered the body with a dry and white scurf. It has its name from a Greek word *lepis*, signifying a scale. There were the strictest laws for keeping separate from it—as the *garments*, Levit. 13. 47, and *houses*, Levit. 14. 34—and in its worst forms it was deemed incurable by human means. The symptoms of the disease, and the Mosaic laws respecting it, are found Levit. 13. and 14. It was a striking emblem of the malady of sin. It was sometimes inflicted by God as a special and signal judgment. Numbers 12. 1–10 (Miriam). 2 Kings 5. 27 (Gehazi). 2 Chron. 26. 16–21. The disease as known at the present day, commences by an eruption of small reddish spots grouped together in a circle. Presently a thin whitish scale forms, glossy like isinglass, and falls off. The circles spread out to a larger size. They are commonly as large as a shilling, or larger, but increase sometimes till they are broad as the palm of the hand. *The disease* of leprosy was the greatest ceremonial uncleanness under the Mosaic law. There was no final excommunication but for leprosy. He that was leprous all over was pronounced clean, because all the poison had come out. If he had yet any live flesh that showed *not* leprous, he was unclean. The priests could not be tainted with it, for they were judges of it. From the strict regulations for keeping aloof from leprosy, it has generally been thought to have been contagious. But this is disproved from abundant facts, the exclusion being wholly regulated by the Mosaic law, and not observed

leper a and worshipped him, saying, Lord, if thou wilt, thou canst make me clean.

3 And Jesus put forth *his* hand, and touched him, saying, I will; be thou clean: and immediately his leprosy was cleansed.

a Mar.1.40, &c. Lu.5.12,&c.

---

where the law did not rule, and the priests who came in contact with it so much, being exempt. As it was a most loathsome disease, it was employed as a *special symbol of sin, and sign of its consequences*—and these strict regulations were meant to *train the people to the great idea of separation from sin as the foul malady of the race*, and of a great deliverer being needed who could cure us only by taking our flesh. " Touch not the unclean thing" (2 Cor. 6. 17). What a striking ordinance was this! The cure could be effected not by any human means, but simply and only by God's expressed pleasure. " Am I a God— to recover a man of his leprosy ?" (2 Kings 5. 7.) The Jews termed it the *finger of God* and the *stroke*. Hence, that " the lepers are cleansed" is a striking mark of the Messiahship (Matt. 11. 5). It generally affects the knees and elbows before it spreads. The spots usually appear first on the face. There were three species known among the Greeks, and three kinds are mentioned under the same generic term (*bahereth*), a white or bright spot. It is hereditary to the third or fourth generation. One may live with it for twenty or thirty years or more. This disease is found to be quite different from that generally known as leprosy in the books of travellers, prevalent in the middle ages, and later in Europe, disappearing about the 17th century. *Kitto.* " W. A. N."

2. *Worshipped Him.* Mark says, " Fell on his knees." Luke, " He fell on his face." The term indicates the outward posture which denoted reverence. And such postures were common in Eastern countries, as we find often in the Old Testament. See Cut, Matt. 2. 11.——
¶ *Lord, if thou wilt.* He ascribed to Christ he ability. This was part of his worship. So we are taught in the Lord's prayer to ascribe the kingdom, power and glory to God, and to regard His will as supreme. " Thy will be done." He believed in Christ as having the *power* to heal him, and he acknowledged Him as sovereign in all his mercies, and made application on these grounds. *Observe:* He did not keep aloof because Christ could do with him as He pleased. The sovereignty of God is no bar to our approach, for we have His offers and promises, and are warranted to trust in Him confidently.

3. *Touched him.* He will use *means* —the touch and command. " He is able, He is willing, doubt no more." We need faith in God the Holy Ghost in all His office work.——¶ *I will.* Here Christ asserted that diseases are subject to His will. His power of course must be divine. The leper acknowledged this, and Christ here claims that His will and command are all that is needed to make the incurable leper clean. And so the result showed. How readily does Christ grant every humble request. This is symbolical of His power over sin, and of His readiness to deliver from its curse.

4. It was the rule under the Mosaic law, that a man cured of leprosy should first present himself to a priest, with a sacrifice of thanksgiving (Lev. 14. 4). Naturally the man would have gone blazing abroad his cure. But the Levitical ceremonies were not yet repealed, and Christ would have this command first attended to.——¶ *See.* From Mark 1. 45, we learn that Christ was obliged to refuse publicity, because of the crowds that sought His miracles and left Him no opportunity to teach and preach; and that by this man's sounding abroad his cure, He was obliged to withdraw to a desert place. Besides, the time had not yet come for

4 And Jesus saith unto him, See thou tell ᵇ no man; but go thy way, show thyself to the priest, and offer the gift that Moses commanded ᶜ for a testimony unto them.

5 And when Jesus was entered into Capernaum, there came unto him a centurion, ᵈ beseeching him,

6 And saying, Lord, my servant lieth at home sick of the palsy, grievously tormented.

7 And Jesus saith unto him, I will come and heal him.

8 The centurion answered and

b c.9.30. Mar.5.43. *c* Le.14.3,&c.   *d* Lu.7.2,&c.

His public manifestation as the Messiah. We are taught to signify our gratitude by careful obedience, rather than blind and headlong zeal. The man was to go and report himself at Jerusalem, according to the command, even before he should report the matter to others. Some have a religion which obeys natural impultes rather than Divine commands. Some people hope they are religious without attending to the appointed ordinances of God's house. Some think it of little account to join the church. But God has appointed His ordinance as a public testimony most important to be made at once. Mark tells us how Christ's work was hindered by this leper's disobeying His commands. How many hinder His work by neglecting the public ordinances.——¶ *For a testimony unto them*—priests and people. The priest was to examine the case and publicly attest the benefit received from God, so that the miracle might be properly certified and circulated, and the man be restored again to society. The Jewish Rabbins allowed that *curing lepers* should be a characteristic of the Messiah. And the testimony therefore was to reach both priest and people for their conviction of Christ's claims. When a man is converted from the power of Satan unto God, it should be made public in the appointed way, for the sake of others. This testifies against them.

§ 42. THE HEALING OF THE CENTURION'S SERVANT.—*Capernaum.*

Matt.	Mark.	Luke.	John.
8. 5–13		7. 1–10	

5, 6. *And when Jesus had entered into Capernaum.* The Evangelist here takes up the narrative. This was the first event after coming down from the mount near Capernaum. Luke records it also.——¶ *A Centurion.* This was a military officer among the Romans. As the name imports (the Latin *centum* meaning a hundred), it was the command of a hundred men. A Roman military force was stationed in Judea because it was now a province of the Roman Empire. It is not a man's *occupation* but his *faith* that gives him standing before God.——¶ *Beseeching.* We must come as suppliants, needy and anxious.——¶ *Lord.* The word here would seem to mean *sir*, as used by a Roman.——¶ *My servant.* The Centurion shows great regard for his servant, being evidently anxious about the case, and taking the same steps, which he would naturally have done for a child. Good masters will pray for their servants, and strive to do their souls good. We ought to beseech Christ for others, especially for our own house.——¶ *Lieth at home.* The word intimates the severity of the disease and the infirmity consequent upon this reduced state.——¶ *Sick of the palsy.* See note, ch. 4. 24.

7. *I will come*—literally, *I am coming*, and will heal him. It falls in with God's eternal purpose, to hear prayer and to grant salvation. So it proved. What free grace! What full offices! Christ had only to signify *His willingness* and this would secure the result. He could even heal him on the way to the house, as He really did. This prompt reply of Christ to the request of this stranger, who was probably born a pagan, and not a Jew, showed His gracious rea-

said, Lord, I am not worthy *e* that thou shouldest come under my roof: but speak the word only, *f* and my servant shall be healed.

9 For I am a man under authority, having soldiers under me: and I say to this *man*, Go, and he goeth; and to another,

e Ps.10.17. Lu.15.19,21. *f* Ps.33.9; 107.20.

Come, and he cometh; and to my servant, Do this, and he doeth *it*.

10 When Jesus heard *it*, he marvelled, and said to them that followed, Verily I say unto you, I have not found so great faith,*g* no, not in Israel.

11 And I say unto you, that *h*

g c.15.28. *h* Is.2.2,3. Lu.13.29. Ac.11.18. Ep.3.6. Re.7.9.

---

diness to bless. It displayed also His conscious Omnipotence, who at His will could heal and save. *Christ has now come*—to Christ we may apply.

8. This gracious language of our Lord was *humbling* to the Centurion. He had great faith, for he could believe in Christ's ability to heal by a word, and now he felt the grace of Christ expressed to him. And this faith affected his views of himself; for he began to feel how unworthy he was to have his house honoured with Christ's presence. Such is the result of genuine faith upon our estimates of self, producing the deepest humility. So Job (42. 6), "I have heard of Thee," &c. Others said he was worthy (Luke 7. 4), but he himself thought he was not. Christ's offers of love abase him and overcome him. He feels that this love is too much, and casts himself upon Divine power.

9. *I am a man under authority*," &c. I am a man of subordinate rank, and yet can order my soldiers who obey me at a word. But Thou, who art Supreme, canst command even diseases and they shall obey Thee. "What manner of man is this, that even the winds and the sea obey Him?" Being under authority, he knew also what it was to be commanded and to obey with strict military precision and promptness. He had experience of this in both ways, and he saw that Christ had absolute authority over disease. How blessed to have Christ's word enough for us, to fly to the power of it, and have it carry Divine authority for our salvation.

10. *He marvelled.* He expressed astonishment or admiration. It was a remarkable instance of one not a Jew, showing the strongest confidence in Christ's ability. It was more signal and illustrious than any instance among the nominal Israel. His faith was probably of a saving nature. And this is the first case of conversion on record among the Gentiles. We learn that while the Jews thought this man worthy (as we find in Luke 7. 4), *on account of his good deeds*, Christ judged of him by *his faith and humility*. A sense of unworthiness should never keep us back from Christ, and will not, if we have right views of Him; we shall cast ourselves on His sovereign ability the more we distrust ourselves. "I am not worthy, but Thou canst perform by a word." Parents and householders who have heard of Christ, ought to seek His blessings on their families and servants. And as all disease and distresses are at the command of God, we ought to mark in all our lot His providence, and cast all our cares submissively on *Him*. We should adore the sovereignty of His will, and in all our prayers should say, "*Thy will be done.*"——¶ *In Israel*—among the Israelites or Jews. Jacob was called Israel (see Gen. 32. 28), meaning Prince of God, because in prayer he prevailed with God. And so his descendants are called Israel and Israelites, after this patriarch of the Jews.

11. *Many shall come.* That the Centurion was a true believer, and had saving faith, and that he was the

A. D. 31.] CHAPTER VIII. 95

many shall come from the east and west, and shall sit down with Abraham, and Isaac, and Jacob, in the kingdom of heaven:

12 But the children of the kingdom *i* shall be cast out into outer darkness: there shall be weeping *j* and gnashing of teeth.

i c.7.22,23.   *j* c.13.42,50.

13 And Jesus said unto the centurion, Go thy way; and as thou hast believed, *so* be it done unto thee. And his servant was healed in the self-same hour.

14 ¶ And when Jesus was come into Peter's house, he saw his

---

first instance of conversion among the Gentiles, would appear from this declaration of our Lord. This case should not be alone. The Gentiles should yet be converted in large numbers, from the east and west and from all quarters of the globe. Isa. 45. 6; 59. 19.——¶ *Shall sit down with*—as at a meal. This is the sense of the word. The benefits of the Gospel were commonly represented by the provisions of a feast. Matt. 26. 29. Luke 14. 15. And this would naturally conciliate the Jew to the Gospel, that it would bring him into happy communion with the patriarchs of his ancient religion.

12. *The children.* The *child* of any thing is a phrase in Hebrew, expressing the special property which such an one has in the thing specified. So in Greek, as in Luke 10. 6, "The Son of Peace." So children of disobedience (Ephesians 2. 2). Here those are meant who have special property in the kingdom, i. e. the *Jews*, to whom it naturally belonged (Rom. 9. 4), and to whom the kingdom had come by hereditary descent, through their fathers. To them "pertained the adoption," &c. They were born into it, and to them it specially belonged by natural associations, and they were related to it by outward covenant. So the baptized children are now called "the children of the church." In Acts 3. 25, the Apostle says to the Jews, "Ye are the children of the prophets and of the covenant which God made with our fathers," &c.——¶ *Outer darkness.* As Abraham and others are represented as sitting down to a brilliant feast, splendidly lighted at night, so those who are excluded are described as being thrust out in the midnight darkness, *which reigned outside.* They were to have the very opposite portion. So the rich man is described as lifting up his eyes in torment and calling upon Abraham in heaven. Darkness is the scriptural image of perdition. It signifies the confinement and distress of a dungeon, the shutting out of cheerful light from the soul, and the shutting up of souls to all the deprivation and despondency and despair of the blackness of darkness forever. There shall be sorrow and torment there which words are unable to portray. See ch. 13. 42, 50. Luke 13. 28. Acts. 7. 54.

13. *As thou hast believed.* According to his faith was his success. This is the Gospel rule—not on this *ground,* but in this *measure.* The healing was performed at once, and his faith was doubtless strong as the grace was signal, and the result sublime. Faith is the *measure* not the *merit* (Ps. 33. 22). "Let Thy mercy O Lord be upon us, according as we hope in Thee." This narrative differs somewhat from that of Luke, but only as the different Evangelists *naturally dwelt upon different points or narrated different features of the transactions.*

[§ 31. THE HEALING OF PETER'S WIFE'S MOTHER, AND MANY OTHERS.—*Capernaum.*]

Matt.	Mark.	Luke.	John.
8. 14–17	1. 29–34	4. 38–41	

Here Matthew brings in another event without regard to the order. This miracle occurred, as we learn from

96 MATTHEW. [A. D. 31.

wife's mother laid, *k* and sick of a fever.

15 And he touched her hand, and the fever left her: and she arose, and ministered unto them.

16 When the even was come, they brought unto him many *l* that were possessed with devils: and he cast out the spirits with *his* word, and healed all that were sick:

17 That it might be fulfilled which was spoken by Esaias *m* the prophet, saying, Himself took our infirmities, and bare *our* sicknesses.

k Mar.1.30,31. Lu.4.38,39.   *l* Mar.1.32,&c.   *m* Is.53.4.   1 Pe.2.24.

Mark and Luke, just after Christ had called Simon and Andrew. Mark's narrative of it leads us to infer that it was on the *Sabbath day*, immediately after coming out of the synagogue, where a demoniac had been healed. See § 30 of the Harmony. Also that it was at the house of Simon Peter and Andrew his brother, whom He had lately called. "*Anon they tell Him of her.*" Blunt notices a coincidence in proof of the veracity of the Gospels, that Matthew and Paul both speak of Peter as married (1 Cor. 9. 5). From this raising of Peter's wife's mother, it is incidentally signified that Peter had a wife, which Paul's statements corroborate. OBSERVE, The Papists claim that Peter is the head of their church, and yet they forbid the clergy to marry. How could he be a Bishop or Pope if he was married? Or how can they forbid marriage if he was their head and married? How inconsistent is such a system with the Scriptures! They who give heed to the doctrine of devils forbid to marry. 1 Tim. 4. 1–3. And in making out testimony of a miracle, would it have been related of a person who did live or had lived (Peter's wife's mother) if there was intent to deceive? The miracle here consisted in Christ's healing by a *touch*, for a miracle is a supernatural work, a suspension or contradiction of nature's laws. It is a wonderful result effected by a power that is utterly beyond that of man. This healing by a touch is a Divine operation, because it is not in the power of man, nor is it according to the constitution and course of nature. Notice the immediate effects of Christ's cure—"Immediately the fever left her;"—and the striking results, "She arose and ministered unto them." Her gratitude included Christ.

16. *When the even was come.* This being on the Sabbath, which they kept from evening to evening—the Jews awaited this time when the sacred day was ended, to bring their sick (Luke 13. 14). Or they might have come after sunset, because the heat of the day would have proved too oppressive to the infirm. OBSERVE, This showed the fame He had acquired among the people and their faith in His healing power. So His fame should spread in the case of every conversion, that many may be induced to apply. "He healed *all* that were sick." This illustrates His abundant grace. How compassionate and kind to sinners. Who need fear to apply? "Come unto me *all*." "For every one that asketh receiveth." His word has healing power.

17. *That it might be fulfilled.* Isa. 53. 4.——¶ *Himself.* Christ Himself. Matthew, writing for the Jews, aims to connect Christ's doings with their own inspired prophecies, and so to identify Him to them as their Messiah. "He that put away sin by the sacrifice of himself," and "bore our sins in His own body on the tree," undertook to put away all the *fruits* of sin. This is the connection of His healing with His atonement. He aimed to remove the curse and restore the ruin of the fall. He took our infirmities and bare our sicknesses, taking the curse and bearing the condemnation of our sin "in his own

18 ¶ Now when Jesus saw great multitudes about him, he gave commandment to depart unto the other side.

body," even in numberless physical sufferings. It may be expressed more generally, "He bore our griefs and carried our sorrows." This Hebrew clause in Isaiah is precisely rendered by the Greek in Matthew here. He took a large share of human woes of every kind, sympathized in the suffering, and provided for the cure. His atoning plan provides as well for the body as the soul. The old versions read, "*He took on Him* our sicknesses," &c. We can suppose that He was a man of pain and ailment in the flesh, so far as would not interfere with His active labours. We know not how He was at Nazareth, the greater portion of His life; but there is authority for saying He "was without form or comeliness." "His countenance was marred more than the sons of men." In the Jewish Talmud is this striking passage: "What is the name of the Messiah? Some say *Leprous*. According is that 'surely he hath borne our sicknesses,' &c., and Messiah sitteth in the gate of the city. And by what sign may he be known? He sitteth among the diseased and poor." It is also said in the Zohar, "That all the diseases, griefs and punishments due to Israel shall be borne by Him." His taking our nature and taking such active part in relieving our woes, is not mere human sympathy, but belongs to His mediatorial work. This lively feeling for our sicknesses, and this prompt and effectual cure of all that were brought, show the reality of His remedial work for sinners, and the hearty interest He has taken in the redemption of men. In undertaking our salvation He took our load of woes *a man of sorrows*. The contemplation of our woes was a living pang to Him—Christ's rule in healing seems to have been to cure applicants and such as He met, where it was asked for. This was in accordance with His redeeming plan: " for every one that asketh receiveth." OBSERVE, The worst cases He can cure as well as any: even the possessed with devils, along with the sick. Our relatives we should bring to Christ's attention. We may go to Him for ailments of the flesh, and for woes of the spirit, for it is His part to cure them both. His control over diseases should satisfy men of His higher work and of all His Divine claims. NOTE, That between verses 17 and 18, there intervene, in the proper order of the history, 3 chapters of events, as recorded in the 11th, 12th and 13th chapters. This crossing the lake (vs. 18), was after a second circuit in Galilee, and after speaking the several parables near Capernaum. (See the Harmony.) In ch. 13. 1, we find our Lord seating Himself *by the sea-side*, giving instructions, "and *great multitudes* were gathered together unto Him," &c. (vs. 2). This explains His giving order here (ch. 8. 18), " to *depart unto the other side*," on account of the multitudes.

	Matt.	Mark.	Luke.	John.
§ 43. The raising of the Widow's son.—*Nain*.	....	....	7. 11–17	
§ 44. John the Baptist in prison, sends Disciples to Jesus.—*Galilee—Capernaum?*	11. 2–19	....	7. 18–35	
§ 45. Reflections of Jesus on appealing to His mighty works.—*Capernaum.*	11.20–30			
§ 46. At Simon the Pharisee's table, Jesus is anointed by a woman who had been a sinner.—*Capernaum?*	....	....	7. 36–50	
§ 47. Jesus, with the Twelve, makes a *second circuit* in Galilee.	....	....	8. 1–3	

98　　　　　　　　　　　MATTHEW.　　　　　　　　　　[A. D. 32.

19 And a certain scribe came, and said unto him, Master, I [n] will follow thee whithersoever thou goest.

n Lu. 9. 57, 58.

20 And Jesus saith unto him, The foxes have holes, and the birds of the air *have* nests, but the Son of man hath not where to lay *his* head.

	Matt.	Mark.	Luke.	John.
§ 48. The healing of a Demoniac. The Scribes and Pharisees blaspheme.—*Galilee.*	12.22–37	3. 19–30	11.14–15 17–23	
§ 49. The Scribes and Pharisees seek a sign. Reflections of our Lord.—*Galilee.*	12.38–45	. . . .	11, 16 24–36	
§ 50. The true disciples of Christ His nearest relatives.—*Galilee.*	12.46–50	3. 31–35	8. 19–21	
§ 51. At a Pharisee's table, Jesus denounces woes against the Pharisees and others.—*Galilee.*	. . . .	. . . .	11.37–54	
§ 52. Jesus discourses to His disciples and the multitude.—*Galilee.*	. . . .	. . . .	12. 1–59	
§ 53. The slaughter of certain Galileans. Parable of the barren Fig tree. *Galilee.*	. . . .	. . . .	13. 1–9	
§ 54. Parable of the Sower. *Lake of Galilee, near Capernaum?*	13. 1–23	4 1–25	8. 4–18	
§ 55. Parable of the Tares. Other parables. *Near Capernaum?*	13.24–53	4. 26–34		
§ 56. Jesus directs to cross the Lake. Incidents.—The Tempest stilled. *Lake of Galilee.*	8. 18–27	4. 35–41	8. 22–25 9.57–62	

18. *Great multitudes.* They came to Christ in crowds, having heard of his healing powers. Some came from curiosity; others came to be healed, or to bring their sick for His cure. He was now at the Lake of Galilee, at or near Capernaum, which was at the north-west coast of the lake or sea. He wished to go to the other side. Observe, the train of intermediate events. The incident does not connect immediately with the previous verses. He wished to go to the other side of the lake; accordingly we find Him next at Gadara, on the opposite or south-east side (see vs. 28–34). He proposed this movement, not to get rid of applicants, but to avoid the suspicion of fomenting disturbance. He also loved to withdraw when He had accomplished His work.

19. *A certain scribe.* A scribe was a writer and teacher of the law; i. e., *a Jewish lawyer.* He came doubtless, as the reply would intimate, from interested and mistaken motives; from worldly ambition or, like others, for the loaves and fishes of the miracles. Such displays of prerogative, and crowds of adherents, were likely to attract such followers. He proposed to throw in his lot with such a wonder-working personage, and go with Him to his place of destination.

20. Our Lord meant to warn him of his mistake, in thinking that he should have earthly ease and privilege from following Him. Even the foxes and birds had better lodging than He. Christ had a home in Nazareth, before He entered on his ministry; but now He was a sojourner and wanderer. How little we know of our hearts! Christ can tell us of them. Some are ready to profess religion with an understanding of temporal ease. Christ proposes the cross. He who rejects it cannot be His disciple.—
¶ *The Son of man.* See 16. 13. 'This is the title which Christ usually gave to Himself. So it occurs sixty-one times in the Gospels. It is a strong assertion of His proper humanity, and of His having a peculiar interest in

[A. D. 32.] CHAPTER VIII. 99

21 And another of his disciples said unto him, Lord, ° suffer me first to go and bury my father.

22 But Jesus said unto him, Follow me; and let the dead bury their dead.

23 ¶ And when he was entered into a ship, his disciples followed him.

24 And behold, ᵖ there arose a great tempest in the sea, insomuch that the ship was covered with the waves: but he was asleep.

o 1 Ki. 19. 20.   p Mar. 4. 37, &c. Lu. 8. 23, &c.

---

man. Yet if He had wished to own Himself a *mere* man, this would have been constrained and unnatural. He was the son of Joseph, the son of David, and also the Son of God; yet His peculiarity was this, that such an one as He should have become man. Therefore He uses the title as distinguishing Him, "The Word *was made flesh.*" He was "found in *fashion as a man.*" He is called the Son of man, because He has a human nature; the Son of *God*, because He has a divine nature; and He is as really God as He was seen to be man. Yet these natures He has mysteriously united in one person, just as Father, Son and Holy Ghost, are one God. How ashamed and grieved should we be for our sins, when we find that Christ on that account had so lowly a condition! and how thankful to Him should we be, and willing to serve Him by all manner of self-denial, when we find Him undergoing such hardships for us.

21. *And another of his disciples.* This alludes to another request made at the same time (Luke 9. 61), to bid a farewell. It is supposed to have been one of Zebedee's children. See *Blunt*, Matt. 4. 21, note. From the narrative in Luke 9. 59, it would seem that this was one who at Christ's call to follow Him made this reserve about what seemed a special filial duty. *Suffer me*—give me this permission. *First*—before following, or as a first obligation, *before* the command of Christ should be obeyed. Elijah permitted Elisha to go and bid adieu.

22. *Let the dead.* Even his most sacred duty as a child, should give way to Christ's call. "They left their nets and father." "He that loveth father or mother more than me is not worthy of me." "Seek first the kingdom of God" is the only rule. Enough can be found to do such services who are not inclined to "follow me." Let the dead in trespasses and sins, who are not of my disciples, attend to this business, and bury the dead. That belongs to a department quite apart from yours. You have no concern with that now. Leave it to those who belong there. This is a kind of proverbial expression. Let the dead in sin have to do with the dead under sin. You have higher concerns. Luke says he was ordered to *go preach.* The duties of this life, our own families, are not to be neglected, but when Christ calls we are bound to *follow*, no matter what may stand in the way. And as there can be no higher claims upon us than this, we must forsake father and mother, if need be, for His sake. If they would hinder our following Him, we must separate from them, rather than from our Lord and Saviour, and His work. This was really a case of half-way service and compromise; for in Luke it is added, in conclusion, "no man having put his hand to the plough and *looking back*, is fit for the kingdom of God."

23. *A ship.*—A fisherman's boat. Mark mentions that there were several boat-loads of followers (4. 36). He had delivered several parables during the day (recorded in Matt. ch. 13), and now He gave commandment to depart, and was detained by the scribe and the disciples. We should always have Christ with us.

24. See Mark 4. 37, for the powerful effects of the storm. It was a sudden and violent squall of wind—

100 MATTHEW. [A D. 32.

25 And his disciples came to *him*, and awoke him, saying, Lord, save us: we perish.

26 And he saith unto them, Why are ye fearful, O ye of little faith? Then he arose, and rebuked ^q the winds and the sea; and there was a great calm.

27 But the men marvelled, saying, What manner of man is this, that even the winds and the sea obey him?

28 ¶ And ^r when he was come to the other side, into the country of the Gergesenes, there met him two possessed with devils, coming out of the tombs,

---

q Job 38.11. Ps.89.9; 107.29.

r Mar.5.1. Lu.8.26.&c.

---

a hurricane. Christ was in the stern of the boat (Mark 4. 38), asleep on a pillow (as it was at night). Difficulties and perils may be expected in the performance of duty. Duties will not exempt us from natural calamities.

25 *Awoke him.* They had seen His marvellous power, and they naturally appealed to Him, seeing Him asleep and unconscious, as it would seem, of the danger.——¶ *Lord save us: we perish.* This is the substance of a prayer for deliverance. Our necessity pleads for God's ability. A proper sense of our inability prompts to earnest prayer. Christ, when He may seem asleep, may always be awaked by His disciples.

26. They should have believed Him as well when He was asleep, as when He was awake. Christ only complains at our fear, not at our confidence, and graciously gives us more demonstrations. They had *little* faith, for they had great *fear*. They had *some* faith, for they flew to Him, and prayed for His help as their only hope. Sharp admonitions and splendid deliverances may go together. Christ spoke first to them—then to the tempest.——¶ *Rebuked* — restrained the fury of the elements, as having them in His power, and even subject to His word.——¶ *A great calm.* This showed the miracle, that the result was so *sudden* and complete. Psalm 107. 23–30.

27. *Marvelled*—wondered, were surprised. The elements would not obey the word of any mere man. He must have been God. This was the impression made on the mind of the beholders. Christ performed miracles by His own power. Moses divides the sea and brings water from the rock by special direction of God, and in dependence on Him—never by his own strength. This difference shows how much greater than Moses is Christ. "Even as he that buildeth the house hath more honour than the house." Christ has given every man sufficient evidence for his belief.

OBSERVE, 1. Christ has embarked in the same vessel with every true disciple. He identifies himself with us, and His interests with ours. 2. Christ is very man—He sleeps. And He is very God—" even the winds and the sea obey Him." 3. The Church is the vessel in which Christ and His disciples are embarked together. It is liable to tempests and perils. "Behold, he that keepeth Israel shall never slumber nor sleep." 4. It is a *great calm* when Christ has rebuked the tempests of the soul. "Peace, be still." Blessed is He "who stilleth the noise of the seas, the noise of their waves, and the tumults of the people."

	Matt.	Mark.	Luke.	John.
§ 57. THE TWO DEMONIACS OF GADARA. SUNDRY MIRACLES. THE PHARISEES MURMUR. . . . . *S. E. coast of the Sea of Galilee.*	8. 28–34 9. 1	5. 1–21	8. 26–40	

A. D. 32.] CHAPTER VIII. 101

exceeding fierce, so that no man might pass by that way.

29 And behold, they cried out, saying, What have we to do with thee, Jesus, thou Son of God? art thou come hither to torment us before the time?

30 And there was, a good way off from them, an herd of many swine, feeding.

31 So the devils besought him, saying, If thou cast us out, suffer ⁸ us to go away into the herd of swine. ᵗ

32 And he said unto them, Go. And when they were come out,

s Job 1.10-12; 2.3-6.   *t* De.14.8. Is.65.3,4.

---

28. The last incident showed His power over the elements; this, over the evil spirits. Together, they exhibit His prerogative in the natural and spiritual world. He came now to the country of the Gadarenes (Mark) or Gergesenes (for the region was called by the name of either Gadara or Gergesa, which lay in the same district) *on the other side*, or S. E. coast of the lake or sea across from Capernaum.——¶ *Two possessed with devils.* Such a case was an awful symbol of depravity in the heart. The devils were allowed such a fearful manifestation on earth, the better to manifest Christ's work of destroying the works of the devil. Mark (5. 2) and Luke (8. 27) mention only one demoniac, because his case was the more special and striking of the two. He was a heathen, as would seem. Josephus says, "it was a Grecian city, and swine were kept there, which was not lawful among the Jews." According to Mark, he was "possessed of an unclean spirit;" and according to Matthew, he was "exceeding fierce." His case was remarkable, too, because he showed his gratitude for the miracle. Luke 8. 35, 38.——¶ *Coming out of the tombs.* This place (Gadara) is remarkable for a great number of tombs, hewn out of the white limestone rocks and richly carved. See "Biblical Geography" S. S. Union.

29. *What have we to do with thee?* was a common form of question, implying some troublesome interference. So the next words explain. The devil here recognizes Christ as the Son of God, and as the Saviour Jesus, but not as their Saviour. Christ has nothing to do with the devils, or with lost spirits for their salvation. The "spirits in prison," to whom Christ preached in the days of Noah (1 Pet. 3. 19), were they who are *now* spirits in prison, but who were waited on then in God's "long-suffering" (vs. 20). This is plain from (1 Pet. 4. 6), where the reference being to these, it is added, "For this cause was the gospel preached also *to them that are dead*," &c.——¶ *Before the time;* that is, the appointed time, as the Greek work is. The devils believe in God and tremble (James 2. 19). From the Epistles of Peter (2 Pet. 2. 4), and Jude 6, we learn that fallen spirits are reserved in chains unto the judgment of the great day. They refer to this time, and doubtless they are kept in constant terror of this time (see Rev. ch. 20. 21). In Luke 8. 31, the devils entreat not to be sent into the *abyss*—or *hell*.

30. *A good way off.* That is, on the same plain, or on the brow of a hill sloping down to the water. Mark says, "*nigh unto the mountains.*" It was "*there,*" that is, in direct view, but some distance from the spot where they stood.——¶ *A herd* (a flock) *of many swine.* Mary says, "about two thousand" (5. 13).

31. Here they entreat permission to be sent into the herd of swine, and Christ's authority over them is here acknowledged.

32. The unbelieving Greeks were wont to ridicule the Jewish laws, especially on account of their prohibiting the use of swine's flesh as food. This entering of the devils into the swine would have a meaning in this respect, and would be likely to show

they went into the herd of swine: and behold, the whole herd of swine ran violently down a steep place into the sea, and perished in the waters.

33 And they that kept them fled, and went their ways into the city, and told every thing, and what was befallen to the possessed of the devils.

34 And behold, the whole city came out to meet Jesus: and when they saw him, they besought *him* that he would depart ^u out of their coasts.

u Job 21.14. Lu.5.8, Ac.16.39.

---

them the sacredness of these laws, and to keep up this awful distinction between the holy and the profane.

The case of the fig-tree—the casting out of the money-changers in the temple, and this, are instances of Christ's vindictive acts, and the only instances of loss attending the exercise of His authority. "These are hints," says Bengel, "of a future punishment.——¶ *Perished*. The devils from these two men fill the whole herd, and the possessed brutes could not live long. It is of mere mercy that men possessed of the devil should not immediately perish.

33. *Fled.* They were terrified at this. They saw this wonderful change in the men that were possessed, and the strange effects upon the swine. Luke says they saw the demoniac "sitting at the feet of Jesus, clothed and in his right mind." They were astonished at the awful power of God over evil spirits, and doubtless it seemed to them a judgment of the God of the Jews upon these animals that were held in abomination by the Jewish laws; and so they feared a judgment also upon themselves, as keepers of swine, which was a business forbidden by those laws.

34. *The whole city.* There was a general turning out at this report of Christ's doings; for it was plain that Christ had power over property and life, and men were universally alarmed. They wished him to go away, lest they might lose their property by this means, or suffer other damage. So many beg Christ to depart from them, "and choose iniquity rather than affliction" (Job 36. 21), or the inconvenience even of attending to His claims. We should desire Christ to be always near us, because He alone can deliver us from difficulties, or support us under trials, and His presence can give peace to our souls. The cured demoniac begs the privilege of following Christ (Luke 8. 38). We should seek this. If He is not near us, we are in danger of being possessed by evil tempers, and thoughts, and desires, and falling under the power of sin. "Deliver us from evil." The true wisdom is to take Him for our portion as He is offered in the gospel, so that we may have Him for a friend at all times, "our refuge and strength, a very present help in trouble." The demoniac was cured, and an interesting account of the result upon him is found in Mark and Luke. He besought Christ to allow of his accompanying Him, but our Lord told him to speak His praises *at home*. Luke 8. 38, 39. OBSERVE, the men who merely saw His *power* were terrified and begged Him to depart. But the poor demoniac, who felt His *goodness* also, begged to remain with Christ. A mere sight of *Divine power* drives us away from God; an insight of *His power and love* draws us near to Him. Such cures of bodily diseases as are *recorded* in the history of Christ are intended to be *symbolical* of the removal of spiritual diseases by the power and grace of the Great Physician (*Ed. Calvin, p.* 436, *note*). All scripture is given for doctrine, for reproof, &c. "Carnal hearts prefer their swine before their Saviour, and had rather lose Christ's presence than their worldly profits."—*Burkitt* Christ often grants the wish of devils and of wicked men, but with calamitous results to themselves.

CHAPTER IX.

AND he entered into a ship, and passed over, and came into his own city.

2 And [a] behold, they brought to

[a] Mar. 2. 3, &c. Lu. 5. 18, &c.

him a man sick of the palsy, lying on a bed: and Jesus, seeing their faith, said unto the sick of the palsy, Son, [b] be of good cheer; thy sins be forgiven thee.

3 And behold, certain of the

[b] Mar. 5. 34.

CHAPTER IX.

1. Our Lord would not obtrude His labours upon the unwilling, and so He yields to the request of the Gergesenes, and leaves their coasts. After He had got into the ship, the demoniac prayed that he might accompany Him. This was asked in a very different spirit from that of the scribe on the other side of the lake.—¶ *His own city.* Capernaum, where he dwelt, and whence he had started out. (See vs. 18, note.)

[§ 34. THE HEALING OF A PARALYTIC] *Capernaum.*

Matt.	Mark.	Luke.	John
9. 2–8	2. 1–12	5. 17–26	

Sick of the palsy. Here Matthew relates a miracle which was wrought at Capernaum, but at a previous period. His object was to tell the works of Christ, though not in their order; and this return of Christ to Capernaum, naturally suggested a miracle previously wrought there, which as yet he had omitted to narrate. §§ 34 and 35 are in parenthesis.

2. They brought to Him—or *offered* to Him. Many such grateful oblations were made to the Saviour. Christ was *in the house* (Mark 2. 1), sitting and teaching a great multitude, who crowded the house and porches. He was probably in the gallery, teaching the crowd that thronged the open court below and filled the doorways (fig. 1). He healed in the presence of Pharisees and doctors of the law, who came from Galilee, Judea and Jerusalem (Luke 5. 17). This paralytic was carried on a couch by four men (Mark). It was a case which fitly represented the *utter helplessness* of the sinner.——¶ *Seeing their faith.* They showed their faith by pressing through difficulties and discouragements. "*Their* faith" included doubtless that of the sick man also, however weakly exercised. The throng was so great that they could not get into the house with the sick man, and they resolved upon this expedient of letting him down through the roof (see Luke). The Eastern dwellings were built in the form of an open square, inclosing a court, with piazzas and rooms on the four sides, and thus securing light and air without exposure (fig. 1). From the front entrance, a stairway led directly to the roof, without the need of passing through any part of the house; which explains the passage, "Let him that is on the housetop not come down to take any thing out of his house" (fig. 2). The "tiling" referred to in Luke, was such as could be removed with some difficulty, and here it was probably the covering of the gallery that was actually taken up. Mark says, "They uncovered the roof;" Luke adds, "They let him down through the tiling in the midst." Faith presses and penetrates through all difficulties till it reaches Christ. The helpless sinner must be let down into His presence.——¶ *Thy sins be forgiven thee.* Christ here attracts attention in a new and startling form to the great truth of His supreme Divinity. He did not say, "*Be healed*," but "Thy sins be forgiven thee." He thus refers sicknesses to sin—hints of this paralytic case as an expressive type of sin, and shows that His work is not merely nor mainly physical, but spiritual. He would even bring His redeeming work distinctly and strikingly before the people, asserting and sealing by a visible sign His authority to forgive sin. He would have His cures al-

The rooms of the house were ranged around this court. The roof was flat, formed often by layers of boughs, matting, and earth laid over the rafters, and trodden down; then covered with a compost, which hardened when dry. This roof was protected by battlements, so that on *the house-top*, persons walked at evening, and sometimes slept at night. 2 Sam. 11. 2, &c.
Kitto.

This cut shows the mode in oriental countries of covering the open court with an awning, stretched upon columns. The sun was thus excluded, and the air was admitted. *Kitto.*

scribes said within themselves, This *man* blasphemeth.

4 And Jesus knowing their thoughts, c said, Wherefore think ye evil in your hearts?

5 For whether is easier to say, *Thy* sins be forgiven thee; or

c Ps.139.2. Jno.2.24,25. He.4.12,13. Re.2.23.

to say, Arise, and walk?

6 But that ye may know that the Son of man hath power on earth to forgive d sins, (then saith he to the sick of the palsy,) Arise, take up thy bed, and go unto thine house.

d Mi.7.18.

ways viewed in this connexion, and men could not fully understand His work otherwise than in this light. See James 5. 14, 15. It would also appear to them, from this language, that the forgiveness of sin was of first consequence and included every blessing. And so also He shows His gospel grace by this visible illustration. He gives before we ask, and then gives more than we ask. The faith here was mostly a deep sense of need, and of Christ as the only helper. Others spoke to Christ, but Christ addressed the paralytic. Forgiveness must be spoken to us, and cannot be spoken to another for us. The sense of personal forgiveness has power with us for a Christian life.

3. The Scribes and Pharisees, in their murmuring, acknowledged that to *forgive sins* was strictly a Divine work. They had always regarded this prerogative as a characteristic of their Messiah when He should come. Hence they were offended in Him. — ¶ *Blasphemeth*. In other writings, blasphemy was evil speaking of any kind, and evil foreboding in regard to any one. In the Scripture, to blaspheme the name of the Lord (Levit. 24. 16), was to impiously profane the Divine titles, attributes or works, and especially to violate the honour of Jehovah by assuming it for the creature. So here, "Who can forgive sins, but God only?" (See Matt. 26. 65. John 10. 36.)

4. *Knowing their thoughts*. Christ here again shows to them His Divinity by showing to them their thoughts. So, with the Samaritan woman, "Come see a man who told me all things that ever I did. Is not this the Christ?" See 1 Sam. 16. 7. 1 Chron. 28. 9. 2 Chron. 6. 30. Jer. 17. 10. Rom. 8. 27. Rev. 2. 23. Mark adds, "Jesus knew by His Spirit," or perceived in His Spirit, their *thoughts*, or carnal reasonings. He might easily say this, thought they, and only blaspheme; for He could safely pretend to a work which admitted no proof. How could we know that the man's sins are forgiven?

5. *Whether is easier*. It was not because it was *easier* to Him, as they supposed, that He so said, but for another reason—to call their attention to His redeeming, sin-forgiving work. And He would presently show them that He could as easily say "*Arise*." His object was to have them know that He—the Son of man—had power on earth to forgive sin, and was therefore God and Saviour. Properly speaking, His prerogative extended equally to both departments, "Who forgiveth all thine iniquities—who healeth all thy diseases" (Psalm 103). But the greater, that included the less, should be put foremost. Disease is but a feature of the curse, and forgiveness virtually removes it, as it takes away its sting, even the sting of death. His object He now declares to be their instruction in His saving work. "But that ye may know," &c. And hence, to convince them that this assumption of His was authorized, and not blasphemous, He will work the miracle in attestation of His claim. He will show them by a visible exertion of Divine power and grace, on His own authority, that He had *power on earth* to forgive sin.

6. *Arise, take up thy bed*. There is a reason for this form of the healing word. As forgiveness of sin is the great substance of blessing which in-

7 And he arose, and departed to his house.

8 But when the multitude saw *it,* they marvelled, and glorified *e* God, which had given such power unto men.

<small>*e* Ac. 4. 21. Ga. 1. 24.</small>

9 ¶ And *f* as Jesus passed forth from thence, he saw a man, named Matthew, sitting at the receipt of custom: and he saith unto him, Follow me. And he arose, and followed him.

<small>*f* Mar. 2. 14. Lu. 5. 27, &c.</small>

---

cludes all good things, so the restoration is most triumphant when it is shown at once in the effects. Christ would deliver the blessing in the form of a command, which He very commonly did, that the first exercise of faith might be an effort of obedience. To the maid he said, "*Arise*" (Mark 5. 41); to Lazarus, "*Come forth*" (John 11. 43); to the paralytic, "*Arise, take up thy bed, and go unto thine house.*"—*Mather on the Types,* p. 140. This incident gave our Lord an opportunity to prove His Messiahship; for a miracle in His own name, "I say unto thee," proved His claim to Divinity; and His claim, if proved, was such as proved Him *their Messiah.* Indeed, in all His miracles, He would assert or illustrate this truth.

8. *Such power unto men.* They saw Divine power in this miracle, but they did not observe how Christ wrought it by His own word, "I say unto thee." They could not conceive or admit His Divinity, though this was proof. They did not own that He was more than man, though sometimes they were forced to say, *What manner of man is this?* Yet here their confessions make them the unwilling witnesses to this truth of His proper *Godhead.* "*The Son of man*" —He whom ye regard only in the light of His humanity, hath Divine power, and thinks it *no robbery* to be equal with God (Phil. 2. 6).

[§ 35. THE CALL OF MATTHEW.]
Capernaum.

Matt.	Mark.	Luke.	John.
9. 9	2. 13, 14	5. 27, 28	

9. *Matthew sitting at the receipt of custom.* This is the call of Matthew as a disciple. Afterward, Christ chose, from all the disciples, *twelve,* for apostles. Every minister of Christ must needs first be a true follower. Church office could not suffice, in His view, without piety. Christ would have, among the twelve, this proof of Judah's low estate—an apostle from the officers of tribute. The custom-house among the Jews, in their subjection to Roman authority, was a place for plundering and extortion. Hence, the call of this apostle was a striking instance of Divine grace. Mark and Luke call him *Levi,* which must have been his common name, as he was so called by the people of the country. But his being a publican, and an officer under the Romans, is a reason why he took a foreign name, though not a foreigner. But he would not here employ the name in which he served as a publican. Christ "calls His servants by another name"—"a new name." The promptness with which he followed Christ, shows us not so much his natural character for decision and promptitude, as the *Divine power of Christ's call.* He was *sitting*—busy at his work. He "*left all,*" adds Luke, and he was made an example of that effectual calling, which renews the heart, and converts the life. Luke gives an account (ch. 5. 29) of a great banquet made by Levi, or Matthew. The freeness of God's grace is such, that he often chooses the worst, and takes the most notoriously wicked as chosen vessels for himself. So with Saul, the persecutor. OBSERVE, The *effectual* calling is seen from the *effects.* 1. The promptness of action at Christ's word—"*He arose.*" 2. The self-denial—"*He left all*" (Luke)—his self-righteousness, and sins, and vain pursuits. 3. The steadfast obedience—"*and followed Him.*"

[A. D. 32.] CHAPTER IX. 107

10 ¶ And it came to pass, as Jesus sat at meat in the house, behold, many publicans and sinners came and sat down with him and his disciples.

11 And when the Pharisees saw *it*, they said unto his disciples, Why eateth your Master with publicans and sinners? ᵍ

12 But when Jesus heard *that*, he said unto them, They that be whole need not a physician, but they that are sick.

13 But go ye and learn what

g c.11.19. Lu.15.2. He.5.2.

---

§ 58. Levi's (or Matthew's) Feast.—*Capernaum.*

Matt.	Mark.	Luke.	John
9. 10–17	2. 15–22	5. 29–39	

There elapsed an interval of some months between Matthew's call and this feast, as will be observed by the Harmony.

10, 11. *As Jesus sat.* This feast Matthew made as an act of gratitude to Christ, and a parting entertainment to his former associates, in which he would at once make them acquainted with his new Master, and make an open profession of his discipleship before them. A convert should surely not be ashamed of Christ: he should not fear to profess Him; nor should he be willing that his own former associates should remain ignorant of Him. And as Christ has made us a great feast in His house, and invited us all, we should pay Him our best honours in our own house, and before all our acquaintances. Luke calls it a *great feast*, which Matthew, in modesty, omits.—¶ *In the house.* Matthew does not call it his own house, though Luke does. "What things were gain to me, those I counted loss for Christ." "Neither said any of them that aught of the things which he possessed was his own" (Acts 4. 32). Christ's excellency makes even a close calculator reckon Him more than all things. How few large entertainments are given where Christ is invited.— ¶ *Publicans and sinners*—or heathens. The Pharisees complained to the disciples that their Master was keeping unhallowed company. *Eating and drinking* with any was a mark of great intimacy and fellowship, which

these proud murmurers, not understanding Christ's work among sinners, sought to lay to His discredit. They were offended at Christ and His claims, and hence they loved to excite prejudice against Him. Their pride revolted at Christ's ways, and at His humiliating, soul-abasing religion. Christ is called on to explain His intercourse with sinners! How the natural man misunderstands the gospel. The very grace is a blot. The love of Christ must be shed abroad in the heart by the Holy Ghost given unto us. Of the sacramental table, the world might ask, why eateth your Master with publicans and sinners?

12, 13. We learn that it belongs to the true spirit and end of the gospel dispensation to seek and save the *lost*, to call *sinners*, to preach glad tidings to the *poor and meek*, and to justify the ungodly. This is most important for us to know; this was our Lord's vindication. Herein lies our hope. The gospel is good news—glad tidings to the weary and heavyladen, and guilty, and undone. This we are to believe. To the self-sufficient, like the Pharisees, the ways of Christ will always be objectionable, and they feel not their need of His help. They objected on the ground of strict ceremonial purity. Christ refers them to their own prophet, Hosea 6. 6. They misunderstood what God proposed and required. He proclaimed mercy to sinners, and not sacrifice; and it was love or mercy that He claimed of men, rather than mere outward observance with severity. Where truth was not found toward God and man, ritual sacrifice was of small account, especially where malice and ill-will toward fel-

MATTHEW. A. D. 32.

that meaneth, I ʰ will have mercy, and not sacrifice: for I am not come to call the righteous, but sinners to repentance. ⁱ

14 ¶ Then came to him the disciples of John, saying, Why do we and the Pharisees fast oft, but thy disciples fast not?

15 And Jesus said unto them, Can the children of the bride-chamber mourn, as long as the bridegroom ʲ is with them? but the days will come when the bridegroom shall be taken from them, and then shall ᵏ they fast.

16 No man putteth a piece of ¹ new cloth unto an old garment; for that which is put in to fill it up taketh from the garment, and the rent is made worse.

h Pr.21.3. Ho.6.6. Mi.6.8. c.12.7. *i* Lu.24.47. Ac. 5.31. 2 Pe.3.9.

j c.25.1,10. Jno.3.29. Re.21.2. k Is.22.12.
1 Or, *raw*, or, *unwrought cloth*.

---

low-men were indulged. God demands mercy or love first of all; and all His *precepts* (even the 4th Command) must have an eye to mercy. See Matt. 12. 7, where this is referred to, as excusing the plucking of corn by the disciples on the *Sabbath*.——¶ *For I am not come*. This was not the object of His mission, to company with such as proud Pharisees who count themselves already righteous, but to *call sinners* and furnish them a perfect righteousness, and thereby lead them to righteousness of life, in genuine repentance. His object was not to get a mere punctilious Pharisaic obedience, but to show mercy, and preach mercy. Here was also a proverbial expression, to signify the consistency of one's course with his object—"*Physicians are with the diseased.*"

14, 15. The disciples of John were drawn into the controversy by the Pharisees, whom Luke represents as speaking, while Mark seems to connect the two. John's disciples were trained to fastings, twice a week at least, in keeping with all that austerity and seclusion which belonged to John's ministry in the wilderness. It served the purpose of Christ's enemies to oppose this strictness against His apparent indulgences. *Fasting* is abstinence from food, either wholly or in part. Its design is to deny the fleshly appetites, and its use is more exclusively to cultivate spiritual dispositions, to humble us at the thought of our dependence for daily food on the goodness of God, and to check the carelessness and sensuality of life. But it was abused to self-righteousness by the Pharisees, and John's disciples had not fully come into the light.——¶ *The bridegroom*. Christ points out the circumstances as justifying this. It was not a time to fast any more than at a wedding. His presence with the disciples was fit to excite joy, as at a marriage feast, where the festivity would seem highly proper. He is the bridegroom; they were the *children of the bride-chamber*—the groomsmen, who conducted the arrangements, and took special part in the joy. *Can they* mourn at such a time? Luke has it, "*Can ye make*" them mourn? It is not fit that they fast, and use the expressions of grief while the marriage is going on and the groom is with them; but when He should be taken away from them, then the expressions of grief would be fit.

16. The illustration here used applies to the same effect, viz.: to show that there is a *fitness of things*. It would be as unfit and hurtful even to put on these forms of sorrow and lamentation, while Christ is present with them, as to patch an old garment with new cloth, or to put new wine into old bottles; for in both cases, there would not only be impropriety, but injury done. So, He would say, my doctrines do not suit the old and legal rites of the Pharisees. They who have embraced Christ, and find Him present, have no right to go in mourning, any more than they have to turn Jews. Because joy is appropriate to

A. D. 32.]   CHAPTER IX.   109

17 Neither do men put new wine into old bottles; else ¹ the bottles break, and the wine runneth out, and the bottles perish: but they put new wine into new bottles, and both are preserved.

18 ¶ While ᵐ he spake these things unto them, behold, there came a certain ruler and worshipped him, saying, My daughter is even now dead: but come and lay thy hand upon her, and she shall live. ⁿ

19 And Jesus arose and followed him, and *so did* his disciples.

l Job 32.19. *m* Mar.5.22. Lu.8.41,&c.   *n* Jno.11.22,25.

---

the believer, and freedom also, he must not go in bondage and sackcloth; for so he does, in heart, return to the old way of the law—*do this and live*—to the beggarly elements. Besides, the day for mourning will soon enough come, and to tender and weak converts there is need of all the joy which comes from the presence of Christ with them.

17. *Bottles.* Bottles made of skins were used, especially for wine. They would become dry and cracked at length, unfit to hold new wine that should ferment greatly; hence there would be impropriety and injury in using old bottles for it. So, everything in its time and place. The law for Pharisees—the gospel for disciples: milk for babes—strong meat for full-grown men: joy in Christ's presence—fasting and grief for His absence. For the form of these skin bottles, see Cut from *Kitto's Bib. Cyclop.*

§ 59. THE RAISING OF JAIRUS' DAUGHTER. THE WOMAN WITH A BLOODY FLUX.—*Capernaum.*

Matt.	Mark.	Luke.	John.
9. 18--26	5. 22--43	8. 41--56	

18. This occurred while our Lord was at Matthew's feast. Mark and Luke speak of this man as a *"ruler of the synagogue,"* and call him by name, *Jairus.* In Mark it is said he was "one of the rulers of the synagogue," which shows that in this office there were more than one (see Acts 13. 15). He was one of those church officers whom we call *Ruling Elders.* "Elders of the Jews" (Luke 7. 3).——¶ *Worshipped.* "*He fell at his feet*" (see Mark and Luke, and note on ch. 2. 11). He paid Him this outward homage as an expression of reverence, which could be done without any hearty worship; yet he humbled himself in prayer. Mark has it, "*he besought Him greatly.*" The ruler was convinced of Christ's marvellous power, and though he regarded his daughter as dead, or dying (Mark 5. 23. Luke 8. 42), he had faith in the *touch* of Christ, though he seemed to think it necessary for the hands of Christ to be laid upon her. He did not feel with the centurion, that a word would be enough.—— ¶ *Even now dead.* Mark has it, "*at the point of death;*" Luke reads, "*she lay a dying.*" Our faith must reach to this: that Christ is able to meet the extremest case—to raise dead souls.

19. *Jesus arose.* Here again we see Christ's willingness to relieve the distressed who called upon Him. This was His work, in a higher sense, that might be shown by these outward and visible doings. The maid was "one only daughter, about 12 years of age" (see Luke 8. 42).

20. Here there occurred, on the

20 ¶ And, º behold, a woman, which was diseased with an issue of blood twelve years, came behind *him*, and touched the hem of his garment:

21 For she said within herself, If I may but touch his garment,ᵖ I shall be whole.

22 But Jesus turned him about; and when he saw her, he said, Daughter, be of good comfort; thy ᵠ faith hath made thee whole.

<small>o Mar.5.25. Lu.8.43.   p Ac.19.12. q Lu.7.50; 17.19; 18.42. Ac.14.9.</small>

---

way, a case which shows the sinner in another light, and exhibits the power and grace of Christ.—— ¶ *And behold, a woman.* Here was a great sufferer, whose disease had been of 12 years' standing. It was held to be unclean by the Jewish law (Levit. 15. 25), and hence she would not give her case publicity if it could be helped. So the sinner, though a sufferer, conceals his sin and shame, and keeps back from Christ and from humble confession to Him. Mark and Luke tell us that she had spent all that she had upon physicians, and was nothing bettered, but only grew worse. " I said unto thee, when thou wast in thy blood, Live."—— ¶ *Touched the hem of His garment.* She thought there must be virtue in *touching* Him, since His touch was seen to give cures. This was as far as she could see of His Divine power. Her faith was full of trembling, yet she did well to think that He was so full of grace, that this touch of His clothes could cure her. She touched the *hem* or fringe on the border, as having peculiar sanctity with the Jews (Matt. 23. 5). This was the hem or fringe of the outer robe, cloak or mantle; and hence it was not at the feet, but below the waist (see fig. and note 5, 40). Fringes on the borders of the garments were commanded (see Numbers 15. 38). The Holy Spirit put this into her mind, and recorded it here that we may see how earnestly Christ must be sought in all circumstances, and how much virtue there is in any contact with Him, and how the power of Christ can make the simplest means efficacious. Many press upon Christ like the care-

The outer and inner garments (coat and cloak) were girt around the loins for a journey (ch 3. 4).

A sword was worn by travel'ers (ch. 26. 51).

And the woman was made whole from that hour.*r*

23. And *s* when Jesus came into the ruler's house, and saw the *t* minstrels and the people making a noise,

24 He said unto them, Give place: for the maid is not dead,*u* but sleepeth. And they laughed him to scorn.

25 But when the people were put forth, *v* he went in, and took her by the hand, and the maid arose.

r Jno.4.53. *s* Mar.5.38. Lu.8.51. *t* 2 Ch.35.25. *u* Ac.20.10. *v* 2 Ki.4.33,&c.

less crowd. *She*, with her heart full, *touched* Him; and the touch of faith was more than the common press upon Him.

22. Jesus inquired after her, as we find from Mark and Luke. He showed an interest in her, and a disposition to encourage her. Then she saw how fully He knew her and her case, and that she could conceal no longer. She came forward and confessed. So every one finds who truly finds Christ. He inquires after such, and emboldens them to speak out, and shows by the very *cure itself*, how ready He is, beyond all that they had dared to think, and then they are impelled by His goodness to "tell Him all the truth." We should not tremble and doubt when we see His readiness to bless, but should "come boldly to a throne of grace." Christ is found to be beforehand with the seeking soul, and shows us His foregoing love. "Before that Philip called thee, when thou wast under the fig-tree, I saw thee."——¶ *Thy faith*. Her faith cured her, because it led her to Him, who alone could cure, and who was so able and ready to heal. It was thus that Abraham's faith was counted to him for righteousness. Faith must take hold, for comfort, upon Christ's power and willingness to save.

23. After this miracle wrought by the way, Christ came to the house of the ruler.——¶ *The minstrels*. These were musicians, hired to play at funerals. It was a method among the Jews of expressing their grief on such occasions. The daughter of the ruler being now dead, the minstrels were already there, to serve at the funeral. In Eastern countries, the people set up a wail for the dead, as a ceremony, and used very noisy demonstrations of their grief. See fig. from *Kitto's Cyclopedia*.

24. *Give place*—make room. He meant to intimate that He had come to show His power, and that to Him it was like raising her out of sleep. They scoffed at this. Thus He obtained their testimony that she was fully dead, and not otherwise, so that when they should see her rise, they could not say she had not been dead, but He should have the credit of raising her from the dead. Sinners scorn the thought of Christ's Divine power with their souls.

24. He chose not to have the multitude present, but only Peter, James and John, and the father and mother of the damsel (Mark 5. 40). He would have quite enough there to witness the miracle, so that it should not be done in secret (see 2 Kings 4. 33). But it would speak for itself.

26. The fame of Christ went abroad, though He did not desire the publicity at present. He charged them (Luke 8. 56) that they should tell no man. "*He charged them straitly*" (Mark). The miracle was manifest—they must all have admitted it; and yet to publish it then, would only excite jealousies against such a power in the state, and throw obstacles in the way

112　　　　　　　　　　MATTHEW.　　　　　　　　　[A. D 32.

26 And ¹ the fame hereof went abroad into all that land.

27 ¶ And when Jesus departed thence, two blind men followed him, crying, and saying, *Thou son of David,*ʷ *have mercy on us.*

1 Or, *this fame.* w c.15.22; 20.30, 31.

28 And when he was come into the house, the blind men came to him: and Jesus saith unto them, Believe ye that I am able to do this? They said unto him, Yea, Lord.

29 Then touched he their eyes,

---

of His work (see Mark 1. 45). It would also encourage the idea of His temporal authority and rule, since He was showing His great work of redemption by these outward and visible doings. Presently, they could better understand, that He came to save sinners, and that this was but incidental, as yet, to His grand object. "Her spirit came again" (Luke), is precisely the same language as in 1 Kings 17. 22, in the Greek version. "He commanded to give her meat" (Luke), to show that it was no phantom, but a real return to life.

OBSERVE, (1.) There are but three miracles of this kind recorded of our Lord; and these, as they are deeply significant of His regenerating power, are different cases. This one had just died—the widow's son was just about to be buried—and Lazarus had been dead four days. (2.) How carefully the proofs are brought forward to show that this was a case of actual death: the father confessed it, the minstrels were there for the funeral, and the people ridiculed any other idea. If men are not dead in sin, Christ's work is shorn of its glory.

§ 60. TWO BLIND MEN HEALED, AND A DUMB SPIRIT CAST OUT.—*Capernaum?*

| Matt. 9. 27–34 | Mark. | Luke. | John. |

27. This miracle is not recorded by the other Evangelists. Christ wrought many wonderful works, that are not narrated, and those that are selected by the Holy Ghost for this inspired narrative, must be told with an object beyond the mere facts. They serve powerfully to illustrate Christ's redeeming work, and to point out to sinners the way of salvation. Every variety of case is therefore given, to show that in all various circumstances, the great business is, to find Christ, and seek His power and grace, as the only hope.

The blind were a numerous class at the East (Levit. 19. 14. Deut. 27. 18). These blind men acknowledged Christ as the Messiah by calling Him the *Son of David.* So He was prophesied of, and so His genealogy had proved as a standing confirmation of His claims, among the Jews.

28. Here Christ allows them to call upon Him till He gets into the house. He would have them earnest enough to follow Him whithersoever He went, and not willing to give up their suit. Who can doubt that they desired sight the more, that they might see Him who was the great object of wonder?——¶ *Believe ye.* He would not only put their faith to the trial of some delay at first, but to this test as to its nature. He would also have their case attract the more public attention. It was most important that He should have credit for His *ability.* This would imply His Divine authority and power, and as yet, this was the great point with the people. His willingness they should also find out. But this could be fully known only when His saving work as Jesus should be revealed. They believed in Him as the Messiah, all-powerful to work bodily cures. But as yet they saw no farther. So some would seem to know of Christ as a Saviour, but only partially as a sanctifier.

29. *According to your faith.* So far as they believed, so far He was willing to show Himself for their cure.

saying, According to your faith be it unto you.

30 And their eyes were opened: and Jesus straitly charged them, saying, See *that* no man know ˣ *it.*

31 But they, when they were departed, spread abroad his fame in all that country.

32 As they went out, behold, they brought to him a dumb man ʸ possessed with a devil.

33 And when the devil was cast out, the dumb spake : ᶻ and

x Is.42.2; 52.13. c.12.16. *y* c.12.22. Lu.11.14.

the multitudes marvelled, saying, It was never so seen in Israel.

34 But the Pharisees said, He ᵃ casteth out devils through the prince of the devils.

35 And ᵇ Jesus went about all the cities and villages, teaching in their synagogues, and preaching the gospel of the kingdom, and healing every sickness and every disease among the people.

36 But when he saw the multitudes, he was moved with

z Is.35.6. *a* c.12.24. Mar.3.22. Lu.11.15. *b* c.4.23.

Yet this formula of speech is rather in the sense of affirming than of limiting. They credited His ability, and this He displayed. The more fully we believe in Christ, the more fully will He deliver us from evil. And what we lack, for the most part, is the implicit and hearty faith in Him. "Let thy mercy, O Lord, be upon us, according as we hope in Thee." (Ps. 33. 22). This faith is the *bucket* let down into the fountain, without which we cannot draw.

30. *Straitly charged them.* The word means, He strictly and positively commanded them, on pain of His displeasure. OBSERVE: We must confess Christ, and cry out to him, and follow Him up, and believe in His mighty and gracious work. See vs. 26.

31. They had no right to publish the miracles, when Christ so positively forbade them. He had His own reasons for charging them with secrecy, and no matter how differently they might think of it, He ought to have been fully obeyed. They thought they knew better than He. This was the sin of Adam : and they had an inconsiderate zeal, which often carries people beyond and contrary to the express word of God.

32. *A dumb man.* The dumbness was doubtless of such a kind as was occasioned by the demon with which the man was possessed, for when he was cast out, the dumb spake. We find Satan and his hosts having to do with diseases. Not merely was it so thought among the Jews, but this is clearly inferred from Scripture, as in the history of Job and here. When Satan is utterly "cast out" (Rev. 20. 10), there shall be no more death, neither sorrow, nor crying, neither shall there be any more pain (Rev. 21. 4).

33. The multitudes confessed that this surpassed all that the prophets had ever done, and that a greater than Moses or Elijah was here—that Israel, who had beheld so many wonders, had never seen the like of this. This was a sudden burst of their admiration.

34. *Prince of the Devils.* This was a charge full of absurdity and blasphemy. They owned the miracles, yet would not ascribe them to His Divinity, but charged Him with infernal intercourse, holding communication with Beelzebub. See ch. 12. 23, 24. The Jews practised exorcisms, or the casting out of evil spirits, in pretence. But they were all amazed at Christ's power over demons, and they made the desperate resort of ascribing *this kind* of miracle to an alliance with the Prince of the Devils. This charge He answered on another occasion (Luke 11. 14), "By whom do your children (or disciples—the exorcising Jews) cast them out ?" &c., ch. 12. 27.

compassion on them, because they ¹ fainted, and were scattered abroad, as sheep ᶜ having no shepherd.

37 Then saith he unto his disciples, The harvest ᵈ truly *is* plenteous, but the labourers *are* few:

<small>1 Or, *were tired and lay down.* c Nu 27.17. 1K. 22.17. Eze.34.5. Zec.10.2. d Lu. 10.2. Jno.4.35.</small>

38 Pray ye therefore the Lord of the harvest, that he will send forth ᵉ labourers into his harvest.

CHAPTER X.

AND when he had called unto him his twelve disciples, he ᵃ gave them power against ¹

<small>e Ps.68.11. a Mar.3.13,14; 6.7, &c. Lu.9.1,&c. 1 Or, *over.*</small>

---

§ 61. Jesus again at Nazareth, and again rejected. . . . .

Matt.	Mark.	Luke.	John.
13. 54–58	6. 1–6		

§ 62. A THIRD CIRCUIT IN GALILEE, &c. See ch. 10.

Matt.	Mark.	Luke.	John.
9. 35–38			

35. *Jesus went about*—doing good, teaching, preaching, and healing. Preaching is something more than teaching—it is proclaiming the good news, and offering the gospel. This general description is given us of His work, to show that much more was done by Him than is narrated. And if we ask why the Spirit dictated these narratives rather than those of other works of Christ, we may suppose, that beyond the facts, there is conveyed important instruction respecting the way of life.

36. *They fainted*—literally, *were faint.* They were *weary in body, and heavy laden* with burdensome rites and doctrines of the Pharisees—without spiritual care from the priests, who were themselves ignorant and heedless of their charge. They were in just such condition as to excite His pity. The people He compared to scattered *sheep,* without a shepherd, or *pastor.* Their case called for help. They needed adequate instruction and care. They needed faithful shepherds, or pastors, to look after them, and tend them.

37. Yet this was the very *harvest* He was designing to reap. He sought the *lost*—" Come unto me all ye that are weary," &c. He points out this great truth to the disciples: The fields were white to the harvest— all was in a state ready for active and faithful labourers. The harvest is the multitude of souls ripe for being gathered in to His kingdom. Labourers are Christian ministers.

38. The disciples' work for the great cause was, first of all, to *pray.* We can help the church by prayers to the great Head of the church. God alone can raise up the men for the ministry in sufficient numbers, and give them the requisite qualifications and put them into the work. OBSERVE: It is *His* harvest, and He must send the men. Ministers must go under *His* commission.

CHAPTER X.

§ 62. (*Continued.*) THE TWELVE INSTRUCTED AND SENT FORTH.—*Galilee.*

Matt.	Mark.	Luke.	John.
10. 1–42 11. 1	6. 6–13	9. 1–6	

Christ was about 32 years old before He commissioned and sent forth His twelve Apostles. He had called them with other disciples at different times and places. He had *chosen* the twelve just after His second Passover. Peter had been called first, and Matthew last. Two of them had been John's disciples. Meantime Christ had been proved to be God, by His numerous miracles wrought in His own name and by His own proper authority. And He was proved to be the Messiah by His fulfilling in Himself the predictions of Him that was to come. He obtained sufficient and proper witnesses of His life and mir-

[A. D. 32.] CHAPTER X. 115

unclean spirits, to cast them out, and to heal all manner of sickness and all manner of disease.

2 Now the names *b* of the twelve apostles are these: The first, Simon, who is called Peter, and Andrew his brother; James *the son* of Zebedee, and John his brother;

3 Philip, and Bartholomew; Thomas, and Matthew the publican; James *the son* of Alpheus; and Lebbeus, whose surname was Thaddeus;

4 Simon the Canaanite; and Judas Iscariot, who also betrayed him.

5 These twelve Jesus sent forth, and commanded them, saying, Go not into the way of the Gentiles, and into *any* city of the Samaritans *c* enter ye not:

b Lu.6.13.

c 2 K.17.24. Jno.4.5,9,20.

acles, by choosing those who should accompany Him in all His course, and receive His private teachings, and such as should be able to give the fullest testimony to His words and works. For this purpose He had chosen and called *twelve*. As there were 12 tribes, and the nation was descended from 12 patriarchs, He would show thus that the church was essentially the same in all ages, and the Head of the church the same, and that it would be restored again, under a new economy.

1. Christ had chosen and called the twelve before the Sermon on the Mount was delivered. Mark 3. 13-19. Luke 6. 12-19. They had been all the time in His special company. Now He summons them to go out to their work. He gave them this power, that they might prove their commission, and have authority with men, as sent by Christ for the promotion of His kingdom. We see that Christ could not only work miracles of Himself, but He could even delegate this power to others. This was His greatest miracle. This clearly proved Him to be God, having life and power in Himself, to give to others.

2, 3, 4. *Apostle*. One that is sent. This is the meaning of our word *Missionary*. Matthew mentions them in pairs, probably as they were sent out " *by two and two*."——¶ The *first*, Simon. Alluding to the fact that Simon Peter was the *first called* as an Apostle. See John 1. 43.——¶ *Matthew the publican*. An humble confession. He does not call James and John the fishermen.—— ¶ *Lebbeus*. The Thaddeus of Matthew, is called by Luke, 'Judas the brother of James.' This is the "Judas not Iscariot." John 14. 22.——*Simon the Canaanite*, or more properly, the *Cananite* or *zealot*, called also " *Simon Zelotes*." There was a Jewish sect called " Zealots."

5. The twelve were sent forth to preach or proclaim the Gospel of Christ. " Ambassadors for Christ." ——¶ *The Gentiles*, were the heathen, who were not born Jews. The Apostles were not now to go *in the way of them*, or *among* them. Their first business was with the Jews.——¶ *The Samaritans*, were inhabitants of the region between Judea and Galilee, the country assigned to the tribe of Ephraim and the half tribe of Manasseh. They were formerly the revolted ten tribes of Israel, who had Samaria for their capital city, and took their name hence, and became most completely separate from the Jews. But subsequently, by the people being carried captive into Assyria, and colonists being sent back from that land, the inhabitants became wholly or mostly *heathen*. They deeply hated the Jews who had no dealing with them (John 4. 9). Their religion was made up of Judaism and heathenism. The twelve were not yet to go among these, because Christ

6 But go ᵈ rather to the lost sheep ᵉ of the house of Israel.

7 And, as ye go, preach, saying, ᶠ The kingdom of heaven is at hand.

8 Heal the sick, cleanse the lepers, raise the dead, cast out devils: ᵍ freely ye have received, freely give.

9 ¹ Provide ʰ neither gold, nor silver, nor brass, in your purses.

d Ac.13.46. *e* Ps.119.176. Is.53.6. Je.50.6,17. Eze. 34.5,6,8. 1 Pe.2.25. *f* c.3.2; 4.17. Lu.9.2; 10.9.

g Ac.8.18,20. 1 Or, *get*. *h* Lu.22.35. 1Cor.9.7,&c.

held a peculiar relation to the Jews through Abraham, and He would first proclaim to them the Gospel salvation, and own them as a peculiar and favourite people, in keeping with the Old Testament prophecies and promises. The Gospel was preached to the Gentiles after His resurrection, and Peter had a vision to authorize him as the Apostle to the Gentiles. But Peter's greater distinction *was his acknowledgment of Christ*. He was called a stone (Cephas and Peter are words which mean a stone), and on this ground of *Christ preached* to Jews and Gentiles, the Christian Church in all nations was to be erected.

6. *The House of Israel.* It was by virtue of a *household* covenant made with the family of Abraham, and extended to Jacob, that this people of the Jews were taken as the Lord's. Jacob was afterward called Israel, in keeping with his family covenant, which was then repeated to him. And so his descendants were called the house of Israel. They were sheep of this fold, but *lost* and scattered sheep. The Jewish Church, though taken into covenant with God, had become estrayed. Yet even in such case, He would have them treated with especial favour, and honoured with signal privilege for the father's sake. All sinners are like lost sheep, as being cared for and sought after by appointment of Christ. But such of them as have been baptized and have come into this outward covenant relation are more especially like the lost sheep of the house of Israel.

7. *The kingdom of heaven.* This was to be the sum of their preaching, to *call attention* to the reign of Christ as the heavenly kingdom—*coming*—drawing near This form of announcement was best fitted to arrest the notice of the Jews, and to express the advance of the Gospel reign. The term "*at hand*" is used in the literal sense of "*presently*"—that is, present here, nigh, even at the doors.

8. *Heal the sick.* Such is the benevolent design of Christ's mission, and by this visible manifestation in bodily diseases was His spiritual work to be set forth, breaking every yoke (Isa. 61. 1). They could do these things only by His divine power, committed to them, but needing to be exercised by Him at every step, in every instance.——¶ *Lepers*—were those defiled with the loathsome disease of leprosy, which excluded the poor sufferers from society, as ceremonially unclean and dreadful, and which nothing but the power of God could cleanse. These miracles they were to work in the name of Christ, not in their own name, nor in any other.——¶ *Freely give.* They were to dispense these benefits as *free gifts*. So they had received them. —and so, in their healing acts, they were to set forth the *free bounty* of God. Simon Magus thought the gift of God, in working such wonders, could be bought and sold for money, and though he was baptized, he was denounced for this. Maintenance, but not *money-making*, by the Gospel, was allowed (1 Cor. 9. 14). The exorcists wrought only for money.

9. *Provide* (margin, *get neither &c.*). They were not to carry any store for themselves. Their journey was not to be *long*, and the office work was to support itself. Though they were to dispense gratuitously, yet they were to look for maintenance from their work, and to cast themselves upon the people.——¶ *In your purses.*

A. D. 32. CHAPTER X. 117

10 Nor scrip for *your* journey, neither two coats, neither shoes, nor yet [1] staves : for [i] the workman is worthy of his meat.

11 And into whatsoever city or town ye shall enter, inquire who in it is worthy ; and there abide till ye go thence.

12 And when ye come into an house, salute it.

13 And if the house be worthy, let your peace come upon it; but if it be not worthy, let your peace return [j] to you.

14 And whosoever shall not receive you, nor hear your words, when ye depart out of that house or city, shake [k] off the dust of your feet.

15 Verily I say unto you, [l] It

1 *A staff.* *i* Lu.10.7,&c. *j* Ps.35.13. *k* Ne.5.13. Ac.13.51; 18.6. *l* c.11.22,24.

They were not to go as other travellers, with a supply of money in their girdle or belt.

10. *Scrip.* Knapsack for provisions.——¶ *Shoes* were here forbidden. In Mark it is said, Be shod with sandals. They were not to make any special preparation, nor take spare clothing.——¶ *Staves* (margin, *a staff*). Mark says, they might have nothing but "*a staff only*," for the journey. They were not to *provide* staves, though they might *take one.* The whole idea is, that they should not make the common provision of travellers, in view of a journey, nor take any thing extra ; but they should rather go empty, and look for the reward of their work. Their business was mainly spiritual, they must feel it to be so, and under the God of Providence, the work should support itself. The people would be bound to supply them with necessities, and they should make this claim upon them as they went. And He that sent them would furnish them, if none others did. Christ's ministers have no right to be secular. Christ commands His servants to come to Him empty rather than full.

11. *Worthy.* Well disposed toward their doctrine and work—such as should be ready to receive them and their doctrine, as is explained by the next verse—those to whom they might hopefully preach the Gospel, as being ready to entertain them and their message. They were to *inquire*, and such an one as was " of good report" in things pertaining to the kingdom, they were to select as their host, and abide with him. Staying in one house, they would better be found, and could more easily despatch their work. Here it was hinted that they were not to make long stay in any one place. The reception of the gospel message is our only worthiness with God. Christ is jealous of the treatment which His ministers receive.

12. *Salute it*—the house. Pay *your address to the family* as ambassadors of Christ, and thus ascertain what reception you shall meet with.

13. *Let your peace.* The common mode of saluting was the simple word "*Peace*," which denotes one's *good wishes.* May peace and prosperity attend you! If the house be favourably disposed, let your peace come upon it—that is, labour to bless them according to the full import of your salutation, and they shall indeed be blessed. But if they should be found unfavourable to you and to your message, withdraw your salutation—leave the house—and your blessing or pronouncing of peace upon them shall return to you again: they shall not be blessed (Luke 10. 6). A cup of cold water given in the name of a disciple shall not lose its reward.

14. *Shake off the dust.* This act was understood, like the *washing of the hands* by Pilate, as signifying innocence of the crime. Accordingly it is a begging to have *no part or lot* in the punishment. The guilt is metaphorically regarded as adhering to the hands or feet (see 1 Kings 2.

shall be more tolerable for the land of Sodom and Gomorrah in the day of judgment than for that city.

16 ¶ Behold, I send you forth as sheep in the midst of wolves: be ye therefore ᵐ wise as serpents, and ¹ harmless ⁿ as doves.

17 But beware ᵒ of men: for ᵖ they will deliver you up to the

---

m Ro. 16.19. Ep.5.15. 1 Or, *simple*. *n* Ph 2 '5. *o* Ph.3.2. *p* c. 24.9. Mar.13.9.

---

5), as the next verse shows. So in Mark 6. 11, it is expressed, "*For a testimony against them.*" Your doom be on yourselves; and let not even the least dust of your sin and condemnation attach to us! Such an act would be most expressive, as testifying the reprobation of the Apostles. They actually did this. Acts 13. 51; 18. 6. Many there are now, who refuse to receive or hear the Gospel. From such, the ministers of Christ can at last only turn away, and disclaim any portion with them. For the punishment will be so complete, that it would seem to reach even the dust trodden by such transgressors. "Have no fellowship with them," "Seeing ye put it from you, and judge yourselves *unworthy* of everlasting life, lo, we turn to the Gentiles." Acts 13. 46, 51. "They shook off the dust of their feet against them."

15. Sodom and Gomorrah were the chief of those cities of the plain which were destroyed by fire raining down from the Lord out of heaven. Gen. 19. 24, 25. They were along the south-east border of Palestine, and their site is now covered by the Dead Sea. Their punishment, though they were so wicked as to be cut off so terribly from the earth, will be more tolerable at the day of final judgment—that is, *more easily endured*, comparatively—than that of such as "obey not the Gospel!" And the reason is, that these neglect and reject so great salvation, and sin against this greater light. For if the word spoken by angels was steadfast, how shall ye escape? (Heb. 2. 2.)

16. These words are spoken more generally of their apostleship, not merely of the particular expedition on which they were at this time sent out, which should be of short duration. The ministers of Christ amongst their enemies are compared to sheep defenceless in the midst of wolves—i. e., the fierce and ravenous foes that should prowl about their path, and seek to devour them. Such were the false prophets; "Inwardly they are ravening wolves." ch. 7. 15. Satan is termed a *roaring lion*. Wicked men that are enemies of Christ's ministers, are here termed *wolves*. The reference is to the *persecutions that they should afterward endure*. (So in Matt. 24. the language is first concerning things *near*, and then concerning things *remote*.) *Therefore* they should require at once to be prudent and discerning, while they should be gentle and meek. This wisdom qualified by the harmlessness, is *wisdom to do good* and not evil. (So David toward Saul.) Christians are, like sheep of the fold, defenceless, and like them they should look to the good shepherd. Christ was led as a lamb to the slaughter, and as a sheep before her shearers was dumb, so He opened not His mouth; and yet He was *wisdom* itself. Proverbs. The word rendered "harmless" here, is the same in Rom. 16. 19, "*simple—concerning evil.*" Its leading sense is, *inoffensive*. It occurs but three times in the New Testament. Serpents are called *wise*, because they have always been the symbols of wisdom. Be full of keen and cautious discernment. The Egyptians expressed their idea of wisdom by the figure of a serpent. Christians are not to abjure true wisdom, but to cultivate it and pray for it. Christian ministers are to have a wisdom as remarkable as that of serpents, only *from God, and for good*.

17. *Beware*. Take good care. Be cautious of the men. Here they were to show their wisdom in dealing with those who are like wolves. They were to expect such enemies, not to

councils, and they will scourge ⁹ you in their synagogues;

18 And ʳ ye shall be brought before governors and kings for my sake, for a testimony against them and the Gentiles.

19 But ˢ when they deliver you up, take no thought how or what ye shall speak; for it shall be given you in that same hour what ye shall speak.

20 For it is not ye that speak, but the Spirit of your Father which speaketh in you.

21 And the brother shall deliver up the brother to death, and the father the child: and the children shall rise up against *their* parents, and cause them to be put to death.

q Ac.5.40. 2Cor.11.24. *r* Ac.24 & 25. *s* Mar.13. 11. Lu.12.11; 21.14,15.

avoid them, nor invite their attack. The caution is explained more fully in vss. 19, 23, &c.——¶ *To the councils.* To the Sanhedrim for trial, where the high priests met.——¶ *Synagogues*, where the people also assembled.
18. *Governors.* See Acts 4. 5–30; 5. 17–33; 12. 1–4; 18. 12; 23. 33; 25. 6, 10; 26. 1, 28, 30. Paul before Nero (2 Tim. 4. 16) fulfilled this forewarning. It was *for the sake* of Christ, because it was on account of Christ's doctrine and cause that they were thus treated. It would be *for a testimony* against these magistrates and the Gentiles, by preaching to them the claims of Christ, and making the gospel known to them, that they might be without excuse, that their unbelief might be rebuked, and that the judgment of God against them might be vindicated. So the gospel is to be preached to all nations, "*for a testimony*" before the end come. See the same phrase where the leper was to offer the gift that Moses commanded *for a testimony unto them.* ch. 8. 4. Though this prediction by Christ was so plain, and though the results so clearly proved His foreknowledge, nothing hindered the apostles from going forward. He who foreknew future events, could foreordain their deliverance; hence they received their persecutions with calmness and trust in God, and rather *rejoiced that they were counted worthy to suffer shame for His name.* Acts 5. 41.
19. *Take no thought*—have no anxiety. So the term occurs in Matt. 6. 25, see note. They would naturally have great terror in coming before kings, as to how and what they should speak, lest they should be unable to vindicate themselves and the truth, in such an embarrassing condition. They were to feel most perfectly at ease on this point; for at the instant, they should have words put into their mouths from God. This would be a most complete relief.
20. *The Spirit of your Father.* A double consolation. It should not depend upon their ability of speech, their rhetoric or discourse, but it should be a question of the Holy Ghost's ability. And this was the Spirit of *their Father*, working in them and speaking in them. For it was He who should give illumination and power of discourse suited to the case. This was not to encourage indolence in attainment of knowledge, or any requisite qualifications, but to fortify their faith in God for all the possible trials of their case.
21. Persecution should be so violent as to break through all the ties of kindred. The opposition to Christ would be so great as to destroy all those natural affections in families, which are the strongest on earth.
22. They are here further encouraged against all their fears, by the assurance that the *result* should be most happy. Their salvation should depend on God, who here beforehand certifies them of the issue. They who should endure should be saved. They had only to hold out in this confidence, and they should see it come to pass as He promised.

22 And ye shall be hated of all *men* for my name's sake; but t he that endureth to the end shall be saved.

23 But when they persecute you in this city flee ᵘ ye into another: for verily I say unto you, Ye shall not ᵗ have gone over the cities of Israel till the Son of man be come.

24 The ᵛ disciple is not above *his* master, nor the servant above his lord.

25 It is enough for the disciple that he be as his master, and the servant as his lord. If ʷ they have called the master of the house ¹ Beelzebub, how much more *shall they call* them of his household?

26 Fear them not therefore: for there is nothing ˣ covered

t De.12.12,13. Re. 2.10 *u* Ac.8.1. 1 Or, *end*, or, *finish*. *v* Lu.6.40. Jno.13.16; 15.20.

w Jno.8.48. 1 *Beelzebul*. *x* Mar.4.22. Lu 12.2,3 1Cor.4.5.

---

23. It should not be their object to *avoid* persecution by fleeing from the reach of it, nor were they to run needlessly into it, nor to lie down and die under it when they could serve the Master more. It should be their object to do others good. They were to flee into another city, not in order to escape all trial, but in order to labour in another place with better success. The plan and prospect contemplated their being driven by persecution through the cities of Israel. So Acts 8. 4, "They that were scattered abroad, went every where preaching the word." Christ here gave them encouragement of a speedy *coming* of His, before they should have gone through this itinerating work. He refers here to the Transfiguration, in which He purposed to reveal Himself by a special manifestation, that should be most important in the history of their work. The apostles owned this to be a special coming of Christ when they asked, why say the Scribes that Elias must *first* come? They fell on their faces when they saw His glory, and heard Him announced as Christ from heaven. Peter refers to it as "the power and coming of our Lord Jesus Christ," that he saw with the rest on the holy mount, when they were eye-witnesses of His majesty. This prospect was given here of a special manifestation, speedily, which should satisfy them of His authority and glory, and should be a great step in the prosecution of His redeeming work (ch. 17. 2 Peter 1. 17).

24, 25. They were to be satisfied with the severities of their lot, when they remembered the greater severities of His, and considered that they could not expect better treatment than He. The servant is not above his lord. If *He* endured privation, and went through drudgery in the cause, though He was the Master, what better lot could be expected for the servants? They should ask no better or easier condition than they saw Him have. This was good enough for them. A family circle is usually called by the same name; and if they have called *me*, the Master of the house, "*Beelzebub*," in derision and scandal, how much more shall they call them of His household by like abusive epithets? (see ch. 9. 34; 12. 24. Mark 3. 22. Luke 11. 15. John 8. 48.) See Jude, vs. 15, "*Hard speeches.*"—¶ Beelzebub (see 2 Kings 1. 2) was chief of the false gods of the Philistines, and was worshipped by the inhabitants of Ekron. The name signifies (from Baal, *god;* and zebub, *fly*) the god of flies—having power over all noxious insects. This was as much as to say, the ' god of idolatry." The worst devil was lord of idols in their view. This alluded to the false worship which they accused Him of setting up in claiming to be God (see *Lightfoot*, vol. II., pp. 185, 196). See 2 Ki. 1. 3. "Is it not because there is not a God in Israel, that ye go to inquire of Baal-zebub," &c.

that shall not be revealed ; and hid, that shall not be known.

27 What I tell you in darkness, *that* speak ye in light : and what ye hear in the ear, *that* preach ye upon the house-tops.

28 And ʸ fear not them which kill the body, but are not able to kill the soul : but rather fear him

ʸ Is.8.12,13 ; 51.7,12. 1Pe.3.14.

which is able to destroy both soul and body in hell.

29 Are not two sparrows sold for a ¹ farthing ? and one of them shall not fall on the ground without your Father.

30 But ᶻ the very hairs of your head are all numbered.

1 In value, *half-penny farthing*, a 10th part of the Roman penny, c.18.28. ᶻ Ac. 27.34.

---

26. *Fear them not therefore.* A reason given for their courage and confidence is the coming development: they should see greater things than these. Their Master should yet appear to them in His glory, and their enemies, and His, should be put to shame. And a final day is coming, when the truth shall come to light, and things shall be called by their true names. Never fear, for truth will prevail.

27. Therefore *speak out* the words of your great Teacher and Master. He taught them privately, as twelve scholars or private pupils. They were to teach these things most publicly, in all the world, without concealment, disguise, or fear. There were many reasons why Christ could not come out openly as the Messiah at first. Men would have prevented His work, or set Him up as a temporal king, or charged Him with treason against the State. Therefore, He would not have those whom He cured tell of Him; nor would He have the transfiguration told of till after the resurrection, when it should be better understood, believed, and appreciated. Both Christ and His apostles were compelled at first to speak privately and in a whisper, for fear of the Jews, and from the weakness and peril of the cause. But they were thus to go abroad to their great public work, and to speak boldly and openly in the face of persecution.

28. They were here emboldened against the fear of death itself. This they should have to meet. But what is this ?—*the body.* Offence against God is the only proper ground of fear, for thereby both soul and body are exposed to eternal death. NOTE: This proves that the wicked shall be sent to hell, and their bodies shall be raised from the grave to suffer forever with their souls. Psalm 9. 17.

29. In Luke we have it that the disciples were charged not only *not* to fear men who were but dust, but to fear and honour Him who has power over body and soul. "Yea, I say unto you, fear Him" (Luke 12. 5). And the verses here seem to follow naturally from that sentiment. The protection of our life is in the hands of God, who has body and soul in His power. And seeing even wicked men who would destroy us, are under His overruling providence, we ought not to fear them as though they could do any thing without His consent. So we also are objects of Divine care.——¶ *Sparrows.* These are insignificant birds, and so unimportant that two of them are sold for a farthing; and yet God's providence is so extensive, so minute and particular, that even one of them shall not fall on the ground, without God being there, allowing it, and ordering it, and arranging that it should be one and not another of them that should fall.——¶ *Your Father.* This God is your Father. And if God gives to them such care, shall He not much more care for you who are of so much more value ?

30. *The very hairs*—the least things that belong to you. This is proverbial language, expressing the most minute and trivial interest connected with any one. The very hairs of your head, for which you care so little, and which you never pretend to

31 Fear ye not therefore; ye are of more value than many sparrows.

32 Whosoever therefore shall confess me before men, him ᵃ will I confess also before my Father which is in heaven.

33 But ᵇ whosoever shall deny me before men, him will I also deny before my Fathe which is in heaven.

a Re.3.5. *b* 2Ti.2.12.

34 Think not that I am come to send peace on earth : ᶜ I came not to send peace, but a sword.

35 For I am come to set a man at variance ᵈ against his father, and the daughter against her mother, and the daughter-in-law against her mother-in-law.

36 And ᵉ a man's foes *shall be* they of his own household.

c Lu.12.49,53. *d* Mi.7.5,6. *e* Ps.41.9.

---

count, are *all numbered*. God's providence is so particular that it reaches to every creature—even to a sparrow or a worm, and to the very separate hairs of the head, and to every thing belonging to and concerning all His creatures, and all their actions.

31. *Fear ye not therefore.* This refers back to vss. 26 and 28. The soul's value, as shown in the priceless work of Christ, is our encouragement.

32, 33. Such a bold, unshaken confidence in Christ, as one is ready to declare openly before men, however they oppose, is demanded. This is the spirit needed for the work: trusting Christ for every thing, and undauntedly boasting Him before the world. There must be an open, earnest espousing of Christ, cleaving to Him, living upon Him—a public confession of His name in the act, and of His all-sufficiency in the life. Such as make Christ their boast will be openly acknowledged by Him as His children in the day of judgment. This word rendered *confess*, is the same word elsewhere rendered *profess* (1 Tim. 6. 12). A profession of religion is a profession not of our extra piety, nor of our worthiness, nor of our being able to stand alone, but a profession of Christ. It confesses our unworthiness and insufficiency, and also His merit and sufficiency. It is confessing or *owning* that Christ is our hope and our all. It professes a determination to follow Him as disciples, and to look to Him alone for salvation. This is to be done before men—publicly in the church, by uniting with this separate body and coming out from the world. It is to be done in all the life, by witnessing for Christ before gainsayers and beholders. Christ will own all such as His, and profess to them that He has known them, and profess to the world that these are His brethren and chosen; while such as deny Him, or are ashamed of Him—refusing to confess Him before men, and practically having no connexion with Him in His Church or His cause—shall be denied and disowned by Him at the judgment.

34, 35, 36. *Think not,* &c. Though the gospel message is peace, yet it introduces collision. Christ's ministers are not to expect worldly ease or advantage. They must not look for peace and harmony with best friends in serving Christ. There would be severe and cruel opposition. The tendency of Christ's doctrines and service, would be to make breaches even in families, because He introduced into a world of sin an opposite element (see Mark 7. 6); and like water upon fire, it would create strife. This was not His object, to make family discords, but it should be the effect of His work; therefore they must not expect easy times in His service. The gospel has produced such results always and every where. Christ's brethren and sisters believed not, and were offended in Him.—¶ *A sword.* Luke reads *division* (ch. 12. 52). This is the idea: strife would ensue where some pro-

37 He *ᶠ* that loveth father or mother more than me is not worthy of me: and he that loveth son or daughter more than me, is not worthy of me.

38 And he that taketh not his cross, and followeth after me, is not worthy of me.

ᶠ Lu.14.26.

39 He *ᵍ* that findeth his life, shall lose it: and he that loseth his life for my sake, shall find it.

40 ¶ He *ʰ* that receiveth you, receiveth me; and he that receiveth me receiveth him that sent me.

41 He *ⁱ* that receiveth a pro-

ᵍ c.16.25. *ʰ* c.18.5; 25.40,45. Jno. 12.44. *ⁱ* 1K. 17.10. He.6.10.

---

fessed Him; hatred would be the consequence, and separation. Christ warns them, therefore, that they must be prepared, even for such painful sacrifice as that of dearest friends.

37. If we love any other more than Christ, though it be father or mother, then He has no claims upon us but such as are subordinate to theirs, and can expect nothing from us, except in a secondary way. We could, in such case, do nothing for Him without their consent, and could not follow Him without first paying the last attentions to them—*seeing them dead and buried first* (ch. 8. 21). But all His claims upon us are for our *supreme love;* and if He receives not this, He receives nothing that He claims. Such as love any being or thing more than Him are *not worthy of Him.* They are not such as He calls for, nor such as His cause demands, and they cannot be His disciples, nor should they be considered such.

38. Since the world is so full of opposition to Christ's cause, as He had just said, and since such strifes and persecutions are to be met, every man will have trials to endure, and sufferings to undergo for the Master. This burden is here called *his cross,* in which language Christ alludes to His own cross which already He bore in secret -a load of trials and reproaches and sufferings. He that taketh not freely the load of worldly condemnations and penalty that is laid upon him for Christ—he that declines duty because of what it costs—he that serves Christ only so far as his convenience and ease will allow, is not worthy of *Him,* who "endures the cross" for sinners "despising the shame." Luke here brings in a paragraph, about building a tower and counting the cost; for every one who professes Christ should count the cost, and this is what Christ here urges. The cross hints here of His death.

39. Here is a general declaration on this whole subject of self-denial. He that *looks after* his life, consulting only his comfort, his profit, his living, shall be disappointed and lose the highest style of living and its highest joys. Luke reads, he that saveth his life, *i. e.,* spareth it and seeketh it as the highest interest, shall fail in his attempt. The selfish man shall not be happy, shall not half live, stinting himself and making his own life miserable to hoard up the means of living. The man always bent upon keeping his health shall often lose his health by his vain devices. So he who looks out for himself supremely, loves himself, and trusts himself rather than God, shall fail of his life, especially of that which is eternal. While he that loseth (or is willing to lose, see ch. 16. 25) his life for my sake—willing to take up his cross and go through trials and perils from supreme devotion to me—shall find his life. He shall find out the true life, and the salvation of his soul. What a terrible loss is it for a man to gain the whole world, if one could do it, and lose his own soul or be cast away (ch. 16. 26). The idea here is, *he that saveth himself* shall lose himself or be lost, while he that loseth himself for Christ's sake shall be saved.

40–42. Here Christ shows them the high claim which they shall have

phet in the name of a prophet, shall receive a prophet's reward; and he that receiveth a righteous man in the name of a righteous man, shall receive a righteous man's reward.

42 And whosoever shall give to drink unto one of these little ones a cup of cold *water* only in the name of a disciple, verily I say unto you, he shall in no wise lose his reward.

CHAPTER XI.

AND it came to pass, when Jesus had made an end of commanding his twelve disciples, he departed thence, to teach and to preach in their cities.

2 Now ᵃ when John

a Lu. 7. 18, &c.

---

on the hospitality of a wicked world. This is for their encouragement. He is with them alway, even unto the end of the world. He held himself identified with his true followers. They in Him and He in them—hence they were to go out with this feeling of identity with the Master. Whoso received *them*, did thereby receive Him (see ch. 25. 40). This alludes to the reception spoken of (ch. 10. 13), receiving their persons and messages with favour. These words also seem to have been spoken as a *passport* given them by Christ to embolden them in presenting themselves and their messages, and to comfort them when cast out. This related to all the course of their work.

41. *In the name of a prophet.* That is, because he is a prophet—from this motive. The principle was first stated, that *Christ was to be treated in them*, for *they were one with Him*. Now the principle is laid down that the sincere reception of a prophet or a righteous man—a religious teacher or a private Christian—from love to Christ and the cause, will secure a share in the reward of such prophet or righteous man; for thus an interest can be shown, making common cause with them in their trials, and such shall have a portion with them in their recompense above. So important is the good treatment of Christ's cause, that often it shows true piety most manifestly, and is a token of the genuine part which such have in the inheritance of the saints.

42. Kindness and hospitality to the servants of Christ, and liberality to the cause of Christ, and cordial sympathy with the church of Christ in all its operations and wants, are here commended, and the principle is such that whoever does the least out of affection for the cause, shall be amply rewarded. Whoever gives a cup of cold water to one of these disciples (or little ones) in the name, or for the sake of a disciple, and because of his being a disciple, he honours Christ in the Christian whom he helps, and he shall in no wise lose his reward (Matt. 25).—¶ *These little ones.* would be easily understood as referring to the disciples, because the term among the Jews for Master was *Rabbi*, which was from a word meaning *Great*.

CHAPTER XI.

1. *He departed thence.* The *Third* circuit in Galilee is here announced. But there are three chapters of *back events* which come in here as a parenthesis, after which this circuit will be detailed (ch. 14. § 63). The twelve had previously been chosen, before the Sermon on the Mount was delivered. They were now instructed and sent forth in Galilee; and from this point Christ departed " to teach and to preach in their cities"—that is, in the cities of Galilee. He did not go into Judea as yet. Here the Evangelist Matthew introduces *back events*, which occupy chapters 11. 12. 13; these belong to His 31st year.

[§ 44. JOHN THE BAPTIST IN PRISON SENDS DISCIPLES TO JESUS.]—*Galilee.*—*Capernaum ?*

Matt.	Mark.	Luke.	John.
11. 2–19		7. 18–35	

A. D. 31.] CHAPTER XI. 125

had heard in the prison the works of Christ, he sent two of his disciples,

3 And said unto him, Art thou he that should come, or do we look for another?

4 Jesus answered and said unto them, Go and shew John again those things which ye do hear and see:

5 The blind receive their sight, and the lame walk, the lepers are cleansed, and the deaf hear, the dead are raised up, and the poor have the gospel preached to them.

6 And blessed is *he*, whosoev-

This is not to be read as directly following upon the former chapter of events. Here, *previous doings* are recited. Soon after the Sermon on the Mount, and the healing of the Centurion's servant, and raising the widow's son, John the Baptist sent this message. In Luke we learn that as John's disciples told him of those miracles, he sent messengers to Christ. John was first put in prison just before our Lord began His work, and came from Nazareth, Matt. 4. 12, to preach, 17. He had been put in prison by Herod for faithfully denouncing, as unlawful and shameful, his marrying his brother Philip's wife. Josephus relates that he was imprisoned in the castle of Machaerus in the south part of Perea, the region east of the Jordan.

3. *Art Thou He that should come?* John knew of Christ enough to serve him in ordinary circumstances. But now he had been detained for some time in a gloomy prison, and could not see or know all that was going on. He had evidently heard of His wondrous works, but he doubtless expected, from the prophecy of Malachi, a somewhat different manifestation, especially a more immediate occurrence of the blessing and punishment promised. So his misgivings were only superficial and such as did but require this explanation of the word and works. Besides, he would send his disciples to Christ as he before pointed two of them to Him.—(John 1. 36). He was sent to herald Christ, and now as his public work was done, he would direct his disciples to Him whom he announced. ——¶ *He that should come.* This refers directly to Malachi's prophecy, by which John was naturally guided; as it was there that he was promised as the Elias, in connexion with Christ the *one that should come.* Mal. 3. the language occurs: "The Lord whom ye seek shall suddenly *come.*" Behold *He shall come.* "The day of His *coming,*" &c. And John's language refers to these prophecies. He inquires for Him that was promised, if Christ were truly He. Christ was expected by the Jews because He was predicted in their Scriptures.——¶ *Or do we look for another?*—that is, to answer the prophet's description of the one that was to come.

4. *Go and tell John again.* From Luke we learn that *at that same hour,* Christ cured many of diseases and plagues, &c., giving John's messengers a specimen, and this only reply to their inquiry. He answered in language that would explain itself, and must be understood by those familiar with the prophet's speaking of the Messiah.

5. He appealed to His miracles wrought in their presence, for a complete attestation of His Messiahship. A miracle is an exertion of Divine power, and therefore is the plainest, highest proof that can be given. These things also had been predicted by Isaiah, ch. 35. 42, and 61. 66, and 29. 18, 19, and they could see that they were now fulfilled in Him.

6. Here Christ shows that though this is good and sufficient ground for believing in Him, yet in His person and doctrine, there would be things at which the natural heart might take offence (or *stumble*). The proofs He brings are not such as to compel the

11*

er shall not be offended b in me.

7 ¶ And, as they departed, Jesus began to say unto the multitude concerning John, What c went ye out into the wilderness to see? a reed shaken with the d wind?

8 But what went ye out for to see? a man clothed in soft raiment? Behold, they that wear soft *clothing* are in kings houses.

9 But what went ye out for to see? a prophet? yea, I say unto you, and more than a prophet.

10 For this is *he* of whom it is e written, Behold, I send my messenger before thy face, which shall prepare thy way before thee.

b Is.8.14,15. 1Co.1.22,23. 1Pe.2.8. c Lu.7.24-30. d Eph.4.14. Ja.1.6.

e Is.40.3. Mal.3.1. Lu.1.76.

---

belief of men, and some, after beginning with Him might break off. Therefore he adds, Blessed is he who shall not *be offended* in me. His humble life was likely to offend the proud, because they would think it mean, and vulgar, and beggared, and off-cast, and unfit for their association. His *death* offends the proud, because it was ignominious and accursed. And in the doctrines which He taught, there is so much that is abasing to men—as, the utter helplessness of fallen nature and the entire dependence on Christ's work for salvation, and the distinguishing grace in our renewal—that they are likely to be offended in Him. It was so with the young ruler, the people of Nazareth and the Pharisees. Persons show that they are ashamed of Christ by refusing to acknowledge Him before men, even when they are persuaded of His claims.

7. Christ takes this opportunity of giving testimony to John, as John had testified of Him. Their work was a joint one, but John was to decrease, while He was to increase. He would have the multitude rightly understand John's mission and character, that they might rightly understand His. Here, then, He tells who and what John was. In ch. 3. 5, we read that Jerusalem, and all Judea, and all the region round about Jordan, went out to John in the wilderness.——¶ *A reed.* A flag that grows around the Jordan. The character which is represented by *a reed shaken with the wind,* is a light, fickle character, "carried about with every wind of doctrine," and of favour. They scarcely knew what manner of person they went out in a vain curiosity to see. But Christ assures them, that John was a firm, substantial character. He showed his firmness by testifying of Christ before He had come, and maintaining his own inferiority to Christ, among so many temptations to exalt himself.

8. *Soft raiment.* They could not have expected to see one different from what this work of John required. No soft clothing would have been appropriate for him. And if they understood his work as a preacher of repentance, they would have understood the rough clothing. He was dressed in a raiment of camel's hair, and a leathern girdle around his waist—dressed for the wilderness, and for his work—not for king's houses; and his preaching was that of repentance, not of ease and self-security. See Luke 7. 25.

9. *A prophet.* This name applied not only to those who predicted future events, but to such as gave religious instructions. The people thought John to be a prophet (ch. 14. 5.). But Christ declares that he was more than an ordinary prophet, since he was His immediate herald and personal forerunner—"*much more.*" Luke 7. 26.

10. In Mal. 3. 1, this had been written of John, that he was to be the *messenger of Christ,* before whom John was sent. This passage is the substance of the prophet's language, and Christ here shows that John had the

11 Verily, I say unto you, among *f* them that are born of women there hath not risen a greater than John the Baptist: notwithstanding, *g* he that is least in the kingdom of heaven is greater than he.

12 And from the days of John the Baptist until now the kingdom of heaven ¹ suffereth violence, and the violent take *h* it by force.

13 For all the prophets and the law prophesied until John.

14 And if ye will receive *it*, this is Elias, which *i* was for to come.

f Jno.5.35. *g* Jno.1.15,27; 3.30.   1 Or, *is gotten by force, and they that thrust men, take it,* &c. *h* Lu.16.16. Ep.6.11-13. *i* Mal. 4.5. c.17.12.

---

honour of its applying to him. Accordingly, the Gospel by Mark opens with direct reference to this prophecy.

11. John was greater than other prophets, because to him it was given to stand personally related to Christ as His forerunner—to prepare His way—to baptize Him, to testify of Him, and to point to Him as the Lamb which the law required.—¶ *He that is least*—or less, inferior. He that is of inferior standing to him in the Christian church is greater than He. The Christian economy is so much in advance of that under which John lived and acted, that he who is of comparatively low rank among the teachers here, is greater than John. He has a more advanced position, and teaches, not merely the Messiah come, but *Christ crucified* (1 Cor. 1. 23). Behold the dignity and excellency of a Sabbath School teacher. Any office of teaching Gospel truth is honourable.

12. *From the days.* All about this time of John's preaching and Christ's, the Christian economy had begun to excite general interest, and to create an extensive zeal for obtaining its privileges.—¶ *The kingdom of heaven.* The new dispensation now preached, in which Christ's kingdom was to be established openly.— ¶ *Suffereth violence*—as though it were attacked. The people were so zealous and earnest; and this would go to show John's superior position above other prophets, and an ordinary Christian teacher's pre-eminence over John. —¶ *The violent.* Those who are earnest, and who strive to get possession of its blessings, succeed. Luke 13, 24; 16. 16.

13. *For all the prophets and the law.* "The Law" was that part of the Old Testament included in the five books of Moses. "The Prophets" comprised the rest, excepting "the Psalms." Sometimes, as here, the Law and the Prophets is a phrase taken for the Old Testament Scriptures. The Old Testament preaching continued until John's time, since which the gospel had been proclaimed. John was himself a herald of Christ, and so came properly under the Old Testament. John's character and rank are understood only by considering his relation to this new economy. In him all the Old Testament prophesying closed. Since his time was the New. At the same time, this responsibility must be weighed, in reference to this altered state of things. In Luke 16. 16, this sentiment is introduced to rebuke the Pharisees, who clung to the Jewish ritual after the gospel was openly proclaimed.—¶ *Prophesied*—taught of Christ. "The testimony of Jesus is the spirit of prophecy" (Rev. 19. 10).

14. *And if ye will receive it.* Our Lord now plainly declares to them that John was no other than the person predicted by the last of their old prophets under the name of Elias. His coming is foretold in Mal. 4. 5. They were familiar with this prophecy, but they had not recognized or received John the Baptist as he that was to come under this name. They had done unto him whatsoever they listed (ch. 17. 12). As in reference to Christ, they had not known Him. John was not Elias, risen from the dead. When they asked him, Art thou Elias? he answered, No; but

15 He *j* that hath ears to hear, let him hear.

16 But *k* whereunto shall I liken this generation? It is like unto children sitting in the markets, and calling unto their fellows,

17 And saying, We have piped unto you, and ye have not danced; we have mourned unto you, and ye have not lamented.

18 For John came neither eating nor drinking; and they say, *l* He hath a devil.

19 The Son of man came eating *m* and drinking: and they

j Re.2.7,&c. *k* Lu.7.31. *l* c.10.25. Jno.7.20. *m* c.9.10. Jn.2.2.

---

he was come in the spirit and power of Elias (Luke 1. 17) or *Elijah*. In declaring to them this truth, He says: "If ye will receive it," meaning that He knew how they would dispute John's being the Elias, as they disputed Himself being the Messiah. They expected that Elias himself would personally reappear in the flesh. He meant by this to show how it was a matter to be believed by them—how it belonged to their disposition, either to believe or not, and if they would not believe it nor receive it, it would be their own fault.

15. *He that hath ears.* This is a phrase used where a truth is conveyed which is not naturally understood, requiring a spiritual penetration and disposition to receive it. It calls special attention as to something not apparent at first view, and requiring more deep examination. It is also used to signify that the truth is of general application. It is spoken to us as well as unto them. We must hear with deep attention, and apply all our faculties to the message received.

16. *This generation*—this people; alluding, as we learn from Luke 7. 30, to the Pharisees and lawyers, who persisted in finding fault, whether with John or with Christ, always having some ground of complaint. "All the people *and the publicans*," it is said, "*justified God*" (instead of finding fault with these declarations); while this other class, the proud opposers of Christ, rejected the counsel of God against themselves. They could not bear to think that John was the Elias that was to come, because he was to come as a reprover and threatener of the curse upon their nation. So that that generation or these opposers of that day, were like children at play, and they treated all these grave matters as child's play. Allusion is here made to the custom of children to assemble for sport in public places.——¶ *Markets*—places of public gathering, in cities and large towns.

17. Piping and dancing were common at festivals (Luke 15. 25), and mourning and lamenting in companies were common at funerals (ch. 9. 23). "Neither the gay nor the grave suits you. Both have been tried, and you are still displeased. Neither and nothing satisfies."——¶ *Piped.* Piping or playing on a wind-instrument, as a shepherd's pipe, was the signal for a dance, and the rest of the company were expected so to respond; hence the complaint, that they had not done *their part.* Or if it were a mourning play, the custom was to set up a wail, and the others would join the lamentation.

18. John had come in the manner of an ascetic, *neither eating nor drinking*, but fasting, or living on coarsest food in the wilderness. And ye say, he *hath a devil;* that is, is possessed by the evil one, like the common demoniacs of that time. It seemed strange, and they called him *a lunatic*—possessed.

19. *The Son of man.* Christ came in the opposite manner, *eating and drinking* as other men, and still you find fault—you make this a ground of complaint. You say, *Behold a man gluttonous*, fond of high living, and a *wine-bibber* (or, *wine-drinker*), one who is fond of wine and given to

A. D. 31.   CHAPTER XI.   129

say, Behold a man gluttonous, and a wine-bibber, a friend of publicans ⁿ and sinners. But ᵒ Wisdom is justified of her children.

20 Then ᵖ began he to upbraid the cities wherein most of his mighty works were done, because they repented not:
21 Woe unto thee, Chorazin! woe unto thee, ᵠ Bethsaida! for if the mighty works which were done in you had been done in Tyre and Sidon, they would have repented long ago in sackcloth and ashes.
22 But I say unto you, ʳ It shall be more tolerable for Tyre and Sidon at the day of judgment, than for you.
23 And thou, Capernaum,

n Lu.15.2; 19.7. *o* Ps.92.5,6. Pr.17.24. *p* Lu. 10.13, &c.   *q* Jno.12.21. *r* c.10.15.

---

drink. They misrepresented Him, because they hated His doctrines and claims.——¶ *But Wisdom.* The proverb means that the truth will always have followers, who will vindicate it in their doctrine and lives. Christ was the wisdom of God—called *Wisdom* in the Proverbs. All the *children of wisdom*, that is, the truly wise, justify the doctrine of Christ. They vindicate it in their words, and in their lives. See Luke 7. 29; where observe, it was the people and the publicans *justifying God*, while the Pharisees and lawyers *rejected the counsel of God* against themselves, that drew from Christ these foregoing remarks.

[§ 45. REFLECTIONS OF JESUS ON APPEALING TO HIS MIGHTY WORKS.]—*Capernaum.*

| Matt. 11. 20-30 | Mark. | Luke. | John. |

20, 21. Our Lord was led now to upbraid—that is, to censure, and rebuke, and condemn the treatment He had commonly received.——¶ '*Wo.*' This is opposed to '*Blessed.*'—Most of our Lord's mighty works were done in the cities round the sea of Galilee, Chorazin and Bethsaida. The site of these towns was not far from Capernaum. Bethsaida was the city of Andrew, and Philip, and Peter. John 1. 44.——¶ *Tyre and Sidon.* These were important and well-known cities of ancient time, on the Mediterranean, celebrated for their commerce and magnificence, but destroyed in accordance with prophecy, for their wickedness. Ezek. 26. 28. Isa. 23. Their remarkable overthrow by the evident hand of God, became notorious and proverbial.——¶ *They would have repented.* (See ch. 21. 31.) This language is to show that the wickedness of these cities in the time of Christ, was greater than that of the worst cities of old. Though those cities were notoriously corrupt, they were ignorant of God, and it could fairly be said, from the facts, that they would not have so despised these mighty works of Christ. They had not sinned against such displays of Divine power and grace. Nineveh repented at the preaching and prophecy of Jonah, and it was allowable to infer that such miracles as had been wrought in these cities would have led *these* to repentance.——¶ *Sackcloth,* was a coarse sacking, worn as a sign of grief with *ashes* thrown on the head, to complete the expression of wo and mourning. These were the well-known badges of desolation and distress, and to repent in " sackcloth and ashes"—"*sitting in*" them, says Luke —means to repent most deeply and bitterly, with all self-abasement.

22. *More tolerable.* (ch. 10. 15,) where this was said of those who reject Christ's ministers. The doom of those ancient cities will be lighter and more endurable, because they had shown less obstinacy, and had not abused such privileges. Those who, at this day, enjoy religious in-

which ᵃ art exalted unto heaven, shalt be brought down to hell: for if the mighty works which have been done in thee had been done in Sodom, it would have remained until this day.

24 But I say unto you, That it shall be more tolerable for the land of Sodom in the day of judgment than for thee.

25 ¶ At ᵘ that time Jesus answered and said, I thank thee, O Father, Lord of heaven and earth. because thou hast hid these things from the wise and prudent, and hast revealed them unto babes.ᵛ

26 Even so, Father: for so it seemed good in thy sight.

27 All ʷ things are delivered unto me of my Father: and no man knoweth the Son but the Father; neither ˣ knoweth any man the Father, save the Son, and *he* to whomsoever the Son will reveal *him*.

s Is.14.13-15. La.2.1. *t* ver.24. *u* Lu.10.21, &c.
v Ps.8.2. Je.1.7,8. 1Cor.1.27. *w* c.28.18. Lu.10 22. Jno.3.35; 17.2. 1Cor.15.27. *x* Jno.1.18. 1Jno. 5.20.

---

structions, and hear the gospel preached, and pass through scenes of great solemnity, without embracing Christ, resemble these cities. The children of pious parents, who have been baptized, and have Sabbath schools, and despise their privileges, must meet a more dreadful doom than the heathen.──¶ *Thou Capernaum.* In this city Christ had tarried much, and performed some of His mightiest works. It was eminently favoured by His presence and power. In this sense, it was *exalted to heaven,* that is, it had the highest privileges. The wo pronounced here is, that it shall meet the very opposite doom. As it had enjoyed more, and abused more, so it should suffer more. It should lose its privileges—Christ would withdraw from it. It should become as desolate as it had been prosperous in temporal things, and its sinful population should perish eternally.

25. *I thank thee.* I confess, or profess. Bengel. Christ began to upbraid these cities, because of the Pharisees, and lawyers, or scribes, who rejected the doctrines He taught about John the Baptist and Himself. They were proud of their own wisdom, and rejected the counsel or wisdom of God. Christ here glorifies the Father for this display of sovereignty. He saw that these things were hid from those who boasted to be wise and prudent, and He recognizes and approves the ways of the Father with men, that having hid these things from such, He had revealed them unto *babes*, that is, to those "*little* children"—the converted, humbled disciples ("little ones" ch. 10. 42), of whom is the kingdom of heaven. (comp. vs. 27.)

26. *Even so.* This is the language of hearty concurrence in the Father's will, and the reason given is merely this: that such was the will of the Father. Luke has these words also at the return of the seventy. This is a temper of implicit and cheerful confidence, which we may all imitate. "*Thy will be done.*" God is glorious in His sovereignty. That gospel truth which the wise reject, babes in Christ can understand—"Born, not of blood, nor of the will of the flesh, nor of the will of man, but of God." In all our times of darkness, we are to trust in God as in one who knows. We are to submit our own wisdom to His, and be resigned, even when we are afflicted, because *so it seems good in His sight.* See Luke 10. 21.

27. *All things.* He had just addressed the Father as Lord of heaven and earth, and as having sovereign control over all men. Now, He presents His own mediatorial relations. Though God is a sovereign, yet God in Christ is a Saviour. Though these differences among men are predestinated, yet Christ is the way, and

28 ¶ Come unto me all *ye* that labour *y* and are heavy laden, and I will give you rest.

29 Take my yoke upon you, and learn *z* of me; for I am meek and lowly *a* in heart: and *b* ye shall find rest unto your souls.

30 For my yoke *is* easy, *c* and my burden is light.

y Is 53.2,3.   *z* Ph.2.5-8. 1Pe.2.21.   *a* Zec.9.9.   *b* Je.6.16.   *c* 1Jno.5.3.

the truth, and the life. So He at once goes on to state the plan of salvation by a Redeemer. The only way that we can know any thing of God's secret purposes of grace, is to come to Christ and embrace eternal life for ourselves. Thus, as elsewhere, He connects faith with the concealed purposes of God. "All that the Father giveth me, shall come to me," &c. We *are of the elect* unless we neglect and reject the great salvation. Let God have all the glory of the sinner's salvation. He maketh men to differ. Christians must trace their conversion to distinguishing grace. Let all men hear the gospel. Behold the only plan! It is proclaimed to all. This is the truth, not concealed or secret, but revealed to us. It is for Christ and not for us, to know the Father—"no man hath seen God," &c. He has control of all things as Mediator (ch. 28. 18). All power is given to Him. But the Father is brought down to us in Christ (Colos. 2. 9), who is the revealer of the Godhead. We must learn of Him. He is head over all things to the church. Yet no being knows the Son but the Father. He had just shown (vs. 25) how the Father reveals the Son to some, and not to others. From Him only who commanded the light to shine out of darkness, can we get the discovery of Christ. OBSERVE, Christ is one with the Father. Our condition is hopeless unless Christ reveal to us the Father, and we see God in Christ reconciled. We are blessed, as having such things revealed to us in Christ, beyond kings and prophets of old, and this favour is inestimable; and all from distinguishing grace.

28. Now He accordingly invites to Himself as the only way.——¶ *Come unto me.* Here His object plainly is, not to show who are *entitled* to come to Him, but who are *invited*, that thus it may appear how He is the fit resort even of the most helpless and forlorn. Not the boasting Pharisees, not John himself was to be their resort, but He, and only He.——¶ *All ye that labour.* There was a class (Luke 7. 29), who justified God, and received His counsel (toward themselves), which the Pharisees and lawyers, or scribes, despised. "*All the people,*" that is, the common mass, "*and the publicans,*" were of this feeling. Seeing this multitude not disposed to cavil, but rather to receive the truth, and fainting with weariness of body and soul, He was moved with compassion toward them, as sheep having no shepherd (9. 36), and these He addresses here, directing them to Himself. Those who are weary and heavy laden in any such sense, who are tired of the world, and of false teaching, and long for the truth: they who have consciences burdened by a sense of sin, and are ready to hear glad tidings, can hear them from *Him.* Only to such can the Gospel be glad tidings or good news. Only to such can it give *rest.* ——¶ *Rest,* is what such want, and He can give it to them and will. It is rest to the *soul* (vs. 29). This you shall *find* in your experience—the peace that flows from free forgiveness, and a sense of *justification* through Christ. So that in Him—coming to Him—looking to Him—finding Him—men shall have *rest.*

29. *Take my yoke.* This is added only as giving a further glimpse of His plan for discipleship. There must be subjection of the understanding—"*Learn of me.*" And of the heart—"*I am meek and lowly in heart.*" This must not be overlooked. None can be saved by Christ, but by im-

CHAPTER XII.

AT that time ª Jesus went on the sabbath day through the corn; and his disciples were an hungered, and began to pluck ᵇ the ears of corn, and to eat.

2 But when the Pharisees saw *it*, they said unto him, Behold, thy disciples do that which is

<small>a Mar.2.23,&c. Lu.6.1,&c. b De.23.25.</small>

not lawful to do ᶜ upon the sabbath day.

3 But he said unto them, Have ye not read what David did, ᵈ when he was an hungered, and they that were with him;

4 How he entered into the house of God, and did eat the shew-bread, ᵉ which was not

<small>c Ex.31.15. d 1Sa.21.6. e Ex.25.30.</small>

---

plicitly submitting to His plan of salvation. Meekness and lowliness of temper are the great characteristics of discipleship. We must be content to *follow Him.* And this temper He patterns for us: " *Not my will but Thine be done.*" And with this, we shall *find rest to our souls. This is rest.* For with this disposition, His yoke upon the feelings is easy—all His restraints are pleasant and welcome—and His burden of service is light. "Wisdom's ways are ways of pleasantness and all her paths are peace."

CHAPTER XII.

[§ 37. THE DISCIPLES PLUCK EARS OF GRAIN ON THE SABBATH.]—*On the way to Galilee.*

Matt.	Mark.	Luke.	John.
12. 1-8	2. 23-28	6. 1-5	

1. *At that time.* OBSERVE, this occurred far back, and just after the call of Matthew. The Jewish sabbath answered to our seventh day of the week. The day was changed after the resurrection of Christ, because He rose from the dead on the first day of the week, and rested from that work, and blessed the day and hallowed it. It is our duty to keep this sabbath holy because it is the Christian sabbath, commemorating the finished work of Christ for us sinners, and an earnest of the eternal sabbath in heaven reserved for the people of God. Luke says (6. 1), that this was *the second sabbath after the first*, literally the *second-first sabbath.* It was known by this name, from the festival appointments. The passover feast was celebrated about our March and April.

On the second day of the paschal week a sheaf of barley was to be offered up as first fruits of harvest, and from this day, which was a day of rest—a sabbath—were to be reckoned *seven weeks* to pentecost or feast of weeks and of harvest. The second sabbath after the first was the second in this series, next after the first or beginning of this reckoning.——¶ *Corn.* This is a general term for grain, and here signifies *Barley,* most probably, which was ripe at that time, and which they rubbed in their hands (Luke 6. 1) to clear it of chaff. The barley harvest in that country commenced in May, and a ripe sheaf of this grain was required to be offered early in *April.*—— ¶ *An hungered*—hungry.

2. The Pharisees complained of them to Christ for this—that it was unlawful to do this on the sabbath day, as though it was a violation of the fourth commandment—not that they *took the grain* in passing through the field, for this was allowed (Deut. 23.25)—but for not treating the sabbath with becoming sanctity.

3, 4. He refers them to a precedent in the example of David (1 Sam. 21. 6). The house of God was then the tabernacle. The *shew-bread* was in twelve cakes renewed every Sabbath, and placed in order on a table covered with gold (Lev. 24. 5–9). This bread was considered holy, and not allowed to be eaten, except by the priests (Ex. 25. 30). When David fled from Saul, he applied to the high priest Ahimelech for food, and could obtain no bread but this, therefore he took it. It was a case of *necessity* which overruled the ceremonial command. They

lawful for him to eat, neither for them which were with him, but only *f for the priests?

5 Or have ye not read in the law, *g* how that on the sabbath days the priests in the temple *h* profane the sabbath, and are blameless?

6 But I say unto you, that in

this place is *one* greater *i* than the temple.

7 But if ye had known what *this* meaneth, *j* I will have mercy, and not sacrifice, ye would not have condemned the guiltless.

8 For the Son of man is Lord even of the sabbath day.

9 ¶ And *k* when he was

f Ex.29.32,33. *g* Nu.28.9. *h* Jno.7.22,23.

i 2 Ch.6.18. Mal.3.1. c.23.17-21. *j* Hos.6.6. *k* Mar.3.1, &c. Lu.6.4,&c.

---

must admit David's example, and a like necessity justified the disciples. The sabbath was not violated in case of "*necessity and mercy.*" (I will have mercy and not sacrifice). Hosea 6. 6.

5. *In the law*—of Moses, prescribing the ceremonies for the sabbath (Num. 28. 9, 10). The Pharisees complained that the disciples by rubbing the grain in their hands had performed labour which violated the sabbath. Christ reminds them that their law even prescribes certain labour on the Sabbath for the priests, which if done by others would have profaned the sabbath. They were to kill two lambs on the sabbath—kindle fires to burn them, which was expressly forbidden otherwise (Exod. 35. 3), &c., and yet were blameless. So that *circumstances* and *cases*-must be considered.

6. Our Lord moreover asserts here His own authority above the temple service — having power over those laws which were of use mostly as referring to Himself. This is an assertion of His supremacy and Divinity, and a hint of His intent to abrogate that cumbersome ritual by His own coming. And if the temple service would excuse the priests' work, much more would His service excuse His disciples' work. In Mark 2. 27, another argument is mentioned. The object of the sabbath must be considered, as it was made for the sake of man, rather than man for its sake. All just ideas of its design would show that it was to subserve man's true advantage, and not to be the means of his destruction. Works of necessity and mercy may be done.

7. This passage Christ had quoted before, to show that His ceremonial requirements must not stand in the way of the weightier matters of the law. A knowledge of the meaning here, would have prevented their condemning the guiltless, because it would have shown them the substance of His requisitions—the general principle of them, and their consistency (1 Cor. 13. 1–3); and it would have shown them too that He requires kind judgments of others, not harsh censures. That which God desires or "*will have,*" is not the letter of sacrifice, so much as the hearty outpouring of love which the sacrifice symbolized (see Heb. 10. 5–10).

8. *Son of man.* This occurs 87 times in the New Testament, always referring to Christ——¶ *Lord even of the sabbath day.* Christ asserts that He has an authority not only higher than that of the temple service, but higher than that of the sabbath itself. He here asserts that He Himself is more to be regarded and trusted than any ceremonial appointments; that the sabbath has its sanctity from His work, and that He has power to alter it, and to direct its observance. He Himself is the end of the law for righteousness to the believer; the end, as that to which it pointed, and that in which it was swallowed up. This is a claim of Divinity.

[§ 38. THE HEALING OF THE WITHERED HAND ON THE SABBATH.]—*Galilee.*

Matt.	Mark.	Luke.	John.
12. 9–14	3. 1–6	6. 6–11	

9. *And when He was departed thence,*

departed thence, he went into their synagogue:

10 And, behold, there was a man which had *his* hand withered. And they asked him, saying, Is ¹ it lawful to heal on the sabbath day? that they might accuse him.

11 And he said unto them, What man shall there be among you that shall have one sheep, and ᵐ if it fall into a pit on the sabbath day, will he not lay hold on it, and lift *it* out?

12 How much then is a man better than a sheep? Wherefore it is lawful to do well on the sabbath days.

13 Then saith he to the man, Stretch forth thine hand. And he stretched *it* forth; and it was restored whole, like as the other.

14 ¶ Then the Pharisees went

l Lu.14.3. *m* De.22.4.

This event occurred in close connexion with the complaint and discussion just noticed. From Luke 6. 6, we learn that it was on another sabbath, and doubtless while this subject was in agitation.

10. A case was brought to Him of a man with a withered hand. Luke tells us that it was his *right hand*. This disease, when seated, is incurable. The Scribes and Pharisees (as we learn from Luke 6. 7) watched Him, to see whether He would heal on the Sabbath; and they questioned Him as to the lawfulness of so doing, that they might accuse Him as "not of God, because He keepeth not the sabbath day" (John 9. 16). Seven cures are recorded as wrought on the sabbath: the demoniac in the synagogue—Peter's wife's mother—the impotent man at Bethesda's pool—the man born blind—the woman with a spirit of infirmity—a man who had the dropsy, and this.

11. He replied by asking whether it was lawful on the sabbath to do good, or to do evil; to save life, or to destroy it? (Luke 6. 8, 9,) for, in His view, the neglect to do good, is the same as to do evil (Mark 3. 4): and He brings up a case, appealing to themselves, if they would not count it lawful to draw a sheep out of a pit: and if so, whether *a man* (so much more important than a sheep) could not be healed on that day. Thus He showed that it was lawful to do good on the sabbath, especially in the way of necessity and mercy.

13. Then looking upon them *with anger* (See Mark 3. 5), that they should have made such a heartless and malicious complaint, He cured the man. This was a miracle, because His word of command gave the man power to stretch forth his hand, *though it was withered*. Thus He proved Himself Lord of the sabbath. This work could have come only from a superhuman source. So, when God commands the helpless sinner, He will give strength if we attempt to obey. We may infer His general rule in regard to the sabbath. Two cases are given: one case was of necessity, the other of mercy. And we infer that works of necessity and mercy may be done on that day, and none other works. We are most likely to err in the way of neglecting such works, from not having a heart in God's service, and not having love to God and man. Where the Sabbath is properly observed, God sends the blessings of His providence and grace. Temporal and spiritual prosperity are to be looked for in this way; but the greatest social mischief and spiritual evils flow from a neglect or contempt of the sabbath.

14. *Held a council;* that is, *planned together*—took counsel. Mark adds, that it was with the Herodians whom they hated. These Herodians were a political party attached to Herod Antipas, of Galilee, and who favour-

[A. D. 31.]   CHAPTER XII.   135

out, and held ¹ a council against him, how they might destroy him.

15 But when Jesus knew *it*, he withdrew himself from thence: and great multitudes followed him, and he healed them all;

16 And charged them that they should not make him known:

17 That it might be fulfilled which was spoken by Esaias the prophet, ⁿ saying.

18 Behold my servant, whom I have chosen; my beloved, in whom my soul is well pleased: I will put my spirit upon him, and he shall shew judgment to the Gentiles.

19 He shall not strive, nor cry, neither shall any man hear his voice in the streets.

1 Or, *took counsel.*   *n* Is. 42. 1.

---

ed his claims as king against Christ. Notice their question proposed to Christ: "Is it lawful to give tribute to Cæsar?" ch. 22. 16, 17.

OBSERVE, (1.) No ordinance of God can be against well-doing. It is lawful, at all times, and in all cases, to do good. (2.) The sinner's inability is quite consistent, in God's view, with the command to obey the gospel; for there is a way provided in which the withered hand can be stretched forth at the word of Christ.

[§ 39. JESUS ARRIVES AT THE SEA OF TIBERIAS, AND IS FOLLOWED BY MULTITUDES.]—*Lake of Galilee.*

Matt.	Mark.	Luke.	John.
12. 15–21	3. 7–12		

15. *He withdrew.* Jesus knew their plans and withdrew, not from fear, but because He also knew that His hour was not yet come. Mark adds that He withdrew with His disciples *to the Sea* (i. e., of Galilee)—that many came from Idumea and from beyond Jordan, and that a great multitude of those here mentioned came from around *Tyre* and *Sidon*, and were of course, *Gentiles* (vs. 21). The crowd, it appears, was so great, that He took a boat, so as not to be pressed down. And here, from the boat, He did His wonders of healing (see Mark) to the throng on the shore.

16. Here again we find Him enjoining silence on them in regard to His being the Christ. It was not yet time for this to be widely known, or loudly asserted with such exciting proofs, any more than it was time for Him to die.

18. And this also was in fulfilment of prophecy (Isaiah 42. 1–4), that His course should be unostentatious and noiseless. They thought the Messiah should be a conquering hero. But instead of *treading down* His enemies, like a renowned conqueror, or shouting as for battle, He should not *tread harshly* on the bruised reed so as to break it, nor on smoking flax so as to quench it, and that it is His plan and characteristic to proceed without noise and parade. He is not to be despised because of His unpretending style, but revered for this, as it is a mark of His mission, according as the prophets had set forth.——¶ *My servant.* This title indicates His mission for a definite work; hence He is also said to be "*chosen*" for that work, and accepted for that work.——¶ *My beloved Son*; "sanctified or set apart and sent." He is promised all the requisites of that work—"the Spirit without measure," and *all success.*——¶ *He shall shew judgment;* that is, He shall make known and *send forth* the established truth in regard to the kingdom of God—God's plan of gospel righteousness extending to the Gentiles (Jer. 16. 19).

19. He shall work by a silent influence in the world, as of the Holy Spirit (vs. 18), not like the sound of a warrior, which is "with shouts and garments rolled in blood."

20. *A bruised reed.* This language indicates His gentle temper and

20 A bruised reed shall he not break, and smoking flax shall he not quench, till he send forth judgment unto victory.

21 And in his name shall the Gentiles trust.

22 ¶ Then °was brought unto him one possessed with a devil, blind and dumb: and he healed him, insomuch that the blind and dumb both spake and saw.

o Mar.3.11. Lu.11.14.

---

course in the world. His object is not to destroy men's lives, like a warrior, but to save; not to break the bruised, but to lift them up. "The Spirit of the Lord God is upon me" (Isa. 61). All His course and His measures shall be of this kind. The humble should be exalted. Tender, troubled consciences should be soothed by His word.——¶ *Smoking flax.* The figure here is of the wick of a smoking lamp, with little or no oil. He should not put out a smothered spark of piety, but rather kindle it to a blaze. His strength is made perfect in weakness. "He giveth power to the faint, and to them that have no might He increaseth strength." *Grace* is the characteristic of Christ's work. ——¶ *Till He.* This form of expression does not refer to a point of time, but to the object in view. This is *His aim*—to send forth judgment or the established truth of God—to proclaim and carry forward the gospel of peace. And it shall be unto victory, causing " mercy to triumph over judgment," showing a plan of judgment, truth, and righteousness by which victory is proclaimed, and secured in consistency with justice. This is the nature of His conquests. He is the Prince of Peace.

21. *In His name.* In His gospel covenant shall the Gentiles trust (who are not Jews). Isaiah has it, "The isles shall wait for His law;" *i. e.*, the regions out of Judea (42. 4).

OBSERVE: It was at this juncture that our Lord delivered the Sermon on the Mount, recorded in the 5th ch. *These* (Mark 3. 7, 8) *are the multitudes* whom He saw when He went up into the mountain and taught (ch. 5. 1). Here a great leading prophecy was fulfilled, *in the Gentiles coming to Him.* And here He naturally took occasion to deliver *His law,* for which the Gentiles (as it had been prophesied) *were waiting!*

OBSERVE, (1.) The reason of Christ's withdrawing from any is, their evident and intense hostility to Him (14). (2.) Christ's purposes cannot be defeated by wicked men, and the gates of hell in council can never prevail against Him. (3.) Of the multitudes who follow Christ, it can always be said, "*He healed them all.*" (4.) Christ's dignity and glory here, are not as an earthly monarch, but as the Saviour of souls.

"Thy noblest wonders here we view,
  In souls renewed and sins forgiven."

[§ 48. THE HEALING OF THE DEMONIAC. THE SCRIBES AND PHARISEES BLASPHEME.]—*Galilee.*

Matt.	Mark.	Luke.	John.
12. 22–37	3. 19–30	11. 14, 15 17–23	

22. The order of this event is at the opening of His second circuit in Galilee, soon after the message of John from prison to Him. See the parallel passages.——¶ *Blind and dumb.* The effect of this demoniacal possession was, that the subject was both blind and dumb. Luke mentions that it was dumb, but does not contradict the blindness.

23. *Amazed*—at this miraculous power, exerted before their eyes. At once they thought of the Messiah prophesied in Isaiah 35. 5. They were struck at once with a conviction that this must be the Christ whom prophets foretold, *the Son of David.* But though this was the honest and natural impression of the common people, the Pharisees would admit no such thing. The multitude alarmed the Jewish rulers by the question, whether Jesus were the

23 And all the people were amazed; and said, Is not this the son of David?

24 But when the Pharisees heard *it*, they said, This *fellow* doth not cast out devils, but by ¹ Beelzebub the prince of the devils.

25 And Jesus knew their ᵖ thoughts, and said unto them, Every kingdom divided against itself is brought to desolation; and every city or house divided against itself shall not stand:

26 And if Satan cast out Satan, he is divided against himself; how shall then his kingdom stand?

27 And if I by Beelzebub ᵠ cast out devils, by whom do your children cast *them* out? Therefore they shall be your judges.

28 But if I cast out devils by the Spirit of God, then the kingdom ʳ of God is come unto you.

29 Or else how can one enter

---

1 *Beelzebul.* p Ps 139.2. Jno.2.24,25.
q ver.24. r Da.2.44. c.6.33. Lu.11.20; 17.21. Ro. 14.17.

Christ. Mark suggests that the Scribes and Pharisees had come from Jerusalem to *watch Him*.

24. They resorted to this impious way of accounting for the miracle: that it was a-wonder wrought by alliance with devils. This would make the people afraid of Christ's influence, and tend to destroy it among them. We can well infer from the incidental hints of the Evangelists, in what spirit this was said. And the Pharisees had no other way of keeping in favour and power, than to attribute these wonderful works of Christ to diabolical agency.—— ¶ *Beelzebub*, the god of flies, or *Beelzebul*, of filth, as they called by this contemptuous name (2 Kings 1. 6) *the arch-demon of idolatry*. It was their name for the very devil of devils—the head and source of all such abominations as were connected with idol worship. They accused Christ of being a base magician, in conference with "the Prince of the power of the air."

25. *Jesus knew their thoughts.* This proves Him God. Ps. 139. 2. Jer. 17. 10. Herein He gives the Pharisees an infallible proof of His being the Messiah, "He shall not judge after the sight of His eyes" (Isa. 11.3).—— ¶ *Every kingdom*, &c. He means by this to show how absurd it would be to suppose Satan leagued with Him, to cast out devils who were his own agents of evil. Satan would thus be set up *against himself*. A contradiction.

27. *Your children.* Those of your family, your disciples: meaning Jews, like themselves, who were *exorcists* (comp. Acts 19. 13), accustomed to cast out evil spirits—in pretence. Why did they not accuse *them* of casting out devils by Beelzebub?—— ¶ *They shall be your judges*, viz., that it is from mere malice that you so accuse me.

28. *By the Spirit of God.* Luke has it—*the finger of God.* The question was, whether it was God's work or Satan's. If God's, it was proof of His Messiahship, for God would not give His miraculous power to establish an imposture. This Christ argues, and claims the argument in His favour.—— ¶ *The kingdom of God* —as opposed to that of *Satan* (vs. 26). The kingdom prophesied as to be set up in the world by God's authority and power.—— ¶ *Is come unto you.* Luke has it: "No doubt the kingdom of God is come upon you." Christ's reign has begun. It makes its appeal, and presents its claim, and if there is any truth in the miracles, you ought to give immediate heed to the gospel of Christ. If the claims of Christ are proved, they are worthy of all our attention. And if they are of *any* importance they are of all importance.

138　　　　　　　　MATTHEW　　　　　　　[A. D. 31.

into a strong man's house and spoil ᵗ his goods, except he first bind the strong man? and then he will spoil his house.

30 He that is not with me is against me; ᵘ and he that gathereth not with me, scattereth abroad.

31 ¶ Wherefore I say unto you, All ᵘ manner of sin and blasphemy shall be forgiven unto men; but the blasphemy *against* the *Holy* Ghost ᵛ shall not be forgiven unto men.

32 And whosoever speaketh a word against the Son of man, ʷ it shall be forgiven him; but whosoever speaketh against the Holy Ghost, it shall not be forgiven him, neither in this world, neither in the *world* to come.

33 Either make the tree good, and his fruit good; or else make the tree corrupt, and his fruit corrupt; for ˣ the tree is known by *his* fruit.

34 O generation ʸ of vipers! how can ye, being evil, speak

ᵗIs.49.24; 53.12.　Re.12.7-10; 20.2,3.　*t* 1Jno.2.19.　*u* Mar.3.28. Lu.12.10.　*v* He.10.29. 1Jno.5.16.
w Lu.7.34. Jno.7.12. 1Ti.1.13.　*x* c.7.16,17.　*y* c.3.7.

---

29. These wondrous works, He says, were done to show that Christ has power over Satan. He "came to destroy the works of the devil." He illustrates His power over Satan himself, by rescuing this man from his possession, and thus showing that He can spoil his goods. So the argument is complete. He proves thus that instead of being in alliance with Satan, He has power over him, and means to break down his kingdom in the earth, and has actually in this miracle begun so to do.

30. In this general language, He shows, *first*, That Satan's reign is directly opposite to His, working contrary results and admitting no collusion or alliance: and *next*, that all Satan's forces, wicked men, and they themselves who oppose Him, are on the opposite side, and so, on the side of Satan. The conclusion is, that instead of *His* co-operating with the devil, *they* are co-workers with him.

31. *Wherefore.* Having proved them so in the wrong, He goes on to show the heinousness of their offence in blaspheming the Holy Ghost. The unpardonable sin is such as they here committed. Mark expressly explains (3. 30), "*Because* they said He hath an unclean spirit." Many mistake in thinking other sins and courses of sin unpardonable. Those who so anxiously fear lest they have committed this sin, do not show the fiendish and malicious contempt of the Holy Ghost which was here exhibited. OBSERVE: It is a deliberate and diabolical blaspheming of the Holy Ghost, and of His work, so as to repudiate it openly, and treat it with impious scorn, that is meant here. "It confounds God, the source *of all good influence*, with the devil, and shows a state of mind utterly given over to Satan, " doing despite unto the spirit of grace."

32. *Neither in the world to come.* This phrase is added for emphasis, like "for ever *and ever*." It was proverbial language. Mark reads, "*hath never forgiveness*, but is in danger of *eternal damnation*." This is the idea which is here most strongly expressed. This gives not the least warrant for inferring forgiveness for any sins in the future world, but the utmost warrant for expecting no forgiveness there. Absolution is publicly pronounced on believers at the judgment, but their sins were forgiven in this life.

33. *Either make.* This is a fair rule laid down for their judgment. Either to *make* (or consider) the tree good and its fruit also, or else, &c. He claims their belief in Him for the *works'* sake. Either lay it down as proved that He and His works are together good or bad. The works are not of Satan as He had shown,

A. D. 31] CHAPTER XII. 139

good things? For out [z] of the abundance of the heart the mouth speaketh.

35 A good man out of the good treasure of the heart bringeth forth good things; and an evil man, out of the evil treasure, bringeth forth evil things.

36 But I say unto you, that every idle word that men shall speak, they shall give account [a] thereof in the day of judgment:

37 For by thy words [b] thou shalt be justified, and by thy words thou shalt be condemned

38 ¶ Then certain of the Scribes and of the Pharisees answered, saying, Master, we would see a sign [c] from thee.

---

z Lu.6.45.

a Ec.12.14. Ep.5.4,6. Jude 15. b Pr.13.3. c c.16. 1. 1Cor.1.22.

Neither is He. They themselves are of Satan, for their opposition to Him and all their works are so.

34. *O generation of vipers—offspring of Satan*, in his worst form. The rule just given is here applied to themselves. Yourselves, *a race* of most malicious, venomous nature, how can good words be expected out of you? This traces evil speaking to the corrupt heart, and shows the dreadful root and source of blasphemy. With their natural, carnal heart, they *could not* speak good things, any more than a bramble bush could bring forth grapes. As it is natural to speak out of the abundance or fulness of the heart, therefore their evil language only proved the overflowing malignity of their natures. The extremity of our sinfulness is our disability. *How can* the Ethiopian change his skin, or the leopard his spots? The power is of God.

35. The same sentiment is further illustrated. Good and bad men act according to their hearts. The one renewed and good, the other unrenewed and evil. All sinfulness does not consist in *action*, for behind the action and anterior to it is the evil, natural heart.

36. They might think their words of small account. But here these are shown to be of serious importance, as speaking out the heart. Hence they shall all be subjected to strict judgment at the final day.—— ¶ *Every idle word*, (αργον) rendered in 2 Pet. 1. 8, '*barren*.' It first means *vain*, then *false*. Every heedless word, even though esteemed most trivial, shall be brought into account.

37. *For by thy words.* A man is to be judged by his own words. "*Take a man as he says*," is a proverb. Words become vastly important in this light. (See James 3. 6, &c.) Besides, at the bar, a man is called on to speak. *Guilty, or not guilty?* The justice and truth of God's judgment is expressed in the declaration, that every mouth shall be stopped, in tacit confession of guilt.

OBSERVE, (1.) The fulness of Christ's power and grace for all wretched sinners. Blindness, dumbness, weakness, hardness He can cure. (2.) An instance of His wonder-working hand in casting out devils from men, is the highest proof of His Divinity. "Many shall see it, and shall fear and shall trust in the Lord" (23). (3.) The malice of the human heart toward Christ and His redeeming, gracious work, is without a bound; ready for the most infernal plots and accusations. (4.) Christ's work and Satan's must not be confounded. Blessed are all they who are one with Christ and His cause.

[§ 49. THE SCRIBES AND PHARISEES SEEK A SIGN. OUR LORD'S REFLECTIONS.]—*Galilee.*

Matt.	Mark.	Luke.	John.
12. 38–45		11. 16 24–36	

38. *We would see a sign from thee.* This seems to have been demanded as settling the question of His claims and to show whether he cast out devils

140 MATTHEW. [A. D. 31.

39 But he answered and said unto them, An evil and adulterous *d* generation seeketh after a sign, and there shall no sign be given to it, but the sign of the prophet Jonas:

40 For *e* as Jonas was three days and three nights in the whale's belly; so shall the Son of man be three days and three nights in the heart of the earth.

41 The men of Nineveh shall rise in judgment with this generation, and shall condemn *f* it: because they repented at *g* the preaching of Jonas; and, behold, a greater than Jonas *is* here.

42 The *h* queen of the south shall rise up in the judgment

d Is.57.3. *e* Jon.1.17.   *f* Ro.2.27. *g* Jon.3.5. *h* Lu.11.31, &c.

---

by the Spirit of God, or by Beelzebub. Luke says (11.16; 24. 36), that it was a "*sign from heaven*" that they sought, and that they did it "tempting Him," asking something more positive than they had yet received—though they had seen miracles and wonders which ought to have satisfied them. They would not believe Him without something more.

39. It was against this stubborn and unreasonable temper in them that Christ exclaims. He therefore charges it upon them that they are an evil and adulterous generation that make this demand. He would point them to their origin while they inquire of His. Their being called *adulterous* would suggest to them the language of the prophets in which this term is so commonly used to represent the unfaithfulness of the Jews to the covenant (Isa. 57. 3. Hos. 3. 1. Ezek. 16. 15, and Malachi).—— ¶ *The prophet.* This should be the only sign. (*Jonas* is the Greek way of writing the Hebrew name *Jonah.*) This idea is explained in what follows. This is the only kind of evidence they should have. Such miraculous proofs attesting his commission as occurred with Jonah. Luke reads, "as Jonah was a sign to the Ninevites," i. e. a wonder, a miraculous messenger. They knew the history of that Old Testament prophet. He was a type of Christ in the matter stated here, of his miraculous deliverance from the whale's belly "*after three days.*" Such evidences He should furnish them for his Divine mission. (See Luke 16.31.)

40. This refers of course to His resurrection from the dead. His rising "from the heart of the earth *after three days;*" (see the book of Jonah.) This event occurred in the Mediterranean sea, and, of course, between Joppa and Tarshish. As to the kind of fish, it is called a whale, though in the Hebrew it is a word that passes for any very large fish. We read that God prepared a great fish for the purpose "to swallow up Jonah." (Jonah 1. 17.)—— ¶ *Three days and three nights.* The Jews reckoned the *parts* of days and nights the same as though they were whole. So in the narrative of Christ's resurrection two nights, with the evening preceding and the morning following, including one whole day, were reckoned as three days. This prophecy, therefore, was never disputed by the Jews on this point, as it would surely have been if they had not owned the computations as correct, according to their mode.

41. *The men of Nineveh.* While the Jews should have as good evidence and of the same kind as the Ninevites, they should be condemned for not repenting as the Ninevites did. The case of the Ninevites shall testify against them. They were heathen. They repented at the *preaching;* and at the preaching of one so much less than He. (For *Nineveh,* see Bib. Geog. S. S. Union.)

42. *The queen of the south.* This is recorded 1 Kings 10. 1: the visit of the queen of Sheba, which was probably in Arabia, south of Palestine.——. ¶ *Uttermost parts,* i. e., the extremest

A. D. 31.] CHAPTER XII. 141

with this generation, and shall condemn it: for she *i* came from the uttermost parts of the earth to hear the wisdom of Solomon; and, behold, a greater than Solomon *is* here.

43 When *j* the unclean spirit is gone out of a man, he *k* walketh through dry places, seeking rest, and findeth none.

44 Then he saith, I will return into my house, from whence I came out; and when he is come, he findeth *it* empty, swept, and garnished.

45 Then goeth he, and taketh with himself seven other spirits more wicked than himself, and they enter in and dwell there: and the last *state* of that man is worse *l* than the first. Even so

i 2Ch.9.1. *j* Lu.11.24. *k* Job 1.7. 1Pe.5.8.

l He.6.4; 10.26. 2Pe.2.20,22.

---

limits of the then known world. *Her* case should give testimony against them. She sought the wisdom of Solomon with the greatest zeal, and at utmost effort. She came a great distance to hear him. But they, instead of seeking Christ and being at effort to hear His doctrine, so much more important, would not even receive His instructions, though He came from heaven to them, and not they to Him.

43–45. *When the unclean spirit.* The discourse here turns upon the matter of His casting out devils, and of His being charged as in league with Satan, when in truth they were co-workers with the devil. He now represents their deplorable case, "*this wicked generation*" (vs. 45). They were naturally possessed with the devil in their hearts, as the possessions talked of here so vividly exhibited. And so much were they a favourite abode of the devil, that though the blind and dumb devils were driven out from them by His miraculous power, Satan would return again with seven-fold dominion to their hearts: and so He applies verse 30.——¶ *Hath gone out.* (See verse 29.)——¶ *He walketh through dry places*, unfrequented by men. There was an ancient and popular belief among the Jews that demons and evil spirits were wont to haunt desert places. The mode of expression here is figurative, and makes use of that common idea. He would merely represent the evil spirit as going out of the person to his natural haunt without. He seeks rest there and finds none. He is dissatisfied *out of* the man. He resolves to return to his *house* and *home* in the heart. He finds it like a house carefully prepared for the reception of its owner, unoccupied by any other, empty and cleansed, swept and garnished, decorated and furnished, all waiting for him. Whatever the outward change with a sinner, if he be not truly renewed, he only grows worse.

45. *Then goeth he.* Finding it ready and waiting, the unclean or depraved spirit resolves on increasing his forces in the bosom. This indicates the case of those only partially and temporarily recovered from Satan's possession. Their usual course is to a worse extremity of sin and opposition to Christ. Such he declared would be the case of the Jews. Such it really proved. They would be only partially, and outwardly, and temporarily benefitted by Christ's work among them. He would cast out devils. But Satan would not become dispossessed of their hearts. They would only become worse and worse.——¶ *Seven other spirits.* This was a *sacred number*, indefinite—denoting *many*, or *sufficient.*

OBSERVE, (1.) Wicked men constantly claim more of God, while they despise what they have at hand. (2.) How shall they who neglect the gospel be condemned by many converted heathen! (3.) Outward reformations often leave men in more settled and stubborn opposition to Christ. Evil men and seducers wax worse

shall it be also unto this wicked generation.

46 ¶ While he yet talked to the people, behold, *his* ᵐmother and his brethrenⁿ stood without, desiring to speak with him.

47 Then one said unto him, Behold, thy mother and thy brethren stand without, desiring to speak with thee.

48 But he answered and said unto him that told him, Who is my mother? and who are my brethren?

m Mar.3.31,&c. Lu.8.19,&c. n c.13.55.

49 And he stretched forth his hand toward his disciples, and said, Behold my mother and my brethren!

50 For whosoever shall do the will ᵒ of my Father which is in heaven, the same is my brother, and sister, and mother.

CHAPTER XIII.

THE same day went Jesus out of the house, and sat by the sea-side.

2 And great multitudes were gathered together unto him, so

o c.7.20. Jno.15.14. Ga.5.6. He.2.11. 1 Jno. 2.17.

and worse, deceiving and being deceived.

[§ 50. THE TRUE DISCIPLES OF CHRIST HIS NEAREST RELATIVES.]—*Galilee.*

Matt.	Mark.	Luke.	John.
12. 46–50	3.31–35	8.19–21	

46. *His mother and His brethren.* From Mark (6. 3), we learn of four brethren, James, Joses, Juda, and Simon. He seems not to have spoken this in their hearing. Others brought the message, while *they* were standing without. He took this occasion to declare to those whom He had been addressing, the true spiritual nature of those relations which He came to institute, as superior, far, to those of flesh and blood. So He left not any opportunity unimproved of declaring His work, and of contrasting it with their common, secular views.

49. This was a most affecting declaration. He showed not the less love for His natural kin but *the more* for His spiritual kindred. His disciples are truly related to Him by bonds nearer and dearer than mother or brethren could be.

50. He sustains these tender relations to all who believe and follow Him, who please Him by exercising faith in His finished work. This was not that He loved His mother less, but His disciples more. He would encourage His faithful follow-

ers.—It will be observed from the Harmony, that Christ does other things here at Galilee which are recorded by Luke. At a Pharisee's table He denounces woes against them and others. Luke 11. 37–54. He discourses to His disciples and the multitude, Luke 12. 1–59, and delivers the parable of the barren fig tree, Luke 13. 1–9. But the next *back item* in order, as given by Matthew is *the parable of the sower.*

CHAPTER XIII.

[§ 54. PARABLE OF THE SOWER.]—*Lake of Galilee—near Capernaum.*

Matt.	Mark.	Luke.	John.
13. 1–23	4. 1–25	8. 4–18	

Here commences a series of SEVEN PARABLES, illustrating the great truths pertaining to the kingdom.

1. *The sea-side.* He had been in Galilee, and now near Capernaum, He passed, "*the same day,*" to the shore of the Sea of Galilee or Tiberias. Luke shows that this *was in His second* circuit in Galilee, as He was traversing the country (8.1). It belongs still to the 31st year of our Lord. See Harmony.

2. *A ship*—the ship. The definite article here intimates that this was the vessel usually there. The crowds of people that came to Him from the cities which He had visited, stood on the beach, where they could be con-

that he went into a ship,ᵃ and sat; and the whole multitude stood on the shore.

3 And he spake many things unto them in parables, saying, Behold, ᵇ a sower went forth to sow:

4 And when he sowed, some *seeds* fell by the way-side, and the fowls came and devoured them up.

5 Some fell upon stony places, where they had not much earth; and forthwith they sprung up, because they had no deepness of earth:

6 And when the sun was up, they were scorched; and be

---

a Lu.5.3. *b* Mar.4.2. Lu.8.5,&c.

---

veniently addressed by Him from the boat. They were "by the sea, on the land" (Mark). Luke mentions (8. 2), that the women of Galilee and the 12 were with Him. The same are mentioned who "followed Him from Galilee" (see Luke 23. 49).

3. *Parables.* This word is from a Greek term, meaning *to bring together for comparison.* This was a method of teaching by *similitudes*, where the truth is presented as in a *picture.* It is a representation of moral or spiritual truth under the likeness or similitude of a natural subject. The advantage of this teaching was, that it secured the attention of the multitudes. It opened and enforced unfamiliar truth by that with which they were now familiar. It was calculated to remove prejudices by gaining a candid, honest judgment on the subject, before the application was made (as Nathan to David); and it tended to test character, leaving the truth veiled from such as would be blinded, and opening it to those who sought instruction.—¶ *A sower*—a man who *sows seed.* This is a common and familiar work; and the lessons from it could easily be understood. It agrees well for an illustration with the work of Christ and His ministers, sowing the seeds of truth.

4. *The way-side*—where the field and the road join—the edge of the field which the plough had not turned up. These are they who hear the word, and do not understand it (vs. 19), and do not care for it. They give it no attention. It falls upon them as upon the hard, unploughed, unprepared edge of the field that skirts the road. Satan takes away the word, by diverting the mind, starting objections, or keeping the thoughts dull, sluggish, and careless about the whole matter, or exciting an interest in any thing else about the sermon or service, rather than the truth itself; or, this seed *is trodden down* (Luke). The young are often prevented from attending to God's commands by gay diversions—companions—pleasures—and by Satan's snatching up, by his temptations, any germ of truth from their minds, just as birds pick up seeds that have lodged on the hard ground. Yet this is no excuse for them, because "they love darkness rather than light."

5. *Stony places* (Luke—"*a rock*"). That is, where there was but a thin surface of soil with rock underneath; a mere covering of ground upon a base of rock, just enough to conceal the rock from view, but not enough to allow of any rooting in the ground.——¶ *Forthwith*—immediately. Though they sprang up the sooner for the lightness of soil, yet they sooner withered, on the same account. There are often hasty conversions and professions that have no depth or genuineness—are gone and vanish as quick as they came. Noisy, boastful converts are often such.

6. See vss. 20 and 21. *Stony ground* hearers, *anon* or promptly receive it (vs. 20) eagerly, "with joy." They differ from the former in going further and yet not getting through. It is not from their being diverted and losing the truth, but from their not being converted to it—not deeply feeling it, but hastily and superficially catch-

cause they had no root, they withered away.

7 And some fell among thorns; and the thorns sprung up and choked them.

8 But other fell into good ground, and brought forth fruit, some an hundred-fold, some sixty-fold, some thirty-fold.

9 Who *c* hath ears to hear, let him hear.

c c.11.15.

ing at it. They spring up in a moment from some exciting impulse. Their hearts are not truly exercised, and not at all changed. Religion has taken *no root* in their bosoms. They cannot *endure* trial or persecution any more than such a hasty sprout can stand the scorching, mid-day sun. *False professors* who sit and hear, but do nothing in Christ's service, and make no advance, *have no root*. Such are *offended* (21). "*Scandalized*" is the Greek term. It refers to a stumbling-block. *They stumble and fall* when a severe trial of temptation or persecution comes; they find it a *stumbling-block* to them, and they turn aside from religion. This furnishes a caution against false hopes, high excitements that soon pass off, and loud professions on light grounds.

7. *Thorns.* Briers and brush in the field, which seemed to grow the faster after the seed had been cast in. These are the natural, wicked desires of the heart. They came up thick and rank—crowded the seed, and shaded them, and took all the sustenance from the ground. In other words, they *choked* them. These thorns that *choke* the truth and prevent sermons and other teachings from coming to any thing in the heart, are *the cares of this world* (vs. 22); i. e., the anxieties and concerns of a worldly kind—of business or pleasure, which occupy men's minds. Their thoughts are so full of these matters that they cannot attend to the word. So, "*the deceitfulness of riches*" (vs. 22)—the planning and worrying to make money—with all the hopes and fears—the successes and disappointments attending it—and even the temptations to unjust gain. This keeps the heart busy and crowds out other and better things. So, "*the lusts of other things*" which Mark adds (ch. 4. 19), "*entering in*" have the same *choking effect*. An appetite for worldliness in various shapes—a hankering after gratifications of sense, in forms nameless and numberless, issue in the same sad result. They keep the soul excited and distracted by the mere frivolities of the hour—passing shows — enjoyments — planning for gratification; and the truth cannot enter in where so much else enters and crowds it out. Those who wish to serve God should treat the cares, and riches, and pleasures of this life, as the seductive baits and snares of Satan, that only mislead the soul and destroy all that is good. "As strangers and pilgrims, abstain from fleshly lusts that war against the soul." And if the hearers of the word produce no fruit, they are known to be lovers of pleasures, more than lovers of God. We should pray against the evils of our own hearts, which will crowd out all good.

8. *Good ground.* Luke explains, "*an honest and good heart.*" The difference turns upon the *state of the heart*. It is not the truth that changes the heart of itself, but like seed it must find a prepared soil, in order to grow and yield fruit. Such a heart as grace has prepared is called here *honest and good*, that is, such as receives the truth soberly and acts upon it—"heareth the word and understandeth it"—"having heard the word, *keep it*"—and does not reject it, nor let it die out.——¶ *A hundred-fold,* &c., i. e., yielding *a hundred grains for one* that was sown, &c. So it is at times with grain. True religion shows a large increase and growth upon the first beginning. "*Much fruit*" is a mark of discipleship (Jno. 15. 8). All true Christians do not produce alike, any more than all good seeds yield ar

10 ¶ And the disciples came, and said unto him, Why speakest thou unto them in parables?

11 He answered and said unto them, Because it is given unto you to ᵈ know the mysteries of the kingdom of heaven, but to them it is not given.

12 For ᵉ whosoever hath, to him shall be given, and he shall have more abundance: but whosoever hath not, from him shall be taken away, even that he hath.

13 Therefore speak I to them in parables: because they seeing, see not; and hearing, they hear not, neither do they understand.

14 And in them is fulfilled the prophecy of Esaias, ᶠ which saith, By ᵍ hearing ye shall hear, and shall not understand; and seeing ye shall see, and shall not perceive:

15 For this people's heart is waxed gross, and *their* ears are dull ʰ of hearing, and their eyes they have closed; lest at any time they should see with *their*

d c.11.25. Mar.4.11. 1Co.2.10,14. Ep.1.9,18; 3.9. Col.1.2ᵌ,27. 1Jno.2.27. *e* c.25.29. Lu.9.26.
f Is.6.9. *g* Eze.12.2. Jno.12.40. Ac.28.26,27. Ro. 11.8. 2Cor.3.14,15. *h* He.5.11.

---

equal product. Yet there is always a harvest.

9. *Who hath ears.* This is the common formula (ch. 11. 15), for calling attention to something that needs special notice to be understood. It intimates, too that all would not understand. And it is an appeal, in general terms, to all who have the natural faculties, as they are bound to hear. It summons the Christian attention of those who understand the gospel by grace. So that this parable is addressed to every one as much as to those disciples.

10. *Why?* The disciples wished to know His reason for adopting this method of teaching the multitudes.

11. *Because,* &c. His sovereign will is the reason given of a difference here made between persons.—— *Unto you it is given,* or it pertains to you (out of mere grace), to know the *mysteries* of the kingdom, i. e., the characteristic doctrines of Christ. But to them it is not given, and hence, these truths are conveyed in a covering of similitude that only the initiated will see through and understand. *Mysteries* here mean, not *things incomprehensible,* but the things *not before revealed,* and not *else revealed* except in Christ.

12. *For.* The reason is here expanded. This is a principle which God adopts. They who improve what opportunities they have, shall have more opportunities and helps. Upon this rule, no desire after truth is ever put up in vain, and none who seek are sent empty away. The promise and threatening, of giving more to those who have any thing at all, and taking all away from those who make no improvement, and treasure nothing up, must apply to those who seek Christ, and shall find help, or who, with all their opportunities, are careless and shall at length have their very opportunities cut off.

13–15. *Because they seeing see not.* The other Evangelists state it in a different form. "*That seeing, they might not see,*" or, "may see, and not perceive." (Mark.) In using the parables, this was the sure result, while their wilful blindness was also a just cause. He gave out the truth in such a way that those of proper disposition toward it would perceive and appreciate the meaning. The fault, therefore, lay in them, for the darkness was their own, and out of their own hearts, and not of the truth. They had not the eyes to see these things, and had not a heart for them at all. He chose to state these things in a way that the disciples would understand and not the Jews. And this

146 MATTHEW. A. D. 31

eyes, and hear with *their* ears, and should understand with *their* heart, and should be converted, and I should heal them.

16 But ¡ blessed *are* your eyes, for they see: and your ears, for they hear.

17 For verily I say unto you, that ɉ many prophets and righteous *men* have desired to see *those things* which ye see, and have not seen *them;* and to hear *those things* which ye hear, and have not heard *them.*

i c.16.17. Lu.10.23.24. Jno.20.29. 2Cor.4.6. *j* Ep. 3.5,6. He.11.13. 1Pe.1.10,11.

18 ¶ Hear ᵏ ye therefore the parable of the sower.

19 When any one heareth the word ˡ of the kingdom, and understandeth *it* not, then cometh the wicked ᵐ *one*, and catcheth away that which was sown in his heart. This is he which received seed by the way-side.

20 But he that received the seed into stony places, the same is he that heareth the word, and anon with joy ⁿ receiveth it:

k Mar.4.14,&c. Lu.8.11,&c. *l* c.4.23. *m* 1Jo.2. 13,14; 3.12. *n* Is.58.2. Eze.33.31,32. Jno.5.35. Ga. 4.15.

could be referred only to His sovereign pleasure, according to this plan of dealing. For to those who had the understanding it was GIVEN, not *deserved, or purchased*——¶ *In them is fulfilled* (Isa. 6. 9, 10). This shows the profound plan. The people are charged by the prophet with grossest insensibility, and the results of all their means of grace were predicted. The Jewish nation was fairly contemplated, and in *these* it is fulfilled. They are even, in irony, commanded to *go and do* the very opposite of what they ought. "Hear indeed," or *hear on*, "but understand not." So sure was it, that this would be the result, and so determined did they seem to be in their unconcern, they are at length dismissed, as it were, with this language of desperation and abandonment. So also, the prophet is charged to do, what all his efforts were foreseen as accomplishing, "*Make fat the heart of this people,*" &c. "Judicial blindness is the thing predicted and ordained as the result of national and personal depravity. This end would be promoted by the preaching of the truth, and so, a command to preach, was in effect, a command to blind and harden them." In this passage the Septuagint (Greek) version is retained, in which the people's guilt is the prominent idea. In John 12. 40, the sentence takes another form in order to bring out the idea of *judicial blindness*. "He hath blinded their eyes," &c. (*See Alexander on Isaiah.*) Mark 8. 17, 18.

16. Those who do see and hear, should bless the *distinguishing grace*. The eyes and ears of the disciples were blessed because their eyes had been opened and their ears unstopped to see and hear the truths of the gospel, which natural men cannot understand. And they were blessed in living to see Christ in the flesh, and to hear His doctrines *from His own lips.*

17. *Many prophets.* Isaiah and all the prophets in some degree looked forward to Christ. They prophesied of Him, and desired to see these gospel realities. So "Abraham rejoiced to see my day; he saw it, and was glad," though it was only by the eye of faith. See John 8. 56. 1 Pet. 1. 10–12. Heb. 11. 13.

18. *Hear ye.* The disciples are here addressed. Christ would explain to them the parable, and asks them to listen. Mark reads (4. 13), "Know ye not this parable. And how then will ye know all parables?" as nothing would seem plainer than this, and this was fundamental.

19. The hardened and careless are here understood—way-side hearers in the unploughed edge of the field, (See notes, vs. 4.)

21 Yet hath he not root in himself, but dureth for a while; for when tribulation or persecution ariseth because of the word, by and by he is offended.º

22 He also that received seed among the thorns, is he that heareth the word; and the care ᵖ of this world and the deceitfulness of riches ᑫ choke the word, and he becometh unfruitful.

23 But he that received seed into the good ground, is he that heareth the word, and understandeth *it*; which also beareth fruit, ʳ and bringeth forth, some an hundred-fold, some sixty, some thirty.

24 ¶ Another ˢ parable put he forth unto them, saying, The kingdom of heaven is likened unto a man which sowed good ᵗ seed in his field:

o c.24.10; 26.31. 2Ti.4.16. p Lu.14.16-24. q Mar. 10.23. 1Ti.6.9. 2Ti.4.10.

r Jno.15.5. s Is.28.10,13. t 1Pe.1.23.

20, 21. *Stony ground hearers*, are the *superficial and outside* converts. Their religion is an impulse, and they are of loose surface and hard, rocky, botttom. (See notes verses 5 and 6.) Hard trials, like the hot sun upon a plant without root, wither it away.

22. *Among the thorns.* The *worldly* converts. Those whose religion is so surrounded and choked by worldliness, that they soon give out (1 Tim. 6. 9-11).

23. The good ground hearers are the *true* converts—the renewed regenerate- where the *heart is really changed*, and it is not all outside, or temporary, or worldly. There may be various degrees of fruitfulness, but all true Christians are fruitful, and we are to aim at much.

[§ 55. THE PARABLE OF THE TARES. OTHER PARABLES.]—*Near Capernaum?*

Matt.	Mark.	Luke.	John.
13. 24-53	4. 26-34		

24. *Put He forth*—παρεθηκεν. The word implies that He proposed it, as one would a riddle. It had a deeply spiritual sense. This parable is intended to exhibit the nature of the *visible church*, the mixture of the members, and the reason of it, and why it must so be till the end.—— ¶ *A man which sowed good seed.* By this is represented " *the Son of Man*" (vs. 37). This title is that most frequently used by our Lord to designate Himself, and never given Him in the New Testament by any other, except in one instance (Acts 7. 56), where Stephen seems to have seen Him in His glorified humanity. The title was already given Him in the Old Testament (Dan. 7. 13), and He claims it as the *Second Adam*, in which capacity He loved to be recognized. The title by which He was popularly named, was " *the Son of David.*"—— ¶ *His field.* This represents the region within which the gospel is properly preached—that is, the world (vs. 38). It is Christ's field for His work of redemption.—— ¶ *The good seed*, " are the children of the kingdom"—the true membership —such as really belong to the kingdom, in distinction from those who are but nominally such. In the last parable, the good seed was the truth; but here, in the progress of the sentiment, the seed is regarded as having entered into the person and having become identical with him. *The field* is called *the world* (vs. 38), because God has ordained to gather His children out of all nations, and because the great preaching commission is, " Go ye into *all the world* and preach the gospel to every creature." The Lord may be said to sow this field, because " of His own will begat He us with the word of truth," and we are born, " not of corruptible seed, but of incorruptible, by the word of

25 But while men slept, his enemy came and sowed tares among the wheat, and went his way.

26 But when the blade was sprung up, and brought forth fruit, then appeared the tares also.

27 So the servants of the householder came and said unto him, Sir, didst not thou sow good seed in thy field; from whence then hath it tares?

28 He said unto them, An enemy hath done this. The servants said unto him, Wilt thou

---

God, which liveth and abideth forever." And, as in this *field*, all these things of the parable occur, so the visible church seems to be described as co-extensive with the world: not confined to Jews, nor brought, as yet, to the strict dimensions of the *church invisible*. The disciples were not prepared to expect this mixture of good and evil—wheat and tares—in the church. Hence Christ warns them beforehand, so that they might not be offended, or think that God's promises had failed, and that they might know how to behave themselves when the mystery of iniquity should begin manifestly to work. What a trial was to come to the faith of the twelve, to find a Judas in their small circle.

25. *While men slept.* This means not so much to censure the neglect of any, as though it were on this account mainly that such mischief was done; but it points to the fact, that this unholy mixture is brought about, *in the night*, as it were, at a time when men cannot see the mischiefmaker or his deeds, but can only tell that it is done, from the result. We cannot always detect Satan's movements, nor expect to see his work in human hearts, and hence we may be the more diffident of our skill in discerning between the precious and the vile.——¶ *Tares. The children of the wicked one* (vs. 38). Such as belong to Satan and are of him. These are the seed of his sowing, as distinguished from the true membership. These are the false professors that must be expected in the visible church. *The enemy is the Devil* (vs. 39). *the wicked one*, as the being, of all, the most emphatically, absolutely, essentially and supremely EVIL, and the *source and sower* of it (John 8. 44). Satan *sows* these seeds, not as though he could create evil beings, but only spoil the good. Therefore Augustine speaks of the origin of evil as not a *generation*, but a *degeneration*—as having not an *efficient* but a *deficient* cause. Satan is here set forth as the enemy of the Son of Man. These tares are rather a *bastard wheat*, says Trench. The *wild grapes* instead of the good (Isa. 5. 2). The mischief here spoken of is well known in the East and elsewhere. Malicious persons sow some bad seed among the grain, that will grow up and choke it. It is not detected at first, or even when it first springs up; and afterward, it is not easy to distinguish the two. The wicked are among the righteous in the church, like tares among the wheat in the same field, because they are of most pernicious influence among professors, and it is impossible, by the strictest discipline, to make a perfect separation of them on earth. This is the point of the parable. Sinners are called the children of the wicked one, because they bear his likeness, and the works of their father they will do.

26. *The blade—the stalk.* It is with the fruits of piety in the Christian life, that a false profession contrasts. There must be *holiness* in the church, *to show the unholiness* in the false membership, and hence, when the church is degenerate, false religion does not so easily appear; the true and false are confounded—discipline is neglected, and the church itself is disgraced.

27. *Whence then hath it tares?* This is the surprise of many, and the world

then that we go and gather them up?

29 But he said, Nay; lest while ye gather up the tares, ye root up also the wheat with them.

30 Let both grow together until the harvest: and in the time of harvest ᵘ I will say to the reapers, Gather ye together first the tares, and bind them in bundles to ᵛ burn them: but gather the wheat ʷ into my barn.

u 1Ti.5.24.   *v* Mal.4.1.   *w* Lu.3.17.

---

affect to wonder at this, and it is a fit topic for earnest inquiry.

28. *Gather them up.* These mischiefs are the direct work of Satan—'an enemy hath done this." It is no part of the church system, or of its design, to harbour bad members. It does not excuse the false professor or the gainsayer. It only points for an explanation to that agency of all evil—the devil. But the zeal of many is at once to rid the church of all imperfection, so that it shall be without spot or wrinkle or blemish, or any such thing. This is often an Eliaszeal, as in Luke 9. 54. Some, like Jehu, call upon others to see their "zeal for the Lord." Some can see no church where they find not perfect purity. But Paul recognized the church of Corinth, though corrupt, because he found there the Christian doctrine with the sacraments, by which the church is to be known.

29. *Lest,* &c. Such a work of rooting out with such an unqualified determination, is perilous in itself, and often suspicious in the spirit of it. Our Lord cautions against such an enterprize. There is danger of rooting up the wheat with the tares, because of our inability to distinguish as perfectly as the case would demand. And a spirit of zealous extermination, that undertakes such a work of *rooting up* and putting out all that seems to them evil, "may be rather a war of the *tares against the wheat,* than *of the wheat against the tares.*"—*Trench.*

30. *Let both grow together.* The tares are to be separated from the wheat, but the householder's servants here are not the ones to do it with exactness, nor is this the time for it to be perfectly done. We cannot expect the church to be wholly rid of false members for the present. Those who lay this to the blame of the church, that it has tares among the wheat, do not know their own hearts, or others'. Discipline is appointed in the church, and wo to those officers who neglect it, and are careless of the flock, or of its purity. But we are to beware of destroying a weak brother, or of indulging an arrogant, Pharisaic zeal, or of pretending, finally, to settle all these differences. There are false professors, but "what is the chaff to the wheat?" OBSERVE: Evil and good are to grow together, to increase and develope side by side, and intermixed, until the end of time. The good is not to choke the evil, but Satan is still to have his work and wages on earth.——¶ *The harvest* represents the end of the world (see vs. 39); because at the last, all results are gathered up—men are judged—fruits are brought to light, and a final disposal is made of the good and the bad.—*The reapers* are *the angels* (vs. 39). They are appointed to this office. Christ is represented as coming to judgment and *all the holy angels with Him*" (Matt. 25).——¶ *To burn them.* Tares are burned so as to destroy most effectually the mischievous seed. Like this, in the end of the world, will be the gathering and effectual destroying of the wicked, beyond the possibility of their propagating evil any more.——¶ *Gather ye together,* &c., or as in vs. 41, *gather out of His kingdom.* This will be the proper purifying process, removing every evil thing from the church (see Zeph. 1. 3) *to " a · furnace of fire"* (vs. 42).—" Whose end is to be *burned"* (Heb. 6. 8). Utterly burned with fire (2 Sam. 23. 6, 7). This ex-

31 ¶ Another parable put he forth unto them, saying, The kingdom of heaven is like to a ˣ grain of mustard-seed, which a man took and sowed in his field :
32 Which indeed is the least

ˣ Mar. 4. 30.

of all seeds; but when it is grown, it is the greatest among herbs, and becometh a tree, ʸ so that the birds of the air come and lodge in the branches thereof.

ʸ Eze. 17. 23.

presses the common idea in the scripture of eternal burning, as the valley of Hinnom (Mark 9. 43–48). This casting into a furnace, which is here the image of hell, was a punishment in use among the Chaldeans (Jer. 29. 22. Dan. 3. 6).——¶ *Wailing*, &c. (vs. 42). The article here, and usually in this phrase in the New Testament, gives a definite and emphatic sense: THE *wailing*, so peculiar and deserved. These are expressions of rage and impatience (Acts. 7. 54).——¶ *Gather the wheat into my barn*. The righteous, in the judgment, shall be admitted and welcomed to the joy of their Lord: *shall shine forth*, as distinct from the rest, "as the sun in the kingdom of their Father" (vs. 43), as if *transfigured* before the universe. "They that be wise shall shine as the brightness of the firmament" (Dan. 12. 3), the children of light and of the day. God permits the evil and the good to dwell together thus, at present, in order to show His forbearance, and to exercise the circumspection and patience of His people, as well as to show the need of a final judgment day, and to make His children look for and pray for His coming kingdom, as prophesied of (Isa. 52. 1), with no more uncircumcised or unclean—Zech. 14. 21, no more the Canaanite in the house of the Lord—His people all righteous Isa. 60. 21. Compare Isa. 35. 8. Joel 3. 17. Ezek. 37. 21–27. Zeph. 3. 13. From this we are encouraged to persuade sinners to repentance, because the long-suffering of our God is salvation and not slackness. It shows His willingness to save. And the goodness of God should lead sinners to repentance. OBSERVE, this parable teaches us how possible it is for false professors to enter the church.

Nothing else can be expected. Nothing else is pretended. This is not to be charged against the church. The self-deceived and deceivers will all be made known at the last. And for the present, how necessary that we examine ourselves, since membership is no guaranty for our new nature. Christ is the final judge. Let all understand: "*Who hath ears to hear, let him hear*" (vs. 43). There are things here that require spiritual discernment, and the parable is worthy to be personally applied by each. In these two parables they had heard of the difficulties and drawbacks which belong to the kingdom. Now He would speak two other parables for their encouragement.

31. *Mustard-seed*. This parable is to show that the kingdom of Christ, though having these hindrances and drawbacks, WILL PROSPER. The growth of a kingdom had been set forth under this image of a tree (Dan. 4. 10–12. Ezek. 31. 3–9), and so of this kingdom (Ezek. 10; 7. 22–24. Psalm 80. 8). This seed is taken to show the greatness of the tree as compared with the smallness of its origin.

32. *The least*. This is not absolutely the case, but comparatively and proverbially so. "Small as a grain of mustard-seed," was a proverb among the Jews. As the church of Christ began in so small a way, and seemed so unpromising at first, but afterward should grow to the greatest size, the image is striking. The mustard-bush becomes the greatest among herbs—becomes a tree. It sometimes grows to the height of ten or twelve feet. This refers to the church in its outward, visible manifestation—and it applies to piety in the individual heart. So adds Theophylact: " Be thou such a grain of

[A. D. 31.] CHAPTER XIII. 151

33 ¶ Another parable spake he unto them: The kingdom of heaven is like unto leaven, which a woman took and hid in three measures¹ of meal, till the whole was leavened.

34 All these things spake Jesus unto the multitude in parables;ᵃ and without a parable spake he not unto them;

35 That it might be fulfilled which was spoken by the prophet, ᵃ saying, I will open my mouth in parables; I will utter things which have been kept ᵇ secret from the foundation of the world.

36 Then Jesus sent the multitude away, and went into the house: and his disciples came unto him, saying, Declare unto us the parable of the tares of the field.

37 He answered and said unto them, He that soweth the good seed is the Son of man:

38 The field is the world :ᶜ the

1 *The Greek word signifies a measure (about a peck and a half, wanting a little more than a pint).* z Mar.4.33. a Ps.78.2.

b Lu.10.14. Ro.16.25,26. Col.1.26. c Ro.10.18. Col. 1.6.

mustard—small, indeed, in appearance, for it becomes thee not to make a spectacle of thy virtue, but fervent, and zealous, and energetic, and armed to reprove."

33. *Leaven.* Under another figure the progress of the church is presented in a new aspect. The kingdom is here compared to that substance which is used to ferment meal. The *hidden, mysterious* working of the gospel is here illustrated. The secret influence in the heart, and in the world, is like that of leaven, which silently works, and pervades the whole mass. How remarkable an ignorance do heathen writers betray of the great work that was going on just below the surface of society, when Christ's kingdom began to spread, even until Christianity had well nigh triumphed. This parable shows how the grace which so effectually operates in the heart, is *imparted*, as the leaven is *put into* the meal. How it is *hidden* away there—spiritual, and not visible except from the effects—"your life is *hid* with Christ, in God"—and how, by the law of its operation, it must go on to spread *until the whole is leavened.* This is the law of Christian progress and perseverance to final perfection in Heaven. So the world shall be filled with the knowledge of the glory of the Lord as the waters fill the seas.

34 This means that Christ adopted this as His favourite and common mode of teaching the multitude. It was by *pictures*, attractive and comprehensive. To those who could not understand the spiritual truth, they were imaged to the eye—and by their vivid impression they might serve as formulas of truth, to recall it in its connexions and relations, if afterward it should be received. Yet they would bring only deeper darkness to the rejecters of the light. It was partly to defeat the malice and vigilant hostility of the Scribes and Pharisees, who, had He now spoken in plainest terms, would have plotted to destroy Him.

35. *That it might be fulfilled.* (Psalm 78). The Psalmist was *Asaph, the seer* (2 Chron. 29. 30). Speaking of the things pertaining to the kingdom of God, he used this language, with an intent in the mind of the Spirit, that it should have an application and fulfilment here, in Christ. The Psalmist is called a *prophet* in this verse, and yet his Psalm is a recital of God's dealings with the church, which can be *prophetic* only as looking forward to Christ, rehearsing the Divine faithfulness in Zion. The terms in the Psalm mean rather " weighty sentences," and " profound sayings." And here Christ shows Himself as using this method of instruction in accord-

152　　　　　　　　　　MATTHEW.　　　　　　　　[A. D. 31.

good seed are the children of the kingdom ; ᵈ but the tares are the children of the wicked ᵉ *one*.

39 The enemy that sowed them is the devil: the harvest is the end of the world ; ᶠ and the reapers are the angels.ᵍ

40 As therefore the tares are gathered and burned in the fire ; ʰ so shall it be in the end of this world.

41 The Son of man shall send forth his angels, and they shall gather out of his kingdom ¹ all things that offend, and ⁱ them which do iniquity ;

42 And ʲ shall cast them into a furnace of fire : there ᵏ shall be wailing and gnashing of teeth.

43 Then shall the righteous shine ˡ forth as the sun, in the kingdom of their Father. Who hath ears to hear, let him hear.

44 ¶ Again: the kingdom of heaven is like unto treasure ᵐ hid in a field ; the which when a man hath found, he hideth, and for joy thereof goeth and selleth

d 1Pe.1.23.　*e* Jno.8.44. Ac.13.10. 1Jno.3.8.　*f* Joel 3.13. Re.14.15.　*g* Re.14.15-19.　*h* ver.30.　1 Or, *scandals*.

i Lu.13.27.　*j* c.3.12. Re.19.20 ; 20.10.　*k* ver.50. c.8.12.　*l* Da.12.3. 1Cor.15.49.　*m* Pr.2.4,5.

ance with this prophetic reference of the Psalm.

37–40. The explanation of the parable of the tares is already given, in connection with the various portions of it as they occur.

41. *All things that offend*—margin, *scandals*. Gr. σκάνδαλα, lit. *stumbling-blocks*. Alluding here to *persons*— "*seducers*."—Campbell. Trench understands the word as from the old form σκανδαληθρον, meaning that part of a trap or snare on which the bait is placed, and which being touched by the animal gives way, and draws the snare suddenly tight. In the New Testament it includes whatever, *entangling* as it were *men's feet*, might cause them to fall. Our Lord having sent the multitude away, *went into the house*, and explained to His disciples that which they had not understood ; and to them also He delivered these other parables of different style from the former.

44. Here it is taught that *the kingdom is not merely a general, but also an individual thing*. Unless it be *personal* with us, it is nothing.— ¶ *Like unto treasure hid*. The point of this and the following parable, seems to be to show how the kingdom of heaven, or the gospel provision, is to be personally laid hold of by faith. That while on God's part, it is destined to spread as leaven, silently, but surely—on our part, it is to be sought and secured. This is the practical portion of the parables. In both these also, the gospel prize is represented as first *found*, then *found out*, and rejoiced in ! *Thus*, says Calvin, *denotes the knowledge of faith*. In both cases it is the joy of the discovery that moves to the earnest and successful appropriation, discarding all things else. In Eastern countries *hid treasure* was not uncommon. Property was often held partly in such valuables as could be buried. Hence these rich deposits were often found where they had been hid by the owners long before. A Greek is said to have bought ground where such treasures were reported to lie. He inquired at the Oracle of Delphi, and was told to "*turn every stone.*" This he did, and found it. So we speak of "*leaving no stone unturned,*" in some great effort. This illustrates what is here taught by the parable. The points are these. The gospel treasure is the rich grace that is found so abundantly in Christ—durable riches and righteousness—"in whom are hid all the treasures of wisdom and knowledge." It is *hid* to the natural man who "discerneth not the things of the Spirit of God." It is "concealed from the wise and pru-

ⁿ all that he hath, and buyeth ᵒ that field.

45 ¶ Again: the kingdom of heaven is like unto a merchantman, seeking goodly pearls;

<small>n Ph.3.7,8.   o Is.55.1. Re.3.18.</small>

46 Who, when he had found one ᵖ pearl of great price, went and sold all that he had, and bought it.

47 ¶ Again: the kingdom of

<small>p Pr.3.14,15: 8.11.</small>

---

dent," but it is "revealed unto babes." "The secret of the Lord is with them that fear Him, and He will show them His covenant." For this discovery every exertion must be put forth, and *no stone left unturned*. The discovery of the treasure which there is in Christ, is the grand gospel *motive* to discard self-righteousness and deny the world.——¶ *When a man hath found, he hideth.* This is his *jealousy* lest it be lost. He would not have it exposed nor endangered, but secured. He covers it *as it was*. He lets it lie where God put it—only marks the spot, and so he hastens and gives all diligence to make his calling sure. The Christian would not have God's plan of grace altered, and he would go to a sovereign God for his hope.——¶ *For joy thereof*, the finder parts with all he hath. The delight at finding Christ, and the riches that are in Christ, make a man renounce all things for Him. So Paul: "I count all things but loss for the excellency of the knowledge of Christ Jesus my Lord," &c. It is by no means a bargaining, but a joyful constraint. He *finds* the *treasure*, and then he *buys the field*—THE TRUTH AS IT IS IN JESUS—and sells it not. This parable represents, therefore, the way in which we actually become partakers of the gospel treasure. It is all *in Christ*, in whom are hid all the treasures of wisdom and knowledge. It is all of grace. Like finding a prize, we know not what it is, until we have found it. So there is no merit of ours in the work. That which is "*set before us in the gospel*," is already *a hope, to be laid hold of* (Heb. 6. 18). So the parable represents it almost as though stumbled upon, or found unawares, lest even the MERIT of *seeking* should have place; as it has in the minds of many. The man who has any discovery of Christ should be jealous, lest he lose Him; and for joy of finding in Him all riches, he should count all things but dross and dung for His sake (Phil. 3. 8). Whatever is a hindrance in the way of having Christ in His fulness, whether it be pleasure, covetousness, indolence or pride, it is to be cast away. And *the joy of Christ is that, in the strength of which it is done.*

45, 46. *A merchantman*. This parable illustrates the way of salvation, in a somewhat different light. The former spoke of the treasure—this speaks of the finder. It shows the man as a seeker, an inquirer, in the lowest sense, of seeking something good—happiness, peace, righteousness, safety, salvation—and finding this one incomparable pearl. In this case you see the man.——¶ *Seeking goodly pearls*. These were *hidden*, also, in the *shell fish*. Men were employed by the pearl-merchant to dive after them in the waters of the East. But when this pearl is found, so transcendent in its excellence and value, this is seen to be the *one thing needful*—the *good part*—the *all in all*—and this discovery leads to a *forsaking of all things else for this*. When we give Christ our *hearts*, we give up our hold on all rival and conflicting interests. This is required of us. And as in the former case, it is our tasting that the Lord is gracious, and finding the one pearl of great price, that makes every other pearl and possession fade and fail to attract us in comparison. *This new affection has an expulsive power*. We throw away the pebbles of earth, for this inestimable pearl. This is represented here, "not as an arbitrary condition, but as a delightful constraint."

48. *Like unto a net*. This par-

heaven is like unto a net that was cast into the sea, and gathered q of every kind:

48 Which, when it was full, they drew to shore, and sat down, and gathered the good into vessels, but cast the bad away

49 So shall it be at the end of the world: the angels shall come forth, and r sever the wicked from among the just;

50 And s shall cast them into the furnace of fire: there shall be wailing and gnashing of teeth.

51 Jesus saith unto them, Have ye understood all these things? They say unto him, Yea, Lord.

52 Then said he unto them Therefore every scribe *which is* instructed unto the kingdom of

q c.22.10.   r c.25.32.

s ver.42.

---

able represents not only the present mixture of good and evil members in the church (as the parable of the tares), but further, the final separation. "As there was a Ham in the ark, and a Judas among the twelve, so there should be a Babylon even within the bosom of the spiritual Israel. Esau shall contend with Jacob even in the church's womb" (Gen. 25. 22.).——¶ *Net.* The word in the original—*sagene*— means a *draw-net,* from which (says Trench) our word *seine* or *sean* is a corruption. It is sometimes half a mile in length, with sinkers at the bottom, and corks at the top, so as to be stretched over a great extent of the waters, and to sweep all the fish, of all kinds, that are there. So Christ's kingdom, or church on earth, will be *spread,* by the preaching of the gospel, all over the world. The field is the world, but in the sea is the net, "a world within a world."——¶ *When it was full*—when the number of God's elect is made up, and His purposes for His church are fulfilled.——¶ *They drew to shore.* The time of final separation is not yet, but at the consummation, when all things will be closed up, and the last judgment will be held— then it shall be.——¶ *Sat down.* This represents the *sitting in judgment.* Christ's ministers are the "fishers of men." But the *angels shall come forth* to the *office work* of final separation, and Christ with them shall come to judgment. In the church, this work is very partially done.

49. *At the end of the world,* the angels shall sever or separate the wicked from among the just (See 2 Tim. 2. 20, 21).——¶ THE JUST are the *justified*—the true disciples. The wicked shall be separated from them, because there shall not enter into the heavenly church, any thing that defileth. They shall be cast out. "Thy people shall be all righteous." "Without are dogs."

50. *The furnace of fire.* Not *a* furnace, but THE furnace. By this is meant that place of torment that is so definitely spoken of in scripture as the abode of lost spirits.——¶ *Wailing.* Bitter, despairing lamentations. Definitely, in the Greek, *the* wailing, and *the* gnashing of teeth, which are deserved, and which belong there. The agony of the lost will spring from self-reproaches at having neglected the great salvation, and now finding, when too late, that there is no escape. They had not heeded the repeated warnings. These seven parables "have a certain unity, succeeding each other in natural order, and having a completeness in themselves."

51. *Have ye understood?* With infinite tenderness our Lord makes this inquiry, whether His explanations had fully enlightened them.——¶ *These things.* That is, the *meaning* of the parables which He had just spoken; the truths pertaining to the kingdom of God which they set forth.

52. *Every scribe,* &c. A *scribe* was, among the Jews, one learned in the

heaven is like unto a man *that is* an householder, which bringeth forth out *t* of his treasure *things* new and old.ᵘ

53 ¶ And it came to pass, *that* when Jesus had finished these parables, he departed thence.

t Pr.10.21; 15.7; 18.4. *u* Ca.7.13.

54 And ᵛ when he was come into his own country, he taught them in their synagogue, insomuch that they were astonished, and said, Whence hath this *man* this wisdom, and these mighty works?

v Mar.6.1,&c. Lu.4.16,&c.

---

law, and an expounder of it. These favoured disciples, who sat under all these teachings of Christ, were *instructed* scribes. The term means, literally, DISCIPLED—made fully acquainted with, or "instructed unto the kingdom, to show forth the praises of Him who called them." He now shows to what they are properly like, as to their position and obligation. They were to be teachers of others.——¶ *An householder.* The teachers of the church are to have stores of knowledge laid up, as those at the head of a house have provisions stored for their families. ——¶ *His treasure.* His storehouse, closet, or treasury of provisions. From this he was to bring out the various supplies, suited to each individual want, and for every occasion; "giving to each a portion in due season," and "rightly dividing the word of truth"—just as a housekeeper brings forth the various stores for each day's meal, and for all. Every teacher and preacher should come before the people with rich stores of useful learning. "Let no man despise thee." "The priest's lips should keep knowledge," that the law may be sought at his mouth. For about three years our Lord gave special instructions to His disciples. He gave here, also, a pattern of gospel teaching, tender and copious in the doctrines of the kingdom. Every well-instructed, or discipled scribe, should thus bring out of his treasure things new and old. We must be able to teach others also. And those who have received of God's free spirit, and the joys of His salvation, should teach transgressors His ways. (Psalm 51.) ——·¶ *Things new and old,* is a pro-verbial expression, taken from the ingathering of the year (Sol. Songs, 7. 13). Compare vs. 35.

53. *These parables.* These SEVEN spoken here in connexion, and containing a series of truths most important for them to know. (See Trench on the Parables.) Here it must be observed from the Harmony, that after finishing the parables near Capernaum, Jesus re-crossed the lake, and healed the demoniacs at Gadara, on the south-east coast, came back to Capernaum, attended Levi's (Matthew's) feast, raised Jairus' daughter, and then He appeared again at "Nazareth, where He had been brought up."

[§ 61. JESUS AGAIN AT NAZARETH, AND AGAIN REJECTED.]

Matt.	Mark.	Luke.	John.
13. 54–58	6. 1–6		

54. *His own country.* That is Nazareth, where He dwelt, until He entered on His public work. Though He was born at Bethlehem, He lived at Nazareth, whither Joseph had returned from Egypt. Hence in fulfilment of prophecy, He was called a Nazarene. Mark says: "And when the sabbath-day was come, He began to teach in the synagogue." This He often did, as when He was before rejected at Nazareth. The synagogues of the Jews were the parish churches, where they worshipped in their various quarters, for ordinary occasions when they need not go up to Jerusalem. We read of the minister and of the rulers of the synagogue. According to the Jewish Talmud, wherever there were ten *Batlanim,* or *men of leisure,* who would be responsible for the synagogue ser-

55 Is not this the carpenter's son? Is not his mother called Mary? and his brethren, James, and Joses, and Simon, and Judas?

56 And his sisters, are they not all with us? Whence then hath this *man* all these things?

57 And they were offended ▼ in him. But Jesus said unto them, A prophet is not without honour, save in his own country, and in his own house.

58 And he did not many mighty works there, because of their unbelief.

<small>*w* Is.49.7; 53.3. Jno.6.42.</small>

---

vice, there a synagogue might be erected. Here again the people brought up against His claims the fact of His low extraction, as known to them, His poor family origin, and His being a common man among them, whose brothers were well known.

55. *The carpenter's son.* Mark has it —*the carpenter.* It would seem clear that our Lord had regularly wrought at this trade, under His father Joseph, until He left Nazareth.—— ¶ *Mary.* Mark has it—"*the son of Mary.*" Though neither of the Evangelists speak of Joseph's death, yet it may be plainly inferred, that Christ was now called "the son of Mary" (see Mark 6. 3), because of her being a widow. (See Luke 8. 19. John 2. 12, and 19. 25–27.)

56. *Whence then?* Here the people of Christ's own town testified that He had had no uncommon advantages. They knew His family well, and knew that they were common people. This was their witness that He could not have received His wisdom from man. The very condescension of our Lord prejudiced the proud against Him. He stooped to save, and His very stooping offended them. They drew from it an argument against His claims. So *many* make Christ's true and proper humanity an argument to disprove His Divinity. But the scripture equally asserts both. And men *beg the question* altogether, when they assume this union of the two natures in one person to be incompatible and impossible with God. Behold the Infinite condescension of our Redeemer! The Creator of the Universe a carpenter!

This dignifies every honest employment of the mechanic, and makes day labour honourable in all.

57. *Offended in Him.* These things, in His case, were an offence or stumbling-block to them. They rejected Him on these grounds. They argued that He could not be any such person as He claimed, because He had grown up among them. They were envious, too, of such superior pretensions by one of their townsmen. Alas, they knew not the wondrous plan of God, in redemption.—— ¶ *A prophet.* This proverb Christ here applies as suiting His own case. He was rejected on natural principles, that belong to the carnal heart. We read that even His brethren believed not on Him.

58. *Mighty works*—miracles. Mark says, "And He could there do no mighty work, save that He laid His hands upon a few sick folk and healed them." According to His plan of grace that required faith, their stubborn unbelief restrained the blessing. This was true, though faith is the gift of God. Obstinate opposers thus even keep back the miracles! Such prejudice, like that of the Gadarenes, besought Him rather to depart out of their coast. Christ would not thrust His benefits upon them unasked. These sick folk, likely, had such a sense of need, as He could properly minister to, and relieve.

OBSERVE, (1.) Unbelief *now*, is equally sinful, and stands equally in the way of His wondrous works. (2.) "Only a spiritual eye can discern beauty in an humbled Saviour."—*Burkitt.* (3.) *We* have seen the fulfilment of His word, and the infallible

A. D. 32.]   CHAPTER XIV.   **157**

CHAPTER XIV.

AT that time ᵃ Herod the tetrarch heard of the fame of Jesus;

a Mar.6.14. Lu.9.7,&c.

proofs of His gospel, as *they* had not. This is more than to have seen Him in the flesh, and so our guilt is greater. (4.) He will not visit Zion with the wonder-working power of the Spirit unless for these things He be inquired of by the house of Israel to do it for them. " Open thy mouth wide and I will fill it." Hardened unbelief will seem to stay His gracious hand. We are not authorized to expect a blessing from God, if we have not faith in Christ as the Divine Redeemer.

CHAPTER XIV.

"While the twelve are absent preaching in the name of Christ, Herod causes John the Baptist to be beheaded in the castle of Machærus, at the southern extremity of Perea, near the Dead Sea. In consequence of the preaching of the apostles, Herod hears the fame of Jesus—is conscience-stricken, and declares him to be John risen from the dead. The disciples of John come and tell Jesus, and the twelve also return with the same intelligence—upon which Jesus retires to the north-east coast of the Lake, not far from the northern Bethsaida, or Julias. All these events seem to have taken place near together. Matthew and Mark narrate the death of the Baptist in explanation of Herod's declaration. According to John 6. 4, the Passover was now at hand, viz., the *third* during our Lord's ministry. John therefore had lain in prison not far from a year and six months, and was beheaded about three years after entering upon his public ministry."—*Robinson's Harmony.* See § 62. ch. 10.

§ 63. Herod held Jesus to be John the Baptist, whom he had just before beheaded.—*Galilee?—Perea.*

Matt.	Mark.	Luke.	John.
14. 1–12	6. 14–16 21–29	9. 7–9	

2 And said unto his servants, This is John the Baptist; he is risen from the dead; and therefore mighty works ¹ do

1 Or, *are wrought by him.*

1. This Herod was one of three sons of Herod the Great, and was surnamed *Antipas*. He ruled over Galilee and Perea; his father, at his death, shortly after Christ's birth, having left his kingdom in three different parts to the three Herods.—— ¶ *Tetrarch*. Literally, the *ruler of a fourth*, is a title not confined to this meaning, but denotes also the ruler of any inferior part. He was called Herod *the king* also, as we find from vs. 9. He heard of the fame of Christ, who had now been engaged the better part of two years in His public ministry, and had twice traversed Galilee, where He had now set out again. But the preaching of the apostles had now made Christ more known, and Herod had in his own house some followers of Christ. (Luke 8. 3, and Acts 13. 1.) Herod was a bad man, of loose character. He was at length banished by Caligula to Spain, and died in exile; and his tetrarchy was given by the same emperor to *Herod Agrippa* (see Acts 12.), who "was eaten up of worms."

2. Herod found that Christ was a remarkable person, and heard that he was possessed of supernatural powers; and his conscience smote him with this idea, that it was John the Baptist, whom he had beheaded, risen from the dead. A sense of guilt, mingled with superstitious fears, had awakened this impression in his mind.—— ¶ *His servants*—or courtiers. "Matthew alone mentions, and without any apparent reason for such minuteness, that Herod addressed his remark to his *servants*. Luke, in the parallel passage, says he *heard of all that was done by him*. But by referring to Luke 8. 3, and Acts 13. 1, we find that Christ had followers from among the household of this prince, with whom Herod was likely to converse on a subject in which they were better in-

shew forth themselves in him.

3 ¶ For Herod had laid hold on John, and bound him, and put *him* in prison for Herodias' sake, his brother Philip's wife.

4 For John said unto him, It [b] is not lawful for thee to have her.

5 And when he would have put him to death, he feared the multitude, because they counted him as a [c] prophet.

b Le.18.16; 20.21. *c* c.21.26. Lu.20.6.

6 But when Herod's birthday was kept, the daughter of Herodias danced [1] before them, and pleased Herod.

7 Whereupon he promised with an oath to give her whatsoever she would ask.

8 And she, being before instructed of her mother, said, Give me here John Baptist's [d] head in a charger.

9 And the king was sorry; [e]

1 *In the midst.* *d* Pr.29.10. *e* Ju.11.31,35. Da.6. 14-16.

---

formed than himself."—*Blunt's Veracity*.——¶ *Mighty works.* Literally, powers or miracles operate in Him—are wrought by Him. Though Herod was a Sadducee, and did not believe in a resurrection or spirit, his conscience here prevailed over his infidel creed. (See ch. 3. 7, note.)

3. John had been in prison, it would seem, about a year and a half. The Evangelist digresses now to narrate that cruelty. When it occurred, we remember Christ opened His public ministry (see notes on ch. 4. 12); and all the time of Christ's preaching until John's beheading, was about two years and a half.

4. *Not lawful.* Herodias, whom this Herod married, was an ambitious and vicious woman, the grand-daughter of Herod the Great, and niece of this man, and was now living in marriage with his own brother, Herod Philip. They had a daughter Salome, who is referred to probably in vs. 6. Of course it was not lawful for Herod to marry this woman, though Philip was his brother by a different mother. It was *adultery* in the first place—and it was besides a case of *incest*, forbidden in Levit. 18. 16—" *brother's wife.*" Christian faithfulness will sometimes cost men their lives.

5. He would have put him to death on account of his reproving him faithfully for this crime. But he feared the multitude, who had great respect for John as a prophet. Good men will gain respect, that will sometimes save them from their enemies.

6. *Herod's birthday.* A great occasion among kings at that time (see Mark 6. 21-29). It was probably kept in the castle of Machærus, where John was imprisoned.——¶ *The daughter of Herodias danced before them*—or, in their midst, on this festive occasion; and it was part of the custom, at such times, for the king to express his special approbation (Esther 5. 6). He made an oath to give her whatsoever she should ask. Mark adds, *even to the half of my kingdom*—a form of royal promise. It was a rash and wicked promise, such as is oftenest made in the company of the gay and revelling. Gay amusements often lead to such crimes. It was such a promise as was wicked in itself, and should therefore have been broken. It was more wicked to keep it than to break it.

8. *Being before instructed of her mother.* This is referred to Herodias, to whom it belonged to instigate the crime. " She went forth and said unto her mother " (Mark). " She came in straightway with haste unto the king " (Mark). " Give me *by-and-by* "—that is, now, immediately, as is the old English sense. This shows us the malignant and depraved character of Herodias, living in sin with Herod, and now ready to call for John the Baptist's head! They wished John put out of the way, that their crimes

[A. D. 32.] CHAPTER XIV. 159

nevertheless, for the oath's [f] sake, and them which sat with him at meat, he commanded *it* to be given *her*.

10 And he sent, and beheaded John in the prison.

11 And his head was brought in a charger, and given to the damsel: and she brought *it* to her mother.

f Ju.21.1. 1Sa.14.28; 25.22. Ec.5.2.

12 And his disciples came and took up the body, and buried [g] it, and went and told Jesus.

13 ¶ When Jesus heard *of it*. he [h] departed thence by ship into a desert place apart: and when the people had heard *thereof*, they followed him on foot out of the cities.

g Ac.8.2. *h* c.10.23; 12.15. Mar.6.32,&c, Lu.9. 10,&c. Jno.6.1,2,&c.

---

might not be reproved or disturbed. It was sometimes demanded that the head be brought, as proof that the person had been executed.——¶ *Give me here*—that is, *now*, before the king should repent his promise.

9. *The king was sorry.* Mark has it, " exceeding sorry." He was troubled, worried, but not sincerely penitent for his crime. He feared the result of this upon his own standing with the people, for they counted John a prophet (vs. 5), and he himself had great respect for him on general grounds (Mark 6. 20). He was not quite prepared, at first, for such a request. It shocked him, and he was uneasy, and felt regret at the circumstance. The world's joy is accompanied with sorrow. Sin has misery. ——¶ *Nevertheless.* He was shamefully inconsistent in first making such an oath, and then regretting it—and then, notwithstanding his conscience accused, carrying it through for the sake of standing to what he had said, and preserving a false honour. He was afraid of being called cowardly or weak—so the king feared his guests!

10. *He sent.* Mark says he sent a " speculator "—a Latin term used by Mark, meaning " executioner."

11. *A charger*—a dish, platter, or waiter. This shows us how corrupt and cruel is the natural heart. A young girl and a base mother conspire to seek so dreadful a gratification as the murder of a good man, a prophet of the Lord, and to triumph over his bloody head, served up to them on a waiter as a luxury! So fiendish, indeed, is human nature, unrestrained, even in its best estate.

12. *Took up the body.* This would look as though the body had been thrown out unburied. John's disciples took pious care of it, and then, knowing how closely John's work and Christ's were related, and how they personally felt toward each other, " they went and told Jesus." Here was incidentally, in the manner of John's death, a proof that he was not the Messiah, for " a bone of Him should not be broken." (John 19. 36.)

OBSERVE, (1.) The terrors and tortures of a guilty conscience. (2.) As is the father, so is the son. Herod the Great sought the life of Christ. Herod Antipas, his son, takes John's life. (3.) To reprove the sins of the great is a minister's duty, though it may lose him his life.

§ 64. THE TWELVE RETURN, AND JESUS RETIRES WITH THEM ACROSS THE LAKE. FIVE THOUSAND ARE FED.— *Capernaum and N. E. coast of the Lake of Galilee.*

Matt.	Mark.	Luke.	John.
14. 13-21	6. 30-44	9. 10-17	6. 1-14

13. *When Jesus heard of it*—i. e., of John's death and Herod's opinion of Himself. He seems to have been affected by the tale of John's death, and to have sought retirement also, from the notice and malice of Herod. Mark says, that He invited the twelve, who had just returned from their mission (see Mark 6. 30. Luke 9. 10), to retire with Him to rest *awhile*. They

14 And Jesus went forth, and saw a great multitude, and was moved with compassion toward them, and he healed their sick.

15 ¶ And when it was evening, his disciples came to him, saying, This is a desert place, and the time is now past; send the multitude away, that they may go into the villages, and buy themselves victuals.

16 But Jesus said unto them, They need not depart; give ye them to eat.

17 And they say unto him, We have here but five loaves, and two fishes.

18 He said, Bring them hither to me.

19 And he commanded the multitude to sit down on the grass; and took the five loaves and the two fishes, and, looking up to heaven, he blessed, and brake; and gave the loaves to *his* disciples, and the disciples to the multitude.

20 And they did all eat, and

i c.9.36; 15.32,&c. *j* He.4.5.

---

must withdraw from the multitude, in order to have time for a meal. He would also instruct them further for their work. From Luke 9. 10, we learn that He went to the vicinity of Bethsaida, known as Bethsaida (Julias).——¶ *A desert place*—thinly populated, on the east of the Sea of Galilee.——¶ *On foot*—as distinguished from His crossing in a boat—"by ship" (see Mark 6. 33). We learn from John 6. 4, that the "*passover* was nigh." Mark says, "there were many coming and going." Such incidental agreements are proofs of the narrations.

14. *Jesus went forth*—in public.—— ¶ *Moved with compassion.* The Greek term is "sympathy." They were doubtless fatigued by their travel, as we judge from its being mentioned that they had gone *on foot*—and this may be noticed in connexion with their having sick among them. Mark notes that His concern for them was, that they "were as sheep not having a shepherd" (Mark 6. 34). The *multitudes*, 5,000, besides women and children (vs. 21), affected Him. They were going to Jerusalem, to keep the feast. "He began to teach them many things" (Mark).

15. *The time is now past.* "It was evening." The day was far spent, and it became necessary to think of the multitudes as to their physical wants. They needed food

16. From John we learn, that Christ had said to Philip, "Whence shall we buy bread, that these may eat?" This was to lead Philip to consider the actual difficulty of providing for so many by human means. "This He said to prove him, for He Himself knew what he would do" (John 6. 6). Philip had expressed the impossibility, and Christ would have it confessed that 200 pennyworth would not suffice.——¶ *They need not depart; give ye them to eat.* A challenge to human power.

17. *But five loaves*—or, *cakes*, usually made in the form of thin biscuits, round, and generally something less than a foot in diameter (see John 6. 9). ——¶ *And two fishes.* All belonging to a lad in the crowd, which could be had, as Andrew ascertained (John 6. 8, 9).

19. *He blessed and brake.* He gave thanks to God, "looking up to heaven." So His followers are taught to receive their food, and our daily bread needs the Divine blessing. As the bread was not in loaves, like ours, but in cakes, it was broken.

20, 21. *Twelve baskets full.* Such baskets as the Jews usually carried with them on a journey, holding their food. There remained more than twelve times the amount that they had at first. This miracle consisted in so increasing the quantity that all were fed (perhaps 10,000 in all), and

A. D. 32.]   CHAPTER XIV.   161

were filled; and they took up of the fragments that remained twelve baskets full.ᵏ

21 And they that had eaten were about five thousand men, beside women and children.

22 ¶ And straightway Jesus constrained his disciples to get into a ship, and to go before him unto the other side, while he sent the multitudes away.

23 And when he had sent the multitudes away, he ˡ went up into a mountain apart to pray: and when the evening was come, he was there alone.

24 But the ship was now in the

k 2K.4.1-7.   l Mar.6.46.

---

more was left than they had at first. This was Divine power, the same as to create a world. John says, that they were convinced by this of His being the Messiah, and Divine (John 6. 14). "How much more (says Bengel) could *all* feed in the Sacred Supper, upon the same Lord." Our Lord thus proclaimed Himself the Bread of the world—the inexhaustible supply for all—only increasing upon the draught on its fulness, and yet showing such a superabundance left. "Yet there is room." "Of His fulness have all we received, and grace for grace" (John). Since there is "bread enough and to spare" in Christ's house, why should any perish with hunger? This was a repetition of Old Testament miracles. "He gave them bread from heaven to eat" (John 6. 30, 31). This was looked for from the Messiah, a prophet like unto Moses. See also Elijah's (2 Kings 4. 42-44) feeding one hundred men with twenty loaves of barley. So also the widow's cruise of oil and barrel of meal (1 Kings 17. 16), and again (2 Kings 4. 1-7). But these only prefigured Christ's. They were only hints of His. These were servants' works, on His authority. His were the works of the Master.

OBSERVE, (1.) Though our Lord would not make bread out of stones for His own hunger, or to meet the impious challenge of the tempter, yet He will make bread out of nothing for His followers' wants, and for proper witness to His work. (2.) "God's blessing through Christ multiplies our supplies, and the food which we eat comes from His grace."

—*Calvin*. (3.) *With Christ, our very leavings are more than all we had without Him.* (4.) Men ought indeed to believe, where they see what ample provisions Christ has for His people within His power, and how abundantly He supplies them. "This is of a truth that prophet that should come into the world." John 6. 14.

§ 65. JESUS WALKS UPON THE WATER.
—*Lake of Galilee. Gennesareth.*

Matt.	Mark.	Luke.	John.
14.22-36	6. 45-56		6.15-21

22. *Constrained*—urged, induced. The word is strong, and means *compelled*. John tells us that this was done because the men would take Him by force and make Him a king. —¶ *A ship*—"*the ship*." Mark.— ¶ *The other side*—i. e. of the Sea of Galilee, "toward Capernaum" (John) to Bethsaida—*not the town* of that name on the north-east coast, but the city of Andrew and Peter, near Capernaum. Philip was of this place.

23. *Apart*—alone, having directed the disciples to go into the ship, and having sent the multitudes away. Mark states that the disciples were ordered to Bethsaida, and there was a town of that name on the west coast.

24. *In the midst of the sea.* John says 25 or 30 furlongs out, or about four miles, reckoning 7½ Jewish furlongs to the mile: and his Sea of Galilee, or Tiberias, was no where three times that width. Christ's ever-watchful love beheld them at a distance, and even at night.

25. *Fourth watch.* The Jews, in the time of Christ, like the Romans,

14*

midst of the sea, tossed with waves: for the wind was contrary.

25 And in the fourth watch of the night Jesus went unto them, walking on the sea.

26 And ᵐ when the disciples saw him walking on the sea, they were troubled, ⁿ saying, It is a spirit; and they cried out for fear.

27 But straightway Jesus spake unto them, saying, Be ᵒ of good cheer; it is I; be not afraid.

28 And Peter answered him and said, Lord, if ᵖ it be thou, bid me come unto thee on the water.

29 And he said, Come. And when Peter was come down out of the ship, he walked on the water to go to Jesus.

30 But when he saw the wind ¹ boisterous, he was afraid; and beginning to sink, he cried, saying, Lord save me.ᵠ

31 And immediately ʳ Jesus stretched forth *his* hand, and

m Job 9.8. Jno.6.19. *n* Lu.24.37. *o* Ac.23.11
p Ph.4.13. 1 Or, *strong*. *q* Ps.69.1.2. La.3.57.
r Is.63.12.

---

divided the night into four watches—evening, midnight, cock-crowing, and morning. The first, from twilight to 9 o'clock; the second, from 9 to 12; the third, from 12 to 3; the fourth, from 3 to day-break. There were *two evenings*, as noted by Matthew and Mark; the first, our afternoon (vs. 15), the other, our twilight (vs. 23).

26. *They were troubled*—at the supernatural sight. Christ is often mistaken by His people when He comes in some unusual and alarming shape—in some affliction, or cross, or mercy. Now they feared not only the *sea*, but Christ the Lord. Mark adds: "For they considered not the miracle of the loaves, and their heart was hardened."

27. *Be of good cheer.* Be cheerful, not disturbed or afraid. This is the gospel message of *peace*, on the ground—the simple ground, "*It is I.*" Christ's presence is *peace* to the soul. "My peace I give unto you." His office work is our trust and rejoicing.

28. *If it be Thou.* This would not really express a doubt, but only in his agitated feeling, and impulsive zeal, would ask a word from Christ for his complete assurance. How perfectly does Christ's word of gospel grace, "*Come,*" embolden us at all times! Yet some make a mystery of even this, and hold back and perish.

29. *Come.* Our simple trust is to be in the *word* from Christ's lips. Christians do not sufficiently find their hope in the express language of the gospel. They build too much on other things, and hence have so little confidence to go forward, and so little steady and confirmed trust. Peter, it would seem, walked for a while on the water! Behold what grace in the Christian can do! What Christ's presence and word can accomplish for us and in us.

30. *But when he saw.* It was only when he saw something besides Christ, and had his fears aroused, that he began to sink. "He saw the wind boisterous and was afraid." How essential is it that we look not even at our own sins for discouragement, nor at Satan's accusations for despair, but so be taken up with Christ as not to be unnerved, even by the worst appearances. "*Lord save me,*" is the language of genuine prayer, prompted by a sense of need, and a sight of Christ at hand.

31. *Wherefore didst thou doubt?* Christ does not find fault with him for *coming*, but for *doubting*. It was not that he trusted the Master too much, but too little. So the Saviour complains never of our confidence, but only of our *diffidence*. Our faith should be firm, even on the troubled wave, when He is near. At once Christ showed His own all-sufficien-

caught him, and said unto him, O thou of little faith, wherefore didst thou doubt?*

32 And when they were come into the ship, the wind ceased. *t*

33 Then they that were in the ship came and worshipped him, saying, Of a truth thou art the Son of God.*u*

34 ¶ And *v* when they were gone over, they came into the land of Gennesaret.

35 And when the men of that place had knowledge of him, they sent out into all that country round about, and brought unto him all that were diseased;

36 And besought him that they might only touch the hem *w* of his garment; and as many *x* as touched were made perfectly whole.

---

s Ja.1.6. *t* Ps.107.29. *u* Da.3.25. Lu.4.41. Jno.1.49; 6.69; 11.27. Ac.8.37. Ro.1.4. *v* Mar.6.53.

w Nu.15.38. c.9.20 Mar.3.10. Lu.6.19. Ac.19.12. *x* Jno.6.37.

---

cy and Peter's groundless distrust. And even as He caught him, and while the terrified Apostle was yet in His arms, He expostulated with him at his doubting. So when Christ stretches forth His hand, and shows us His salvation, He makes us wonder that we could have doubted His power and grace at all.

32. *When they were come into the ship.* John says, "they willingly received Him," and on account of the wind abating, they came at once to port. Christ's getting in the ship was their salvation. He can both calm the tempest round us, and carry us safe to heaven.

33. *Worshipped Him.* "They that were in the ship," may mean the crew, who were moved by this display of Divine power over the elements (Psalm 77. 19. Hab. 3. 15). They were satisfied that He was God, and this was what He claimed to be. No mere man could have done this. And He both walked on the sea Himself, and saved Peter from sinking.

34. *Gennesaret.* This land or region of country was on the northwest shore of the Lake of Galilee, sometimes called the Lake of Gennesaret. John states that the disciples went to or about Capernaum, and Mark says that they were to go to Bethsaida on the west, which was a town in the land of Gennesaret. (See Map.) From John we learn (6. 25), that the people wondered how Christ came thither. They had seen the disciples go in the boat without Christ, and the storm would not have allowed His crossing afterward—"*for the wind was contrary*" (vs. 24). So the gospels explain each other. See *Blunt's Veracity.*

35, 36. Here the people expressed their confidence in Christ as divine, bringing to Him their sick for a cure. They were now persuaded that only *a touch* was requisite! And even at this they were *made perfectly whole.* It could not be in the *touch*, but in the fulness of *Christ.* See note, 9. 20.

OBSERVE, (1.) That when the disciples were in a situation to feel their helplessness, and perishing need of Him, He came near. So is it always. Here, too, He would show them the plan of His grace. Christ puts them forth unto the danger alone, even as some loving mother-bird thrusts her fledgelings from the nest, that they may find their own wings, and learn to use them.— *Trench.* "God is our refuge and strength, a very present help in trouble, therefore will not we fear." (2.) It is further taught that the church, though as that little bark upon the stormy sea, buffetted and struggling, and making little headway, and even ready to be swallowed up, is not lost sight of nor forsaken by Christ. In her extremity He does appear to save. *He descries her at a distance, and at*

CHAPTER XV.

THEN *a* came to Jesus Scribes and Pharisees, which were of Jerusalem, saying,

a Mar. 7. 1, &c.

2 Why do thy disciples transgress the tradition of the elders? for they wash not their hands when they eat bread.

night. "When the Lord shall build up Zion He will appear in His glory. He will regard the prayer of the destitute and not despise their prayer." He is on the mountain apart praying, ever living to make intercession for us. He suddenly appears in the time of urgent necessity, and anon the toiling rowers are at the haven where they would be.—*Trench.* Mark relates that "*He would have passed them by.*" This appearance of things to them, served only to draw out their entreaties. So is it often with the church. He never has an intent like this; for He will not depart from us to do us good, but He will often hide His face, or seem to *turn aside.* The bride must say, come! "Though Christ appeared at the proper time for rendering assistance, yet the storm did not immediately cease till *the disciples* were more fully aroused to desire and expect His grace."—*Calvin.* (3.) They who trust the more, are the more powerfully kept. They who have begun to trust in grace, says Bengel, can the less use nature. Peter feared. He had not thought to *swim,* but to *walk* to Christ, the Lord helping.

§ 66. Our Lord's Discourse to the multitude in the synagogue at Capernaum. Many Disciples turn back. Peter's profession of faith. *Capernaum.*

Matt.	Mark.	Luke.	John.
			6. 22–71 7. 1.

PART V.

From our Lord's third Passover until His final Departure from Galilee at the Feast of Tabernacles.

Time—six months.

CHAPTER XV.

§ 67. OUR LORD JUSTIFIES HIS DISCIPLES FOR EATING WITH UNWASHEN HANDS. Pharisaic traditions.—*Capernaum.*

Matt.	Mark.	Luke.	John.
15. 1–20	7. 1–23		

1. *Of Jerusalem.* The most distinguished of their body from Jerusalem came, probably, to watch and ensnare Him.

2. *Tradition of the Elders.* By the *Elders* here, is meant the ancients; and their "*tradition*" is what they *handed down;* any precept or custom as taught to them, and to be observed by their successors. The Jews held that there was an oral or verbal law, of indefinite antiquity, unwritten, but delivered by God to Moses, and by Moses to Joshua, and so down to their time. A collection of these they pretend to have in the Mishna, containing various precepts and customs of the *elders,* handed down as binding on their generations. This was one of the traditions: That it was unlawful to eat with unwashen hands. And one Rabbi asserted that neglect of washing was a greater sin than whoredom; another, that it was better to die than to omit it. *Traditions* cannot be of equal authority with *documents* written by inspiration, as the *Scriptures.* (See *Greenleaf on the Evangelists.* Appendix, No. 2.) The very existence and use of Scripture is to dispense with traditions.

3. *Why do ye?* Christ replied that these traditions were themselves unlawful, and violated the command-

3 But he answered and said unto them, Why do ye also transgress the commandment of God by your tradition?[b]

4 For God commanded, saying, [c] Honour thy father and mother: and, He [d] that curseth father or mother, let him die the death.

5 But ye say, Whosoever shall say to *his* father or *his* mother, *It is* a gift, by whatsoever thou mightest be profited by me:

6 And honour not [e] his father or his mother, *he shall be free.*

Thus have ye made the commandment of God of none effect by your tradition.

7 *Ye* hypocrites! well did Esaias prophesy of you, saying,

8 This [f] people draweth nigh unto me with their mouth, and honoureth me with *their* lips: but their heart is far from me.

9 But in vain they do worship me, teaching *for* doctrines [g] the commandments of men.

10 ¶ And he called the multitude, and said unto them, Hear, and understand:

[b] Col.2.8,23. Tit.1.14. [c] Ex.20.12. De.5.16. [d] Ex. 21.17. Le.20.9. [e] De.27.16.

[f] Is.29.13. [g] Col.2.22.

ments of God. He gives an instance as to the fifth commandment. Men are willing to make void God's law. They are prone to be governed more by current maxims than by Divine precepts. The use of traditions among men, is mostly to set *aside the Scriptures.*

4. *Honour.* This includes respect, obedience and support.——¶ *Curseth. Revileth.* (Exodus 21. 17. Levit. 20. 9.) God's law has always been most rigorous and severe against filial ingratitude or disrespect. The language is here the strongest possible, "denoting a capital punishment of the worst sort."—*Bloomfield.*——¶ *Let him die the death.* "Let him be put to death without mercy." God commanded. Exod. 20. 12–17. They pleaded for traditions, the honour due to their ancestry. Christ takes this very commandment on this point.

5. *A gift. Corban,* is the Hebrew word meaning *gift,* and Mark has the word as it is in Hebrew; that is, their word which they used. It means a consecrated offering, a thing devoted to God. When they put any thing out of their power for a sacred use, they called it *corban, dedicated.* And this tradition was, that they who, to avoid doing their parents a benefit, should say, as a pretext, that what they had and might help them with, was *corban,* that is, devoted to God, *should go free.* Thus they encouraged filial ingratitude and hypocrisy, by authorizing the use of a religious term, as a release from filial obligation.

7. *Hypocrites.* Because both in their zeal for forms of worship and in their pious pretensions for an excuse of pious actions they were full of hypocrisy. God hates filial ingratitude. Christ was a son. He hates vain worship.

8, 9. *People.* (Isa. 29. 13.) Though the prophet spoke of the Jews in his own time, his language still applied prophetically to these, for they were one with those ancient hypocrites. It was a prophecy, remotely, of their character as a nation. 1st. They were insincere and heartless in their worship. It was with their *lips*—no lack of profession and words. This made it more hypocritical as there was so little in deed and truth. 2d. They followed the commandments (or institutions, ordinances) of men, as the *doctrines* and law of God. "Their *fear toward me* is taught by the precept of men" (Isa. 29. 13). The commandments of God are to be distinguished from the traditions of men in this, that they are found in the Scripture. Traditions, however, are now enjoined and regarded as authoritative, by the Romish church.

11 Not ʰ that which goeth into the mouth defileth a man; but that which cometh out of the mouth, this defileth a man.

12 Then came his disciples, and said unto him, Knowest thou that the Pharisees were offended, after they heard this saying?

13 But he answered and said, Every plant ⁱ which my heavenly Father hath not planted, shall be rooted up.

14 Let them alone: they ʲ be blind leaders of the blind. And if the blind lead the blind, both shall fall into the ditch.

15 Then answered Peter, and said unto him, Declare unto us this parable.

16 And Jesus said, Are ye also yet without understanding?

17 Do not ye yet understand, that whatsoever entereth in at the mouth ᵏ goeth into the belly, and is cast out into the draught?

18 But those things which proceed out of the mouth come forth from the heart; and they defile the man.

19 For ˡ out of the heart proceed evil thoughts, murders, adulteries, fornications, thefts, false witness, blasphemies:

h Ac. 10.15. Ro. 14.14–20. 1Tim, 4.4. Tit.1.15.
i Jno.15.2,6. *j* c.23.16. Lu.6.39.

k Lu.6.45. Ja.3.6. *l* Ge.6.5; 8.21. Pr.6.14; 24.9. Je.17.9. Ro.3.10–19. Ga.5.19–21. Ep.2.3. Tit.3.3.

Their error is, that they set up something as binding on the conscience and practice which God has not enjoined, and these usually have the effect to set aside the precepts of revelation. The word of God in the scriptures of the Old and New Testament is the only infallible rule of faith and practice.

11, 12. Christ here states a general truth, that it is not the *eating* or *not*, in itself, which is the moral pollution, but something from within the man; that is, that sin is not *from without*, a thing of externals and ceremonies, of contact and observance, or uncleanness of the flesh, but a thing of the *heart*. The source of all our corruption is in the evil nature within. Yet Pharisees and proud formalists of every age are offended at this sentiment.

13, 14. As they were offended, and the disciples seem to have been disturbed by this (vs. 12), Christ took occasion to lay down this doctrine: that only the truth can ultimately triumph, and that such a course of infatuation and delusion as the Pharisees pursued, would issue in ruin. Christians need not be over-much concerned, nor make battle always upon error. Blind leading the blind are doomed to the ditch. Errorists are offended at being exposed. But error must ultimately fail.——¶ *Ditch*, or *pit*, such as was dug for holding rain water.

15. *This parable*—or *saying*, viz.: this last about meats. "*When He was entered into the house* (says Mark) *from the people, His disciples asked Him*"—especially Peter, who was deeply attached to the law and its injunctions.

16, 17. *Are ye also yet*, &c. Mark has it, "Are ye *so* without understanding also?" Christ means to represent by this distinction, that the pollution of sin comes from the heart, and not from outside distinctions of clean and unclean, washings, &c.

19. *Out of the heart*. These dreadful sins have their origin in the heart. They spring from depraved principles deeply seated within. An evil *nature in us*, is the root of all corruption. All evil is there before it breaks out into acts.——¶ *Evil thoughts*. The word means reasonings or "*contrivances.*"—*Campbell*. This is a general declaration that actual transgressions, of all kinds, even the most horrid and malignant, come from this seat in the bosom. Who can deny

20 These are *the things* which defile a man: but to eat with unwashen hands defileth not a man.

21 ¶ Then^m Jesus went thence, and departed into the coasts of Tyre and Sidon.

22 And, behold, a woman of Canaan came out of the same coasts, and cried unto him, saying, Have mercy on me, O Lord, *thou* son of David! ⁿ my daughter is grievously vexed with a devil.

23 But he answered her not a word. ᵒ And his disciples came and besought him, saying, Send her away, for she crieth after us.

24 But he answered and said, ᵖ I am not sent, but unto the lost sheep of the house of Israel.

m Mar.7.24. *n* Lu.18.38,39. *o* Ps.28.1. La.3.8. *p* c.10.5,6. Ac.3.28.

---

man's native depravity, or that it is entire?

20. *These are*, &c. The natural state of the human heart is desperately wicked, "deceitful above all things," an unknown depth of iniquity. Evil acts have their character from the inward tempers. Bad deeds springing from an evil nature are the real defilement. Such being the disease, the remedy must be Divine and Omnipotent. No power but that which made the soul, can renew its fallen nature. We are urged by this to an immediate seeking of Christ for the new birth—"Create in me a clean heart, O God" (Psalm 51). It is not man's will that renews, for it is the will *that is renewed*. "Thy people shall be *willing*." "Born, not of blood, nor of the will of the flesh, nor of the will of man, but of God" (John 1).

Observe, (1.) The maxims that sanction filial ingratitude or disrespect, God especially hates. The Apostle notes it as a mark of perilous times, when youth *shall be disobedient to parents* (2 Tim. 3. 1), and yet he prophecies that in the last days such times "*shall come.*" Wo to the children of such a character. (2.) Men may adopt a religion of rites and vows, even, to escape a religion of the heart and life, and these hate Christ's doctrine, which exposes them. But the true religion will at length prevail. (3.) So far from all sin consisting in acts, all acts of evil have their sinfulness in the heart.

§ 68. The daughter of a Syrophenician woman is healed.—*Region of Tyre and Sidon.*

Matt.	Mark.	Luke.	John.
15. 21–28	7. 24–30		

21. *The coasts of Tyre and Sidon.* These cities were of Phenicia, in the north-west part of Palestine, on the sea-coast. They were in the northwest direction from Jerusalem, and distant from it some 90 to 100 geographical miles. He departed to the confines (or "borders," Mark) of that heathen country.

22. *A woman of Canaan.* Mark calls her a Greek, and says she was "a Syrophenician by nation" (among whom she dwelt); that is, from Phenicia, which was connected with the province of Syria, under the Roman government: yet a *Canaanite*, that is, belonging to the people of Canaan. The country was taken by Alexander the Great, and in the time of Christ, these were Greek cities. They called all foreign nations Greeks. Our Lord's fame was abroad in Syria (4. 24). Attention is here called to her nation, because this is a remarkable instance of grace to the Gentiles. It appears from Mark that He had gone into a house, wishing not to be known; *But the ointment bewrayeth itself.*—— ¶ *Came out of.* For Christ did not enter those coasts.

24. *I am not sent but unto*, &c. He meant that His mission was first of all to the Jews, rather than to the Gentiles, of which she was one. (Comp. ch. 10, 5 and 6.) This refer-

25 Then came she, and worshipped him, saying, Lord, help me!

26 But he answered and said, It is not meet to take the children's bread, and to cast *it* to dogs.*q*

27 And she said, Truth, Lord: yet the dogs eat of the crumbs

_{*q* c.7.6. Re.22.15.}

which fall from their masters table.

28 Then *r* Jesus answered and said unto her, O woman, great *is* thy faith, be *s* it unto thee even as thou wilt. And her daughter was made whole from that very *t* hour.

_{*r* Job 13.15; 23.10. La.3.32. *s* Ps.145.19. *t* Jno. 4.50-53.}

---

red to His own personal ministry on earth. (Rom. 15. 8, 9.)

25. *Worshipped Him*, &c. She promptly paid Him divine honour, and acknowledged Him as *Lord*. This was remarkable for a Gentile.

26. *It is not meet*, or proper.——¶ *The children's bread.* The Jews' peculiar privileges. They were ranked as the *children* of God—His peculiar people—His house. The gospel blessings were termed *their bread*, not to be wasted upon others; and as compared with them, the Gentiles are here termed *dogs* (See Psalm 87. 6). See the commission to the twelve: "Go rather to the lost sheep of the house of Israel," not to the *Samaritans* (10. 5, 6). This was designed not merely to test and draw out her earnestness and faith, but also to show the true order of His work. He would not vex her, but He would call public attention to the fact that she was a heathen and that His work was first with the Jews, yet not so as utterly to exclude the Gentiles, but to receive them by faith.

27. *Truth, Lord.* "Certainly, let the Jews have the *children's bread;* this will not prevent my getting the crumbs, if I am a dog, as is true also." Or the rendering may be, "*I beseech Thee, Lord, for indeed the dogs,*" &c. See Phil. 3. 2. Rev. 22. 15. Be it so, that I am a dog, and let me be served as such, with *the leavings* or *the overflowings.*

28. *Great is thy faith.* He pronounced her confidence uncommon, notable! It persevered so. It hoped against hope. It would take no denial. Mark has it: "*for this saying*, *go thy way*, the devil is gone out of thy daughter." He who said, "I will not let Thee go except Thou bless me," was called by that peculiar name, "*Israel,*" "*a Prince of God.*" He is not a Jew who is one outwardly. This is the true Israel. This case illustrated to the people the precise relations of Christ's work. Here, as with the Centurion and the Samaritan leper, He hinted that the Gentiles would more readily receive the gospel than the Jews. Strong faith prevails with God for Christ's sake, and lo! the faithful Gentiles are now of Abraham's seed, and heirs according to the promise.

OBSERVE, (1.) That Christ doth sometimes delay to return an answer to a well-qualified prayer. Sometimes His people do not pray earnestly enough. Sometimes they pray too earnestly for an outward and temporal mercy. Sometimes the mercy they pray for is not good for them, or may be is not *yet* good for them. Let us not then judge of God's hearing prayer by His present answer (vs. 23). (2.) Christ puts the strongest faith of His own children upon the severest trials. The trial had never been so sharp if her faith had not been so strong.—*Burkitt*. He who seemed to *repel*, in words, still *drew* her by His Spirit. (3.) Christ loves to be followed with faith and importunity. (4.) Humility grants the very worst as to our case, and yet the faith in Christ triumphs.

A.D. 32.] CHAPTER XV. 169

29 And ᵘ Jesus departed from thence, and came nigh unto the sea of Galilee; and went up into a mountain, and sat down there.

30 And great multitudes came unto him, having with them *those that were* lame, blind, dumb, maimed, and many others, and cast them down at Jesus' feet; and he healed them;ᵛ

31 Insomuch that the multitude wondered, when they saw the dumb to speak, the maimed to be whole, the lame to walk, and the blind to see: and they glorified the God of Israel.

32 ¶ Then ʷ Jesus called his disciples *unto him*, and said, I have compassion on the multitude because they continue with me now three days, and have nothing to eat: and I will not send them away fasting, lest they faint in the way.

33 And ˣ his disciples say unto him, Whence should we have so much bread in the wilderness, as to fill so great a multitude?

34 And Jesus saith unto them, How many loaves have ye? And they said, Seven, and a few little fishes.

35 And ʸ he commanded the multitude to sit down on the ground.

36 And he took the seven loaves and the fishes, and ᶻ gave thanks, and brake *them*, and gave to his disciples, and the disciples to the multitude.

37 And they did all eat, and were filled; and they took up of the broken *meat* that was left seven baskets full.

38 And they that did eat were four thousand men, beside women and children.

39 And he sent away the mul-

---
u Mar.7.31. *v* Ps.103.3. Is.35.5,6. *w* Mar.8.1, &c.

x 2K.4.43,44. *y* c.14.19,&c. *z* 1Sa.9.13. Lu.22. 19; 24.30.

---

§ 69. A DEAF AND DUMB MAN HEALED—also many others. FOUR THOUSAND ARE FED *The Decapolis. Sea of Galilee, same as Tiberias or Gennesaret.*

Matt.	Mark.	Luke.	John.
15.29–39	7. 31–37 8. 1–9		

29. *Jesus departed.* Mark says that from the borders of Tyre and Sidon, He came through the midst of the coasts of Decapolis, that is, in the district of those "*ten cities*," and around the Sea of Galilee.

30. *Cast them down.* The crowds that brought their sick to be healed, took this method with them—casting them down at Jesus' feet, throwing them entirely upon His power and grace for the cure.——¶ *And He healed them.* What numbers were compassed in this operation! The multitude were with Him "*three days*" (Mark 8. 2). Mark narrates one notable case among the many, *a deaf and dumb man*, whose amazing cure astonished the people!

31. *When they saw.* His miracles wrought such an effect upon beholders, that they glorified the God of Israel. Such evidence it was to which our Lord referred John's disciples. (See ch. 11. 4, 5.)

37. The miracle here consisted in a miraculous provision. The disciples had expressed their surprize at any such idea as the feeding of so many on so little, and it was a work as much beyond human power, as creating something out of nothing. They had already forgotten the previous miracle of five thousand (ch. 14. 15). How soon we forget our deliverances, and the resources of grace.

titude, and took ship, and ᵃ came into the coasts of Magdala.

CHAPTER XVI.

THE Pharisees also with the Sadducees came and tempting, desired him that he would shew them a sign ᵃ from heaven.

2 He answered and said unto them, When it is evening, ye say, *It will be* fair weather; for the sky is red:

3 And in the morning, *It will be* foul weather to-day: for the sky is red and lowering. O ye hypocrites! ye can discern the face of the sky; but can ye not

a Mar.8.10. *a* c.12,38,&c. Mar.8.11,&c. Lu.11. 16; 12.54-56. 1Cor.1.22.

discern the signs of the times?

4 A wicked and adulterous generation seeketh after a sign : and there shall no sign be given unto it, but the sign of the prophet Jonas.ᵇ And he left them, and departed.

5 ¶And when his disciples were come to the other side, they had forgotten to take bread.

6 Then Jesus said unto them, ᶜ Take heed, and beware of the leaven ᵈ of the Pharisees and of the Sadducees.

7 And they reasoned among

b Jon.1.17. *c* Lu.12.1. *d* 1Cor.5.6-8. Ga.5.9. 2Tim.2.16,17.

---

39. *Coasts of Magdala.* The *coasts* here means the *regions* round about. Mark says, He came to the *parts* of Dalmanutha. These towns adjoined. It was to the vicinity of these towns, probably on the west coast of the sea, as judged by the latest authorities. From the Decapolis, which was on the *east*, He took ship to reach them.

CHAPTER XVI.

§ 70. THE PHARISEES AND SADDUCEES REQUIRE A SIGN.—*Near Magdala.*

Matt.	Mark.	Luke.	John.
16. 1-4	8. 10-12		

1. All parties now demanded some special, visible token from heaven. It was an unreasonable demand, and this they did "*tempting* Him," that is, *trying* Him. From Mark we learn that they disputed with Him.

3. *Foul weather*—stormy, tempestuous.——¶ *Hypocrites.* See note, ch. 6. 2.——¶ *Discern the face of the sky*, i. e., they could judge of the weather. This they did, too, from appearances founded on observation. He asks if they cannot perceive what is going on and coming to pass around them, by watching the aspects of things.

4. *A wicked and adulterous generation.* It is the character of such an evil generation to seek a sign. He referred to their generation (the Jews)

and to their own evil intent in making such a demand. (See note, Matt. 12. 38-40.)——¶ *Sign of the prophet Jonas.* (See on 12. 39.)

§ 71. THE DISCIPLES CAUTIONED AGAINST THE LEAVEN OF THE PHARISEES AND SADDUCEES.—*North-east coast of the Lake of Galilee.*

Matt.	Mark.	Luke.	John.
16. 5-12	8. 13-21		

5. *The other side*, i. e., of the lake or sea. See Mark. They had been on the west side, and now came to the north-east coast.——¶ *To take bread*. i. e., they had neglected to take a supply. They had but one loaf, as we learn from Mark.

6. *Take heed, and beware.* This repetition of terms is emphatic.—— ¶ *Leaven of the Pharisees.* Mark adds, *and of the leaven of Herod.* The Jews were well acquainted with this simile. Leaven was in certain cases to be carefully put out of their houses. (See Exod. 13. 7.) It was used in making bread, to swell the flour and make it puff and light. It was very silent and effectual in its working. It would finally ferment and pervade the whole mass. "A little leaven leaveneth the whole lump." Under this familiar figure therefore, He represents the *doctrines* of these power-

[A. D. 32.] CHAPTER XVI. 171

themselves, saying, *It is* because we have taken no bread.

8 *Which* when Jesus perceived, he said unto them, *e* O ye of little faith, why reason ye among yourselves, because ye have brought no bread?

9 Do ye not yet understand, neither remember the five *f* loaves of the five thousand, and how many baskets ye took up?

10 Neither the seven *g* loaves of the four thousand, and how many baskets ye took up?

11 How is it that ye do not understand, that I spake *it* not to you concerning bread, that ye should beware of the leaven of the Pharisees and of the Sadducees?

12 Then understood they how that he bade *them* not beware of the leaven of bread, but of the doctrine *h* of the Pharisees and of the Sadducees.

13 ¶ When Jesus came into the coasts of Cesarea Philippi,

e c.6.30; 8.26; 14.31. *f* c.14.19,&c. *g* c.15. 34, &c.

h c.15.1-9.

ful sects who were false teachers. (vs. 12.)

7. *Because we have taken no bread.* They supposed the caution somehow connected with their lack of a supply, and perhaps as warning them against using bread made by such.

8. *O ye of little faith.* Their thoughts ran altogether upon their temporal supply, and so they misapplied His teachings. For this He rebukes them. His cautions are not of this kind. If they had full faith on this point, they would not have mistaken His word. "Have ye your heart yet hardened?" Mark 8. 17.

9. *Neither remember.* Mark represents Christ as questioning them on the miracles of feeding the multitudes. They should have remembered those miracles so appropriate to their case, and they should have felt at ease on this subject of a supply.

See 14. 15-21, and 15. 22-38. Past experience should give us confidence. Temporal anxieties will often lead us to mistake God's word. "I will remember the years of the right hand of the Most High."

11. *The leaven of the Pharisees* and Sadducees, had reference to their insidious but powerful efforts at spreading false doctrine. A little of it mixed with the mass soon *works, spreads,* and pervades the whole lump.

12. *The doctrine of the Pharisees* and Sadducees, was their false teaching about true religion, formal and carnal: the one, not believing in regeneration: the other, not holding to the resurrection, and departing altogether from the truth as it is in Jesus. So we are to guard against the *beginnings* of error. The influence of it will be gradual and silent, but mischievous and pervasive in our minds.

| § 72. A blind man healed.—*Bethsaida (Julias)*. . . . . | Matt. | Mark. 8. 22-26. | Luke. | John. |

§ 73. PETER AND THE REST AGAIN PROFESS THEIR FAITH IN CHRIST. (See § 66.)—*Region of Cesarea Philippi.*

| Matt. 16. 13-20 | Mark. 8. 27-30 | Luke. 9. 18-21 | John. |

13. *Coasts of Cesarea Philippi.* So called to distinguish it from Cesarea on the Mediterranean coast, and in honour of the Roman emperor Tiberius Cesar, and of Philip the tetrarch, son of Herod, who enlarged it. It was in Naphtali, near the ancient Dan, and was formerly called *Paneas.* The "coasts" here means the vicinities. Mark has it, "the *towns* of" or adjacent to this—in this district, of which it was the chief city.——¶ *He asked his disciples.* Mark says it was on the journey—"by the way;" Luke

he asked his disciples, saying, Whom ¹ do men say that I, the Son of man, am?

14 And they said, ʲ Some *say that thou art* John the Baptist; some, Elias; and others, Jeremias, or one of the prophets.

15 He saith unto them, But whom say ye that I am?

16 And Simon Peter answered and said ᵏ Thou art the Christ, the Son of the living God.

i Mar.8.27. Lu.9.18,&c. *j* c.14.2. Lu.9.7-9. *k* Ps. 2.7. c.14.33. Jno.1.49. Ac.9.20. He.1.2,5.

17 And Jesus answered and said unto him, Blessed art thou, Simon Barjona: for ˡ flesh and blood hath not revealed *it* unto thee, but ᵐ my Father which is in heaven.

18 And I say also unto thee, That thou art Peter;ⁿ and ᵒ upon this rock I will build my church; and the gates ᵖ of hell shall not prevail ᑫ against it.

l 1Cor.2.10. Ga.1.6. Ep.2.8. *m* 1Jno.4.15; 5.20. *n* Jno.1.42. *o* Ep.2.20. Re.21.14. *p* Ps.9.13. *q* Is. 54.17.

---

says it was as He was alone with them, praying, that He asked the question. On His way, it would seem, He had retired to pray, and then had put this query to them, to test and confirm their knowledge of Him.——¶ *Son of man.* He calls Himself by this name, because this was the point of the mystery of which He would ask them—"God manifest in the flesh."

14. *John the Baptist*—i. e., risen from the dead! This was Herod's thought! This supernatural rising of the beheaded John, whom they counted as a prophet, would seem to explain his miracles and mighty works to some, as to Herod; and Christ appeared among them after John had deceased——¶ *Jeremias.* The Greek mode of writing *Jeremiah.* It was one of the Jewish traditions that he would appear when the Messiah came.

16. *Simon Peter*—here showed the forwardness of his faith and zeal.—— ¶ *The Christ*, &c.—i. e., *the Anointed*, meaning the same in Greek as *the Messiah* in Hebrew. Mark has it, "Thou art the Christ;" Luke has it, "Thou art the Christ of God."—— ¶*Son of the living God.* This expressed His Divinity. Christ had just called Himself the *Son of man.* Peter declares their conviction that ·he was also the *Son of the living God!* As truly then as He was *a man* before them, did they believe Him to *be God*. "The living God" was a term used in the Old Testament to distinguish Jehovah from dead idols (Jer. 10. 9, 10, &c.). This, therefore, expressed a full belief in Christ as the promised Messiah. This was the point which Christ aimed at in His inquiry. But when believing in Christ is spoken of, more than this is meant. We must *receive His merits for our own souls, and trust in His atoning blood.*

17. *Barjona*—means the son of Jona. The word *bar* is Syriac, signifying *son.* Peter's father was named Jona, or Jonas (John 1. 42; 21. 16, 17). "Simon, son of Jonas."—— ¶ *Flesh and blood*—i. e., human means. It was not natural, or of human agency, that this truth of the Divine Messiahship of Christ had been disclosed to Him. "Born, not of blood, nor of the will of the flesh, nor of the will of man, *but of God*" (John 1. 13). So in 1 Cor. 2. 12, "We have received, not the spirit of the world, but the Spirit which is of God, that we might know the things that are freely given to us of God." Christ has declared, that thus to know Him is eternal life (John 17. 3).

18. *And I say also unto thee.* In return to this language of Peter, calling Him *the Christ*, He calls this apostle "a stone," as in John 1. 42. This name, Peter, or *Cephas*, as the word is in Syriac (both meaning *stone*), had been given to the apostle at his conversion, with reference to this confession of his faith, and to the work he should perform (John 1. 42).——

A. D. 32.]   CHAPTER XVI.   173

19 And I will give unto thee the keys of the kingdom of heaven; and whatsoever ʳ thou shalt bind on earth, shall be bound in heaven; and whatsoever thou shalt loose on earth, shall be loosed in heaven.

20 Then ˢ charged he his dis-

ʳ c. 18. 18.   ˢ Mar. 8. 30.

¶ *Upon this rock.* Not upon *thee*, nor upon *this Peter*—but (with the term now in a different gender—*petra*—keeping the sense, but shifting the subject) upon this *doctrine*—this *confession of faith*, as the foundation truth, will I build *my church.* As in 1 Cor. 3. 11, "Other foundation can no man lay than that is laid, which is Jesus Christ." It could not refer to Peter, personally or officially, for in no sense could he be the foundation to build upon—a *founder* even, is not the *foundation.* Yet the *allusion* is to Peter, and the sense is—UPON THIS DOCTRINE, CONFESSED AND PREACHED, will I build my church—alluding to Peter's prominent part in preaching the gospel to Jews and Gentiles, and gathering a visible Christian church. This corresponds precisely with the great apostolic commission, "Go ye into all the world, and *preach the gospel* to every creature;" and the promise annexed here, "the gates of hell shall not prevail against it," agrees entirely with Christ's parting promise, "Lo, I am with you alway"—and "All power is given unto me in heaven and on earth" (Matt. 28. 18–20). As to Peter's work, this indicated the part he should have in Providence, and not any *primacy* or prerogative among the apostles. He first planted the church among the Jews, after Christ's resurrection, by his preaching at Pentecost, where the first thousands were gathered in (Acts 2. 41–47), and he carried the gospel to the Gentiles, and founded the Gentile church. (See the conversion of Cornelius, Acts 10. 5; 15. 7.) Peter does not claim to have been the foundation, personally or officially. He himself gives this honour to Christ (1 Pet. 2. 6, 7). We read nothing in Scripture, even in the Acts of the Apostles, of such a primacy. The true and only foundation to build upon is Jesus Christ (1 Cor. 3. 11. Eph. 2. 20), upon whom apostles and prophets are built, and all Christians. ——¶ *The gates of hell.* As in the walled cities of old, the gates were the places of concourse for public business, the word is here used for *counsels, enterprises, combinations,* and so the phrase means the schemes and powers of hell, &c.

19. *The keys.* A key is that which keeps the door, opening it or locking it. I will make thee the instrument of opening the door of the kingdom to the Gentiles (Acts 10). The act was *future.* Christ would soon devolve the authority in the visible church upon the twelve, and all its affairs for the establishment and government of the church visible.——¶ *And whatsoever thou shalt bind.* This language, in ch. 18. 18, is addressed to the *twelve.* As Christ gave the keys to them at the Ascension, and not to Peter alone, so we find them charged there to "preach the gospel" which they professed, and to exercise this official authority in the visible church. Disciple all nations—baptize—bind and loose. As Peter answered for the twelve, so he might be addressed for the twelve, as having a certain prominence. He was first to preach to the Jews after Christ's death (Acts 2. 14), and to the Gentiles (Acts 10). Peter answered for all the apostles, as Christ had asked, "Whom say *ye* that I am?" The *binding* and *loosing* refers to the ministerial authority in Christ's house, common to Peter with the rest of the twelve, and all Christian ministers. As Christ had just spoken of building His church, this visible body would require government, for which He here provides. So Peter addresses his fellow-ministers (1 Pet. 5. 1), " The elders or Presbyters which are among you, I exhort, who am also a *presbyter* (as the word is), Feed the

15*

ciples, that they should tell no man that he was Jesus the Christ.

21 ¶ From *t* that time forth began Jesus to shew unto his

t Lu.9.22; 18.31; 24.6,7. 1Cor.15.3,4.

flock of God," &c., as a *pastor*. The terms *binding* and *loosing* were commonly in use to denote *forbidding* and *allowing*. They should have authority to found and govern the Christian church on earth, prescribing and prohibiting according to Divine direction, and so their acts should have Divine authority (see Acts 15. 20). This binding and loosing extended to *things*, as doctrine and discipline Acts 10. 28, and 21. 24), and to *persons* (John 20. 23). In ch. 18. 18, a case is given, and the church court is thus spoken of. But we find James' advice taken rather than Peter's. He could not have been regarded as necessarily Head, and less, an infallible Head (see Gal. 2. 11). Christ calls him *Satan*, immediately after! Alas, too fallible was Peter! The *stone* can soon become a *stumbling-block*. Put before Christ, it stands in His way, and must *get behind Him*.

20. *Then charged He*, &c. After this very special conversation, He thought fit to enjoin upon them secrecy respecting His Messiahship, which they had admitted. It was not that He wished now to promulgate it, that He had inquired for men's opinions and theirs. He wished to confirm them in the great truth, but the time had not come for its open dissemination. The Jews would only seek His life, and their malice would only hinder His work.

OBSERVE, (1.) The authority given to Christ's ministers in the Church, is based upon the confession of Christ in His person and offices, as the truth is in Jesus. Hence the true and only succession of the ministry cannot be traced independently of this requisite (vss. 16 and 17). (2.) Grace from Heaven is essential to this ministerial work, even before office (vs. 17).

disciples, how that he must go unto Jerusalem, and suffer many things of the elders and chief priests, and scribes, and be killed, and be raised again the third day.

22 Then Peter took him, and

(3.) Christian doctrine is the stability of the Christian Church (vs. 18). (4.) The government of the Church comes from Christ, as the Head, and looks for the ratification of its acts in Heaven (vs. 19).

§ 74. OUR LORD FORETELLS HIS OWN DEATH AND RESURRECTION, AND THE TRIALS OF HIS FOLLOWERS.— *Region of Cesarea Philippi.*

Matt.	Mark.	Luke.	John.
16. 21–28	8. 31–38 9. 1	9.22–27	

21. *From that time forth.* Having now signified to them their office-work, He speaks of His own, and would have them understand what was to come. This language calls attention to the fact that now, for the first, He discloses to His disciples the particulars of His cruel death. This belongs to the year 32, in His 33d year, some nine months before His death.——¶ *Elders and chief priests and Scribes*, as of the Sanhedrim. See note, 5. 22. He showed these things to them beforehand, that when they should come to pass, their faith in His Divine character and claims might be most fully established (John 13. 19). He had always known all that was to happen (John 18. 14), and He could have avoided death if He had so preferred. It was entirely a voluntary offering of Himself. " Lo I come." This proved His love to men, that He should have willingly laid down His life. " Therefore doth my Father love me, because I lay down my life that I might take it again."

22. *Then Peter took Him*, &c. The word is expressive, having the same force as our word *assume*.——¶ To *rebuke* is to blame, and here, to *reply harshly*. We have his language, de-

began to rebuke him, saying, 1 Be it far from thee, Lord: this shall not be unto thee.

23 But he turned, and said unto Peter, Get thee behind me, Satan; u thou art an offence v unto me: for thou savourest not the things that be of God, but those that be of men.

24 ¶ Then said Jesus unto his disciples, If any w man will come after me, let him deny himself, and take up his cross, and follow me.

25 For x whosoever will save his life shall lose it: and whosoever will lose his life for my sake, shall find it.

26 For what is a man profited, if he shall gain the whole world,

1 *Pity thyself.* u 2Sa.19.22. v Ro.14.13.

w c.10.33. Mar.8.34. Lu.9.23; 14.27. Ac.14.22. 1Th.3.3. x Jno.12.25. Est.4.14.

---

claring what Christ had said impossible, and vouching that it should not come to pass. Peter said this, doubtless, because of his surprize at such a statement, and because he thought he could warrant its not occurring, as he afterward offered to lay down his own life for Christ. The Apostles did not know before this, these particulars of Christ's death.——¶ *Be it far from thee*, (ἵλεώς) translated Heb. 8. 12, "*merciful.*" It is an exclamation invoking mercy. Let God in mercy avert such a thing.

23. *Satan.* This word means an *accuser*, an *adversary*, and so Christ applies it here, intimating that Peter knows not his own heart in all this, but accuses and contradicts Christ with something of Satan in him, that shall yet appear in connexion with this very event of His crucifixion. He orders him to stand back and not to interrupt or cross His designs. So He ordered Satan himself (ch. 4. 10) to get behind Him. See also John 6. 70.——¶ *Offence.* This word means a *stumbling-block.* Bengel remarks, it is an antithesis to the name just given him, ' *a stone.*' You are now *a stone in my way.* All this outcry of Peter against such an event, is in truth against the plan of Christ's great work, for which He came into the world.——¶ *Thou savourest not.* Thou *mindest* not the things Divine and spiritual, but the things human and carnal. He did not discern as yet the mystery of the cross.

24. *Then.* The doctrines of the cross are not the things of men, but of God. Christ took this opportunity to lay down the requisitions of discipleship—denial and perseverance. He was to suffer indeed for them. They were to suffer with Him. It was not to be a life of ease. Christians are called the followers of Christ, as His disciples and adherents. "*Follow me*," was the call to each of them. To forsake all and follow Him, was the substance of duty, to take Him instead of all things else.——¶ *Deny himself.* Sacrifice your self-indulgence, give up worldly ease, labour and suffer, and endure reproach, if need be. "Even Christ pleased not Himself" (Rom. 15. 3). The same word is used for Peter's *denying* Christ—disclaim, disown.——¶ *Take up his cross.* Cheerfully bear all the burdens of Christ's service, as they come, *daily.*

25. He that has for his object to *spare himself*, shall be at last the loser, and shall sacrifice himself, while he that spares not himself, but gives up his own will and pleasure for Christ, shall have salvation. By losing one's life for Christ's sake, is meant the enduring of all personal sacrifice and loss, "not counting his life dear," and "*counting all things* but loss" (Phil. 3. 8), and laying down one's life even, for Christ. Many of the first disciples actually lost their lives for Christ's sake.——¶ *Shall find it.* Bengel remarks, that the soul which is saved is *found.*

26. *For what is a man profited?* Christ here passes to estimate the profit and loss. To *lose* the soul, is to lose all the opportunities of its sal-

and lose his own soul? or *y* what shall a man give in exchange for his soul?

27 For *z* the Son of man shall come in the glory of his Father, with his angels, and *a* then he

y Ps.49.7,8. *z* Da.7.9,10. Zec.14.15. Jude 14. *a* Re.22.12.

shall reward every man according to his works.

28 Verily I say unto you. There *b* be some standing here which shall not taste *c* of death, till they see the Son of man coming in his kingdom.

b Mar.9.1. *c* He.2.9.

vation, and die eternally. This will be the result, if Christ is not followed, because He is *the way and the truth and the life* (John 14. 6). And of course the soul is more valuable than the world, because even with all that a man can have of the world, he cannot enjoy any thing here if his soul be in distress. And the soul will live forever, after all that is of earth has passed away. So that if a man should possibly gain all the world (which men would like to do, but cannot), he could keep it only for a few years at longest. And if his soul is lost, it is lost for ever and ever. A man runs great risk of losing his soul if he loves the world, because his heart cannot be set upon two opposite objects at a time. "Where the treasure is, there will the heart be also" Mat. 6. 21). He cannot serve God and mammon. And one that is devoted to worldliness and in pursuit of its joys, cannot follow Christ, or seek his soul's concerns. "If any man love the world, the love of the Father is not in him."—¶ *Give in exchange for his soul?* To redeem it, buy it back. The word means, give as *a ransom*. No man can redeem his own soul, and "none can by any means redeem his brother, or give to God a ransom for him."

27. *The Son of man.* This points to the judgment, and refers to Christ's *exaltation*, as an offset to all His humiliation which so *offended* Peter. The Lord Jesus Christ, who has an interest in men and is related to our nature, has "authority given Him to execute judgment because He is the Son of man." The works of people are to be brought up in the day of judgment, that every mouth may be stopped, and that God's justice may be

fully vindicated. Men will be rewarded *according* to their works. They shall receive such a measure of retribution and reward as will comport with their respective works, the strictest equity being observed in every case. "We must all appear (on that day) before the judgment seat of Christ."
—¶ *The glory.* Christ here opened to their view His future and final glory, that they might not despond at His coming death.

28. This verse gives a hint of the *transfiguration* which was about to take place, when Peter, James, and John should see Christ in His glory so soon, for their encouragement. Peter speaks of that sight (2 Pet. 1. 16), as "the power and COMING of our Lord Jesus Christ," when they were eye-witnesses of His majesty.—¶ *Not taste of death.* A Hebraic idiom for *shall not die.*—¶ *In His kingdom.* Mark has it: "Till they have seen the kingdom of God come with power." Luke reads it: "Till they see the kingdom of God."

OBSERVE, (1.) We more readily receive the doctrine of Christ's *person* than that of His *cross*. Peter could profess Christ as the *Son*, but not as the *sacrifice*. (2.) OFFICE in the church is nothing but an offence without Christian doctrine and conduct. (3.) The doctrines of the cross are not of men, but of God, and those sentiments which spring from men's own wisdom and natural choice, are false. The word of God must be beyond human reason in substantiating doctrine.

CHAPTER XVII.

§ 75. THE TRANSFIGURATION. Our Lord's subsequent discourse with the three disciples.—*Region of Cesarea Philippi.*

CHAPTER XVII.

AND ᵃ after six days Jesus taketh Peter, James, and John his brother, and bringeth them up into a high mountain apart.

2 And was transfigured before them: and his face did shine as the sun, ᵇ and his raiment was white as the light.

_{a Mar.9.2,&c. Lu.9.28,&c.   b Re.1.16.}

3 And, behold, there appeared unto them Moses and Elias, talking with him.

4 Then answered Peter and said unto Jesus, Lord, it is good for us to be here: if thou wilt, let us make here three tabernacles; one for thee, and one for Moses, and one for Elias.

Matt.	Mark.	Luke.	John.
17. 1–13	9. 2–13	9. 28–36	

Our Lord was still in the vicinity of Cesarea Philippi, in the northernmost part of Palestine.

1. *Jesus taketh Peter, James and John.* (He would have two or three witnesses. Deut. 17. 6.) These three He selected also to go with Him to Gethsemane, Mark 14. 33, and to the house of the ruler of the synagogue, whose daughter He raised from the dead (Mark 5. 37). He would specially train them for their special work.—— ¶ *After six days.* Luke says *about* an eight days after, that is inclusive of the two which bounded the reckoning. This was a common mode of computing time.——¶ *A high mountain apart.* Apart from the rest of the twelve. Mark has it, "*apart by themselves.*" Luke adds that He went up there *to pray* (9. 28). This high mountain is not mentioned to us by name. Most have thought it to be mount Tabor. But we find Him afterward still in this region farther north. He was near the mountain range of *Hermon*.——¶ *Transfigured.* The word is "*metamorphosed.*" The meaning of the term is, that His *appearance* was changed, as is afterward described. His face shone as the sun. The same word is rendered in Romans 12. 2, *transformed.* And in 2 Cor. 3 18, *changed* into the same image, &c. So Moses is spoken of when he came down from talking with God on Sinai. Exod. 24. 29, 30. ——¶ *His raiment*, or clothing, was white as the light. Mark has it: "White as snow, so as no fuller (or clothes bleacher) on earth can white them." His body underwent no change.

3. *Moses and Elias.* These were prominent characters of the Old Testament dispensation, that was now coming to an end. It was fit that they should appear. *Moses* as the mediator of the old Covenant and giver of the Law from Sinai, and a type of Christ, represented the Old Law.—— ¶ *And Elias.* (See Matt. 21. 13.) For all the prophets and the law were until John, and if ye will receive it, this is Elias, which was for to come. Elias, or Elijah, the symbol of Christ's forerunner, John, represented the prophets. The Law and the Prophets waited here upon Christ the Redeemer, for they all had an eye to His work. They talked with Him. Luke says, they conversed about His decease which He should accomplish at Jerusalem (Luke 9. 31). Moses had now been dead nearly 1500 years. He died on the top of Pisgah, over against Jericho, and was buried in an unknown spot, in a valley, Deut. 34. Elijah had not died, but had been *translated*, or taken to heaven without death (2 Kings 2. 11). This occurred about 900 years before Christ's birth. This appearance of two that had gone to eternity, shows us that a resurrection of the body is no impossible thing. Moses' dead body was raised, and both these were the identical persons they had been on earth.

4. *Tabernacles*, tents, booths (see Levit. 23. 34), for shelter, and a dwelling. This expressed Peter's desire to abide there. Yet he would build *three*, not six. He would plan

178 MATTHEW. [A. D. 32.

5 While he yet spake, behold, a bright cloud overshadowed them: and behold, a voice ᶜ out of the cloud, which said, This is my beloved Son, in ᵈ whom I am well pleased; hear ᵉ ye him.

6 And when the disciples heard *it*, they fell on their face, and were sore afraid.

7 And Jesus came and touched ᶠ them, and said, Arise, and be not afraid.

_{c c.3.17. Mar.1.11. Lu.3.22. 2Pe.1.17. d Is.42.1, 21. e De.18.15,19. Ac.3.22,23. He.1.1,2; 1.1-3. f Da.10.10,18. Re.1.17.}

8 And when they had lifted up their eyes, they saw no man, save Jesus only.

9 And as they came down from the mountain, Jesus charged them, saying, Tell the vision to no man, until the Son of man be risen again from the dead.

10 And his disciples asked him, saying, Why ᵍ then say the scribes that Elias must first come?

11 And Jesus answered and

_{g Mal.4.5,6. c.11.14.}

---

only to keep these glorious personages there, "not knowing what he said" (Luke). Mark: "For he wist not what to say, for they were sore afraid."

5. *A bright cloud overshadowed—spread over them*, all light and glorious. A cloud of glory was God's symbol of His presence in former times. Ex. 24. 16, 17. "*Upon the mercy seat*," Levit. 16. 2. Such a cloud was the shechinah which abode in the temple. 1 Kings 8. 10, 11.——¶ *A voice.* Of Jehovah, which formerly spoke out of the cloud that symbolized His presence.——¶ *Hear Him.* The same had been declared at Christ's baptism. (3. 17.) (See also John 12. 28.) This gave another attestation of Christ's divine glory and authority, and placed Him *before* Moses and the prophets. See 2 Peter 1. 17, 18. They needed this confirmation of their faith, and this reiteration of Divine testimony to His mediatorial person and work, in order to be strengthened for the events of His death.——¶ *Hear Him.* This is to attend upon His instructions and obey Him. The same word in Hebrew, means to hear and to obey. If we disobey this command, refusing to acknowledge, receive and follow Christ, we must perish.

6. *They fell on their face*, with reverence and fear. At once prostrate and enveloped in the cloud. Luke 9. 34. The exceeding (excellent) glory made them afraid. Men should fear the voice of God, because they are sinners and lost, and to Christ Jesus they must attend if they would live. Adam was afraid of God's voice as soon as he had sinned, but not before. And if God should now so utter His will, as He did at Sinai, men would tremble as they did there, where even Moses said, "I exceedingly fear and quake," and the multitude begged that God's voice be not spoken to them any more, lest they die (Heb. 12. 19–21).

9. *Tell the vision.* A vision is a supernatural exhibition to the sight— "*the things which they had seen.*" Luke. They were not to tell it until He had risen, for then it would be understood, and not till then could it have its full force, but would be only abused to the hindrance of His work. Mark says, they kept this saying with themselves, questioning what the rising from the dead should mean. (Mark 9. 10.) Luke says, they kept it close, and *told no man* "*in those days.*"

10. *Why then?* i. e., If, as now plainly appears, Thou art the Messiah, why do the scribes say that Elias must come first? They knew this to be a received doctrine among the Jews, and they thought it involved a contradiction—for here was Christ and where was Elias? They had not known of *his* coming in John the Baptist. The prophecy is found in Malachi, *the last verses.* And as the

said unto them, Elias truly shall first come, and restore all things.

12 But I say unto you, that Elias is come already, and they knew him not, but have done unto him whatsoever they listed. Likewise shall also the Son of man suffer ʰ of them.

13 Then the disciples under-

ʰ c.16.21.

stood that he spake unto them of John the Baptist.

14 ¶ And ⁱ when they were come to the multitude, there came to him a *certain* man kneeling down to him, and saying,

15 Lord, have mercy on my

ⁱ Mar.9.14,&c. Lu.9.37,&c.

---

scribes were writers and teachers of the law, and familiar with the Old Testament scriptures, they were quoted as good authority. They held, however, that the prophet Elijah would personally re-appear.

11. *Elias truly shall first come.* That is, this is true as it was prophesied.—— ¶ *And restore all things*, as was predicted by Malachi, " turning the hearts of the fathers unto the children," &c., reforming the people in their scriptural views, and in their relations to the covenant made with their fathers, and doing this *thoroughly*, as the parallel form of expression imports, fathers to children and children to fathers.

12. *Elias is come already*, i. e., John the Baptist, who came " *in the spirit and power of Elias*" (Luke 1. 17), and who was the one prophesied as to come in the character of Elijah of old. So Christ had declared, ch. 11. 14, that John was the Elijah mentioned by Malachi.—— ¶ *Knew him not*, did not recognize or acknowledge him.—— ¶ *Whatsoever they listed*, or *chose*. They had treated John according to their inclinations, reckless of his character and office. They had imprisoned and beheaded him, Matt. 14. 10, "*as it is written of him*." Mark.—— ¶ *Likewise*. What is more amazing, He Himself, their Lord, should share of the people a similar treatment! So He afterward did! (See Mark 9. 12. Isa. 53d ch.)

13. *That He spake unto them of John the Baptist.* Their question was fairly answered. Christ passed through all these scenes in order to establish them in the faith, and we see how

He is gradually bringing them into the light.

OBSERVE, (1.) Christ manifests Himself and His work to His people, as their case demands, and as their training will bear. (2.) The thrice reiterated testimony from the Father is that in Christ and not in the sinner God is well pleased. Hence Christ is all in all to us—His vicarious sacrifice, His perfect obedience, His finished work. (3.) How fearful yet delightful is the presence of God in Christ! how ample is Christ's revealing of Himself in His word and works, yet how slow are we at best, to understand or believe the glorious reality!

§ 76. THE HEALING OF A DEMONIAC, whom the disciples could not heal. —*Region of Cesarea Philippi.*

Matt.	Mark.	Luke.	John.
17.14–21	9. 14–29	9. 37–43	

14. *To the multitude.* It is to be remembered that only three of the twelve had gone up into the mount of transfiguration with Christ. The rest had remained below where they were now found, " the next day," Luke 9. 37, surrounded by a crowd of people, and by scribes questioning with them, as we learn from Mark 9. 15. They ran to Him *amazed* to see Him, and *saluted* Him. Jesus asked them why they questioned thus with the disciples, involving them probably in disputes and puzzling queries.

15. *My son.* An " *only child*" (Luke) possessed with a devil, " *hath a dumb spirit.*" Mark. So that he was lunatic or crazy, and *sore vexed*—in a

son; for he is lunatic, and sore vexed: for oft-times he falleth into the fire, and oft into the water.

16 And I brought him to thy disciples, and they could not cure him.

17 Then Jesus answered and said, O faithless and perverse generation! how long shall I be with you? how long shall I suffer you? Bring him hither to me.

18 And Jesus rebuked the devil, and he departed out of him: and the child was cured from that very hour.

19 Then came the disciples to Jesus apart, and said, Why could not we cast him out?

20 And Jesus said unto them, Because of your unbelief: *j* for verily I say unto you, if *k* ye have faith as a grain of mustard-seed, ye shall say unto this mountain, Remove hence to yonder place, and it shall remove; and nothing shall be impossible unto you.

21 Howbeit this kind goeth

j He.3.19. *k* c.21.21. Mar.11.23. Lu.17.6. 1Cor. 13.2.

---

rage, mad, furious. Mark adds: "wheresoever he taketh him he teareth him, and he foameth and gnasheth with his teeth, and pineth away." Luke also adds other symptoms, as that the devil *tore* him, *bruised him*, &c., "hardly departed from him."

16. *To thy disciples.* Their failure during Christ's absence, doubtless gave the scribes ground to gainsay and reproach them and their Master. This accounts for Christ's rebuke, not of the man but of His disciples.

17. *O faithless!* Addressing the multitude He asked how much longer He must give them evidence of His Messiahship which yet the scribes were disputing, and which all were so slow fully to believe. So with Philip (John 14. 9). So Moses was shocked at the weak Israelites when he came down from the mount. See the account in Mark for fuller particulars.

18. *Rebuked the devil.* As He had full authority over these emissaries of the pit, He displayed it signally here, as another proof of His Divinity. The other Evangelists state more particularly. The man had come with a doubt, "*If Thou canst do any thing, have compassion on us.*" Christ had challenged his faith, "all things are possible to him that believeth," and so He had helped the delivery in that difficult birth. "Lord I believe, *help thou mine unbelief.*" Only he who truly believes (though in the smallest measure) conceives aught of the *unbelief* of his heart.

19. *To Jesus apart.* The disciples who had been baffled in an effort to cast out this evil spirit, came now to Christ apart, or in *private*, to inquire the cause of their failure. Mark says, "when He was come into the house." And they sought a private interview because they were abashed and would have a familiar explanation of the case, as it might even involve some secrets of His plan.

20. *Because of your unbelief.* This faith here alluded to is the faith of miracles. It was something more than a common belief in Christ, and was peculiar to the Apostles' age. It was a faith for such miraculous works as they were commissioned to perform. If they had this in the smallest degree, or in the proverbial phrase, "as a grain of mustard-seed," they should accomplish the most difficult things, or proverbially, should remove mountains.

21. *This kind* of difficulties expressed by the term mountains, or this kind of evil spirits, so malignant, departs not, removes not, but by prayer and fasting. The most special religious exercises were needed for so special a purpose.

OBSERVE: Great degrees of devo-

not out, but by prayer and fasting.

22 ¶ And ¹ while they abode in Galilee, Jesus said unto them, The Son of man shall be betrayed into the hands of men:
23 And they shall kill him, and the third day he shall be raised again. And they were exceeding sorry.

24 ¶ And when they were come to Capernaum, they that received ¹ tribute-*money* came

l c.16.21; 20.17. Mar.8.31; 9.30,31; 10.33. Lu.9. 22,44; 18.31; 24.6,26,46. 1 *Didrachma*, Ex.38.26.

to Peter, and said, Doth not your master pay tribute?
25 He saith, Yes. And when he was come into the house, Jesus prevented him, saying, What thinkest thou, Simon? of whom do the kings of the earth take custom or tribute? of their own children, or of strangers?
26 Peter saith unto him, Of strangers. Jesus saith unto him, Then are the children free.
27 Notwithstanding, lest we should offend ᵐ them, go thou to

m Ro.14.21; 15.1-3. 2Cor 6.3.

tion attain special measures of Divine strength and of power with the hosts of evil.

§ 77. JESUS AGAIN FORTELLS HIS OWN DEATH AND RESURRECTION. See § 74.—*Galilee.*

Matt.	Mark.	Luke.	John.
17. 22–23	9. 30–32	9. 43–45	

22, 23. *While they abode in Galilee.* The term rather means, "*as they were travelling,*" &c., on their way to Capernaum, and thence to Jerusalem The country called Galilee, it should be remembered, stretched about equally above and below (north and south) of the Sea of Galilee.——¶ *Shall be betrayed.* This is the first disclosure of the *means* by which He should fall into cruel and deadly hands. He should be handed over—delivered up —by a friend. Who would think it should be a *disciple*, an apostle! All that was now hinted to them of this, further than had been before, was, that He should be delivered up to death by a most criminal breach of confidence.——¶ *Exceeding sorry.* Mark and Luke add that they understood not that saying, and it was hid from them and they were afraid to ask Him.

§ 78. THE TRIBUTE MONEY MIRACULOUSLY PROVIDED —*Capernaum.*

Matt.	Mark.	Luke.	John.
17. 24–27	9. 33		

24. *Tribute-money,* literally, the *didrachmas,* the name for the yearly temple-tax, being a coin equal to a half shekel, or about twenty-five cents. This was allowed in the Mosaic law (Exod. 30. 11-16). It resembles the stated church collections for expenses, as it was additional to the regular church rates or tithes.

25. *Prevented, anticipated* him—began to speak of it before Peter had told Him. He was beforehand with this question. Christ knew what had been said to Peter, because He knew all things, "and needed not that any should testify to Him of man, for He knew what was in man.——¶ *Tribute.* (*kenson,* Gr.) Latin *census,* a tax. "*Custom*" was for lands, *tribute* for persons.——¶ *Their own children,* their sons and daughters of their own royal family.——¶ *Strangers,* those not of their own family.

26. Peter replied, *Of strangers,* meaning that kings do not tax their own sons. And Christ applies the conclusion to Himself, that then the *children* are free. The temple is His Father's house (John 2. 16), and as He is the Son, and greater than the temple (ch. 12. 6), why should He be taxed for the service? It was only another assertion of His Divine SONSHIP, with which He would make them every way familiar.

27. *Lest we should offend them.* He

the sea, and cast a hook, and take up the fish that first cometh up; and when thou hast opened his mouth, thou shalt find ¹ a piece of money; that take, and give unto them for me and thee.

CHAPTER XVIII.

AT ᵃ the same time came the disciples unto Jesus, saying,

1 *A stater*, which was half an ounce of silver.
a Mar.9.33,&c. Lu.9.46,&c.; 22.24,&c.

Who is the greatest in the kingdom of heaven?

2 And Jesus called a little child unto him, and set him in the midst of them,

3 And said, Verily I say unto you, except ye be converted, ᵇ and become as little children, ᶜ ye shall not enter into the kingdom of heaven.

4 Whosoever therefore shall

b Ps.51.10-13. Jno.3.3. *c* 1 Cor.14.20. 1 Pe.2.2.

pays, under a protest, for expediency's sake (1 Cor. 8. 13); and lest a scandal should be put upon the temple service and upon Himself among the people, He would pay what He was not bound to, of right.——¶ *Go to the sea*—*of Galilee*, near by.——¶ *A piece of money*, a stater, a Roman coin, equal to a shekel, enough, of course, for the *tax of two*. The miracle consisted in His so ordering all the circumstances as to show a power over all things equal to that of creation itself. If He could make one of the numberless fish in the sea come first to Peter's hook, with a piece of money in its mouth, and just such a piece of money, He could as well have created the money and the fish for the purpose.

OBSERVE, (1.) Christ meets the law's demands for Himself and for His people. He pays for Himself and for Peter, "*for me* and *for thee.*" Christ would put Himself in the disciples' place, to pay the law's price for them. He came under the same yoke with men, that men might enter into the same freedom as His. "My father and your Father, my God and your God." John 20. 17. (2.) Christ confirms His gracious words by His gracious works. He protests His rightful exemption from the ceremonial tax, as much by the mode of His furnishing the money, as by His express declaration. In the miracle He proves Himself the Divine Being whom He claimed to be in words. (3.) We see how God's most holy, wise and powerful preserving and governing all His creatures, and all their actions, can help in every extremity.

CHAPTER XVIII

§ 79. THE DISCIPLES CONTEND WHO SHOULD BE THE GREATEST. JESUS EXHORTS.—*Capernaum.*

Matt.	Mark.	Luke.	John.
18. 1-35	9. 33-50	9. 46-50	

1. *The greatest in the kingdom of heaven.* This may have arisen from the preference just shown, at the transfiguration, for Peter, James and John (see Luke 7. 46), and from Christ's allusion to His royalty in the tribute. They were thinking of the kingdom as one of earthly kind, and were now speculating about its preferments and offices. But it is a kingdom that "cometh not with observation" (Luke 17. 20), and one which is not meat and drink, but righteousness (Rom. 14. 17). It appears from Mark and Luke, that they had disputed about it among themselves on the way to Capernaum, and that Christ had perceived the thoughts of their hearts, and questioned them, so as to elicit this distinct query from themselves. They often started such inquiries.

2, 3. *A little child.* He taught them by this *symbol*, for such was the method of teaching in the East.——¶ *Be converted*—changed, turned from such tempers, in such a thorough way as to become, instead of *aspirants*, like *little children*. It is the lowly, dependent, simple disposition of a *little*

humble himself [d] as this little child, the same is greatest in the kingdom of heaven.

5 And whoso shall receive one such little [e] child in my name receiveth me.

6 But whoso shall offend [f] one of these little ones which believe in me, it were better for him that a millstone were hanged about his neck, and *that* he were drowned in the depth of the sea.

7 Wo unto the world because of offences! for [g] it must needs be that offences come; but [h] wo to that man by whom the offence cometh!

[d] Lu.14.11. Ja.4.10. [e] Mat.10.42. [f] Mar.9.42. Lu.17.1,2.

[g] 1Cor.11.19. Jude 4. [h] Jude 11.

---

child, that is set forth as the symbol of piety. It is not as a pattern, but as an *image* or *figure*, that a child is set forth. It is not that children are patterns of innocence, for they are depraved, but that they are *pictures* of it to the eye. We must become as such, having a child-like spirit, happy in our dependence on God, our heavenly Father. They had asked for high places and proud stations, and had enviously inquired which of them should be first (see Mark 9. 34). This showed in them a worldly, ambitious, unhumbled character, and Christ, instead of encouraging them with such expectations, set before them a little child. Humility, teachableness, trustfulness of spirit, are necessary, because so only can we enter in at the strait gate, and by the living way.

4. *Shall humble himself*, in true humility—whosoever shall come down to this level of a little child, in the unaspiring temper of his heart—he shall be greatest, or, *the greater*, among Christians. The deepest humility is the highest honour and joy. Lowly thoughts of self, as to merit, and sufficiency and ability, coupled with a hearty trust in Christ, make up the true Christian characteristics.

5. *Whoso shall receive one such*. One of this character may be despised among men; Christ therefore makes this special provision for such, and for those who favour such.——¶ *In my name*—on Christ's account, because he is Christ's, and resembles Him (ch. 7. 22; 10. 22), for it is the nature of true piety to love this child-like disposition, wherever it is found; while vain men often treat it with contempt. Christ not only regards such as His, but regards Himself as received and favoured in them (Matt. 25. 40); "Ye have done it unto me." Those who love Christians for their Christian temper, as like Christ, shall be rewarded accordingly. Mark and Luke here record a conversation omitted by Matthew. John told Him that they had seen one casting out devils in His name, and they forbade him, because he was not of their company. Jesus answered that there was a principle by which all such should be judged. If they did such things as He alone could have instigated and produced, and if so they wrought with Him, they were of needs His. "He that is not against us is for us. (See Mark and Luke.) These are proverbial sayings, like Prov. 26. 4, 5.

6. *Shall offend one*—shall put a stumbling-block or an occasion to fall in his brother's way—shall tempt to sin any of these Christian, child-like ones—" disciples "—" that believe in me" (Mark 9. 42), he is worthy of severest punishment. He sins against the Holy Spirit's work in the heart. ——¶ *Millstone*. The term means a millstone large enough to be turned by an ass—not the *hand-stones*.

7. *Offences*. Occasions of sin—temptations to do wrong, as a hand or foot even may be, are a wo to the world, and wo to any one by whom they may come.——¶ *It must needs be* —it is necessary or unavoidable, as things are, that such temptations come.——¶ *But wo*—that is, curse or condemnation on that man by

8 Wherefore, *i* if thy hand or thy foot offend thee, cut them off, and cast *them* from thee: it is better for thee to enter into life halt or maimed, rather than, having two hands or two feet, to be cast into everlasting fire.

9 And if thine eye offend thee, pluck it out, and cast *it* from thee: it is better for thee to enter *j* into life with one eye, rather than, having two eyes, *k* to be cast into hell-fire.

10 Take heed that ye despise not one of these little ones; for I say unto you, that in heaven their angels *l* do always behold *m* the face of my Father which is in heaven.

11 For the Son of man is come

i c.5.29,30. Mar.9.43,45. *j* He.4.11. *k* Lu.9.25. *l* Ac.12.15. *m* Ps.17.15.

---

whom the temptation cometh. He that leads others into sin, is a child of the devil, who is the great seducer and deceiver of men. Yet this is often done, by example, or enticement to a first step of evil doing. This teaches us that evil communications corrupt good manners, and that bad company is a wo and curse to any one.

8, 9. *If thy hand or thy foot.* Whatever is an occasion to sin, however dear it be, and valuable, though the hardest to be parted with, must be given up. This enforces the sentiment just laid down (see ch. 5. 29, 30). —— ¶ *Halt*—lame.—— ¶ *Maimed*—mutilated, as by a hand cut off. This means, that it is better to get to heaven *without* any such enjoyments, however dear, as are a snare, than to have them here, and perish at last. See the case of the rich man and Lazarus: "Thou in thy life-time receivedst thy good things, and likewise Lazarus evil things; but now he is comforted, and thou art tormented" (Luke 16. 25).—— ¶ *Into hell-fire.* This is the eternal consequence of cherishing evil passions and habits, and idol objects of sin (see ch. 5. 29, 30). We should be willing to abandon the dearest object or pursuit, rather than to sin ourselves, or lead others to sin. "Hell-fire" is torment *without end*, represented by the fire of Hinnom, near Jerusalem. "These shall go away into everlasting punishment" (ch. 25. 46), "*everlasting fire*," vs. 8.

10. Christ now warns more particularly against such treatment of meek-minded, child-like Christians, as men of the world are prone to, who understand nothing of the true dignities and proprieties of His kingdom.—— ¶ *That ye despise not* — or treat with disrespect and scorn, as though they were mean, and silly, and contemptible.—— ¶ *Their angels*—that is, such persons are objects of interest and care to angels in heaven (Heb. 1. 14), and this is a reason for respecting them.—— ¶ *Do always behold the face.* This, in Eastern courts, was a mark of special honour, to be admitted into the presence of the king. The *servants* of these disciples are the special favourites of the Heavenly King. Servants of Eastern kings also stood in their presence, to wait their orders and watch their motions of command. The angels are *theirs*—ministering spirits to them—and always intent to execute the orders of the Heavenly King.—— ¶ *My Father*—" and their Father" (John 20. 17). The angels serve these disciples by Divine warrant and command. This shows a greater dignity. Hence these lowly-minded Christians, though sneered at, often, by men of the world, are true dignitaries—they have the angels of God for their servants; not each having *one*, but *more*—and as many as his case should at any time require. The ministry of angels is a scriptural doctrine, and deserves to be more thought of and looked for (Ps. 34. 7. Dan. 6. 22. chs. 1. & 2).

11. *The Son of man,* &c. Christ's work has regard to just such. The humble, obscure, and *lost,* He comes to save. This is another reason for

A. D. 32.] CHAPTER XVIII. 185

to save ⁿ that which was lost.

12 How think ye? If ᵒ a man have an hundred sheep, and one of them be gone astray, doth he not leave the ninety and nine, and goeth into the mountains, and seeketh that which is gone astray?

13 And if so be that he find it, verily I say unto you, He rejoiceth more of that *sheep*, than of the ninety and nine which went not astray.

14 Even so, it is not the will of your Father which is in heaven that one ᵖ of these little ones should perish.

15 ¶ Moreover, if ᑫ thy brother shall trespass against thee, go and tell him his fault between thee and him alone: if ʳ he shall hear thee, thou hast gained thy brother.

16 But if he will not hear *thee*, *then* take with thee one or two more, that in the mouth of two or three ˢ witnesses every word may be established.

17 And if he shall neglect to hear them, tell *it* unto the church: but if he neglect to hear the church, let ᵗ him be unto thee as an heathen man and a publican.

n Mat.1.21. Lu.9.56; 19.10. Jno.3.17; 10.10; 12.17. 1Ti.1.15. *o* Lu.15.4,&c. *p* 2Pe.3.9.
q Le.19.17. Lu.17.3. *r* Ja.5.20. *s* De.19.15. *t* Ro.16.17. 1Cor.5.3-5. 2Th.3.6,14.

---

their not being despised. By the lost, are meant sinners. This shows His condescension, which may well be pattern to all sinners among themselves. Men are said to be lost, because they are ruined and undone by sin, and need now to be saved, or they perish forever. Christ, the Son of man—the Mediator—saves the lost, by giving His life *in exchange*—a ransom—for the ruined soul. He has died, and obeyed the law in His life, and gone to intercede in heaven —all that He might save sinners. Hence, their views of greatness were altogether wrong. If they could keep in view the plan of salvation, they would see that none can boast in themselves, and that they who are *lost*, may boast in Christ.

12. Our Lord further illustrates this sentiment by a *parable*, recorded by Matthew, and not by the other evangelists. By the sheep gone astray, our Lord means, sinners strayed from Him, and, like sheep, wandering from the fold and helpless, exposed to destruction. By the owner's going into the mountain to seek *one*, He would have us understand Himself *coming into the world* (among us) *to save sinners* (1 Tim. 1. 15). He is our Shepherd (Ps. 23. 1), the good Shepherd (John 10. 14), the Shepherd and Bishop of our souls (1 Pet. 2. 25).

13. *He rejoiceth more.* This is to show the peculiar joy to Christ of saving that which was lost—like the joy of the father in receiving home a prodigal son. God pursues wandering sinners, and when any would repent and return, they may be sure of His tenderness toward them, and His joy in their reception. See parable of the lost sheep and son, Luke 15. Therefore, whom God thus honours and cares for, sinners should not despise; and distinctions of least and greatest should be referred to this standard.

14. *Even so.* As in this case, God signifies it as His disposition that *not one* of these, though despised by men, should perish, or be eternally destroyed. John 12. 28.

15–17. *Thy brother.* Our Lord now proceeds to enjoin *brotherly kindness* and charity. He sets forth the Christian and Christ-like method of dealing, as instead of jealousy and envy. "Brother" here means fellow-disciple, or Christian brother.——¶ *Trespass against thee*—injure thee, transgress or sin against thee.——¶ *Go and tell*

16*

18 Verily I say unto you, ᵘ Whatsoever ye shall bind on earth, shall be bound in heaven; and whatsoever ye shall loose on earth, shall be loosed in heaven.

19 Again I say unto you, That if two of you shall agree on earth, as touching any thing that they shall ask, it ᵛ shall be done for them of my Father which is in heaven.

20 For where two or three are gathered together ʷ in my name,

u c.16.19. Jno.20.23. Ac.15.23-31. 2Cor.2.10. *v* Mar.11.24. Jno.16.24. 1Jno.5.14. *w* Jno.20.19. 1Cor.5.4.

---

him his fault—expostulate with him, strive to convince him. This was the rule under the old law (Levit. 19. 17).——¶ *Alone*—to give private opportunity of making explanations or confession, without a disposition to expose him, previously to such face-to-face interview.——¶ *One or two more*, for influence with him, and as *witnesses*, if the case should require to come before the church. This was the law (Deut. 19. 15).——¶ *The church*. The court of Christ's house, charged with such matters. In the Jewish synagogue, which was the parish church in that time, there was a bench of elders for such trials, &c. ——¶ *As an heathen man*, &c.—as not a Christian. Do not own him any longer as such. The Jews did not own the heathen, nor have intercourse with them. So let him be to thee.

18. (See note, ch. 16. 19.) These words are addressed to the twelve. The constituted court of Christ's church has authority to pronounce upon all such cases; and their decisions, on scriptural grounds, shall have sanction from above. These important words had been spoken to Peter (ch. 16. 19), but here they are addressed to all the apostles, showing that Peter was not there set over the rest, as the Romish church asserts. These words imply that the church officers are to act in Christ's name, and their decisions, under direction of His word, are to be revered as His, though they be few men in number.

19. The meaning is, that Christ's presence and authority would give power and success in the administration of His church on earth, even to the fewest—that the whole body of members was not contemplated as sitting in judgment, or ordering church affairs—but that if two of the twelve should agree in any case, especially as to binding and loosing, and they should ask counsel of God, it should be done for them (see Acts 1. 14-26). Church discipline is to be approached with united prayers to the Great Head of the church (1 Cor. 5. 3, 4).

20. *For*. It is not the numbers, but Christ's *name*, that gives the validity. Two or three, met according to His appointment, may be considered as sufficient—for His presence is pledged to be in their midst—Himself as one with them, and efficiently present to bless. This has, of course, a special reference to the authority granted in vs. 18 to the apostles. Yet it applies also to the discipleship. This identifies a Christian church.

OBSERVE, (1.) True greatness consists in being Christ's—sheep of His fold—freemen of Christ—children of God by faith in Christ—made kings and priests unto God and the Father (vss. 1-10). (2.) The true dignity and value of man is shown by God's redeeming work (vss. 10, 11); "the redemption of their soul is precious, and it ceaseth for ever"—and by the joy of Christ in their recovery (vs. 13), and by His eternal covenant, securing their salvation (vs. 14). (3.) How commonly would personal disputes between men be settled, by following strictly this rule of our Lord! Christians especially owe it to one another, and much more the ministers of Christ. (4.) Church discipline is provided by the Great Head of the church, as a final, but salutary resort. (5.) Christ is GOD (vs. 20),

A. D. 32.] CHAPTER XVIII. 187

there am I in the midst of them.
21 ¶ Then came Peter to him, and said, Lord, how oft shall my brother sin against me, and I forgive ˣ him? till seven times?
22 Jesus saith unto him, I say not unto thee, Until seven times; but, Until seventy times seven.
23 ¶ Therefore is the kingdom of heaven likened unto a certain king, which would take account ʸ of his servants.

x Mar.11.25. Lu.17.4. Col.3.13. *y* Ro.14.12.

24 And when he had begun to reckon, one was brought unto him which owed him ten thousand ¹ talents:
25 But forasmuch as he had not to pay, his lord commanded him to be ᶻ sold, and his wife and children, and all that he had, and payment to be made.
26 The servant therefore fell down, and worshipped ² him,

1 *A talent is 750 ounces of silver, which, at 5s. the ounce, is 187l.10s.* z 2K.4.1. Is.50.1. 2 Or, *besought him.*

21. *Then came Peter.* Our Lord having thus discoursed about the treatment of personal offenders, Peter makes an inquiry as to how often we should forgive the *same person.* To forgive is to *pass by* an offence and treat the offender as though he had not done wrong. And by a brother is meant here a fellow-Christian, as in verse 15.

22. *Until seventy times seven.* The Jews taught that three times, but not the fourth one, should be forgiven, grounding their idea on Amos 1. 3; 2. 6. "Seven is the number in the Divine law, with which the idea of *remission* is ever linked."—*Trench.* Peter had extended his ideas to the seventh time. Christ in this strong expression goes far beyond his farthest thoughts, and evidently means that it should have no such limit, but that we should be disposed to repeat it, *times without number.* (Luke 17. 3, 4.)

23. Our Lord on this occasion delivered the *first* of His Moral Parables, and first appears in the character of king.——¶ *A certain king.* A parable is here introduced to illustrate and set in a strong light the duty of forgiving injuries. On this point He discoursed at large in the Sermon on the Mount. The kingdom of heaven here means God's plan of dealing in His church (see Matt. 5. 20), and the case proposed has reference to the mutual forgiveness of *fellow-Christians,* which, accordingly, our Lord argues on the ground of their being more largely forgiven.——¶ *Would take account—make settlement* with his servants, not the final settlement, but such as in Luke 16, of stewardship. All the king's officers are usually called his servants, but here the collectors of revenue are probably meant. It was customary to sell out to certain tax-gatherers the revenue of a district at a round sum. This made them responsible to the king for the gross amount agreed upon. Such a contract may have brought such a servant or officer so largely in debt, say ten to fifteen millions of dollars. Yet the whole is stated in round numbers, and in the language of a parable. Or he was a satrap, who should have remitted the revenues of his province to the royal treasury. The amount is put at the highest, to express an indebtedness of the largest possible kind, representing the magnitude of our account before God. "This sum is exactly that with which Darius sought to buy off Alexander the Great, that he should not prosecute his conquests in Asia, and this was the amount imposed by the Romans on Antiochus the Great, after his defeat by them."—*Trench.*

25. *His lord commanded him to be sold.* This was allowed by the Jewish laws. A debtor could be sold into bondage with wife and children until the debt should be satisfied. (Levit. 25. 39-46. 2 Kings 4. 1. Amos 8. 6.) ——¶ *And payment to be made.* Not

saying, Lord, have patience with me, and I will pay thee all.

27 Then the Lord of that servant was moved with compassion,[a] and loosed him, and forgave him the debt.

28 But the same servant went out, and found one of his fellow-servants which owed him an hundred [1] pence, and he laid hands on him, and took *him* by the throat, saying, Pay me that thou owest.

29 And his fellow-servant fell down at his feet, and besought him, saying, [b] Have patience with me, and I will pay thee all.

30 And he would not; but went and cast him into prison, till he should pay the debt.

31 So when his fellow-servants saw what was done, they were very sorry, and came and told unto their lord all that was done.

32 Then his lord, after that he had called him, said unto him,

[a] Ps 78.38. [1] *The Roman penny is the 8th part of an ounce, which, at 5s. the ounce, is 7d. half-penny.* c.20.22.

[b] ver.26.

---

as though the sale would pay the claim.

26. *Fell down, and worshipped him.* That is, prostrated himself as a worshipper in a posture of humblest entreaty, and as was customary for Eastern subjects before their king. He asked indulgence, and declared his disposition, *pledged all for the future,* and pleaded his present inability. The hardest sinners, and even infidels, do cry for mercy when death and judgment are at hand. Convinced sinners, not yet aware of the immensity of their debt, are ready to promise full satisfaction.

27. *Moved with compassion.* This represents the tender pity of God toward sinners in their destitute and helpless case, and His prompt response to the prayer of suppliants. God's severity endures only till the sinner, burdened under his debt, seeks forgiveness. Then it proves, like Joseph's harshness, only love in disguise. So, the reckoning was good for the man (Isa. 1. 18). The parable would show that men's sins against us, cannot compare in magnitude with ours against God. Therefore we should be lenient toward them, even as we hope for mercy from God. But see.

28. *But the same servant.* The grace was not received aright.——¶ *Went out.* It is thus from *going out* of the presence of our gracious Lord that we are ready so to act. This very man, just treated with such lenity by his lord, finds a fellow-servant who owes him the merest trifle in comparison—" *a hundred pence.*" A Roman penny was equal to about 12½ of ours. This debt would be about 12½ dollars. Trench makes the proportion of the two debts to be " One million two hundred and fifty thousand, to *one.*" As a *drop* (says Chrysostom) to the *ocean.* He asked for the debt in a most severe and abusive way. The gospel grace demands a "*benign retaliation,*" to forgive as we are forgiven.

29. *Besought — entreated, begged.* Observe, he promised the same as this man had just promised to his lord! But with what different success! Only the truly '*spiritual*' can restore one " overtaken in *a fault.*" Gal. 6. 1.

31. This was a mode of treatment even beneath the common feelings of humanity. How base when one who professes to have been pardoned, out of mere grace, should show himself a monster of cruelty and severity to others.——¶ *Told.* The Greek word is expressive, *told fully.*

32. *Then his lord.* We are now brought to see what judgment such conduct may reasonably expect of our Lord and Master. Christ, the Saviour, is also the Judge! As to this man, his lord had forgiven him, not a part but the whole of his debt, and that not a small debt but im-

O thou wicked servant, *c* I forgave thee all that debt, because thou desiredst me;

33 Shouldest not thou also have had compassion on thy fellow-servant, even as I had pity on thee?

34 And his lord was wroth,

c Lu. 19. 22.

and delivered him to the tormentors, till he should pay all that was due unto him.

35 So *d* likewise shall my heavenly Father do also unto you, if ye from your hearts forgive not every one his brother their trespasses.

d Pr. 21. 13. c. 6. 12. Ja. 2. 13.

---

mense. And he refers him also to his own feelings, when he desired the release in his destitution and extremity. Infinite grace has come to sinners, in the gospel of Christ, and now the great question is, whether we have so received it, as that it has power with us in our lives, fashioning our conduct. "If any man have not the Spirit of Christ, he is none of His." (See James 2. 13.)

33. *Shouldest not thou also?* The man is judged out of his own mouth. He had besought forgiveness and it was granted, and all this bound him to grant it to the fellow-servant, on his own principles. Besides, that was a debt of 12 dollars, the merest pittance, compared with the infinite sum which he had been forgiven. The golden rule applies here, "As ye would that men should do to you, do ye even so to them likewise, for this is THE LAW."

34. *Tormentors.* In early times of Rome, the debtor was condemned to wear a chain of fifteen pounds weight, and to live on the scantiest fare, that he might be brought to terms. In the East, those who appear the poorest will often have secret hoards of wealth. Hence the torture would be applied to elicit information. He was to be treated for *crime* now, which was worse than *indebtedness*. He was to be delivered up to the tormentors. These were executioners who applied all kinds of tortures. This iniquity of his incurred a penalty which the selling of himself, and wife, and children could not pay.——¶ *Till he should pay.* Now he was to be treated, not merely as a criminal, but as a criminal and *debtor* also. All his debts were to be rigorously exacted of him, because he thus testified that he had never been a true recipient of the pardon.

35. *So likewise.* A sinner is like the servant in question, because he is utterly unable to satisfy God's infinite claims upon him. Men are in debt to God for every thing they have received, because they have deserved nothing but punishment. And they are in debt to Him in the way of numberless sins, of which they must give account. They owe Him thanks and service beyond account, and the debt they have incurred by constant transgression none can estimate. It is for ten thousand times ten thousand; and " he cannot answer for one of a thousand." Job. They are not only unable to pay, but if called to account, they could give no excuse for this inability, which is wilful and wicked. Yet God forgives us for Christ's sake. Therefore we should forgive men their sins, never forgetting how much greater crimes we have had forgiven. We should forgive, not merely in the act, but *from the heart*, that is, sincerely, meaning to pass by the offence, and to treat the offender as though he had not done us the wrong. There is a forgiveness *in name*, which retains the ill feeling, and forgets not the injury. This is a mere pretence, and if we should be *so* forgiven by our heavenly Father, how different were our case!

OBSERVE, (1.) How FREELY Christ forgives, NOT because we have forgiven others, or done any other good thing, but THAT WE MAY. (2.) How FULLY He forgives us the most immense indebtedness, " *all that debt*"

CHAPTER XIX.

AND it came to pass, *that* when Jesus had finished these sayings, he ᵃ departed from Galilee, and came into the coasts of Judea beyond Jordan:

a Mar.10.1. Jno 10.40.

(vs. 32), and accepts not our vain promises to pay Him all in future. (3.) How completely we are in the power of the law for eternal punishment, except we find forgiveness in Christ Jesus. (vs. 25.) (4.) How unwarranted must be that man's hope of pardon, who is himself unforgiving (vs. 35).

(5.) Christ forgives us freely that we may be moved, by gratitude, to serve and follow Him, and that, by the power of this forgiveness in our lives, we may be actuated to forgive others and in all things imitate His gracious example.

	Matt.	Mark.	Luke.	John.
§ 80. The Seventy instructed and sent out.—*Capernaum.*	....	....	10. 1–16	
§ 81. Jesus goes up to the Festival of Tabernacles. His final Departure from Galilee. Incidents in Samaria.	....	....	9. 51–56	7. 2–10
§ 82. Ten Lepers cleansed.—*Samaria.*	....	....	17.11–19	

PART VI.

Festival of Tabernacles, and the subsequent transactions until our Lord's arrival at Bethany, six days before the fourth Passover.

Time—six months, less one week.

	Matt.	Mark.	Luke.	John.
§ 83. Jesus at the Festival of Tabernacles. His public teaching.—*Jerusalem.*	....	....	....	7. 11–53 8.1
§ 84. The woman taken in adultery.—*Jerusalem.*	....	....	....	8. 2–11
§ 85. Further public teaching of our Lord. He reproves the unbelieving Jews, and escapes from their hands.—*Jerusalem.*	....	....	....	8. 12–59
§ 86. A Lawyer instructed. Love to our Neighbour defined. Parable of the Good Samaritan.—*Near Jerusalem.*	....	....	10.25–37	
§ 87. Jesus in the house of Martha and Mary.—*Bethany.*	....	....	10.38–42	
§ 88. The Disciples again taught how to pray.—*Near Jerusalem.*	....	....	11. 1–13	
§ 89. The Seventy return.—*Jerusalem.*	....	....	10.17–24	
§ 90. A man born blind is healed on the Sabbath. Our Lord's subsequent Discourses.—*Jerusalem.*	....	....	....	9. 1–41 10. 1–21
§ 91. Jesus in Jerusalem at the Festival of Dedication. He retires beyond Jordan.—*Jerusalem. Bethany beyond Jordan.*	....	....	....	10.22–42
§ 92. The raising of Lazarus.—*Bethany.*	....	....	....	11. 1–46
§ 93. The Counsel of Caiaphas against Jesus. He retires from Jerusalem.—*Jerusalem. Ephraim.*	....	....	....	11.47–54

2 And great multitudes followed him; and he healed them there.

3 ¶ The Pharisees also came unto him, tempting him, and saying unto him, Is it lawful for a man to put away his wife for every cause?

CHAPTER XIX.

§ 94. JESUS BEYOND JORDAN, IS FOLLOWED BY MULTITUDES. The healing of the infirm woman on the Sabbath.—*Valley of Jordan. Perea.*

Matt.	Mark.	Luke.	John.
19. 1, 2	10. 1.	13. 10–21	

The Evangelist here gives, at a glance, the course of our Lord, as seen in the Harmony, declaring in a word, that He had departed from Galilee after His discourse (see § 81), and that at length He came into the coasts of Judea beyond Jordan, where we now find Him. It was in this quarter, that he healed the woman who had an infirmity (see Luke 13. 10–21). We find that He had passed through Samaria (see § 81 and 82) to Jerusalem, where He was present at the feast of tabernacles (§ 83), and at the feast of dedication (§ 91), when He retires beyond Jordan (§ 91 and 93). We find now many incidents related of Him in Perea. Perea was a region belonging to Judea, and so called from a word which signifies *beyond*, as it lay beyond Jordan, and was formerly part of the tribes Reuben, Gad and Manasseh.

	Matt.	Mark	Luke.	John.
§ 95. Our Lord goes teaching and journeying toward Jerusalem. He is warned against Herod.—*Perea.*	....	....	13.22–35	
§ 96. Our Lord dines with a chief Pharisee on the Sabbath. Incidents. *Perea.*	....	....	14. 1–24	
§ 97. What is required of true Disciples. *Perea.*	....	....	14.25–35	
§ 98. Parable of the Lost Sheep, &c. Parable of the Prodigal Son. *Perea.*	....	....	15. 1–32	
§ 99. Parable of the Unjust Steward. *Perea.*	....	....	16. 1–13	
§ 100. The Pharisees reproved. Parable of the Rich Man and Lazarus. *Perea.*	....	....	16.14–31	
§ 101. Jesus inculcates Forbearance, Faith, and Humility. *Perea.*	....	....	17. 1–10	
§ 102. Christ's Coming will be sudden. *Perea.*	....	....	17.20–37	
§ 103. Parables. The importunate Widow. The Pharisee and Publican. *Perea.*	....	....	18. 1–14	
§ 104. PRECEPTS RESPECTING DIVORCE. *Perea.*	19. 3–12	10. 2–12		

The Evangelist thus passes over other incidents to relate the conversation respecting divorce. The Pharisees came to Him "*tempting Him,*" desiring to entangle Him in His talk. As on other occasions, so here, they wished to commit Him against one of the two parties, who took opposite sides on this question. So on the point of paying tribute to Cesar (ch. 22. 16, &c.), they sought to commit Him either against the friends or the enemies of the Roman government. But in both cases, He confounded their hypocrisy by His answer.——¶ *For every cause,* i. e., for *any* reason. Christ had laid down the true doctrine on this subject, in His Sermon on the Mount (ch. 5. 32), viz.: that there was but one sufficient cause, and *that* such as was in its very nature fatal to the marriage relation.

4 And he answered and said unto them, Have ye not read, that ᵇ he which made *them* at the beginning, made them male and female?

5 And said, For ᶜ this cause shall a man leave father and mother, and shall cleave to his wife; and they twain shall be one flesh.

6 Wherefore they are no more twain, but one flesh. What ᵈ therefore God hath joined together, let not man put asunder.

7 They say unto him, Why ᵉ did Moses then command to give a writing of divorcement, and to put her away?

8 He saith unto them, Moses, because of the hardness of your hearts, suffered you to put away your wives: but from the beginning it was not so.

9 And I say unto you, Whosoever ᶠ shall put away his wife, except *it be* for fornication, and shall marry another, committeth adultery: and whoso marrieth her which is put away doth commit adultery.

10 ¶ His disciples say unto him, If the case of the man be

b Ge.1.27; 5.2. Mal.2.15. *c* Ge.2.24. Ep.5.31.
d 1Cor.7.10. *e* De.24.1. Is.50.1.

f c.5.32. Lu.16.18.

4. *Have ye not read?* Literally, "Do ye not know?" that is, by reading. He here refers them to their scriptures, and to the original institution of marriage. Mark has it, "What did Moses command you?"

5. *And said.* By the mouth of Adam (Gen. 2. 24).——¶ *Shall cleave.* Shall adhere firmly. The Greek word is from a noun, signifying *glue.*

6. *Joined together.* The term is from a metaphor taken from the yoking of oxen.

7. *Why did Moses?* They now appeal to Moses' regulations in Deut. 24. 1. Yet it was not a '*command*,' but only a *permission*, the spirit of which was still in the line of our Lord's legislation, making a writing of divorcement requisite, and thus giving a lower testimony to the essential sanctity of marriage. See note on ch. 5. 31, 32. But Moses' permission had been abused, until, as in the text, they called it a *command*, and without reference to the original institution of marriage, they held among them, that divorce might be for *any and every* cause. There were two schools or sects among the Jews who took opposite sides on this subject. The school of *Shammai* interpreted Moses, as allowing divorce "only for the cause of fornication." The school of *Hillel* construed it as referring to any cause or pretext. And instead of being entangled, by siding with either, our Lord declares that Moses' permission only showed *their hardness* which had gone so much beyond this allowance; so that this civil regulation of that day, was meant as a check upon their worse habits, and that from *the beginning*, as Moses himself had recorded (Gen. 2), "*it was not so.*"——¶ *Hardness of your hearts*—intractable disposition.—*Campbell.*

9. This verse is almost in the same language as ch. 5. 32, and states again the Christian law of marriage and divorce. Marriage has special sanctity as the shadow of that great mystery, Christ's union with His church. Mark adds (ch. 10. 12) "And if a woman shall put away her husband," &c. The practice of divorcing the husband unwarranted by the law, had been introduced (says Josephus) by Salome, sister of Herod the Great, who sent a bill of divorce to her husband Coslobarus, which had example was afterward followed by Herodias and others.—*Campbell.*

10. An objection is here urged making against the very institution of marriage, if such strictness is to be observed.

so with *his* wife, it is not good to marry.ᵍ

11 But he said unto them, All *men* cannot receive this saying, save *they* to whom it is given.

12 For there are some eunuchs, which were so born from *their* mother's womb: and there are some eunuchs, which were made eunuchs of men: and there be eunuchs, which have made themselves eunuchs for the kingdom of heaven's ʰ sake. He that is able to receive *it*, let him receive *it*.

13 ¶ Then were there

---
g Pr.19.13; 21.9,19.   h 1Cor.7.32.
---

11. Our Lord replies that such a doctrine as the expediency of living unmarried, could not be received by men at all, save by a certain limited class. It is not natural with men.——¶ *All men cannot receive.* That is, *none can receive.* This use of terms is peculiar in the New Testament. So in Rom. 3. 20: "There shall no flesh be justified," reads in the Greek, "All flesh shall not be justified." It is an emphatic negative, "*All* shall *not* be." That is, the impossibility is universal and extends positively to ALL. The sense of this passage then is, none can receive this sentiment, suggested in verse 10, save those few to whom it is given, who are spoken of in verse 12. He meant to say that men have a different principle implanted in their very constitution. Marriage is natural as well as honourable in all. See 1 Cor. 7. 7, 26.—— ¶ *To whom it is given*, by nature or by grace.

12. Our Lord here speaks of a certain class fitted to live unmarried. *Eunuchs.* The term means, literally, *a bed-keeper*, chamberlain. Either such as are so born, or such as are so made by men, for the purpose commonly, of attending on females. There was such a class in the East, who served in the harem. They were sometimes promoted to high office, whence the word comes to mean also *a minister of state, a high officer*, whether a eunuch in fact or not. So Potiphar is called a eunuch, Gen. 39. 1. Comp. Acts 8. 27, the eunuch, a grandee under *Candace*, queen of the Ethiopians.——¶ *Made themselves eunuchs.* This is hyperbolical language, like ch. 5. 29. 30, cutting off a right hand, &c. Such as by mortification and denial have virtually made themselves so. That is, they willingly live unmarried, for the kingdom of heaven's sake, with the intent of more exclusively devoting themselves to the services of religion. Origen fell into sad error on this point, carrying out the literal purport of this clause. And some forbid marriage to the clergy, which is denounced by the Apostle as "a doctrine of devils" (1 Tim. 4. 1, 3). See Paul's teachings "by permission and not of commandment," in 1 Cor. ch. 7. They embody the general sentiment here annexed.——¶ *He that is able*, &c. *It is good to abide even as I. But*, &c. 1 Cor. 7. 8, 9. All the Apostles did not receive it, that is, did not live unmarried. 1 Cor. 9. 5. *An obligation to celibacy* (says Calvin) is a great mistake. It is a foolish imagination that celibacy is a virtue, especially if in it a man only consults his own ease and convenience.

OBSERVE, (1.) The sanctity of the marriage institution is proved to be "*from the beginning*" (4–8). (2.) Moses legislates in the same line with Christ, and gives a lower testimony in those civil regulations which must have respect to the state of society (8). (3.) The gospel of Christ restores the marriage relation to all its original sanctity and value. *For this*, even modern civilization is indebted to the gospel. And society in Christian lands owes all its domestic blessings to the religion of Jesus Christ.

§ 105. JESUS RECEIVES AND BLESSES LITTLE CHILDREN.—*Perea.*

Matt.	Mark.	Luke.	John
19. 13–15	10. 13–16	18. 15–17	

brought unto him little children, that he should put *his* hands on them, and pray : and the disciples rebuked them.

14 But Jesus said, Suffer *i* little children, and forbid them not, to come unto me, for of such *j* is the kingdom of heaven.

15 And he laid *his* hands on them, and departed thence.

i Mar.10.14. Lu.18.16,&c.

j c 18.3.

13. *There were brought unto Him.* As it had been customary among the Jews to apply to children the seal of the Abrahamic covenant in circumcision, they came naturally enough, with their *little children*, under the new dispensation. This is the most obvious mode of accounting for a presentation of such children by the parent's act. In Luke we find that these were *infants.*——¶ *That He should put His hands on them.* This was the customary sign of a blessing. In the act of pronouncing it, the hand was laid on the head of the person, expressing by such a gesture, the idea of conveying the benefit. See Gen. 48. 14. Matt. 9. 18. It has always been natural to seek such a communication of good, or sign of it, from the excellent whom we venerate. Especially was this done among the Jews. Num. 22. 6 ; 27. 18. Acts 8. 18. 2 Kings 5. 11.——¶ *And pray.* They sought His prayers for them, it appears, looking upon Him as "the messenger of the covenant" (Mal. 3.1) —the Christ of God.——¶ *Rebuked*—that is, *reproved* those who brought them, found fault with them, and signified their displeasure at this. They thought it a small matter or a mere obtrusion of the parents, interrupting Christ to show their children, or that *children* had nothing to do with Christ, nor He with them. This last would have seemed the point aimed at in Christ's reply, and it is the sad mistake of many.

14. *Suffer little children*, allow them. Do not cast them off as though they had no interest in my work, "*and forbid them not*," adds Mark, who also says that Christ "*was much displeased*" at the disciples for rebuking the parents. Luke has it further that Christ "*called them* unto Him." Our Lord's remark here means that *of such* as these is the church on earth. He meant to signify (1.) that infants of believing parents have an interest in the covenant, and are therefore to be respected and allowed this blessing from Christ. Also, (2.) That of *such like*, persons of childlike temper and character, the church consists, (rebuking their haughtiness by the way) (ch. 18. 1-5, 10), as He adds (see Mark and Luke), "Whosoever shall not receive the kingdom of God *as a little child*, he shall not enter therein" (ch. 18. 3, 4). This language gives encouragement to children who would seek Christ, that He pays them such marked attention and is much more willing to receive them, than men would think. They can go to Christ now, for they can pray to Him, and believe these words that He has said. And they should go now whilst they are children, because He shows here and elsewhere a special readiness to receive the young. "They that seek me early shall find me" (Prov. 8. 17).

15. *He laid His hands on them.* He complied with the parental request. Mark adds, that "*He took them up in His arms and blessed them.*"

OBSERVE, (1.) *Christian* parents, who seek in prayer the Divine blessing on their children, and so bring them now to Christ, are here encouraged. It is the way of His plans for Zion to comply with their request, for He perpetuates the church on earth by means of *a godly seed.* He can and will bless them, for of such is the kingdom of heaven. (2.) Infant baptism falls in with this sentiment of our Lord. "*Suffer*" such to come. He *rebukes* such as *forbid* them. Many, like those disciples, think that children have nothing to do with Christ, and are to be held back, because unable to understand. But of such is the visible church. "The

16 ¶ And behold, one came, and said unto him, Good master, what ᵏ good thing shall I do, that I may have eternal life?

17 And he said unto him, Why callest thou me good? *there is* none good but one, *that is* God: but if thou wilt enter into life, keep the commandments.

k Mar.10.17. Lu.10.25; 18.18.

18 He saith unto him, Which? Jesus said, Thou ˡ shalt do no murder, Thou shalt not commit adultery, Thou shalt not steal, Thou shalt not bear false witness;

19 Honour thy father and *thy* mother; and, Thou ᵐ shalt love thy neighbour as thyself.

20 The young man saith unto

l Ex.20.13. De.5.17,&c. *m* Le.19.18.

---

promise is unto you and to your children."

§ 106. THE RICH YOUNG MAN. PARABLE OF THE LABOURERS IN THE VINEYARD.—*Perea.*

Matt.	Mark.	Luke.	John.
19.16–30	10.17–31	18.18–30	
20. 1–16.			

This was " a certain *ruler*," as we learn from Luke. He "came *running* and kneeled to Him," as we learn from Mark. He was doubtless a ruler of the synagogue. Though he is here called a young man he belonged to the Jewish eldership, which was filled, like the same office now, not according to age always, but according to the standing in the church. He was no doubt of high repute.——¶ *Good Master.* A title usually given to distinguished Jewish Rabbis.——¶ *Eternal life,* that is, salvation, heaven.

17. *Why callest thou?* &c. Our Lord would take him up, upon the title he gave Him, "*good master,*" and would show him that his real views of Him did not agree with this. He would thus more directly attack his low ideas of the Master. " You give me a title which properly belongs to God alone, yet you do not even receive my doctrine, much less regard me as God." Christ did not mean to say that He was not God, but rather *that He was;* and that the young man ought so to esteem Him, even to be consistent with the title which he gave Him. But he denied at heart the Divinity of Christ, and our Lord here calls attention to His own claims, which he rejected. And this was a striking and appropriate way of reproving the young man.——¶ *Keep the commandments.* Christ now presents him with the claims of the Divine law upon him, charging him with his obligation to keep the commandments. He does not say that any man ever kept them so as to deserve heaven, as none ever did (Rom. 3. 20, 28; 4. 6. Gal. 2. 16. Ephes. 2. 9. 2 Tim. 1. 9). But by these he is to be judged; and only by seeing his inability to do this, and his short coming, could he feel the need of Christ's salvation. If any one is to gain eternal life by his works, he must, in all his life, keep the whole law, and not offend in one point—else he is *guilty of all*—that is, condemned by the whole law (James 2. 10).

18, 19. *Which?* Our Lord here points the inquirer to certain of the commandments. These were not all, yet quite enough for a trial (See Ex. 20. 12–16). These had relation to the common relative duties, and were all summed up in the last clause, " Thou shalt love thy neighbour as thyself" (Matt. 22. 39). He would have him judged now by his daily conduct, to see if he had kept, *in the spirit,* these commandments; and by using the last clause as a comprehensive summary, he points him to the great truth, that there is the *spirit,* beyond the *letter,* which is to be observed.

20. He holds himself unimpeached on all these points, and thought he had fully kept these requirements. So narrow had been his views of what the law of God demands of men.

him, All these things have I kept from my youth up: what lack I yet?

21 Jesus said unto him, If thou wilt be perfect, go ⁿ *and* sell that thou hast, and give to the poor, and thou shalt have treasure in heaven; and come *and* follow ᵒ me.

22 But when the young man heard that saying, he went away sorrowful: for he had great possessions.

23 ¶ Then said Jesus unto his disciples, Verily I say unto you, that ᵖ a rich man shall hardly enter into the kingdom of heaven.

24 And again I say unto you, It is easier for a camel to go through the eye of a needle, than for a rich man to enter into the kingdom of God.

n Lu.12.33; 16.9. Ac.2.45; 4.34,35. 1Ti.6.18,19.
o Jnu.12.26.

p 1Ti.6.9,10.

—— ¶ *From my youth up* — rather, from my childhood.

21. Our Lord now puts to him an unexpected test, yet the most allowable.—— ¶ *If thou wilt be perfect.* See note, ch. 5. 48. "One thing thou lackest" (Mark, Luke). The law he had not kept. If we really had kept the ten commandments, we should be ready to obey whatever God enjoins; and the ten commandments, rightly understood, do really cover all possible duties. Though love to our neighbour does not require of us, ordinarily, to give away all we have to the poor, yet here Christ commanded it; and if He commanded it of us, we should not hesitate, else we love ur possessions better than Himself. Had he *done this,* he could not have *deserved* eternal life, for it could not be bought by any amount of money or of self-sacrifice. It must needs be received by sinners as a free gift. Yet this young man could have claimed Christ's promise to him. But now, the heart is shown to be *worldly,* and needing to be changed. To part with wealth for Christ, and to give to the poor, were beyond his attainments. Mark says that "Jesus, beholding him, loved him" (vs. 21). As a man, He felt an interest in his amiable and ingenuous qualities; and He who loves sinners, even his enemies, so as to die for the vilest, could not be destitute of love toward this youth, though it was not his covenant love. God has a love *to the world.* But it is expressed in the plan of salvation by a Redeemer. "God *so* loved the world, that He gave His only-begotten Son, *that* whosoever believeth in Him should not perish, but have everlasting life."

22. It appears here, that he had great struggles and sorrows on account of such a test being applied. He could not bear to give up his worldly possessions. They were the idol of his heart, and the more wealth he had, the harder it was to yield to such a demand. "*Covetousness* is IDOLATRY."

23. *Hardly*—with great difficulty. Christ here teaches what was shown in this case, that it is *hard*—not impossible, but extremely difficult—for a rich man to get to heaven—because it is found to be hard to put Christ's will before his worldly possessions. Mark has it, "How hard is it for them that trust in riches." Luke, "They that have riches."

24. *It is easier for a camel to go through the eye of a needle.* Lord Nugent, in his recent publication, "Lands Sacred and Classical," has given an application of these words which strikingly shows their fitness and point. Lord N. describes himself as "about to walk out of Hebron, through the *large gate,* when his companions, seeing a train of camels approaching, desired him to go through *the eye of the needle*"—in other words, the small side of the gate. This Lord N. applies as explanatory of the Saviour's words; for he adds, "the sumpter camel cannot pass through unless

A. D. 33.] CHAPTER XIX. 197

25 When his disciples heard *it*, they were exceedingly amazed, saying, Who then can be saved?

26 But Jesus beheld *them*, and said unto them, With men this is impossible; but ^q with God all things are possible.

27 ¶ Then ^r answered Peter, and said unto him, Behold, we have forsaken all ^s and followed

thee: what shall we have therefore?

28 And Jesus said unto them, Verily, I say unto you, that ye which have followed me, in the regeneration, when the Son of man shall sit in the throne of his glory, ye ^t also shall sit upon twelve thrones, judging the twelve tribes of Israel.

q Ps.3.8; 62.11. Zec.8.6. *r* Mar.10.28. Lu.18.28. *s* Ph.3.8.

t c.20.21. Lu.22.28-30. 1Cor.6.2,3. Re.2.26.

with great difficulty, and stripped of his load, his trappings, and his merchandize." This language was proverbial among the Jews, to denote an impossibility. Literally it meant, that it was easier for a huge camel, with all his load of goods, to go through this small side gate, than for a rich man to enter into the kingdom of heaven—of course one who loves riches, and trusts in them (as Mark has it), is meant. This should warn us not to covet wealth, nor too eagerly to pursue what may prove to us such a serious obstacle in the way to heaven. This young man lacked *one thing* (see Mark's language); Christ had put to him this test—if he would be *perfect*—that is, if he had a disposition to be complete and entire—*wanting nothing*. But here was the lack of *one thing*—of a disposition to serve Christ fully, and to make His favour more than wealth or life. He lacked the *essential, vital thing*. So there is some one thing that keeps many from following Christ. They have too large possessions, or too many gay friends and amusements, or a self-righteousness, which they cannot consent to part with, *even for Christ Himself*. The most common thing among the young is this *love of the world*, which the scripture declares is so inconsistent with true love to God (1 John 2. 15). "They that *will* be rich, fall into temptation," &c. (1 Tim. 6. 9.)

25. *Exceedingly amazed.* Mark has it. "were astonished out of measure."——¶ *Who then can be saved?*

They are startled at such a rule laid down, and think it must exclude many —*or* ALL.

26. *With men, &c.* Our Lord replies, that this only shows the impossibility by human power—that by human means, indeed, this is quite impossible. The impotency of all human effort, and even of the *means of grace*, in themselves, to change and save the soul, is most apparent. In God is the only hope. But *with Him*, it is *possible!* "Born, not of blood, nor of the will of the flesh, nor of the will of man, but of GOD" (John 1. 13). "I can do all things through Christ, which strengtheneth me" (Phil. 4.13).

27. *Then answered Peter.* Peter is induced by this language of our Lord, to mention the case of the twelve, and to ask what special reward they may expect *for having left all*. Their boats, and nets, and fish, and father, were *every thing* to them. They might, indeed, look for a reward, for it had been promised. But this temper is wrong, so far as it puts forth *claims* for our good deeds, as though we deserved the reward at Christ's hands. What *pay* does a man deserve for giving up a copper, or pepper-corn, for a palace?

28. *Ye which have followed me.* The words "*in the regeneration*" belong to the remainder of the verse, and are not to be read with the preceding words. Christ tells of the reward that shall be revealed for his humble followers. A time of *regeneration* is coming. The term means *renovation* —literally *new birth*—and refers to

29 And ᵘ every one that hath forsaken houses, or brethren, or sisters, or father, or mother, or wife, or children, or lands, for my name's sake, shall receive an hundred-fold, and shall inherit everlasting life.

30 But ᵛ many *that are* first shall be last; and the last *shall be* first.

u Mar.10.29,30. Lu.18.29,30. 1Cor.2.9.

v c.20.16. c.21.31,32. Mar.10.31. Lu.13.30. Ga.5.7. He.4.1.

the *new creation* prophesied as the glory of the latter days, "when the Son of man shall sit on the throne of his glory" (ch. 25. Isa. 65. 17; 66. 22. Rev. 21. 1). In this new state of things, wherein all things *shall become new*, ye shall enjoy a glorious distinction. When Christ shall come to judgment, sitting on the throne of His glory—or His glorious throne—as Mediator and Judge, then, as great kings have officers around them, dignitaries of the kingdom, ye, the twelve apostles, shall be exalted to special honour, and shall sit on twelve thrones of majesty, judging the people of God —the twelve tribes of Israel. The language is used to express most strongly to them, in a way which they could appreciate, the special glories *reserved for them*, in connexion with Christ's exaltation. See Luke 22. 28, 29, 30, where it is "eating and drinking at His table" that is the figure used to enforce this.

29. *Forsaken.* The forsaking here intended is such as accords with the spirit of the discourse. We must have our affections weaned from the pleasures and riches of the world, so as willingly to part with any thing and every thing for Christ. The early Christians actually gave up houses, and lands, and friends. This is not always called for; but where it is called for we are not to hesitate. The disposition—the *heart* is all-important.——¶ *A hundred-fold.* Such shall receive a hundred-fold of *real good.* Mark reads, a hundred-fold (that is, a hundred times as much) of the same things. But the meaning is rather, in substantial, essential value. Mark adds, "with persecutions," showing that it is not *worldly ease* that is promised, but what shall be a hundred times better.

30. This verse is thrown in, as a caution against indolence or presumption. Though great honours and rewards awaited them, they were not such as they had thought; for the *last* might come out *first*, on His plan of reckoning, and the *first* be *last* in those distributions. Also He would teach, by a proverbial saying, that this future exaltation will not be according to appearances or prospects here. The highly honoured here, will often be the most degraded and sunk, in those future awards. Hence they should not covet earthly distinctions, as Peter seemed to have sought for, in his question. This language applies to all! Those of best advantages for obtaining true religion, often turn out the worst; while those of humble opportunities are often found entering the kingdom first. Publicans and harlots enter, while the children of the kingdom are cast out. Those who seem nearest the kingdom, are often the farthest from entering in, and seem to find it most difficult to see the way, or continue most careless about it. The moral and correct in life, who are not true Christians, often seem most fixed and settled in their neglect of Christ.

OBSERVE, (1.) Many inquire what they must *do* to be saved, with the most mistaken views of Christ's person and claims. (2.) Those who would get to heaven by *doing some good thing*, must be held to a perfec obedience of the Divine law. "Do this and live." (3.) How easy is it for men to be mistaken as to their keeping the commandments. So Paul the apostle, in Romans ch. 7, "The law is spiritual." (4.) Duties to God are of superior rank—but duties to our neighbour will sufficiently test our dispositions. (5) Christ will

CHAPTER XX.

FOR the kingdom of heaven is like unto a man *that is* an householder, *a* which went out early in the morning to hire labourers into his vineyard.

2 And when he had agreed with the labourers for a penny *b*

a Ca.3.11,12.

b c.18.28.

teach men their utter impotency to reach heaven by *their works*. (6.) There is no salvation but by *embracing Christ*, acknowledging His claims, trusting to His offices, and following His gracious commands (vss. 17–21).

CHAPTER XX.

1. *For.* This parable, on the principle of rewards in the kingdom of God, is to be read in close connexion with the preceding context. It is given to illustrate the last verse of the former chapter. Peter had asked, in view of the young ruler's shrinking, and of their forsaking *all*, "What shall we have therefore?" Christ told them that their reward should be great. But he adds a sentiment in the last verse of ch. 19., and enforces it by this parable—warning them against a *hireling spirit*.——¶ *The kingdom of heaven*—here means the church of Christ. This general doctrine is most important: SALVATION IS ALL OF GRACE—"not of works, lest any man should boast." Many shall come out very differently from their haughty expectations and claims. But God will do justly by all, and yet will do what He will with His own; and if nothing of works, but all of grace to all, then no glorying of one over another could find place—no judging of one against another—no claim as of right on the part of any. (See Rom. 4. 1–4.) As addressed to Peter, and in him to all true believers, the parable is rather aimed against their carnal calculations of reward. The same legal spirit that worked for wages (the penny a day) looked for *temporal* preferments, and asked *who* should be *greatest*. In all these things they should be disappointed. And though "they expected to have received more," they would get nothing but the substance of the gospel promise—eternal life—with persecutions; and this according to the plan of grace. So the last shall be first, &c. Peter's pay should so disappoint his carnal hope, that at the moment he would deny the Master. It could not be by self-complacent comparisons with others, nor by laying their demands upon God, that they could ever stand. The spirit of that question, "What shall we have therefore?" shall only, if carried out, bring itself sadly behind those who, like the other and later labourers, humbly wait upon God for all that He hath promised. Again: it is altogether a false principle in Christian duty, to have an eye always to *others'* services and rewards—comparing ourselves among ourselves. This hinders Christian engagedness. We are to work, not with eye-service, but as unto the Lord and not to men—to walk worthy of God. This Peter, at last, when told of his final trials, thought immediately of *the other disciple*, and asked the Master, "And what shall this man do?" Jesus answered, "If I will that he tarry till I come, what is that to thee? *Follow thou me*" (John 21. 18–22). The parable would precisely meet his case, as it was foreseen. *Each man to do his own duty, irrespective of others' duties or rewards, is the true principle.* Only this can lead us to the great idea of aiming at God's will on earth—not as other men do it here, but *as angels do it in heaven.* "Go work to-day in my vineyard," is the call. "Follow THOU me."——¶ *An householder.* The head of a family who keeps house, and has work done in his vineyard. The vineyard was a farm for raising *grape-vines*, to make *wine;* and this was a common business in Judea. God calls the visible church His vineyard, as a well-cultivated spot. Isa. 5. 7. Christ is this householder in God's house.——¶ *Went out.* God seeks His labourers, rather than they

200 MATTHEW. [A. D. 33.

a day, he sent them into his vineyard.

3 And he went out about the third hour, and saw others standing idle in the market-place,

4 And said unto them, Go ye also into the vineyard, and whatsoever is right, I will give you. And they went their way.

5 And again he went out about the sixth and ninth hour, and did likewise.

6 And about the eleventh hour he went out, and found others standing idle, and saith unto them, Why stand ye here all the day idle? *c*

7 They say unto him, Because no man hath hired us. He saith unto them, *d* Go ye also into the vineyard; and whatsoever is right, *that* shall ye receive.

8 So when even was come, the lord of the vineyard saith unto his steward, Call the labourers, and *e* give them *their* hire, beginning from the last unto the first.

9 And when they came that *were hired* about the eleventh *r* hour, they received every man a penny.

10 But when the first came, they supposed that they should

c Pr.19.15. Eze.16.49. Ac.17.21. He.6.12.   *d* Ec.9.10. Jno.9.4.   *e* Lu.10.7.   *f* Lu.23.30-43.

Him. "Ye have not chosen me, but I have chosen you." The Son of man is come to seek and to save that which was lost.

2. *He had agreed.* God has recorded His promises, which are to be the basis of our transactions with Him. What He will do, He has told us beforehand; and on this ground we are called to act. And His promises never fail.——¶ *A penny a day.* This Roman coin was equal to about 12 cents, or our shilling, and was the common price of labour then when every thing else was in proportion. There was a *positive agreement, at fair wages.*

3. *The third hour.* Nine o'clock in the morning.

4. This shows the understanding with others. They were standing idle in the *market-place,* where the people generally gathered for business, or to see what work could be had. In this case there was no definite price fixed, but they were hired for what was right, and they must have confidence in the employer. When we find not a definite promise personal to ourselves, we must work for our Master, and TRUST HIM for a reward.

5. *The sixth and ninth hour.* 12 and 3 o'clock. The Jews divided their days into twelve parts, from sunrise to sunset; and there were four chief divisions, third, sixth, ninth and twelfth hours.

6. *The eleventh hour.* Just upon the close of working time—one hour only left.

8. *When even was come*—that is, the close of the day, at sunset; or the 12th hour having arrived, and the working time being finished, the settlement must be made.——¶ *His steward.* This was the man-servant or overseer who took the house under his charge—provided meals, and attended to house business—keeping accounts, &c., so as to relieve the householder. ——¶ *Beginning from the last.* He had a right to *begin* the *payment* where he chose—and beginning at the bottom of the list, the others first hired found what these received. This order was chosen to illustrate the doctrine, and bring out the point of the parable.

10. *Supposed that they should have received more.* The parable would meet such false and self-complacent expectations as they evidently had, after all that had been told them. How disappointed were they to be, at their Master's trial, and at their own per-

have received more; and they likewise received every man a penny.

11 And when they had received *it*, they murmured ᵍ against the good man of the house,

12 Saying, These last ¹ have wrought *but* one hour, and thou hast made them equal unto us, which have borne the burden and heat of the day.

13 But he answered one of them, and said, Friend, ʰ I do thee no wrong: didst not thou agree with me for a penny?

14 Take *that* thine *is*, and go thy way: ⁱ I will give unto this last even as unto thee.

15 Is ʲ it not lawful for me to do what I will with mine own? Is ᵏ thine eye evil because I am good?

16 So ˡ the last shall be first, and the first last: for ᵐ many be called, but few chosen.

g Lu.15.29,30. 1 Or, *have continued one hour only.*
h c.22.12. *i* Jno.17.2. *j* Ro.9.15-24. Ja.1.18. *k* De.15.9. c.6.23. *l* c.19.30. *m* c.22.14. 1Th.2.13. Ja.1.23-25.

---

secuted lot! How Peter was to shrink at the announcement, by his Lord, of the outstretched hands—the girding—and violent carrying away in his old age (John 21. 18)! How James and John were to revolt at the cup (vs. 23)! No earthly throne—no right and left hand station, should be theirs in a temporal kingdom.

11. *Murmured*—at others being made equal to them—at their having no higher emolument such as they had expected, and comporting with their close personal connexion with the Master. So Peter himself should soon murmur that, instead of earthly dignity, he should have violent death—and that John should have had, at the same time, no such hard lot assigned him. But Christ should then reply substantially as here: "What is that to thee?" see John 21. 18-22, "I do thee no wrong."

13. *Friend.* As we say, "My friend." Christ vindicates His equity.

14. *I will give*—literally, "It is my will to give."

15. *Is it not lawful.* Has not God a perfect right to dispense His favours, and especially His gifts of grace, as He will?——¶ *Is thine eye evil?* Does my goodness to others give you an envious eye, or alter my fairness toward yourself? It was His *extra goodness,* after all, and nothing else, that they could complain of. "An evil eye" was one not *single* but *double* (Matt. 6. 23)—not principled and honest—double-sighted, full of duplicity and envy. In this expression, "*an evil eye,*" there lies, says Trench, the belief—one of the most wide-spread in the world—of the eye being able to put forth positive powers of mischief. "So long as I am *just* to you, may I not be *good* and liberal to them?" This distinction in the words "*righteous*" and "*good*" occurs in Romans 5. 7.

16. *So.* This proverbial language—where the parallel form of expression is for intensity—gives the opening sentiment (ch. 19. 30), illustrated by the parable. Christians shall often be greatly disappointed in the temporal rewards of Christ's service. The poverty, crosses, persecutions, are hard to understand, and harder to bear. It is yet so. We murmur at others who fare better. But is not God *faithful?* And is not salvation of *grace?* And is not Christ enough? And is it not enough for us, if we be *chosen,* from among the many that are called? Should not this one thought of God's distinguishing grace to us in Christ, quell our rising murmurs, and make us rejoice in persecutions for His name.——¶ *For many.* This sentiment enforces the moral of the parable. Amidst so much that is unworthy and mistaken, we see how the salvation of any must be of MERE GRACE. This looking after rewards

17 ¶ And ⁿ Jesus going up to Jerusalem, took the twelve disciples apart in the way, and said unto them,

n c.16.21,&c. Mar.10.32,&c. Lu.18.31,&c. Jno.12.12,&c.

18 Behold, we go up to Jerusalem; and the Son of man shall be betrayed unto the chief priests and unto the scribes, and they shall condemn him to death,

---

prematurely, and wrongfully—making invidious comparisons and claims—having an envious eye to others' pay—and disposed to act so little on the high principles of individual duty—will lead to disappointment. It will make the last first and the first last—confounding all such unworthy expectations and estimates. And let it be known that, amidst many deceptions and delusions, the truly Christian are a few—chosen; for this evil spirit will reign in many that shall be found outside. "Many will say to me in that day, Lord, Lord, have we not prophesied in thy name," &c. Matt. 25.

OBSERVE, (1.) A legal temper looks for reward on wrong grounds, and looks for the wrong kind of wages. It must therefore be disappointed and fall short. (2.) God is just and faithful. He will not fail of all that He has promised. (3.) It is altogether a false principle of Christian duty to compare ourselves among ourselves, or have an eye to others' duty and reward. "Follow *thou* me." (4.) Every Christian inherits the promises, and gets *Christ*. They all are "heirs according to the promise." God is a sovereign. He is not indebted to any. What He grants to some is no injury to others. His electing love, whereby some are plucked as out of the burning, does not make His proclamation of grace *insincere* to others. The true convert sees and adores His distinguishing grace, displayed in his salvation. (5.) Salvation is possible to the aged and to the dying; yet this parable is not spoken to teach this doctrine. They have been called long before the eleventh hour, and therefore are not like these in the parable (vss. 6 and 7). They who neglect religion, planning to come into the kingdom at the eleventh hour, may tremble at *God's sovereignty*, as it is here taught. He will do what He wills with His own. "Because I called and ye refused, &c., I will laugh at your calamity."

§ 107. JESUS A THIRD TIME FORETELLS HIS DEATH AND RESURRECTION. (See § 74 and § 77.)—*Perea.*

Matt.	Mark.	Luke.	John.
20.17–19	10.32–34	18.31–34	

17. *Jesus going up to Jerusalem.* He had been on the way from Galilee, on the other side Jordan, having left Galilee finally; and now He sets out more particularly in the direction of Jerusalem. He was probably now bending His course across from Perea to Judea, about in the line of Jerusalem. They always spoke of *going up* to Jerusalem, no matter from what quarter they went. Mark says, that "Jesus went before them, and they were amazed; and as they followed, they were afraid."——¶ *Apart in the way.* He took them aside. There may have been others in the company, as the Passover was approaching, and many must have been going up to the feast. All the males were required to attend (Exod. 23. 17). The ground of their fear was likely His setting His face toward Jerusalem, where they knew He had enemies. He had also announced to them His coming death, which they dreaded. Accordingly He declares His intention to visit the holy city, and reveals to them more than their fears. This was a farther disclosure of the circumstances that should attend His death than He had yet made. (See ch. 17. 22.) Luke has it, that He declared to them now the fulfilment of all the prophecies, and that they understood none of these things.

18. *Betrayed unto the chief priests,* &c. So Judas did betray Him into the hands of the Sanhedrim, who also condemned Him to death; for

19 And ⁰ shall deliver him to the Gentiles, to mock, and to scourge, ᴾ and to crucify *him:* and the third day he shall rise again.

20 ¶ Then ᑫ came to him the mother of Zebedee's children, with her sons, worshipping *him*, and desiring a certain thing of him.

o c.27.2,&c. Mar.15.1,16,&c. Lu.23.1,&c. Jno.18. 28,&c. Ac.3.13. 1Cor.15.3-7. p Is.53.5. q Mar.10. 35.

21 And he said unto her, What wilt thou? She saith unto him, Grant that these my two sons may sit, the one on thy right hand, and the other on the left, in thy kingdom.

22 But Jesus answered and said, Ye know not what ye ask. Are ye able to drink of the cup that I shall drink of, and to be baptized with the ʳ baptism that I am baptized with? They

r Lu.12.50.

they were the highest court of the nation. (Matt. 26. 66; 27. 2.)

19. *And shall deliver Him to the Gentiles*, i. e., the Romans—because the Jews had no longer the right of executing sentence of death for crime. This should literally come to pass. Accordingly He was handed over to Pilate and the soldiers (Matt. 27. 2, 27, 30).——¶ *To mock*—with insulting looks and words.——¶ *Scourge*—or whip, with lashes made for the purpose of whipping criminals.——¶ *Crucify*. This was the severe extremity to which things should be carried. It was a Roman punishment, not Jewish.——¶ *And the third day.* There was nevertheless this consolation, that He should after all triumph and rise again. (See Mark and Luke, Harmony.)

§ 108. JAMES AND JOHN PREFER THEIR AMBITIOUS REQUEST.—*Perea.*

Matt.	Mark.	Luke.	John.
20. 20–28	10. 35–45		

From Luke 19. 11, it is plain that they expected the kingdom would immediately appear. He had hinted of what was to take place soon at Jerusalem, and He was drawing toward it.

20. *The mother of Zebedee's children.* The father of James and John was now in all probability dead. Hence Salome is called by this striking title, which indicates that she was now a *widow*.——¶ *With her sons.* She joined in the request, and would seem to have prompted it, as *they* are addressed in reply.

21. *Grant that these.* Mark has it that James and John made the request. Doubtless they did it in connexion with their mother, and chiefly through her. Having learned from the parable of the labourers that the reward is not of debt, but of grace, they come with the petition, "*Grant.*" "We would that thou shouldest do for us whatsoever we shall desire" (Mark 10. 35); and this paragraph closes with the same sentiment of the parable, farther enjoined (vss. 26 and 27); "Whosoever shall be great among you," &c.——¶ *Thy kingdom.* They were expecting an earthly kingdom, and they wished its honours and comforts, especially the elevation and ease of a seat beside Himself—*right and left hand stations*—the two places of greatest dignity and power. (See 1 Kings 2. 19.)

22. *The cup.* In the arrangement of feasts, in ancient times at the East, the *cup* and *dish* with their portion, expressed the personal esteem of the Master of the feast, for the guest. This term, in scripture, is used to denote a portion, especially of sorrow. So Christ speaks of *the cup* which His Father gave Him to drink (John 18. 11), and the cup at the sacramental feast, represented His suffering unto death, while it was the sign of covenant blessings to be partaken by the disciples: "Drink ye all of it, this cup is the new testament in my blood." By the cup that he should drink of, He means here the measure

say unto him, We are able.

23 And he saith unto them, Ye *shall drink indeed of my cup, and be baptized with the baptism that I am baptized with; but to sit on my right hand, and on my left, is not mine to give, but *it shall be given to them* for whom it is prepared of my Father.

24 And when the ten heard *it*, they were moved with indignation against the two brethren.

25 But Jesus called them unto him, and said, Ye *know that the princes of the Gentiles exercise dominion over them, and they that are great exercise authority upon them.

26 But it shall not be ᵘ so among you : but ᵛ whosoever will be great among you, let him be your minister ;

27 And whosoever will be chief among you, let him be your servant :

28 Even as the Son of man came not to be ministered unto,

s Ac.12.2. Ro.8.17. 2Cor.1.7. Re.1.9.

t Lu.22.25,26. u 1Pe.5.3. v c.23.11. Mar.9.35; 10.43.

---

of His agonies, in the garden, and on the cross for sinners. (See Isa 51. 17, 22. Psalm 75. 8; 16. 5; 23. 5.) So the *baptism* under another figure, expresses the same idea. Baptism represents the *outpouring* of Divine influence upon the soul. But *this* baptism was one of suffering, and tears, and blood. The cup and baptism which they understood Him to mean, was that of an outward profession and adherence to Him, as baptism was the open profession of faith.

23. *Ye shall drink.* Our Lord here assures them, that it shall be indeed as they so promptly agree to, and beyond what they yet conceive. James was slain by Herod (**Acts** 1 . 2), and John was banished to Patmos, a sufferer for Christ (Rev. 1. 9).

——¶ *Not mine to give, but.* Observe that the words in Italics have no authority, and should be left out, because they mar the sense. These rewards (He would say) are not mine to give *except* for whom it is prepared of my Father. They should have their measure of suffering, and the reward should come to them according to Infinite equity and love. These were not matters of favouritism, but of Divine grace, and of eternal counsel. The Greek word αλλα, " *but*," is here for " except," as in Mark, 9. 8.

24. *When the ten.* The other ten apostles, when they heard it—that is, this ambitious request of the two brethren for a superiority, which would disparage themselves—were indignant.

25–27. *But Jesus called them.* Here our Lord took occasion to lay down the true principle on the whole subject, to show what were the true honours of His kingdom, &c. That it was unlike earthly courts, where the princes of the nations (Gentiles) are set over the subjects, and (great) men of noble rank exercise authority. Not so in His kingdom (vs. 26). The rule of pre-eminence which He would prescribe is the very opposite of earthly courts. The true greatness in His kingdom, is to *serve* or *minister.*

28. *Even as.* They had Christ's own example for this. He took the form of a servant, though He was the greatest of beings, God over all. Phil. 2. 7. This was His very object, to serve men.——¶ *And to give His life a ransom for many.* This was the most striking evidence of His coming to serve men—rather than to be served by them—that His object was to give His own life in the stead of others The language is altogether the strongest possible. " *A ransom*" was the price of redemption which should actually buy back out of evil hands. *For*, in the Greek, is (αντι) *anti—over*

but ʷ to minister, and ˣ to give his life a ransom for many.

29 And as they departed from Jericho, a great multitude followed him.
30 ¶ And ʸ behold, two blind men, sitting by the way-side, when they heard that Jesus passed by, cried out, saying,

<small>w Lu.22.27. Jno.13.4,14. Ph. 2.7. x Is.53.5,8,11. Da.9.24,26. 1Tim.2.6. Tit.2.14. He.9.28. 1Pe.1.18,19. Re.1.5. y c.9.27. Mar.10.46. Lu.18.35.</small>

Have mercy on us, O Lord, *thou* Son of David!
31 And the multitude rebuked them, because they should hold their peace: but they cried the more, saying, Have mercy on us, O Lord, *thou* Son of David!
32 And Jesus stood still, and called them, and said, What will ye that I shall do unto you?
33 They say unto him, Lord, that our eyes may be opened.

---

against, instead of. Besides, the sense of a ransom is a price paid for the redemption of a captive. That price was His own life. He died *in the stead of* "*many*," that is, of multitudes.
OBSERVE, (1.) Ambition, in the church, mistakes the nature of Christ's kingdom, and overlooks the spirituality of His service. (2.) Ambitious sons, even in the church, have often been put forward by ambitious mothers. Maternal training makes a sad mistake, when it seeks earthly preferment and station for children, rather than the solid graces of the Christian life. (3.) Christ's example in giving Himself, should always plead with a Christian for humility and self-sacrifice in the church and in the world. (4.) Christ declares His sacrifice to be *vicarious*. This makes it purely and only *gracious*. If it is in the *room* and *stead* of the sinner, it must be altogether of grace.

§ 109. THE HEALING OF TWO BLIND MEN NEAR JERICHO.

Matt.	Mark.	Luke.	John.
20.29-34	10.46-52	18.35-43 19. 1	

29. *As they departed*—or "*went out of Jericho*," as Mark has it, in the same Greek words, though Mark had also just before said, "*and they came to Jericho.*" We suppose that as Jericho was a prominent city, which He had not visited before, He took up a temporary abode there, choosing to *go out* of the city occasionally for His work and labour of love, among the crowds that were already making their way toward Jerusalem for the feast. "He went out with His disciples, and a great number of people"—Mark—and on His return, "as He was come nigh unto Jericho" (that is, on the road, *near the city*), Luke 18. 35, He restored the blind men to sight. It would seem that *after this miracle,* He entered and passed through Jericho (Luke 19. 1), passing on toward Jerusalem; or Luke's account may include in one brief sentence, the approach, and stay, and departure. Jericho was a city next in importance to Jerusalem, about 20 miles east, and a little north of it.
30. *Two blind men.* Mark and Luke mention but one—the more noted Bartimeus (chap. 10. 46)—just as Matthew soon speaks of the ass and colt, and Mark of the colt only. So Luke speaks of two angels who appeared, Matthew and Mark of one only, who spake. So of the two possessed among the tombs, there was one specially mentioned as the more noted.——¶ *Heard.* Luke says, "hearing the multitude pass by, he asked what it meant." Being informed that it was Christ, and having doubtless heard His fame, and seeming, too, to know of the scripture concerning Him, this blind man called to Him, recognizing Him as the son of David, which was the common title for the Messiah.——¶ *Cried out.* Being re-

34 So Jesus had compassion on them, and touched their eyes; and immediately their eyes received sight, and they followed him.

buked by the crowd, for what seemed an unmannerly clamour, they cried out the more. Jesus at length, after putting their earnestness to open test, halted and called them—addressed them—asking what they would have Him do to them. This elicited their more definite prayer. It was, that their eyes might be opened.

34. *Touched their eyes.* The multitude had become interested. They had seen the earnestness of the blind men, and had heard them plead for their recovery, and now to show the greatness of the miracle, He cures them by His *touch.* They received sight, and immediately became His followers.

OBSERVE, (1.) It is with the seeking soul, as with these *blind men*—when one cries out after Christ, at first, he finds from the multitude, nothing but hindrances and oppositions. But a true desire only *cries the more*, the more it is so rebuked. (2.) Then it is, that Christ shows Himself most ready to meet the earnest application. Jesus stood still and commanded him to be called (Mark); and then it is, too, that the multitude who first rebuked, are interested, and seem to fall in with the work as a mighty reality. *They call the blind man, saying unto him,* " *Be of good comfort—rise, He calleth thee.*" (3.) Jesus is always arrested by the cry of need—nay, He

CHAPTER XXI.

AND ª when they drew nigh unto Jerusalem, and were come to Bethphage, unto the

a Mar.11.1. Lu.19.29.

not only stands still, but *calls them* (vs. 32), not only waits on their request, but beckons them near, and powerfully constrains them. (4.) He whose cry was before a vague call for mercy, now becomes particular in his petition, and states his most definite want. The effect of hearing Christ's call is always to make our prayer more pointed and definite. (5.) The sinner whose eye-sight is restored, uses his new vision in following Christ.

From this narrative of the blind men, we have useful lessons. For such miracles were wrought, not merely to heal these maladies, but in them also to illustrate the great spiritual work of Christ in His cure of souls. We are taught then, that as respects our sinful case by nature we are blind—as respects Christ for a Saviour He is now passing by, and may be applied to, and be sought with success. He is always ready to hear and cure. As respects our present duty we should cry out to Him—own Him as the Messiah, the only Saviour —and beg for salvation from Him alone. And as respects the nature and grounds of the salvation, we should seek it, as bringing us " out of darkness into God's marvellous light;" " opening blind eyes," and all of *mere mercy; of grace* and not of *debt.*

	Matt.	Mark.	Luke.	John.
§ 110. The visit to Zaccheus. Parable of the ten Minæ.—*Jericho.*	....	....	19. 2–28	
§ 111. Jesus arrives at Bethany six days before the Passover.—*Bethany.*	...	....	....	11. 55–57 12.1,9–11

This (§ 111) brings us to the LAST WEEK of our Lord's history prior to the crucifixion. " Six days before the Passover" (John 12. 1)—which, by the Jewish reckoning, is " *the sixth day* before the Passover"—He arrived at Bethany. It was the Jewish sabbath, our Saturday. *See Appendix,* 314.

[A. D. 33.] CHAPTER XXI. 207

Mount of Olives, then sent Jesus two disciples,

2 Saying unto them, Go into the village over against you, and straightway ye shall find an ass tied, and a colt with her: loose *them*, and bring *them* unto me.

3 And if any *man* say aught unto you, ye shall say, The Lord hath need of them; and straightway he will send them.

4 All this was done, that it might be fulfilled which was spoken by the prophet, [b] saying,

[b] Zec. 9. 9.

PART VII.

Our Lord's Public Entry into Jerusalem, and the subsequent transactions before the fourth Passover.

Time—Five days.

	Matt.	Mark.	Luke.	John.
§§ 112, 113, and 114. OUR LORD'S PUBLIC ENTRY INTO JERUSALEM... First *day of the week*.	21. 1-11 14-17	11. 1-11	19. 29-44	12 12-19
THE BARREN FIG-TREE. CLEANSING OF THE TEMPLE.—SECOND *day of the week*. Bethany. Jerusalem.	12, 13 18, 19	11.12-19	19.45-48 21. 37,38	
THE BARREN FIG-TREE WITHERS AWAY.—THIRD *day. Between Bethany and Jerusalem.*	20-22	11. 20-26		

CHAPTER XXI.

These verses (1-6) introduce us to the week in which Christ suffered the death of the cross.

1. *They drew nigh to Bethphage.* This village on the road from Jericho, lay very near Jerusalem to the East, separated from the city chiefly by the Mount of Olives. Luke says, "nigh to Bethphage and Bethany." Mark has it, "nigh to Jerusalem, unto Bethphage and Bethany." These villages were near to each other, and Bethphage was reached first. So that "the village over against them," from Bethphage was Bethany, where Lazarus and his two sisters dwelt. See John 12. Bethphage means "the house of figs." (Comp. Sol. Song 2. 13.) No trace of it now exists.

2. *The village over against you*—viz. Bethany, which place lay beyond them toward Jerusalem, a little above Bethphage to the west.——¶ *Ye shall find an ass tied.* The princes of the Jews were forbidden to multiply horses to themselves. Deut. 17. 16, and 20. 1. This law was imposed as a standing law of distinction between them and other nations, to show their confidence as being not in horses but in God. (To ride on an ass, was also an emblem of peace—as opposite to the warlike aspect of riding on a horse.) David rode on a mule, and Solomon also on the day of his coronation. 1 Kings 1. 33, 34. 2 Sam. 18. 9. Subsequently this command was violated by the kings of Israel and Judah. The Messiah was predicted as coming on an ass, bringing deliverance, and salvation, and peace, and coming in the strength of the Lord. Zech. 9. 9. Judges rode on asses, and it was a mark of dignity. 1 Sam. 25. 20. Judges 10. 4; 12. 14. See Note in Greenleaf on the Evangelists. Mark and Luke speak only of the *colt*, for on this Christ rode, as it had never been rode before. Such were used for sacred purposes.

3. *The Lord hath need of him.* God has power over all things. He has a right to every thing, and He can so control men's hearts as to make them willing to obey Him.

MATTHEW. [A. D. 33.

5 Tell ye the daughter of Sion, *Behold, thy king cometh unto thee, meek, and sitting upon an ass, and a colt the foal of an ass.

6 And the disciples went, and did as Jesus commanded them.

7 And brought the ass, and the colt, and put on them their

c Is.62.11. Mar.11.4,&c. Jno.12.15.

clothes, and they set *him* thereon.

8 And a very great multitude spread their garments in the way; others cut down branches from the trees, and strewed them in the way.

9 And the multitudes that went before, and that followed, cried, saying, Hosanna to the Son of

---

4, 5. *Spoken by the prophet.* Zech. 9. 9. Here Matthew again, writing for the Jews, points out the fulfilment of their prophecies. This passage was uniformly understood by the Jews, as applying to the Messiah: though they would not acknowledge Christ. ——¶ *Daughter of Sion.* — Among the Jews, in their figurative mode of speech, the towns were often represented under the figure of a woman — and the population of any place was called the daughter of that place. (Isa. 37. 22. Ps. 45. 13; 137. 8. Isa. 10. 30. Jer. 46. 19. Lam. 4. 22.) Here then is meant the people of Sion, or the inhabitants of Jerusalem. ——¶ *Thy King.* Christ claimed to be the *King of the Jews* (Matt. 27.11).——
¶ *Meek.* Not warlike—nor revengeful—but bringing peace and salvation. He came in the way of the ancient kings, who rode in the strength of God, *like David*.——¶ *Sitting upon an ass, even* (and) *a colt*, &c. This is the force of the conjunction *and* here, as elsewhere often in the New Testament.

6, 7. *And put on them their clothes.* This was the custom of the people, as an acknowledgment of an appointed king. So when Jehu was anointed king by Elisha the prophet (2 Kings 9. 13), *every man took his garment and spread it under him on the top of the steps and blew the trumpet, saying, Jehu is king.*——¶ *Thereon;* literally, *upon them,* that is, properly, on *one* of them, as we say, "*He sprang from the horses.*"—Winer's Idioms. Or it may refer to the *garments.* Mark tells us that He rode upon the colt (11. 7).

8. *A very great multitude.* This was the crowd, that was going to the Passover, and many who came out of the city to see Him, and to see Lazarus whom He had raised from the dead. See John 12. 9.——
¶ *Branches from the trees.* Besides the outer garments or mantles, which were thrown on the animal, and in the road, branches of trees were strewed all along the way. These were *palm branches,* which were symbols of joy (John 12. 13), and this was a mark of welcome and gladness often paid to Kings of the East on triumphal occasions.

9. *Cried*—shouted.——¶ *Hosanna to the son of David.* Hosanna is taken from two Hebrew words, meaning "*save now.*" It was an acclamation specially used at the *Feast of Tabernacles,* when the palm branches were used also. This feast was mainly symbolical of Christ's advent to "*tabernacle* with men ;" and this feast was called " *Hosanna,*" as they sung Ps. 118. 25, 26, which prominently introduces this word. So it was well understood by the people. This was an ascription to Christ as the appointed Saviour, and as the son of David—for under this last title, they knew and spoke of the Messiah. So the next clause further imports; " *Blessed be,* &c. This was part of the Paschal Hymn, which in a few days they were about to recite. The words were used when the priests offered the victims. This refers also to the verses of the Psalm from which they sang at the feast of Tabernacles, Ps. 118. 26. To " come in *the name of*" or by *the authority of,* is expressed by Mark as " the kingdom of our Father David that cometh

[A. D. 33.] CHAPTER XXI. 209

David! Blessed ᵈ is he that cometh in the name of the Lord; Hosanna in the highest!ᵉ
10 And when he was come

ᵈ Ps. 118. 26. c. 23. 39.   ᵉ Lu. 2. 14.

in the name of the Lord." They recognized Him as the Messiah, of David's line, whose kingdom was to come of Divine authority.——¶ *Hosanna in the highest.* Luke has it, "Peace in heaven, and *glory in the highest.*" See also Luke 19. 38. Glory and salvation be ascribed to Him in the highest heavens. It was at this time, descending the Mount of Olives to Jerusalem, that He uttered His lamentation over the city. Luke 19. 41, 42. This actual entry into Jerusalem, was on the *first day of the week.* This was the *tenth* day of Nisan (or Abib, the first month), and on this day the PASCHAL LAMB WAS TO BE SELECTED. Exod. 12. 3. For the better understanding of the whole history, here, we insert Dr. Robinson's harmony and schedule of the days. The Jewish day, of twenty-four hours, was reckoned from sunset to sunset, as is still the case in oriental countries. The Paschal Lamb was killed on the fourteenth day of Nisan, toward sunset; and was eaten the same evening, after the fifteenth day of Nisan had begun. Exod. 12. 6, 8. Our Lord was crucified on the day before the Jewish sabbath, that is, on Friday, Mark 15. 42; and as he had eaten the Passover on the preceding evening, it follows that the fourteenth of Nisan fell that year on Thursday, reckoning from the preceding sunset. Hence, the sixth day before the Passover, or as John reads, "Six days before the Passover" (John 12. 1), when Jesus came to Bethany, was the Jewish Sabbath, or Saturday—and the transactions of the following week are to be understood thus:

See Appendix, p. 314.

Day of Nisan. Day of the week.

9 .... 7. SAT..... *Reckoned from preceding sunset.* The Jewish Sabbath. Jesus arrives at Bethany. (John 12. 1.)

10 .... 1. SUND... *From preceding sunset.* Jesus makes his public entry into Jerusalem (§ 112), and returns at night to Bethany. (Mark 11. 11.) On this day the paschal lamb was to be selected. (Exod. 12. 3.)

11 .... 2. MOND... Jesus goes to Jerusalem. On His way the incident of the barren fig-tree occurs. He cleanses the temple (§ 113), and again returns to Bethany. (Mark 11. 19.)

12 .... 3. TUES.... *From preceding sunset.* Jesus returns to the city. On the way the disciples see the fig-tree withered. (Mark 11. 20.) Our Lord discourses in the temple (§§ 115–126)—takes leave of it—and when on the Mount of Olives, on His way to Bethany, foretells His coming to destroy the city, and proceeds to speak also of His final coming to judgment (§§ 127–130).

13 .... 4. WEDN... The rulers conspire against Christ on the eve of this day (*i. e.,* the evening following Tuesday). Our Lord had partaken of the supper at Bethany, where Mary anointed Him, and where Judas laid his plan of treachery, which he made known to the chief priests in the course of this day. Jesus remained this day at Bethany.

14 .... 5. THURS.. Jesus sends two disciples to the city to make ready the Passover. He himself repairs thither in the afternoon, in order to eat the paschal supper at evening,

18*

210   MATTHEW.   [A. D. 33.

15........6. Frid....At evening, in the very beginning of the fifteenth of Nisan, Jesus partakes of the paschal supper—is betrayed and apprehended (§§ 133–143). He is brought first before Caiaphas, and then, in the morning, before Pilate—is condemned, crucified, and before sunset laid in the sepulchre (§§ 144–158).

16........7. Sat.....The Jewish Sabbath. Our Lord rests in the sepulchre.

17........1. Sund....Jesus rises from the dead, at early dawn. (§ 159.)

10. This wonderful sensation among such multitudes, created great excitement in the city, and led to an inquiry after the cause of it all. *Who is this?*——¶ *Was moved.* Was in commotion.

11. This description of Him by the multitude merely alludes to His fame, taking for granted that He had been heard of. " Art thou only a stranger in Jerusalem? (Luke 24. 18.)—— ¶ *Prophet of Nazareth.* This was a common appellation. "He shall be called a Nazarene" (Matt. 2. 23).

12. *Jesus went into the temple of God.* This, as we infer from Mark, was the *next day after* His reaching Jerusalem, having gone out to lodge at Bethany for the intervening night, and having cursed the fig-tree on His return to Jerusalem in the morning. At the first entrance into the temple Marks speaks only of His "looking round about upon all things." His first *work* there, was to clear out the temple, as Matthew relates. (See Mark 11. 12–15.) He may have taken a first step towards this on the preceding day.

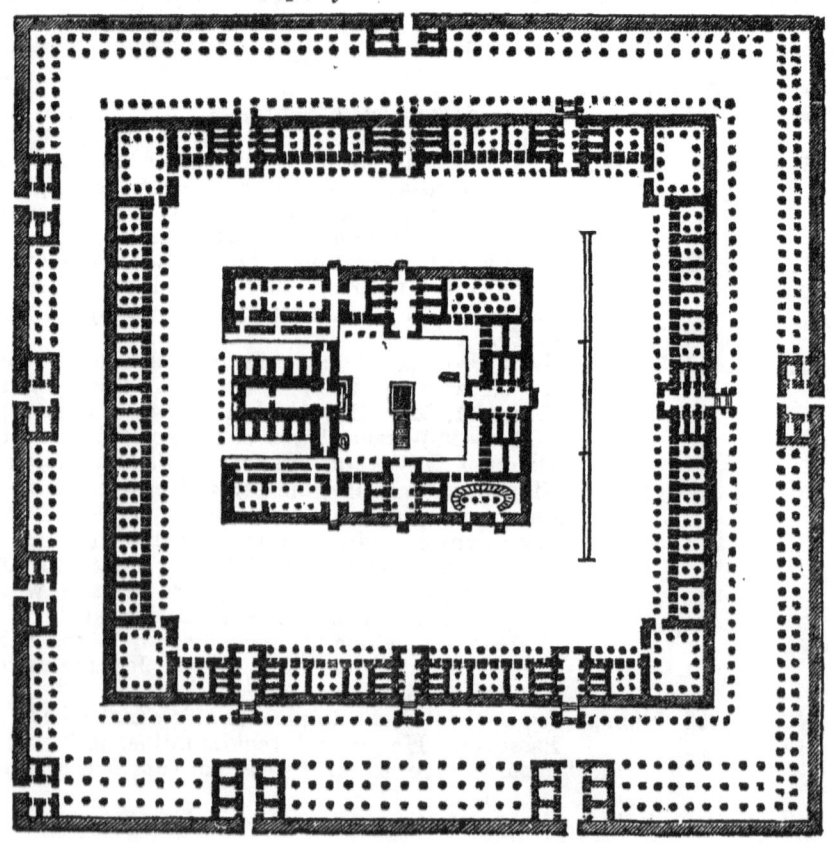

into Jerusalem, all the city was moved, saying, Who is this?

11 And the multitude said, This is Jesus, the prophet of Nazareth of Galilee.

12 ¶ And ᶠ Jesus went into the

f Mar.11.11. Lu.19.45,&c. Jno.2.15,&c.

THE TEMPLE OF GOD. In Malachi 3. 1, it was prophesied, "The Lord whom ye seek shall suddenly come to HIS TEMPLE." This was the sacred structure at Jerusalem, set apart for the service of God, and recognized as His House. The temple of Solomon, or the first temple, was built about 1000 years before Christ, on Mount Moriah. It is described in 1 Kings chs. 6. and 7., and 2 Chron. 3. and 4. This costly and magnificent edifice was destroyed by the Chaldeans, 584 years before Christ (2 Chron. 36. 6, 7).

THE SECOND TEMPLE. This structure, rebuilt by Zerubbabel, 70 years afterwards, at the close of the Babylonish captivity, was called the Second Temple. It was on the same site. The old men who had seen the first temple, were moved to tears on beholding this, which seemed so inferior (Ezra 3. 12. Haggai 2. 3); yet not really so much in dimensions, as in glory—not having the ark of the covenant, which had been burnt with the temple of Solomon. This building was desolated and profaned during the wars from B. C. 175, and was stormed by Herod, with the Roman troops, B. C. 37. This HEROD THE GREAT, being anxious to ingratiate himself with the Church and State party, undertook to repair and renew the temple. He commenced it in the eighteenth year of his reign, about twenty or twenty-one years before the Christian era. Priests and Levites finished the temple itself in a year and a half. The outbuildings and courts required eight years. However, building operations were long afterward in progress, under his successors, and it is in reference to these that the Jews said to Jesus, "Forty and six years was this temple in building." A Mohammedan mosque (of Omar) now occupies this site. (See plate of modern Jerusalem.)

All the premises occupied half a Roman mile in circumference. This temple hill was terraced by means of massive walls thrown up; and the ground for the courts was made and laid out by this artificial means, each rising above the other, reached by a staircase, and the temple at the top, showing in all its splendour from every point of view.

COURTS. The outermost enclosure walled in, nearly square, was called the Court of the Gentiles, and also "the Mountain of the House." None but Jews could go beyond this court. On its east side was the Beautiful Gate (Acts 3. 2 and 10). Around the outer wall were halls, or covered porches, for the Levites' residence, and a synagogue, in which the Talmudic doctors might be asked questions (Luke 2. 46). Here Jesus had various opportunities for addressing the people and refuting cavillers. Here also the first Christians could assemble daily, with one accord (Acts 2. 46). One of these porches, called Solomon's (Acts 3. 11), was noted. It probably stood near that celebrated part of the outer wall, where the immense stones (some of them 45 cubits long, six wide and five high) are thought to have remained since Solomon's time. They form the base of that part of the wall whose eastern angle rests on the rocky precipice of Jehoshaphat. From the pinnacle or summit of the building that surmounts this point, our Lord was dared by the tempter to cast Himself down, a height of seven hundred feet in all, to the ravine below. Within this Court of the Gentiles were the tables of the money-changers, and the seats of them that sold doves, &c., for sacrifice, which our Lord cast out—cleansing the temple premises of these traffickers.

The *Court of the Women* was the next enclosure, reached by a staircase from the Court of the Gentiles. This

temple of God, and cast out all them that sold and bought in the temple, and overthrew the tables of the money-changers, and the seats of them that sold doves;

13 And said unto them, It is *g* written, My house shall be called

g Is. 56. 7.

---

was not devoted to the women, but they might advance thus far, with others, yet no further, save when they brought a sacrifice. Lest the Gentiles should advance so far, there was a stone balustrade, some ten hands high, erected on a terrace; and still within this, were columns, having Greek and Latin inscriptions, warning off all heathens under penalty of death to enter farther (Eph. 2. 13, 14). Compare Acts 21. 28, where Paul is accused of having brought Greeks into the temple. In this court was the ordinary worship of the Jews (Luke 18. 10-14. Acts 21. 26-30). Here was *the treasury*, consisting of small chests along the wall (Mark 12. 41), where the gifts of worshippers were cast for the temple service. It contained the sums annually paid in by the Israelites (half a shekel each), besides donations, great and small, of rich men and poor widows.

Beyond this court, and on a still higher level, was the *Court of Israel*—i. e., of the *males*—whither all the men might come up, except such as were ceremonially unclean, &c. Our Saviour, being of the tribe of Judah, entered no farther than any common Israelite. *Within* this space, as a kind of inner half of the court, and surrounded by a stone balustrade, was the *Court of the Priests*, where they performed the daily temple service. Here was the altar of burnt offering and the brazen laver. This court directly surrounded the *Sanctuary*, or *temple proper*, which stood on still higher ground, and was reached by a staircase of twelve steps. A stately porch rose in front of the temple, at the highest point, to 180 feet. Within were two grand apartments—the *Holy Place*, with the altar of incense, golden candlestick, and table of show-bread; and the *Most Holy Place*, or Holy of Holies, separated from it by a rich *veil*, or curtain (Matt. 27. 51).

This immense and costly structure was the pride and glory of the Jew. Built of white marble, and overlaid with silver and gold, it was an object of dazzling splendour. Yet it was utterly destroyed in the siege of Titus (Sept. 7, A. D. 70), as our Lord foretold (ch. 24. 2). The apostate emperor Julian undertook (A. D. 363) to rebuild it, defying the Divine purpose; but after much preparation and expense, he was compelled to desist by flames, which burst forth from the foundations, as historians abundantly testify.

12. *Drove out them that sold and bought.* Such an expelling of traders is recorded in John, 2d chapter. It was symbolical of his work in purifying the covenant people. This was done in the outer court (of the Gentiles), the least sacred. Animals for sacrifice were sold here, and all that was necessary for the worshippers, many of whom being strangers in the city, would find this an accommodation. There were *stands*, or "seats" of *them that sold doves*. But this business was afterward a mere matter of gain and exaction. The buying and selling became a sad profanation of the sacred place. The house of God should not be devoted to secular purposes.——¶ *Tables of the money-changers.* As the worshippers came up from all quarters—and especially as in Judea, now a Roman province, the money in use was a Roman currency, it needed to be exchanged for the Jewish coin which they were required to present for the sanctuary service. This made a business for Jewish brokers. It was often quite extensive, and was made a source of gain. The term here for *money-changers* is from a small coin, "*change*." These brokers sat in the outer court.——

the house of prayer: but ye have made it a den of ʰ thieves.

14 And the blind and the lame came to him in the temple; and ⁱ he healed them.

15 And when the chief priests and scribes saw the wonderful things that he did, and the children crying in the temple, and saying, Hosanna ʲ to the Son of David! they were sore displeased,

16 And said unto him, Hearest thou what these say? And Jesus saith unto them, Yea: have ye never read, Out ᵏ of the mouth of babes and sucklings thou hast perfected praise?

17 ¶ And he left them, and went out of the city into Bethany: and he lodged there.

18 Now in the morning, as he returned into the city, he hungered.

h Je.7.11. *i* Is.35.6. *j* ver.9.   *k* Ps.8.2.

¶ *Sold doves*—which were used for sacrifices (Levit. 12. 6–8).

13. *It is written* (Isa. 56. 7). Christ charges them with having made His house *a den of thieves*, or *plunderers* (see Jer. 7. 11), though, in this prophecy, it was declared and destined to be a *house of prayer!* These traders in religious things probably cheated the people; and this added to the profanation. The scribes and chief priests now sought to kill Him, because He was destroying their gains (as the apostles at the temple of Diana, Acts 19. 25–28), and drawing the world after Him. "If the multitude should hold their peace, the stones would cry out." They confessed that they *could prevail nothing*, and that the world had gone after Him (Luke 19. 39, 40). They dared not kill Him, for they feared the people; but they were ready to plot for His destruction. (See John 12. 19.)

14. *The blind and lame.* Here it is stated, that in the temple, to which Malachi had prophesied he should come, He did His works of healing mercy. As His purging the temple was symbolical of His work in purifying the covenant people, so this has a symbolical aspect—to teach the great truth of His coming to be a Prince and a Saviour. Besides, He would prove His work by miracles.

15. *The chief priests.* They were jealous of this great popularity which He had—and were annoyed at the acclamations, especially at those of the children, for it indicated a most extensive and deep feeling in the community, that the children should fall in with the Hosannas. Hence they would turn this especially to His reproach, that it was children's work.

16. *And Jesus saith.* Our Lord understood all this in a most important light—and herein He found that passage in the psalm fulfilled (Ps. 8. 2), where the Psalmist spoke of God's glorifying Himself in creation, providence, and redemption. So He takes it up, exults in it—(*Yea!*) and refers them to the scripture, which they ought to know, that these are the ways in which God was to perfect praise. (In the Hebrew, thou hast *established*, founded, ordained *strength*.) "For His strength is made perfect in weakness." He has ordained, or appointed, strength from infant praises—contrary to the ways of men. This is a symbol of His gracious plan. Christ honoured infancy by being Himself a little babe. Thus He has "set His glory above the heavens" (Ps. 8. 1); because in the arrangements of grace, He gets a glory greater than from the firmament which He has made.

17. *Into Bethany*—"*house of dates*"—about 15 furlongs east from Jerusalem, toward Jericho, and reaching along to within 8 furlongs of the city being a sabbath day's journey from it. Luke 24. 50. From John, we learn that the family of Lazarus (with his

19 And when he saw ¹ a fig-tree in the way, he came to it, and found nothing thereon, but leaves only, and said unto it, Let no fruit grow on thee henceforward for ever. And presently the fig-tree withered ᵐ away.

l Mar.11.13. 1 One fig-tree. *m* Jude 12.

20 And when the disciples saw it, they marvelled, saying, How soon is the fig-tree withered away!

21 Jesus answered and said unto them, Verily I say unto you, If ⁿ ye have faith and doubt not, ye shall not only do this

n c.17.20. Lu.17.6. Ja.1.6.

two sisters) was often visited by our Lord. (See John, chap. 12.)

18, 19. *As He returned.* This was on the *second day* of the week. It occurred in the morning, that is, after He had lodged for the night at Bethany, that on His return to the city, He hungered, and met a barren fig-tree, which He immediately cursed and withered, as a token of His displeasure, that it should offer Him no figs for His hunger. This occurred before His fully cleansing the temple (12, 13). We are to observe in this transaction, and its relation here, a higher object than would appear at first. It was not merely to express His indignation at the barren tree, nor any such exciting disappointment at not finding fruit when He knew it was barren. But He took this occasion of teaching them symbolically certain great truths. That leaves without fruit, or a form of godliness without the power, or a profession without the practice would be accursed. And especially that His barren church of the Jewish people, would soon be stricken and withered on account of its giving Him no fruit now, as He came to Jerusalem. This incident is quite in keeping with all the parables spoken in this connexion. They are all meant to show that He came now to the temple as a King, and in like manner as Malachi had prophesied, to call His covenant people to account, and to sit as a refiner's fire.—— ¶ *Presently.* This word means *immediately*—but it has obtained in common use a different sense. The term here used, is commonly rendered *immediately* in the New Testament. Sometimes,

straightway (Acts 5. 10)—*forthwith* (Acts 9. 18), and in the next verse it is the same word, translated *soon !* meaning *how instantly !* Mark mentions that "the time of figs was not yet," and seems to give it as a reason for His finding nothing. But it may be understood rather as a reason for His disappointment. At that early period of the year, March or April, (says Trench,) neither leaves nor fruit were to have been expected. But this tree had leaves, and it is to be observed that with figs, "the fruit appears before the leaves." This tree therefore made pretension of being so much more than the rest, that our Lord approached it. It had put forth leaves, though "the time of figs was not yet." And this symbolized exactly the sin of Israel, in boasting, vaingloriously. They counted themselves the peculiar people of God, though rejecting Christ; they claimed to be saved without Christ the only Saviour, and to be whole without need of this only physician. They were blamed therefore, less for being *barren* than for being *false.* It is remarkable that it was with the *fig leaves* in the garden, that Adam attempted to cover his nakedness before God. (S. Micah 7. 11.)

20. *They marvelled.* It is here n° that the disciples observed the sudde. effect of His curse upon the barren tree (see Mark 11. 21). This was on "Tuesday"—the "third day of the week."

21. *If ye have faith.* The faith here alluded to was connected with the working of miracles, in confirmation of the Christian religion. They wondered at this miracle wrought by

which is done to the fig-tree, but also if ye shall say unto this mountain, Be thou removed, º and be thou cast into the sea, it shall be done.

22 And all things whatsoever ye shall ask ᵖ in prayer, believing, ye shall receive.

23 ¶ And ᵍ when he was come into the temple, the chief priests and the elders of the people came unto him as he was teaching, and said, By ʳ what authority doest thou these things? and who gave thee this authority?

24 And Jesus answered and said unto them, I also will ask you one thing, which if ye tell me, I in likewise will tell you by what authority I do these things.

o c.8.12. p c.7.7. Mar.11.24. Ja.5.16. 1Jno.3.22; 5.14. q Mar.11.27. Lu.20.1.

r Ex.2.14.

Christ. He shows them, that they could even expect to work such wonders and greater, in their official capacity, if they had the faith of miracles, requisite in such case.——¶ *Ye shall say to this mountain.* They were passing over the Mount of Olives.— It was a common saying among the Jews, when they would commend one of their doctors as dexterous in solving difficult questions, that he was a *rooter up of mountains.* And so our Lord tells the disciples that they should be able to do the most difficult things in confirmation of the Christian religion, if they had this kind of faith peculiar to the time of the Apostles, and belonging to their work.

22. *And all things.* This seems addressed specially to the twelve, and with some reference to their wide prerogative in going forth to establish the religion of Christ. Yet it would seem from the passage in Mark, that it was spoken with a wider reference. And, doubtless, whatever is asked by any true believer, in a genuine exercise of faith, with all its humility and confidence in God, will be granted. Accordingly, in Mark, our Lord is said to have conjoined Christian *forgiveness*, as essential *in order to* obtain this promise. It is not supposable that a Christian in true faith could ask, what, in the substance of the prayer, God would be unwilling to grant—for He is more willing to grant, than we are to ask the true Christian benefits and gifts.

OBSERVE, (1.) In due time, Christ asserts His Kingly authority and office, whether men will hear or forbear. So He will come at last, as King of Kings, before friends and foes. (2.) Christ's triumphal entry is joined in by multitudes. So shall it be at last —" a very *great multitude*" (vs. 8). (3.) Christ comes to His temple and asserts His authority over it. He is Head of the Church, and he will yet purge it from all defilements (vss. 12, 13). (4.) In wrath He remembers mercy. Grace reigns with justice. He heals the blind and lame there. Sinners in the sanctuary can now be healed by Him (vs. 14). (5.) Children should join in Christ's praise, and should be trained with a view to their early uniting with God's people. Nothing more delights Christ, or offends the wicked, than youthful piety. Christ not only allows this, but plans for it. He will perpetuate His church by a godly seed. These children in the temple shouting Hosanna, should encourage sabbath-school instruction and domestic religion. (6.) Proud pretenders, like the barren fig-tree, Christ will curse.

§ 115. CHRIST'S AUTHORITY QUESTIONED. PARABLE OF THE TWO SONS.—(THIRD *day of the week.*) *Jerusalem.*

Matt.	Mark.	Luke.	John.
21. 23–32	11. 27–33	20. 1–8	

23. *When He was come into the temple.* " As He was teaching." Mark has it, " as he was walking in the temple "—Luke, " as He taught the

25 The baptism of John, whence was it? from heaven, or of men? And they reasoned with themselves, saying, If we shall say, From heaven; he will say unto us, Why did ye not then believe him?

26 But if we shall say, Of men: we fear the people; for ᵃ all hold John as a prophet.

ᵃ c.14.5.

27 And they answered Jesus, and said, We cannot tell. And he said unto them, Neither tell I you by what authority I do these things.

¶ 28 But what think ye? A certain ᵗ man had two sons: and he came to the first, and said, Son, go work to-day in my vineyard.

ᵗ Lu.15.11,&c.

---

people in the temple, and preached the gospel." He came now into the court of the Israelites, next within that of the Gentiles.——¶ *By what authority.* He had taken such bold measures, that we cannot wonder at this question of those who were in authority, and did not own His claims.

25. *The baptism of John.* That is the religion of which the baptism was a profession. He answers their question by proposing another, which involved the answer to His own. There was a close connexion between John's work and His. If they recognized John's baptism (or ministerial work) to be from heaven, and Divinely authorized, then they must own Him whom John preached, and His work which John introduced. But if they did not own John's work, they would not believe in Him. Every way this reply was calculated to silence them. They could not say it was of God, for this would convict themselves for rejecting Christ. They dared not say it was of men, for the people would rebel at this—as they held, or considered John to be a prophet. They so conceived the question. Hence they made no answer, except to own themselves *shut up.*

27. He refused to answer their question directly, because it would have done them no good. Had they been honest inquirers, His reply would have directed them to the true solution.——¶ *We cannot tell.* Literally, "We do not know."—— ¶ *Neither.* If they knew not this preliminary point, they could not fairly require to know further.

28. *But what think ye?* Our Lord in the temple, now, having met their malicious question, turns upon the chief priests and elders, and becomes Himself the assailing party, and commences that series of JUDICIAL PARABLES, which set before them as in a glass, their obdurate case. Remembering Malachi's prophecy, we find 'the Lord,' whom the rebellious Jews sought in their murmurings, " suddenly come to His temple." " But who may abide the day of His coming." He here states to them their own wicked case, under a parable, and draws from them an opinion which convicted themselves. The point of the parable is given in vs. 31, last clause, and vs. 32. It does not primarily refer to Jew and Gentile, but to the two classes among the Jews—Pharisees and Publicans.——¶ *My vineyard.* My field for raising grapes — as we would say, my farm—grapes being in Judea a chief article of cultivation. The church is often set forth under this figure in scripture. To work in the Lord's vineyard, means to perform Christian duty in His church.

29. The *first* son represented the publicans, and notoriously wicked people—such as made no promises and received religious things with contempt. These afterward *repented*—altered their mind — changed their course—and did what was demanded, so that the result was their obedience. It was wrong to re-

[A. D. 33.] CHAPTER XXI. 217

29 He answered and said, I will not; but afterward ^u he repented and went.

30 And he came to the second, and said likewise. And he answered and said, I *go*, sir; and went not.

31 Whether of them twain did the will of *his* father? They say unto him, The first. Jesus saith unto them, Verily I say unto you, that the publicans and the harlots go into the kingdom of God before you.

32 For John came unto you in the way of righteousness, and ye believed him not; but the publicans ^v and the harlots ^w be

u 2Ch.33.12,13. 1Cor.6.11. Ep.2.1-13.   *v* Lu.3.12. *w* Lu.7.37, &c.

---

fuse at first. It was right to be candid and honest; and not promise and profess *with no intention* to perform. And especially it was right to repent of a wrong course, and promptly to turn from the evil ways and do well. The wicked, who have had no religious education, and have never been baptized—without Christian parents or advantages—who after all that is unpromising in their case and character, do repent and obey the Master, are like the first son. There were many such in the time of Christ.——¶ *I will not.* The representative of open, reckless sinners —who flatly refuse God's claims, and calls.

30. *Said likewise.* That is, He commanded the *second* son, as he had done the first. He replied favourably.——¶ *I go, sir.* That is, *I will go and do as you require.* By such, our Lord meant these Pharisees, who claimed to be the special people of God (see Par. Luke 18.11), and who professed to be "the church of God." They made fair promises — large pretensions — and had all the externals of an abundant piety — the form, and show, and noise. But they did not obey, after all. They said and did not. They had the form of godliness, but denied the power thereof. False professors now are like them. Those who boast aloud, and do little or nothing for the cause of Christ, and the spread of true Christianity, are like them—formalists, bigots, hypocrites. But this does not disparage an honest profession—nor excuse any who do not profess. Some decline to profess religion, as though they avoided the obligations thus. But will they class with publicans and harlots?

31. *Which of them twain,*—that is, *which of the two sons.* The will of His father, was the order given to *work in the vineyard*—like God's command to every man, to obey and serve Him in His church on earth. The first son, as they confessed, was the obedient one—for though he declined at first, he went at last. He was better than he promised. The other was not so good as he promised. Those who are full of fair promises and professions, but do nothing, are often outdone by the most unpromising characters, who become true Christians before them. So Christ declared to the Jews that the publicans and harlots, that is, the notoriously wicked— those who, as a class, had the poorest repute, and were most unlikely to follow Christ—go into the kingdom of God, or become Christians before them. This does not disparage morality, or make it worse than impiety. But there is no such fault as counting we have no fault, and fortifying ourselves against Christ.

32. *For John came.* Christ thus explains His remark. It had been proved true in their recent history. For *John*—that is, John the Baptist— came unto them (from God) *in the way of righteousness* (in the right way, strict in the law, and pointing out the way of righteousness), and like the second son, though they professed to serve God more than any other people, and were full of fairest professions toward God, yet they believed

lieved him: and ye, when ye had seen *it*, repented not ˣ afterward, that ye might believe him.

33 ¶ Hear another parable: There was a certain household-

ˣ Re.2.21.

er, which ʸ planted a vineyard, and hedged it round about, and digged a wine-press in it, and built a tower, and let it out to husbandmen, and went into a far country:

ʸ Ps.80.8-16. Ca.8.11,12. Is.5.1-7. Je.2.21. Mar.12. 1. Lu.20.9,&c.

---

not (Matt. 15. 8). They *said,* and *did not* (Matt. 23. 3). But the publicans and harlots, who had taken no such prominence in religious things, but had been openly profane, believed John—and these were like the first son; and though their case had been most unpromising, yet they went into the service of Christ before the Pharisees—and what is worse, they, *when they had seen this,* did not even yet repent, were not yet provoked to jealousy, and did not enter into Christ's kingdom at all.

OBSERVE, (1.) While some think it an advantage not to have professed religion, it is not the *refusing,* but the *after repenting of that refusal,* which is here commended; while it is still shown that an insincere profession may be the most abhorrent and vile before God. Professing, with no intent to serve God, is indeed odious— but the true course is to say, "I go, sir; so help me God." (2.) To obey, *without* promising or professing, is now impossible; since we are COMMANDED TO PROFESS: "*This do.*" "With the mouth confession is made unto salvation" (Rom. 10. 10). (3.) Morality is not worse than immorality. But it may be more hopeless, if it proudly and studiously fortifies itself against Christ; not only *neglecting,* but positively *rejecting* His salvation.

§ 116. PARABLE OF THE WICKED HUSBANDMEN.—THIRD *day of the week. Jerusalem.*

Matt.	Mark.	Luke.	John.
21. 33–46	12. 1–12	20.9–19	

33. *Hear another parable.* Our Lord now presses them still more closely, and signifies their ultimate rejection as a nation. Mark says,

"He began to speak unto them by parables." He would not let them go.——¶ *A vineyard.* These several steps in laying out a vineyard, and fitting it for cultivation and production of grapes, so common in Judea, are here used to represent God's attention to His covenant people. This image runs through the whole Old Testament. The vine-stock often appears on the Maccabean coins as the emblem of Palestine. (See Deut. 32. 32. Psa. 80. 8. Isa. 5. 1. Ezek. 15. 2.)——¶ *Hedged it round*—that is, *fenced* it, most likely, with a hedge stout and thorny. A stone fence was also used, which makes a most secure enclosure.——¶ *Digged a wine-press in it.* Mark says, "digged a place for the wine-fat." Both are referred to, in either case—they were connected. There was a *wine-press,* in which the grapes were trodden by men, to press out the juice; and under this was the *vat,* or reservoir, into which the juice ran, through a close grating——¶ *And built a tower.* This was a tall observatory, on the premises, for watching the grounds. It served also as a lodge for the keepers. ——¶ *Let it out*—hired it, so that the owner was to get a share of the products. The husbandmen were to raise grapes, and make the most profit from the vineyard. This householder, or head of a family, represents God, who chose the Jews as His house and people, "to whom pertaineth the adoption, and the glory, and the covenants, and the giving of the law, and the service of God, and the promises" (Rom. 9. 4). The *vineyard,* then, is this *covenant relation and privilege,* given to be cultivated —"the good olive stalk and root" (Rom. 11. 24). The Gentiles, in these

A. D. 33.] CHAPTER XXI. 219

34 And when the time of the fruit drew near, he sent his servants ᶻ to the husbandmen, that they might receive the fruits of it.

35 And ᵃ the husbandmen took his servants, and beat one, and killed another, and stoned another.

36 Again, he sent other servants more than the first: and they did unto them likewise.

37 But, last of all, he sent unto them his son, saying, They will reverence my son.

38 But when the husbandmen saw the son, they said among themselves, This is the heir: ᵇ come, let us kill him, and let us seize on his inheritance.

39 And they ᶜ caught him, and

z 2K.17.13,&c. a 2Ch.36.16. Ne.9.26. Je.25.3-7, c.5.12; 23.34-37. Ac.7.52. 1Th.2.15. He.11.36,37. Re. 6.9.

b He.1.1,2. c Ac.2.23; 4.25-27.

days, share all these privileges. "Whose house are we, if we hold fast," &c. (Heb. 3. 6.)——¶ *A far country.* After the Theocracy, when God so openly manifested Himself, He dealt more distantly with them in Canaan. Luke adds, "for a long while."

34. *When the time of the fruit.* The time of Christ's coming to His temple.——¶ *Sent his servants.* He had reason to expect fruit, because all the arrangements and agreements were to this effect. So with the Jews. He had chosen them as a covenant people, to show forth His praise—to bring forth grapes—not wild grapes (Isa. 5. 4). He had given them all the means of grace, and at a suitable time, He sent His servants, the *prophets*, raised up and specially sent, calling upon them for the good results. Not that God has done every thing to His vineyard *that He could,* as some construe the passage in Isaiah, limiting His power. But "what more is there to be done?" (Isa. 5. 4.) "Why, when He waited for it to bring forth grapes, brought it forth wild grapes?" "I will tell you what I will do to my vineyard" (vs. 5). For us He has done much—has given us the gospel, and the Spirit—has sent His messengers—and He has a right to expect from us all the fruits of piety.

35. *They beat one,* &c. The word means, literally, to *skin,* or *flay.* Mark and Luke relate these modes of treatment more particularly. They indicate the reception which God's prophets met at the hands of the Jewish people: "entreated shamefully"(Heb. 11. 37. Jer. 44. 4-6. 2 Chron. 36. 16. Neh. 9. 26. 2 Chron. 24. 20, 21). Jeremiah was stoned by the exiles in Egypt; Isaiah sawn asunder by king Manasseh. "They were stoned, sawn asunder," &c. (Heb. 11. 36.)

37. *Last of all.* This contains the point of the parable. That the various messengers and messages had been followed up at length by such an one as this. After the prophets had been abused and rejected by the Jews, God sent His Son, Jesus Christ. Mark says that this was the ONE, only Son— His well-beloved.——¶ *They will reverence*—that is, they will respect and treat with due esteem such a messenger (John 3. 16, 17).

38. *This is the heir.* They had a selfish motive, even for killing the Son! When Christ came to the Jews, their low ideas, and their pride of heart, and His own offices—caused them to reject Him. (Comp. Joseph's brethren, Gen. 37. 19.) An *heir* is one to whom property is left, called an *inheritance:* (one who is yet a minor, and coming to possess His estate.) Christ was Heir of all things, as the Son of Man—and Maker of all things, as the Son of God.

39. *Slew Him.* The Jews caught Christ, arrested Him, cast Him out of their midst, and slew Him, that the inheritance might be theirs, demanding the covenant privileges ("We be Abraham's seed,' &c.) in

220 MATTHEW. [A. D. 33.

cast *him* out of the vineyard, and slew *him*.

40 When the Lord therefore of the vineyard cometh, what will he do unto those husbandmen?

41 They say unto him, He will miserably destroy ᵈ those wicked men, and will 'let out *his* vineyard unto other ᵉ husbandmen, which shall render him the fruits in their seasons.

42 Jesus saith unto them, Did ye never read in the scriptures,

The ᶠ stone which the builders rejected, the same is become the head of the corner: this is the Lord's doing, and it is marvellous in our eyes?

43 Therefore say I unto you, The kingdom ᵍ of God shall be taken from you, and given to a nation ʰ bringing forth the fruits thereof.

44 And whosoever shall fall ⁱ on this stone shall be broken: but on whomsoever it shall fall, it ʲ will grind him to powder.

ᵈ Ps. 2.4,5,9. Zec.12.2 Lu.21.24. Ro.9.26; 11.11.
ᶠ Ps. 118.22. Is. 28.16. 1 Pe.2.6,7. ᵍ Is. 28.2.
ʰ 1Cor.13.2. ⁱ Is.8.14,15. ʲ He.2.2,3.

their own way—rejecting Christ as the Messenger of the covenant.

40. *What will he do?* See the same idea applied to the vineyard (as the Jewish church), in Isa. ch. 5. 4th vs. This subject was put to them in parable, that they might decide without knowing that they would condemn themselves.—¶ *Will give the vineyard.* The covenant relation and privilege should be given to the Gentiles, who should bring forth the fruits (Rom. 11. 7, 17).

41. *They say unto Him.* They did not yet discern the application of the parable. So they pronounced judgment against their own conduct, and declared beforehand the justice of that destruction which was coming on their city and people. He was about to take their privileges from them and give them to the Gentiles (other husbandmen), who should cultivate the ground on which they were placed, and render Him the fruits. So, swift destruction may be expected by us, at the final coming in judgment, if we reject Christ as our Lord and Saviour.

42. *Have ye never read.* Christ now brings out the application of the parable, by referring them to a prediction in their own scriptures, showing that this concerns themselves (Psalm 118. 22, 23). See Acts 4. 11, and 1 Peter 2. 7. Ephes. 2. 20. By the *stone* is meant Jesus Christ, and the *builders* were the Jews. The Psalm is prophetic of Christ, as the whole context beautifully shows! They would not have Christ in their building—they set Him aside, as builders would reject a stone too rough-looking or too unwieldy—or too different from the rest of the fabric. But this same stone is become the *corner-stone* of the true building! (Isa. 28. 16.) "Behold, I lay in Zion for a foundation a stone, a tried stone, a precious corner-stone, a sure foundation." Christ is called the *corner-stone*, because the whole building of the true Church rests upon Him, and is held together by Him. He unites Jew and Gentile in one building. This image is added, to show that Christ will triumph to their shame.

43. The doom about to be executed on their nation, is here definitely stated. See Rom. 9. 25.

44. *Whosoever shall fall*, &c. To come in violent contact with Christ, even as one stumbles carelessly or blindly over a stone, shall be ruinous. They fall on this stone who are offended at His low estate. But He is Judge—He falls on obdurate opposers. But to bear the weight of His condemnation, and to suffer the penalty of openly rejecting Him, will be a crushing doom (Isa. 8. 14. Luke 2. 34. 1 Pet. 2. 8). This curse of

45 And when the chief priests and Pharisees had heard his parables, they perceived that he spake of them.

46 But when they sought to lay hands on him, they feared the multitude, because they ᵏ took him for a prophet.

k Lu.7.16. Jno.7.40.

rejecting Christ shall fall like a millstone on the heads of those, who, amidst the privileges of the gospel, refuse to accept the salvation.

45. *Perceived that He spake of them.* He had gradually brought out the application in its full force.

46. *Sought to lay hands on Him.* True to the parable, the chief priests and Pharisees already seek to kill Him. And if they had taken Him, the multitude would probably have cried, "Away with Him!" (See ch. 27. 25.)

OBSERVE, (1.) The amazing and distinguishing goodness of God to such as have the gospel—its ordinances—ministers—calls and offers—especially his goodness to *a church.* (2.) If fruit is not brought forth, the candlestick will be taken out of its place (Rev. 2. 5). (3.) The *baptized,* who have been born in such outward relations to the church, and with such privileges, will be utterly cast off if they reject Christ. "Ye are the children of the prophets and of the covenant," &c. (See Acts 3. 25.)

CHAPTER XXII.

§ 117. PARABLE OF THE MARRIAGE OF THE KING'S SON. THIRD *day of the week.—Jerusalem.*

Matt.	Mark.	Luke.	John.
22. 1-14			

Our Lord was still in the temple. It is to be observed that there is here a series of parables bearing upon one point, and all tending to set forth one practical sentiment. The case of the two sons, and of the wicked husbandmen, exhibited the wickedness of the Jews, that deserved their utter rejection as a people—and they were calculated to forewarn them of this

CHAPTER XXII.

AND Jesus answered and spake unto them again by parables, and said,

2 The ᵃ kingdom of heaven is like unto a certain king, which made a ᵇ marriage for his son.

3 And ᶜ sent forth his servants

a Lu.14.16. b Re.19.7,9. c Ps.68.11. Jer.25.4; 35.15. Re.22.17.

result. The boasting Pharisees were worse than the common despisers—and the nation were worse than the Gentiles; they were false to their common engagements. Moreover they had enjoyed eminent privileges, which they had only abused, and had at length been ready to slay the only son of Him whose vineyard they were set to keep, and who asked only a proper return from it at their hands. Now, in this parable of the marriage feast, He more fully opens the subject of their rejection: of His *royalty,* and their radical delinquency. They had plainly refused His offers, and the result was to be their rejection. Our Lord gave so many of His teachings by parables, partly to conceal the application of the truth, until it should gain their concurrence—(as Nathan to David), and as in the parable of the two sons (see chap. 21. 31)—and partly to represent the truth in pictures, calculated to interest and impress. He seemed at times also to have an object of showing the blindness of those who could not see the truth even in the picture, and so to let the picture be seen instead of the truth it portrayed. God's revelation is a test to men, and so it is variously received and construed.

2. *A certain* KING. This represents the gospel of grace, given by God the Father to the world, through His Son Jesus Christ. It is called here the *kingdom;* and the picture is that of the king making a marriage feast for His Son. Christ is the great personage—the Son of God. This brings to view their relations to Himself, as not only the son of the householder,

to call them that were bidden to the wedding: and they would not come.

4 Again, he sent forth other servants, saying, Tell them which are bidden, Behold, I have prepared my dinner; my oxen and *my* fatlings *are* killed, and all things *are* ready: come unto the marriage.

5 But they made light ᵈ of *it*, and went their ways, one to his

d Ps. 106. 24, 25. Pr. 1. 24, 25. Ac. 24. 25. Ro. 2. 4.

but the King's son. This hints also of the covenant between the Father and the Son; and of Christ, as having His claims founded on that eternal covenant with Jehovah, whom they worshipped. It was also a *marriage feast*, representing the *relations of love*, revealed in the gospel (see Isa. 25. 6; 65. 13. Sol. Song 5. 1. Isa. 61. 10; 62, 5. Hosea 2. 19. Matt. 9. 15. John 3. 29. Ephes. 5. 32. 2 Cor. 11. 2).

3. *His servants.* These represent ministers of the gospel, whose work is to urge men to come, though they have been already bidden, or invited, in the word of God, the gospel message. The Jews had had invitations from the prophets before the nuptials. Now, on the nuptial day, when Christ had come, these other messengers were sent. God was not bound to make any such arrangement as this, for a ministry of reconciliation to urge His own offers upon the reluctant. The impenitent treat the gospel now, in the same manner—with all their invitations, first and last, they are disinclined to come. Men will not come to Christ because of their wicked hearts. It is not enough to say that they stay away because they *will not come* —but further than this, they will not come, because of their utterly depraved hearts.——¶ *That were bidden.* This would show that as they had been invited to this very feast long before, so, Christ was no new claimant, and His kingdom nothing sudden, but all in the line of previous calls and claims. He was Himself the end of the law. This custom of repeating the message, or after the first invitation, sending a summons when all was ready, is common at the East (comp. Esth. 5. 8. and 6. 14). This band of servants represents particularly John the Baptist, and the seventy, and the apostles, preaching Christ in His lifetime.

4. *Again.* This second band may represent the renewed invitation before and after the crucifixion, by another company, including Stephen, Barnabas, and Paul, and others, preaching "Jesus and the resurrection."——¶ *All things are ready.* This represents the substance of their preaching to the Jews—that the fulness of time had come—the Messiah prophesied had appeared. Obstacles were all removed—all provisions were made (see Acts 2. 38–39; 3. 19–26; 4. 12). The *end* of the law was Christ. *It is finished.* This conduct of the King represents the gospel offer, which *repeats* its messages, and multiplies its messengers. Various preachers, different providences, and the Holy Ghost Himself, reiterate the call, and press it for immediate action. Sinners are entreated to come to Christ, by every gospel sermon, every good tract, every providence, and every motion of the Holy Spirit in the heart. Every thing is prepared for them inasmuch as Christ has actually died, and the redeeming work is done, and now they are invited as to a feast, spread and waiting on the table. Pardon is proclaimed. The grace is free. It is most important for sinners to understand this: "Behold I have prepared my dinner." Let them see what God has done—and how the benefits are all waiting their reception.

5. *They made light of it.* There are two classes of despisers noticed here. *These first* treated it lightly as an unimportant thing. So many men do now. They show no interest in its

A. D. 33.] CHAPTER XXII. 223

farm, and another to his merchandise:

6 And the remnant took his servants, and entreated [e] *them* spitefully, and slew *them*.

7 But when the king heard *thereof*, he was wroth: and he sent forth his armies, and destroyed [f] those murderers, and burned up their city.

8 Then saith he to his servants, The wedding is ready, but they which were bidden were not worthy.[g]

9 Go ye therefore into the highways; and as many as ye shall find, bid to the marriage.

10 So those servants went out into the *high*ways, and gathered together all, [h] as many as they found, both bad and good: and the wedding was furnished with guests.

11 And when the king came

e 1Th.2.15. *f* Da.9.26. Lu.19.27.   *g* c.10.11,13. Ac.13.46. Re.3.4; 22.14. *h* c.13.47.

---

most solemn warnings, or most momentous privileges. They care more for their "farms" and "merchandizes" than for this.

6. *Entreated them spitefully*—treated them severely. This was true of the Jews who slew the prophets, and "stoned them that were sent to them." (See Acts 4. 3; 5. 18; 8. 3; also Acts 5. 40; 14. 5-19, 17. 5; 21. 30; 23. 2.) ¶ *And slew them.* (Acts 7. 58; 12. 2. Comp. Matt. 23. 34.) And it represents also the conduct of many who revile, and abuse, and persecute the ministers of Christ and His messages.

7. *Wroth*— angry. The sending forth of the king's armies, here applies to the destruction of Jerusalem by Roman armies, which they are thus forewarned should come to pass. (See Isa. 10. 5; 13. 5. Ezek. 16. 41. Jer. 25. 9.) Those who thus shamefully abuse the servants of God or their messages may expect swift destruction.——¶ *Their city.* Jerusalem is here intended. Matt. 23. 34, 35. Luke 13. 33, 34. See Acts 7. 39; 12. 2, 3. "Your house is left unto you desolate." Chap. 23. 38.

8. *Not worthy.* The unworthiness consisted in their rejecting the provisions, as the worthiness of the guests lay in their *accepting it*. This indicates the sentence passed upon the despisers and neglecters of the gospel, whether Jews or Gentiles. The Jews in rejecting the message proved that they were not worthy of their high privileges. Seeing ye put it from you and judge yourselves unworthy of everlasting life—lo, we turn to the Gentiles (Acts 13. 46).

9. *Highways*— thoroughfares. This word is translated by the Wicklif version, A. D. 1380, "*the ends of ways.*" It means literally the *outlets* of streets where several ways meet, and where people pour out through some gate, or into some open square. This is the multitude. And it is meant here, that the gospel is now made universal in its call, without distinction as before. And it forewarns the Jews of its being addressed thenceforth to the Gentiles. So now, the gospel is to be preached to all, and all are invited to come. So Philip went down to Samaria (Acts 8. 5)—Peter to Cornelius—Paul to the men of Athens. The calling of the Gentiles, by occasion of the Jews' disobedience is here plainly set forth. (See Rom. 11.)

10. *Both bad and good.* That is, in *men's* estimate—for the gospel takes in all classes, on one common platform— merging all distinctions in this, of accepting or rejecting Christ and His provisions. By grace alone are we called and saved.——¶ *Guests* —partakers of the feast. That these were "*good and bad*" only means that they were of all characters, some better, some worse.. None come to Christ's provisions on the ground of their goodness. All must come on

in to ¹ see the guests, he saw there a man which had not on a wedding ʲ garment:

12 And he saith unto him, Friend, how camest thou in hither, not having a wedding garment? And he was ᵏ speechless.

i Zep.1.12. j Ps.45.14. Is.61.10. 2Cor.5.3. Ep.4. 24. Re.16.15; 19.8. k Je.2.26.

13 Then said the king to the servants, Bind him hand and foot, and take him ¹ away, and cast *him* into outer darkness: ᵐ there shall be weeping and gnashing of teeth.

14 For ⁿ many are called, but few *are* chosen.

l Is.52.1. Re.21.27. m c.8.12. n c.7.14; 20.16. Lu.13.23,24.

the same footing—and whatever their character.

11. *A wedding garment.* That is, a dress provided for the purpose. This was the custom of Eastern kings on special occasions. Changes of raiment were reckoned as an article of wealth (Job 27. 16. Isa. 3. 6. James 5. 2. 2 Kings 10. 22), and kings made much of presenting favourites with a dress in which they might appear before them. (See 1 Sam. 18. 4. 2 Kings 5. 5. Dan. 5. 7. Esth. 6. 8.) Not to wear it in such case would be the most pointed contempt. Sir John Chardin relates an instance where such a refusal cost a vizier his life. It was a custom calculated to show at once the king's liberality and the subject's dependence on the king. It had a very important meaning in this connexion. (See Zechariah 3. 4.) Such are they in the church, who make a false profession. They who come to the gospel feast without Christ's robe of righteousness upon them, and are not clothed with humility, are represented here. No matter what be our professions, or stations in the church, if our hearts are not changed, if our lives be not Christian, and if our hope be not in Christ alone. This figure of a dress or clothing, runs through the whole scripture. We are bidden to *put on* the Lord Jesus Christ (Rom. 13. 14. Gal. 3. 27), to *put off* the old and put on the new man (Col. 3. 10. Ephes. 4. 22), to put on the whole armour of God (Ephes. 6. 13–16. 1 Thess. 5. 8). *Be clothed with humility.* "Clothed upon with our house which is from heaven." By faith we recognize a righteousness out of and above us, wherewith our spirits can be clothed, which righteousness is in Christ, who is "the Lord our Righteousness." "And this righteousness we so appropriate by faith as to make it ours, so that it becomes, in that singularly expressive term our HABIT." —*Trench.* So, in heaven—"white robes," "like a bride adorned for her husband." The term here for *wedding garment* seems to denote rather that of the bridegroom. It is Christ's righteousness that is put on. As He is, so are they in the world. *Tavernier* mentions a king of Persia who was so pleased by the conduct of a *nazar* that he caused himself to be unrobed, and gave his own habit to the *nazar*, "*which is the greatest honour a king of Persia can bestow on a subject.*" p. 43.

12. *How camest thou,* &c. Our Lord is represented as detecting every false professor. We may learn that our true character is known to Him, and will not escape His judgment. The man was *speechless,* because he was clearly without excuse—self-condemned and his own destroyer. No man can offer any excuse at the judgment-day. "Every mouth shall be stopped" (Rom. 3. 19).——¶ *Speechless;* literally, *muffled* or *gagged.*

13. *Bind him hand and foot.* Here the punishment is denoted that shall come upon all, Jew and Gentile, who so contemptuously refuse Christ's salvation. The hypocrite's hope shall perish (Job 8. 13).——¶ *Outer darkness.* is exclusion from the blissful presence of God. As the wedding feast was usually at night, and all was brilliancy *within* the house, so, *outside,* it was the deepest contrast of dark

15 ¶ Then º went the Pharisees, and took counsel how they might entangle him in *his* talk.

16 And they sent out unto him

o Mar. 12. 13, &c. Lu. 20. 20, &c.

their disciples, with the Herodians, saying, Master, we know that thou art true, and teachest the way of God in truth, neither carest thou for any *man*; for

ness. (See note, ch. 8. 12).——¶ *Weeping and gnashing of teeth* are terms, expressive of the severest rage, agony, and despair. This there will be. A sense of the self-destruction and a memory of the free grace, will make this eternal as the mind in its future estate. The previous parables had been against the avowed opposers; this is directed further against the false pretenders—those among the actual comers to the feast, who have rejected Christ, the only way. This is a second sifting and separation. This fulfils John's forewarning, "Whose fan is in his hand, and he will thoroughly purge his floor;" and the sifting by the fan was the last process of purging. See note, ch. 3. 12.

14. *Many are called*. This verse is the general application given to the parable by our Lord. It was true in respect to the Jews, since the great mass of them that were addressed with gospel offers did not and would not come, and hence were not the true Israel (see vs. 3). This is also true of many others (see vs. 11), who even enter the church, and are not truly of Christ's chosen.

OBSERVE, (1.) Under the gospel, men are repeatedly bidden to the feast of grace. (2.) All things are now ready. It is a *feast* which is spread. Sinners are invited to partake what Christ has freely and fully furnished. The gospel is glad tidings. (3.) Men prefer the world to Christ and heaven. (4.) Many who have had fewer calls and privileges will be saved, while those most favoured with religious opportunities will often stand aloof and be lost. (5) It is not enough to accept the message formally. Every man must have on the *wedding garment* of Christ's righteousness, and must put on Christ. None can

object that they have it not. It is freely furnished them. (6.) The church will yet be sifted. He will thoroughly purge His floor. False professors have a fearful doom, as well as open opposers. *The King will soon come in to see the guests.*

§ 118. INSIDIOUS QUESTIONS OF THE PHARISEES. TRIBUTE TO CESAR.

Matt.	Mark.	Luke.	John.
22.15–22	12.13–17	20.20–26	

15. *Entangle him,* or ensnare him in talk. The term is properly used of ensnaring birds, leading them into a trap by some bait. The meaning is that they planned to see how they might draw Him into some conversation that would work His ruin.

16. *The Herodians.* The old versions have it "the servants of Herod." They were doubtless his adherents, and as he was tetrarch of Galilee under the Romans, Christ was at once under his civil jurisdiction and a rival to his claims. These, therefore, were brought forward to entrap Christ in a political matter. They proposed a question which would be likely to involve a dispute *either* with the Pharisees or the Herodians. The Pharisees condemned the practice of paying tribute to a foreign power, as contrary to the laws of Moses (Deut. 17. 15). But the Herodians approved it, since *Herod* held his office under the Romans. Therefore if Christ declared it unlawful, He would be complained of as undermining the authority of Cesar. If He declared it lawful, He would be represented as a foe to the Pharisees and Jewish people. We see that though the Pharisees hated the Herodians, they could league with them to overthrow Christ.——¶ *Master, we know that thou art true.* Luke mentions more particularly (ch. 20 20), that these were "spies, which

thou regardest not the person of men.

17 Tell us therefore, What thinkest thou? Is it lawful to give tribute unto Cesar, or not?

18 But Jesus perceived their wickedness, and said, Why tempt ye me, *ye* hypocrites?

19 Show me the tribute-money. And they brought unto him a [1] penny.

20 And he saith unto them, Whose *is* this image and [1] superscription?

21 They say unto him, Cesar's. Then saith he unto them, Render [p] therefore unto Cesar the things which are Cesar's, and unto God [q] the things that are God's.

22 When they had heard *these words*, they marvelled, and

---

1 In value, 7 pence halfpenny.

1 Or, *inscription*. *p* c.17.25,27. Ro.13.7. *q* Mal. 1.6-8; 3.8-10.

---

should feign themselves *just men*, that they might take hold of His words so that they might deliver Him unto the power and authority of the governor." Of course they had no such exalted opinion of Christ as they here express, but used the most wicked flattery, intending to deceive Him. They therefore praised Him for an *independent* course, as not afraid of any man, hoping thus to have Him speak disrespectfully of the king.—¶ *Regardest not the person*. A Hebrew idiom. Literally, thou *lookest not upon the face*.

17. *Tribute*. A tax paid by the Jews as a conquered people to the Roman government or Cesar.—— ¶ *Cesar* was a common title for the Roman emperors at this time, as Pharaoh was for the Egyptian kings. This Cesar was Tiberius.

18. *Their wickedness*. It was their malice and hypocrisy. Our Lord perceived it. He was the searcher of hearts. The temptation which they used was an artful device to have Him say something to His injury. It was no temptation in the sense of an inclination of His, as we often use the word. He showed His knowledge of their artifice by calling them deceivers, pretenders, *hypocrites*.

19. *Tribute-money*. The Roman coin with which they paid their tax. ——¶ *A penny*. It was a silver coin, the principal money at the time. It was formerly of 8½ pence value, afterward 7½ pence, say about 14 cents of ours. See note, ch. 20. 2.

20. *Image and superscription*. Literally, *epigraph*. In the time of our Lord it bore the image and titles of the emperor, as common Spanish or English coin at this day, though formerly it was impressed with the symbols of the republic. The inscription was Καισαρ Αυγουστ. Ιουδαιας εαλωκυιας.

21. *Render therefore*. The general rule prescribed here is to give every one his due, or what belongs to him. Their coin, having Cesar's impress on it, showed that they were in his dominions and under his government. Their ordinary currency acknowledged him as their civil ruler, and they should pay to him a rightful obedience as such. This was aimed at the Pharisees, who resisted the Roman authority. At the same time God had His claims, and they were bound to render to Him His due. He came not to settle their political disputes, nor to interfere with the civil affairs of the country, nor would He be embroiled in such questions. Their duties to God did not absolve them from duties to the state (Rom. 13. 1), nor were their civil duties to release them from religious obligations. This was aimed at the Herodians, and all at both.

A. D. 33.] CHAPTER XXII. 227

left him, and went their way.

23 ¶ The ʳ same day came to him the Sadducees, which ˢ say that there is no resurrection, and asked him,

24 Saying, Master, Moses said, If ᵗ a man die, having no children, his brother shall marry his wife, and raise up seed unto his brother.

25 Now there were with us seven brethren: and the first, when he had married a wife, deceased, and, having no issue, left his wife unto his brother:

26 Likewise the second also, and the third, unto the ¹ seventh.

27 And last of all the woman died also.

28 Therefore, in the resurrection, whose wife shall she be of the seven? for they all had her.

29 Jesus answered and said unto them, Ye do err, not ᵘ knowing the Scriptures, nor the power of God.

ʳ Mar.12.18,&c. Lu.20.27,&c. ˢ Ac.23.8. ᵗ De. 25.5. Ru.1.11.

¹ *Seven.* ᵘ Jno.20.9.

---

22. *They marvelled.* They were taken by surprise at such an answer, which so utterly defeated their design against Him. Luke says *they marvelled at His answer, and held their peace.*

OBSERVE, (1.) It is a favourite device of opposers, to bring the religion of Christ into conflict with the state, hoping to harm the cause. But the position of Christ is plain: that Christians are to be good citizens— *and they are*—and that properly understood, the church and the state may have their respective dues without their union, or their opposition. But Christ is head of the church, and head over all things to the church. (2.) We are to be subject to civil rulers—the powers that be are ordained of God. But "the things that are Cesar's" do not include an infringement on "the things that are God's." (3.) All malicious opposers of Christ's cause will be fearfully silenced and shamed.

§ 119. INSIDIOUS QUESTION OF THE SADDUCEES. — *The Resurrection.* THIRD *day of the week.*

Matt.	Mark.	Luke.	John.
22. 23–33	12. 18–27	20. 27–40	

23. *The Sadducees.* This was another attempt to entangle Him in conversation by another party, whose doctrine was known to be a denial of the resurrection of the body, and of the soul's immortality. They proposed to Him a difficulty that would grow out of their law, if the relations which it prescribed were to be extended beyond the grave. It was the case of a woman having seven husbands, all brothers of each other, according to a Mosaic provision in special circumstances, by which a woman might marry a husband's brother, and several brethren might come by the law to have successively the same woman to wife. The question was, who should claim her, of these seven, in the future world? They conceived this an insuperable objection to the doctrine of a future state. Deut. 25. 5.

29. *Ye do err.* The difficulty was not in the case proposed, but in their mistake of the future estate and its relations. They were ignorant of the scriptures which plainly enough in the Old Testament, taught the resurrection (see vs. 32), also (Dan. 12. 2. Isa. 26. 19. Job. 19. 25–27): and they knew not the *power of God*, which men overlook when they say that the body cannot be raised.—" Thou fool " (1 Cor. 15. 36), why should we reason that a thing cannot be done by God Himself, because we have never seen it done, and because we cannot conceive it possible to be done? Why bind God to laws of nature, when nature's laws are only His ordinary modes of action, which He

228 MATTHEW. [A. D. 33.

30 For in the resurrection they neither marry nor are given in marriage, but are as the angels ᵛ of God in heaven.

31 But as touching the resurrection of the dead, have ye not read that which was spoken unto you by God, saying,

32 I ʷ am the God of Abraham, and the God of Isaac, and the God of Jacob. God is not the God of the dead, but of the living.

33 And when the multitude heard *this*, they were astonished ˣ at his doctrine.

34 ¶ But when the Pharisees had heard that he had put the

v c.18.10. 1Jno.3.2. *w* Ex.3.6,15,16. He.11.16. *x* c.7.28. Mar.12.17.

---

chooses for the present to adopt? His word is *above* all the teachings of nature, wherever the authorities may seem to us to conflict.

30. *In the resurrection.* In that future estate, about which they were so puzzled, there are none of these temporal and temporary arrangements; but they are as the angels of God, or, as Luke says, equal to the angels; that is, in like circumstances, as concerns these points. They are above these mere temporal and temporary conditions, not dying any more (as Luke adds), but fixed in a superior state.

31, 32. *As touching the resurrection.* Our Lord appeals here to a passage from their scriptures with which they ought to have been familiar, and which they were bound to credit as spoken unto them by God. It was found in Exod. 3. 6, 15. It was in the conversation of Jehovah and Moses at the burning bush (see Mark and Luke). This was a common title which Jehovah assumed to Himself, and which the ancient saints accorded to Him. Hundreds of years after the death of Abraham, Isaac, and Jacob, God is found claiming to be their God, and this shows that *then* they must have been *living*, for He is not the God of the *dead*. This proved a future existence which the Sadducees denied, and which was the great point. They said there was no resurrection, neither angel, nor spirit. Acts 23. 8. But a future *personal* existence, where Abraham is Abraham still, involves a resurrection of the body, though that body may have gone through important changes, as it does on earth, while it continues essentially and personally the same.

OBSERVE, (1.) They who understand the scriptures will find the resurrection of the body sufficiently taught in the Old Testament. So many passages, as this that is quoted, teach it plainly *by implication.* (2.) They who know the *power of God*, will not think it a thing incredible that God should raise the dead. He brought Adam into life full grown—out of the dust—and Eve out of a rib—and Lazarus out of the sepulchre—and brought Moses and Elias—one of whom was buried in an unknown place, and the other translated without death—both in their bodies to the *transfiguration.* (3.) The *scripture* is the authority, and God's *power* the warrant, for this belief. (4.) How glorious shall be the resurrection estate of believers! Who can conceive it? No longer these fleshly and dying relations, but as the angels—pure and celestial, our relations shall be higher and more extensive. "We shall sit down with Abraham, and Isaac, and Jacob." "It doth not yet appear what we shall be."

§ 120. A LAWYER QUESTIONS JESUS. THE TWO GREAT COMMANDMENTS.— THIRD *day of the week.*

Matt.	Mark.	Luke.	John.
22 34–40	12. 28–34		

34. *When the Pharisees heard.* It seems to have been the great object of these rival parties only to entrap Christ: and the Pharisees would have

A. D. 33.   CHAPTER XXII.   229

Sadducees to silence, they were gathered together.

35 Then *y* one of them, *which was* a lawyer, asked *him a question,* tempting him, and saying,

36 Master, which *is* the great commandment in the law?

37 Jesus said unto him, Thou *z* shalt love the Lord thy God with all thy heart, and with all

y Lu.10,25,&c.   *z* De.6.5; 10.12.

thy soul, and with all thy mind.

38 This is the first and great commandment.

39 And the second *is* like unto it, *a* Thou shalt love thy neighbour as thyself.

40 On these two commandments *b* hang all the law and the prophets.

41 ¶ While the

a Le.19.18.   *b* Ro.13.9. Ja.2.8.

been glad if the Sadducees had succeeded in so doing. But now that they had failed, some new device must be raised.

35. *A lawyer.* That is, one of the *scribes* (see Mark), whose business it was to expound and write the laws.

36. *The great commandment in the law.* That is, the most important commandment in the Mosaic law. Mark has it, "Which is the first commandment of all?" This question was put to Him to get an opinion on *a disputed point,* so that He might come into collision with one or the other party. The Jews divided the commandments of their law into *greater* and *lesser* (see ch. 5. 19; "one of these *least* commandments"), but they were not agreed in the particulars. Some contended for the law of circumcision; others for that of sacrifice; others for that of phylacteries.

37. *Jesus said unto him.* This reply was not what the scribe had desired, but from particulars it ascended to the general and comprehensive spirit of obedience. Supreme love to God, which is at the basis of all the commandments, was given as the chief requirement. Heart, soul, mind and strength, all of each, and all together, is the entire obedience required (Deut. 6. 5. Levit. 19. 18).

39. *The second.* Our Lord adds the second commandment, which is equally broad and comprehensive. These two agree with the two tables of the moral law. The first four commandments of the decalogue have respect to our duties toward God. The last six commands respect our duties toward fellow-men. This last table is here given in a summary, and is called the *second commandment.*

40. *On these two.* These are represented as the grand fundamental principles on which all the law and all religion depend. Duties to fellow-men are not enough without duties to God, and these latter are essential to the former.——¶ *Hang*—that is, *depend.* Mark adds, that the scribe owned this as *truth,* and that upon this, Christ declared that he was "*not far from the kingdom of heaven*"—nearly understanding and embracing the gospel doctrine. This whole conversation (vss. 15–40) had quite confounded all parties that came against Him. And none of them, after that, durst ask Him any questions. (See Mark and Luke.)

OBSERVE, (1.) Many raise questions about specific points of duty, and give them a prominence beyond the great question of love to God—neglecting thus the gospel, and the gospel plan of salvation. (2.) Love to God and to man are kindred precepts of the same law—nor can we properly and fully love our neighbour, without first of all, and above all, loving God. They who boast a religion of *social piety,* and reject Christ, and have no supreme regard to God's will, do not understand the commandments.

§ 121. HOW IS CHRIST THE SON OF DAVID?—THIRD *day of the week.*—*Jerusalem.*

Matt.	Mark.	Luke.	John
22. 41–46	12 35 37	20.41–44	

Pharisees were gathered together, Jesus asked them,

42 Saying, What *c* think ye of Christ? whose son is he? They say unto him, *The Son* of David.

43 He saith unto them, How then doth David in spirit call him ¹ Lord, saying,

44 The LORD said unto my Lord, Sit thou on my right hand, till I make thine enemies thy footstool.

c Mar.12.35,&c. Lu.20.41,&c. *d* Ps.110.1. Ac.2. 34,35. He.1.13 ; 10.12,13.

45 If David then call him Lord, how is he his son?

46 And *e* no man was able to answer him a word; neither *f* durst any *man*, from that day forth, ask him any more *questions*.

CHAPTER XXIII.

THEN spake Jesus to the multitude, and to his disciples,

2 Saying, The *a* scribes and the Pharisees sit in Moses' seat:

e Lu.14.66. *f* Mar.12.34. Lu.20.40. *a* Mal.2.7.

42. *What think ye of Christ?* Our Lord now in turn (while He was yet teaching in the temple—Mark) puts a question to them, which should show their ignorance of the scriptures, and of the Christ whom they professed to look for. The difficulty which this question involved, had reference to the two natures of Christ in one person; and because they could not understand how He could be God and man at the same time, they rejected Jesus of Nazareth, who was the son of David (Matt. 1. 1), and also David's Lord, as the co-equal Son of God. David "in spirit"—that is, by inspiration of the Holy Ghost—calls Him "Lord" (Ps. 110. 1).

45. *How is He his Son?* This is substantially the difficulty which Socinians find in the doctrine of Christ's divinity. They ask how Christ can be equal with God, and be the Son of God, at the same time? Yet their own scripture plainly asserts that *He is both*, just as it asserts that He was David's Son and Lord. And where the scripture testimony is acknowledged, as it was by the Jews, the result must be the same as in their case—"No man was able to answer Him a word," &c. (vs. 46.) Mark adds, beautifully, "The common people heard Him gladly."

OBSERVE, (1.) From these repeated triumphs over His most cunning enemies, we infer Christ's Divinity. He was beyond the power of His most bitter and venomous assailants to overthrow Him in doctrine, or ensnare Him in conversation. He could read their hearts, and so He could well adapt His replies to their inquiries, so as to foil them in their base attempts. (2.) The scripture is full of authority for the doctrine of Christ's Divinity—and on this ground it must irrefragably stand. They who deny it, must be silenced from the plain word of God. (3.) "Common people" receive this doctrine with joy, while disputers of this world reject it. Hath not God made foolish the wisdom of this world? "Thou hast hid these things from the wise and prudent, and hast revealed them unto babes."

CHAPTER XXIII.

§ 122. WARNINGS AGAINST THE EVIL EXAMPLE OF THE SCRIBES AND PHARISEES. — THIRD *day of the week. Jerusalem.*

Matt.	Mark.	Luke.	John.
23. 1-12	12.38,39	20. 45, 46	

1. *Then spake Jesus.* Our Lord now takes occasion to expose those who had laboured to entangle Him. He had utterly foiled them in their attempts, and overthrown them in His questions, and now He would expose their real character and standing. Mark has it, "*Beware of the Scribes.*" Luke has an instructive clause, introductory, "*Then in the audience of all the* people, He said unto His disciples," &c.

2. *Sit in Moses' seat.* As Moses was

3 All therefore, whatsoever they bid you observe, *that* observe and do: but do not ye after their works: for *b* they say, and do not.

4 For they bind heavy burdens, *c* and grievous to be borne, and lay *them* on men's shoulders; but they *themselves* will not move them with one of their fingers.

5 But *d* all their works they do for to be seen of men: they make broad their phylacteries *e* and enlarge the borders of their garments,

6 And *f* love the uppermost rooms at feasts, and the chief

b Ro.2.21-23. *c* Ac.15.10.

d c.6.1-16. *e* Nu.15.38. *f* Mar.12.38,&c. Lu.1 43,&c.

the law-giver, so these were the public expounders of the law. In this sense they sat in His seat, or chair, as teachers.' This alludes to the fact that the Jewish Doctors *sat* when they taught.

3. *All therefore.* On account of their holding this place as authorized teachers of the Mosaic law, they were to be respected. But as it was expressly on *account of* this relation in which they stood to Moses and his seat, that they were to be followed, it must be only so far as their teachings were consistent with Moses' law. Their *works* were to be avoided, for they practised inconsistently with their instructions.

4. *They bind heavy burdens.* As the loads were packed on beasts of burden, so they imposed the heaviest requisitions of the ritual, with all their grievous additions. This was the yoke upon the neck, which neither their fathers nor they were able to bear (Acts 15. 10). They were intolerant and exacting. Those rites, however numerous and costly, they loved to enforce upon others, but would not touch for themselves " with one of their fingers "—that is, in the least. They would not carry " the burdens, no not even touch them." They sought indulgence and applause rather.

5. *All their works,* &c. They loved the praise of men more than the praise of God. They practised not self-denial, but self-exaltation. Some of their self-sufficient practises are here mentioned. ——¶ *They make broad their phylacteries.* These were scraps of parchment containing certain passages from the law, which they rolled up in a leathern case, and bound by leather thongs to the hand and forehead—according to the letter of that direction in Deut. 6. 8; 11. 18. The passages so carried about the person were, Exod. 13. 1-10, 11-16. Deut. 6. 4-9; 11. 13-21. These parchments *they* made broader than common, in order to seem more religious than others. (*See cut.*)

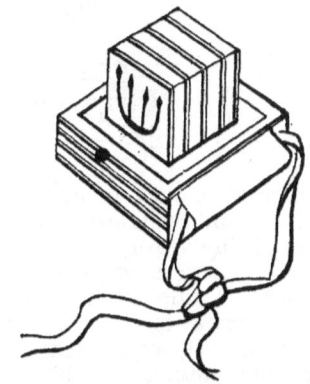

——¶ *Borders of their garments.* These were fringes on the edges of their garments, called the hem, (ch 9. 20,) which they were commanded to have, as a distinction from other nations, and as a memorial of God's statutes, and which He also wore (ch. 14. 36. Num. 15. 32–41). These people made them wider than others, to seem extra religious (ch. 5. 40; 9. 26).

6. *Uppermost rooms.* Rather the uppermost *places.* The Jews *reclined* at table instead of sitting as we

seats in the synagogues,

7 And greetings in the markets, and to be called of men, Rabbi, Rabbi.

8 But ᵍ be not ye called Rabbi, for one is your Master, *even* Christ; and all ye are brethren.

9 And call no *man* your Father upon the earth: for one is

<small>g Ja.3.1.</small>

your ʰ Father, which is in heaven.

10 Neither be ye called masters: for one is your Master, *even* Christ.

11 But ⁱ he that is greatest among you, shall be your servant.

12 And ʲ whosoever shall ex-

<small>h c.6.9. i c.20.26,27. j Pr.15.33. Ja.4.6.</small>

---

do. The table was composed of three parts—forming two sides and an end. The couches were ranged along the three sides—and the uppermost room or place, was that at the head of the table—looking down the two sides. It was the place of the most honoured guest. John reclined on Christ's bosom. (*See cut.*) —— ¶ *The chief seats in the synagogues.* In the Jewish synagogues there was a class of officers called Elders, whose seats were conspicuous near the minister, under the pulpit and fronting the people. These seats they loved, as bringing them into notice.

7. *Greetings*, &c. The markets were public places where a large concourse usually met for business,

and here also, they loved show and distinction and applause. They were fond of being saluted and greeted there by the crowd. —— ¶ *Rabbi.* This was a title of honour given to the doctors of the law in the time of Christ, equivalent to our *doctor* and *master*, combining the sense of both. They loved to be saluted by men as their superiors. It is from a word meaning *great*.

8. *Be not ye.* Such fondness for titles was forbidden by our Lord. It showed a wrong heart. The custom made invidious distinctions and fostered pride, and was unfit among the apostles, as He had previously shown, when they asked who should be the greatest. And there was this broad reason against it, that Christ claimed to be their Master, and no other should be owned as such.

9. *Call no man your Father*, &c. Neither treat others so, nor demand so to be treated. They who own a religious head on earth as infallible and supreme, violate this precept. So the Papists own the Pope as their *papa* or *father*, and they call other religious dignitaries by this title. They who make ranks in the clergy, who are set to be equal, foster this spirit.

11, 12. *But he that is greatest*, &c. The highest honour in the church is not superiority of station, but of service. Humility is the most excellent distinction of the truly great and good. Only they who are humble shall be exalted, and they who seek earthly exaltation, whose hearts are proud and presumptuous, shall be abased. The spirit of ambitious rivalry and proud self-seeking is rebuked.

alt himself, shall be abased; and he that shall humble himself, shall be exalted.

13 ¶ But wo unto you, scribes and Pharisees, hypocrites! for ye shut up the kingdom of heaven against men: for ye neither go in *yourselves*, neither suffer ye them that are entering to go in.

14 Wo unto you, scribes and Pharisees, hypocrites! for ye devour widows houses, [k] and for a pretence make long prayer: therefore ye shall receive the greater damnation.

15 Wo unto you, scribes and Pharisees, hypocrites! for ye compass sea and land to make one proselyte; and when he is made, ye make him twofold more the child [l] of hell than yourselves.

16 Woe unto you, *ye* blind [m]

k 2Ti.3.6. Tit.1.11. *l* Jno.8.44. Ac.13.10. Ep.2.3. *m* c.15.14.

---

§ 123. Woes against the Scribes and Pharisees. Lamentation over Jerusalem. — Third *day of the week.*

| Matt. | Mark. | Luke. | John. |
| 23.13-39 | 12. 40 | 20. 47 | |

13. *Wo unto you.* Our Lord now puts forth the severest denunciations against those who had so attacked Him, and of whom He had just warned the people. They were guilty of shutting up the kingdom of heaven. All their influence was turned against the gospel, so as to prevent the multitude from receiving it. They professed to be guardians of the church, and this had been their office. But they abused it to exclude men from this salvation. Holding the keys in this sense, they locked the door and kept men from entering. They persecuted the true Messiah, and they taught for doctrines the commandments of men.

14. *Devour widows' houses.* Cruelty, avarice, and hypocrisy, are here charged upon them. Such was their greedy avarice, that they even swallowed up the 'houses' (or property) of widows, as they went about seeking whose estates they could devour. They often took advantage of the unprotected, and perverted their office as ecclesiastics and lawyers, to get possession of their property.——¶ *For a pretence*—for a disguise. In Luke, we read "*for a show*," but the same Greek word. With all this, they pretended the greatest piety, so they made long prayer (see ch. 6. 5), "standing in the synagogues and in the corners of the streets," and continuing several hours in these showy devotions. For this hypocrisy, doing the most despicable deeds under the show of piety, they should be the more severely punished in the future world.

15. *Ye compass sea and land*—or traverse. This is a proverbial phrase, expressing the most extensive and assiduous efforts. They would leave no stone unturned, and would spare no pains to make *one proselyte*—that is, to convert one man to their religion, more or less fully.——¶ *Two-fold more.* The result was, that those whom they so won over to the Jewish rites, were made twice as bad as themselves.——¶ *A child of hell*, is a Hebrew mode of speech, to denote one who belongs to hell — the offspring and heir of perdition. So in Sam. 20. 31, marg., "Son of death"—devoted to death. And it was notorious that their adherents became more awfully wicked than themselves—doubly so. The proselytes were called "the scabs of Israel, as hindering the coming of the Messiah, being ignorant of the law and bringing in revenge." Their zeal for proselyting was proverbial among the heathen. The Latin poet Horace speaks of it.

16, 17. *Ye blind guides.* Here they are denounced for their mischievous

234 MATTHEW. [A. D. 33.

guides, which say, Whosoever shall swear by the temple, it is nothing; but whosoever shall swear by the gold of the temple, he is a debtor.

17 *Ye* fools, [n] and blind! for whether is greater, the gold, or the temple that sanctifieth the gold?

18 And, whosoever shall swear by the altar, it is nothing; but whosoever sweareth by the gift that is upon it, he is [1] guilty.

19 *Ye* fools and blind! for whether *is* greater, the gift, or the altar that sanctifieth [o] the gift?

20 Whoso therefore shall swear by the altar, sweareth by it, and by all things thereon.

21 And whoso shall swear by the temple, sweareth by it, and by him [p] that dwelleth therein.

22 And he that shall swear by heaven, sweareth by the throne [q] of God, and by him that sitteth thereon.

23 Wo unto you, scribes and

---

[n] Ps.94.8. [1] Or, *debtor*, or, *bound*.

[o] Ex.29.37; 30.29. [p] 2Ch.6.2. Ps.26.8. [q] Ps.11.4. Is.66.1. c.5.34.

---

doctrines in the community—calculated to lead men sadly astray. As to the obligation of oaths, they were wont to swear by a variety of objects most foolishly. They made the most arbitrary distinctions, calculated to confound all such obligations. To swear by the temple, was to take an oath by the temple that what was said or promised was *truth*. The folly of it was, that it was no test of sincerity, and that it confounded a building with God Himself, who alone could search the heart. If one sware by the temple, it was nothing, that is, of no account —having no force in their esteem. But if he sware by the gold of the temple, his oath was solemnly binding. Whereas no reason could be given why there should be more force in one oath than in the other; and if either was greater, it was the temple greater than the gold: for all the golden vessels and furniture had their sanctity from the temple itself. (See ch. 5. 33, &c.)

18, 19. *Shall swear by the altar.* The altar of *burnt-offerings* (2 Chron. 4. 1). This, men could swear by, without the oath having any force; but if they sware by the gift upon the altar, they were "*guilty*," that is, *liable to condemnation*, for breaking the oath. This is the force of the words "guilt" and "guilty" in the old English. This figure shows an altar, thought by many to be the form of that in the temple. The horns of the altar are seen here.

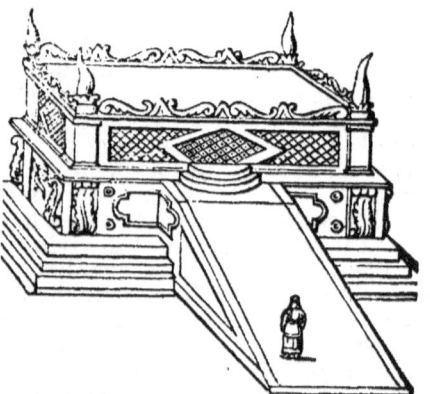

20, 21. *Whoso therefore.* Here the true doctrine is laid down in regard to the solemnity and sanctity of oaths. The Jews had many foolish oaths that they regarded as having no force. But they are here declared to be solemn and awful appeals to Jehovah, though they did not so regard them. (See ch. 5. 34, &c.) Hence (as in the 5th chap.) they were shown that this was profane jesting, for God was concerned in it all. Hence it was the subject of *profanity* that was here treated of, for it prevailed extensively among the Jews. The sin of profane swearing consists in using lightly terms of the greatest solemnity—when

A. D. 33.] CHAPTER XXIII. 235

Pharisees, hypocrites! for *r* ye pay tithe of mint, and anise, *¹* and cummin, and have omitted the weightier *matters* *s* of the law, judgment, mercy, and faith: these ought ye to have done, and not to leave the other undone.

24 *Ye* blind guides! which strain at a gnat, and swallow a camel.

25 Wo unto you, scribes and Pharisees, hypocrites! for *t* ye make clean the outside of the cup and of the platter, but within they are full of extortion and excess.

26 *Thou* blind Pharisee!

r Lu.11.42. 1 *Dill.* *s* 1Sa.15.22. Je.22.15,16. Ho.6.6. Mi.6.8. c.9.13.

t Mar.7.4,&c.

ther God's names, titles, attributes, words, works, or any thing relating to His worship. It is a frivolous trifling with holy things.

23. *Ye pay tithe.* A tithe means a *tenth part.* The Jews were required strictly to pay a tenth of all their yearly produce of corn, cattle, &c., to the Levites, and after that, a second tenth or tithe to the sanctuary service, and then, a third tenth, that is, of the remainder, to the poor widows, the fatherless, &c. There seems to have been no law for a tithe of herbs; but in this the Pharisees would show an extra devotion. They paid tithe, even to the merest herbs, and were exact to the very smallest items. (Numb. 18. 20-24. Deut. 14. 22-29.) These herbs, here mentioned, are from the garden and of little value, except for odour or flavour. They represent here, the minor matters in which the Pharisees were so strict. It was not condemned. They did right to pay tithes to the utmost. But, with all this attention to smallest matters, they neglected things of more importance —their *social and religious duties.*— ¶ *Judgment*—or justice, for they were great extortioners, and unjust.—— ¶ *Mercy*—for they were unfeeling and cruel.—— ¶ *Faith*—for they were the grossest unbelievers, and had not piety towards God; and so also they were *unfaithful.* These things were their first duty, while the others should have been done also.

24. *Blind guides.* The allusion may here be to some of the more ostentatious of the sect, who wore *bandages* on their eyes in public, as not looking on iniquity, lest they should be defiled. They claimed to be leaders in morals, and undertook to be instructors of the people. But Christ shows their utter incapacity for this, and the mischief they must do in such a work. They lacked the very quality which a guide should have. Hence they must lead into evil.——
¶ *" Which strain at a gnat."* The word means *filter.* This is a proverbial expression. The term refers to the straining of wine, or water, to get it pure. (See Amos 6. 6.) Their conduct is represented by this: straining their drink to avoid swallowing a gnat, and yet swallowing—gulping down—a camel;—particular about little sins, but careless about great ones—seeing *motes,* but overlooking *beams*—affecting the greatest dread of trivial improprieties, but committing the grossest crimes. This was the spirit that could see the mote in another's eye, and think nothing of the *beam* in its own. The old versions read it, *" Strain out a gnat,"* and *" Strain a gnat."* This, *" Strain at a gnat,"* may be understood in the same sense—straining over and over to get out the last gnat in the wine. The Jews had a proverb of *swallowing an elephant,* analogous to this.

25, 26. These verses are properly connected with the 24th, as explaining it, and showing the danger of their guidance. They were careful of outside ceremonies, but at heart (within), they were full of extortion and excess. The washing of pots and cups, and other such things they did (Mark 7. 8) careful about ex-

cleanse first that *which is* within the cup and platter, that the outside of them may be clean also.

27 Wo unto you, scribes and Pharisees, hypocrites! for ye are like unto [u] whited sepulchres, which indeed appear beautiful outward, but are within full of dead *men's* bones, and of all uncleanness.

28 Even so ye also outwardly appear righteous unto men, but within ye are full of hypocrisy and iniquity.

29 Woe unto you, scribes and Pharisees, hypocrites! because

[u] Lu.11.44. Ac.23.3.

---

ternal niceties, but careless about the heart. Even their cups and platters, which they would so ceremoniously wash, were filled with the fruits of extortion and with all excess.—— ¶ *Cleanse first.* They are here exhorted to pay first attention to the things *within* their cup and platter. How ridiculous for one to be careless of what was within his dish, and only to see that it have a clean outside.

27, 28. Still further warning the people against the deceits of their wicked teachers, our Lord here further likens them to whited sepulchres. The Jews were accustomed yearly, on the 15th day of Adar, to whiten the vaults or tombs which they had built. This was the season for it, *just before the Passover*, and the fresh white paint would now be conspicuous on the adjoining hills and valleys. This gave them a bright, beautiful appearance, and was a token of their attention and respect. It also served to keep them visible to passers by, that they might not touch them and be polluted. (See Numb. 19. 16. Luke 11. 44.)——¶ *Beautiful outward* (ωραιοι). The Jews paid great respect to burial. The more opulent had ornamented tombs, and the women visited them, especially a few days after the burial, to strew flowers, or to weep. So the sisters of Lazarus (John 11. 31). (*See cut, from Kitto.*) So the Pharisees kept up their own appearance by mere whitewash, while at heart, they were full of rottenness and corruption. Outwardly they seemed righteous *unto men*, but to God they were known to be full of hypocrisy and iniquity. This is the character of all hypocrites.

29. *Ye build the tombs of the prophets.* Another deception which they practised was this of affecting the greatest respect for the deceased prophets This would make them seem to the Jews to be zealously devoted to their religion. They showed the greatest zeal in preserving their memory and honour, by erecting tombs of stone sacred to their names.——¶ *And garnish* —that is, *decorate, adorn.* By adding various ornaments to the sepulchres of eminent saints, they affected a great reverence and love for the piety of such. Josephus tells us of the splendid manner in which Herod repaired David's sepulchre, mentioned Acts 2. 29.

30. *And say.* They further pretended by these and other acts, and in their language, that they abhorred the crime of those who killed the pro-

ye build the tombs of the prophets, and garnish the sepulchres of the righteous,

30 And say, If we had been in the days of our fathers, we would not have been partakers with them in the blood of the prophets.

31 Wherefore ye be witnesses unto yourselves, that ye are the children of them which killed ᵛ the prophets.

32 Fill ʷ ye up then the measure of your fathers.

33 *Ye* serpents, *ye* generation ˣ of vipers! how can ye escape the damnation of hell?

34 Wherefore, behold, I send unto you prophets, and wise men, and scribes: and *some* of them ye shall kill ʸ and crucify; and *some* of them shall ye scourge ᶻ in your synagogues,

v Ac.7.52. 1Th.2.15.   *w* Ge.15.16., 1Th.2.16.   *x* c.3.7.   *y* Ac.7.59.   *z* Ac.5.40. 2Cor.11.24,25.

---

phets: and all this was a mere hollow parade—a vain pretence of hypocrites. People often talk against other sinners, while they are just as bad themselves: "Thou that judgest, doest the same things."

31. *Ye be witnesses unto yourselves.* Their own consciences and conduct told them that they were the genuine offspring of those who murdered the prophets—that they were like them, as children are like their parents, and not only naturally descended from them, but really of the same sort. So their persecutions of the apostles would soon prove.

32. *Fill ye up then.* This is as much as to say, Go on, then, as you are going, and you will only do as your wicked fathers have done, and will fill up their measure of iniquity—that is, in other words, will complete the iniquity which they have begun. There is an air of irony in the language. Yet it is spoken with the force of a judicial abandonment, as if, at length ordering them to do, what it was so certain they would do; like the language in Isaiah 6. 9, 10 (quoted in Matt. 13. 14, 15—see note), where the prophet's word to that people was to be, "Hear ye, indeed, but understand not," and the prophet is commanded, "Make the heart of this people fat." (See Alexander on the passage in Isaiah.) Comp. Acts 7. 57.

33. *Ye serpents.* This further expresses their specious hypocrisy. "The old serpent," is a scriptural name for the devil, who is also called "the father of lies."——¶ *Generation of vipers.* This alludes again to their being the true children of those who murdered the prophets, and like them in heart—and so they are called a family or brood of vipers, instead of being such a generation as they claimed. As the *serpent* expressed their wicked deceitfulness, so the *viper* expressed their mischievous, poisonous power. They were plainly rushing to destruction, and in the strongest terms, Christ charges them that eternal damnation was most sure to be their lot. He who knew the end from the beginning could predict the result.

34. *Wherefore, behold*—Accordingly, He now shows how their perseverance in iniquity like this, should even now go on and bring them to such a fearful end. Luke speaks of this, as a previous prediction. "Behold the wisdom of God *hath said.*" The gospel teachers should go among them—that is, the apostles, and others—and they should treat *them* as cruelly as their fathers had treated their prophets. The Jews called their doctors by these names, *prophets, wise men* and *scribes;* and Christ so calls His gospel teachers who ought to supersede them. These things were fulfilled after Christ's death. Stephen was stoned (Acts 7. 59); James was killed with a sword (Acts 12. 1, 2), see Acts 5. 40. Acts 22. 19–24. 2 Cor. 11. 24, 25; and persecution was re-

238 MATTHEW. [A. D. 33

and persecute *them* from city *a* to city.

35 That *b* upon you may come all the righteous blood shed upon the earth, from the blood of righteous Abel *c* unto the blood of Zacharias *d* son of Barachias, whom ye slew between the temple and the altar.

36 Verily I say unto you, All these things shall come upon this generation.

a He.11.37. *b* Re.18.24. *c* Ge.4.8. *d* 2Ch.24.20,21.

37 O *e* Jerusalem, Jerusalem, *thou* that killest the prophets, and stonest them which are sent unto thee, how often would I have gathered *f* thy children together, as a hen gathereth her chickens under *her* wings, and ye would not!

38 Behold, your house is left unto you desolate.*g*

39 For I say unto you, Ye shall not see me henceforth, till

e Lu.13.34. *f* De.32.11,12. Ps.91.4. *g* Zec.11.6.

---

alized by all the gospel teachers—as *Peter* (Acts 12. 3), *and the brethren* (Acts 14. 2). Paul and Barnabas were persecuted from city to city.

35. *That upon you.* This was the *result* to which all their wicked conduct should tend. They should fill up their cup, or measure of iniquity, until *the nation should suffer at length the punishment due for all this continued sin.* As they had always been bent on slaying the righteous, so, the blood of righteous Abel, though he was not slain by them (Gen. 4. 8), is laid to their charge. Their spirit was just such as would have slain him also. This is a striking contrast with their pretence in vs. 30.——¶ *Zacharias*—or Zechariah. This is another case of ancient date, recorded in 2 Chron. 24. 20, 21. The object is to show that, as the nation had persisted in like cruelties, they were to be fairly held accountable for those long ago perpetrated by their fathers. This Zacharias was stoned in the porch of the temple, in sight of every thing sacred, which their fury would not allow them to regard. He is mentioned as the son of Jehoiada; but it was customary among the Jews to have two names.——¶ *Whom ye slew*—that is, *the Jewish people.* Between the temple, or sanctuary, and the altar—i. e., of burnt-offerings.

36. *Upon this generation.* This refers to the coming destruction of Jerusalem, which was prophesied as to come upon the city for the sins of the nation. It occurred in about forty years after this time, and would come upon many then living. See Matt. 27. 25.

37. *O Jerusalem.* The holy city of the Jews is here taken for the nation—and this served to set forth more strongly the shocking case—that God's chosen city should have become used to such crime and blood, as killing the prophets.——¶ *That killest.* This is a present participle, and has a special force expressing *constant practice.* The case of Isaiah, Jeremiah and others, is here referred to. "They were stoned, they were sawn asunder," (see Heb. 11).——¶ *How often!* Our Lord here declares that He had cherished toward them the most tender affection, and would often have taken them under His protection and care, as His children.——¶ *Thy children.* The population of a city or country are spoken of in Scripture as the *children* of that place. This declaration of our Lord, shows to what a pitch of obduracy and impiety they had attained (Isa. 65. 2). They had refused His fondest love (see Deut. 32. 11. Isa. 31. 5. Psalm 17. 8).

38. *Your house*—especially *the temple,* and generally, including *all their estate.* The temple was desolate, because God now forsook it in righteous judgment, and it would pass into the hands of their Roman invaders and be destroyed, according to the predictions of the next chapter.

39. *For I say.* Their destruction

ye shall say, [h] Blessed *is* he that cometh in the name of the Lord.

CHAPTER XXIV.

AND [a] Jesus went out, and departed from the temple; and his disciples came to *him* for to shew him the buildings of the temple.

2 And Jesus said unto them, See ye not all these things? Verily I say unto you, There [L] shall not be left here one stone upon

[h] Ps.118.26. c.21.9. [a] Mar.13.1. Lu.21.5.
[b] 1Ki.9.7. Je.26.18. Lu.19.44.

should be certain, because He should depart from them in just judgment—and they should yet see the day when they would hail a Deliverer—the Messiah from God.—¶ *Blessed.* This they sung daily in their Psalm (118. 26), and their nation would yet call for HIM as their Messiah, before He should come again. This is prophetic of their restoration, and presents their obdurate unbelief under this striking aspect as a thing yet to be bitterly repudiated by themselves.—¶ *He that cometh.* "He that should come," as John's disciples termed the Messiah. It was a title by which the predicted Messenger of the Covenant was known. See Mal. 3. 1.

OBSERVE (1.) The sins of religious teachers are most odious before God. (2.) Ostentatious hypocrisy is abominable in God's sight, and shall be visited with terrible woes, here and hereafter. "Behold the goodness and severity of God" (Rom. 11. 22).

	Matt.	Mark.	Luke.	John.
§ 124. The Widow's Mite.—THIRD *day of the week.—Jerusalem.*	. . . .	12.41–44	21. 1–4	
§ 125. Certain Greeks desire to see Jesus. *Same day.*	. . . .	. . . .	. . . .	12.20–36
§ 126. Reflections upon the Unbelief of the Jews. *Same day.*	. . . .	. . . .	. . . .	12.37–50

CHAPTER XXIV.

§ 127. JESUS ON TAKING LEAVE OF THE TEMPLE FORETELLS ITS DESTRUCTION.—THIRD *day of the week. Jerusalem. Mount of Olives.*

Matt.	Mark.	Luke.	John.
24. 1–14	13. 1–13	21. 5–19	

1. *And Jesus went out.* This departure from the temple, expressed in immediate action, what should more fully and fearfully come to pass. He had "*come to His temple,*" as the prophet had said, and now He was about to *leave* it to destruction. He was passing now out of the city to the Mount of Olives. This temple was of most costly and solid structure. The several buildings included courts, towers, walls, porches, &c. Mark speaks of the *stones* as being pointed at *by the disciples.* Luke also speaks of their calling attention to the massive and magnificent materials. Some of these stones were forty cubits long, six wide, and five high—or about sixty feet in length, about nine in height, &c. Some such enormous blocks are thought to have remained in the north-east wall toward Olivet, since Solomon's time. They regarded this building as beyond possible destruction. And it was the boast and glory of the Jewish nation.

2. *Verily I say unto you.* He now takes occasion to foretell the utter ruin of the temple, buildings, &c. The massive structure should be levelled with the ground. This was literally fulfilled to such an incredible extent. The Roman conqueror *Titus* sought to spare the temple, but the Jews would not come to terms. He even gave orders to extinguish the flames. And after its fall, the foundations were actually ploughed up, in search of the treasure that so abounded in the furniture and vessels. See Josephus—Alexander's Evidences. It is estimated that in the erection of the first temple (Solomon's), 183,000 men were employed seven years—48,000 tons of gold and silver used, computed at $35,520,000, besides immense quantities of brass, iron and stone.

another, that shall not be thrown down.

3 ¶ And as he sat upon the mount of Olives, the disciples came unto him privately, saying, Tell us, when shall these things be? And what *shall be* the sign of thy coming, and of the end of the world?c

4 And Jesus answered and said unto them, Take d heed that no man deceive you.

5 For many shall come in my e name, saying, I am Christ; and shall deceive many.

6 And ye shall hear of wars, f and rumours of wars: see that ye be not troubled: for all *these things* must come to pass, but the end is not yet.

7 For g nation shall rise against nation, and kingdom against kingdom: and there shall be famines, and pestilences, and earthquakes, in divers places.

8 All these *are* the beginning of sorrows.

9 Then h shall they deliver

c 1Th.5.1,&c.   d Col.2.8. 2Th.2.3.   e Je.14.14.   f Da.ch.11.   g Hag.2.21,22.   h Lu.21.12.

3. *The Mount of Olives*—is one of "the mountains round about Jerusalem." It overlooked the city, and was about 625 paces east. Between lay the valley of Jehoshaphat—the brook Cedron—and the garden of Gethsemane. Mark mentions Peter, James, John, and Andrew, as inquiring of Christ. They went to Him *privately* as Nicodemus did, because they were amazed, and in the dark, and full of secret misgivings and doubts which they would have Him relieve. They asked of the signs of His coming and of the end of the world, because they had always believed that the temple would stand till the world should end. His coming here refers to the last verse of the last chapter, where He had hinted of such an event. The answer is such as applies both to the destruction of Jerusalem and to the end of the world.

4, 5. *Take heed*, &c. Beware of deceivers. Many should come in His name—that is, claiming to be Christ, and bearing His name. As the Messiah was generally looked for at that time, and as Jesus was disbelieved by the Jews, many deceivers would naturally claim to be the true Messiah. Josephus tells us that this was actually the case, and that many went after them and followed their false teachings. See Alexander's Evidences.——¶ *In my name*. Not by my authority, but *claiming* it.

6–8. *Wars*, &c. The world was now at peace, therefore this marked change in affairs should be a sign. And though wars and commotions, were not peculiar to any age or clime, yet men should remark these things as precursors of the end. They were mentioned here, rather to show that such commotions must be met first—that these were not *the end*—that the disciples must not be soon shaken in mind, nor troubled at such agitations as though the end had come (2 Thess. 2. 2). But they must prepare for the rest and worst, that should follow. Wars and rumors (or reports) of wars abounded throughout the Roman empire, prior to the destruction of Jerusalem. (See Josephus and Tacitus.) ——¶ *The end is not yet*. Luke has it, " is not *by and by*," that is, not *immediately*, as the phrase meant.

7. *Famines and pestilences*. The terms and things are often connected. Comp. Acts 11. 28. In Greece, and Rome, and Palestine, there were famines prior to the end.——¶ *Earthquakes*. Pompeii was nearly destroyed by an earthquake, and several cities are mentioned in Asia Minor as being overthrown—also in Greece. Earthquakes presaged times of distress. (See Joel 3. 16: 2. 10.

A. D. 33.] CHAPTER XXIV. 241

you up to be afflicted, and shall kill *i* you: and ye shall be hated of all nations for my name's sake.

10 And then shall many be *j* offended, and shall betray one another, and shall hate one another.

11 And *k* many false prophets shall rise, and shall deceive *l* many.

12 And because iniquity shall abound, the love of many shall wax *m* cold.

13 But *n* he that shall endure

i Jno.16.2. Ac.7.59. *j* c.13.21. *k* 2Pe.2.1. 1Jno.4.3. *l* 1Ti.4.1. *m* Re.3.15,16. *n* Re.2.10.

8. *Sorrows.* This term signifies the pangs of childbirth, to which severe afflictions and judgments are frequently compared in the scriptures —also in other writers.

9. *Then.* Luke has it, " before these things." The persecutions of the Christians commenced shortly after Christ's ascension, and continued after the city's destruction.—— ¶ *Deliver you up,* &c., i. e. to the authorities. Mark has it, " to councils " or the Sanhedrim.——¶ *To be afflicted,* literally *to tribulation,* to be tried and punished—" and ye shall be beaten in the synagogues, and ye shall be brought before rulers and kings for my sake," &c.; and all this shall be for a testimony in behalf of the gospel and against the persecutors (Mark 13. 9). These things happened after our Lord's resurrection, and are recorded in the Acts of the Apostles. Peter and John suffered imprisonment (Acts 4. 3). So did Paul and Silas (Acts 16. 24), and they were beaten (16. 23). James was killed by Herod (Acts 12. 2). Peter was put to death in the persecution under Nero, before the destruction of Jerusalem, as Christ forewarned (John 21. 18). It was also considered a crime to be a Christian, and adherence to Christ was a sufficient cause for persecution to death.

10. *Shall be offended.* Many shall be turned away from this religion, because of its trials; and many who had professed to follow Christ should fall away and desert His cause.—— ¶ *Betray one another.* Tacitus states that in Nero's persecution, several were seized at first who confessed, and by their information a multitude of others were convicted and slain. Such shall be the bitterness and severity that shall prevail. Many, to save themselves, will prove treacherous to their fellow-professors—not only deserting them, but handing them over to their persecutors. Luke says " that this shall be done by parents and brethren, and kinsfolk and friends.' And the hatred against Christians would be such as to destroy all natural affection. Phygellus and Hermogenes forsook Paul (2 Tim. 1. 15). Hymeneus and Philetus were apostates (2 Tim. 2. 17, 18).

11. *Many false prophets.* Of such also, Josephus is found to testify. Many such appeared during the siege, predicting help from God, to embolden the Jews, and make them obstinate.

12. *And because iniquity.* A caution to the disciples. This is mentioned in this way to show that those times of persecution should be calculated to overthrow the faith of some, and, if possible, destroy the love and trust of the very elect. The general prevalence of iniquity (literally *lawlessness,*) would be such as to discountenance Christianity, and it would have a fearful effect upon the love of many, which would wax (or grow) cold on this account. So the fear of persecution and of desertion by friends, would cool the ardor of Christians.

13. *He that shall endure,* &c. No Christian professor could expect salvation unless he endured to the end. Luke adds encouragements and exhortations. " There shall not an hair of your head perish. In your patience possess ye your souls." This however is a *principle* of universal appli-

242 MATTHEW. [A. D. 33

unto the end, the same shall be saved.

14 And this gospel of the kingdom shall be °preached in all the world for a witness unto all nations; and then shall the end come.

15 When ye, there-

o c.28.19. Ro.10.18. Re.14.6.

cation. Those that fall and endure only for a while, cannot expect to be saved. The promise is " to him that overcometh" (Rev. 3. 12).

14. *This Gospel.* All the world, means the whole Roman empire, as referring to that time, and in its more extended application, means the entire globe. In its narrower and wider sense, it is true. The offer of salvation would first be made to them in every part of the world where they should be dispersed, so that by all, their punishment should be acknowledged just. *The Gospel of the kingdom*, is the gospel of Christ, who sets up the kingdom of grace upon earth. This shows them the kind of universal kingdom He is to have and the wide extent to which it should be promulgated.

This message of grace was first to be preached for a testimony or witness to all nations concerned. It was to bear a special witness or manifestation of God to the world. To the Roman empire, it was to go forth as a witness, before the Romans should be embattled with the Jews in the destruction of the city and temple; and to the then known world it was to go abroad within thirty years after the crucifixion (see Rom. 1. 8; 15. 24-28), and before the final coming of Christ and the end of the world, it was to be universally made known.

§ 128. THE SIGNS OF CHRIST'S COMING TO DESTROY JERUSALEM. THIRD day. Mount of Olives.

Matt.	Mark.	Luke.	John
24. 15-42	13. 14-37	21. 20-36	

A. D. 33.] CHAPTER XXIV. 243

fore, shall see the abomination of desolation, spoken ᵖ of by Daniel the prophet, stand in the holy place, (whoso readeth let him understand :)

16 Then let them which be in Judea flee into the mountains :

17 Let him which is on the house-top not come down to take any thing out of his house :

p Da. 9. 27 ; 12. 11.

18 Neither let him which is in the field return back to take his clothes.

19 And ᑫ wo unto them that are with child, and to them that give suck in those days !

20 But pray ye that your flight be not in the winter, neither on the sabbath day :

21 For ʳ then shall be great

q Lu. 23. 29. *r* Da. 12. 1.

---

15. Daniel (12. 11) speaks of the *abomination that maketh desolate*, in connexion with the abrogation of the legal services. The abomination set up was to be the sign of final desolation to Jerusalem. And the allusion of the prophet and of this passage is to the standards of the Roman armies, which bore idolatrous ensigns—eagles. The images of the emperor were carried in front and treated with divine honours; and Josephus relates that in Jerusalem sacrifice was paid by the Romans to their idols after the conquest of the city. (*See cut.*)——¶ *In the holy place*—" where it ought not" (*Mark*)—i. e., in the temple (see Isa. 60. 13. Acts 6. 13; 21. 28). "When ye shall see Jerusalem compassed with these (heathen) armies" (Luke 21 20), as was predicted by Daniel long ago to occur in a specified time.——¶ *Whoso readeth*—i. e. the prophecy. This calls attention to the fulfilment.

16. *Then let them*, &c. These warnings indicate the suddenness of the destruction, and the haste which should be made in flight. Here were directions for the escape of the Christians. These directions were followed, and it is believed that not a single Christian perished in the siege. (Eusebius.) They were to flee to the mountains as was often done for security, and they were not to delay for any articles of furniture or clothing, but to hasten their escape. Many fled to Pella and elsewhere, beyond Jordan, and were safe. A warning is here included of the suddenness of death and the last judgment

and of our need of timely preparation.

17. *Not come down.* (See figure ch. 19.) The houses were so constructed that by an outside stairs persons could get from the house-tops to the street without entering the house. Mark has it, "not go down into the house, neither enter therein."

18. *His clothes.* They always laid aside or left behind their upper garments when at work.

20. *But pray ye.* Though the particulars were ordered, they might pray, and ought, for all such things as would relieve their flight. Two seasons they should specially deprecate.——¶ *The winter.* The winter because of the cold and the state of the roads, and the short days.——¶ *The sabbath day*—they would be restricted in their journeyings on that day more than on others, either by the Jewish law limiting the distance to five furlongs (Exod. 16. 29), or by the gates of the cities being closed (Nehem. 13. 19-22), or by their religious scruples or engagements. We may pray for easy circumstances in our death.

21. *Great tribulation.* (See Luke 21. 24.) The destruction of the city took place during the passover feast, when some three millions of people were usually gathered there from all Judea. Josephus relates that in the siege about 1,100,000 perished, and the whole city ran with blood, and altogether in and about Jerusalem, there were slain fully a million three hundred and fifty thousand. Famine prevailed with all its horrors. Women ate their own children, as was

tribulation, such as was not since the beginning of the world to this time, no, nor ever shall be.

22 And except those days should be shortened, there should no flesh be saved: but *s* for the elect's sake those days shall be shortened.

23 Then *t* if any man shall say unto you, Lo, here *is* Christ, or there; believe *it* not.

24 For *u* there shall arise false Christs, and false prophets, and *v* shall shew great signs and wonders; insomuch that, if *w it were* possible, they shall deceive the very elect.

25 Behold, I have told you before.

26 Wherefore if they shall say unto you, Behold, he is in the desert; go not forth: Behold, he is in the secret chambers, believe *it* not.

27 For as the lightning *x* cometh out of the east, and shineth even unto the west; so shall also the coming of the Son of man be.

s Is.65.8,9. *t* De.13.1-3. *u* ver.5,11. *v* 2Th.2.9-11. Re.13.13.

w Jno.10.28,29. *x* Zec.9.14. Lu.17.24,&c.

---

prophesied. (See Deut. 28. 53, 56, 57. Alexander's Evidences.) 97,000 were carried captive, of whom 11,000 perished from want.——¶ *No, nor ever.* Here is a most emphatic expression, being a *triple negative* in the Greek.

22. *For the elect's sake.* Those days of distress should be shortened on account of the Christians (Isa. 1. 9), who are God's elect, "*whom He hath chosen*" (Mark), and whom He will always regard. If those dreadful horrors should not be stopped before their natural time, none of the nation could be kept alive. The pestilence, famine, and war, would have swept them all away. (Compare Abraham's prayer for Sodom, "*for ten's sake,*" Gen. 18. 32.)

23. *Then if any man*, &c. As the Jews looked forward for a Messiah, as a temporal Prince and Deliverer, they could easily be imposed upon by false pretenders at such a time. Here was a warning against any such who should arise and claim to be the Christ—for the Messiah had already come.

24. *False Christs and false prophets.* Such persons did arise, and led many after them. They even pretended to work miracles. Josephus says they were magicians and sorcerers. Their deceptions were so plausible that they would have prevailed with the Christians—if it had been possible—to draw them from their faith in Christ.

25. *I have told you before*—that is, *beforehand*, that they might mark the prediction in its fulfilment.

26. *In the desert.* This was the plan. The impostors announced that Christ was in the desert, and sought to draw the people out. Josephus, though a Jew, and an enemy of *Christianity*, and not intending to verify the Scripture, speaks of such. "Many impostors persuaded the people to follow them into the wilderness, promising to work miracles there"– "one led out thus 4,000 men."—— ¶ *Secret chambers.* The word means, properly, a store-house, or treasury, and so any private chamber. It is here spoken of the Temple chambers, where they actually looked for the appearing of these false Christs. They were warned against all this device.

27. *As the lightning.* The true Christ should come, but suddenly and manifestly as the lightning. He could be known by His works. The coming, here refers immediately to the visitation of Jerusalem—and the language is so constructed, as to include also His final coming for the destruction of the world.——¶ *The east.* The Roman army entered Judea

A. D. 33.]   CHAPTER XXIV.   245

28 For ʸ wheresoever the carcass is, there will the eagles be gathered together.

29 Immediately after the tribulation of those days shall ᶻ the sun be darkened, and the moon shall not give her light, and the stars shall fall from heaven, and the powers of the heavens ᵃ shall be shaken.

30 And then shall appear the sign of the Son of man ᵇ in heaven: and then shall all the tribes of the earth mourn, and ᶜ they shall see the Son of man coming in the clouds of heaven, with power and great glory.

31 And he shall send his angels ¹ with a great sound ᵈ of a trumpet; and they shall gather

y Job 39.30. *z* Is.13.10. Eze.32.7. Am.5.20. Ac.2.20. Re.6.12. *a* 2Pe.3.10.

b Da.7.13. Re.1.7. *c* c.16.27. Mar.13.26. Lu.22.69. 1 Or, *with a trumpet and a great voice* *d* 1Th.4.16.

at the east, and carried its conquests westward. This may be hinted here.

28. *For wheresoever.* This explains the coming of Christ. It should occur in accordance with established laws, so as to have its explanation in the circumstances. When the people's iniquity was full, and in the fulness of time He should come. And not more naturally did eagles and vultures appear in that country, wherever dead carcasses were cast out in the field, than the coming of Christ in judgment should occur just where and when the guilty transgressors spoken of were found, and when the circumstances were suited. See Job 39. 30. It was more than hinted also, that the Jewish nation were the *carcass* soon to be a prey for the *Roman eagles.*

29. *The tribulation of those days.* The same as alluded to in vss. 19, 21 and 22. The days here intended, are those of the siege in which these tribulations should be suffered. Mark has it, "In those days after that tribulation."——¶ *The sun shall be darkened,* &c. This is figurative language. Changes should occur in the government, and ruin should fall upon the cities of the nation, that should be like the putting out of the sun and moon. Fifty years later, under Adrian, occurred the overthrow and complete extirpation of the Jewish people, when they were sold as slaves, and utterly driven out from the land of their fathers. Luke adds other particulars. Similar language is found in Isa. 13. 9, 10, where the destruction of Babylon is spoken of—and this very destruction of Jerusalem is foretold by Joel 2. 31, 3. 15, in the same language. There should be a destruction of their ecclesiastical and civil state, and of the rulers of them both, as well as of their chief cities and of the nation. This actually took place. And the language *further* looks to the final judgment and the universal catastrophes of that day.——¶ *Powers of the heavens.* See Deut. 4. 19—all the host of heaven.

30. *The sign of the Son of man.* The manifestation and open display of His coming (Luke 17. 30). It shall then plainly appear, as by a standard raised in the clouds, that He has come. This alludes to the prophecy in Dan. 7. 13, from which the Jews had expected a visible appearance of the Messiah in the clouds. He attaches the correct meaning to that language which they had mistaken.——¶ *And then shall all the tribes of the earth.* This is applicable both to the people of Judea, in that judgment—and to the world at the final day (Zech. 12. 12).——¶ *Mourn.* The word means *to beat the breast* in token of sorrow. It occurs in Rev. 1. 7.

31. *And He shall send His angels.* This shows the care that shall be had to the welfare of God's people As they are His elect, His chosen, so He will choose to defend and deliver them. They shall not suffer harm with the wicked; but their deliver-

together his elect, *e* from the four winds, from one end of heaven to the other.

32 Now *f* learn a parable of the fig-tree: When his branch is yet tender, and putteth forth leaves, ye know that summer *is* nigh:

33 So likewise ye, when ye shall see all these things, know that it ¹ is near, *even g* at the doors.

34 Verily I say unto you, This generation shall not pass till all these things be fulfilled.

35 Heaven *h* and earth shall pass away, but my words shall not pass away.

36 But *i* of that day and hour knoweth no *man*, no, not the angels of heaven, but my Father only.

37 But as the days of Noe *were*, so shall also the coming of the Son of man be.

38 For as in the days that were

e Zec.14.5. *f* Lu.21.29. 1 Or, *He.* *g* Ja.5.9.   *h* Ps.102.26. Is.51.6. *i* Zec.14.7. 1Th.5.2.

ance shall be certain and manifest. This was also fulfilled in the gathering of the Gentile church by the trumpet of Gospel messengers. See Rev. 2. 1, where the minister is called "the *angel* of the church of Ephesus." This is also applicable to the last judgment day. See Matt. 25. 31, 32. *Christians* who are here called Christ's *elect*, or chosen ones, shall be gathered from the four winds—that is, from the four quarters of the globe (see 1 Chron. 9. 24. Ezek. 37. 9). None of them shall be overlooked.

32, 33. *A parable.* This was spoken to show the nearness of these events, so far as they relate to the destruction of Jerusalem. The disciples had asked of the *time* in vs. 3. Here is a parabolical answer. The sprouting of the fig-tree and the putting forth of leaves would show that summer is nigh. So you can even now observe the indications of this event being near—that is, the destruction foretold, or, as Luke has it, "*the kingdom of God* (21. 31) *is nigh at hand*"—His coming with power and glory. These tokens which He had given them, should show that it was *even at the doors.*

34. *This generation.* (See ch. 23. 36.) A generation of men is understood to cover a space of thirty to forty years, which was the time that elapsed before the city was destroyed, or about forty years. Lest they should put off the evil day, He assured them how imminent was the destruction which should come upon their land, and that there were none of these things which people then living should not experience. This does not forbid an extension of the prophecy to the last judgment day. For the language has a secondary reference to that event, and that alone exhausts the meaning. The judgment immediately referred to, should occur within that generation. Some, as John the Evangelist, doubtless lived to see these things come to pass. The last judgment is *substantially* passed upon all at death.

35. *Heaven and earth*, &c. God's immutability is beyond the steadfastness of the natural world. This language is proverbial. Nothing seems more permanent than the solid earth. So we say a thing shall not occur while the world stands, or the world shall pass away sooner. See Matt, 5. 18. The material world shall finally pass away; but God's words shall not pass away or all. God's truth cannot possibly fail. "Yea, let God be true, but every man a liar."

36. *Knoweth no man.* This is to declare, in the strongest language, that the precise time in unknown. Mark adds, "neither the Son," that is, *as man.* It is utterly hidden from human knowledge.

37. *As the days of Noe.* Here He likens His coming, to the judgment that occurred in the days of Noah by

before the flood, they were eating and drinking, marrying and giving in marriage, until j the day that Noe entered into the ark,

39 And knew not, until the flood came, and took them all away; so shall also the coming

j Ge.6.2.

ing of the Son of man be.

40 Then shall two be in the field; the one shall be taken, and the other left.

41 Two *women shall be* grinding at the mill; the one shall be taken, and the other left.

42 Watch *k* therefore; for ye

k Lu.12.39,40. Re.3.3; 16.15.

the flood. (*Noe* is the Greek.) Their coming destruction should be equally sudden and surprizing to the unbelieving Jews, as also the final coming to judgment should surprize the unbelieving world.

38. *For.* The people in Noah's time, though so abundantly forewarned, were giving attention to worldly things, and indulging in common gratifications up to the very day of the flood, as though nothing would occur. See 1 Pet. 3. 20.

39. *Knew not*—the real truth of the case, until they experienced the destruction. So far did they persist in their wilful ignorance and unbelief—and so it should be with the Jewish nation.

40. *Then shall two be in the field.* So Christ's coming whether to the Jewish nation then, or to the world hereafter, should overtake men at their accustomed avocations, and so it should break up connexions without a moment's warning — and so, the providence of God should *distinguish,* and take one and leave another, sparing His people, and sweeping away the wicked from their side. The doctrine of distinguishing grace is here also taught.

41. *At the mill.* Mills among the Hebrews were driven by the hand; and **two** persons, commonly women, were employed in the operation. It was laborious work, and belonged to the lowest maid-servants. See Job 31. 10. The mill itself consisted of two circular stones, commonly two feet in diameter, and half-a-foot thick. The lower is called " the *nether millstone,*" Job 41. 16, which was fixed firmly to the floor or ground, while the upper was turned upon it, by a

stick or handle—one of the **women** turning it half round—the other driving it the rest of the way. As the nether stone had an elevation in the centre, which fitted in a corresponding hole in the upper stone, the corn was ground by the revolutions, and came out at the edges.

42. *Watch therefore.* All this was calculated to make them watchful and anxious.

§ 129. TRANSITION TO CHRIST'S FINAL COMING AT THE DAY OF JUDGMENT PARABLES—*Ten Virgins. The five Talents.*

Matt.	Mark.	Luke.	John.
24. 43–51			
25. 1–30			

know not what hour your Lord doth come.

43 But know this, that if the good man of the house had known in what watch the thief would come, he would have watched, and would not have suffered his house to be broken up.

44 Therefore be ye also ready: for in such an hour as ye think not, the Son of man cometh.

45 Who then is a faithful and wise servant, whom his lord hath made ruler over his household, to give them [1] meat in due season?[m]

46 Blessed *is* that servant, whom his lord, when he cometh, shall find so doing.

47 Verily I say unto you, that he shall make him ruler [n] over all his goods.

48 But and if that evil servant shall say in his heart, My lord delayeth his coming:

49 And shall begin to smite *his* fellow-servants, and to eat and drink with the drunken;

l Je.3.15.   *m* c.13.52.   *n* c.25.21.

That our Lord here makes a transition and proceeds to speak of His final coming at the day of judgment, appears from the fact, that here the parallel reports of Mark and Luke end, and that which in Luke is parallel to this paragraph (Luke 12. 39), has obvious reference to this final coming at the last day. And that it has here the same reference is apparent from the subsequent warnings, and their intimate connexion with Matt. 25. 31–46. See Robinson's *Harmony—Notes.* The destruction of Jerusalem was a proper emblem of the dissolution of the world, and the warnings which had just been delivered in reference to impending national judgments, would naturally lead to a caution against a more awful surprize by His coming at the final day.

43. *But know this.* As with a man whose house is robbed, he would certainly have watched, if he had known the hour when it would be, so every one that is overtaken by Christ's coming, if he had known the *time* of it would have *watched.* There is really *every motive* for watchfulness; and here is exposed the folly of that man who does not watch, merely because he does not know the time. This would rather be a reason for keeping *constant* watch—and this is urged by our Lord in the next verse.

44. *Be ye also ready.* That is, be fully prepared, so as not to be taken by surprize—because death will come without warning, even as a thief. 1 Thess. 5. 2. 2 Pet. 3. 10. Rev. 3. 3. A deathbed is no place for preparation. And none can count on having timely notice. Commonly we find that men are called to eternity in most unexpected times and ways. See Luke 21. 36; 12. 36.

45–47. *Who then.* This duty of vigilance and diligence is illustrated by the case of a servant in his master's absence. A faithful servant looks out for the master's return, and acts in his absence as though he were there, or would any moment appear. A wicked servant takes advantage of the delay, and abuses his trust. The good servant is rewarded by his master's increased confidence. The evil servant represents the careless professor or minister, who acts as though God would not see him, or call him to account. These acts here mentioned indicate dishonesty and cruelty —worthy of severest punishment. Professing Christians or ministers may act so unfaithfully, when they forget their Lord and His promised return.—— ¶ *Wise*- discreet—prudent —— ¶ *Household*—family of servants. Provisions were distributed monthly.

50. *When he looketh not for him.* Be-

[A. D. 33.] CHAPTER XXV. 219

50 The lord of that servant shall come in a day ᵒ when he looketh not for *him*, and in an hour that he is not aware of.

51 And shall¹ cut him asunder, and appoint *him* his portion with the hypocrites: there ᵖ shall be weeping and gnashing of teeth.

CHAPTER XXV.

THEN shall the kingdom of heaven be likened unto ten virgins, ᵃ which took their lamps, and went forth to meet the bridegroom.ᵇ

o 1Th.5.3. Re.3.3. 1 Or, *cut him off*. *p* c.25.30.

a Ps.45.14. Ca.6.8,9. 2Cor.11.2. *b* Jno.3.29.

cause he has forgotten his Master, and has not believed that he would soon return, and so has given himself up to sinful pleasure.——¶ *Day and hour*—are here used, to denote the suddenness. It might occur the next hour of this day, as easily as the next *day*.

51. *Shall cut him asunder.* A most severe punishment. It was sometimes practised. (Daniel, ch. 3. 29. 1 Sam. 15, 33.) And the term is used here only to show that the retribution will be of *the severest kind*. Unfaithful servants of God, ministers or members, who take such advantage, and so abuse their trust, shall have the most dreadful doom.—— ¶ *With the hypocrites.* This is to show that hypocrisy is the foulest crime; and that all hypocrites shall dwell in everlasting torment; "all liars shall have their part in the lake that burneth with fire and brimstone." (Rev. 21. 8.)——¶ *Weeping and gnashing of teeth*—is a phrase often used to denote the bitterest agony and convulsions of pain and rage. (See Matt. 8. 12, note.) Death to each of us is the same as Christ's coming, for at death we are separately judged. And from this passage we learn how wise it is to be prepared *now*, so that whenever death may come we may be ready.

Observe, (1.) Christ's second coming is purposely concealed as to the precise time, and they who presume to fix its date, go counter to the express warning of God. Our business is to be ready, and count practically in our living, that it may come immediately. As of the former coming, we are to reckon that "the end of all things is at hand," and by faith, we are to consider it "nigh, even at the doors." It will burst upon the world, in the midst of other calculations. (2.) Christ's coming *to us*, in death and judgment will be the most sudden —requiring the utmost readiness. (3.) If we knew just when He will come to us, in death, and could know the very date, we should be watching now. (4.) The professed servants of Christ are blessed only as they are watchful and faithful, looking for, and hasting unto, the coming of the day of God. They who make His delay to be slackness, and live like the careless world, must have their portion with the hypocrites. (See 2 Pet. 3. 9.)

CHAPTER XXV.

1. *Then shall the kingdom of heaven*, &c. This parable is now introduced to enforce the duty of watchfulness, to warn against declension, and to show the danger of neglect. He had spoken of His coming in judgment upon their city and nation, and then He had passed to speak of His final coming.——¶ *The kingdom of heaven*, here refers to the results of the Christian economy among men, and the closing up of means of grace at the end. Christ's relation to the Church is compared in Scripture to the marriage relation, and symbolized by it. (Matt. 9. 15. Rev. 21. 9. Ephes. 5. 25–32.) This parable refers to the circumstances attending the final consummation, when Christ shall come to be glorified in His saints, and admired in all them that believe. Allusion is here made to the Jewish customs at a wedding. The bridegroom was the newly married husband. Af-

2 And ᶜ five of them were wise, and five *were* foolish.

3 They that *were* foolish took their lamps, and took no ᵈ oil with them:

4 But the wise took oil • in their vessels with their lamps.

5 While the bridegroom tarried, they all slumbered ᶠ and slept.

c Je.24.2-9. c.22.10. *d* Is.48.1.   *e* 1Jno.2.20. *f* 1Th.5.6.

ter the marriage feast, which occupied a week, the husband, with the children of the bridechamber, led the bride to his own home. (Ps. 45. 10.) She is accompanied from her father's house by her young friends and companions, while others of these (the virgins here), at some convenient place, meet and join in the procession, and enter with the *rest of the bridal* company into the hall of feasting. There were usually ten for this ceremony. This number was the number of completeness among the Jews. Where there were "ten men of leisure," a synagogue might be built.
—— ¶ *Lamps.* As this was done commonly at night, they had lamps or torches—a bunch of rags wound thickly round the end of an iron rod, and dipped in oil, was the common torch.
—— ¶ *The bridegroom.* By this is meant the Lord Jesus Christ, whose coming is here illustrated, with its results, when the New Jerusalem shall come down from heaven as a bride adorned for her husband.

2. *Wise*, &c. Some were wise enough to take oil, and others foolish enough to neglect it. These two classes represent the faithful and unfaithful professor—the one prepared for Christ's coming, the other unprepared.

3. *Took no oil.* Whatever is merely outward in the Christian profession, is the lamp; whatever is inward and spiritual, is the oil in the vessel. Oil is in the Scripture a standing symbol of the Spirit. (Exod. 30. 22-33. Zech. 4. 2, 12. Acts 10. 38. Heb. 1. 9.) They should have taken oil, because their torches were of no use without it. They had only a show of preparation, but no substance; lamps without oil, or a form of godliness without the power. They had rather expected His coming in the day-time—for this life—or had a religion for this world and for the demands of society, with no reference to death or the judgment. There are many such, who have made no substantial or adequate preparation for Christ's coming *at length* and *at night*.

4. *The wise.* True Christians, who made suitable and special preparation for Christ's coming, and had regarded His coming as needing a special provision—as not in the common course of things, and as requiring the spirit in them—these had graces of the Spirit, and good hope through grace. They who prepare for the future are wise, that they may be always prepared—ready at all times for whatever may occur.

5. *Tarried.* That is, *delayed to come.* He did not come as soon as some had expected. They had only a *day-time provision* in fact—only for *this world*—not for the deep night—the *hereafter*—the midnight of death and judgment.—— ¶ *Slept.* This represents the time—as now at length the night, and not the day—the future, and not the present—when, as in a city at midnight, the populace have put aside the business of the day, and are asleep; and now, only, this special coming is the great concern with the church. This is the ground-work on which the picture is painted. It is Christ's coming, as that ultimate event that shall come *at length*—beyond all other things; not as other secular comings—in the day—but at *night*, as needing the most special preparation—lamps and oil, trimmed and burning—that were not needed if this had been a common matter, or provided for by natural morality.——
¶ *All slumbered and slept*—not *they all*, as though speaking of the virgins—but "*all*," as indicating the time of sleep—the night.

6 And at midnight *g* there was a *h* cry made, Behold, the bridegroom cometh: go ye out *i* to meet him.

7 Then all those virgins arose, and trimmed their lamps.

8 And the foolish said unto the wise, Give us of your oil; for

g Re.16.15. *h* 1Th.4.16. *i* Am.4.12.

our lamps are gone ¹ out. *j*

9 But the wise answered, saying, *Not so;* lest there be not enough for us and you: but go ye rather *k* to them that sell, and buy for yourselves.

10 And *l* while they went to buy, the bridegroom came; and

1 Or, *going out.* *j* Lu. 12.35. *k* Is. 55.1,6. *l* Am.8.12,13.

Ward (View of the Hindoos, v. 2. p. 29), describing the parts of a marriage ceremony in India, of which he was an eye-witness, says: "After waiting two or three hours, at length near midnight, it was announced, 'Behold the bridegroom cometh, go ye out to meet him.' All the persons employed now lighted their lamps, and ran with them in their hands to fill up their stations in the procession. *Some of them had lost their lights and were unprepared, but it was then too late to seek them,* and the cavalcade moved forward."

6. *At midnight.* This was the custom, to have a crier go before the bridegroom, and give notice aloud of his coming. Sometimes part of the retinue ran before and gave the public tidings. This is done by Death, the last messenger. We know not when we shall hear that cry. We can be prepared to meet the Lord, only by embracing His offers, and accepting His gospel for our hope, and getting all our supplies of grace from Him. We must prepare *now*, if we would be ready, and we must be ready before we are called, because then, we are obliged to go whether prepared or not. Concerning the second coming of Christ, it belongs essentially to the doctrine that the time be unknown and uncertain, so that there may be this constant and ever-increasing motive to watch, because we know not the time.

7. *Then.* When the call came, all were anxious to have their lights burn. The most careless begin to examine their hopes and preparation at last, but often find their lack, not until it is too late. The best need to trim their lamps, examine their hopes, and refresh their faith in Christ.——
¶ *Trimmed.* The hand-lamp was naturally small, and would not contain a supply for many hours' burning. The margin reads, lamps "*going out*"—needing to be constantly watched and replenished. The trimming implied two things—the infusion of fresh oil, and the removing whatever had gathered round and was clogging the wick.

8. *Give us.* The foolish now saw their deficiency. They wanted oil now, because they must go, and they applied to their fellows; but the best furnished had no oil to spare. They needed all they had for their own use. So the unprepared sinner finds he has nothing that will do for the trying hour. He calls upon Christians, but they cannot give him grace, nor pardon, nor hope. God alone can give saving grace; men cannot convert their fellow-men. The *wise have not* grace enough for themselves and others. "If the righteous scarcely be saved, where shall the ungodly and the sinner appear?"

9. *Go ye rather.* The dying sinner must be directed for pardon to Christ alone. The wise virgins gave Christian counsel, though they could not give oil; they directed to Christ and the means.

10. *While they went to buy.* This they had put off till it was too late: verifying vs. 33, ch. 24. If they had known beforehand just when He would come, they would have looked to their timely preparation. Those that were ready were the wise who had oil

they that were ready went in with him to the marriage: and the door was shut. ᵐ

11 Afterward came also the other virgins, saying, ⁿ Lord, Lord, open to us.

12 But he answered and said, Verily I say unto you, I ᵒ know you not.

13 Watch ᵖ therefore, for ye know neither the day nor the hour wherein the Son of man cometh.

14 ¶ For ᑫ *the kingdom of*

m He.3.18,19. Re.22.11. *n* c.7.21-23. He.12.17. *o* Hu.1.13. *p* c.21.42,44. Mar.13.33,35. Lu.21.36. *q* Lu.19.12,&c.

True Christians, who have supplies in Christ, are prepared, whenever their summons may come. If they have repented, and have laid hold on the hope set before them, they are ready.——¶ *The door was shut*—because the marriage company had entered to the marriage, that is, to the celebration or wedding party, that took place in the bridegroom's house, after the ceremony and festal week. We are not sure of having any other season than the present, for this great, momentous work.

11. *Afterward came.* They had not obtained oil; but, knowing now their extremity, they came to plead for mercy on general grounds. But though God is Love, He has expressed His Love to sinners in the gospel plan, where the door of grace stands open in Christ (Jno. 3.16).——¶*Lord, Lord.* The impenitent often cry out for mercy when it is too late—when they have so long cavilled and neglected, that their fear cometh as desolation, and because they cannot lay hold of the hope—they can only call in vain (Prov. 1. 28).

12. *I know you not.* I do not own or acknowledge you. They are not recognized as believers. The good shepherd knows His sheep, and as they also always know Him, this is as much as to say, Ye never knew me.

13. *Watch therefore.* Be on your guard—looking out for his coming,—that is, for His summons at death, and His coming to you in judgment. The reason is, that you know not when He shall come to you with a call to eternity. You know not the day, nor can you be secure even of the hour of the day: for *in an hour* you may be cut off out of robust health. To be ready, you must be a *true Christian*: loving, believing, and following Christ, and resting on Him alone for salvation, as he is offered to you in the gospel. The only certain plan for being ready on *that* day, is, to be ready *every* day—and unreadiness for that day is without a remedy. In the marriage of the King's Son, the unfurnished guest could get admission, and could be thrust out. It referred therefore to the church on earth. Here, the reference is to the church in heaven—into which nothing unholy can enter, and where they go no more out. This parable shows the mistake of those who make Christ's coming a mere social melioration. Infidels make it a mere matter of the day-time—a high state of advancement in society—a consummation of civilized culture. But it is beyond the day, and past all common changes It belongs to the *hereafter.*

OBSERVE, (1.) There are those who go out to meet the Bridegroom, professors of religion in the church, who have no grace in their hearts These are they who have lived without thinking of the night of death, or considering well their latter end—and religion has been to them a matter of very inadequate preparation. No new heart—no new conduct—no watching—no prayer. (2.) Such find their deficiency and lack when it is too late. Only the prepared, who have been truly changed—who have embraced Christ, and watched for His appearing—are saved. (3.) The lifeless, careless professor may awake to anxiety and earnest seeking at last, and may call on others for help, but in vain. He may seek for a good hope, but with perverted views and

heaven is as a man travelling into a far country, *who* called his own servants, and delivered unto them his goods.

15 And unto one he gave five ¹ talents, to another two, and to another one : to every man according to his several ability ; *r* and straightway took his journey.

16 Then he that had received the five talents, went, and traded with the same, and made *them* other five talents.

1 *A talent is* 1871. 10s. c.18.24.

r Ro.12.6. 1Cor.12.4,&c. Ep.4.11.

false calculations, he is in danger of being overtaken in his alarm by the judgment!

14. This is not the same parable as the one recorded in Luke 19. 12, though many of the terms are similar. That was spoken in the house of Zaccheus, this on mount Olivet. The last parable brought to view the possibility and danger of a *false profession,* having lamps without oil. This pursues the subject, and shows the duty of active service in Christ's cause, and the reward that awaits the faithful, as well as the doom that must come upon unfaithfulness. There they are *watching* for Him—here they are *working* for Him.——¶ *As a man.* By this, is represented our Lord. His servants are His disciples who profess to follow and serve Him—more especially His ministers—and to them He delivers his goods or property, that is, the interest of His cause on the earth, and their powers of usefulness. Christians are entrusted with the concerns of His kingdom, and for this end, they have the gifts of the Spirit. Ephes. 4. 8. We are not to be idly waiting the time of His return, but are to be actively and usefully employed for Him. ——¶ *Far country.* They were to look beyond the present temporal state. He was not to come in a temporal kingdom, nor immediately was His great final coming to occur. He would extend and expand their views. Those who think that the end of the world is to be at a given time, as next year or month, become distracted in their appropriate religious duties. They do not lay plans for long and laborious work.——¶ *His own servants.* Slaves of masters, at that time, were often allowed to use their masters' money in trade, and were to bring him in a share of the profits.——¶ *His goods*—his property.

15. "Talent" now has come to signify any mental endowment or faculty whatever—for these are the gifts that are to be accounted for. Time, wealth, reputation, intellect, and *calls*, are all talents which we are bound to improve. A talent of silver was, at largest calculation, fifteen hundred dollars of our money. Here the five talents are meant to signify the largest share of gifts and means of doing good- and this includes also the highest stations in the church. He gave them different sums to take care of and employ—that is, different stations to fill, and different gifts to use—powers of body and mind, means of grace and goods.——¶ *According to his several ability*—that is, each one's *ability* is his *talent.* Religion does not make all men alike, nor put them in the same circles of society. But each has his own measure of talents to improve, and this is all that is asked of any one. The one-talent men in the church, who bury the goods they have, are guilty.——¶ *Straightway*—immediately. None could complain of inferior gifts, for they were fairly distributed, and no account was asked for more than each had received. Men receive all that they have of natural and spiritual, and temporal gifts, from God alone, for who maketh us to differ from another, and what have we that we have not received (see 1 Cor. 4. 7). The master has a right to expect from us all a profitable employment of all we have and are, in advancing the interests of His cause, which are entrusted to us.

17 And likewise he that *had received* two, he also gained other two.

18 But he that had received one, went, and digged in the earth, and hid his lord's money.

19 After a long time, ^s the lord of those servants cometh, and reckoneth ^t with them.

20 And so he that had received five talents, came, and brought

s c.24.48. *t* c.18.23,24.

other five talents, saying, Lord, thou deliveredst unto me five talents ; behold, I have gained besides them five talents more.

21 His lord said unto him, Well done, *thou* good and faithful servant : thou hast been faithful over a few things, I will make thee ruler ^u over many things : enter thou into the joy of thy lord.

u Lu.12.44; 22.29; Re.3.21.

---

16. The faithful servants doubled their means, by a useful occupation of them. We get more graces— more means of doing good—and we gain more for Christ's cause, in proportion as we are faithful in the use of what we have. We shall find sure direction in God's word for the use of our means in His service. If a man has property he should wisely employ it in promoting true religion among men. So if he has time, or any other talent, he should use it in serving God. And whatever religious opportunities he has for increasing in knowledge and grace, he should diligently improve.

18. *He that had reccived one.* Those who have received but few gifts and graces are in danger of pleading excuse on this ground. But he should have put these to some profitable use. It was only this one talent that he was responsible for. Hence he could not plead his small ability or opportunity. Many will do nothing because they cannot do more. Many think themselves excused because they have not as many talents as others. But it is 'according to what a man hath, and not according to what he hath not," that God demandeth (2 Cor. 8. 12). The Lord requires fidelity in the little as well as in the much.

19. *After a long time.* Though the master long delays, He will come at last. Concerning this subject, see 2 Pet. 3 ch.——¶ *Reckoneth with them.* Makes a final settlement of accounts (see ch. 18. 23). Christ will come at last to the final judgment (Rom. 14.

10. 2 Cor. 5. 10). " We must all appear before the judgment seat of Christ." The Lord will come to reckon with us *in death.*

20. *Five talents more.* He had gained this by trading (vs. 16)—by active and careful employment of his talents.——¶ *I have gained.* It was the servant's industry applied to God's property. The faithful servant acknowledges God's grace in himself. " *Thou deliveredst unto me,*" &c. (vs. 20). And yet he rejoices in the day of Christ that he has not run in vain, neither laboured in vain (Phil. 2. 16). This that he has to show is not his desert, but the results by God's grace. As Paul, " What is our hope or joy, or crown of rejoicing ? Are not even ye in the presence of our Lord Jesus Christ, at His coming ?" (1. Thess. 2. 19.) " I—yet not I, but CHRIST LIVETH IN ME."

21. *Faithful.* Dutiful — having aimed to do one's duty. I will exalt thee to higher stations, and to the use of more abundant gifts (Rom. 2. 7). Such do rest from their labours and their works do follow them (Rev. 14. 13.——¶ *Joy of thy lord,* i. e., the entertainment provided on occasion of their lord's return, to which the faithful servants were to be admitted as the highest token of his favour. This represents the reward of faithful Christians. They shall enter into the joy of Christ upon His mediatorial throne, sitting with Him there, and sharing His bliss. " To him that overcometh, will I grant to sit with me in my throne, even as I overcame

22 He also that had received two talents, came, and said, Lord, thou deliveredst unto me two talents: behold, I have gained two other talents besides them.

23 His lord said unto him, Well done, good and faithful servant: thou hast been faithful over a few things, I will make thee ruler over many things: enter thou into the joy of thy lord.

24 Then he which had received the one talent, came, and said, Lord, I knew thee that thou art an hard ᵛ man, reaping where thou hast not ʷ sown, and gathering where thou hast not strawed:

25 And I was afraid, ˣ and went, and hid thy talent in the earth: lo, *there* thou hast *that is* thine.

26 His lord answered and said unto him, Thou wicked ʸ and slothful servant, thou knewest that I reap where I sowed not, and gather where I have not strawed:

27 Thou oughtest therefore to

---

v Job 21.15. *w* Je.2.31. *x* Pr.26.13. Re.21.8. *y* Job 15.5,6. c.18.32. Lu.19.22. Jude 15.

---

and am set down with my Father in his throne" (Rev. 3. 21). " Here we have a few drops of joy which enter into our bosoms, but there we shall *enter into joy*, as vessels put into a sea of happiness."—*Leighton*. Among the Romans, the master's inviting his slave to sit down with him at table, did constitute in itself an act of manumission—henceforth he was free. Henceforth I call you not servants but friends (John 15. 15. Luke 12. 37. Rev. 3. 20).

23. The master will reward men not *for* their works, but *according* to their works. " According to the deeds done in the body," shall all be judged. These two received the same approbation, and virtually the same reward.

24. *Then*. This one came *reluctantly*, and *last of all*.——¶ *I knew thee*, &c. He meant to say by this, that the master demanded more of him than he had any right to require, as if a man should look for a crop from a field which he had not sown, or should look for clean grain where he had not *strawed* or scattered the chaff.——¶ *Strawed*. This was the process of fanning, to cleanse the grain from the chaff (chap. 3. 12). He pleaded his inferior gifts, and poor opportunities. There was a show of humility in this. But at the bottom of his excuse, was *his false view of* *the character of God.*——¶ *An hard man*. Severe—*hard-hearted*, requiring bricks without straw (Exod. 5. 7). " They who know thy name will put their trust in thee."

25. He pleaded that God called to a labour for which He gave no ability; and so he feared Him.——¶ *I was afraid*. So utterly false were his views of the master, and of his own duty. He had the spirit of bondage. The legal spirit that *looks upon God* as an exacting master, and does not see His grace, will always bury its talent. He was afraid lest by employing the one talent in business (so small a sum), he might lose it, and so incur the severity of this harsh master. There are none who have no means of usefulness committed to them — and that obscure station which they occupy is honourable. The blame is in not serving God according to what we have. But this servant laid the blame of his unfaithfulness upon God.——¶ *That is thine*. He claimed to be strictly honest, and to be dealing justly with God. But it is proved against him. Such a slavish fear of God, and such unworthy views of Him as He is in Christ, must lead to all infidelity.

26. *Slothful*—indolent, *lazy*. He is here called " *wicked and slothful*,' for his indolence was sinful, and led

have put my money to the exchangers, and *then* at my coming I should have received mine own with usury.

28 Take therefore the talent from him, and give *it* unto him which hath ten talents.

29 For ᶻ unto every one that hath shall be given, and he shall have abundance: but from him that hath not shall be taken away ᵃ even that which he hath.

30 And cast ye the unprofitable

z c.13.12. Mar.4.25. Lu.8.18; 19.26. a Lu.19. 42.

---

to sin. He was charged only with neglecting his duty. But for this we are justly condemned, because it is a contempt of God, and a neglect of our best interest. "How shall ye escape if ye NEGLECT so great salvation" (Heb. 2. 3). Mere neglect of Christ, or mere indifference to religion is as certain of perdition as open sin itself, because the only way of escape is despised, and contempt is thrown upon the very grace of God. "Inasmuch as ye *did it not*" (vs. 45). ——¶ *Thou knewest.* This is spoken in retort, taking him up at his word. "*Thou knewest?*" Thou oughtest *therefore.*" "Out of thine own mouth will I judge thee. (See Job 15. 6.) If you did know me to be such as you say, you should *on this very account* have been careful to serve me.

27. *Exchangers — money-dealers — bankers*, who allowed interest for the use of money. Very high rates of interest were paid for money by the ancients. Why did he not put out the money to such use, *if he was afraid* of using it in business ? And especially *if he was afraid* of a strict and harsh dealing from his lord, this would have been the natural course to take. His lord did not recommend this, but thus condemns the man on his own showing. He might have known that lawful interest or *usury* would be demanded by a severe master. This was his inconsistency. Sinners in all their excuses are grossly inconsistent with themselves. They plead their inability yet they do not pray (as they are urged to do) for greater ability, nor do they honestly employ their common powers, or use the means. From those Christians who have few means and small opportunities, God demands earnestness, prayerfulness, and growth in grace.——¶ *With usury* — with increase, or interest, as the word *usury* signified in the old English.

28. *Take therefore,* &c. The money was taken from him because he had made such bad use of it, and shown such contempt of the master. It was given to him that had ten talents, as part of his reward for his eminent improvement. The good shall be raised as high as the wicked are cast low. Dives' measure of good things is taken away from him and given to Lazarus. The slothful servant claims to have given back all that he got as in strictest justice. But not so. The law allows a rate of interest that can be *claimed*, equally with the principal. The just return would have been at least the original sum with interest added. The man who despises his talent from God, forfeits it, and shall be stripped of it at length.

29. *Every one that hath.* (See note Matt. 13. 12.) A disposition to improve his talents is here meant. The man of one talent had it not —for he buried it—he put it to no use, he only seemed to have it. To him *that hath to purpose* shall be given an increase, and he shall have *abundance.* But from him that hath not, with such a disposition for improvement, shall be taken away even the talents which he neglected and misimproved—" that *which he seemeth to have.*" If we neglect the time and opportunities given us of God, we may expect to be cast off beyond the reach of mercy (Heb. 6. 7).

30. *Outer darkness.* This is always the opposite to the brilliant festivities

servant into outer darkness:[b] there shall be weeping and gnashing of teeth.

31 ¶ When[c] the Son of man shall come in his glory, and all the holy angels with him, then

b c.8.12. *c* Da.7.13. Zec.14.5. c.16.27; 19.28. Mar. 8.38. Ac.1.11. 1Th.4.16. 2Th.1.7. Jude 14. Re.1.7.

shall he sit upon the throne of his glory:

32 And[d] before him shall be gathered all nations; and he shall separate[e] them one from another, as a shepherd[f] divideth *his* sheep from the goats:

d Ro.14.10. 2Cor 5.10. Re.20.12. *e* Eze.20.38. c. 13.49. *f* Ps.78.52. Jno.10.14,27.

of the faithful, to which they are admitted, as to an entertainment — while outside, all is utter darkness — sin and misery.

The parable of the virgins and this of the talents would seem to meet two different but common cases in the church among professed disciples. The foolish virgins were over bold and presumptuous. This *one-talent-man*, was suspicious and backward. The former counted the service easy and themselves safe; within reach of full preparation at any time. The latter regarded the Master as one not able to be pleased. The former represent a class that need to be urged and plied by the *alarming* motives. Strait is the gate (ch. 7. 14). Let a man deny himself (16. 24). The latter represents such as need the spirit of *adoption*, instead of that other spirit of *bondage*. Rom. 8. 15. Heb. 12. 18, 22, 24.

Observe, (1.) We are to *work* for Christ as well as to *wait* for Him. (2.) Christians have very different talents entrusted to them for His service. Some have very many endowments and opportunities and means — others have very few. (3.) Those of moderate means and powers are the great majority, and it is of utmost consequence that such feel their high responsibility, and that every one be brought into active and faithful service. This would give prosperity to the churches. (4.) *The joy of our Lord*, is our common inheritance. "If we suffer with Him we shall also reign with Him." There is fellowship of service here — and partnership of glory hereafter. (5.) Mistaken views of God are at the bottom of unfaithfulness in the church.

Chiefly the legal spirit — the spirit of bondage and a lack of the spirit of adoption — which fails to apprehend the *grace* of the gospel, leads to a hiding and burying of the talent. Such are the inactive, backward, and slothful servants. (6.) God claims an improvement of what we have received. The slothful will be cast off: to others He gives the increase.

§ 130. Scenes of the Judgment day. Third *day of the week.*

Matt. 25. 31-46	Mark.	Luke.	John.

31. *When the Son of man.* From the parables in regard to final retribution, He now passes to *describe* the judgment day — the scenes — the parties. The *Son of man* is Christ. This is a title which Christ generally applies to Himself, and it expresses His glorious Humanity — the mystery of His Divine and Human natures It occurs often in connexion with something that expresses His proper Divinity. So here, "*in His glory*," in His proper authority and majesty as Governor of the universe and Judge of all. To Him is given "the authority to execute judgment, because He is the *Son of man*" (Jno. 5. 27). This authority as Mediator, is *the throne of His glory*. This makes Him the proper Judge.——¶ *The holy angels*, as distinguished from *fallen* angels (Jude 6), are attendants of His majesty.——¶ *All nations.* All mankind every where, that have ever lived. John 5. 28, 29. The Jews had a notion that the Gentiles would form no part in the resurrection. "For we must all appear before the judgment seat of Christ, that every one may receive the things done in his body[h]

258 MATTHEW. [A. D. 33

33 And he shall set the sheep on his right *g* hand, but the goats on the left.

34 Then shall the King say unto them on his right hand, Come, ye blessed *h* of my Father, *i* inherit the *j* kingdom *k* prepared for you from the foundation of the world:

35 For *l* I was an hungered, and ye gave me meat: I was thirsty, and ye gave me drink: I was a stranger, *m* and ye took me in:

36 Naked *n* and ye clothed me: I was sick, and ye visited *o* me: I was in prison, *p* and ye came unto me.

g He.1.3. *h* Ps. 115.15. *i* Ro. 8.17. 1Pe. 1.4. *j* 1Th.2.12. Re.5.10. *k* 1Cor.2.9. He.11.16.

l Is.58.7. Eze.18.7. *m* 1Pe.4.9. 3Jno.5. *n* Ja.2 15,16. *o* Ja.1.27. *p* 2Ti.1.16. He.13.2.

(2 Cor. 5. 10). "He hath appointed a day in which He will judge THE WORLD." We shall be there at that day.—¶ *Separate them.* This He will do, because they are of different characters—as the *sheep* in a flock are different from the *goats*—and are divided on that account. This is an allusion to the practice of shepherds in early times, to keep the sheep and the goats in different flocks. By the sheep, are meant true *Christians.* Christ calls Himself the Shepherd, and He has *a flock.* "He calleth *His own sheep* by name, and leadeth them out." John 10. 3. By the *goats* are meant the wicked. He will know the characters of each, because He is the searcher of hearts. Wicked children shall be separated from their pious parents on that day, and so they shall remain apart for ever.

33. *On His right hand.* This denotes the favour and protection of the Sovereign and Judge. (Psalm 110. 1.) "Sit thou at my right hand." Only those who are followers of Christ shall be set there. The goats or wicked shall be placed on the left hand, which denotes the place of rejection and condemnation.

34. *The King.* This refers them back to the Parables, where in the character of King He had set forth Himself. The Lord Jesus Christ is King of Kings (Rev. 19. 16. Psalm 2. 6). He must be God, as well as man. The righteous are called "blessed of the Father," as chosen and called from eternity, and given to Him by the Father (John 17. 6), and now approved by Him, and admitted to glory. The earnest expectation of the creature waiteth for the *manifestation* of the sons of God." Salvation is all of grace.—¶ *Inherit the kingdom.* This is to take possession of it, as heirs take possession of their estate.—¶ *Prepared for you.* It was made ready long beforehand. It was provided for them and intended to be theirs. It did not come to them of chance or of their own superior goodness—or of their sovereign will—but of God's free choice, "according to the election of grace." (Rom. 8. 29-30. 1 Pet. 1. 2.) And this was ordained in God's gracious purposes.—¶ *From the foundation of the world*—that is, from all eternity. Comp. Ephes. 1. 4, 5. This points back before the world was, to a founder, builder, designer of it. The same God wrought their salvation. This shows that on God's part their salvation is all of grace. No man deserves it—none can have any claim—and if He has chosen to save some, and so has sent Christ into the world, none can complain, for it is a *free gift*—and He can do what He will with His own (Matt. 20. 15). Besides, while it is of free grace on God's part, it is shown to be *according* to their works. Without holiness no man shall see God. These acts of charity and friendship were in great estimation among the Jews, though confined to their kin.

35. *For I was an hungered,* &c. They had a tender regard for Him, and for His cause, and improved the means and talents entrusted them. Favours shown to His people He regards, and will reward as fa-

37 Then shal. the righteous answer him, saying, Lord, when saw we thee an hungered, and fed *thee*? or thirsty, and gave *thee* drink?

38 When saw we thee a stranger, and took *thee* in? or naked, and clothed *thee*?

39 Or when saw we thee sick, or in prison, and came unto thee?

40 And the King shall answer and say unto them, Verily I say unto you, Inasmuch ᑫ as ye have done *it* unto one of the least of these my brethren, ye have done *it* unto me.

41 Then shall he say also unto them on the left hand, Depart ʳ from me, ye cursed, into ˢ everlasting fire, ᵗ prepared for the devil and his angels:

42 For I was an hungered, and

q Pr.19.17. Mar.9.41. He.6.10. *r* Lu.13.27. *s* c. 13.40,42 Re.14.11. *t* Jude 6. Re.20.10.

---

vours shown to Himself. " *These my brethren*," He calls them (vs. 40). Christ and His children are *one*. (John 17. 21.) " Pure religion and undefiled is this." James 1. 27.

36. *Naked*—that is, badly clothed.
—¶ *Ye visited* — more literally, *looked after*.

37. *Then shall the righteous*. They were only amazed at such a notice of their meanest services. They could not have thought that small favours shown to the obscurest Christian would be mentioned at the judgment to their praise. They could not have thought that Christ would consider it as done to Himself in person. The true Christian is always humble, and feels himself unworthy of God's favours. God will praise him, where he would be silent.

40. *The least of these my brethren*. The most insignificant of His followers are His brethren (Mark 3. 35), because they do His will, and are His brethren also in tribulation. To do a kindness to His disciples is to do it to Him, because they are one with Him (Matt. 10. 42). So with injuries. Saul persecuted Him thus. (Acts 9. 4.) We should help the hungry, and thirsty, and stranger—we should attend and supply the naked and sick and imprisoned, as we are able. And especially should we regard the wants of Christians in distress, for we are to " do good to all men, especially to them that are of the household of faith " (Gal. 6. 10). These things can be done for Christ's sake—that is, out of hearty love to Him, and a desire to do good to others because they are His—or because He requires it. Kindness to the poor is not always a sign of grace in the heart. To please Christ it must have His will and His service for the motive, " for without faith, it is impossible to please Him." (Heb. 11. 6.)

41. *Depart from me*—that is, from the presence and favour of Christ. They are *cursed*—that is, condemned, and not acquitted, nor blessed. They must *dwell*, that is, have their home, in everlasting fire. This torment was *prepared*, that is, made ready beforehand, for the devil and his angels —that is, for fallen spirits, and all the wicked who are " the children of the evil one." (Jude 6. Rev. 12. 8, 9.) The wicked must dwell with all the apostate and vile beings in the universe, and their torment must be indescribably awful. It must be real and inevitable, for the devils are already under the condemnation. And it must be eternal. It is expressly said to be *everlasting*. " Gather not my soul with sinners." (Ps. 26. 9.) *Fire* was the common image of punishment to the Jews, expressing severest suffering with all that is loathsome and outcast—as in the valley of Hinnom. *Note*—Matt. 5. 22. The fulness of the idea cannot be given in language—and it cannot be found out any more than " the *worm* that never dies." Isa. 66. 24.——¶ *Prepared for the devil*, &c. Some have argued hence that it was not prepared for

ye gave me no meat: I was thirsty, and ye gave me no drink:

43 I was a stranger, and ye took me not in: naked, and ye clothed me not: sick, and in prison, and ye visited me not.

44 Then shall they also answer him, saying, Lord, when saw we thee an hungered, or athirst, or a stranger, or naked, or sick, or in prison, and did not minister unto thee?

45 Then shall he answer them, saying, Verily I say unto you, Inasmuch *u* as ye did *it* not to one of the least of these, ye did *it* not to me.

46 And *v* these shall go away into everlasting punishment: but the righteous into life eternal.

u Zec.2.8. Ac.9.5. *v* Da.12.2. Jno.5.29.

---

sinners. But Judas went "*to his own* PLACE." (Acts 1. 25.) They to whom Christ is a stone of stumbling and a rock of offence are not more truly disobedient, than inheritors of a doom whereunto also they were appointed (1 Pet. 2. 8)—"and all liars shall *have their part* in the lake," &c. Rev. 21. 8. The force of the language therefore is, that the left hand company should inherit the doom of fallen angels, and go to that torment which is already entered on by lost spirits—who are, "for an example, suffering the vengeance of eternal fire." (Jude 6, 7.)

45. *One of the least of these*—that is, those on the right hand. The wicked will be condemned, for not serving Christ in His cause, or in His people—as the man of one talent was condemned for what he neglected to do. If omission of duty is enough to send men to perdition, how shall they answer for the sins committed? The actions of the wicked shall be brought forward in the final day to vindicate God's judgment, and to show that they cannot answer a word. *That every mouth* may be stopped. Rom. 3. 19. What vast crowds shall be compassed by such terms, of all grades of morality!

46. *These shall go away.* These individuals on the left hand just commanded to depart from His presence and favour, *shall go into everlasting punishment.* So saith Christ the Lamb —the Judge! It is into *punishment*, or torment, inflicted on them for crime, that they are to go — called "*the lake of fire.*" (Rev. 20. 14.) This punishment is *everlasting.* The word is the same in the Greek that is rendered *eternal* in the next clause. So that if the *life eternal* means *eternal life*, this everlasting punishment means punishment that is everlasting. The word is used forty-four times in the New Testament in the phrase, "everlasting life," or "eternal life." It is used frequently in phrases kindred, as, "everlasting covenant." Heb. 13. 20. "Eternal inheritance." Heb. 9. 15. "His eternal glory" (*i. e.* God's, which cannot be finite). 1 Pet. 5. 10. "Eternal salvation." Heb. 5. 9, &c. And it is used quite as distinctly, seven times, in phrases like these: "everlasting punishment"—"eternal fire." Jude 7. "Everlasting destruction." 2 Th. 1. 9. And that it can mean nothing less than eternal, without end, is proved from its use in Rom. 16. 26, "The commandment of the EVERLASTING GOD;" and in Heb. 9. 14, of God the Holy Ghost, "the ETERNAL SPIRIT." If the Divine Existence is eternal, so will be the wicked's doom. As the punishment of the wicked will be eternal or everlasting, so also will be the joy of the righteous. They enter into *the joy of their Lord.* vs. 21. This eternal life God hath given to us, in His Son. 1 John 5. 11. Christ is the author of eternal salvation. (Heb. 5. 9.) The *life* includes all that is opposite to the death of the wicked. It is perfect and eternal holiness and happiness in God's presence. "Seeing we look for such things, we should be diligent, that we

CHAPTER XXVI.

AND it came to pass, when Jesus had finished all these sayings, he said unto his disciples,

2 Ye^a know that after two days

<small>a Mar. 14. 1, &c. Lu. 22. 1, &c. Jno. 13. 1, &c.</small>

may be found of Him in peace, without spot, and blameless" (2 Pet. 3. 14). Who of us shall dwell with *everlasting burnings?* Isa. 33. 14.

OBSERVE, (1.) Christ, who is now neglected and rejected, will come to judgment, in inconceivable majesty and glory—" the great white throne "—" *all* the holy angels." (2.) Mere morality will not be enough at His bar. There are men *who have whereof to glory, but not before God*. A mere negative religion—a barren profession—a faith that is without works—will not be accepted there. (3.) The righteous will be surprized at their good deeds being mentioned — and the wicked at their omissions being taken into account. How mistaken are the multitude in regard to God. How the men of fairest morality must be confounded on this plan of trial. How shall ye escape if ye *neglect* so great salvation. (4.) Christ is on earth now, in His church, as truly as He was here in the flesh. (40.) (5.) The righteous are children of God, and the wicked are children of the devil. (6.) The doom of the wicked will be eternal as the bliss of the righteous, or the existence of God. (7.) The righteous will have their smallest good works mentioned by Christ. (8.) There is no middle, or moderate doom. They who are not absolutely welcomed and rewarded, will be absolutely cast off and destroyed for ever.

CHAPTER XXVI.

§ 131. THE RULERS CONSPIRE. THE SUPPER AT BETHANY. TREACHERY OF JUDAS.—FOURTH *day of the week.* *Bethany. Jerusalem.*

Matt.	Mark.	Luke.	John.
26. 1-16	14. 1-11	22. 1-6	12. 2-8

On the fourth day of the week, the

is *the feast of* the passover, and the Son of man is betrayed to be crucified.

3 Then assembled together the chief priests, and the scribes, and the elders of the people,

chief priests and others, after deliberation, came to the formal conclusion to seize Jesus and put Him to death.

1. *When Jesus had finished,* &c. These sayings had been preparatory to the closing up of His ministry. And the final scenes are now coming on.

2. *The feast of the passover.* This was the great festival among the Jews, in celebration of their deliverance from Egypt, when the destroying angel that slew the Egyptian firstborn, had *passed over* the houses of the Israelites marked with blood, and they escaped from Pharaoh. Exod. 12. This was associated in the type, and to be associated in the fact with a greater deliverance of God's people by the blood of Christ. This joyous festival lasted seven days. In Luke and elsewhere, it is called "the feast of unleavened bread," because the people were forbidden to allow any *leaven*, or fermented food or yeast, in their houses during this time. Exod. 12. 18.——¶ *The Son of man.* Here again Christ calls Himself by this name, as belonging to this narrative of His humiliation, and of His mediatorial work.——¶ *Is betrayed*— is *about to be* betrayed, or surrendered by treachery. Here the idea of His death by foulest means, even by violated friendship, is associated with all their ideas of the passover, as a memorial of deliverance. Sinners are delivered from death, only by the sacrifice of Christ. Observe this most definite announcement now of His coming death—the mode of it, and the means by which it shal be brought to pass. The *mode* is crucifixion—the *means* is betrayal by a friend.

3. Here is noted, at the same time, a conspiracy of the Sanhedrim and chief religious officers of the people. How perfectly Jesus knew before-

MATTHEW. [A. D. 33.

unto the palace of the high priest, who was called Caiaphas.

4 And [b] consulted that they might take Jesus by subtilty, and kill *him*.

5 But they said, Not on the

feast *day*, lest there be an uproar among the people.

6 ¶ Now when Jesus was in Bethany, in the house of Simon the leper,

7 There [c] came unto him a

---

b Ps.2.2.   *c* Jno.11.1,2; 12.3.

---

hand all things that should come upon Him. They met at the palace or office of Caiaphas, who was high priest that year, as is noted also in John 11. 51. The high priest's office, that used to be hereditary in the family of Aaron, was now an office in the gift of the Romans, and filled without any sacred regard to its institution.

4. *By subtilty*—by cunning and deceit, so that He could not escape their foul purposes, and so that they should not be detected in their malicious intent.

5. *Not on the feast day*. They would have preferred another time; but God chose the passover season, and His counsel stood against their preference. Their reason against this time was, that such crowds—about three millions—assembled in Jerusalem; and in such a case, where various opinions prevailed respecting Christ, a tumult and outbreak might

be the result. God chose this season, to have this not done in a corner—and also to have the shadow merge into the substance at the meridian. It was fit that Christ *our passover*, should be crucified at the passover festival.

6. *In Bethany*. Mark has it, "*and being in Bethany*," as though at this very time, or about the same time. John says that Christ came to Bethany six days before the passover. Yet this supper seems to have been made on the evening following the third day of the week, which, as they reckoned the day from evening to evening, was the beginning of the *fourth* day, viz.: after sunset on Tuesday. This house was that of Simon, who had *once been* a leper, and probably had been cured by Christ. Lazarus was one of those who reclined at the table—*a guest* (see John 12).

7. *A woman*. This was Mary, sister of Martha and Lazarus. John 12. 3.

woman having an alabaster box of very precious ointment, and poured it on his head, as he sat *at meat.*

8 But when his disciples saw *it,* they had indignation, saying, To what purpose *is* this waste?

9 For this ointment might have been sold for much, and given to the poor.

10 When Jesus understood *it,* he said unto them, Why trouble ye the woman? for she hath wrought a good work upon me.

11 For ᵈ ye have the poor al-

---

d De.15.11.

——¶ *Alabaster box* — αλαβαστρον. These were either jars or vases, called *alabasters*, and made of different materials. More generally, they were long-necked flasks or bottles sealed at the top. The woman is said by Mark, to have *broken* it—that is, probably, the seal. (*See cut.*)——¶ *Very precious ointment.* Mark and John say, *spikenard.* It was very rare and costly, being a most rich perfume, " so that the house was filled *with the odour.*" John 12. 3. Ointment was used for anointing the body. Ps. 104. 15. It was believed to contribute to health and cleanliness, and to protect from the intensity of the sun. It was used for the perfume in paying visits and at home. It was omitted in mourning. Deut. 28. 40. Ruth 3. 3. It was a token of welcome to guests — among the Egyptians at least; and to be " anointed with the oil of gladness" was so understood. The practice of anointing the dead is hinted at. Mark 14. 8. Luke 23. 56. It was supposed to check the progress of corruption. —— ¶ *On His head.* This was the common mode. John states also the fact that she anointed His *feet* (12. 3). She did *both.* She had *a pound* of it, and used it in abundance, as the house was filled with the odour—and it would have brought three hundred pence (see Mark and John), that is, about $40. As people *reclined* at the table, having their feet spread out on their couch behind them (see note, ch. 23. 6), this anointing of the feet was easily done, and was only an extra mark of her humility and affection.

8. *Indignation* — displeasure and anger. It was *Judas* to whom this reference is thus generally made (John 12. 4-6), and this feeling he had, because he *had the bag* or *purse,* of the twelve. He carried the money and was a *thief*, and *bare* (that is, as the word may mean), " *carried away* what was put therein." He grudged this expense, for he had rather have had the amount given to them, and put in the bag where he could get it. But she had a right to do with her money as she pleased. The avarice that would complain and murmur at this Christian charity and call it a waste, would steal from the disciples' bag, and sell Christ for thirty pieces of silver, *one third as much!*

9. *Given to the poor.* Not that he cared for the poor. See John 12. 6. What hypocrisy!

10. *Why trouble ye.* This outcry of Judas had, no doubt, grieved and agitated her delicate feeling.——¶ *A good work*—good in itself as prompted by the tenderest affection for Christ, and good as being seasonable for His burial. Mary's motive was to express her hearty welcome at the supper (John 12. 2), and her strong personal devotion to Christ. Nothing is a waste or too costly that is bestowed upon Him—and such benevolent acts will always be vindicated by Christ, and abundantly honoured (vs. 13) and rewarded.

11. *For ye have the poor.* Judas had pleaded that the expense were better laid out upon the poor, and Christ replies that this opportunity of serving and honouring Him was very special—whereas the poor could *always* be served. As He was to die soon, what was done for His person must be done *then.* Personally, He should soon be absent from them— not to be known " after the flesh,"

ways with you; but *me ye have not always.

12 For in that she hath poured this ointment on my body, she did *it* for my burial.

13 Verily I say unto you, Wheresoever this gospel shall be preached in the whole world, *there* shall also this, that this woman hath done, be told for a memorial of her.

e John 14.19; 17.11.

14 ¶ Then one *f* of the twelve, called Judas Iscariot, went unto the chief priests,

15 And said *unto them*, What will ye give me, and I will deliver him unto you? And they *g* covenanted with him for thirty pieces of silver.

16 And from that time he sought opportunity to betray him.

f c.10.4.   *g* Zec.11.12,13. c.27.3.

though spiritually He would be present with them always.

12. It was so timely, because (as He now declares) it would serve for a *burial anointing*, though Mary knew it not. And it was not thought extravagant to lay out large expense upon the dead body, for its anointing and embalming. (Christ cannot be present *bodily* in the sacrament of the Supper.) Nicodemus (John 19. 39) brought a hundred pounds weight for Christ's emoalming. It was no loss therefore, in respect of the poor (vs. 11), nor of the disciples (Mark 14. 7), nor of the woman (vs. 13), nor *of Christ* (vs. 12). Christ here further warned of his death as *so near.*

13. *This gospel*—which Christ preached, and which was destined to be promulgated throughout the world. This narrative, He says, should go with the narratives of His sufferings and death, as a memorial—for the remembrance of her—to celebrate this act of piety. It should show what true Christian devotion will do for Christ, as well as what Christ has done for us. This has proved true. The scripture is inspired by God, and everything is told by Divine direction. Three of the evangelists have recorded this account of Mary.

14. *Then.* This rebuke of Judas for his interference with Mary's piety, prompted him to plot for the betrayal of Christ, though it was not the sole impulse. He was urged on by his covetousness and worldly ambition.——¶ *To the chief priests.* Luke adds, "*and captains*"—or leaders of the temple guards—heads of the watch. He went to bargain with them. He may have heard of their meeting together (vs. 3) at that time, and for the purpose of taking Christ and putting him to death.

15. *Deliver Him*—hand Him over. Such a proposal directly fell in with their wishes, and the objects of their meeting. It does not seem to have been their plan, but that of Judas. They wished to take him and kill Him (vs. 4), but they had planned to defer it, lest it might raise a tumult at the passover. This hastened the work.——¶ *They covenanted*—literally, *they placed* (in a scale), *weighed or paid:* bargained and agreed at once. Mark says, "*promised* to give him money"— to pay him the amount when the deed was done.——¶ *Thirty pieces of silver* —or shekels. This was the price of a slave. Exod. 21. 32. And this is probably the ground on which the sum was fixed. The amount is computed at fifteen or sixteen dollars (?). The prophecy was also fulfilled (Zech. 11. 12), "So they weighed for my price thirty pieces of silver." So was every minute particular the same as had been foreseen and predicted. Nothing in the death of Christ was without design or calculation If the *silver pieces* were numbered beforehand, why not the souls that should be saved?

16. *To betray Him*—to deliver Him over to the chief priests, by treachery. The opportunity sought was "the absence of the multitude." Luke 22. 6.

OBSERVE, (1.) A man without the

A. D. 83.]   CHAPTER XXVI.   265

17 ¶ Now ʰ the first day of the *feast of* unleavened bread, the disciples came to Jesus,
h Ex. 12. 6, 18.

saying unto him, Where wilt thou that we prepare for thee to eat the passover?

---

wedding garment. A slothful servant—a foolish virgin—a *hypocrite* is nere. Under a pious pretence was concealed the most base malignity. He was a *thief* (John 12. 6)—a *traitor*—a *murderer of Christ*—and yet the *treasurer* of the *twelve!* Our being in the church does not make us safe—but our being in Christ. (2.) He who talks of *loss* upon Christ, is himself the *son of perdition*. He who thinks forty dollars too much to waste on Christ's anointing, will take sixteen dollars to betray Him to death! (3.) Behold the depth of human depravity! Judas, who had lived with Christ, and had seen His miracles, and had ranked with the apostles, and must declare *Him innocent* at last, could hand him over to a cruel death, for the paltriest price. (4.) Temptation to sin is no excuse for sin, no matter how strong it be—no matter if by Satan himself. Judas *volunteered* to betray Christ. It was his own proposal to the chief priests. Sinners act willingly in yielding to temptation, and this is the condemnation. (5.) Those who are in danger from temptation, should mark the dreadful lengths to which they may be carried, if they yield at all. They should resist at the onset. And while we resist we should pray, "*lead us not into temptation.*" And we have the promise, "Resist the devil and he shall flee from thee." (6.) Money is a snare. They who set their hearts upon it, fall into "many foolish and hurtful lusts, that drown men in destruction and perdition."

§ 132. PREPARATION FOR THE PASSOVER.—FIFTH *day of the week. Jerusalem. Bethany.*

Matt.	Mark.	Luke.	John.
26. 17-19	14. 12-16	22. 7-13	

17. *Feast of unleavened bread.* It was so called, because, as the bread had not time to be leavened when the Lord appeared for their deliverance

out of Egypt, they baked unleavened cakes out of the dough. (Exod. 12. 39.) And so, bread made with leaven or yeast, was strictly forbidden during the feast. The feast lasted from the 14th to the 21st (evening to evening), and the evening of the 14th was called the *first*—the fermented things having been removed during the day. (Exod. 12. 6, 15.) This feast was called the *Passover*, because, at that time, the paschal lamb was slain and eaten, in commemoration of their deliverance in Egypt. Luke says, "the day of unleavened bread, in which the *passover* must be killed." Thus, the lamb was also called "*the passover;*" as Christ says, "This is my body." They were wont to keep the feast in companies—a family or two together. The houses in Jerusalem were thrown open, for the immense crowd from all the land. How remarkable a company was this of the twelve, with the Master, in a guest-chamber, or spare room. The feast took place in the month Abib, which is our April. After the usual washings or purification, the master of the family, or chief guest, proceeded to give thanks, after which, the first cup of wine was partaken by all present. Then came the washing of hands, with a blessing. Next came the provisions for the table—bitter herbs, unleavened bread, the lamb roasted whole (no bone broken), and the sauce. Then another thanksgiving, taking an herb and dipping it in the sauce, to eat it with all present. (vs. 23.) The table was then removed *from before the master of the feast only*, who rehearsed openly the deliverance from Egypt. (1 Cor. 11. 26. Exod. 12. 17; 13. 8.) Then the second cup of wine was filled, and the question was asked by the children (Exod. 12. 26, 29), to which the master of the feast would respond, as the dishes were returned—repeating Ps. 113 and 114. Then the second cup of wine was

18 And he said, Go into the city to such a man, and say unto him, The Master saith, My time is at hand; I will keep the passover at thy house with my disciples.

19 And the disciples did as Jesus had appointed them; and

---

partaken, after the usual blessing. Then followed the blessing for the washing of hands, and a second washing took place. (John 13. 4, 5, 12.) Then he took two cakes and brake one of them, and, with the usual form, *blessed the bread.* The bread was then distributed, saying: " *This is the bread of affliction, which our fathers did eat in the land of Egypt;*"—instead of which, Christ said, " *This is my body broken.*" Then all ate, such as chose dipping their portion into the sauce. (vs. 23. John 13. 26.) The master next blessed God, and ate of the paschal lamb, in which the whole company joined. Then the third cup was blessed and drank, called " *the cup of blessing.*" (26, 27. 1 Cor. 10. 16.) And this was followed by thanksgiving for their fathers' deliverance, for the covenant of circumcision, and for the law of Moses. Hence, at this cup the Saviour said, " This cup is the *new* testament," or covenant. A fourth cup was then usually filled, and a song or hymn sung. (vs. 30.)

The Jews were to remember at this feast, their deliverance, in the destruction of the firstborn in Egypt, when they were *passed over*—and their departure out of the land of bondage. The lamb slain at the passover, represented Christ, " the Lamb of God." A room for the feast was necessary to be prepared, and it could be had, for the houses in Jerusalem on this great occasion, were always thrown open to the public.

18. *Into the city.* Jerusalem was *the* city by eminence, among the Jews. The festival was kept there by law. The paschal lamb must be slain by the priests at the temple (Ezra 6. 20), and each company received it slain, from their hands, for the solemnity. —— ¶ *To such a man.* Mark and Luke say, " there shall meet you a man." Luke adds, " when ye are entered into the city." This, like the case of the ass tied (Matt. 21. 2), showed the omniscience of Christ. They were to identify the man by such a coincidence which none but a Divine mind could foresee. Luke says that *Peter* and *John* were sent. They must needs be impressed with the fact, that the Master knew, beforehand, all the minutest particulars. Their faith needed all strengthening for the trial at hand.——¶ *The Master saith.* The man was probably a *disciple.*—— ¶ *My time.* That which He had called *His hour.* He had often said, " Mine hour has not yet come." In John 7. 6, 8, this word is used in the same sense as here. " My time is not yet come," and " not yet full come."

19. *They made ready.* They obtained the lamb and all the articles necessary for keeping the feast. The room was found furnished and prepared (Mark 14. 16). Our Lord partook the passover on the same night in which He was betrayed. This was His last meal with His disciples, the regular and ordinary paschal supper of the Jews, on the evening after the 14th day of Nisan. But this introduced the *festival* of unleavened bread, which lasted seven days. This is what John refers to (13. 17), the feast, or rather festival (εορτη), of the passover. (See Numb. 28. 16, 17.) This is distinct from the paschal supper, but from not noticing the terms, has been confounded with it. The passage in John 18. 28, might seem to decide that on the day of the crucifixion, the paschal supper had not yet been eaten. But as the term " passover " was often used to include all the feasts and festivals appertaining to it, and especially the festival of unleavened bread, and as here, there is nothing to restrict the sense to the eating of the paschal lamb, it is warrantably taken in the wider sense. (See Luke 22. 1. Matt. 26. 2. John 2. 13.) There were other paschal

they made ready the passover.

20 Now when the even was come, he sat down with the twelve.

21 And as they did eat, he said, Verily I say unto you, that one of you shall betray me.

22 And they were exceeding sorrowful, and began every one of them to say unto him, Lord, is it I?

---

sacrifices connected with the passover, but less public. Special daily sacrifices were appointed for the seven days—and there was a voluntary private sacrifice—a festive thank-offering. It is observed that in the phrase, "the preparation of the passover," John 19. 14, the word παρασκευη (preparation) refers, as elsewhere, to the Jewish sabbath, which actually occurred the next day after the crucifixion. It was at length employed as the term for the whole sixth day of the week, or Friday. It was the weekly παρασκευη or προσαββατον that John referred to. (See Robinson's Harmony. Notes.)

PART VIII.

The Fourth Passover. Our Lord's Passion and the accompanying events until the end of the Jewish Sabbath.

Time—two days.

§ 133. THE PASSOVER MEAL. CONTENTION AMONG THE TWELVE. *Evening introducing the* SIXTH *day of the week. Jerusalem.*

Matt.	Mark.	Luke.	John.
26.20	14. 17.	22. 14-18, 24-30	

20. *The even.* Between 3 o'clock and 9 was the time for killing the lamb, called also, *between the evenings* (Exod. 12. 6) in the Hebrew.—— ¶ *The twelve* were the apostles.—— ¶ *Sat down*—literally, *reclined*, as was the posture at table. (See Exod. 12.3,4, as to the number who generally ate the feast together.) Though the passover was at first eaten "standing," the posture was afterward changed to reclining, as a token of rest and security. Luke records the contention of the twelve at this time, and our Lord's instructions to them, at the same time.

§ 134. *Jesus washes the feet of his disciples. Same evening.*

Matt.	Mark.	Luke.	John.
			13. 1-20

§ 135. JESUS POINTS OUT THE TRAITOR. JUDAS WITHDRAWS. *Same evening.*

Matt.	Mark.	Luke.	John.
16.21-25	14.18-21	22.21-23	13.21-35

21. *One of you shall betray me—* "which eateth with me." John says, "He was troubled in spirit." He knew who it was, as He knew all the particulars with utmost exactness, because He was God as well as man, "knowing all things that should come upon Him." (John 18. 4.) Still He did not conceal Himself, because He designed to die, and for this cause He came unto this hour. The eternal purposes of God are accomplished thus by wilful and wicked men. (Acts 2. 23.) "Him being delivered," &c.

22. This was the most definite announcement of His death, in the diabolical manner of it, and they were sorry—"*exceeding sorrowful*"—on every account—both that He should die, and that it should be by such means. That it should be by any one of *them*, amazed and overcame them. Like innocent men, the whole eleven were agitated, and not knowing what they were to be left to, began to inquire most earnestly. It was worse for one of *them* than for any other, because they had seen His miracles and character, and had professed the closest attachment to Him. One of them knew who the betrayer was, and he, Judas himself, was the last to inquire about the guilty person.

MATTHEW. [A.D. 33.

23 And he answered and said, *i* He that dippeth *his* hand with me in the dish, the same shall betray me

24 The Son of man goeth as it is written *j* of him : but wo unto that man by whom the Son of man is betrayed! it had been good for that man if he had not been born.

25 Then Judas, which betrayed him, answered and said, Master

i Ps.41.9; 55.12-15. *j* Ps.22. Is.53.

---

23. *He that dippeth*, &c. The Jewish mode of eating was to take the food from the dish with the hand. Spoons and knives and forks were not then in use. This reply of our Lord was intended to designate the betrayer. He sat near the Lord—John on one side, and Judas on the other, as is supposed. Peter beckoned to John that he should ask the Lord who the traitor was; and Christ, it appears, gave a most distinct sign (John 13. 26): "He it is to whom I shall give a sop when I have dipped it." This was from the thick sauce, made of dates, figs, raisins, vinegar, &c., and prepared to represent the *clay* which their fathers used in Egypt in making brick. (See vs. 2, note.) That Judas was present at the *passover meal* appears from Luke 22. 21: "The hand of him that betrayeth me is with me on the table." But that he was *not* present at the Lord's Supper, appears from John 13. 30.

24. *Goeth as it is written*, &c. Luke —"as it was determined." All the steps in the course of our Lord, even through the betrayal and through death, were appointed and prophesied. It was not of chance, nor without design. This was all in the Divine intention, and it was eternally purposed so to be; and so all the *results* of this atoning sacrifice were purposed. He was delivered up to die by the determinate counsel and foreknowledge of God. (Acts 2. 23.) This was spoken for their consolation, who were already so agitated, and would soon be so overwhelmed. How consoling to view all our afflictions as ordered by the wise and good counsel of our God. How important to behold God's eternal purposes in all the steps and issues of Christ's death. (Acts 4. 27, 28.) Christ's death was foretold in Isaiah, 53d chap. Dan. 9. 26, 27, &c.——¶ *But wo unto that man.* Let him be accursed. It was none the less criminal, because it was predicted, or because it fulfilled God's purposes. It was so great a crime, because it was the treachery of a professed follower and friend—it was against the purest being that the world ever saw—it was for the meanest objects and from the lowest motives—it was against greatest light—for he had seen His miracles, and had heard the heavenly testimonies of His being the Son of God. Jesus knew perfectly (John 6. 64) what Judas was about to do. But He made no attempt to escape. He showed no fear. He came on earth with a full understanding of all He was to suffer, and He was prepared to meet it. He was ordained to suffer all these things, to make expiation for sinners. (See Luke 24. 26,

A. D. 33.] CHAPTER XXVI. 269

is it I? He said unto him, Thou hast said.

26 ¶ And ᵏ as they were eat-ing, Jesus took bread, and ¹ blessed *it*, and brake *it*, and gave *it* to the disciples, and said, Take, eat; this is my body.

k 1Cor.11.23,&c.

1 Many Greek copies have, *gave thanks.*

" *Ought not Christ,*" &c.) This shows the dreadful nature of sin, that required such a sacrifice for atonement.—— ¶ *It had been good for that man if he had not been born*—because in a lost eternity, he should for ever have occasion to lament his existence. This shows that his punishment would be *eternal* (see Luke 23. 29). This was a proverbial expression among the Jews. The Divine decree did not excuse Judas, because it neither forced him nor induced him to the act.

25. *Then Judas.* The wicked study concealment, and Judas was the last to say anything of the criminal, for he felt the crime in his heart. He had already engaged to betray Jesus.—— ¶ *Master.* Judas is remarked not to have called Jesus *Lord*. He asked this question only to escape singularity, for all the rest had now asked it.—— ¶ *Thou hast said,* or, It is as thou hast said. Whether Judas now went out, or whether he ate the supper with the rest, has been questioned. He ate the regular paschal meal, but withdrew at the giving of the sop (John 13. 30), leaving Christ and the eleven at the Sacramental Supper. The order of items in the narrative will appear from § 133 to § 137. Matthew aims to bring out the connexion between Judas' conviction and the institution of the Supper. It was a most impressive transition. It will be seen from the sections 136 and 137 that Christ foretold the fall of Peter, &c., before proceeding to the solemnity.

§ 136. JESUS· FORETELLS THE FALL OF PETER AND THE DISPERSION OF THE TWELVE.—*Evening introducing the* SIXTH *day of the week.*

Matt.	Mark.	Luke.	John.
26.31–35	14.27–31	22.31–38	13.36–38

§ 137. THE LORD'S SUPPER.—*Same evening. Jerusalem.*

Matt.	Mark.	Luke.	John.
26.26–29	14.22–25	23.19, 20	

Observe, Christ foretold Peter's fall, and His desertion by the twelve, before the Sacramental Supper. (See § 136.)

26. *As they were eating,* i. e., the passover. It was of the unleavened bread or cakes there used, that our Lord took for the Sacramental Institution. ——¶ *Blessed it.* The same is meant as in vs. 27, " *Gave thanks.*" This was in conformity with the Jewish custom at meals (comp. Luke 9. 16, with John 6. 11).——¶ *Brake it.* As a significant type of His body, which should be broken on the cross.—— ¶ *This is my body.* This form of expression grew out of the passover forms. That feast was a memorial—and when it was asked in the ceremonies what these things meant, the method of reply was, " This *is* the body of the lamb which our fathers ate in Egypt." Not the *same*, but this is meant to represent and commemorate that. He could not have meant that the bread was His real body, because His body was present at the table breaking the loaf, and he was speaking and acting in person among them. Observe, too, He broke it *after* it was blessed, when Papists think it was transubstantiated. See also Exod. 12. 11. Gen. 41. 26. John 15. 1, 5. So Luke 22. 20, " *This cup is* the new testament in my blood." The bread represented His body, as an expressive emblem. " I am *that bread* of life," and *broken,* as His body should be, the next day by the crucifixion. (See 1 Cor. 11. 23, 25.) This breaking of bread in all after time, would vividly call to mind His violent and cruel death, who " by wicked hands was crucified and slain " (Acts 2. 23). Christians can weep that they have slain the Lord. But they can also partake the emblems of their deliverance and subsistence, with joy—and so *by faith* they can feed upon *Him.*

27 And he took the cup, and gave thanks, and gave *it* to them, saying, Drink ye all of it:

28 For this is my blood of the new testament, ¹ which is shed for many for the remission of sins.

29 But I say unto you, I will not drink henceforth of this fruit of the vine, until that day

¹ Je. 31. 31.

27. *The cup.* This was the passover cup, at the *third* filling—called "the cup of blessing" (see note on vs. 2.) This cup was taken after supper (see Luke), that is, after the regular passover meal was gone through. The Jews drank wine at the paschal feast—and this wine our Saviour used as He found it, called "the fruit of the vine." Mark 14. 35. Jesus gave the wine to His disciples as He had done with the bread.——¶ *Drink ye all.* The Greek reads "ALL YE," in the plural, referred to the disciples, and not possibly to the wine.

28. *This is my blood*—a sign or emblem of my blood. This formula occurs again from the forms of the passover feast. They praised God for the covenant of circumcision, and spoke of the cup as a thanksgiving for that covenant, and here the form is followed. "This is my blood of the *new* testament," or as the word properly reads, "*new* COVENANT." In the old covenant made with the Jewish nation, the blood of the sacrifices was sprinkled (Exod. 24. 8. Jer. 31. 31–33). His blood was shed on the cross, as His heart was pierced, and He died a sacrifice appointed of God. *The blood is the life.* Levit. 17. 14. He laid down his life. It pleased the Lord to bruise Him. Isa. 53. Sinners cannot be saved in any other way—for "other foundation can no man lay" (1 Cor. 3. 11). The object of the Lord's Supper is, 1st, a memorial—"This do in remembrance of me." Ye do show the Lord's death till He come. 2d. A seal—"a sacrament whereby Christ and the benefits of the new covenant are represented, sealed and applied to believers." It is a perpetual ordinance in the church, to be observed by Christians till He come. 1 Cor. 11. 26. The friends of Christ should love to partake of it, because it commemorates His love, and seals to them, through faith, the benefits of the covenant. It is the lively representation of Christ crucified, and the nearest approach on earth to the Lamb. It is also His dying ordinance—most important for the visible church, and most sacred to every follower of Christ. Here we feel His preciousness and our sins, and His amazing love to sinners, most deeply, as we are brought most closely in contact with the lively symbols, and with our living Lord.——¶ *Shed for many for the remission of sins.* This language refers back to John the Baptist's preaching, viz., the baptism of repentance *for the remission of sins* (Mark 1. 4), and this explains *that.* John heralded this new dispensation of Christ, which they professed to embrace, in his baptism. Yet that baptism looked forward to this plan of remission by Christ's blood. He preached Christ, through whom was to come this remission—and here it is announced and explained. "For without shedding of blood is no remission" (Heb. 9. 22).

29. *I will not drink henceforth.* He meant by this, to say that henceforth He should no more have to do with these ceremonies. They were about to have their accomplishment in His death, and the great future participation with them would be in heaven, where they should enjoy together the blessings represented in this feast. There all the disciples of Christ will be with Him.——¶ *Fruit of the vine.* (See Deut. 22. 9. Isa. 32. 12.)—— ¶ *New,* i. e., different from that which they were then partaking. The term has the same force as in the phrases "*new* heavens and *new* earth," "all things *new,*" "*New Jerusalem.*"—— ¶ *My Father's kingdom.* This is something different from the common

when I drink it new with you in my Father's kingdom.ᵐ

30 And when

m Is. 25. 6.

they had sung an ¹ hymn, they went out into the Mount of Olives.

1 Or, *psalm.*

---

phrase, kingdom of God, and refers to the final consummation in glory. Christ intimates the perfect fellowship and friendship in heaven, between Himself and His people. He shall sit down and feast with them, as a guest with them.

OBSERVE, (1.) This blood-shedding was for PERSONS, not for THINGS—"FOR MANY." (2.) It was IN THEIR ROOM, not merely *for their possible advantage.* The term "*for*" in the Greek, means INSTEAD OF (ὑπερ)—AS A SUBSTITUTE FOR MANY, that is for all His people. Luke has it, "*which is shed for you.*" And this was His work and design, as announced by the angel at His birth. He gets His precious name from this, "*Thou shalt call his name* JESUS, *for He shall* SAVE HIS PEOPLE *from their sins.*" (See John 17. 9. Ephes. 5. 2. Heb. 7. 27. Isa. 53. 10. Rom. 8. 33. ch. 1. 21. 1 John 4. 10.) " For even Christ, OUR PASSOVER, is sacrificed for us." (1 Cor. 5. 7.) Though this precious blood is of infinite value, and amply sufficient for all, as appears in the proclamations of grace, and the calls of the gospel which it brings, yet plainly Christ died not in the same sense for all. That some are saved and others not, is traceable to distinguishing grace, and to the sovereign purpose of God, and not ultimately to men's different choosings, because their will is not the sovereign power in salvation, but God's—" Born, not of blood, nor of the will of the flesh, nor of the will of man, but of God. (John 1. 13.) It cannot be man's will that renews, because it is his will that is renewed. " *Thy people shall be willing in the day of thy power* " (Psalm 110.3). Hence we learn that all true believers may apply to their full advantage the shedding of Christ's blood. None else can do it. Let every believer approach the table, and feel that satisfaction has been made thus for his sins.

	Matt.	Mark.	Luke.	John.
§ 138. Jesus comforts His Disciples. The Holy Spirit promised.—*Evening introducing the* ¹SIXTH *day of the week.—Guest-chamber.*	....	....	....	14. 1–31
§ 139. Christ the true Vine. His Disciples hated by the World.—*Same evening.*	....	....	....	15. 1–27
§ 140. Persecution foretold. Further Promise of the Spirit.—*Same evening.*	....	....	....	16. 1–33
§ 141. Christ's last Prayer with His Disciples. *Same evening.*	....	....	....	17. 1–26
§ 141½. DEPARTURE TO THE *Mount of Olives.*	26. 30,	14. 26	22.39	18. 1

30. *And when they had sung an hymn*—or having hymned (literally). It was customary to commence the Passover service with singing or chanting Psalms 113 and 114, and to conclude the services with the 115th to the 118th from the Scripture, in which not only the events of the Exodus are commemorated, but there is a direct reference to the sorrows of the Messiah, and His resurrection from the dead. Observe that vs. 36 is a continuation of the narrative, where they come to Gethsemane, at the foot of the Mount of Olives, passing out from the city. The foretelling of Peter's fall (vs. 31–35) should occur earlier in the narrative, viz., just before the Supper. See Harmony.

OBSERVE. " For THE JOY that was set before Him He endured the cross, despising the shame" (Heb. 12. 2).

31 Then saith Jesus unto them, All ye shall be offended because of me this night: for it is written, ⁿ I will smite the Shepherd, and the sheep of the flock shall be scattered abroad.

32 But after I am risen again, ᵒ I will go before you into Galilee.

33 Peter answered and said unto him, Though all *men* shall be offended because of thee, yet will I never be offended.

34 Jesus said unto him, Verily

n Zec. 13. 7.

o c. 28. 7, 10, 16.

[§ 136. JESUS FORETELLS THE FALL OF PETER.]

Matt.	Mark.	Luke.	John.
26. 31-35	14. 27-31	22. 31-33	

31. *Then saith Jesus.* This was a direct and startling declaration of our Lord, which may have been called forth by Peter's inquiry, "Whither goest thou?" (John 13. 36.) Or which more likely was brought suddenly upon them. ——¶ *All ye shall be offended* (that is, shall *stumble*, as the word means) because of me—on my account; you will be staggered in your faith on account of my betrayal and delivery into the hands of my enemies. It shall prove an offence, or occasion of stumbling to you, that I, your Leader, shall seem to fall under the power of the wicked. ——¶ *For it is written.* This refers them to one of their own prophets' predictions fulfilled in this event. Zech. 13. 7. This represents the Father as smiting Christ, the shepherd of His people. So Isa. 53, "*It pleased the Lord to bruise Him.*" The plan had the highest authority, and His covenant was with the Father. And as a substitute and sacrifice, He was accepted, and in Him the Father was well pleased. Now, when the time had come for Christ the shepherd to be smitten, the flock—that is, the disciples — would be scattered abroad, and would flee for fear (vs. 56). (See Ps. 23. 1.)

32. *But after.* This was to give them the strongest assurance of His actual rising from the dead. Here was a positive appointment made for a meeting after His burial and rising again. It was fulfilled. (See Mark 16. 7. Matt. 28. 16.) Galilee was the spot of His principal ministrations.

33. *Though all.* This is the strong language. "Though all should be offended" (the word "*men*" is added), meaning all the apostles beside, and all others. This is characteristic of Peter—bold, forward, fearless, hearty. He had strong feeling, too much self-confidence, too little spirit of dependence. Such men are very likely to find themlseves weaker and worse than they had thought. "Let him that thinketh he standeth take heed lest he fall."—— ¶ *Will I never.* The phrase in the Greek is intensive — and " is used of that which in no way is or can be."—*Winer.* Luke records a warning that Christ gave first to Peter, "Satan hath desired to have thee, that he may sift thee as wheat." Still he went forward, and with all this forewarning he found himself the guilty man, before he was aware. The prediction had nothing to do with inducing his wilful denial—it would rather have prevented it—nor did it alter the crime. "Lead us not into temptation."

34. *Before the cock crow.* The daybreak is here meant, commonly called *cock-crowing*, though the cock crows also at midnight, which accounts for Mark and Luke reading, "*Before the cock crow twice.*" This denial was thrice repeated (see vss. 70-74). He denied being a disciple of Jesus, and denied again and again any acquaintance with Him, or approbation of Him. Our Lord plainly foreknew all this, even in the nicest particulars, and hence, we see His divinity.

35. *Though I should die with thee.* This was the strongest form in which Peter could put his expression of confidence. It was a proverbial expression. This shows us Peter in himself

I say unto thee, that this night, before the cock crow, thou shalt deny me thrice.

35 Peter said unto him, Though I should die with thee, yet will I not deny thee. Likewise also said all the disciples.

36 ¶ Then ᵖ cometh Jesus with them unto a place called Gethsemane, and saith unto the disciples, Sit ye here, while I go and pray yonder.

37 And he took with him Peter and the two sons of Zebedee, and began to be sorrowful and very heavy.

38 Then saith he unto them,

p Mar.14.32,&c. Lu.22.39,&c. Jno.18.1,&c.

OBSERVE. The strength of man is weakness. However positive we may be of our principles, we should never be above praying against temptation, nor above taking the warnings which Christ gives. Christians may fall into sin, but cannot fall away, for Christ, the Great Intercessor, *prays for them, that their faith fail not* (Lu.22.52).

§ 142 THE AGONY IN GETHSEMANE.—*Evening introducing the* SIXTH *day of the week. Mount of Olives.*

Matt.	Mark.	Luke.	John.
26.36–46	14.32–42	22.40–46	

36. *Then cometh Jesus.* John has it, "when Jesus had spoken these words," viz. the discourse to them, which he had just recorded (chap. 14–17 inclusive), encouraging them in the gospel—laying down the great practical principles upon which they should stand—opening the plan of His gracious economy, and promising them the Spirit—and concluding with the intercessory prayer. That interesting and parting address to them was made probably before they left the room—"the *guest* chamber"—which is quite consistent with the general terms of vs. 30, where it is meant that they sung a hymn (according to the custom) and *afterward* went out to Olivet. They went out probably before midnight. John mentions that Christ's parting words were spoken before they crossed the brook Cedron. This brook ran just under the city wall on the east, before rising the slope of Olivet, where Gethsemane was. (See plate of Modern Jerusalem.) John further mentions (18. 2), that "Judas knew the place—for Jesus ofttimes resorted thither with His disciples." It was not for concealment, but according to His known custom. His obedience unto death was purely *voluntary*. The place was hallowed, doubtless, to that band, for meditation, converse and prayer.—— ¶ *Gethsemane.* Matthew and Mark read, "*a place.*" The term means "*a place of oil presses,*" from two Hebrew words. John has it, "*a garden;*" gardens were not allowed in the holy city. A cluster of eight old olives is still found on this consecrated ground of Christ's prayers and agonies.—— ¶ *The disciples.* He directed them to remain where they had entered, while He went on farther to pray alone. Luke says that He charged them to pray against entering into temptation, and "was withdrawn from them about a stone's cast." Matthew gives only the general narrative (22. 41), but speaks of His singling out three disciples and going on, and then withdrawing a short distance from *these*, to pray.—— ¶ *Sit ye here.* This same direction Abraham addressed to his servants when he went to sacrifice Isaac (Gen. 22. 5).

37. *Peter and the two sons of Zebedee*, viz. James and John (Matt. 10. 2). These three our Lord had taken with Him before on rare occasions. We know not why, unless it was to prepare them, by special experience, for special duties and sufferings, such as fell to their lot. They were chosen to accompany Him at the cure of the ruler's daughter (Luke 8. 51), and at the transfiguration. (Matt. 17 1.) —— ¶ *Began to be sorrowful.* He entered now into the special griefs of

My *q* soul is exceeding sorrowful, even unto death: tarry ye here, and watch with me.

39 And he went a little farther, and fell on his face, and *r* prayed,

q Ps.116.3. Is.53.3,10. Jno.12.27. *r* He.5.7.

saying, O my Father, if it be possible, let this cup *s* pass from me! nevertheless, *t* not as I will, but as thou *wilt*.

40 And he cometh unto the

s c.20.22. *t* Jno.5.30; 6.38. Ro.15.3. Ph.2.8.

His approaching death, and it was as though they had just begun, though He had been a "man of sorrows." The context shows that He suffered now and was "*very heavy*"—oppressed and burdened. He had no sins of His own to make Him sorrowful, but He had assumed the responsibilities of sinners. He had undertaken to be "*made a curse for us.*" Mark says, "He began to be sore amazed and to be very heavy." He bore the curse of sin—the weight of His people's condemnation lay upon Him.

38. *My soul is exceeding sorrowful,* &c. Here He broke out in an expression of His inward agony. As yet all was quiet in the garden—no one had bruised Him—the mere dread of dying could not so have distressed Him, for martyrs have triumphed at the stake—but he was pouring out His soul unto death. (Isa. 53. last vs.) He stood already in the sinner's place, and hence, His *exceeding sorrow* of spirit, "*even unto death*"—reaching the measure of *death sufferings* before physical death came on. Observe, it was *soul-sorrow unto death!*—¶ *Watch with me.* This means substantially the same as Luke's language, "Pray that ye enter not into temptation" (22. 40); yet, including, besides this vigilance and prayer for themselves, the idea of sympathizing with Him. He called for their liveliest interest. He was brought to that point of shrinking where He called in their help. It was near midnight.

39. *A little further*—that is, beyond them—removing from the three disciples so as to be quite alone in His grief. Luke's words, "about a stone's cast," refer to this.——¶ *Fell on his face.* Luke says, He "kneeled down and prayed." But Matthew mentions this more distressed and prostrate attitude which His prayer took, expressive of a most overwhelming wo. All these attitudes of earnestness and anguish He took. This was the natural gesture of his emotion——¶ *If it be possible.* Luke has it, "If thou be willing." Mark refers it also to the Father's pleasure, and speaks of all things being possible with God. Here is the conflict and agony in the Redeemer's breast, showing the extremity to which he was brought, even to the point of shrinking! Here is His FILIAL spirit under the heaviest suffering. Here it is proved *how necessary* it was that Christ should *take this cup,* and not only that *He* should die, and none other, but that He should take THIS CUP, and not another cup— even *this cup of the curse!* It was not possible that He should be released from *this*—for in this there was substitution and expiation. "He hath borne our griefs," &c.——¶ *Cup,* or chalice. As a cup contains something to drink, it is used to express a draught of bitter experience.— ¶ *Nevertheless.* This he refers at last to the Father's appointment, and thus He defers to the Father's pleasure. It was not more important that Christ should be *voluntary* in His sacrificial work, than that in Him the Father should be "*well pleased*" (Isa. 42. 21). This was expressed at His baptism. "This is my beloved Son in whom I am well pleased." "It pleased the Lord to bruise Him. He hath put him to grief." (Isa. 53. 10.) "Thou shalt make His soul an offering for sin" "The Lord hath laid on Him the iniquities of us all." (Isa. 53. 10.) "A body hast thou prepared me," he says; and now, in the sacrifice, the flesh that was taken in order to die, scarcely survives this agony; and the hu

disciples, and findeth them asleep, and saith unto Peter, What! could ye not watch with me one hour?

41 Watch, ᵘ and pray, that ye ᵛ enter not into temptation; ʷ the spirit ˣ indeed *is* willing, but the flesh *is* weak.

42 He went away again the second time, and prayed, saying, O my Father, if this cup may not pass away from me, ex-

u Mar.13.33; 14.39. Lu.22.40. Ep.6.18. Re.16.15.
v Pr.4.14,15. *w* Re.3.10.

x Is.26.8,9. Ro.7.18-25. Ga.5.17.

man soul shudders and shrinks at the endurance. This "*Nevertheless*" hints at the covenant which Christ had entered into with the Father, which bound Him to its terms. Though the curse was awful, yet the will of the Father was supreme. Though Christ shrunk, yet He was voluntary, in consideration of that covenant engagement.

40. *Asleep.* Luke has it, He "found them sleeping for sorrow." (ch. 22. 45.) This refers to the three whom He had taken apart. No other Evangelist mentions the cause of their drowsiness. But Luke was a physician (Col. 4. 14), and he was prepared to speak on this point, and he would be likely so to do. So he notices the bloody sweat (22. 44), and the cure of Malchus' ear (22. 51). Persons condemned to die are often waked from sound sleep by the executioner. Excessive sorrow *brings on* sleep. This is hinted at by our Lord in the next verse.──¶ *Saith unto Peter.* Peter had *boasted*, but now he was to see and feel his weakness. How feeble are our best resolutions or dispositions towards God. How easily are we overcome by the world, the flesh and the devil. What could we do but for upholding, and strengthening, and reclaiming grace.

41. *Watch and pray, that ye enter not;* or, in Mark, "*lest ye enter into* temptation. They were in danger of losing their confidence in Christ, when they should see Him betrayed into the hands of sinners. And here they are directed to watch against this temptation, which He saw to be coming on. A concern for their own souls in this coming trial, should keep them watching against Satan's power in their hearts. We should always watch, knowing that the adversary is always ready to ensnare and destroy us. They were to pray against being overcome, and lest they should be overcome by that temptation. So we are to pray that we may not run into temptation, nor come in the way of it—especially that we may not yield to it. And *if we do not pray*, the tempter will gain the advantage.──¶ *The spirit indeed is willing* (προθυμον). Mark has the same Greek word, but it is there rendered "*ready*." They were in danger from the infirmities of the flesh. These are a fruitful source of temptation. Satan attacks us through the flesh, and takes advantage of our weaknesses. Therefore we are the more earnestly to pray for all needed supports and helps in the trying hour. We should take this passage (says Bengel), not to excuse our torpor, but to sharpen our vigilance (see Heb. 5. 7).

42. *He went away again.* The tenor of His prayer seems altered now, and it is rather a devout submission. He returns now to give in His *free and full consent* to the endurance. The sufferings are here shown to have been well understood beforehand. This was most important. This is distinctly declared by John (18. 4), "Jesus knowing all things that should come upon him." Yet, "*drinking the cup*," that is, taking all the load of our condemnation, and going through the bitter experience, was full of agony, from which the flesh could not but shrink. Luke notes that an angel from heaven here appeared and strengthened Him (vs. 43), and that "His sweat was, as it were, great drops of blood falling down to the ground," (vs. 44,) occasioned, as in other instances on record, by the extreme suffering. Yet he

cept I drink it, thy will be done.

43 And he came and found them asleep again: for their eyes were heavy.

44 And he left them, and went away again, and prayed the third ʸ time, saying the same words.

45 Then cometh he to his disciples, and saith unto them, Sleep on, now, and take *your*

y 2Cor.12.8.

rest: behold, the hour is at hand, and the Son of man is betrayed into the hands of sinners.

46 Rise, let us be going: behold, he is at hand that doth betray me.

47 ¶ And while he yet spake, lo, ᶻ Judas, one of the twelve, came, and with him a great mul-

z Ac.1.16.

---

does not say *blood*, but "*as it were*" *blood—bloody—*or large as drops of blood. And this was from anguish of soul—from burdens laid upon His spirit. Already He lay under the tremendous weight of the curse, and stood charged with the iniquities of such as He had undertaken for in covenant with the Father. Yet, in the midst of it all, He declares His willingness to *drink the cup*, because this was His part in the eternal covenant of redemption, and by this means Jesus was to "save His people from their sins."

43. *Asleep again.* Mark adds, "neither wist they what to answer Him" (ch. 14. 40). They were in the extremest heaviness, completely overpowered, and *not fully awaked* by our Lord's address to them. So at the transfiguration, Peter and they that were with him (the same company of disciples, Peter, James and John) were heavy with sleep, and probably from the overpowering excitement (Luke 9. 32). How poorly able are our weak natures to enter into Christ's sufferings, or His glory.

44. *The same words* (vs. 42). This wrestling was continued, and the utmost earnestness was shown. Repeated praying is a different thing from vain repetition in prayer. From His earnestness we learn not to be discouraged or to grow weary, for '*He was heard, in that He feared*" (Heb. 5. 7). He was enabled to say, "not my will, but thine be done." We are heard as much by being enabled to endure, as by having the affliction spared us. Paul was heard, not by having the thorn removed, but by

having the promise come to Him in all its consoling power—"My grace is sufficient for thee" (2 Cor. 12. 9).

45. *Sleep on now.* In perfect consistency with the foregoing narrative, He comes up to them at last, declaring that He has no longer that special need for their *watching with Him* there as at first—that He had come to the point of peace and triumph, where He had sweetly put all fears to rest, and now He could dispense with their watchings with Him, for He felt not alone as before. Besides, their watching could do Him no good any longer. For scarcely has He uttered these words, when He sees the traitor approach, and, as in the same breath, He cries out, "Rise, let us be going." Here would come in Mark's additional language, "It is enough." Luke's, "Why sleep ye?" (22. 46.) would seem to have been at His *first* rising from prayer, corresponding with Matt. 26. 40.

OBSERVE, (1.) How sluggish and unworthy are the best, the favourite three among the twelve. (2.) How insupportable is the curse of sin. (3.) Christ's sufferings are seen to be vicarious—in the stead of others—and the grace free without any desert of others—all according to a *particular plan*, and an eternal covenant with the Father.

§ 143. JESUS BETRAYED AND MADE PRISONER.—*Mt. of Olives. Evening introducing the* SIXTH *day of the week.*

Matt.	Mark.	Luke.	John.
26.47-56	14.43-52	22.47-53	18.2-12

47. *While He yet spake.* The dis-

[A. D. 33.] CHAPTER XXVI. 277

titude, with swords and staves, from the chief priests and elders of the people.

48 Now he that betrayed him gave them a sign, ª saying, Whomsoever I shall kiss, that same is he: hold him fast.

49 And forthwith he came to Jesus, and said, Hail, Master; and kissed ᵇ him.

50 And Jesus said unto him, ᶜ Friend, wherefore art thou come? Then came they and laid hands on Jesus, and took him.

51 And, behold, one of them which were with Jesus stretched out *his* hand, and drew his sword, and struck a servant of the high priest, and smote off his ear.

52 Then said Jesus unto him, Put up again thy sword into his place: for ᵈ all they that take the sword shall perish with the sword.

a Ps.38.12. *b* 2Sa.3.27; 20.9. Ps.28.3. *c* Ps.41. 9; 55.13.

d Ge.9.6. Eze.35.5,6. Re.13.16.

ciples must have marked this striking prediction of Christ and His full foresight of the events. This would naturally strengthen their confidence. Since Judas went out from the supper, He had been bargaining with the chief priests and completing the arrangements for Christ's delivery into their hands.——¶ *With him a great multitude.* John says, "a band and officers from the chief priests and Pharisees." Some have supposed that Judas was entrusted with the command of a cohort stationed in the castle of Antonia, or with the guard which attended near the temple at the time of the great feasts. These were likely Roman soldiers and Jewish guards, carrying "swords and clubs" (translation 1582). The Wicklif translation, 1580, has it 'swordis and battis." Besides these, they had " *lanterns and torches.*" See John 18. 3. Guilty consciences led them to make large preparations, and to take a strong force.

48. *A sign.* That there might be no mistake or failure in seizing Christ, he gave them a mark by which they might know which was HE; he was *to kiss* the person, and on his kissing Him, they were to seize Him. The *kiss* was a customary mode of friendly salutation among the Jews and early Christians. See Luke 7. 45. Hence the "holy kiss" of Paul. 1 Cor. 16. 20. Rom. 16. 16. This custom still prevails in the Eastern church. What foul hypocrisy. A kiss, the signal to hold Him fast, or as Mark has it, to "take Him and lead Him away safely," or cautiously.

49. *Hail, Master.* This was part of the salutation — "Hail, Rabbi." Health to thee!

50. *Friend*—as we say, "my friend." This is the substance of the conversation which John more particularly details (18. 4-9)—Christ's question, whom seek ye? and their reply—the overpowering effect of His answer, "I am He," &c.—all as preliminary to their seizing Him. Luke has it, "Judas, betrayest thou the Son of man with a kiss?" The term here, is meant as the language of recognition—that Christ *knew* Him well, and knew his object—and that the traitor could not deceive Him by his hypocrisy. Judas was not alone—but Christ accosted *him* personally—and to his amazement.

51. *One of them.* This was *Peter*, as John informs us (John 18. 10).— ¶ *A servant.* His name was Malchus. The gracious Saviour healed the wound immediately. (Luke. See Fig. ch. 18. 20.)

52. *Put up again,* &c. This was a rebuke to Peter. The sheath was the place for the sword. Such a deed was even a reflection upon the nature of His kingdom. See John 18. 36. "My kingdom is not of this world, else would my servants fight." Christ needed no such defences, and *they that take the*

24

278 MATTHEW. [A. D. 33.

53 Thinkest thou that I cannot now pray to my Father, and he shall presently give me more than twelve legions of ᵉ angels.

54 But how then shall the scriptures be fulfilled, that ᶠ thus it must be?

55 In that same hour said Jesus to the multitudes, Are ye come out, as against a thief, with swords and staves for to take me? I sat daily with you teaching in the temple, and ye laid no hold on me.

56 But all this was done, that the scriptures ᵍ of the prophets

e 2K.6.17. Da.7.10. c.4.11. *f* Lu.24.26,46.
g Ge.3.15. Ps.22.69. Is.53. La.4.20. Da.9.24,26. Zec.13.7. Ac.1.16.

sword render themselves liable to the same weapons, and the aggressors in such violence will be the sufferers. Compare Gen. 9. 6, "Whoso sheddeth man's blood, by man shall his blood be shed—for in the image of God made He man." Here again Christ shows His willingness to suffer—and the covenant grounds of it all—and John has it here, "The cup which my Father hath given me, shall I not drink it?" (John 18. 11.)

53. *Thinkest thou.* Such a resort betrayed an unworthy trust, and a poor understanding of His higher dependence. It was like getting bread out of stones, instead of living by every word that proceedeth out of the mouth of God (Matt. 4. 3). It was not for want of helpers that He gave Himself up to Judas. But "for this cause He came unto this hour."—— ¶ *My Father.* Here is still the filial temper and confidence. It was not a conflict between the Father and the Son.—— ¶ *Twelve legions.* A legion was a body of the Roman army, varying from about 4,000 to over 6,000 men. It is taken for an indefinitely large body, as in Luke 8. 30, where the demoniac gave his name as "*Legion*, because *many* devils were entered into him." The number *twelve* is to the same effect. The *hint* is, that He could have a legion of angels in the place of each disciple for a body guard—and that He did not choose the twelve for such a purpose as a defence with *swords.*

54. *But how then.* Here the whole subject is explained. The Saviour plainly had *undertaken* to die (Bengel). His death was not a common death or any casual event. It had been predicted in the Scriptures, and an eternal covenant now demanded it as the great prescribed condition of man's redemption. OUGHT not Christ to have suffered these things (i. e. was it *not necessary*). (Luke 24. 26. 27.) He labours to show throughout that His death in all these cruel circumstances, was both predetermined and voluntary. For the prophecies, see Psalms 17. 22. 69. Isa. 53. Dan. 9. 24, &c.

55. *Are ye come out,* &c. The three Evangelists have these same words, and they, doubtless, were spoken in a way to leave the strongest impression. This brings out the secret of such preparations for His seizure. It was rendered necessary only in their troubled conscience and disturbed imagination. "The wicked flee when no man pursueth."—— ¶ *As against a thief*—or rather robber. Here again He declares a voluntary surrender, and the *ground* of it, in the predictions which must be fulfilled. What a tremendous word to them was this, that it was not at all their strong force, but rather the hand of God, even in His arrest. What a thought to the apostate, infamous traitor, that he was fulfilling the Scripture, and that a sovereign God was higher than he—so that even in this, he could not contravene the Divine purpose, nor escape the judgment of God. Here, also, Christ vindicates His peaceable course, and His open, public manner among them. Why all this arming as against a thief, except in their own wicked thoughts? Judas might have feared His power, from the impressions he had of His

A. D. 33.]   CHAPTER XXVI.   279

might be fulfilled. Then all the disciples forsook him, and fled.

57 ¶ And ʰ they that had laid hold on Jesus led *him* away to Caiaphas the high priest,

h Mat.14.53.&c. Lu.22.54,&c. Jno.18.12.&c.

where the scribes and the elders were assembled.

58 But Peter followed him afar off, unto the high priest's palace, and went in, and sat with the servants, to see the end.

---

wondrous works. Had he not seen His omnipotence?

56. *But all this was done.* Here again occurs this phraseology of the Evangelists, and especially of Matthew, who refers the Jews constantly to their own prophecies. There was a *purpose* in all this that the scriptures should be fulfilled. Gen. 3. 15. Ps. 22. 69. Isa. 53. Dan. 4. 24, 26. Zech. 13. 7. Luke expresses it, "This is your hour, and the power of darkness." (22. 53.)——¶ *Forsook Him.* Then—at this juncture—when He was actually seized, their alarm overpowered them. Natural sense was overcome, and faith failed. The effect was the same with *all of them,* and even this fulfilled His prediction, (26. 31,) and see Zech. 13. 7. Here an incident is related of a young man who followed Him, and was seized by the guard, but escaped. (Mark 14. 51.) Christ should *not be utterly without a follower,* even in that extremity. No suffering was ever so awful as Christ's, even in the garden. We can only judge what it must have been beyond all our thought, by knowing what it was *for*—the curse FOR SIN. "*He was made sin for us*"—i. e., He stood in the sinner's place. Those who continue to sin, after all that has been done for them, He will visit with heaviest retribution; and at the judgment He will utterly reject those who here reject Him. OBSERVE, Christ gave Himself up to death voluntarily. He was delivered up by the determinate counsel and foreknowledge of God; yet, *by wicked hands He was crucified and slain* (Acts 2. 23).

	Matt.	Mark.	Luke.	John
§ 144. JESUS BEFORE CAIAPHAS. PETER THRICE DENIES HIM. — NIGHT *introducing the* SIXTH *day of the week.*	26. 57,58 69-75	14. 53,54 66-72	22.54-62	18.13-18 25-27
§ 145. JESUS BEFORE CAIAPHAS AND THE SANHEDRIM—IS THE CHRIST— IS CONDEMNED AND MOCKED.— *Morning of* SIXTH *day—Jeru'lem.*	26.59-68	14.55-65	22.63-71	18.19-24

57. *Led Him away.* Our Lord was in the garden, seized now by Judas' band. The mob gave no reason for seizing Him.——¶ *Caiaphas.* John states that they led Him to *Annas* first. This was out of compliment, for he had been high priest, and those who had held the office retained some of their authority, sat in council, &c. He may have been President of the Sanhedrim at this time. The house of Annas was also a stopping place, until the Sanhedrim should be assembled at the high priest's house. The business of the high priest was to sit in judgment with the Sanhedrim (the scribes and elders), and to exercise judicial authority. Deut. 17. 8, 9. Though the higher jurisdiction was now taken from the Jews, yet the *form* remained, and it was preliminary to a presentment before the Roman governor. Annas sent Him bound to Caiaphas. (18. 24.)

58. *Peter.* His conduct is here noted, since he had so boldly and boastfully pledged himself for the worst. He followed Christ—for he really loved Him, and was anxious for the result; but his fears had overcome him, and *sight* was before *faith,* so that he followed "*afar off.*" Christ has followers, but, oh! their usual *distance* from Him—their shameful

280   MATTHEW.   [A. D. 33.

59 Now the chief priests and elders, and all the council, sought false witness against Jesus, to put him to death;

60 But found none: yea, though many false witnesses came, *yet* found they none. At the ⁱ last came two false witnesses,

i Is. 27. 12; 35. 11.

distance—afraid of sacrifices for Him, even when He goes to sacrifice Himself for them—afraid of taking any burdens of His blessed cause, when He bore the burden of THEIR SINS! How little do they know that their happiness and safety lie in keeping near to Him.——¶ *Palace* (αυλη). This is rather the open square of the dwelling—the court which Eastern houses had in the centre (see Fig. ch 9). John here notes the fact, that another disciple (which was he himself) also followed Christ, and *went in with Jesus* into the high priest's house. But Peter stood at the door without. Matthew states that the maid in the porch recognized Peter. But John shows us how this occurred. Peter had been noticed, doubtless, standing outside—and then John (who was known at the high priest's house) went out and spoke to the maid and brought in Peter. This undesigned coincidence is an incidental proof of the veracity of the Evangelists.—*Blunt.*

59. Though Matthew and Mark record Peter's denials, *after* Christ's condemnation, yet they occurred, doubtless, *while the* council was sitting in judgment. Luke mentions the denial first, and so does John.——¶ *False witness.* The Sanhedrim sought testimony that could be urged against Him, not in the way of sheer fabrication, for such stood ready, but would not be admitted. They sought to have the show of right, though they had prejudged the case, and had resolved on putting Him to death. But the false witnesses did not agree in their testimony (Mark 14. 56). It is very difficult for two or three (which the law required) to agree in all particulars where the whole is false. Hence we see the strong proof of truth we have in the harmony of the four Evangelists.

60. *Two false witnesses.* The law required two witnesses to convict a man (Deut. 19. 15).

61. *I am able to destroy.* Here was something which they could take hold of. He had spoken of His death and resurrection, and had said that the temple of His body which they should destroy, He would raise again in three days. This language they perverted to a declaration that He would destroy their temple, "*the temple of God,*" &c. (Mark 14. 58). "*But neither so did their witness agree together*" (Mark 14. 59). Therefore *this* FIRST PLAN FAILED. This could have been proved a capital crime, if it had so been said, since it amounted to the claim of the power of working miracles.

62. *The high priest arose.*

¶ *Answerest thou nothing?* Here sundry conversations passed, as related

61 And said, This *fellow* said, I am able to destroy the temple of God, and to build it in three days.

62 And the high priest arose, and said unto him, Answerest thou nothing? What *is it which* these witness against thee?

63 But [k] Jesus held his peace. And the high priest answered and said unto him, I adjure [l] thee by the living God, that thou tell us whether thou be the Christ, [m] the Son of God.

64 Jesus saith unto him, Thou hast said: nevertheless I say unto you, Hereafter [n] shall ye see the Son of man sitting on the right hand [o] of power, and coming in the clouds of heaven.

65 Then the high priest rent his clothes, saying, He hath

j Jno.2.19-21. *k* Is.53.7. c.27.12,14. *l* 1Sa.14.26, 23. 1Ki.22.16. *m* c.1.6.16. Jno.1.34. *n* Da.7.13. Jno.1.51. 1Th. 4.16. Re.1.7. *o* Ps.110.1. Ac.7.55.

---

some by one, and some by another Evangelist. The high priest wished to draw from Him something which should give ground of procedure—as thus far nothing was shown—accordingly He pressed Him most solemnly on the great point of His alleged Divinity. Satan and the Sanhedrim both battled Him on this point, "IF THOU BE THE SON OF GOD" (ch. 4. 3, 6). *Buxtorf*, in his Talmudic Lexicon, cites a Rabbinical testimony, which admits the subornation of false witnesses against Christ, and which vindicates it by law, on the ground of His introducing *a new worship* (that is, *of Himself as Divine*), which they counted *idolatry*. See Hales' *Analysis of Chronology*, vol. 3. p. 209.

63. *He held His peace.* He made no reply, because the witnesses disagreed, and the whole matter was contradictory. The law required the concurrent testimony of two or three examined *apart.* See Numb. 35. 30. Deut. 17. 6. And He was not intent on a self-vindication against their malice.——¶ *I adjure thee*—that is, I demand of thee, upon thine oath—*by the living God.* This was the usual form of administering an oath, and when the accused was thus sworn, it was called the *oath of adjuration.* See Numb. 5. 19, 21. Josh. 7. 19.—— ¶ *Whether thou be the Christ*—that is, the Messiah—"*the Son of God*"—whom the Jews expected (Mark reads "the Son of the Blessed"). The Jews had stoned Him for this claim, and they understood it to mean an assertion of divinity and equality with the Father, as they declared at the time (John 10. 31). Now, if He would confess to such a claim, they would charge Him with *blasphemy* (Levit. 24. 16). If He would deny it, they could charge Him with deceiving the people. Comp. Luke 22. 67, 68.

64. *Thou hast said.* This is the same as to say—Yes, *it is so.* Caiaphas indeed had prophesied of a vicarious death for the people. "It is expedient for us that one man should die for the people." John 11. 50.—— ¶ *Nevertheless.* Though you disbelieve it, yet *you shall see!* Wicked men have no idea of Christ as the Judge, or of their dismay at His final coming. He here boldly declared how that tribunal of the Almighty should confound all their judgments, and how He, though now under arrest, and bound, should be seen on the right hand of power, enthroned in majesty and might.——¶ *Coming in the clouds.* According to His predictions (Matt. 24. 30), referring primarily to His coming for their destruction, as a city and nation, and also threatening the great final judgment.

65. *Rent his clothes.* This was a customary expression of amazement or grief, though it was a mere form, as the rent was usually *in the seam.* The question now arises upon the justice of the trial and sentence according to the Jewish law. It is plain that they understood the title, *Son*

spoken blasphemy; what further need have we of witnesses? behold, now ye have heard his blasphemy.

66 What think ye? They answered and said, He is guilty of death.p

67 Then q did they spit in his

p Le.24,16. Jno.19.7.   q Is.50.6.

God (vs. 63), as implying divinity, for so alone could it be blasphemy and worthy of death. Blasphemy was a capital crime, regarded by the Jews with peculiar horror. And if Christ had been a mere man, this claim *would have been blasphemy*, and the death-sentence would have been lawful (see John 10. 31–33). They who deny Christ's true and proper divinity make Him out a blasphemer, and join the Jew in His condemnation and death. The law of blasphemy, as it existed among the Jews, extended not only to the offence of impiously using the name of the Supreme Being, but to every usurpation of His authority, or arrogation by a created being of the honour and power belonging to Him alone. The crime was held in such horror that whoever heard it, was obliged to rend his garments; but not the high priest, except in very special cases. So the high priest's act was an open and exciting testimony to the multitude, of His being found guilty. BUT IT WAS NOT BLASPHEMY IN CHRIST, BECAUSE HE WAS GOD.

66. *He is guilty of death.* The usual form of giving sentence—i. e., He has incurred the penalty of death. (Levit. 24. 11–16.) The high priest, as presiding over the Council or Sanhedrim, called for their verdict. They gave it unanimously, *guilty!* The judgment was now passed in their own supreme court. The next step was to present the case to the Roman government, in whose hands was the power of capital punishment. The sceptre had departed from Judah, since the Shiloh had come. The Jewish prejudice was most bitterly roused against Him, on the most religious point—and now they had only to bring the matter before the Roman authority, for their consent to His death. "Pilate was now Vice-President of Judea with capital jurisdiction." (Greenleaf.) Thus far, however, the charge and condemnation was purely on Jewish grounds, in which a Roman could not be expected to sympathize. The God of the Jews, against whom the offence had been committed (as alleged), was neither respected nor recognized by the Romans. This will account for the new form under which the accusation is now made. They shifted the charges, and came before Pilate with a new specification, founded on Roman law, and from that moment, no farther allusion was made to the charge of blasphemy. (See ch. 27. 11.) "It was now a charge of high treason against the Roman State and Emperor, which was wholly within Pilate's cognizance, and which no officer of Tiberius would venture lightly to regard." This led to Pilate's arraignment of Christ. It should be remarked that trials were usually held in the morning, (Jer. 21. 12,) and by the later Jews it was held unlawful to try a capital cause in the night—or to issue a cause of this nature on the same day. This last point was entirely disregarded in the case of our Lord. Before noon He was crucified. To see the *haste* in this transaction, consider that the supper was on Thursday evening—at midnight He was arrested and led before the high priest and Sanhedrim—at *six* o'clock on Friday morning He was brought before Pilate—was crucified at *nine* o'clock—darkness reigned from *twelve* to *three*—and He was buried the same evening!

67. *Spit in His face.* This was a mark of the most utter contempt and abhorrence. See Numb. 12. 14. Deut. 25. 9. By this time the utmost bitterness of the people had been stirred up against Christ.——¶ *Buffeted* cuffed Him with the fist—Mark adds

face, and buffeted him, and others smote *him* with [1] the palms of their hands

68 Saying, Prophesy unto us, thou Christ, who is he that smote thee?

[1] Or, *rods*.

69 ¶ Now *r* Peter sat without in the palace: and a damsel came unto him, saying, Thou also wast with Jesus of Galilee.

70 But he denied before *them*

r Mar. 14. 66, &c. Lu. 22. 55, &c. Jno. 18. 16, &c.

"*and began to cover His face.*" Luke says, "*blindfolded Him.*" And though Matthew does not mention these things, he says they challenged Him to *prophesy who smote Him*—which intimates that He was *first* blindfolded. This shows how the Evangelists undesignedly coincide in their statements, and thus prove their honest truth.——¶ *Smote Him with the palms of their hands (errapisan,* Gr.)—rapped or slapped Him. This was expressly predicted. (Isa 50. 6; 53. 3, 7.)

68. This was a taunting challenge of His divinity—"*Thou Christ.*" He would not confound them now, as He had it in His power to do. (See John 18. 19–23.) No such impious tests of His claims would He gratify. Luke adds, "Many other things blasphemously spake they against Him." *They were the blasphemers, and not He.*

69. The narrative now connects properly with verse 58. Our Lord was most shamefully treated—and He had prophesied at the supper that during that night, "before the cock crow," Peter should deny Him thrice (Matt. 26. 34). Mark and Luke have it, "*before the cock crow twice.*" The Jews in the time of our Lord divided the night into four periods, *even, midnight, cock-crowing, and morning.* But often it was reckoned from midnight to day-break, by three crowings of the cock—and of this period our Lord spake. Peter indeed believed it not, and all the disciples protested their steadfast adherence unto death. ——¶ *Peter sat without.* Mark has it, *beneath.* This was in the hall or open court of Caiaphas' house. An oriental house is usually built around a quadrangular interior court, into which there is a passage, sometimes arched through the front part of the house, closed next the street by a heavy folding gate, with a smaller wicket for single persons, kept by a porter, usually male, sometimes female. (See Acts 12. 13.) In the text the interior court, often paved or flagged and open to the sky, is the αυλη where the attendants made a fire, and the passage beneath the front of the house from the street to this court is the προαυλιον or πυλων (porch). The place where Jesus stood before the high priest may have been an open room or place of audience on the ground-floor in the rear or on one side of the court—such rooms, open in front, being customary. (See Fig. ch. 9. vs. 2.) It was close upon the court, for Jesus heard all that was going on around the fire, and turned and looked upon Peter. Luke 22. 61. Peter's *first* denial took place in the middle of the court, on his being questioned by the female porter. Peter then, according to Matthew and Mark, retreats into the passage leading into the street (or porch), where he is again questioned, and makes his *second* denial. Luke and John do not specify the place. As to the person who now questioned him, Mark says the maid saw him again and began to question him (vs. 69). Matthew has it another maid (vs. 71). Luke writes another person or man (vs. 58), while John uses the indefinite form, "they said," which gives us a key to the fact that Peter was here at length questioned and charged by *several.* The *third* denial took place an hour after, probably near the fire, or at least within the court, where our Lord and Peter could see each other (Luke 22. 61). Though the denials are narrated together, it is to be remembered that during the intervals between them, and all along,

all, saying, I know not what thou sayest.

71 And when he was gone out into the porch, another *maid* saw him, and said unto them that were there, This *fellow* was also with Jesus of Nazareth.

72 And again he denied with an oath, I do not know the man.

73 And after a while came unto *him* they that stood by, and said to Peter, Surely thou also art *one* of them; for thy speech bewrayeth thee.

74 Then began he to curse and to swear, *saying*, I know not the man. And immediately the cock crew.

75 And Peter remembered the *ᵃ* word of Jesus, which said unto him, Before the cock crow, thou shalt deny me thrice. And

ᵃ ver.34. Lu.22.31-34.

---

the examination of Christ was going on before the high priest, the progress of which is given in § 145.—Robinson's Harmony, Notes.——¶ *Jesus of Galilee.* This was a title of reproach, as *Jesus of Nazareth*, which Mark reads.

70. *But he denied*, &c.—as though he was perfectly ignorant even of what was meant by the charge. " I know not what thou sayest." This was the grossest, most unblushing falsehood. Mark now testifies that he went out into the porch, and *the cock crew.* (14. 68.)

71. *Into the porch.* After this first denial, Peter withdrew into the porch or vestibule of the *front entrance.* It was now about the time of the first cock-crowing, or about midnight. He was at once met by another, who repeated the charge. It would seem to have been confirmed by others, who insisted on its truth (Luke 22. 58. John 18. 25). Amidst these charges he came up again toward the fire, embarrassed and confused.

72. *Again he denied, with an oath*— more emphatically, and even profanely. This second denial followed soon upon the first—" after a little while." Luke 22. 58.

73. *After a while*—" about the space of an hour after." (Luke 22. 59.) He had now denied twice. Peter was now in or near the court-room. He had drawn nearer within sight of Christ, (Luke 22. 61,) and now " another confidently affirmed " (Luke 22. 59), and they that stood by pressed it on him that they knew him from his speech. His language was Galilean.——¶ *One of them* (of the company).——¶ *Bewrayeth thee.*" (Mark, " *agreeth thereto.*") This enraged him, as it sealed his conviction.

74. Now he denied more vehemently—" *began to curse and to swear.*" This was about the second cock-crowing, or about 3 o'clock. ——¶ *And immediately the cock crew.* This made good to the letter the prediction of our Lord. Mark says, " and the second time the cock crew." Peter was now within sight of Christ. " The Lord turned and looked upon Peter." Luke 22. 61.

75. *Peter remembered.* " When he thought thereon he wept." Mark 14. 72. " The Lord turned and looked upon Peter." Luke 22. 61. " To the voice of the cock was added the look of Christ."—*Calvin.* This last was requisite. That personal notice and direct attention of Christ, causing us to remember his word (Luke 22. 61), gives the word pungency to us. The truth as it is in Jesus, is flashed upon the mind, by seeing the Saviour face to face. Peter went bitterly because he remembered Christ's love, Christ's warnings, and that tender assurance, " Simon, Satan hath desired to have thee that he might sift thee as wheat, but I have prayed for thee that thy faith fail not." Luke 22. 32. No one can keep himself from sin without the help of God. Behold this forward, zealous apostle *thrice* denies in so brief a period, and would have gone on to deny with viler oaths, if others had arisen to the accusation.

[A. D. 33.] CHAPTER XXVII. 285

he went out, and wept bitterly.

CHAPTER XXVII.

WHEN the morning was come, all the chief priests and elders of the people took counsel ᵃ against Jesus to put him to death.

2 And when they had bound him, they led *him* away, and delivered him ᵇ to Pontius Pilate the governor.

a Ps.2.2. *b* c.20.19.

Christ restrained the tongues of enemies, else Peter's denials had been thirty rather than three. Peter thought he could walk alone on the sea of Galilee, or go upon his own strength in the midst of temptations. But here he was taught his weakness, as there he was taught his need of Divine help. Being left of God, he cries, "Lord save, I perish." This teaches us the danger of presumption and self-confidence, and the danger especially of carnal influence. In the midst of Christ's foes, Peter thought of their power and number, and his heart failed. We should not forget the word of Christ, nor should we lose sight of the Master. Alas! for those who follow Him afar off. When shall a look from Him melt and reclaim His backsliding followers? Peter's tears did not merit salvation, but they were drawn from him by the covenant look of Christ. Repentance flows from Christ's looking at us in a way to remind us of our sins and of His word, and from our looking at Him in a way to catch this subduing glance of His. Peter after this followed out the charge of Christ—"When thou art converted, strengthen thy brethren." We never read of his being any more afraid to be known as a Christian. He was the bold and intrepid champion of the infant cause after the Master was removed; and the two Epistles which bear his name, he wrote full of ripe instruction.

CHAPTER XXVII.

§ 146. THE SANHEDRIM LEAD JESUS AWAY TO PILATE.—SIXTH *day of the week. Jerusalem.*

Matt.	Mark.	Luke.	John.
27. 1, 2	15. 1	23. 1	18. 28

1. *When the morning was come.* At early dawn of the crucifixion day. All the procedure, up to this point, had been carried on at night. Though this was illegal, they disregarded the law. Luke (ch. 22. 66) introduces some of these events in a kind of parenthesis, as if he had said, "As soon as it was day, our Lord having acknowledged that he was the Son of God, they pronounced their sentence of His death." These events, therefore, are to be viewed in their rapid succession, from the paschal supper to the arrest of Christ, and sentence of the Sanhedrim—ALL IN A NIGHT. *Now,* they consulted how to bring the matter successfully before Pilate, for His death. The events being of such rapid occurrence and sequence, and all within so short a time, the Evangelists cannot be expected to speak very precisely of the time. John says "*it was early,*" and "*they led Jesus from Caiaphas unto the hall of Judgment*"—that is, Pilate's. Here, again, it is noted how the religious officers plotted for the death of Christ, and how all the show and formality of trial was with *full intent* to put Him to death. They saw that a charge of blasphemy would amount to nothing before Pilate, as he had no sympathy with the Jewish law. They must therefore frame an accusation upon grounds of Roman law. Having consulted, therefore, "*they began to accuse Him, saying, We found this fellow perverting the nation and forbidding to give tribute to Cesar, saying that He himself is Christ, a king.*"

2. *When they had bound Him.* "Annas had sent Him bound unto Caiaphas." John 18. 24. But in the examination He had been partly or wholly loosed, and now was rebound, or more strongly bound, as being considered more certainly condemned.——¶ *Pontius Pilate the gov-*

3 ¶ Then Judas, which had betrayed him, when he saw that he was condemned, repented himself, and brought again the thirty pieces of silver to the chief priests and elders,

4 Saying, I have sinned, in that I have betrayed the innocent blood. *c* And they said, What *is that* to us? See thou to *that*.

5 And he cast down the pieces

c 2K.24.4.

ernor, or rather, the *procurator*. He was a Roman officer, and not Jewish. And as he had jurisdiction in cases of capital crime, and the Jews had no power to put any man to death, they must needs bring the case to his bar.

Tacitus, the Roman historian, gives an account of Christ's being condemned and executed in the reign of Tiberius Cesar, Pontius Pilate being procurator.

	Matt.	Mark.	Luke.	John.
§ 147. Jesus before Herod. . . . . *Jerusalem*.	. . . .	. . . .	23. 6–12	
§ 148. Pilate seeks to release Jesus. The Jews demand Barabbas.	27.15–26	15. 6–15	23.13–25	18. 39,40
§ 149. Pilate delivers up Jesus to death. He is scourged and mocked. .	27.26–30	15.15–19	. . . .	19. 1–3
§ 150. Pilate again seeks to release Jesus.	. . . .	. . . .	. . . .	19. 4–16
§ 151. Judas repents and hangs himself. *Jerusalem*.	27. 3–10			

3. *When he saw that He was condemned*, viz.: that Christ was condemned. Perhaps till this time he had thought to satisfy his evil intent without the guilt of his Master's blood. This is often the effect upon a guilty conscience of seeing the contemplated deed of iniquity *done*. So the murderer often goes frantic at the sight of his victim, or at the thought of what has been perpetrated by his bloody hands. This repentance of Judas was a sorrow of the world that worketh death. He went and hanged himself. His eyes were opened to the horrible enormity the moment he saw it enacted, and Christ actually condemned. Peter's repentance flowed from the melting look of Christ, reminding him of Christ's word. Judas' sprang from the horrors of a guilty conscience, reminding him of his own deed. The latter only drove the miserable man for solace to the parties whom he had served in his sin. The former came from a sense of the injury done to Christ; it caught a sight of His gracious face, and it led to His feet.——¶ *Thirty pieces*. This was the price of betrayal—the money that he had received from the Sanhedrim for his traitorous work.

4. *I have sinned*, &c. He now confesses to them this sin. He thinks not of a sinful *heart and life*, but of a sinful *act*. He confesses, not to Christ, but to the *chief priests*.——¶ *Betrayed the innocent blood*—or been guilty of bringing this innocent being to death. The *blood* he thinks of—and that blood *innocent*. His testimony is most important. Judas had been with Christ nearly two years, as one of His constant attendants. If He had been a malefactor or impostor, he would have known it. He had now no motive to exculpate Him, but rather the contrary. Yet against himself—against his own recent act—and in a way to condemn himself before those whom he had just now served, he declares that Christ is innocent, and that the blood that should flow on Calvary, was innocent blood. The chief priests did not let Christ go, because they were bent on His death. ——¶ *What is that to us?* They cared not for Judas' remorse—nor could they cure it. His own cup of iniquity

of silver in the temple, and departed, and went and hanged ᵈ himself.

6 And the chief priests took the silver pieces, and said, It is not lawful for to put them into the treasury, because it is the price of blood.

d Ps.55.23. 2Sa.17.23. Ac.1.18.

7 And they took counsel, and bought with them the potter's field, to bury strangers in.

8 Wherefore that field was called, The field of blood, unto this day.

9 Then was fulfilled that which was spoken ᵉ by Jeremy

e Ze.11.12,13.

---

was full. They only cared to have their victim — and they would put Christ to death, though Judas were to hang himself for betraying Him. How often do wicked men sacrifice their partners in sin, and treat the agonies of the sufferers with the most utter hardness and contempt.

5. *Cast down the pieces.* Now he would throw away the infamous and bloody bribe; but that could not put away his sin, nor his suffering. Who can imagine this fire of torment in his soul? He went to the temple, with this desperate intent of hanging himself—and as if this would help to satisfy his mind, he threw the money on the temple floor.——¶ *Hanged himself.* On his way to this suicidal act, he cast away the silver. Entrapped by this bait, he cares no longer for the bait, but only for an escape! Alas, it is from himself and from his own undying thoughts, that he would seek a refuge. Eternity gives him only a prison. Luke has written, in the Acts 1. 18, that Judas "falling headlong, burst asunder in the midst, and all his bowels gushed out." This was the tragic result. In a hasty attempt to hang himself, he fell so as to be dashed in pieces like a potter's vessel (Psalm 2).

6. *Not lawful.* The chief priests, who had so wickedly plotted for Christ's death, are now very scrupulous about this point of ceremonial law. What hypocrites! They who are most rigid in mere formalities, and who find all their religion in the outward rites, can sometimes perpetrate the blackest crimes.——¶ *The treasury.* This was the chest (or chests) in the court of the women, for receiving the offerings of worshippers (see ch. 15. 5). They found a law against putting this money into the treasury of the temple. It was not allowable to offer to God what was regarded an abomination (Deut. 23, 18).——¶ *The price of blood*—that which had been the means of death.

7. *They took counsel*—that is, about what should be done with the money—as the next clause shows.——¶ *The potter's field.* A field near Jerusalem, that had been used for making earthenware. The size of it is not mentioned; but it was evidently a spot which was valuable for little else than a grave yard, and it was considered a charitable use of the money, to purchase this ground "to bury *strangers in*"—such as died at Jerusalem, not belonging there—as when they came up from all quarters to the feast. *Strangers* are provided for in death by the price of Christ's blood. They that were far off are brought nigh by the blood of Christ, even "aliens from the commonwealth of Israel, and strangers from the covenants of promise."

8. *Wherefore.* This field gets a name in Providence, that commemorates the bloody deed. That measure which the chief priests used as *a mock charity,* is made a memorial of their impiety. It was called *Aceldama,* which means this, Acts 1. 19, (see View of Mod. Jerusalem)—and it was so called at the time of Matthew's writing this history, several years after, at least.

9. *Jeremy the prophet.* Jeremiah's prophecy, as it anciently commenced that division of the Old Testament Scriptures, called *the prophets,* was

the prophet, saying, And they took the thirty pieces of silver, the price of him that was valued, ¹ whom they of the children of Israel did value;

10 And gave them for the potter's field, as the Lord appointed me.

11 ¶ And Jesus stood before

¹ Or, *whom they bought of the children of Israel.*

the governor: and the governor asked him, saying, Art thou the King of the Jews? And Jesus said unto him, Thou sayest.

12 And when he was accused of the chief priests and elders, he answered ᶠ nothing.

13 Then saith Pilate unto him, Hearest thou not how many things they witness against thee?

ᶠ c.26.63.

often a name for the whole—and under this name, quotations from the prophets were made. This will account for these words, which are found in Zechariah, being quoted as if from Jeremiah. See Zech. 11. 12, 13. Jer. 32. 6, &c. The exact language is not recited; but the application of the idea is made. The prophet found the people ungrateful. He asked of them *his price,* or the wages they were willing to allow him. They contemptuously fixed it at thirty pieces of silver, which was the *price of a slave.* He indignantly casts it to a potter. The whole transaction was most clearly intended to presignify the train of events here narrated. The prophecy or vision would seem to relate almost alone to Christ, and the Jews refer it to the Messiah. So our Lord came to an ungrateful people, who expressed their slight of Him, by naming *this as his price,* which was the value of a slave! "They of the children of Israel did value," or estimate Him at this menial rate. We see from this history of Judas how wicked counsels may be prospered, only to the ruin of the soul—how all plotting against Christ must end in destruction—how sin brings its own punishment, and is often visited on earth with speedy and signal vengeance—the money gave him no pleasure. The pain of a guilty conscience he had—that is, the bitter sense of having done wrong. Men may now deny their Lord as Peter did—by being ashamed of Him, and refusing to bear their cross, and appearing among His despisers—and

they may betray His cause as Judas did, by giving the enemy an advantage, and being the means of reproach to religion and of triumph to Christ's foes.

[§ 146¼. CHRIST BEFORE THE GOVERNOR.]

Matt.	Mark.	Luke.	John.
27. 11–14	15. 2–5	23. 2–5	18. 29–38

Christ having been seized in Gethsemane, was taken first to Annas and Caiaphas, high priests. He was afterward led before the Sanhedrim, who decided that He was guilty, and worthy of death. They then sent Him to Pilate. Pilate was a severe and mercenary man. His administration as procurator was oppressive. The Jews complained of this, which led to his removal. He was banished to Vienne in Gaul, A. D. 36, and committed suicide, having been in office ten years.

11. *And Jesus stood,* &c. (see vs. 2) He was charged before the Roman governor, with subverting the nation, and forbidding to give tribute to Cesar, saying that He Himself is Christ, a KING (Luke 23. 2). This was a thing of which Pilate could take cognizance, and this was the charge now pending. To this point, Pilate directs his questioning.——¶ *Thou sayest.* This is a form of reply which means, *It is so.* He was the king of the Jews (John 18. 36); but His kingdom was not of this world, but spiritual (Ps. 110). John 18. 36.

12. *He answered nothing.* He knew their malignant designs; and in meekness, as He knew their charges to be ungrounded, He held His peace.

A. D 33.] CHAPTER XXVII. 289

14 And he answered him to never a word; insomuch that the governor marvelled greatly.

15 ¶ Now ᵍ at *that* feast the governor was wont to release unto the people a prisoner, whom they would.

g Mar.15.6,&c. Lu.23.17,&c. Jno.18.39,&c.

16 And they had then a notable prisoner, called Barabbas.

17 Therefore, when they were gathered together, Pilate said unto them, Whom will ye that I release unto you? Barabbas? or Jesus which is called Christ?

13. *They witness against thee* (see Luke 23. 5). "He stirreth up the people, teaching throughout all Jewry, beginning from Galilee to this place."

14. *To never a word*—not even to the extent of a word—not so much as one word—"as a sheep before her shearers was dumb, so He opened not His mouth" (Isa. 53. 7). This was in accomplishment of prophecy. It showed His meekness and willingness to suffer—the innocent for the guilty. This made an impression on Pilate.——¶ *Marvelled.* He wondered that Christ should be so silent, and seemingly so indifferent about His acquittal. Pilate declared that he found no fault in this man—and the chief priests and people grew fierce, and pressed the charge that He "*stirred up the people* (seditiously), *beginning from Galilee* to this place" (Luke 23. 5). The mention of Galilee, led Pilate to ask if Christ was a Galilean; and when he found that he was, he gladly put Him off upon Herod, who was Governor of Galilee, and was then at Jerusalem, at the feast. Luke 23. 7.

[§ 148. PILATE SEEKS TO RELEASE JESUS. THE JEWS DEMAND BARABBAS.—SIXTH *day of the week.*]—*Jerusalem.*

Matt.	Mark.	Luke.	John.
27.15-26	15.6-15	23.13-25	18.39,40

15. *The governor was wont to release*—was accustomed. This custom with the Roman government in Judea, we learn, grew out of a Jewish regulation, in connexion with that feast. "*Ye have a custom.*" John 18. 39. And we infer that there was something very special in this practice. "For of necessity he must release one unto them at the feast." As it was only "at THAT feast"—the passover—we infer that this was a symbolical act, and embodied to the constant view of the people, the great fundamental idea of RELEASE, as connected with the Paschal sacrifice. A MAN was by a formal ceremony SET FREE—A MALEFACTOR—an elect malefactor—"whom they would"— "whomsoever they desired" (Mark). And the people were trained by such an expressive symbol, to the great doctrine of justification—the guilty released from the hands of justice—the condemned—the prisoner—dismissed as a freeman by governmental authority. So by the great Paschal sacrifice ("Christ our Passover")—the condemned, who are prisoners of law—but yet the chosen of Christ are freely and fully RELEASED.

16. *A notable prisoner*—notorious—as *famous* in the sense of *infamous*. From Mark it appears that he was the ringleader in an insurrection, and the band were bound with him in prison, and he had added murder to his sedition (Mark 15. 7).

17. *Gathered together*—in expectation of the customary release (see Mark 15. 8).——¶ *Whom will ye.* From Mark 15. 8, we learn that the multitude were clamorous for Pilate to act upon this established principle, and to release one. He then proposes Christ for this release—"the king of the Jews" (Mark)—or puts the question as between Christ and Barabbas. Pilate was evidently willing to obtain for Christ the privilege of this custom (Luke 23. 20). Already, perhaps, he had received the message

25

18 For he knew that for envy ʰ they had delivered him.

19 ¶ When he was set down on the judgment-seat, his wife sent unto him, saying, Have thou nothing to do with that ⁱ just man, for I have suffered many things this day in a dream because of him.

ʰ Pr.27.4. Ec.4.4. *ⁱ* Is.53.11. Zec.9.9. Lu.23.47. 1Pe.2.22. 1Jno.2.1.

20 But the chief priests and elders persuaded the multitued that they should ask ʲ Barabbas, and destroy Jesus.

21 The governor answered and said unto them, Whether of the twain will ye that I release unto you? They said, Barabbas.

ʲ Ac.3.14.

from his wife (vs. 19), that she had "suffered many things in a dream, because of Him—'*that just man.*'" It is also stated by two Evangelists, that Pilate "knew that the chief priests had delivered Him for envy." He also states to them openly, his own impressions of His innocence upon a thorough examination, in which opinion, also, Herod concurred. Luke 23, 14, 15. It was really the fear of sedition on the part of the multitude (vs. 24), and his dread of the jealousy of Tiberius, which prevailed with him, against his conscience, to deliver Christ to be crucified.

18. *For envy*—" that the chief priests had delivered Him for envy" (Mark)—that is, for uneasiness and opposition at His popularity. He had drawn away the people after Him, and had unsettled the public confidence very much in their doctrines and claims. Pilate should have let Him go if he would have judged justly. But he deferred to the voice of the people. And here it is shown, 1st, that the very authority which condemned Christ also declared him innocent; and 2d, that it is the voice of men- -of the multitude—of *the people*, that Christ should be put to death. "They cried out *all at once.*" Men are naturally opposed to Christ, to His claims and offers.

19. *His wife sent unto him.* This tribunal was in a place that is called the Pavement (see John 19. 13), in the open court before the palace. Here was a most remarkable and direct warning to Pilate from his wife, through a dream, just at this juncture. This incidental notice of her being now at Jerusalem, is a strong proof of the Evangelist's veracity, as it was only in the reign of Tiberius that the governors of provinces had been permitted to take their wives with them. (Tacitus' Ann. 3. 33, Horne's Introduction, Vol. III., p. 109.) What strange incidents hang around all the steps in the procedure. They who are tempted to give up Christ, against all their judgment and conscience, shall have many a direct warning to desist. She had strong and special convictions that Christ was a *just* or righteous man, not a transgressor against the law— "*That just man*" (see ch. 1. 19); and so she was deeply exercised respecting Him, and anxious that Pilate should not be implicated in His condemnation.

20. *Ask Barabbas.* Influences were brought to bear upon the multitude for preferring Barabbas to Christ. Observe—in this significant matter of a release, that represents the justification of the sinner through Christ, it is not the more innocent, but the more guilty, that shall illustrate the gracious plan. "*Not Christ but Barabbas.*" Yet, Barabbas, but for Christ.

21. *Whether of the twain*—or of the two. The question is now distinctly put to the people. Every thing now turns upon their decision between these opposite parties. The sinner chooses Barabbas the *robber*, before Christ the *Redeemer*. But it is not the righteous, but the sinner—the malefactor—that is released at the Passover. Christ came not to call the righteous, but sinners to repentance.

22 Pilate saith unto them, What shall I do then with Jesus, which is called Christ? *They* all say unto him, Let him be crucified.

23 And the governor said, Why, what evil hath he done? But they cried out the more, saying, Let ᵏ him be crucified.

k c 21.38,39.

24 ¶ When Pilate saw that he could prevail nothing, but *that* rather a tumult was made, he took water, and washed ¹ *his* hands before the multitude, saying, I am innocent of the blood of this just person : see ye *to it.*

25 Then answered all the people, and said, His ᵐ blood *be* on

l De.21.6. *m* De.19.10. Jos.2.19. c.21.44. Ac.5.28.

---

22. *What shall I do then.* Pilate presents, now, this difficulty. How should they dispose of Christ—"Jesus which is called Christ"—"whom ye call the King of the Jews?" (Mark.) This was designed to remind them of His claims, and to hint to them of the difficulties which they must find in His case. The question turned only incidentally upon His getting the benefit of the paschal release. He was upon His trial. He had been condemned by the Sanhedrim, but not as yet formally by Pilate. Yet the governor, finding himself in straits, would gladly be availed of this provision. But Christ must be counted as a culprit, before He can have the benefit of a release that applies only to the condemned. Pilate would fain put the responsibility upon the people. So, many a one who decides not positively for Christ, tries to shift the blame upon others, and pleads that he does only as he is impelled by necessity or stress of circumstances.

23. *And the governor said, Why?* This question Pilate asked them even to the *third time* (says Luke), and proposed a punishment that might satisfy their worst passions. "I will therefore chastise Him, and let Him go." This *chastising*, or scourging with rods, was inflicted upon those who were to be crucified. It was a first step in their punishment. Pilate wished them to be satisfied with this. This was an abandonment of the former ground. If he could not get the paschal privilege for Him, he would have them stop at their usual scourging, and *upon that*, would let

Him go. They could not even tell of any evil which He had done. They only called clamorously for His crucifixion. They were instant with loud voices, requiring that He might be crucified.

24. *Took water.* The timid, unprincipled, unjust judge who sets the popular clamor before the solemn demands of justice, would now fain find a solace for his conscience in a poor ceremony. But this profession of innocence did not acquit him of his crime. No outward profession of religion, nor administration of solemn rights can expiate sin, or stand against wilful transgression. This *washing the hands* of this capital offence, was an expressive sign, which the Jews understood. Deut. 21. 6. It was a Jewish custom. He would publicly declare himself to them *as having nothing to do with this just man;* and so he testified in words. "I am innocent of the blood of this just person." And as he would formally roll the blame upon them, he adds, "*See ye to it.*" It is your business, and you must answer for it, not I.

25. *His blood be on us,* &c. This was their open assumption of all the consequences. They would take the responsibility, and would invoke it even upon their families. Little did they think what they were doing. I. was a solemn imprecation upon themselves and their posterity, of all that the Divine vengeance should recompense for His blood. The destruction which was prophesied in their Scriptures (Malachi), and forewarned by Christ Himself, was to be at their

us, and on our children.

26 Then released he Barabbas

---

call. Soon, their city was destroyed, with most peculiar horrors of the siege—of famine—of disease—and even of crucifixion itself (see Josephus' Jewish War, 7. 1).

[§ 149. PILATE DELIVERS UP JESUS TO DEATH—HE IS SCOURGED AND MOCKED.]—*Jerusalem.*

Matt.	Mark.	Luke.	John.
27. 26–30	15. 15–19		19. 1–3

26. *Then released.* This is the conclusion of the whole matter—the tragic act of Pilate—washing his hands of the crime, and delivering up Jesus to their will. He was an unjust judge—a self-deceiver—bound to have pronounced Christ innocent, and to have set Him free as such, without any resort to the provision of that festival. Behold, **then,** how Christ is at once acquitted and condemned by the same parties! He dies for sin—yet He is not a sinner—He is under condemnation in the sinner's place; but He is without fault. The Father calls Him His beloved, yet lays on Him our iniquities. How strangely wonderful, yet essential! Barabbas must have been executed, but for **His** stepping in where Barabbas, the sinner, should have died. He stood in his stead. And now Barabbas may go free, and trust in Christ. He may feel thankful for such an one to stand in his room, and his sins—seditious, murderous—sins as scarlet and red like crimson—may be washed in the blood of that Paschal sacrifice, which gives release and cleanses from all sin.——¶ *Scourged Jesus.* This was customary where a *slave* was to be crucified. Christ, then, was not *merely* crucified, but most ignominiously—as a common *slave.* This scourging was inflicted on the back with a rod, sometimes sharpened by points of iron (see note, Matt. 10. 17).——
¶ *Delivered Him*—i.e., officially—"*gave sentence that it should be as they required.*" Luke shows his education

unto them: and when he had scourged [n] Jesus, he delivered *him* to be crucified.

n Is.53.5. Lu.18.33.

---

in his accurate statement here, of the formal judgment pronounced by Pilate, which is only implied in the other Evangelists. The release of Barabbas involves the condemnation of Christ. The choice of "the multitude" is a rejection of the Saviour. "If any man love the world, the love of the Father is not in Him;" yet the interposition of Christ to take the sinner's place, is the only hope of the world. We annex here, in a note, a most singular document, entitled the *Death Warrant of Christ.*

Pilate at last condemned Christ.

Sentence rendered by Pontius Pilate, acting Governor of Lower Galilee, stating that Jesus of Nazareth shall suffer death on the cross.

"In the year seventeen of the empire Tiberius Cæsar, and the 25th day of March, the city of holy Jerusalem, Anna and Caiaphas being priests, sacrificators of the people of God, Pontius Pilate, Governor of Lower Galilee, sitting on the presidential chair of the Prætory, condemns Jesus of Nazareth to die on the cross between two thieves—the great and notorious evidence of the people saying—
1. Jesus is a seducer.
2. He is seditious.
3. He is an enemy of the law.
4. He calls himself falsely the Son of God.
5. He calls himself falsely the King of Israel.
6. He entered into the temple, followed by a multitude bearing palm branches in their hands.
Order the first centurion, Quillus Cornellus, to lead him to the place of execution.
Forbid to any person whomsoever, either poor or rich, to oppose the death of Jesus.
The witnesses that signed the condemnation of Jesus are, viz.:—1. Daniel Robani, a Pharisee; 2. Joannes Rorobable; 3. Raphdel Robani; 4. Capet, a citizen.
Jesus shall go out of the city of Jerusalem by the gate of Struenus."
The above sentence is engraved on a copper plate; on one side are written these words:—"A similar plate is sent to each tribe." It was found in an antique vase of white marble, while excavating in the ancient city of Aquilla, in the kingdom of Naples, in the year 1820, and was discovered by the Commissariats of Arts, attached to the French armies. At the expedition of Naples, it was found enclosed in a box of ebony, in the sacristy of the Chartrom—the vase in the chapel of Caserta. The French translation was made by the members of the Commission of Arts. The original is in the Hebrew language. The Chartrom requested earnestly that the plate might not be taken away from them. The request was granted as a reward for the sacrifice they had made for the army. M. Denon, one of the savans, caused a plate to be made of the same model, on which he had engraved the above sentence. At the sale of his collection of antiquities, &c., it was bought by Lord Howard for 2,890 francs.

27 Then the soldiers of the governor took Jesus into ¹the common hall, and gathered unto him the whole band *of soldiers.*
28 And they stripped him, and put on him a scarlet robe.
29 And when they had platted a crown of thorns, they put *it* upon his head, and a reed in his right hand: and they bowed the knee before him, and mocked ᵒ him, saying, Hail, King of the Jews!
30 And they spit ᵖ upon him, and took the reed, and smote him on the head.

1 Or, *governor's house.*   o Ps.69.19,20.   p Is.49.7; 50.6; 53.3,7.

"He was vacillating—fearful for his office, and even for his life—for he served 'the dark and unrelenting Tiberius.'" The charge against Him was of treason against the state. Hence the people accused Pilate of opposition to Cesar, in showing lenity toward Christ (John 19. 12). Pilate gave Him up to the people.

27. *The common hail*—called (πραιτωριον) Pretorium—the governor's palace or house (αυλη) (Mark 15. 16.) Pilate's judgment seat was in an open, public place, from which Christ was now led to the house of Pilate. The Jews would not enter in there, because contact with the heathen soldiers would defile them for the passover (John 18. 28).——¶ *The whole band.* This was a cohort in the Roman army of from 4 to 600 men—the tenth part of a legion.

28. *A scarlet robe.* This was put upon Him in mockery, because He claimed to be king, and this was the kind of robe worn by Roman officials. Mark says it was *purple.* The former was a military cloak—the latter was worn by the Roman emperors. Very probably in their deep derision, an old cast-off general's cloak was put on Him, as a MOCK PURPLE, to deride His claims as king. This intent appears from next verse. Hence it is said by Mark, "*they clothed Him with purple,*" &c.

29. *A crown of thorns.* This was a chaplet or wreath of the thorn bush, woven or platted so as to fit upon His head, and further to mock His kingly pretensions. Instead of His crown of glory, they assign Him a crown of thorns. Instead of adorning His brow, it pierces His temples.——¶ *A reed.* This mocks His *sceptre.* Instead of a golden or ivory staff of office, which kings commonly bore, they put *in His right hand a frail reed*, that would bruise and break almost at the touch.——¶ *They bowed the knee.* This was further mockery, tantalizing Him with such pretence of subjection, and thus playing off the ridiculous farce to show how thoroughly they despised His claims as king. How vile is the human heart! What was the ground of all this bitter enmity that could not possibly be satisfied with mockeries or cruelties? "The carnal mind is ENMITY against God, for it is not subject to the law of God, neither indeed can be." Human nature, at best, can only present a mock subjection—a profane bowing of the knee, more scoffing, than spiritual or sincere. To crown all the derision, they shout aloud a mock salutation—"Hail, King of the Jews"—which they used toward their emperors.

30. *Spit upon Him.* This was the mark of utmost spite and contempt, both in ancient and modern times (see ch. 26. 67). Compare Isa. 50. 6. This indignity would show us the abhorrence of which our sins are worthy, and men may now see, in all this, the infinite dishonour which they deserve, as the curse of sin; for it was in the capacity of the sinner's substitute that our Lord passed through all these bitter experiences.——¶ *Smote Him.* This despite was further shown the Sufferer. John has it "they smote Him with their hands." Matthew and Mark speak of a reed being also used, and *on the head.* Mark also adds that "bowing their knees they worshipped Him." All this was in mingled spite and derision.

294 MATTHEW. [A. D. 33

31 And after that they had mocked him, they took the robe off from him, and put his own raiment on him, and led ᑫ him away to crucify *him*.

32 And as they came out, they found a man of Cyrene,

ᑫ Nu.15.35. 1K.21.10,13. Ac.7.58. He.13.12.

Simon by name: him they compelled to bear his cross.

33 And when they were come unto a place called Golgotha, that is to say, A place of a scull,

34 They gave him vinegar to drink, mingled ʳ with gall: and

ʳ Ps.69.21.

OBSERVE, (1.) Pilate delivers Christ to be crucified, but He is delivered up also by the determinate counsel and foreknowledge of God (Acts 2. 23). (2.) The enmity of the heart against the claims of Christ is unprovoked and unmitigated. (3.) Men call for Christ to be crucified, and when this death is shown to be for the salvation of sinners, they reject Him even in this. (4.) Some shall awake to shame and everlasting contempt (Dan. 12. 2).

§ 152. JESUS IS LED AWAY TO BE CRUCIFIED.—SIXTH *day of the week. Jerusalem.*

Matt.	Mark.	Luke.	John.
27.31-34	15.20-23	23.26-33	19.16,17

31. *The robe.* Mark says, the *purple*, viz., the mock purple.

32. *As they came out*—viz., of *the city;* for the execution of criminals was commonly outside the gates. The soldiers led Him out, for they were the common executioners under the Roman governors.——¶ *A man of Cyrene.* Mark and Luke both speak of this man as "*coming out of the country*" towards the city, which would show that they found him as they passed out of the city gate. Mark adds that he was "the father of Alexander and Rufus." *Cyrene* was in Africa, where there were Jews residing. The district was called Pentapolis Cyrenaica. It is stated by John (19. 17), that Christ went forth "*bearing His cross*," which was the custom for criminals. They impressed this man Simon, "and on him they laid the cross, that he might bear it after Jesus." (See Luke 23. 26.) The *cross* was a *high post* with a *cross-beam* near the top, and fastened firmly in the ground. It usually stood some ten feet out of ground, and was in size and weight such as a man could carry *with difficulty.* A small seat belonged to it (about the middle), that the crucified person might rest upon it, and not hang entirely by the hands. The hands and feet were sometimes fastened to the cross with spikes, and sometimes bound fast to it with ropes. In our Saviour's case, the former method was used, as the most cruel. Christ is to be crucified for His people. Yet He would bring men into a mysterious and glorious partaking with Him of His sufferings and of His glory. The place of execution lay to the north-west, and near the city. As the bodies of the beasts that were sacrificed as types of Him were burned without the camp, so He suffered without the gate (Heb. 13. 11, 12). See Map of Mod. Jerusalem, where the spot standing outside the old walls, but afterwards enclosed, is indicated by the site of "the Holy Sepulchre." (K.) *On the swell of Acra, beyond the Second Wall,* (see " View of Jerusalem as besieged by Titus,") the crucifixion took place.—*Bartlett's " Walks about Jerusalem,"* p. 38.

33. *Golgotha*—"a place called the place of a skull, which is called in the Hebrew *Golgotha* "(John)—" *the place Golgotha*" (Mark)—" *the place which is called Calvary*" (Luke). This was also the meaning of Calvary in the Latin—"*a skull.*' Though called *Mount Calvary,* it was rather a *knoll,* just sufficient to designate the spot. It received its name, doubtless, from its being used for the execution of criminals. Comp. 2 Kings 9. 35.

34. *Vinegar mingled with gall.*

A. D. 33.]	CHAPTER XXVII.	285

when he had tasted *thereof*, he would not drink.

35 And ᵃ they crucified him, and parted his garments, casting lots: that it might be fulfilled

<small>ᵃ Ps.22.16. Mar.15.24,&c. Lu. 23,34,&c. Jno.19,24, &c.   *l* Ps.22.18.</small>

which was spoken ᵗ by the prophet, They parted my garments among them, and upon my vesture did they cast lots.

36 And sitting down, they watched him there;

37 And set up over his head

This was a mixture offered in derision, it would seem. Mark speaks of another potion, viz. *wine*, or wine-vinegar, *mingled with myrrh*, which was the usual stupefying drink for criminals about to suffer death. It served as an opiate, like laudanum, to relieve the extreme sufferings. This fulfilled the prophecy in Psalm 69. 21.——¶ *He would not drink.* Here again He was to show how willingly he endured the curse. If He had sought relief, He could have had it from heaven, or could have destroyed His enemies at His will. He would now refuse any alleviations which His murderers would administer. He would drink the *cup* to the *dregs*, for it was given Him of His Father. He endured the curse voluntarily and fully.

OBSERVE, (1.) Christ must needs die, not by the scourging, nor by the sinking under the cross, but by crucifixion itself. (2.) The smallest matter in all this work entered into the particular plan. The Scriptures were fulfilled, and God's purposes were carried out.

§ 153. THE CRUCIFIXION.—SIXTH *day of the week. Jerusalem.*

Matt.	Mark.	Luke.	John.
27. 35–38	15. 24–28	23. 33 34, 38	19. 18–24

35. *They crucified Him.* The manner of crucifixion was briefly this. The sentenced man was first stripped of all his clothing, saving a strip about the loins, and then severely whipped, so that he sometimes died under this. Smarting and exhausted, he was compelled as soon as possible to bear his cross to the spot. Four soldiers of the Prætorian guard, under the superintendence of a centurion, were the common executioners. These drove each a nail into the hand or foot of the man, sometimes before, and sometimes after the cross had been set up in its place in the ground. Resting on the small seat which was fixed about the middle of the cross, the person could be nailed to it after it was set up. It was a slow and severe death, not exceeded in physical suffering, perhaps, by any method of torture. It was also the most ignominious punishment, "as it is written, Cursed is every one that hangeth on a tree." Robbers and slaves were generally doomed to this kind of death. Hence "the *offence of the cross.*" Hence the wonder of Christ's humiliation, "EVEN *the death of* THE CROSS." Such suffering must needs be short, showing how poorly our weak nature can bear the curse of sin. A person generally lived on the cross till the third, fourth, or fifth day—the nails poisoning and inflaming the whole system, and through the nerves among which they were driven, making the pain indeed EXCRUCIATING, a term which is derived from the word *crux*, a cross. With the Jews it was not lawful that a malefactor's body hang on the cross over night (Deut. 21. 23). Hence the soldier tried with the spear to see if He was yet dead, else they would break his bones to hasten His decease.——¶ *Parted His garments.* The soldiers who acted as executioners were entitled to the garments of the deceased. They "made four parts, (says John), to every soldier a part," and for His coat they *cast lots.* This was a method of deciding such a doubtful point by appealing to what was ostensibly regarded in the case

his accusation written, THIS IS JESUS THE KING OF THE JEWS.

38 Then were there two thieves *u* crucified with him; one on the right hand, and another on the left.

u Is. 53. 12.

as an expression of God's will. See Acts 1. 26, in the case of choosing an apostle who should stand in the room of Judas, and fill up the fixed number.——¶ *That it might be fulfilled.* This prophecy is found in Psalm 22. 18, which shows that the Psalm refers to Christ as a striking detail of His sufferings, in that *crucifixion experience.* Men — wicked men — may have the *raiment* of Christ. Even the *most wicked* may wear His robe of righteousness and salvation by Divine grace.

36. *They watched Him.* This they did, as *guards,* lest anything might occur to obviate their cruel purpose. This is recorded to show us how certainly and without any failure, all the malicious designs of men for His death were accomplished. Nothing failed of all His endurance on the accursed tree.

37. *His accusation* — the charge upon which He was condemned. Mark and Luke speak of the superscription, and John of the *title.* It was customary to set over the head of the criminal the crime for which he had been condemned and was about to suffer. It was usually graven on a metal plate, with black characters on a white ground. This was in order that the people might know the case. Hence we find this written in three languages, Hebrew, Greek, and Latin, that the Jews, Greeks, and Romans, who were in the crowd, might understand. These were the three sacred languages of the world. John says that *Pilate* wrote it (19. 19). The title itself is given differently by all the Evangelists, though it is the same in substance. The ground of His condemnation was that He claimed to be "the King of the Jews." It may have been variously written in the different languages. But it was not necessary that the precise words should be stated, so long as they agreed most perfectly in the substance of the accusation. In John's narrative we find that the chief priests expostulated with Pilate, and they themselves quote the title defectively, leaving out a part (19. 21). The harmless disagreement here in the very words, would only show that the Evangelists had not copied from each other, or conspired with each other to fabricate their narrative. Here, also, by this custom of stating publicly the ground of sentence, we have an open declaration that He "had done nothing amiss." This was the *third* hour, when they crucified Him, or 9 o'clock (Mark).

38. *Two thieves*—robbers, or highwaymen, with which Judea then abounded. All the Evangelists mention this, that two malefactors were crucified with Him, one on each side. Mark notices this as in fulfilment of the prophecy (Isa. 53. 12), "And He was numbered with the transgressors." Executions were appointed at passover time, for the impression upon the greatest number. (See Deut. 17. 13.) For the same purpose, several were usually executed together. Our Lord ranked now as a capital transgressor, for He stood in the stead of sinners—*made a* CURSE FOR US."

OBSERVE, (1.) The accusation on the cross shows Christ to have been innocent. (2.) Sinners will not have this man to reign over them (see Luke 19. 14). This is their guilt, and this procures the death of Christ. So Adam in the garden disdained subjection to God. (3.) He was numbered with the transgressors, as Mark notices (Isa. 53. 12), standing in sinners' place to save sinners (4.) Behold *Jesus in the midst of malefactors* (John). He is also in the midst of the throne (Rev. 5. 6), and in the midst of the Church. Matt 18. 20.

[A. D. 33.] CHAPTER XXVII. 297

39 ¶ And they that passed by reviled him, wagging their heads,

40 And saying, Thou that destroyest the temple, and buildest *it* in three days, save thyself. If thou be the Son of God, come down from the cross.

41 Likewise also the chief priests mocking *w him*, with the scribes and elders, said,

v Ps.22.7; 109.25. *w* Job.13.9. Ps.35.16. Is.28.22. Lu.18.32.

42 He saved others, himself he cannot save. If he be the King of Israel, let him now come down from the cross, and we will believe him.

43 He trusted in God; let *x* him deliver him now, if he will have him: for he said, *y* I am the Son of God.

44 The thieves also, which were crucified with him, cast

x Ps.3.2; 22.8; 42.10; 71.11. *y* Jno.5.17,18; 10.30,36.

§ 154. THE JEWS MOCK AT JESUS ON THE CROSS. *He commends His mother to John.*—(SIXTH *day of the week.*)

Matt.	Mark.	Luke.	John.
27.39-44	15.29-32	23.35-37 39-43	19.25-27

39. *Reviled Him*—literally, "blasphemed." They heaped vile epithets upon Him, shaking and tossing the head in scorn (see Job 16. 4. Psalm 109. 25). People and rulers joined in this, as we learn from Luke. Human insult was part of the bitter curse which He endured.

40. *Thou that destroyest.* This claim of His was brought up now in derision. His boast of power was challenged, dared, defied now. How easily He might have used that power to hurl them into perdition; but He forbore. He could have come down: but He came to die. He would not have Himself now, else He could not save sinners.——¶ *If thou be the Son of God. Like* SATAN in the wilderness, they challenge HIS CLAIM TO DIVINITY.

41. This scoffing was universal among all classes of the multitude—chief priests, scribes and elders, and soldiers and the thieves, are mentioned.

42. *He saved others.* This was an allusion to His miracles, which pretended even to raise the dead; but which they obstinately discredited or attributed to Beelzebub. They dared Him now to do this conclusive miracle for their belief; but this would neither have convinced them—nor would it have served His purpose of grace—nor could they demand any further sign. "A wicked and adulterous generation seeketh after a sign, but there shall no sign be given them, but the sign of Jonas the prophet." The wondrous miracle to be wrought lay in the purposes of God, and was soon to come on, in HIS RESURRECTION, according to Jonah's type and the ample prophecy. Nor was this a sincere demand of theirs, but only in mockery.

43. *He trusted in God.* These words are remarkably predicted in Ps. 22. 8. This also recalled His declarations of confidence in the Father and of oneness with Him, which now they would have Him test, and manifest (ch. 25. 53). So did Satan in the wilderness—"*If thou be the Son of God, cast thyself down,* for it is written, He shall give His angels charge over thee," &c. (ch. 4. 6). But would He meet such insulting challenges? Had they not had the most abundant proofs, which they utterly despised? And would the Father arrest His gracious plans to satisfy, or stop such raillery? Behold in the midst of all this, Christ had rather die to offer them salvation, than *decline* to die, to induce their conviction.

44. *The thieves.* Luke says, "*One of the malefactors,*" while Matthew and Mark speak in general of *the thieves,* as doing this. One of them was more conspicuous in the history, and upon his case Luke dwelt.——

the same in his teeth.

45 Now from the sixth hour there was darkness *z* over all the land unto the ninth hour.

46 And about the ninth hour

z Am. 8. 9.

¶ *Cast the same in His teeth*—literally, reproached Him to *the same effect*—or, *in like manner*. Luke alone tells us of the *penitent* one (23. 40). Here around the cross, Christ would illustrate the power of that grace which the cross should procure even for the vilest of sinners, even in the worst case, and to the last. This is no encouragement to put off repentance till death. That *one* is rescued amidst extremest *perils*, is no encouragement *to take the risk*, especially when this must be, by despising the grace till the last. It is not probable that this thief had enjoyed the means of knowing the Saviour. At this time, our Lord commended His mother Mary (now a widow, doubtless) to the affectionate care of the beloved disciple; as John himself narrates (19. 25-27).

Observe, (1.) How much of Satan's language and spirit was in this bitter trial of Christ on the cross. (See the temptation in the wilderness, ch. 4.) (2.) Christ's claim to Divinity, was that against which Satan and all God's enemies vented their malicious spite. They challenged and tantalized His Sonship. (3.) The pardoning grace is signally illustrated.

§ 155. Darkness prevails. Christ expires on the Cross.—Sixth *day of the week. Calvary.*

Matt.	Mark.	Luke.	John.
27.45-50	15.33-37	23.44-46	19.28-30

45. *The sixth hour.* It was our *noon*, or *twelve o'clock*. Darkness at noon-day was the most striking and palpable work of God, as it could not have been a common eclipse, for the passover was always at *full-moon*. The darkness also lasted *three hours*, as an eclipse never could. Tertullian (Apolog. ch. 21) appeals to the

Jesus cried with a loud voice, saying, Eli, Eli, lama sabachthani? that is to say, *a* My God, my God, why hast thou forsaken me?

47 Some of them that stood

a Ps. 22. 1. Is. 53. 10. La. 1. 12.

accounts of this event, contained in the Roman archives. *Phlegon*, a Roman astronomer, A. D. 140, speaking of this very time, testifies of this——
¶ *All the land*—or "*all the earth*," as Luke (same Greek word). This phrase was often applied to *Judea* alone. See Bp. Watson's Reply to Gibbon, Let. 5.

46. *My God.* These words are from Psalm 22. 1, and are quoted not from the Hebrew, but from the Chaldee paraphrase. Mark gives the words in the Syro-Chaldaic (ch. 15. 34), his object not being to give the dialect in which they were spoken; but the exclamation itself. This language was spoken in Judea at that time. Here our great sacrifice cried out under the dreadful sense of the Divine wrath against sin, as He bore its load and curse. Compare the 22d Psalm, which He applied now to His case, and which the Jews had always applied to the Messiah. As He stood in the sinner's place, He saw and felt the Father's wrath, not toward Himself as a personal transgressor, but toward Himself as the *sinner's Substitute.* He still cried, *My God*, and retained His filial confidence. But here was the *sting of death* to Him, that He, the holy Lamb of God, should occupy such a place, and sustain for a moment such a relation to His Father. He cried out at this point! as He did not under His other sufferings. His human soul was left to shudder at the thought of standing under the curse, even for others, and here He felt the awful dread of sinking under such a load. "He was heard in that He feared." Heb. 5. 7.

47. *Calleth for Elias.* It is not declared that they *thought* He called for Elias, but this they *said*, in taunt. And, as it was intended, it was a

[A. D. 33.] CHAPTER XXVII.

there, when they heard *that*, said, This *man* calleth for Elias, 48 And straightway one of them ran, and took a sponge, and filled *it* with ᵇ vinegar, and

ᵇ Ps.69.21.

put *it* on a reed, and gave him to drink.
49 The rest said, Let be, let us see whether Elias will come to save him.
50 ¶ Jesus, when he had cried

---

most severe and cruel mockery—tantalizing Him, as now, in vain, calling for Elias, who was prophesied of, as the Messiah's forerunner, and whom the Jews expected as first to appear. He had laboured to show that John the Baptist was he, but they rejected this with disdain. (See ch. 11. 14, 18.) They expected Elijah the prophet to appear in person, and hence they sneeringly adverted here to the want of this testimony to His being the true Messiah. Greenleaf notices this incidental allusion by Matthew and Mark to the popular opinion as additional evidence of their veracity.

48. *Gave Him to drink.* This was not from any misunderstanding of the outcry, as might seem from the connexion, and as some have supposed, but from another cry which John reports—"*that the Scripture might be fulfilled He saith, I thirst.*" John 19. 28. See Psalm 69. 21. This was the rich man's outcry in torment (Luke 16. 24.) It expressed the severity of perdition. As the gospel benefits are represented by "the waters" and by drink, so the bitterness of sin's curse and punishment is represented by THIRST. This vinegar, or *sour wine*, was the soldier's drink, of which a vessel full was there (John 19. 29). They put the sponge on a reed, or hyssop-branch (John), that thus they might reach it to His mouth as He hung upon the cross.

49. Others expressed their rage and venom thus—repeating the taunt about Elias. There was all manner of scorn and reviling among the malignant crowd.

50. *With a loud voice.* This was another cry. His voice was *loud* in death. He was heard to say "Father, into thy hands I commend my spirit" (Luke), showing His relations to the Father as undisturbed. Stephen the martyr died crying, "LORD JESUS *receive my spirit*" (Acts 7. 59), worshipping the risen Lamb. Christ also said, "*It is finished*" (John), which expressed what John had just before noticed (ch. 19. 28)—"*Jesus* KNOWING *that* ALL THINGS *were* NOW ACCOMPLISHED." The prophecies of His sacrificial death were fulfilled—the covenant with the Father was met—the cup given Him to drink was taken to the dregs—the types and shadows of the old dispensation were answered in Him, and now by His finished work satisfaction was made for believers.——¶ *Yielded up the ghost*—or in Greek, *the spirit*. He expired, as Mark has it literally (εξεπνευσε). He laid down His life to take it again. His soul was made an offering for sin.

OBSERVE, (1.) Christ's sufferings were more in soul than in body, and this mysterious, unknown anguish of spirit, was THE CUP—the STING of *death* —the CURSE for us. (2.) The ATONEMENT of Christ cannot be explained except we find here the *punishment* due to sin suffered by the innocent for the guilty. This accounts for all the history; and the last dying cry; "*It is finished*," brings peace to the troubled soul, from the *finished work* of Christ. The Lord provides a lamb for the burnt-offering, and the son of Abraham, though already bound and laid upon the altar, and now even under the knife, may go free (Gen. 22. 13), may even worship there. (3.) The *crucifixion experience* of Christ, as expressed from the cross, exhibits the whole truth. The FORSAKING and the THIRST show the CURSE. The words of LOVE, and FORGIVENESS, and PROMISE to sinners, there also expressed, show the GRACE. "Behold thy mother." "Father for-

again with a loud voice, yielded up the ghost.

51 And, behold, the vail *c* of the temple was rent *d* in twain, from the top to the bottom;

c Ex.26.31. Le.16.2,15 ; 21.23. 2Ch.3.14. *d* Is.25. 7.

and the earth did quake, and the rocks rent;

52 And *e* the graves were opened; and many bodies of the saints which *f* slept, arose,

53 And came out of the graves *g*

e Is.25.8 ; 26.19. Ho.13.14. Jno.5.25,28. *f* Da.12. 2. 1Th.4.14. *g* 1Cor.15.20.

give them." "To-day shalt thou be with me in paradise." And the DYING WORDS show the ACCEPTANCE of His work in heaven. "*It is finished.*" "Father into thy hands I commend my spirit."

§ 156. THE VAIL OF THE TEMPLE RENT. THE GRAVES OPENED. THE WOMEN AT THE CROSS.—SIXTH *day of the week.*

| Matt. | Mark. | Luke. | John. |
| 27.51-56 | 15.38-41 | 23.45,47-49 | |

51. *The vail of the temple.* This was the interior vail in Herod's temple, which separated the holy place from the Holy of Holies (see Temple, ch. 21). Exodus 26. 33. Paul refers to this event, and to the important symbolical purport of it. See Heb. 9. 8. and 10. 20. It was rent in two parts, torn from top to bottom, exposing all the sacred mysteries of the Most Holy Place. Thus, "*the way into the holiest of all was (now) made manifest,*" and laid open to all nations. The sacred ceremonies of the day of atonement, when the high priest entered into the Most Holy Place—viz., once a year—were now to be dispensed with, as the great high priest had furnished His own blood and offices, and gone within the vail to show His blood in heaven; and thus, also, believers have boldness to enter into the holiest by a new and living way which He hath consecrated for us through the vail, that is to say, His flesh. The priest was probably burning incense in the holy place at this hour of the evening sacrifice.—— ¶ *The earth did quake*—or shake. The ground that was cursed sympathizes. There are traces of this remarkable earthquake in Judea, and heathen writers speak of one which occurred in this reign of Tiberius that destroyed twelve Asiatic cities (see Macrobius). Tacitus' Ann. II. 47. Suetonius in Tib. 48. That it was great, would appear from the additional clause, "*the rocks rent.*" This was entirely miraculous, in testimony to Christ's work: and so it impressed the centurion (54).

52. *The graves were opened.* This was another testimony to Christ's work. As the rending of the vail symbolically showed the mysteries of the ritual opened, and the way to heaven opened, and Christ's office opened as superseding that of the Levitical law—so this demonstrated that the power of death and the grave was vanquished, and an earnest was given of a general resurrection.—— ¶ *The saints*—the pious dead. These were probably such as old Simeon, who was known in Jerusalem, and who had but recently died.——¶ *Which slept.* Believers are said to *sleep in Jesus.* Death is to them a calm and sweet repose, which the softest slumber of the pillow only typifies. They are said to sleep also, because for them there is a blest awaking when the resurrection day shall dawn. See 1 Thess. 4. 14. John 11. 11. 1 Cor. 15. 20.

53. *Came out of the graves after His resurrection.* Though the graves were shaken and torn open by the earthquake, it was not until after He arose (day after next), that their tenants came forth. This, therefore, showed that there was POWER in His DEATH TO OPEN THE GRAVES of believers—and POWER in His RESURRECTION TO BRING THEM FORTH. Christ was Himself "the first-fruits of them that slept." 1 Cor. 15. 20. Col. 1. 18.——¶ *The holy city*—Jerusalem. The burial grounds were around the city, in the

after his resurrection, and went into the holy city, and appeared unto many.

54 Now ʰ when the centurion, and they that were with him watching Jesus, saw the earthquake, and those things that were done, they feared greatly,

h Mar. 15. 39. Lu. 23. 47, &c.

saying, Truly this was the Son of God.

55 And many women were there, (beholding afar off,) which ⁱ followed Jesus from Galilee, ministering unto him;

56 Among which was Mary Magdalene, and Mary the moth

i Lu. 8. 2, 3.

valleys, or along the slopes adjacent. For a remarkable prophetic delineation of Christ's sufferings on the cross, see the 22d Psalm. And for a sound and devotional exposition of the language, see Stevenson's work, entitled, "*Christ on the Cross.*" Behold the Lamb of God, our Passover, sacrificed for us. Though the cross was of all punishments most ignominious, yet Christians find here their hope. This was the shame due to their sin. Christ is the power of God, and the wisdom of God unto salvation to every one that believeth (1 Cor. 1. 24). They glory in the cross. For hereby Christ spoiled principalities and powers, and made a show of them openly, triumphing over them in His cross (Col. 2. 15). Behold! Jews and Gentiles (Sanhedrim and Pilate) condemned Christ—the Roman soldiers crucified Him—the mixed multitude, rapacious and malignant, called for His sentence and crucifixion, until they prevailed on Pilate—and all without a reason. No reason can be given for the death of Christ, except that thus it behooved Him to *suffer the punishment due to sin,* in order to the salvation of any.

54. *The centurion.* As the name imports, this officer had command of a hundred soldiers. He superintended the crucifixion.——¶ *Watching.* This was the Pretorian guard who attended to keep watch throughout. ——¶ *Truly,* &c. He knew the alleged blasphemy for which Christ suffered; and these tokens from Jehovah were most convincing. All "those things that were done"—the miraculous darkness, and rending of the vail, and the opening graves,

had power as testimonies from the Most High. They were evident attestations of His claims, and proved Him to be the Son of God, by setting a seal to His work. Luke records another saying of the centurion— " Truly this was a righteous man"— as Pilate's wife had warned the governor before this very guard—" that just man." See Acts 3. 14; 7. 52; 22. 14.

55, 56. *Many women.* John speaks of Mary His mother, and His mother's sister, Mary the wife of Cleopas, and Mary Magdalene. Mark omits our Lord's mother, and adds Salome. These were afterward prominent in the resurrection scenes (Mark 16. 1). This last is she whom Matthew calls the mother of Zebedee's children— John alone making mention of our Lord's mother, who was so specially entrusted to his care. These followed Him from Galilee, ministering to Him—that is, waiting upon Him and serving Him. Mary Magdalene was so called, because she was from the district of Magdala (see ch. 15. 39, note), near the sea of Tiberias, and not far from Capernaum, on the same side. These at first came near the cross, and Christ spoke to His mother, "Behold thy son," referring to John, whom He commended to her as protector and son (John 19. 26). Afterward, as the terrors of the dying moment came on, and the awful tokens from Heaven appeared, they retired from the horror of the scene. See Wall's Critical Notes, p. 116, and Watson's Reply to Gibbon, Let. 5, and Newcome.

OBSERVE, What follows upon the death of Christ. (1.) The temple

er of James and Joses, and the mother of Zebedee's children.

57 ¶ When ʲ the even was come, there came a rich man of Arimathea, named Joseph, who

ʲ Mar.15.42. Lu.23.50. Jno.19.38.

also himself was Jesus' disciple
58 He went to Pilate, and begged the body of Jesus Then Pilate commanded the body to be delivered.
59 And when Joseph had ta-

---

vail is rent—the ritual is abolished. Heaven is opened, and Christ the forerunner enters for us within the vail—and there we may cast our hope—sure and steadfast—as an anchor that takes hold upon the rock (Heb. 6. 19, 20). (2.) Death is vanquished for believers—and a resurrection is secured, and the glorious rising of the saints is demonstrated. (3.) Sinners are convinced by His death. The preaching of the cross and the scenes of His *blood-shedding* shall yet powerfully convince the most obdurate hearts. Jehovah's inflexible justice—Christ's dying love—the awful cup of the curse, and the acceptance of the work in heaven, are the great truths which shall always have convincing power, by the Holy Ghost. (4.) His people are willing. The last at the cross and the first at the sepulchre are the women — ministering — following from far — and when they can do nothing more, bringing sweet spices to embalm His corpse.

§ 157. The taking down from the cross. The Burial.—*Jerusalem.*

Matt.	Mark.	Luke.	John.
27.57-61	15.42-47	23.50-56	19.31-42

57. *Joseph.* A rich man, and a disciple. Not many such were found among Christ's followers. But the Scripture was to be fulfilled in this, "He made His grave with the wicked *and with the rich in His death.*" Isa. 53. 9. This man is called by Luke, "a counsellor—a good man and a just. The same had not consented to the counsel and deed of them (i. e., who condemned and crucified Him)—who also himself waited for the kingdom of God." John says of him, "being a disciple of Jesus, but *secretly,* for fear of the Jews."——¶ *Arimathea.* This is supposed by some to be the same as Ramah, six miles north of Jerusalem. It is more likely the same as Ramleh, near Lydda, about thirty miles north-west of Jerusalem. This was Samuel's birth-place (see 1 Sam. 1. 1). "Ramathaim-Zophim."

58. *Begged the body.* This incidental allusion to existing customs, shows the veracity of the narrative. Those crucified by the Romans, are said to have been usually exposed to the birds of prey—and a guard was set to prevent their friends from burying the bodies. The body of Jesus, therefore, could not be obtained for burial, without leave from Pilate. The Evangelists only relate that it was applied for.—See "*Greenleaf's Testimony of the Evangelists.*" With the Jews, it was not lawful for the bodies of criminals to remain all night upon the tree, "but thou shalt in any wise bury him that day." Deut. 21. 23. Mark says that Joseph "*went in boldly unto Pilate.*" This is expressive, considering what John says of him, that he was a disciple *secretly* for fear of the Jews. The most timid Christians do sometimes show the greatest courage, and accomplish the boldest things for Christ. Who would not plead for Christ's body? But *the church* is now *His body* (Col. 1. 24). Who will go forward before governors and kings for it? Pilate ordered the body to be given up. But, the most completely to forestal any allegation of His being yet alive, in order to account for His rising, Mark records (15. 44), that "Pilate marvelled if He were already dead, and calling unto him the centurion, he asked him if He had been any while dead. And *when he knew it of the centurion*, he gave the body to Joseph." John gives another confirmation of His actual death (19. 31), that because it was the (παρασκευη,

A. D. 33.] CHAPTER XXVII. 303

ken the body, he wrapped it in a clean linen cloth,

60 And ᵏ laid it in his own new tomb, which he had hewn out in the rock : and he rolled a great stone to the door of the sepulchre, and departed.

61 And there was Mary Magdalene, and the other Mary, sitting over against the sepulchre.

62 Now the next day, that followed the day of the preparation, the chief priests and Pharisees came together unto Pilate,

k Is.53.9.

---

day of preparation (see ch. 26. 19, note), and the bodies were not allowed to remain on the cross on the sabbath day, they asked to have the legs of all the bodies broken, and the corpses removed. And the manifest fact of Jesus' death (dead already), kept them from breaking His legs, and thus fulfilled the Scripture (Ps. 34. 20), and answered to the type, for the paschal lamb was to have no bone broken. Exod. 12. 46.

59. *Clean linen cloth.* This was a large square wrapper, in which the body was shrouded, and then bound by linen bandages, with spices. This was the Jewish mode of burying. John 19. 40. So also the Egyptians embalmed—and it seems of Egyptian origin. John tells us, in this connexion, of the *Nicodemus*—whose night visit to Christ he records also (chap. 3)—that he came at this time, and "brought a mixture of myrrh and aloes, about a hundred pounds weight," to embalm the Saviour.

60. *In his own new tomb.* John tells us more precisely, that this sepulchre was in *a garden* adjoining the place where Christ was crucified—i. e., in the near vicinity of Calvary, outside the city—where, in the rocky slopes, tombs were excavated (see ch. 23. 27, 29, note). Gethsemane was called "a garden." No other tenant occupied this tomb.——¶ *Rolled a great stone.* It was customary to close the mouths of tombs and caves thus, to preserve from wild beasts.

61. While this was doing, and after it was done, Mary Magdalene and the other Mary, in their warm and undying affection, sat *over against*, or opposite the sepulchre, gazing at the sacred spot. Luke says, they " beheld the sepulchre and *how the body was laid.*"

OBSERVE, (1.) These particulars are so fully given—viz., of Christ's ascertained death and of His being alone in the tomb, so that the rising could not have been another's—that we shall have the fullest evidence of His resurrection. (2.) We see the Scripture fulfilled in this case, to the last and least details, and we may look for all Scripture to be equally made good. (3.) Christ shall never be without some faithful followers. (4.) Timid faith is drawn out and emboldened by contact with the realities of *Christ's death*—e. g. *Joseph* and *Nicodemus.*

§ 158. THE WATCH AT THE SEPULCHRE. —SEVENTH *day of the week, or Jewish* SABBATH. *Jerusalem.*

| Matt. 27.62–66 | Mark. | Luke. | John. |

62. *The day of the preparation.* The *fore-sabbath* (see ch. 26. 19, note). The day *after* preparation-day was therefore the sabbath. Because this was a sabbath occurring amidst the the great festival season, " that sabbath lay was a *high day*" (John 19.

63 Saying, Sir, we remember that that deceiver ᶩ said, while he was yet alive, After ᵐ three days I will rise again.

64 Command therefore that the sepulchre be made sure until the third day, lest his disciples come by night, and ⁿ steal him away, and say unto the people, He is risen from the dead: so the last error shall be worse than the first.

65 Pilate said unto them, Ye have a watch: go your way, make *it* as sure as you can.

66 So they went, and made the sepulchre sure, sealing º the stone, and setting a watch.

---

l Jno.7.12,47. 2Cor.6.8. *m* c.16.21; 17.23; 20.19. Lu.24.6,7. Jno.2.19. *n* c.28.13.

o Da.6.17.

---

31). As the Jews reckoned their days *from evening to evening*, this day spoken of, means *not* the next morning, but *after sunset* of Friday, when the Jewish day commenced. Saturday was the Sabbath at that time. Hence they took the *very promptest* measures, before a night should intervene.

63. Here we find the utmost precaution of Christ's enemies taken against His rising, and against any possible deceptions to that effect. Hence they call Him "*that deceiver*"—or impostor. They speak of Him as an impostor, because they have not the least confidence in His rising from the dead. See ch. 12. 40; 26. 61.

64. *Until the third day.* This is the sense in which the Jews evidently understood the time, "after three days" in the preceding verse. The period for Christ's remaining in the grave, was the intervening time *until the third day*, taking in the parts of three days. They supposed that His disciples would steal away His body, as the only means of making His word seem good—deceiving the people, by declaring Him risen. This is introduced to show that they were on the sharpest look out for any deception. ——¶ *The last error*, or fraud—imposition. If this should succeed, and they could pretend that He had risen, this last pretence would more powerfully influence the people than the first, or His pretending to be the Messiah. This confession of theirs is their *testimony*, that *if He should really rise*, it would carry the most overpowering conviction.

65 *A watch.* (κουστωδιͅν)—Latin—*Custodia.* The guard from the castle of Antonia—used at the festivals for any service needed in the city. "A watch" consisted, usually, of about *sixty* soldiers. This watch had already been in use in the trial and crucifixion.——¶ *As sure as you can*—literally (ωσ οιδατε), *as ye know*, or *know how.*

66. *Sealing the stone.* This was the utmost security that could be given. Pilate's signet was stamped on a seal set to the extremities of a leathern band, that passed round the stone. This was done probably to prevent the guards being bribed by the disciples, as they suspected to be possible. Daniel's den was sealed (Dan. 6. 17). ——¶ *Setting a watch.* They stationed this military guard at the sepulchre, and gave them charge to duty.

OBSERVE, (1.) It is plain that all deception was most thoroughly guarded against, as to the resurrection of Christ. At the earliest moment—*before night*—in a way utterly to prevent His leaving the tomb, except by Divine power—the *stone*, the *guard*, the *seal*, and the active *suspicion* of any possible fraud, all invested the sepulchre with the utmost possible security. Let us see whether He will rise again. This will settle the evidence of His work. (2.) Every sinner should weep at the sufferings and death of Christ, both in penitence for his own sins, and in gratitude for the grace of our Lord Jesus. (3.) Christians have comfort in looking forward to death, because Christ went through the grave for them, to make its darkness bright with hope, and its repose

CHAPTER XXVIII.

IN ª the end of the sabbath, as it began to dawn toward the

a Mar.16.1. Lu.24.1,&c. Jno.20.1,&c.

first *day* of the week, came Mary Magdalene, ᵇ and the other Mary, to see the sepulchre.

b c.27.56.

sweet in Him—and to take away its victory. (4.) He needed to lie under the power of death for a time, to taste death for others, that so also He might vanquish and despoil the last enemy.

"O Death, where is thy sting? O Grave, where is thy victory? Thanks be unto God who giveth us the victory through our Lord Jesus Christ" (2 Cor. 15. 55, 57).

PART IX.

Our Lord's Resurrection. His subsequent appearances and His Ascension.

Time—Forty days.

	Matt.	Mark.	Luke.	John.
§ 159. THE MORNING OF THE RESURRECTION.—FIRST *day of the week. Jerusalem.*	28. 2-4	16. 1		
§ 160. VISIT OF THE WOMEN TO THE SEPULCHRE. Mary Magdalene returns.—*Same day.*	28. 1	16. 2-4	24. 1-3	20. 1, 2

CHAPTER XXVIII.

1. *In the end of the sabbath*—literally (ὀψὲ), *in the evening* of the sabbath. And as in Jewish reckoning, the day ended at six o'clock, P. M., this phrase refers to the opening of the subsequent day. The next clause more exactly specifies the time. Quite as soon as the sabbath time had passed, and the earliest dawn of the following day was breaking, these anxious and affectionate followers of Christ hastened to the sepulchre. John says, "*early.*" Luke, "*very early.*" Mark, "*very early, at the rising of the sun.*" Matthew, "*as it began to dawn.*" The time was early dawn, or at day-break. This early movement shows their devotion to the Master; for as the other Evangelists tell us, they came "bringing the spices which they had prepared" (Luke). They had "bought sweet spices, that they might come and anoint Him" (Mark). The women reached the sepulchre, *after the* incidents recorded in the next verses (2-4).——¶ *The first day of the week*—an unusual phrase (μιαν σαββατων)— literally, "*one of the Sabbaths.*" The same phrase and no other is used by each of the Evangelists, in their mention of this *first Christian sabbath.* Mark uses it twice; Luke once, as Matthew and John twice, and only in the records of the resurrection. Besides, it is used in Acts 20. 7, and in 1 Cor. 16. 2, both to designate the Christian sabbath. Bengel remarks, that "with the resurrection of our Lord, is associated the first remarkable mention of the Dominical day." The Cranmer version of the New Testament (A. D. 1539) reads, "*Upon an euening of the sabbothes which dawneth the fyrst daye of the sabbothes.*" Wicklif (A. D. 1380) reads, "*In the euentide of the saboth, that bigynneth to schyne in the first dai of the wike.*" The evening of the old dispensation is the dawning of the new.——¶ *Mary Magdalene, &c.* Besides, there are mentioned in all, the other Mary, wife of Alpheus, and mother of James and Joses—Salome, the mother of Zebedee's children—viz. James and John—and Joanna, the wife of Chuza, Herod's steward.— —¶ *To see* (θεωρησαι)

2 And, behold, there ¹ was a great earthquake: for the angel of the Lord descended from heaven, and came and rolled back the stone from the door, and sat upon it.

3 His ᶜ countenance was like lightning, and his raiment white as snow:

4 And for fear of him the keepers did shake, and became as dead *men.*

5 And the angel answered ᵈ

1 Or, *had been.* c Ps.104.4. Eze.1.4-14. Da.10.6. Re.1.14-16.

d He.1.14.

— to *visit.* Bengel remarks here, " that they came for such offices as belonged to those who were not near relatives—viz., of embalming—and hence it is not wonderful that our Lord's mother was not in the company."

2. *Great earthquake.* This had taken place before their arrival. Such an event had accompanied the *death* of Christ, and the graves of His people were opened. Much more shall it occur at His own rising, when His own sepulchre is burst.—¶ *The angel of the Lord.* He came with *authority* "from heaven." Matthew describes him as sitting. Luke speaks of *two* that were seen *standing.* Twelve legions of angels could have been there at Christ's command. These were *His* angels ("of the Lord"). Theophylact remarks, that "the stone was removed, *not to let Jesus out, but to let the disciples in.*"

3. *His countenance*—literally, his *form or appearance.* This was heavenly apparel. Christ at His transfiguration had His face shining as the sun, and His raiment white and glistening. This dazzling whiteness was the symbol of joy and purity and glory. Bengel remarks, that we do not read of celestial messengers appearing before this, in such dress; but afterward they so appeared. Acts 1. 10, and 10. 30.

4. *For fear of him*—i. e., of the angel.——¶ *Did shake*—or *quake.* The verb here has the same force as the noun, vs. 2—"*earthquake.*" The military guards were struck with tremor and terror, and fell down as dead. Mark records the query of the women on the way, about who should roll away the stone for them, and of their finding the stone rolled away (16. 3, 4). Luke tells further of their entering into the sepulchre (24. 3). John tells further still, of Mary Magdalene's returning with the message to Simon Peter (20. 2).

§ 161. VISION OF ANGELS IN THE SEPULCHRE.—FIRST *day of the week. Jerusalem.*

Matt.	Mark.	Luke.	John.
28. 5–7	16. 5–7	24. 4–8	

5. *And the angel answered.* Mark says that this address of the angel was as they had entered the sepulchre—the heavenly messenger "*sitting on the right side*"—viz., on the stone, as Matthew records. There was an inner vault where the bodies were laid, and the stone was at the mouth of this, while there was also an *outer* enclosure, into which the women entered, as stated by Mark—and saw the angel sitting, as told by Matthew. This reconciles the seeming discrepancy. Mark further describes him as "a young man (that is in form), clothed in a long white garment, and *they were affrighted.*" This last statement by Mark, of the women's fear, accounts for the conciliatory address of the angel, here given. The angel knew whom they sought, because he was sent on this Divine commission. In vs. 8, Matthew intimates by the Greek term rendered "*departed*" (or having gone out from), that they had been inside. The fact that Luke records the appearing of *two* angels who stood by them, is not inconsistent with the other statements; because Matthew and Mark speak only of the one who addressed the women. This is natural, and occurs elsewhere· as in

and said unto the women, Fear not ye : for *e* I know that ye seek Jesus, which was crucified.

6 He is not here; for he is risen, as he said. *f* Come, see the place where the Lord lay.

7 And go quickly, and tell his disciples that he is risen *g* from the dead; and, behold, he goeth before you into Galilee; there *h* shall ye see him : lo, I have told you.

8 And they departed quickly

---

e Ps.105.3,4. *f* c.27.63.   *g* Lu.24.34. 1Co.15.4. *h* ver.16,17.

---

regard to the blind men at Jericho, and the demoniacs at Gadara. And as to the *standing* posture, the word rendered "*stood*" in Luke, means more literally, "*appeared suddenly*." Besides, they might easily have both sat and stood, during the interview— might have been both outside and inside at different moments—and they might have been seen both singly and together in tne sudden and shifting apparition. When infidels would make war against the Scripture on such slight grounds, they show alike their zealous hostility, and their lack of better weapons.

6. *He is not here.* This was the consoling message to the affrighted disciples — that Christ, though not there, was where His promise had appointed—not dead and buried any longer, but alive and faithful. They needed an angel message to remind them of Christ's word. They were looking for Him other than in the way of His appointment—and they should not find Him there. They were guided by natural expectations, and not by the calculations of faith grounded on the express word of promise.——¶ *See the place.* This was a niche in the inner chamber of the tomb. The angel thus convinces them of Christ's having actually risen, and of his own Divine commission to assure them of the fact. He calls the Saviour "*the Lord*."—A glorious appellation, says Bengel. The object of the angel was to remind them of Christ's promise to *rise on the third day*, which was fulfilled, and of His appointment to meet them in Galilee, which was ready to be fulfilled. So our finding one promise made good, increases our faith in all the promises.

The body of Christ was laid in the tomb before sunset on Friday—and he rose early on the morning of Sunday. He therefore rose *on the third day*, having lain in the tomb during one whole day and a part of two others— in all, not far from thirty-six hours.

7. *Go quickly.* Bengel remarks that the apostles especially ought to have believed before they had the sight. Therefore, they shall be informed of these scenes by the *women*, and their faith shall be tried.——¶ *Tell His disciples.* Mark adds, emphatically, "and *tell Peter.*" What a tender care had Christ for the faith of this unfaithful apostle, who had so lately denied Him. This accords well with His praying for him, that his faith fail not—an angel message now to rally his faith.——¶ *He is risen.* This was the animating word—"risen from the dead."——¶ *He goeth before you.* How faithful was Christ, though they were so unbelieving. Why had they not hurried to Galilee instead of to the tomb? Alas, notwithstanding the very word of promise, they had gone to the sepulchre with spices to *embalm His corpse!* Yet Christ is *faithful!* He went where He had appointed, and waited for them there. How He goes before us—anticipates our promptest movements. This was only a hint of what His anticipating, foregoing grace should always do—going before us even where we have promises— and being *beforehand* with us. "Before that Philip called thee, &c., Jno. 1. 48.

§ 162. THE WOMEN RETURN TO THE CITY. JESUS MEETS THEM.—FIRST *day of the week.*

Matt.	Mark.	Luke.	John.
28. 8-10	16. 8	24. 9-11	

from the sepulchre, with fear and great joy, and did run to bring his disciples word.

9 ¶ And as they went to tell his disciples, behold, Jesus met them, saying, All hail.^i And they came and held him by the feet, and worshipped him.

10 Then said Jesus unto them,

i Jno. 20. 19.

Be not afraid : go tell my brethren ^j that they go into Galilee, and there shall they see me.

11 ¶ Now when they were going, behold, some of the watch came into the city, and shewed unto the chief priests all the things that were done.

j He. 2. 11.

---

8. *And they departed quickly*—literally, *went out of, or from* the sepulchre. This is a hint in the language, that they had been *inside*, as the other Evangelists mention.——¶ *Fear and great joy. Fear*, at the astounding sights of the angels and the vacant sepulchre—and *great joy*, at the Divine messages, and at their new views of the promises. So "*we tremble and rejoice*" in our discoveries of Christ's gracious words and ways.——¶ *Quickly.* At the thought of *seeing* Christ as had been promised (vs. 7), and with zeal to convey the glad news to the rest.

9. *And as they went.* This was plainly our Lord's *first* appearing, for though Mark speaks of His having appeared *first* to Mary Magdalene (16. 9), yet the term is used relatively. It was the first of those several appearings, which Mark records. Mary Magdalene was not with the other women at this appearing, as we infer from her language to Peter and John (John 20. 2). She had not yet seen the Lord. (See the narratives harmonized at the end.)——¶ *All Hail*—or rather, *Hail.* A term of salutation. The literal meaning of the Greek word is, *rejoice*—i. e., *joy to thee !*——¶ *Held Him by the feet.* This phrase, with the next term which signifies the act of prostration on the ground in reverence (see note 2. 2), describes their earnest and overjoyed devotion. They cast themselves before Him, and took Him by the feet. So promptly did they find that He was verily the same Lord that was crucified. And if He was indeed their RISEN LORD they must needs pay Him Divine homage. It is intimated that their holding Him by the feet was an expression of their dread of separating from Him again, even for an instant. This explains the opening of vs. 10.

10. *Be not afraid*—that is, to part from me on this errand, especially, when it is to *meet me with the rest*, in a place *beyond*. This meeting now by the way was more than Christ had promised. He will sometimes do *more than He has said* for His people, to confirm them in all that *He has said*. We may go out from our closet interviews on our errands of Christian duty—for he has appointed to meet us *beyond.* In the way of our cheerful obedience He will often meet us, crying, *Hail ! Peace !*——¶ *My brethren.* How tender the message It was not enough to have *promised*—He must every way remind and assure them that He would *keep His promise.* Surely this was Christ, "*Thy speech bewrayeth thee !*" He is "the first-born among many brethren" (Rom. 8. 29. comp. Heb. 3. 11).——¶ *Galilee.* He went up to Jerusalem to be crucified. He would now go to Galilee, where most of His mighty works were done. There was His nativity, and the place where He had been brought up. It was Galilee of the Gentiles where *the light* had sprung up upon the region and shadow of death. ch. 4. 13–16.

OBSERVE, (1.) "The sign of the prophet Jonas" is given (ch. 16. 4). Let us enter the vacant sepulchre, and, like John, SEE AND BELIEVE (John 20. 8). (2.) Christ *proves* to us His resurrection, by meeting us, and confirming to us His promises.

12 And when they were assembled with the elders, and had taken counsel, they gave large money unto the soldiers,

13 Saying, Say ye, His disciples came by night, and stole [k] him *away* while we slept

14 And if this come to the governor's ears, we will persuade him, and secure you.

15 So they took the money, and did as they were taught:

k c.26.64.

	Matt.	Mark.	Luke.	John.
§ 163. Peter and John run to the Sepulchre.—First *day of the week. Jerusalem.*	....	....	24. 12	20. 3-10
§ 164. Our Lord is seen by Mary Magdalene at the Sepulchre.—*Same day.*	....	19. 9-11		20.11-18
§ 165. Report of the Watch.—First *day of the week. Jerusalem.*	28.11-15			

11. *When they were going*, or rather when they had gone. The guard (or keepers, vs. 4), having now recovered sufficiently from their stunning fright, and seeing their own liability to charges for not having kept the tomb safely, went to make report of all that had occurred.——¶ *Unto the chief priests.* The *chief priests* were well understood to be the parties interested, and the active agents in Christ's death, though the charge and condemnation before Pilate had been one which concerned the state. Moreover the guard had been put at command of the chief priests (ch. 27. 65). The guards themselves were convinced of a miraculous work at the sepulchre.

12. At this astounding news, they convene the Sanhedrim.——¶ *Large money*—literally *sufficient*, in the sense of abundant. They could think now only of lying and bribery. The statements of the guards satisfied them that there was no need of searching for the body, or investigating the case. They did not think of possible collusion. And now if He had risen, the last point was harder to kick against than the first (ch. 27. 64).——¶ *Unto the soldiers.* Ordinarily the soldiers might have been open to bribe. But in this case, they would expose themselves to the penalty of the Roman law, which was *death*, if it should appear that they had been asleep at their posts, and with such fatal results. The conduct of the chief priests here, showed their perfidy—their eagerness to contradict the facts, even after they were convinced—their extreme corruption that would resort to such iniquitous means—and especially their unhappy extremity, that could find no possible escape from the overwhelming proofs, and must bribe the soldiers to lie, against all probability, and in peril of their own life, to get a shadow of pretence against the resurrection. Yet what a gross absurdity was involved in this falsehood. *If the guards were asleep, how could they know of the body's being stolen away by the disciples?* Their very lack of fidelity so confessed, would destroy their testimony.

14. *The governor's ears.* They must give the soldiers this warrant against the fatal consequences of such a confession. The penalty of being asleep would be death—and yet, this pledge is given of influencing Pilate, so that they should escape the law.——¶ *Persuade.* It was well understood that money could operate with Pilate, so that the soldiers need not fear. The governor was evidently known as being open to this kind of persuasion. Philo testifies to this point in his character.

15. *So they took the money and did as they were taught!* What a record of *guilt and shame!*——¶ *This saying,* referring to vs. 14. The saying of the soldiers.——¶ *Among the Jews.* This became the common *Jewish* ver-

and this saying is commonly reported among the Jews until this day.

16 Then [l] the eleven disciples went away into Galilee, into a mountain where Je-

[l] c. 26. 32.

---

sion of our Lord's disappearance from the sepulchre. This fabrication was most industriously circulated by the Jews in distant countries, as Justin Martyr certifies. (Dialogue with Trypho, p. 202 and 335.) The same story is related in the Jewish Talmudical writings.——¶ *Until this day*, viz., the date of Matthew's gospel. Such an event as Christ's rising from the tomb, was seen to be so confounding an argument for all His claims, that the chief priests took utmost precaution against the shadow of any pretence to this effect (ch. 27. 63, 64). They had provided most completely against the very measures which they afterwards declare to have been taken, viz., the *stealing of the body by the disciples*. It was to prevent all possibility of this, that they had a guard of *sixty men* stationed around the tomb. Could all their laborious and abundant precautions have been defeated by these disciples? But the disciples carried spices to the sepulchre to *embalm* the body in death! Besides, could a Roman guard of sixty men have been all so soundly asleep at the same time and throughout such a transaction? This would have been a miracle. Could the disciples have *given life* to the body? It was abundantly testified that He appeared alive, by many infallible proofs (Acts 1. 3). Besides, what motive could His followers have had for removing His dead body out of so honourable a sepulchre? Did the *chief priests believe* that His body was in possession of the disciples? They would surely have instituted search in the morning, so short a time after the event. The very report of the transaction given by the soldiers, and currently circulated among the Jews, carries its own refutation. And notwithstanding the false witness of the Jews, and their industrious circulation of it, multitudes of Jews and Gentiles believed. And this was no more wonderful an event than many of His miracles had been.

OBSERVE, The resurrection of Jesus Christ from the dead must be admitted as the crowning proof of His claims—and the highest token of the acceptance of His work in heaven. It establishes our faith (John 20. 8), and gives believers a pledge of their resurrection and redemption, since He is risen for us (1 Cor. 15. 20–23). It shows that Christ died not as others, but for a specific purpose as covenanted with the Father. And at once upon the accomplishment of this great end of His death, He triumphantly rose again (Heb. 1. 3). This therefore proves the object of His death to have been substantially attained. We are begotten again unto a lively hope by the resurrection of Jesus Christ from the dead (1 Pet. 1. 3–5).

	Matt.	Mark.	Luke.	John.
§ 166. Our Lord is seen of Peter—then by two Disciples on the way to Emmaus.—FIRST *day of the week*. *Emmaus*.	....	16. 12,13	24.13–35	
§ 167. Jesus appears in the midst of the Apostles, Thomas being absent.—*Evening following the* FIRST *day of the week.* *Jerusalem.*	....	16·14–18	24.36–49	20.19–23
§ 168. Jesus appears in the midst of the Apostles, Thomas being present.—*Evening following the* FIRST *day of the subsequent week. Jerusalem.*	....	....	....	20.24–29

A. D. 33.]　　　　　　CHAPTER XXVIII.　　　　　　311

sus had appointed them.
17 And when they saw ᵐ him, they worshipped him: but some doubted.

m c. 16. 28.

18 And Jesus came and spake unto them, saying, All ⁿ power is given unto me in heaven and in earth.

n Ps. 2. 6; 89. 19; 110. 1-3. Is. 9. 6, 7. Da. 7. 14. c. 11. 27. Lu. 1. 32. Jno. 17. 2. Ro. 14. 9. Ep. 1. 20, 21. He. 2. 8. 1 Pe. 3. 22. Re. 11. 15.

	Matt.	Mark.	Luke.	John.
§ 169. THE APOSTLES GO AWAY INTO GALILEE. JESUS SHOWS HIMSELF TO SEVEN OF THEM AT THE SEA OF TIBERIAS　*Galilee.*	28. 16	....	....	21. 1-24
§ 170. JESUS MEETS THE APOSTLES AND ABOVE FIVE HUNDRED BRETHREN ON A MOUNTAIN IN GALILEE.	28. 16-20			

16. *Away into Galilee.* Here it is recognized that the apostolic circle was now reduced by the apostacy and death of Judas, so as to number but *eleven.* Referring to John's record, which supplies mainly the deficiencies of the rest, we find those interesting narratives of the fishing, and Christ's appearing after their unsuccessful night, directing them where to cast—the prompt and marvellous success in following His directions—Peter's springing out from the fishers' boat into the sea—their feeding afterward on the fish, where Christ showed His identity and humanity, by eating with them—and His special conversations with Peter, testing his love, and forewarning him of his violent death.——¶ *A mountain where Jesus had appointed.* This appointment is recorded in ch. 26. 32, but no mountain is spoken of either there or in His promise (vs. 10), or by the angel (vs. 4). Our Lord may have designated a mountain, though the apostles make no record of it. Or, the Transfiguration Mount may have been understood as the spot. Many ("above five hundred brethren at once") had assembled there (1 Cor. 15. 6), as was natural enough from the report of such an appointment among Christ's followers, circulating more than eight days before the time, and the lively expectations excited both in Jerusalem and Galilee. He appointed this meeting in GALILEE, because there were but few disciples in Jerusalem (the number of the names being about a hundred and twenty, Acts 1. 15), and Galilee had been the principal sphere of His labours, and was the chief seat of His followers.

17. *When they saw Him.* What a sight! What a glorious confirmation of their faith! John entered within the sepulchre and "*saw and believed*" (ch. 20. 8), not only that Christ had risen, but that His work was stamped with the seal of Divine authority and acceptance, and that He was a Divine Saviour. Now, at the *sight* of their identical Master, and at this fulfilment of His promise to meet them, how could they avoid worshipping Him as their Divine Lord?——¶ *But some doubted.* There were some there doubtless, who had not before beheld Him, nor had palpable proofs of His real appearance. All the natural doubts, therefore, now rose and struggled in their breasts. They doubted the evidence of their senses, that this could be the same Lord and Master risen. How plainly all the narrative implies that it was Christ in His identical flesh, as they had before known Him. The print of the nails and the very open wounds, were shown to Thomas. He ate "the broiled fish and honeycomb" before them (Luke 24. 42), to show them that it was really and personally He, in the same flesh, for "*they believed not* yet for *joy, and wondered*" (vs. 41).

18. *Then Jesus came and spake unto them*—i. e., the *eleven* (vs. 16), of whom alone Matthew has spoken. The apostolic commission is given by

19 ¶ Go * ye therefore, and ¹ teach ᵖ all nations, baptizing them in the name of the Father, and of the Son, and of the Holy Ghost.

20 Teaching ᵍ them to observe

c Mar.16.15. 1 Or, *make disciples,* or *Christians, of all nations.* p Is.52.10. Ro.10.18.

q Ac.2.42. 1Cor.11.2.

Mark at the appearing of Christ to the disciples, in Thomas' absence (16. 15–18). Then, also, John records the *breathing* on them, with the words, "*Receive ye the Holy Ghost*, &c. Our Lord repeats publicly here, in the presence of all His disciples, the solemn charge which He had already given, in private, to the apostles. This was the great ministerial commission, that looked beyond the apostles' age, and beyond their extraordinary office, to the preaching of the Gospel by the ministers of Christ, ALWAY *even unto the end of the world.*——¶ *All power is given unto me.* This cannot imply any inferiority, for "ALL POWER" is OMNIPOTENCE, which is an incommunicable attribute of God. And that it was "GIVEN" Him, refers only to the exaltation upon which He was just now to enter. As Mediator, He was now to take all power on earth and in heaven—as COVENANTED WITH THE FATHER—for the purpose of gathering in His people—ruling and defending His church—and subduing all His and our enemies. As to His original power over all things, as the second person in the Godhead, and God the Son, see John 1. 1–3. Romans 9. 5. Col 1. 16, 17. Heb. 1. 3, 8.

19. *Go ye therefore.* This commission given to the Gospel ministry, is on the basis of Christ's all-sufficient power.——¶ *Teach*—literally, "*make disciples of.*"——¶ *All nations.* This gave the widest sphere for the ministerial work.——¶ *Baptizing them.* Thus the people of different and distant lands were to be gathered into a visible church by a formal and credible profession of Christ, the baptism and instruction in Christ's truth being enjoined as requisites of a church. To those of that time, the belief that Jesus of Nazareth was the true Messiah, involved all fundamental points, and was the substance of a good profession. Now, this Christian baptism as we see from what follows, involves more than the avowal of such a commonly confessed belief. From the Acts of the Apostles we learn, too, that *household baptism* was understood (see 3. 39; 16. 33).——¶ *In the name.* This does not mean, "*by the authority.*" It is "*into* the name," or *unto,* involving a profession of this Christian religion, in which alone the Father, Son, and Holy Ghost, can be made known to men. One so baptized into the name of the Triune God, professes to receive the Father, Son, and Holy Ghost, in all the offices in which they act for the government and salvation of men; and engages to walk in all the commandments and ordinances of the Lord. In infant baptism, this engagement is made by the believing parent for the child, with the view of the child's assuming the obligation for itself at discretionary years. The baptism is the child's privilege. The after profession is its solemn Christian duty.——¶ *Of the Father, and of the Son, and of the Holy Ghost.* Observe, it is in THE NAME of these three persons AS ONE GOD, not in their NAMES as though they were three Gods. The same phraseology is used, when speaking of any *one being,* as 1 Cor. 1. 13, "were ye baptized in the name of *Paul?*" This language therefore gives the NAME of God—*Three Persons in one Godhead.* How absurd that the Son and the Holy Ghost should be thus named, if they be not *persons.* How impossible that any inferior being could be ranked thus with the Father, in the sacred form of this perpetual ordinance—or if the Spirit were only an *attribute,* how trifling would be such a formulary! The Father, and the Son, and the Holy Ghost, must be *equal in power and glory.*

20. *Teaching them,* &c. Christ's

all things whatsoever I have commanded you: and lo, I ʳ am with you alway, *even* unto the end of the world. Amen.

ʳ c.18.20. Re.1.18.

commands are to be taught in the church. The church is set to be a grand TEACHING institution. Its business is educational. The scriptures are to be taught. There is sufficiency in these, and exclusive authority as a rule of faith. To gather into the church all nations—baptizing them into the Christian faith—to preach the gospel to every creature, and to teach the church Christ's commandments, were the substantial points of the great commission.——¶ *Lo I am with you.* This implies His essential *presence and assistance.* He had said before, "*there am I in the midst of them*," promising to be so especially present where two or three of them were gathered together in His name (ch. 18. 20). He here again asserted His Divinity—able to be omnipresent, and upholding all things by the word of His power—sitting down on the right hand of the majesty on High.—— ¶ *Alway.*—literally (πάσας τὰς ἡμέρας), ALL THE DAYS. He is with His faithful ministers *always.* He does not say "*all your days,*" as though speaking only of the apostles, or of their times, but of all future time.——¶ *End of the world.* The former phrase sufficiently shows that this can have no limited signification, as "*end of the age.*" And even such a construction could prove nothing for the opponents of Christ's Divinity, since to have been everywhere present with them from His ascension to the destruction of Jerusalem—some forty years after—would have required the same Divine attributes. How speedily and signally was this presence given at Pentecost to succeed the preaching of Christ—at the temple gate to cure the lame man, at the word of Peter and John—and in prison, to loose and deliver Paul and Silas—though these last were not of the eleven. And now, eighteen hundred years after the promise, it can be testified that Christ has been and is with His faithful ministers, to cheer, and counsel, and strengthen, and direct, and defend them. And so shall it be to the *very end.* "And they went forth and preached every where, the Lord working with them."

§ 171. Our Lord is seen of James, then of all the Apostles.—*Jerusalem* (See Acts 1. 3–8, and 1 Cor. 15. 7.)

	Matt.	Mark.	Luke.	John.
§ 172. The Ascension. *Bethany*	....	16. 19,20	24.50–53	
§ 173. Conclusion of John's Gospel. .	....	....	....	20. 30,31 21.25

We subjoin Dr. Robinson's Harmony of our Lord's appearances.
1. To the Women returning from the Sepulchre—*Matthew.* See § 162.
2. To Mary Magdalene, at the Sepulchre—*John* and *Mark.* § 164.
3. To Peter, perhaps early in the afternoon—*Luke* and *Paul.* § 166.
4. To the two disciples going to Emmaus, towards evening—*Luke* and *Mark.* § 166.
5. To the apostles (except Thomas), assembled at evening—*Mark, Luke, John,* and *Paul.* § 167.
N. B. These five appearances all took place at or near Jerusalem, upon the first day of the week, the same day on which our Lord arose.
6. To the apostles (Thomas being present) eight days afterward, at Jerusalem—*John.* § 168.
7. To seven of the apostles on the shore of the Lake of Tiberias—*John.* § 169.
8. To the eleven apostles, and to five hundred brethren besides, on a mountain in Galilee—*Matthew* and *Paul.* § 170.
9. To James, probably at Jerusalem—*Paul.* § 171.
10. To the eleven at Jerusalem, immediately before the ascension—*Luke in the Acts,* and *Paul.* § 171.
Then follows the ASCENSION § 172.

APPENDIX.

We have not thought it needful to depart from Dr. Robinson's Harmony in "The Schedule of Days," immediately preceding the crucifixion. Dr. Simon Greenleaf of Harvard University, in his "Testimony of the Evangelists," has adopted the same arrangement. No important points are involved, if we may except the question which might be considered important by some, whether Christ's triumphal entry to Jerusalem was on *Sunday*—hence called "*Palm Sunday.*"

We subjoin the Harmony of this portion, which *Mimpriss* (London, 1845) adopts, after Greswell, which is generally conceded now, as the most authorized "Schedule of the Days."

CLOSE OF THE SEVENTH DAY.—After the expiration of the Jewish Sabbath (or Saturday), "six days before the Passover," John 12. 1 (meaning, in the Jewish reckoning, *the sixth day before*), Jesus arrives at Bethany.

FIRST *day of the week*, SUNDAY.—The Jews resort to Bethany, to see Jesus and Lazarus.

SECOND *day*, MONDAY.—Jesus goes in procession from Bethany to Jerusalem, to appear in the temple, four days before He suffers. He makes His *public entry*—after which, He goes to Bethany to lodge there.

THIRD *day*, TUESDAY.—Jesus, in the way from Bethany, curses a fig-tree; and on the same day He cleanses the Temple.

FOURTH *day*, WEDNESDAY.—Jesus returns to the city, and the conversation is held with the disciples about the fig-tree now withered. He discourses in the Temple and on Mount Olivet. He foretells His coming to destroy the city, &c.

FIFTH *day*, THURSDAY (*toward evening*).—The disciples make preparation for the Paschal Supper, which is eaten in the evening, which would be the beginning of Friday, as the day began after sunset.

We need only remark, that the sixth day before the Passover, according to the Jewish phraseology and reckoning, would rather be Sunday, as the sixth day before Friday—for the first and last day of the reckoning would be strictly included. So the other expression, "*after three days,*" or "*the third day*" from Friday, confessedly meant *Sunday*—the day when our Lord appointed to rise again. But if the Sunday previous was the day of His arriving at Bethany, His public entry to Jerusalem was "*on the next day*"—Monday--(John 12. 12).

JEWISH MONEY REDUCED TO DOLLARS AND CENTS.

	Dollars.	Cents
A *Shekel*, or "piece of silver," which was equal to 2 Pekahs and 20 Gerahs..		50.187
A Gold *Shekel*..	8	03.
A *Maneh* or *Mina* (called "*Pound.*" Luke 19. 13)............	25	9.35
A *Talent of Silver*...	1,505	62.5
A *Talent of Gold*	24,309	

Roman money mentioned in the New Testament, reduced to Dollars and Cents.

A *Mite*, about one-third of a cent.
A *Farthing*, about two-thirds of a cent.
A *denarius*, or *Penny*, about one-eighth of a dollar.

www.ingramcontent.com/pod-product-compliance
Lightning Source LLC
Chambersburg PA
CBHW021803220426
43662CB00006B/167